SOMETHING ABOUT THE AUTHOR®

Something about
the Author *was named
an "Outstanding
Reference Source,"
the highest honor given
by the American
Library Association
Reference and User
Services Division.*

something about the author®

Facts and Pictures about Authors
and Illustrators of Books for Young People

volume 118

GALE GROUP

Detroit
New York
San Francisco
London
Boston
Woodbridge, CT

STAFF

Scot Peacock, *Managing Editor, Literature Product*
Mark Scott, *Publisher, Literature Product*

Katy Balcer, *Editor;* Sara L. Constantakis, Kristen A. Dorsch, Shayla Hawkins, Motoko Fujishiro Huthwaite,
Simone Sobel, Denay Wilding, *Associate Editors*

Alan Hedblad, *Managing Editor*
Susan M. Trosky, *Literature Content Coordinator*

Victoria B. Cariappa, *Research Manager;* Tracie A. Richardson, *Project Coordinator;* Maureen Emeric, Barbara McNeil, Gary J.
Oudersluys, Cheryl L. Warnock, *Research Specialists;* Tamara C. Nott, *Research Associate;* Nicodemus Ford, Tim Lehnerer, Ron
Morelli, *Research Assistants*

Maria L. Franklin, *Permissions Manager;* Edna Hedblad, Sarah Tomasek, *Permissions Associates*

Mary Beth Trimper, *Composition Manager;* Dorothy Maki, *Manufacturing Manager;* Stacy Melson, *Buyer*

Michael Logusz, *Graphic Artist;* Randy Bassett, *Image Database Supervisor;* Robert Duncan, *Imaging Specialist;* Pamela A. Reed,
Imaging Coordinator; Dean Dauphinais, Robyn V. Young, *Senior Image Editors;* Kelly A. Quin, *Image Editor*

Library of Congress Catalog Card Number 72-27107

ISBN 0-7876-4036-0
ISSN 0276-816X

Printed in the United States of America

10 9 8 7 6 5 4 3 2 1

Contents

Authors in Forthcoming Volumes viii
Introduction ix
Acknowledgments xi

Authors in Forthcoming Volumes

Below are some of the authors and illustrators that will be featured in upcoming volumes of *SATA*. These include new entries on the swiftly rising stars of the field, as well as completely revised and updated entries (indicated with *) on some of the most notable and best-loved creators of books for children.

Te Ata: Born in the late 1800s, Te Ata was a famous storyteller during the early twentieth century who performed throughout the United States, including the White House. New York's Lake Te Ata is named in her honor, and her compilation *Indian Tales* reflects Te Ata's Chickasaw ancestry and remains in print over one hundred years after her birth.

Joseph S. Bonsall: Best known as the lead singer of the country music band The Oak Ridge Boys, Bonsall has a second career as a children's author. His inspirational "Molly" series of books describes the adventures of a calico kitten and is based on Bonsall's experiences with his five cats.

Amelia Lau Carling: A talented illustrator, Carling depicted her childhood as the daughter of Chinese immigrants making a new home in South America in her picture book *Mama and Papa Have a Store*. Named a Pura Belpre Honor Book for its illustrations, *Mama and Papa Have a Store* offers readers a view of everyday life in early twentieth-century Latin America.

Gael Cresp: Australian writer Cresp is a professional storyteller and librarian. The title character of her critically acclaimed book *The Biography of Gilbert Alexander Pig* is a musically gifted black pig who plays the trumpet. Cresp based the character on a friend who uses his musical talents to inspire and educate others.

Tony De Saulles: Since quitting his job as an advertising executive almost twenty years ago, English author De Saulles has found his true calling as an artist and children's writer. De Saulles has illustrated nearly thirty books, including many for Nick Arnold as well as his own *Ridiculous Rhymes*.

Nigel Hawkes: Hawkes is an Oxford graduate and prolific science writer renowned for his straightforward nonfiction titles for young adults. He has written numerous books that present young and adolescent readers with a wealth of scientific information on a great variety of subjects, ranging from space exploration to the perils of drug use.

*Monica Hughes: Considered one of the premier science fiction writers in Canada, Hughes has earned numerous awards as well as popular and critical acclaim for her vivid and socially relevant writing. She has written over thirty books, including the modern classic *Hunter in the Dark* and a number of picture books and easy readers for children.

Veda Jones: Jones began her successful career as a children's writer when her three sons asked her to write a story for them. Since then, Jones has published more than fifteen children's books, including *Native Americans of the Northwest Coast* and *Adventure in the Wilderness*.

*Gordon Korman: Korman is an award-winning Canadian author whose humorous books, including *The Twinkie Squad* and *Nose Pickers from Outer Space*, are inspired by his teenage experiences as a self-described "gutless troublemaker" at school. Korman's first novel, *This Can't Be Happening at Macdonald Hall!*, was published when he was just fourteen years old.

Soinbhe Lally: Irish writer Lally writes children's books inspired by her family and her country. One of Lally's most recent works is *The Hungry Wind*, which serves as a memorial for those who died anonymously in Ireland's great potato famine.

*George Ella Lyon: Lyon is a prolific writer who has achieved success in many literary genres. She has won several awards for her children's books, including the Golden Kite Award from the Society of Children's Book Writers and Illustrators for *Borrowed Children*.

*Gayle Pearson: Noted for her realistic coming-of-age stories, Pearson has been writing children's novels for more than a decade. Her books, including *One Potato, Tu* and *The Secret Box*, adeptly portray the adolescent struggle for self-understanding amid the emotional turbulence of puberty.

Introduction

Something about the Author (*SATA*) is an ongoing reference series that examines the lives and works of authors and illustrators of books for children. *SATA* includes not only well-known writers and artists but also less prominent individuals whose works are just coming to be recognized. This series is often the only readily available information source on emerging authors and illustrators. You'll find *SATA* informative and entertaining, whether you are a student, a librarian, an English teacher, a parent, or simply an adult who enjoys children's literature.

What's Inside SATA

SATA provides detailed information about authors and illustrators who span the full time range of children's literature, from early figures like John Newbery and L. Frank Baum to contemporary figures like Judy Blume and Richard Peck. Authors in the series represent primarily English-speaking countries, particularly the United States, Canada, and the United Kingdom. Also included, however, are authors from around the world whose works are available in English translation. The writings represented in *SATA* include those created intentionally for children and young adults as well as those written for a general audience and known to interest younger readers. These writings cover the entire spectrum of children's literature, including picture books, humor, folk and fairy tales, animal stories, mystery and adventure, science fiction and fantasy, historical fiction, poetry and nonsense verse, drama, biography, and nonfiction.

Obituaries are also included in *SATA* and are intended not only as death notices but also as concise overviews of people's lives and work. Additionally, each edition features newly revised and updated entries for a selection of *SATA* listees who remain of interest to today's readers and who have been active enough to require extensive revisions of their earlier biographies.

New Autobiography Feature

Beginning with Volume 103, *SATA* features three or more specially commissioned autobiographical essays in each volume. These unique essays, averaging about ten thousand words in length and illustrated with an abundance of personal photos, present an entertaining and informative first-person perspective on the lives and careers of prominent authors and illustrators profiled in *SATA*.

Two Convenient Indexes

In response to suggestions from librarians, *SATA* indexes no longer appear in every volume but are included in alternate (odd-numbered) volumes of the series, beginning with Volume 57.

SATA continues to include two indexes that cumulate with each alternate volume: the Illustrations Index, arranged by the name of the illustrator, gives the number of the volume and page where the illustrator's work appears in the current volume as well as all preceding volumes in the series; the Author Index gives the number of the volume in which a person's biographical sketch, autobiographical essay, or obituary appears in the current volume as well as all preceding volumes in the series.

These indexes also include references to authors and illustrators who appear in Gale's *Yesterday's Authors of Books for Children, Children's Literature Review,* and *Something about the Author Autobiography Series.*

Easy-to-Use Entry Format

Whether you're already familiar with the *SATA* series or just getting acquainted, you will want to be aware of the kind of information that an entry provides. In every *SATA* entry the editors attempt to give as complete a picture of the person's life and work as possible. A typical entry in *SATA* includes the following clearly labeled information sections:

• *PERSONAL:* date and place of birth and death, parents' names and occupations, name of spouse, date of marriage, names of children, educational institutions attended, degrees received, religious and political affiliations, hobbies and other interests.

• *ADDRESSES:* complete home, office, electronic mail, and agent addresses, whenever available.

• *CAREER:* name of employer, position, and dates for each career post; art exhibitions; military service; memberships and offices held in professional and civic organizations.

• *AWARDS, HONORS:* literary and professional awards received.

• *WRITINGS:* title-by-title chronological bibliography of books written and/or illustrated, listed by genre when known; lists of other notable publications, such as plays, screenplays, and periodical contributions.

• *ADAPTATIONS:* a list of films, television programs, plays, CD-ROMs, recordings, and other media presentations that have been adapted from the author's work.

• *WORK IN PROGRESS:* description of projects in progress.

• *SIDELIGHTS:* a biographical portrait of the author or illustrator's development, either directly from the biographee—and often written specifically for the *SATA* entry—or gathered from diaries, letters, interviews, or other published sources.

• *FOR MORE INFORMATION SEE:* references for further reading.

• *EXTENSIVE ILLUSTRATIONS:* photographs, movie stills, book illustrations, and other interesting visual materials supplement the text.

How a SATA Entry Is Compiled

A *SATA* entry progresses through a series of steps. If the biographee is living, the *SATA* editors try to secure information directly from him or her through a questionnaire. From the information that the biographee supplies, the editors prepare an entry, filling in any essential missing details with research and/or telephone interviews. If possible, the author or illustrator is sent a copy of the entry to check for accuracy and completeness.

If the biographee is deceased or cannot be reached by questionnaire, the *SATA* editors examine a wide variety of published sources to gather information for an entry. Biographical and bibliographic sources are consulted, as are book reviews, feature articles, published interviews, and material sometimes obtained from the biographee's family, publishers, agent, or other associates.

Entries that have not been verified by the biographees or their representatives are marked with an asterisk (*).

Contact the Editor

We encourage our readers to examine the entire *SATA* series. Please write and tell us if we can make *SATA* even more helpful to you. Give your comments and suggestions to the editor:

BY MAIL: Editor, *Something about the Author,* The Gale Group, 27500 Drake Rd., Farmington Hills, MI 48331-3535.

BY TELEPHONE: (800) 877-GALE

BY FAX: (248) 699-8054

Acknowledgments

Grateful acknowledgment is made to the following publishers, authors, and artists whose works appear in this volume.

ARNOSKY, JIM. From an illustration in *All about Turtles*, by Jim Arnosky. Scholastic Press, 2000. Copyright © 2000 by Jim Arnosky. Reproduced by permission./ From an illustration in *Crinkleroot's Visit to Crinkle Cove*, by Jim Arnosky. Aladdin Paperbacks, 1999. Text and illustration copyright © 1998 by Jim Arnosky. Reproduced by permission.

ARTHUR, ROBERT. Dodge, Bill, illustrator. From a cover of *The Three Investigators in The Mystery of the Fiery Eye*, by Robert Arthur. Random House, 1998. Cover art copyright © 1998 by Bill Dodge. Reproduced by permission of Random House Children's Books, a division of Random House, Inc./ Dodge, Bill, illustrator. From a cover of *The Three Investigators in The Mystery of the Silver Spider*, by Robert Arthur. Random House, 1998. Cover art copyright © 1998 by Bill Dodge. Reproduced by permission of Random House Children's Books, a division of Random House, Inc./ Dodge, Bill, illustrator. From a cover of *The Three Investigators in The Mystery of the Vanishing Treasure*, by Robert Arthur. Random House, 1998. Cover art copyright © 1998 by Bill Dodge. Reproduced by permission of Random House Children's Books, a division of Random House, Inc.

ASHER, SANDRA FENICHEL. Asher, Sandra Fenichel, photograph. Reproduced by permission of Sandy Asher./ Martinez, John, illustrator. From a cover of *But That's Another Story*, edited by Sandy Asher. Walker and Company, 1996. Copyright © 1996 by Sandy Asher. Reproduced by permission.

BLACKWOOD, GARY L. From an illustration in *Life in a Medieval Castle*, by Gary L. Blackwood. Lucent Books, 2000. North Wind Picture Archive. Copyright © 2000 by Lucent Books, Inc. Reproduced by permission.

BRADSHAW, GILLIAN. Bradshaw, Gillian, photograph by David Bradshaw. Reproduced by permission.

BURGAN, MICHAEL. Trego, Keith, illustrator. From a cover of *Dominik Hasek: Ice Hockey Legends*, by Michael Burgan. Chelsea House Publishers, 1999. Copyright © 1999 by Chelsea House Publishers, a division of Main Line Book Co. Cover Photos: AP/Wide World Photos. Reproduced by permission.

BUSBY, CYLIN. Busby, Cylin, photograph by Damon Ross. Reproduced by permission.

CAMBURN-BRACALENTE, CAROL A. From an illustration in *Twist and Ernest*, by Laura T. Barnes. Barnesyard Books, 1999. © 1999 by Laura T. Barnes. All rights reserved. Reproduced by permission.

CARRICK, CAROL. Carrick, Carol, photograph by Sara Piazza. Reproduced by permission./ Bouma, Paddy, illustrator. From an illustration in *Upside-Down Cake*, by Carol Carrick. Clarion Books, 1999. Illustrations copyright © 1999 by Paddy Bouma. Reproduced by permission of Houghton Mifflin Company./ Carrick, Donald, illustrator. From an illustration in *What Happened to Patrick's Dinosaurs?*, by Carol Carrick. Clarion Books, 1986. Illustrations copyright © 1986 by Donald Carrick. Reproduced by permission of Houghton Mifflin Company./ Carrick, Paul, illustrator. From an illustration in *Mothers Are Like That*, by Carol Carrick. Clarion Books, 2000. Illustrations copyright © 2000 by Paul Carrick. Reproduced by permission of Houghton Mifflin Company.

CHARBONNEAU, EILEEN. Charbonneau, Eileen, photograph. Reproduced by permission./ Doughty, Thomas, illustrator. From a cover of *The Randolph Legacy*, by Eileen Charbonneau. Tom Doherty Associates, LLC., 1997. Reproduced by permission./ Royo, illustrator. From a cover of *Rachel LeMoyne*, by Eileen Charbonneau. Tom Doherty Associates, LLC, 1998. Copyright © 1998, by Eileen Charbonneau. Reproduced by permission./ Waldman, Neil, illustrator. From a cover of *The Ghosts of Stony Clove*, by Eileen Charbonneau. Tom Doherty Associates, LLC., 1995. Copyright © 1988 by Eileen Charbonneau. All rights reserved, including the right to reproduce this book, or any portion thereof, in any form. Reproduced by permission.

CHEESE, CHLOE. Cheese, Chloe, photograph by Barbara Bellingham. Reproduced by permission.

COVILLE, BRUCE. Coville, Bruce, photograph by Jules Fried. Reproduced by permission of Photography by Jules./ Oberheide, Heide, illustrator. From the cover of *Fortune's Journey*, by Bruce Coville. BridgeWater Paperback, 1995. Cover illustration © Heide Oberheide. Reproduced by permission of Troll Communications, LLC./ Vojnar, Kamil, illustrator. From a jacket of *Armageddon Summer*, by Jane Yolen and Bruce Coville. Harcourt Brace & Company, 1998. Copyright © 1998 Jane Yolen and Bruce Coville. Jacket photograph © by Kamil Vojar/Photonica. Reproduced by permission of Harcourt, Inc.

COWLEY, JOY. All photographs reproduced by permission by permission of the author.

CUTLER, JANE. Karas, G. Brian, illustrator. From an illustration in *Mr. Carey's Garden*, by Jane Cutler. Houghton Mifflin Company, 1996. Illustrations copyright © 1996 by G. Brian Karas. Reproduced by Houghton Mifflin Company./ Pearson, Tracey Campbell, illustrator. From an illustration in *'Gator Aid*, by Jane Cutler. Farrar Straus & Giroux, 1999. Illustrations copyright © 1999 by Tracey Campbell Pearson. Reproduced by permission of Farrar Straus & Giroux, a division of Farrar, Straus and Giroux, LLC.

SOMETHING ABOUT THE AUTHOR

ALLEN, Alex B.
  See HEIDE, Florence Parry

*   *   *

ARNOSKY, Jim 1946-

Personal

Full name, James Edward Arnosky; born September 1, 1946, in New York, NY; son of Edward J. (a draftsman) and Marie (maiden name, Telesco) Arnosky; married Deanna L. Eshelman, August 6, 1966; children: Michelle, Amber. *Hobbies and other interests:* Collecting old fishing tackle and old boats, "not classic boats—just lovely old boats."

Addresses

Home—South Ryegate, VT 05069.

Career

Draftsman in Philadelphia, PA, 1964; Braceland Brothers (printers), Philadelphia, art trainee, 1965-66, creative artist, 1968-72; freelance illustrator and writer, 1972—. *Exhibitions:* Cricket's Traveling Illustrators' Exhibitions. *Military service:* U.S. Navy, 1966-68; U.S. Navy Reserves, 1968-72.

Awards, Honors

Outstanding Science Book Award, American Association of Science Teachers, 1978, for *Possum Baby;* Outstanding Science Books of 1979, National Science Teachers Association and the Children's Book Council, for *Crinkleroot's Animal Tracks and Wildlife Signs* and *Moose Baby;* Christopher Award, Children's Science Book honorable mention, New York Academy of Sciences, both 1983, both for *Drawing from Nature; Washington Post*/Children's Book Guild nonfiction award, 1988; Eva L. Gordon Award, American Nature Study Society, 1991.

Writings

SELF-ILLUSTRATED CHILDREN'S BOOKS

I Was Born in a Tree and Raised by Bees, Putnam, 1977.
Outdoors on Foot, Coward, 1978.
Nathaniel, Addison-Wesley, 1978.
Crinkleroot's Animal Tracks and Wildlife Signs, Putnam, 1979, revised edition published as *Crinkleroot's Book of Animal Tracking,* Bradbury, 1989.
A Kettle of Hawks and Other Wildlife Groups, Coward, 1979.
Mudtime and More: Nathaniel Stories, Addison-Wesley, 1979.
Drawing from Nature, Lothrop, 1982.
Freshwater Fish and Fishing, Four Winds, 1982.
Mouse Numbers and Letters, Harcourt, 1982, reprinted as *Mouse Numbers* and *Mouse Letters,* Clarion, 1999.
Secrets of a Wildlife Watcher, Lothrop, 1983.
Mouse Writing, Harcourt, 1983.

Drawing Life in Motion, Lothrop, 1984.
Watching Foxes, Lothrop, 1985.
Deer at the Brook, Lothrop, 1986.
Flies in the Water, Fish in the Air: A Personal Introduction to Fly Fishing, Lothrop, 1986.
Raccoons and Ripe Corn, Lothrop, 1987.
Sketching Outdoors in Spring, Lothrop, 1987.
Sketching Outdoors in Summer, Lothrop, 1988.
Sketching Outdoors in Autumn, Lothrop, 1988.
Sketching Outdoors in Winter, Lothrop, 1988.
Gray Boy, Lothrop, 1988.
Come Out, Muskrats, Lothrop, 1989.
In the Forest, edited by Dorothy Briley, Lothrop, 1989.
Crinkleroot's Guide to Walking in Wild Places, Bradbury, 1990.
Near the Sea: A Portfolio of Paintings, Lothrop, 1990.
Fish in a Flash! A Personal Guide to Spin-Fishing, Bradbury, 1991.
Crinkleroot's Guide to Knowing the Birds, Bradbury, 1992.
Otters under Water, Putnam, 1992.
Long Spikes: A Story, Clarion, 1992.
Crinkleroot's Guide to Knowing the Trees, Bradbury, 1992.
Every Autumn Comes the Bear, Putnam, 1993.
Sketching Outdoors in All Seasons, Countryman, 1993.
Crinkleroot's 25 Birds Every Child Should Know, Bradbury, 1993.
Crinkleroot's 25 Fish Every Child Should Know, Bradbury, 1993.
Crinkleroot's 25 Mammals Every Child Should Know, Bradbury, 1994.
Crinkleroot's 25 More Animals Every Child Should Know, Bradbury, 1994.
All about Alligators, Scholastic, 1994.
All Night Near the Water, Putnam, 1994.
I See Animals Hiding, Scholastic, 1995.
All about Owls, Scholastic, 1995.
Little Champ, Putnam, 1995.
All about Deer, Scholastic, 1996.
Nearer Nature, Lothrop, 1996.
Rabbits and Raindrops, Putnam, 1997.
Crinkleroot's Guide to Knowing Animal Habitats, Simon & Schuster, 1997.
Crinkleroot's Guide to Knowing Butterflies and Moths, Simon & Schuster, 1997.
All about Rattlesnakes, Scholastic, 1997.
Animal Tracker, Random House, 1997.
Bird Watcher, Random House, 1997.
Bring 'Em Back Alive!: Capturing Wildlife on Home Video, Little, Brown, 1997.
Bug Hunter, Random House, 1997.
Shore Walker, Random House, 1997.
Watching Water Birds, National Geographic Society, 1997.
Little Lions, Putnam, 1998.
All about Turkeys, Scholastic, 1998.
Watching Desert Wildlife, National Geographic Society, 1998.
Crinkleroot's Visit to Crinkle Cove, Simon & Schuster, 1998.
Arnosky's Ark: Beginning a New Century with Old Friends, National Geographic Society, 1999.
The Wild Coast, Morrow, 1999.
The Wild Desert, Morrow, 1999.
The Wild Plains, Morrow, 1999.

Crinkleroot's Nature Almanac, Simon & Schuster, 1999.
Big Jim and the White-Legged Moose, Lothrop, 1999.
All about Turtles, Scholastic, 2000.
Rattlesnake Dance, Putnam, 2000.
Wild and Swampy: Exploring with Jim Arnosky, Morrow, 2000.
A Manatee Morning, Simon & Schuster, 2000.
Climbing Crinkle Mountain, Simon & Schuster, 2001.

ILLUSTRATOR

Melvin Berger and Gilda Berger, *Fitting In: Animals in Their Habitats,* Coward, 1976.
Miska Miles, *Swim, Little Duck,* Atlantic Monthly Press, 1976.
Miles, *Chicken Forgets,* Atlantic Monthly Press, 1976.
Miles, *Small Rabbit,* Atlantic Monthly Press, 1977.
Marcel Sislowitz, *Look: How Your Eyes See,* Coward, 1977.
Berniece Freschet, *Porcupine Baby,* Putnam, 1978.
Freschet, *Possum Baby,* Putnam, 1978.
Kaye Starbird, *The Covered Bridge House, and Other Poems,* Four Winds, 1979.
Freschet, *Moose Baby,* Putnam, 1979.
Eloise Jarvis McGraw, *Joel and the Great Merlini,* Knopf, 1979.
(With Lydia Dabcovich and Charles Mikolaycak) Richard Kennedy, *Delta Baby and Two Sea Songs,* Addison-Wesley, 1979.
Michael New, *The Year of the Apple,* Addison-Wesley, 1980.
Betty Boegehold, *Bear Underground,* Doubleday, 1980.
Ann E. Weiss, *What's That You Said?: How Words Change,* Harcourt, 1980.
A. R. Swinnerton, *Rocky the Cat,* Addison-Wesley, 1981.
Freschet, *Black Bear Baby,* Putnam, 1981.
Margaret Bartlett and Preston Bassett, *Raindrop Stories,* Four Winds, 1981.
Boegehold, *Chipper's Choices,* Coward, 1981.
Joan Hiatt Harlow, *Shadow Bear,* Doubleday, 1981.
Anne Rockwell, *Up a Tall Tree,* Doubleday, 1981.
Freschet, *Wood Duck Baby,* Putnam, 1983.
Honore de Balzac, *A Passion in the Desert,* Creative Education, 1983.
Freschet, *Raccoon Baby,* Putnam, 1984.
Dale H. Fife, *The Empty Lot,* Sierra Club, 1991.

Adaptations

A four-part television series, *Drawing from Nature,* featuring Jim Arnosky and based on his books *Drawing from Nature* and *Drawing Life in Motion,* was produced by the Public Broadcasting Service (PBS) in 1987; Crinkleroot, Arnosky's fictional character, has been featured on PBS's *Backyard Safari* series.

Sidelights

An inveterate observer of nature and a skilled artist, Jim Arnosky has blended these proclivities and talents to create almost seventy picture book titles about wildlife and nature. His informal and anecdotal style has been put to the service of fictional renderings, but primarily Arnosky is an informational and instructional writer-illustrator. His books present facts from how to fish to how to draw nature; from tracking deer to observing raccoons. His popular Crinkleroot character, adopted in his very first children's book, has proven to be a staple for Arnosky, appearing in sixteen of his books, introducing animal facts to young readers through the guise of a grandfatherly woodsman. Arnosky's books on sketching from nature, including *Drawing from Nature* and *Drawing Life in Motion,* also inspired a four-part television series from Public Broadcasting Service (PBS).

Arnosky has detailed the life cycle of animals from manatees to rattlesnakes, and has been praised by critics for his clear explanations and finely detailed drawings. Critics have also frequently observed that although Arnosky's books initially set out to introduce a particular outdoor activity, their end result is to fully reorient their readers to the natural world by presenting new ways of seeing and participating in it. *Booklist* critic Linda Callaghan commented in her review of *Flies in the Water, Fish in the Air: A Personal Introduction to Fly Fishing:* "Blending the beauty of nature with the joy of sport, Arnosky leaves no doubt that fishing is an art form, a reverent pilgrimage in which the respectful and observant are rewarded." Callaghan added that this book is "a pleasure to the eye, the mind, and the soul." Similarly, *School Library Journal* contributor Patricia Homer wrote that Arnosky's *Drawing from Nature* is "a spiritual sharing of ideas and techniques by a gifted wildlife artist.... Arnosky's goal seems to be to teach young readers how to see as an artist would, and observe as a naturalist would. He succeeds beautifully."

Arnosky, a naturalist in both private and professional life, makes little distinction between work and leisure. He lives in northern Vermont with his wife and two daughters, where the family grows its own food and spins yarn from the wool of the sheep they rear. Arnosky spends most of his days rambling through whatever habitat he is observing for his books. "The life I live is a reward in itself," the author remarked in *Horn Book.* "I have no weekdays or weekends. I look forward to every day. Except for family events and rare occasions, my schedule is determined by the activities of the animals I choose to study. Few people are able to follow their instincts as truly as I follow mine. I write about the world I live in and I try to share all I see and feel in my books."

In 1977, Arnosky introduced the character of Crinkleroot in *I Was Born in a Tree and Raised by Bees.* In this debut book, old Crinkleroot, a forest dweller, takes the reader through four seasons of life in the wild, pointing out bits of that life which most observers would miss. "Crinkleroot is a backwoods gnome who introduces readers to simple nature information and experiences," according to Susan Sprague in her *School Library Journal* review. The subject matter of *I Was Born in a Tree and Raised by Bees* is very inclusive; according to a *Kirkus Reviews* contributor, "Crinkleroot's tour mixes ... hidden pictures with project suggestions ... a mini-lecture on interdependence ... and random notes" on a variety of subjects. Arnosky once commented that

"Crinkleroot is a vehicle I use to express the teacher and father in me. He is an old grandfatherly woodsman who knows endless wonders about the natural world and teaches them to his readers through activities they can join in."

Crinkleroot has continued in this function in several subsequent works, including *Crinkleroot's Guide to Knowing Butterflies and Moths* which *Booklist*'s Carolyn Phelan has called an "appealing, practical cross between a picture book and field guide." Such books deal with birds, trees, mammals, and tracking, all told by the benevolent, Santa-like woodsman. "Arnosky's text is a felicitous blending of spare, elegant description and homey conversation," noted Margaret A. Bush in a *Horn Book* review of *Crinkleroot's Guide to Walking in Wild Places.* With his 1992 *Crinkleroot's Guide to Knowing the Birds,* "Arnosky has created another wonderful nature guide featuring his lovable woodsman," according to *Booklist* critic Chris Sherman. Of the 1997 *Crinkleroot's Guide to Knowing Animal Habitats,* Helen Rosenberg wrote in *School Library Journal* that the book was "crammed full of information and delightfully presented with appealing watercolor illustrations." Reviewing Arnosky's *Crinkleroot's Visit to Crinkle Cove,* Rosenberg noted in *Booklist* that "everyone's favorite woodsman and nature guide" takes a different approach. Instead of focusing on one aspect of nature or one animal, he looks at a cross-section and sees how nature is interconnected.

Arnosky observes nature by participating in it, while fishing, drawing, or walking. In the introduction to his 1990 book, *Near the Sea: A Portfolio of Paintings,* he

Old Crinkleroot, the forest-dwelling protagonist of several Arnosky books, provides readers with a lesson in the interconnection of all living things through his detailed observation of a small, special habitat in which he searches for his friend, Sassafrass the Snake. (From Crinkleroot's Visit to Crinkle Cove, *written and illustrated by Arnosky.)*

provides a glimpse of the working relationship he developed with the environment he was painting during a two-week visit to a Maine island. "The first few days, beginning a painting at low tide, I found myself having to move my easel ever backward as the tide returned and flooded the land around me. Eventually, timing my outings according to the ebb and flow of the tide, I was able to work in the slow, sure, deliberate rhythm of life near the sea." Constant interaction has given Arnosky the special connection with nature that is so frequently noted in his work. "Over the past twenty years I have developed an intimate relationship with my subject matter," he commented in *Horn Book.* "Through my study of nature I have become convinced that every little thing is part of some whole and that if you look closely enough and think well enough, you will recognize the scheme of things. You may even find a place for yourself in that order. I have found my place. It is outdoors near the earth and its waters, near the birds and beasts."

In most of his books, Arnosky's personal approach manifests as an invitation to readers to see and understand nature through his eyes. His award-winning 1982 book, *Drawing from Nature,* received accolades from reviewers for its well-presented insights into how a naturalist and artist views his subject matter. Reviewing the companion book, *Drawing Life in Motion, Booklist*'s Denise M. Wilms remarked that the text "cultivates an appreciation for careful observation of the natural world." Writing of both volumes in *Voice of Youth Advocates,* Delia A. Culberson noted, "Every page ... is a lesson not only in the fine art of drawing but also in careful, almost microscopic, observation."

The television series spawned by these books featured Arnosky at work, spontaneously drawing various natural subjects. Arnosky told Kimberly Olson Fakih of *Publishers Weekly* that he chose to demonstrate his work via television because "a real person is always much more interesting to a reader than the book, someone who is in *love* with nature and wants to share that love." But Arnosky does not see himself as the focus of this series any more than he is the focus of his "autobiographical" books; rather, he feels that he functions as a link between his audience and nature. He introduces and explains his subject to his viewers, he told Fakih, "and then I'll fade out of their minds, and they'll be left looking. The best nonfiction lets the reader knock on the door, and you let them in. Then you go away."

Other how-to drawing books from Arnosky include his seasonal "Sketching Outdoors" titles. Reviewing *Sketching Outdoors in Spring, Horn Book* reviewer Anita Silvey claimed the book "celebrates ... the artist's craft and this artist's method of drawing what he sees." Arnosky's *Sketching Outdoors in Autumn* and *Sketching Outdoors in Winter* complete "his splendid cycle of seasons," according to *School Library Journal* contributor Eleanor K. MacDonald, "guiding young artists and naturalists through the delicate growth of spring to the freezing depths of winter."

Other popular how-to titles from Arnosky include his three books of fishing techniques, *Freshwater Fish and Fishing, Flies in the Water, Fish in the Air: A Personal Introduction to Fly Fishing,* and *Fish in a Flash! A Personal Guide to Spin-Fishing.* Reviewing the last title, *Horn Book* critic Bush wondered, "Who but Jim Arnosky could convey such a sense of excitement and fun in an instructional guide to spin-fishing?" Bush further observed that Arnosky's writing is marked by "a measured economy and with great respect for his subject and audience."

Arnosky continues to lead young readers to a heightened awareness of the natural world with his instructional books. In his 1983 publication, *Secrets of a Wildlife Watcher,* Arnosky shares some of his nature-watching methods, providing "how-to" tips as well as information on animal behavior. In her *Appraisal: Children's Science Books* review, Carolyn Noah remarked that "Arnosky's delight in wildlife, and the effectiveness with which he conveys it, conspire to lure the young naturalist, book in hand, out into the wild." A quote from physicist Albert Einstein that serves as the epigram to *Secrets of a Wildlife Watcher*—"Joy in looking and comprehending is nature's most beautiful gift"—has been cited by several critics as a singularly well-suited motto for Arnosky's work.

Arnosky's "All About" series continues this blending of entertainment with instruction. In a spate of books dealing with various animals from rattlesnakes to turtles, Arnosky provides young readers with pertinent information from behavior to structure. *Booklist*'s Hazel Rochman commented favorably on *All about Alligators,* the first book in the series, noting that "Arnosky's clear text and handsome watercolors convey a sense of wonder." Susan Oliver, writing in *School Library Journal,* remarked of *All about Deer* that the "author's wonderfully simple and enticing style ensures that children will look at these wild animals with both wonder and understanding." And reviewing the sixth book in the series, *All about Turtles, Booklist*'s Kay Weisman concluded, "Succinct, yet full of details, this is a good introduction for browsers and young researchers." Arnosky also provides excellent introductions to water fowl and desert habitats in his *Watching Water Birds* and *Watching Desert Wildlife.* Reviewing the latter title, *Horn Book* critic Bush wrote, "Jim Arnosky here makes his first foray into the desert and creates an exquisite introduction to desert wildlife."

In his many picture books about animals, Arnosky conveys his subjects as he observes them in his studies, relying more on his accurate and detailed illustrations than on his sparse and well-chosen words to tell the story of the animal's existence. Although a few reviewers have regretted the lack of a conventional story line in these books, Arnosky is often praised for telling animals' stories without romanticizing or humanizing them. The raccoons in his picture book *Raccoons and Ripe Corn,* for example, are considered captivating subjects by critics, but they are not presented as cute or cuddly animals. "These raccoons are greedy and some-

In All about Turtles, *a title from his series of self-illustrated instructional books about various animals, Arnosky discusses many facts about turtles, from physical attributes to life cycles and habitat.*

what destructive," *Booklist* contributor Denise M. Wilms commented. "A close-up of one of them gnawing an ear of corn has an undercurrent of ferocity."

A bear that arrived near his Vermont home each year is the subject of *Every Autumn Comes the Bear,* "real natural history in a lovely book," according to a contributor for *Kirkus Reviews.* A mother mountain lion and her young provide the focus for *Little Lions,* a picture book that is "a fine combination of dignity and playfulness," according to *Booklist*'s Phelan. Arnosky tells a tall tale in his 1999 *Big Jim and the White-Legged Moose,* in which the author has a close encounter with a moose. *Booklist* reviewer Susan Dove Lempke commented, "Arnosky has written a ballad and put it into picture-book form."

A departure for Arnosky, who writes mainly picture books, is his *Nearer Nature,* a collection of essays chronicling part of a year in the life around his home in Vermont. "Arnosky's very special insights, patient observations, and fluent writing make this a book to learn from, delight in, and savor," wrote Diane Tuccillo in a *Voice of Youth Advocates* review. "There are few authors who write this kind of material for a teen audience," Tuccillo further commented. "A treat for the eye and the spirit, this is a book for the unique young adult who enjoys nature writing."

Realizing that many of his readers do not have ready access to the kind of wilderness in which he lives and works, Arnosky often writes about natural environments that can still be found in or near urban areas. Although he is concerned about water and air pollution and the destruction of the wilderness and its inhabitants, Arnosky is more intent on helping his young readers discover

the existing wonders of the natural world than on warning them of the dangers that face it. He once told *SATA:* "I feel strongly that, contrary to present feelings about the future—about wildlife, ourselves, and our environment and the popular illusion of seeing everything headed down some vast drain in a hurry—that the first part of a better tomorrow is the awakening to our problems today. Our children, and their children, are headed for an even better future—where man may have a closer, working relationship with his natural world." Such a view is also present in *Arnosky's Ark,* in which Arnosky "celebrates a century of conservation efforts," according to Shelle Rosenfeld, writing in *Booklist.* Arnosky writes of thirteen types of animals he loves which are or were once on the endangered species list. "In engaging, reader-friendly prose, he relates survival stories," Rosenfeld wrote.

Works Cited

Arnosky, Jim, "The Moon in My Net," *Horn Book,* September-October, 1989.

Arnosky, Jim, introduction to *Near the Sea: A Portfolio of Paintings,* Lothrop, 1990, p. 7.

Bush, Margaret A., review of *Crinkleroot's Guide to Walking in Wild Places, Horn Book,* November-December, 1990, p. 757.

Bush, Margaret A., review of *Fish in a Flash!, Horn Book,* September-October, 1991, pp. 608-09.

Bush, Margaret A., review of *Watching Desert Wildlife, Horn Book,* November-December, 1998, p. 751.

Callaghan, Linda, review of *Flies in the Water, Fish in the Air: A Personal Introduction to Fly Fishing, Booklist,* July, 1986, p. 1618.

Culberson, Delia A., review of *Drawing from Nature* and *Drawing Life in Motion, Voice of Youth Advocates,* October, 1987, p. 183.

Review of *Every Autumn Comes the Bear, Kirkus Reviews,* October 15, 1993, p. 1325

Fakih, Kimberly Olson, "Watching the Artist Watch Nature," *Publishers Weekly,* May 29, 1987, pp. 43-44.

Homer, Patricia, review of *Drawing from Nature, School Library Journal,* January, 1983, p. 70.

Review of *I Was Born in a Tree and Raised by Bees, Kirkus Reviews,* December 1, 1976, p. 1261.

Lempke, Susan Dove, review of *Big Jim and the White-Legged Moose, Booklist,* August, 1999, p. 2062.

MacDonald, Eleanor K., review of *Sketching Outdoors in Autumn* and *Sketching Outdoors in Winter, School Library Journal,* December, 1988, p. 114.

Noah, Carolyn, review of *Secrets of a Wildlife Watcher, Appraisal: Children's Science Books,* winter, 1984, p. 7.

Oliver, Susan, review of *All about Deer, School Library Journal,* September, 1996, p. 195.

Phelan, Carolyn, review of *Crinkleroot's Guide to Knowing Butterflies and Moths, Booklist,* May 1, 1996, p. 1508.

Phelan, Carolyn, review of *Little Lions, Booklist,* March 1, 1998, p. 1139.

Rochman, Hazel, review of *All about Alligators, Booklist,* August, 1994, p. 2045.

Rosenberg, Helen, review of _Crinkleroot's Guide to Knowing Animal Habitats, School Library Journal,_ June, 1997, p. 105.

Rosenberg, Helen, review of _Crinkleroot's Visit to Crinkle Cove, Booklist,_ August, 1998, p. 2012.

Rosenfeld, Shelle, review of _Arnosky's Ark, Booklist,_ November 15, 1999, p. 630.

Sherman, Chris, review of _Crinkleroot's Guide to Knowing the Birds, Booklist,_ October 15, 1992, p. 432.

Silvey, Anita, review of _Sketching Outdoors in Spring, Horn Book,_ May-June, 1987, p. 355.

Sprague, Susan, review of _I Was Born in a Tree and Raised by Bees, School Library Journal,_ March, 1977, p. 128.

Tuccillo, Diane, review of _Nearer Nature, Voice of Youth Advocates,_ April, 1997, p. 50.

Weisman, Kay, review of _All about Turtles, Booklist,_ February 1, 2000, p. 1024.

Wilms, Denise M., review of _Drawing Life in Motion, Booklist,_ October 1, 1983, p. 214.

Wilms, Denise M., review of _Raccoons and Ripe Corn, Booklist,_ September 1, 1987, p. 58.

For More Information See

BOOKS

Authors of Books for Young People, 3rd edition, Scarecrow, 1990.

Children's Books and Their Creators, edited by Anita Silvey, Houghton Mifflin, 1995.

Children's Literature Review, Vol. 15, Gale, 1988, pp. 1-11.

PERIODICALS

Booklist, September 1, 1995, p. 79; September 15, 1996, p. 243; May 1, 1997, p. 1489; June 1, 1997, p. 1708; December 1, 1997, p. 625; October 15, 1998, p. 423.

Bulletin of the Center for Children's Books, July-August, 1978; May, 1986; March, 1988; April, 1992, p. 198; March, 1997, p. 239; May, 1999, p. 307.

Horn Book, September-October, 1990, p. 616; March-April, 1995, p. 219; March-April, 1996, p. 220; September-October, 1997, p. 589; January-February, 1998, p. 88.

New York Times Book Review, August 30, 1995, p. 19.

Publishers Weekly, March 19, 1982, p. 70; September 12, 1994, p. 89; October 27, 1997, p. 79; August 3, 1998, p. 87; January 18, 1999, p. 341; March 29, 1999, p. 106; May 31, 1999, p. 92.

School Library Journal, November, 1990, p. 102; November, 1992, pp. 81-82; April, 1995, p. 121; November, 1996, p. 127; March, 1997, p. 148; June, 1997, p. 130; March, 1998, p. 166; August, 1998, p. 132; November, 1998, p. 101; June, 1999, p. 110.*

ARTHUR, Robert (Jr.) 1909-1969 (Andrew Benedict, Andrew Fall, A. A. Fleming, Robert Forbes, Andrew McCullen, Anthony Morton, The Mysterious Traveler, Jay Norman, Andrew Saxon, Pauline C. Smith, Andrew West, John West, Mark Williams)

Personal

Born November 10, 1909, at Fort Mills, Corregidor Island, the Philippines; died May 2, 1969, in Philadelphia, PA; son of Robert Arthur, Sr. and Sarah Fee Arthur; married Susan Smith Cleveland, 1938 (divorced, 1940); married Joan Vaczek, 1946 (divorced, 1959); children (second marriage): Robert Andrew and Elizabeth Ann. _Education:_ Attended William and Mary College, 1926-28; University of Michigan, B.A. (English, with distinction), 1930, M.A. (journalism), 1932.

Career

Contributor of short stories to pulp fiction magazines; editor of _Pocket Detective_ (magazine), Street & Smith, 1936-37; copy editor and head writer, _Parade_ (magazine), 1942-44; scriptwriter, producer, and director, Mutual Broadcasting System, 1944-52; managing editor, Waverly Publishing Company, 1946-48; producer, _Dark Destiny_ (television series), 1948-51; co-producer, _Mystery Time_ (radio series), 1952-53; _The Mysterious Traveler_ (magazine), editor, 1951-52; scriptwriter and story editor, _The Twilight Zone_ (television series) and _Alfred Hitchcock Presents_ (television series), 1959-62.

Awards, Honors

Edgar Award for Best Mystery Radio Show, Mystery Writers of America, 1952 and 1953, for _The Mysterious Traveler;_ New Jersey Authors Award, 1967, for _Spies and More Spies._

Writings

"ALFRED HITCHCOCK AND THE THREE INVESTIGATORS" MYSTERY SERIES

The Secret of Terror Castle, Random House, 1964.

The Mystery of the Stuttering Parrot, Random House, 1964.

The Mystery of the Green Ghost, Random House, 1965.

The Mystery of the Whispering Mummy, Random House, 1965.

The Mystery of the Vanishing Treasure, Random House, 1966.

The Secret of Skeleton Island, Random House, 1966.

The Mystery of the Fiery Eye, Random House, 1967.

The Mystery of the Silver Spider, Random House, 1967.

The Mystery of the Screaming Clock, Random House, 1968.

The Mystery of the Talking Skull, Random House, 1969.

The Three Investigators match wits with master criminals in their search for a stolen jewel-encrusted Japanese belt in this installment of Robert Arthur's popular series. (Cover illustration by Bill Dodge.)

OTHER

Moon-Up (play), Samuel French, 1947.
Epitaph for a Virgin (novel), Mercury Mystery Book-Magazine, 1956, published as *Somebody's Walking on My Grave*, Ace, 1961.
Ghosts and More Ghosts (short stories), Random House, 1963.
Mystery and More Mystery (short stories), Random House, 1966.

Uncredited author of *Alfred Hitchock's Solve-Them-Yourself-Mysteries*, a collection of short stories, published by Random House, 1963.

Contributor of hundreds of short stories to periodicals, including *Argosy, Wonder Stories, Thrilling Wonder Stories, Astonishing Stories, Astounding Science-Fiction, Unknown Worlds, A. Merritt's Fantasy Magazine, Asteroid, Detective Novels Magazine, MacLean's Magazine, Household Magazine, Detective Fiction Weekly, Popular Detective, Weird Tales, Mystery, The Illustrated Detective Magazine, Street & Smith's Detective Story Magazine, Amazing Stories, The Shadow, Street & Smith's*

Mystery Reader, Detective Tales, Thrilling Detective, Double Detective, Startling Stories, Collier's, The Phantom Detective, Unknown Worlds, and *Black Mask*. Many of Arthur's short stories appeared under the pseudonyms Andrew Benedict, Andrew Fall, A. A. Fleming, Robert Forbes, Andrew McCullen, Anthony Morton, The Mysterious Traveler, Jay Norman, Andrew Saxon, Pauline C. Smith, Andrew West, John West, and Mark Williams.

Arthur also wrote more than five hundred radio scripts, some adapted from his own short stories, for *The Mysterious Traveler, Adventure into Fear, The Shadow,* and *Nick Carter*. Additionally, in the early 1960s, he wrote teleplays for *Alfred Hitchcock Presents* and *The Twilight Zone*.

EDITOR

Davey Jones' Haunted Locker: Great Ghost Stories of the Sea, Random House, 1965.
Cloak and Dagger: Ten Thrilling Stories of Espionage, Dell Mayflower, 1967.
Spies and More Spies, Random House, 1967.
Thrillers and More Thrillers, Random House, 1968.

Uncredited editor for many of the "Alfred Hitchcock Presents" anthologies for Random House, including *Stories for Late at Night,* 1961, *Stories My Mother Never Told Me,* 1963, *Stories Not for the Nervous,* 1965, *Stories That Scared Even Me* (with Thomas Disch), 1967, and *Stories They Wouldn't Let Me Do on TV,* 1968. Also uncredited editor of a series of anthologies for young readers published by Random House, including *Alfred Hitchcock's Haunted Houseful,* 1961, *Alfred Hitchcock's Ghostly Gallery,* 1962, *Alfred Hitchcock's Monster Museum,* 1965, *Alfred Hitchcock's Sinister Spies,* 1966, *Alfred Hitchcock's Spellbinders in Suspense,* 1967, and *Alfred Hitchcock's Daring Detectives,* 1969.

Sidelights

American author Robert Arthur is best known as the creator of the popular young-adult mystery series "Alfred Hitchcock and the Three Investigators" (now known as "The Three Investigators"). The culmination of his long experience as a mystery writer, and inspired in part by Arthur Conan Doyle's Sherlock Holmes stories, Arthur's mysteries are strictly logical. Many readers, now adults, have credited the series with both their love of reading and their interest in science, mathematics, and systematic thought.

The heroes of "The Three Investigators" series are unusually distinctive and feature a depth of character that is not normally associated with children's series fiction. Jupiter Jones, First Investigator, though extremely smart—the "brains" of the operation—is overweight, and sometimes condescending; his intellect is matched by his energy, and once on a case he is tenacious and determined. Pete Crenshaw, Second Investigator, although good-looking and athletic, is easily frightened; he is loyal, however, and always comes through in the end. Bob Andrews, Records and Research, is slight and studious. All three boys come from middle-class or blue-collar backgrounds.

The three young sleuths rely on cunning, creativity, and logic to solve complicated crimes and intrigues involving lost treasures, eccentric clients, evil criminals, and apparent supernatural menaces that prove to have rational explanations. In some ways, "The Three Investigators" book series has proven, in the years since its original publication, to have been ahead of its time. When the first books were originally published in the 1960's, reviewers of the books were guarded in their comments. "Entertaining and somewhat melodramatic adventures, enhanced as usual with the methods of real detective work," was how a reviewer for *Library Journal* described the 1967 publication of *The Mystery of the Fiery Eye,* in which the trio helps a young friend decipher a cryptically worded will and claim a fabled jewel for his inheritance.

The same commentator, appraising a plot built around the theft of an exotic royal family heirloom in *The Mystery of the Silver Spider,* wrote: "This author has the knack of making the outrageous seem plausible." Even

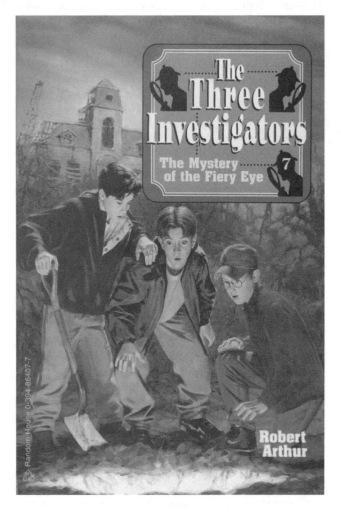

Jupiter, Pete, and Bob race against fortune hunters to solve a riddle and uncover a treasure for a friend. (Cover illustration by Bill Dodge.)

an "unlikely" tale such as *The Mystery of the Vanishing Treasure,* in which the detectives solve a mystery involving an author of children's stories who is bedeviled by gnomes out of the illustrations for her books, impressed the reviewer as "amusing and strictly logical."

Readers of the books have been decidedly more enthusiastic. In response to the 1998 reprinting of the Arthur books, purchasers of copies at the bookseller *Amazon.com* have posted notes on-line. Adults who read the books at the time of their original publication remember waiting impatiently for library copies of new books to become available. Some recall forming their own detective agencies, and printing business cards similar to the ones the boys used. Though the heroes of "The Three Investigators" were male, the fans of the series seem to have had a large number of girls in their ranks. In their comments on the series, readers repeatedly credit "The Three Investigators" books with giving them a life-long love of reading, and many state that they continue to enjoy the books as adults.

From 1964 until his death, Arthur wrote two titles a year for the series. In 1968, he brought in Dennis Lynds as an additional author, and after Arthur's death in 1969, "The Three Investigators" series was continued in the United States until 1987 by several writers, including Dennis Lynds, under the pseudonym William Arden; Mary Carey, under the pseudonym M. V. Carey; and Marc Brandel. All in all, there are forty-three titles in the original series. These were followed by the "Find-Your-Fate" mysteries—of which four were "Three Investigators" titles—and by the unsuccessful "Crimebusters" series.

Because "The Three Investigators" books are old-fashioned mystery adventures, they have proven to be remarkably durable. Arthur's titles were reissued by Random House beginning in 1998. The series' titles have sold over thirty million copies worldwide, and have been translated into Spanish, French, German, Japanese, Swedish, and many other languages. In 1993, the series was revived in Germany as "Die Drei Fragezeichen," and between 1993 and 2000 thirty-seven new books were published, all German language originals. It wasn't until well after Arthur's death that "Alfred Hitchcock," who appears as a minor character and the "author" of a short introduction, was dropped from the title and the series. He was replaced by the fictitious Hector Sebastian.

Before he began writing "The Three Investigators" series, Arthur had a long and varied career as a professional mystery writer working in a number of different mediums. Arthur was born on November 10, 1909, at Fort Mills, a United States Army base on Corregidor Island in the Philippines, where his father, Robert Arthur Sr., then a lieutenant in the Army, was stationed. His mother was Sara Fee Arthur, formerly of New Orleans. Arthur's childhood was spent on the move as his father was transferred from one Army base to the next. While Col. Arthur was stationed at Fort Monroe, in Hampton Roads, Virginia, Robert attended Hampton

High School, where he was elected President of his senior class. After high school, Arthur was admitted to both West Point and Annapolis but decided against a career in the military.

Instead, in the fall of 1926, he enrolled at William and Mary College in Williamsburg, Virginia. Two years later, he transferred to the University of Michigan in Ann Arbor, where he earned a bachelor's degree in English with distinction in 1930. He returned to Ann Arbor for graduate studies in journalism and completed his master's degree in 1932, after which he moved to New York City. Arthur's short story "The Terror from the Sea," which appeared in the December 1931 issue of *Wonder Stories,* was the first of hundreds of short stories he published over the next three decades in leading science-fiction, mystery, horror, and fantasy magazines like *Weird Tales, Amazing Stories, Black Mask, Thrilling Wonder Stories, The Magazine of Fantasy and Science Fiction,* and *Astounding Science-Fiction.* He also wrote a play and a novel for adults, and edited numerous anthologies of short fiction.

Some of the best of Arthur's short stories are charming fantasies with clever twists. A number of them are narrated by a character named Murchison Morks, a member of an exclusive mens' club who tells fantastic tales about people he supposedly knows. Morks' tales feature postage stamps from imaginary countries that can magically transport letters there, obstinate men who disbelieve people and places out of existence, and similar whimsical and comic premises. Originally published in *Argosy* in the 1940s, the Morks stories garnered favorable comparisons to Lord Dunsany's tales of Jorkens and Arthur C. Clarke's *Tales from the White Hart,* and were praised by the editors of the *Magazine of Fantasy and Science Fiction* as fantasies that provide the reader with "a fresh imaginative frame for his own daydreams of escape."

Arthur revised several of the Murchison Morks stories for inclusion in *Ghosts and More Ghosts,* a collection of stories for young readers published in 1963. In 1966, he published a second collection of his work revised for young readers, entitled *Mystery and More Mystery.* Anthony Boucher, reviewing this collection for the *New York Times Book Review,* wrote: "Arthur is easily one of the best puzzle-gimmick men in the business and has written an undue proportion of my own favorite detective short stories. A collection of his work (for any age) has long been overdue." A contributor in *Publishers Weekly* stated: "Robert Arthur's *Ghosts and More Ghosts* established itself with ease as one of the most popular collections of stories on bookstore shelves. His new one *Mystery and More Mystery* ... contains 10 more well-knit, well-told stories . . . . "

In 1944, Arthur turned his attention to radio and became a producer-director for the Mutual Broadcasting System, for which he wrote—with his partner David Kogan—the weekly radio show *The Mysterious Traveler. The Mysterious Traveler* was on the air from 1944 to 1952, and during that time it was rated at the top of all shows

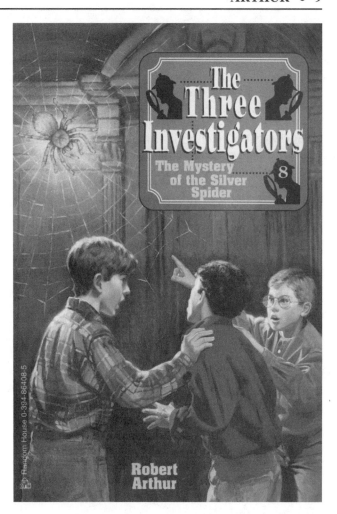

The Three Investigators need to find a jeweled silver spider in order to save the prince of Varania from his political enemies in the eighth book in the series. (Cover illustration by Bill Dodge.)

heard over the Mutual Broadcasting System, consistently outranking CBS and NBC programs broadcast in the same time slot. In a report from the Research Department of WOR Radio dated July 31, 1950, *The Mysterious Traveler* ranked first out of the sixteen most popular shows on radio. Arthur and Kogan were honored for their work on *The Mysterious Traveler* with an Edgar Allan Poe Award from the Mystery Writers of America for the Best Mystery Radio Show of the Year in 1952 and 1953.

In 1959 Arthur moved to Hollywood to work in television. He wrote scripts for *The Twilight Zone,* and he worked as a story editor and script writer for Alfred Hitchcock's TV show, *Alfred Hitchcock Presents.* Because of his work with Hitchcock, Arthur was approached by Random House to edit a series of literary anthologies designed to capitalize on Hitchcock's popularity. Drawing on his background of mystery and suspense writing, as well as his knowledge of the pulp magazines in which so many of the classic stories first appeared, Arthur put together a series of popular adult anthologies, the first of which was published in 1961.

The "Alfred Hitchcock Presents" series included *Stories for Late at Night, Stories My Mother Never Told Me, Stories Not for the Nervous, Stories That Scared Even Me,* and *Stories They Wouldn't Let Me Do on TV.* In 1962, he moved to Cape May, New Jersey.

While editing the "Alfred Hitchcock Presents" titles, Arthur was also involved in editing a series of anthologies for younger readers that included *Alfred Hitchcock's Haunted Houseful, Alfred Hitchcock's Ghostly Gallery, Alfred Hitchcock's Monster Museum, Alfred Hitchcock's Sinister Spies, Alfred Hitchcock's Spellbinders in Suspense,* and *Alfred Hitchcock's Daring Detectives.* The success of the early anthologies led Arthur to suggest to Walter Retan, an editor at Random House, a new children's book series that would use Hitchcock's name. The result was *Alfred Hitchcock and the Three Investigators in The Secret of Terror Castle,* published in 1964.

In addition to "The Three Investigators" series and the "Alfred Hitchcock Presents" anthologies, Arthur also edited under his own name anthologies of supernatural and suspense fiction aimed at younger readers, including *Davy Jones' Haunted Locker, Cloak and Dagger, Spies and More Spies,* and *Thrillers and More Thrillers.* Their eclectic blends of classic and contemporary fiction by writers that appeal to younger and mature readers alike prompted the reviewer of *Thrillers and More Thrillers* in *Publishers Weekly* to remark that "Arthur knows a good story when he sees it."

Works Cited

Arthur, Elizabeth and Steven Bauer, *Three Investigators Headquarters* Web site, located at http://www.threeinvestigators.net.

Boucher, Anthony, review of *Mystery and More Mystery, New York Times Book Review,* November 6, 1966, p. 68.

Magazine of Fantasy and Science Fiction, August, 1951, p. 15.

Review of *The Mystery of the Fiery Eye, The Mystery of the Silver Spider,* and *The Mystery of the Vanishing Treasure, Library Journal,* November 15, 1967, p. 4269.

Publishers Weekly, June 9, 1969, p. 46.

Russ, Lavinia, review of *Mystery and More Mystery, Publishers Weekly,* November 7, 1966, p. 66.

Review of *Thrillers and More Thrillers, Publishers Weekly,* October 7, 1968, p. 54.

For More Information See

BOOKS

Cook, Michael, *Mystery Detective and Espionage Magazines,* Greenwood Press, 1983.

Reginald, Robert, *Science Fiction and Fantasy Literature, Volume 1: A Checklist, 1700-1974,* Gale, 1979.

Tuck, Donald, *The Encyclopedia of Science Fiction and Fantasy,* Volume 1, Advent, 1974.

ON-LINE

The *Three Investigators* Readers' Web site, located at http://www.3investigators.homestead.com.

*   *   *

ASHER, Sandra Fenichel 1942- (Sandy Asher)

Personal

Born October 16, 1942, in Philadelphia, PA; daughter of Benjamin (a doctor) and Fanny (Weiner) Fenichel; married Harvey Asher (a professor), January 31, 1965; children: Benjamin, Emily. *Education:* Attended University of Pennsylvania, 1960-62; Indiana University, B.A., 1964; graduate study in child development at University of Connecticut, 1973; Drury College (now Drury University), elementary education certificate, 1974.

Addresses

Home—721 South Weller Ave., Springfield, MO 65802. *Office*—Department of Literature, Drury University, 900 North Benton, Springfield, MO 65802. *E-mail*—sasher@lib.drury.edu. *Agent*—Harold Ober Associates, Inc., 425 Madison Ave., New York, NY 10017.

Sandra Fenichel Asher

Career

WFIU-Radio, Bloomington, IN, scriptwriter, 1963-64; Ball Associates (advertising agency), Philadelphia, PA, copywriter, 1964; *Spectator,* Bloomington, drama critic, 1966-67; Drury University, Springfield, MO, instructor in creative writing, 1978-85, writer in residence, 1985—. Instructor, Institute of Children's Literature, 1986-92. Instructor in creative writing for children's programs, Summerscape, 1981-82, Artworks, 1982, and Step-Up, 1998—. Speaker at conferences, workshops, and schools. *Member:* American Alliance of Theatre and Education, International Association of Theatre for Children and Young People, Dramatists Guild, National Council of Teachers of English Assembly on Literature for Adolescents (member of board of directors, 1989-1992), Society of Children's Book Writers and Illustrators (Missouri advisor, 1986-1989; member of Board of Directors, 1989-1997), Phi Beta Kappa.

Awards, Honors

Award of excellence, Festival of Missouri Women in the Arts, 1974, for *Come Join the Circus;* honorable mention, Unitarian Universalist Religious Arts Guild, 1975, for play *Afterthoughts in Eden;* creative writing fellowship grant in playwriting, National Endowment for the Arts, 1978, for *God and a Woman;* first prize in one-act play contest, Little Theatre of Alexandria, 1983, and Street Players Theatre, 1989, for *The Grand Canyon;* first prize, Children's Musical Theater of Mobile contest, and first prize, Dubuque Fine Arts Players contest, both 1984, both for *East of the Sun/West of the Moon;* Mark Twain Award nomination, 1984, for *Just Like Jenny;* Outstanding Books for Young Adults citation, University of Iowa, and Best Books citation, Child Study Association, both 1985, both for *Missing Pieces;* best new play of the season, Maxwell Anderson Playwriting Series, 1985-86, and Ellis Memorial Award finalist, Theatre Americana, 1988, both for *Little Old Ladies in Tennis Shoes;* first prize, Center Stage New Horizons contest, 1986, first prize, Mercyhurst College National Playwrights Showcase, 1986-87, and first prize, Unpublished Play Project of the American Alliance for Theatre in Education, 1987-88, all for *God and a Woman;* Iowa Teen Award nomination, and Young Hoosier Award nomination, both 1986-87, both for *Things Are Seldom What They Seem;* Children's Theatre Indianapolis Children's Theatre Symposium playwriting awards, Indiana University/Purdue University, 1987, for *Prince Alexis and the Silver Saucer,* 1989, for *A Woman Called Truth,* and 1995, for *The Wolf and Its Shadows;* Joseph Campbell Memorial Fund Award, The Open Eye: New Stagings for Youth, 1991-92, and AATE Distinguished Play Award, 1994, both for *A Woman Called Truth;* New Play Festival Award, Actors' Guild of Lexington, 1992, for *Sunday, Sunday;* first prize, TADA! play writing contest, 1991, and first prize, Choate Rosemary Hall play writing contest, 1993, both for *Dancing with Strangers;* Outstanding Play for Young Audiences, U.S. Center of the International Association of Theaters for Children and Young People, 1993, for *A Woman Called Truth;* AATE Unpublished Play Project winner, 1994, and IUPUI/Bonderman Award, 1995, both for *The Wolf and Its Shadows;* Kennedy Center New Visions/New Voices Forum selected play, 1995, and AATE Unpublished Plays Project National Award, 1996, both for *Across the Plains;* Honorary Life Membership, Missouri Council for the Social Studies, 1998; Celebrate Literacy Award, International Reading Association, 1998-1999; Pittsburgh One-Act Play Festival winner, 1999, for *Thunder Mountain;* IUPUI/Bonderman semi-finalist and Unpublished Play Project National Award, both 1999, both for *Joan of Ark;* Pick of the Lists and National Jewish Book Award, both 1999, both for *With All My Heart, With All My Mind;* Aurand Harris Playwriting Fellowship grant, Children's Theater Foundation of America, 1999; Charlotte Chorpenning Award for a body of distinguished work in children's theater, American Alliance for Theatre and Education, 1999.

Writings

PLAYS

Come Join the Circus (one-act), produced in Springfield, MO, at Springfield Little Theatre, December, 1973.

Afterthoughts in Eden (one-act), first produced in Los Angeles, CA, at Los Angeles Feminist Theatre, February, 1975.

A Song of Sixpence (one-act), Encore Performance, 1976.

The Ballad of Two Who Flew (one-act), *Plays,* March, 1976.

How I Nearly Changed the World, but Didn't (one-act), produced in Springfield, MO, at National Organization for Women Herstory Women's Fair, November, 1977.

Witling and the Stone Princess, Plays, 1979.

Food Is Love (one-act), first produced in Springfield, MO, at Drury College, January, 1979, published in the anthology *A Grand Entrance,* Dramatic Publishing, 1999.

The Insulting Princess (one-act; first produced in Interlochen, MI, at Interlochen Arts Academy, May, 1979) Encore Performance, 1988.

The Mermaid's Tale (one-act; first produced in Interlochen, MI, at Interlochen Arts Academy, May, 1979), Encore Performance, 1988.

Dover's Domain, Pioneer Drama Service, 1980.

The Golden Cow of Chelm (one-act; produced in Springfield, MO, at United Hebrew Congregation, December, 1980), *Plays,* 1980.

Sunday, Sunday (first produced in Lafayette, IN, at Purdue University, March, 1981), Dramatic, 1994.

The Grand Canyon (one-act), first produced at the Little Theatre of Alexandria, Virginia, 1983.

Little Old Ladies in Tennis Shoes (two-act; first produced in Philadelphia, PA, at the Society Hill Playhouse, 1985), Dramatic, 1989.

East of the Sun/West of the Moon (one-act), first produced at the Children's Musical Theatre of Mobile, AL, 1985.

God and a Woman (two-act), first produced in Erie, PA, at the National Playwrights Showcase, 1987.

Prince Alexis and the Silver Saucer (one-act), first produced in Springfield, MO, at Drury College, 1987.

A Woman Called Truth (one-act; first produced in Houston, TX, at the Main Street Theatre, 1989), Dramatic, 1989, revised as *A Woman Called Truth: A Play in Two Acts Celebrating the Life of Sojourner Truth,* Dramatic, 1993.

The Wise Men of Chelm (one-act; first produced in Louisville, KY, at the Jewish Community Center, 1991) Dramatic, 1992.

Blind Dating (one-act), first produced in New York City at TADA!, 1992.

Perfect (one-act), first produced in New York City at The Open Eye: New Stagings for Youth, 1992.

Where Do You Get Your Ideas? (adapted for stage from book of same title), first produced in New York City at The Open Eye: New Stagings for Youth, 1992.

All on a Saturday Morning (one-act), first produced in Columbia, MO, 1992.

Dancing with Strangers (three one-acts, first produced in Wallingford, CT, 1993), Dramatic, 1994.

Once, in the Time of Trolls, first produced in Lawrence, KS, by the Seem-to-Be Player, 1995; Dramatic, 1995.

Across the Plains, first produced in Kansas City, MO, by the Coterie Theater, 1996; Dramatic, 1997.

Emma (two-act), first produced in Springfield, MO, at the Vandivort Center Theatre, 1995; Dramatic, 1997.

The Wolf and Its Shadows, first produced in Omaha, NE, by the Omaha Theater Company for Young People, 1995; Anchorage Press, 1999.

I Will Sing Life: Voices from the Hole in the Wall Gang Camp, first produced in Springfield, MO, by the Good Company Theatre, 1999; Dramatic, 1999.

FICTION FOR CHILDREN; AS SANDY ASHER

Summer Begins, Elsevier-Nelson, 1980, published as *Summer Smith Begins,* Bantam, 1986.

Daughters of the Law, Beaufort, 1980, published in England as *Friends and Sisters,* Gollancz, 1982.

Just Like Jenny, Delacorte, 1982.

Things Are Seldom What They Seem, Delacorte, 1983.

Missing Pieces, Delacorte, 1984.

Teddy Teabury's Fabulous Fact, Dell, 1985.

Everything Is Not Enough, Delacorte, 1987.

Teddy Teabury's Peanutty Problems, Dell, 1987.

Princess Bee and the Royal Good-night Story (picture book), illustrated by Cat Bowman Smith, A. Whitman, 1990.

With All My Heart, With All My Mind, Simon & Schuster, 1999.

Stella's Dancing Days, illustrated by Kathryn Brown, Harcourt, 2001.

NONFICTION

The Great American Peanut Book, illustrated by Jo Anne Metsch Bonnell, Tempo, 1977.

(As Sandy Asher) *Where Do You Get Your Ideas? Helping Young Writers Begin,* illustrated by Susan Hellard, Walker, 1987.

(As Sandy Asher) *Wild Words! How to Train Them to Tell Stories,* illustrated by Dennis Kendrick, Walker, 1989.

"BALLET ONE" SERIES; AS SANDY ASHER

Best Friends Get Better, Scholastic, 1989.

Mary-in-the-Middle, Scholastic, 1990.

Pat's Promise, Scholastic, 1990.

Can David Do It?, Scholastic, 1991.

SHORT STORY COLLECTIONS

Out of Here: A Senior Class Yearbook, Dutton/Lodestar, 1993.

(Editor) *But That's Another Story: Famous Authors Introduce Popular Genres,* Walker, 1996.

(Editor and contributor) *With All My Heart, With All My Mind: Thirteen Stories About Growing Up Jewish,* Simon & Schuster, 1999.

Contributor of plays to anthologies, including *Center Stage,* Harper, 1990, and *Scenes & Monologues for Young Actors,* Dramatic, 1999. Contributor of stories and articles to books, including *Performing the Text: Reading, Writing, and Teaching the Young Adult Novel,* edited by Virginia Monseau and Gary Salvner, Heinemann-Boynton/Cook, 1992; *Authors' Perspectives: Turning Teenagers into Readers and Writers,* edited by Donald Gallo, Heinemann-Boynton/Cook, 1992; *Collins Book of Ballet and Dance,* edited by Jean Ure, Harper-Collins, 1997; *Theatre for Young Audiences: Twenty Great Plays for Children,* edited by Coleman Jennings, St. Martin's Press, 1998; *Two Decades of the ALAN Review,* edited by Patricia P. Kelly and Robert C. Small, Jr., NCTE Press, 1999. Contributor of stories and articles to magazines, including *Highlights for Children, Humpty Dumpty's Magazine, Parents Magazine, ALAN Review, Journal of Reading, Spark!, Theater for Young Audiences Today, Writers Digest, The Writer,* and *National Geographic World.*

Work in Progress

If You Lived in China and *If You Lived in Mexico* for Marshall Cavendish, due in 2002.

Sidelights

Sandra Fenichel Asher, a playwright and children's author who is probably best known for her young adult novels written under the name Sandy Asher, gets many of the ideas and characters for her writings from her childhood memories. Growing up in Philadelphia, Pennsylvania, the active and observant author-to-be absorbed the abundant sights and sounds and varieties of people in her neighborhood. But while young, Asher also learned to be alone even when there were lots of people around. She explained in an essay for *Something about the Author Autobiography Series* (*SAAS*) that, while living with her older brother, parents, aunt, uncle, cousin, and grandparents in a large row house that also served as office space for her father's medical practice, "I learned early that inner space is worth exploring and that even when alone, you can find yourself in fascinating company. Much of the time was spent in a fantasy world where I grew up to be the people I saw in movies and read about in books: a dancer, actor, circus juggler, magician, world traveler, puppeteer...."

As she grew up, Asher recalls that the difference between the social world and her own private "inner space" became increasingly pronounced, making it more and more difficult to communicate her dreams and insecurities to those around her. Although she aspired to be a professional writer from an early age, her efforts at writing were "considered amusing by my family, but certainly not significant," she wrote in *SAAS*. Looking back, Asher understands why her parents were not more encouraging. "I can't blame them for the way they saw me. They were products of their time. They were good, decent people trying to raise a good, decent female child." Since her parents believed that for a woman marriage was the only key to a secure future, they viewed her interests in writing, drama, and dance as harmless pastimes or hobbies. As a young woman, Asher had to learn to separate her own sense of identity from her parents' perception of her.

Asher's relationships with friends at school also became strained in early adolescence. Although she was an excellent student, the author recalled in *SAAS* that secondary school was "like a forced visit to a strange planet." Growing increasingly shy in a social environment she did not always understand, she responded to her peers with "a sarcastic sense of humor" and "a sharp tongue." Realizing later that other young people around her were probably as insecure as she was, Asher perceived that adolescents are often socially isolated at just the time they are developing their deepest concerns about identity. A young child, she once observed in *Something about the Author (SATA),* can take his or her questions to a parent, an older adolescent can talk to a boyfriend or girlfriend, an adult can confide in a spouse, close friend, or psychiatrist. But friendships in early adolescence are often tenuous. "So you're alone with your fears and confusions at the very point in life when frightening and confusing changes are happening to you every day," she once said in *SATA*. "You tell no one the truth about how you feel, no one tells you, and everyone ends up thinking, 'I am the only person this crazy in the whole world.'"

However uncomfortably, Asher thrived in her adolescence, pursuing youthful dreams into challenging experiences in ballet, the theater, and finally into writing—professionally. She credits teachers and role models from books (Jo March of Louisa May Alcott's *Little Women* in particular), for her perseverance in the things she loved. But she also believes that adolescence is not just a difficult time, it is a "time of hope," she once told *SATA*. "You *can* solve problems. You *can* learn how to live well. No one can tell children that life is not worth living. They just got here and they're rarin' to go."

After an eventful high school and college career that included performing in plays with La Salle College Masque and Indiana University Theatre, musicals on the traveling showboat, the *Majestic,* and ballet with the Philadelphia Civic Ballet Company, the author graduated from Indiana University and married her husband, Harvey Asher. Within a span of several years, her parents and her grandparents died, and her husband's job necessitated a move to Missouri. During these years she worked as a scriptwriter for a radio station, a copywriter

In a continued attempt to encourage budding writers, Asher edited this anthology of short fiction representing twelve genres including humor, suspense, folktales, and science fiction. (Cover illustration by John Martinez.)

in advertising, and a drama critic for an alternative newspaper before having two children and beginning graduate studies in child development. "My twenties, in short," Asher said in *SAAS,* "were a decade of turmoil, and I had to learn how to deal with it, how to sort it all out and survive it, far from old friends and what little was left of my family."

In 1969, a year after the birth of her second child, she began to write her first novel, *Daughters of the Law,* a story about a young girl trying to understand her Jewish heritage in light of her mother's unexpressed but painful memories as a survivor of the Holocaust of World War II. As Asher became more familiar with her genre, she reworked the novel many times over the next ten years before its publication. During these years she also began to write plays that have been produced throughout the country, winning numerous awards.

Before she finalized *Daughters of the Law,* Asher wrote and published *Summer Begins,* a novel about an eighth-grade girl named Summer who submits an article to her school newspaper suggesting that the holiday celebrations at her school should include Buddhist and Jewish traditions along with the exclusively Christian ones currently observed. Summer finds herself the unwilling center of attention when the principal demands that she retract her article, and her teacher resigns in protest of this violation of Summer's civil rights. *Summer Begins* raises important issues of censorship and religious freedom, but many critics noted that the book's strength lies in its focus on Summer's development toward maturity, related in invitingly human and often humorous terms. A *Washington Post Book World* reviewer commented that "Summer is a winningly self-aware 13-year-old and her reluctance to take on the heroine's role is often very funny."

In her 1982 novel, *Just Like Jenny,* Asher explores the friendship between Stephie and Jenny, two talented young dancers. When they are both asked to audition for a semi-professional dance group, Stephie, who is under pressure from her parents and envious of Jenny's classic skills, decides that she is not good enough to try out. The resolution of Stephie's loss of nerve, according to Judith S. Baughman in her *Dictionary of Literary Biography Yearbook: 1983* essay, entails lessons in "the nature of real friendship and the motivation underlying commitment to hard but fulfilling goals." A *Times Literary Supplement* reviewer of *Just Like Jenny,* although criticizing the story for "relying on inevitable disappointments and triumphs," commended Asher for her knowledge of teenagers, claiming "Sandy Asher knows about the dreams and aspirations of young people.... She understands also the stubborn crises of confidence which afflict adolescents who do not know how they compare in ability and maturity with others."

In later novels, Asher continued to raise social issues while focusing on her adolescent characters' development of identity. In her award-winning 1983 book *Things Are Seldom What They Seem,* she examines the effect a teacher's sexual abuse—and the silence of the adult world about what he has done—has on some of his students. Baughman noted that the significant focus in this story is "how these complexly developed fourteen- and fifteen-year-olds deal with their discovery that things are seldom what they seem, that deceptions or misperceptions do undermine relationships." In *Missing Pieces,* noted Virginia Marr in a *School Library Journal* review, Asher "deals with such adolescent concerns as lack of communication within families, loss, loneliness and the constant need for emotional support." Asher's 1987 novel, *Everything Is Not Enough,* the story of a seventeen-year-old boy's move toward independence, tackles the theme of violence against women in a similar manner. In this story, a supportive friendship arises between a young man and a female coworker at a restaurant when, together, they confront the fact that a friend is being beaten by her alcoholic boyfriend. And in her 1993 work *Out of Here: A Senior Class Yearbook,* Asher uses nine interconnected stories about a series of problems such as teen pregnancy, abusive parents, and alcoholism to highlight dilemmas faced by graduating seniors at a high school in a small town. "The cumulative effect," *School Library Journal* reviewer

Doris A. Fong concluded, "is an accurate portrayal of high school, with concerns and activities that give Asher's work the texture of a yearbook...."

Asher shows additional sides to her writing in other children's books. Her 1990 picture book, *Princess Bee and the Royal Good-night Story,* takes a lighthearted look at separation anxiety. Princess Bee cannot go to sleep when her mom, the Queen, goes out of town. Her siblings' stories come up short and Bee has to look within herself to solve the problem. In a review for *Booklist,* Julie Corsaro called the work a "soothing offering with potential for repeat late-night performances." With the "Teddy Teabury" books, Asher gets inside the head of a sixth-grader who becomes involved in his hometown's tourist trade. She finds a humorous way to make "some important points about honesty and being true to oneself," according to *School Library Journal* critic Cindy Darling Codell in a review of *Teddy Teabury's Peanutty Problems.*

Asher pursued another area of interest in the late eighties—encouraging children to write—by penning companion nonfiction books *Where Do You Get Your Ideas? Helping Young Writers Begin* and *Wild Words! How to Train Them to Tell Stories.* These books, suited for children in grades three to eight, tackle the problems of how to begin writing and then how to edit stories to make them more effective. In *Where Do You Get Your Ideas?,* chapters alternate between idea-generating activities and "stories behind the stories," with quotes from popular children's authors. *Wild Words!* gets more specific, offering advice on shaping plots and characters, then explaining the editing process that allows authors to "tame" words. "The examples," comments Martha Rosen, writing in *School Library Journal,* "are right on target, and the original writing samples by junior- and senior-high-school students provide interest and incentive for others who are trying to hone their writing skills."

In a continued attempt to encourage budding writers, Asher edited *But That's Another Story: Famous Authors Introduce Popular Genres* in 1996. Eleven genres, including adventure, suspense, horror, and science fiction, are represented in short stories by well-known authors. "This brief volume answers language arts teachers who have dreamed of an accessible collection of genre explanations, short stories, author interviews, and story commentaries all rolled into one pleasure-reading package," summarized Patti Sylvester Spencer in her *Voice of Youth Advocates* review.

Asher says that writing, for her, has been a means to "take control, puzzle things through, and work them out." In her novels she continues to reflect on what happened to her in her own early years. She wrote in *SAAS,* "In a word, what happened was 'adolescence,' but there don't seem to be enough words in the world to illuminate that murky tunnel. To reach adulthood, a child must become more like his or her parents. To establish an individual identity, that same child must become *less* like his or her parents. It's a difficult passage, hard on parents and young people alike. Slowly but surely, as I write my books and plays, I find I've repaired broken bridges to my past and laid old sorrows to rest. I hope I also show readers that this does happen, that it can be done in their own lives. It takes time and understanding, and a willingness to forgive—oneself and others—and move on. A sense of humor also comes in handy."

Works Cited

Asher, Sandy, *Where Do You Get Your Ideas? Helping Young Writers Begin,* Walker, 1987.

Asher, Sandy, essay in *Something about the Author Autobiography Series,* Volume 13, Gale, 1991, pp. 1-16.

Baughman, Judith S., article on Sandy Asher, *Dictionary of Literary Biography Yearbook: 1983,* Gale, 1984, pp. 179-86.

Codell, Cindy Darling, review of *Teddy Teabury's Peanutty Problems, School Library Journal,* December, 1989, p. 98.

Corsaro, Julie, review of *Princess Bee and the Royal Goodnight Story, Booklist,* February 1, 1990, p. 1084.

Fong, Doris A., review of *Out of Here: A Senior Class Yearbook, School Library Journal,* July, 1993, p. 98.

Review of *Just Like Jenny, Times Literary Supplement,* September 7, 1984, p. 1006.

Marr, Virginia, review of *Missing Pieces, School Library Journal,* May, 1984, p. 86.

Rosen, Martha, review of *Wild Words! How to Train Them to Tell Stories, School Library Journal,* January, 1990, p. 110.

Spencer, Patti Sylvester, review of *But That's Another Story: Famous Authors Introduce Popular Genres, Voice of Youth Advocates,* August, 1996, p. 176.

Review of *Summer Begins, Washington Post Book World,* July 11, 1982, p. 12.

For More Information See

BOOKS

Major Authors and Illustrators for Children and Young Adults, Volume 1, Gale, 1993, pp. 123-26.

PERIODICALS

Booklist, May 1, 1986, p. 1307; January 1, 1990, p. 907.
Bulletin of the Center for Children's Books, February, 1981, p. 106; September, 1982; May, 1983, p. 162; June, 1984; December, 1987.
Horn Book, December, 1982, p. 654.
Kirkus Reviews, June 15, 1987, p. 921.
Publishers Weekly, February 13, 1987, p. 94; June 14, 1993, p. 72.
School Library Journal, October, 1980, p. 164; February, 1983, p.72; April, 1986, p. 83; August, 1987, p. 88-89; September, 1987, p. 184-85; March, 1990, p. 184; July, 1996.
Times Literary Supplement, September 17, 1982.
Voice of Youth Advocates, June, 1984, p. 94; June, 1987, p. 74; December, 1993, p. 286.

ON-LINE

Asher's Web site is located at http://www.redrival.com/mowrites4kids/asher/.

*   *   *

ASHER, Sandy
See ASHER, Sandra Fenichel

B

BENEDICT, Andrew
See ARTHUR, Robert (Jr.)

* * *

BEYNON, John
See HARRIS, John (Wyndham Parkes Lucas) Beynon

* * *

BLACKWOOD, Gary L. 1945-

Personal

Born October 23, 1945, in Meadville, PA; son of Roy W. and Susie (Stallsmith) Blackwood; married Jean Lantzy, October 3, 1977; children: Gareth, Giles, Tegan. *Education:* Grove City College, B.A., 1967. *Hobbies and other interests:* Music, outdoor pursuits.

Addresses

Home—6031 CR 105, Carthage, MO 64836. *E-mail*—gblackwood@hotmail.com.

Career

Writer of fiction and nonfiction books, playwright, and writing teacher. Missouri Southern State College, teacher of playwriting, 1989-93, 1997—; Trinidad State Junior College, teacher of writing-for-publication course, 1995. *Military service:* U.S. Army, Sergeant, E-5, 1968-70.

Awards, Honors

Friends of American Writers Best YA Novel, 1989, for *The Dying Sun;* Best Book for Young Adults citation, American Library Association, 1998, for *The Shakespeare Stealer.*

Writings

NOVELS

The Lion and the Unicorn, Eagle Books, 1983.
Wild Timothy, Atheneum (New York City), 1987.
The Dying Sun, Atheneum, 1989.
Beyond the Door, Atheneum, 1991.
The Masters, EPB Publishers, 1995.
The Shakespeare Stealer, Dutton, 1998.
Moonshine, Cavendish, 1999.
Shakespeare's Scribe, Dutton, 2000.
Pirates, Benchmark, 2001.

NONFICTION

Rough Riding Reformer: Theodore Roosevelt, Benchmark, 1997.
Life on the Oregon Trail, Lucent, 1999.
Life in a Medieval Castle, Lucent, 1999.

"SECRETS OF THE UNEXPLAINED" SERIES; ALL PUBLISHED BY BENCHMARK

Alien Astronauts, 1999.
Extraordinary Events and Oddball Occurrences, 1999.
Fateful Forebodings, 1999.
Long-Ago Lives, 1999.
Paranormal Powers, 1999.
Spooky Spectres, 1999.

"THE BAD GUYS" SERIES

Pirates, Benchmark, 2001.
Highwaymen, Benchmark, 2001.

OTHER

Also producer of original plays; author of *Futures: A Dining-Room Comedy-Drama in Three Acts,* Players Press, 1996.

Sidelights

Gary L. Blackwood was a book lover from an early age. "While I was still young enough to be sleeping in a crib," he once commented, "I struck a deal with my mother: I'd give up sucking my thumb if she bought me a series of Gene Autry comics I'd seen advertised on the back of a cereal box." Blackwood, who grew up in Cochranton, a small town in northwestern Pennsylvania, attended one of the last remaining one-room school-houses in the state. He remembers that the school library "consisted only of a single set of bookshelves, but it did contain a full set of the Dr. Doolittle books. I had a competition going with one of my classmates to see who could read the entire series first."

Considering the sharpness of Blackwood's memories of reading as a child, it is no surprise that the audience he writes for is mainly school children through young adults. Blackwood has published prodigiously in both fiction and non-fiction, but the book that has captured the most critical attention by far is *The Shakespeare Stealer,* published in 1998. The idea for the story came to Blackwood in the late 1960s, from an item he came upon in the newspaper. "It informed me that, in the sixteenth century, an English doctor named Timothy Bright had invented an early system of shorthand," he once said. "I knew something of that time period already, from studying Shakespeare in college. The elements of shorthand and Shakespeare melded in my mind, and expanded to become my first novel, which I called *An Art of Short, Swift, and Secret Stealing.*"

Blackwood never found a publisher for the book, so he gave up on it for a number of years. But looking back on this first effort of novel-writing, Blackwood decided to rewrite it "as a book for kids." "For a long time," Blackwood stated, "it looked as if the new improved version of the book, now called *The Shakespeare Stealer,* would be consigned to oblivion like its predecessor. Most of the editors who saw it liked it a lot, but didn't feel it would sell well.... After being turned down sixteen times over a period of seven years, the book finally found a home at Dutton." The work has received substantial critical recognition.

The Shakespeare Stealer concerns Widge, a fourteen-year-old boy who has spent his life in a Yorkshire orphanage. Soon after the story opens Widge is apprenticed to Dr. Bright, a minister who teaches Widge his system of "charactery" (or shorthand) for the purpose of stealing other ministers's sermons. But before long, Bright sells his young apprentice for the sum of tens pounds to Simon Bass, a London theatrical manager. Bass plans to use the boy's skills to have him steal Shakespeare's new play, *The Tragedy of Hamlet, Prince of Denmark,* so that Bass's own theater can produce it without having to pay royalties.

Blackwood's text provides information on the history and use of medieval castles, as well as descriptions of the inhabitants. (*From* Life in a Medieval Castle.)

Widge has not gotten very far with his copy when he is discovered hiding in a balcony by the Globe players; thinking fast, he pretends to be stagestruck, and is so convincing that the group take him on as an acting apprentice. At first Widge thinks he will use his new position to steal the Globe's own copy of the play, but the "brave new world of friendship, fun, and backstage intrigue," in the words of a *Kirkus Reviews* critic, make him question his unethical quest. Instead, Widge practices lines, learns the arts of stagecraft and swordfighting, and works to evade Bass's brutal henchmen. Jennifer M. Brabander, writing in *Horn Book,* points out that "like *Hamlet,* Blackwood's story focuses on its protagonist's doubt and deliberation about his interrupted quest." By the end of the story, Widge plays Ophelia for the Queen.

Critics were nearly uniformly charmed by Blackwood's tale. Deborah Stevens, in her review in *Bulletin of the Center for Children's Books,* noted that "there's a pleasing air of high adventure to Widge's escapades that is enhanced by Blackwood's careful but never dry use of period and theatrical detail." Brabander, in *Horn Book,* credited Blackwood with "set[ting] the stage for future reading and play-going" for its young readers. The *Kirkus Reviews* critic called the book a "delightful and heartwarming romp through Elizabethan England," and Carolyn Phelan, writing in *Booklist,* opined that "this historical novel makes an exciting introduction to the period and to Shakespearean theater."

A *Publishers Weekly* reviewer, however, complained that the story was marred by "[a] myriad of anachronisms," including Widge's reference to London's square city blocks, to having his supper warmed on a stove, and to the recovery of an injured man in a hospital—all apparently imprecise. But the reviewer did admire Blackwood's "lively depictions of Elizabethan stagecraft and street life." Sally Margolis, who reviewed the book for the *School Library Journal,* wrote that "Blackwood puts a young boy in a sink-or-swim predicament in alien territory where he discovers his own strength. It's a formula with endless appeal."

Works Cited

Brabander, Jennifer M., review of *The Shakespeare Stealer, Horn Book,* June, 1998, p. 353.

Margolis, Sally, review of *The Shakespeare Stealer, School Library Journal,* June, 1998, p. 140.

Phelan, Carolyn, review of *The Shakespeare Stealer, Booklist,* June 1, 1998, p. 1763.

Review of *The Shakespeare Stealer, Kirkus Reviews,* April 15, 1998, p. 576.

Review of *The Shakespeare Stealer, Publishers Weekly,* June 1, 1998, p. 63.

Stevens, Deborah, review of *The Shakespeare Stealer, Bulletin of the Center for Children's Books,* July-August, 1998, p. 483.*

For More Information See

PERIODICALS

Booklist, September 1, 1999, p. 131.
English Journal, December, 1989, p. 77.
Horn Book, July-August, 1989, p. 485.
School Library Journal, October, 1987, p. 137; May, 1989, p. 124; March, 1991, p. 192; March, 1999, pp. 216-17; August, 1999, p. 166; October, 1999, p. 144.
Wilson Library Bulletin, January, 1990, p. 99; March, 1990.

*   *   *

BLADE, Alexander
See HAMILTON, Edmond

*   *   *

BLUTIG, Eduard
See GOREY, Edward (St. John)

*   *   *

BODE, Janet 1943-1999

OBITUARY NOTICE—See index for *SATA* sketch: Born July 14, 1943, in Penn Yan, NY; died of breast cancer, December 30, 1999, in Manhattan, NY. Author. Bode (BOE-dy) wrote numerous nonfiction books for teenagers and young adults that dealt with such explosive subjects as rape, teen pregnancy, immigration, and interracial dating. Her works struck a chord with readers, and were noted among the books most frequently stolen from school and public libraries. Bode attended schools in London during the 1950s when her father worked at the American Embassy there. Upon returning to the United States, she attended Northwestern High School and the University of Maryland, graduating with a Bachelor's degree in 1965. After college, Bode taught school in Europe, Mexico, and Florida for a time before beginning work in public relations. Her first book, *Kids School Lunch Bag,* was published in 1972, the same year Bode was gang raped in the woods of Kansas. After the attack, the author found writing therapeutic; her painful experience led her to write several books on the topic of rape: *Fighting Back: How to Cope with the Medical, Emotional and Legal Consequences of Rape, Rape: Preventing It; Coping with the Legal, Medical and Emotional Aftermath,* and *The Voices of Rape.* Bode's books were lauded by librarians and other commentators for their thorough and straightforward examinations of such weighty and important material. When preparing her texts, Bode generally interviewed hundreds of teenagers, using their specific stories and words to tell a tale, whether the topic was rape or eating disorders or juvenile crime. Many of those stories were used in such works as *Death Is Hard to Live With: Teenagers Talk about How They Cope with Loss* and *Heartbreak and Roses: Real Life Stories of Troubled Love.* Bode's book *The Colors of Freedom: Immigrant Stories,* was published weeks before her death and her last book, *For Better, for Worse: Kids Tell the Truth about Divorce and Remarriage,* is to be published in 2001. Bode received numerous awards throughout her career, including The Outstanding Social Studies Book Award from the National Council for Social Studies for *Rape: Preventing It* and Best Books for Young Adults citations from the American Library Association for *Kids Having Kids: The Unwed Teenage Parent, New Kids on the Block: Oral Histories of Immigrant Teens, The Voices of Rape, Beating the Odds: Stories of Unexpected Achievers, Heartbreak and Roses: Real Life Stories of Troubled Love,* and *Hard Time: A Real Life Look at Juvenile Crime and Violence.*

OBITUARIES AND OTHER SOURCES:

PERIODICALS

New York Times, December 31, 1999, p. A19.
Washington Post, December 31, 1999, p. B6.

*   *   *

BRADSHAW, Gillian (Joan) 1949-

Personal

Born January 6, 1949, in Brisbane, Queensland, Australia; daughter of Edward Thomas Moriarty (an executive bank officer) and Joan Maitland (a bookkeeper and shop owner; maiden name, Steele) Moriarty; married David Graham Bradshaw (an electrician), August 24, 1985; children: Duncan David Edward, Emily Joan Beatrix.

Gillian Bradshaw

Education: Brisbane Technical College, Associate Diploma of Fine Art, 1973; Queensland Dept. of Education, Certificate of Early Childhood Education, 1976, and Support-A-Reader Certificate in tutoring, 1999. *Politics:* Labor. *Religion:* "Reverence for nature." *Hobbies and other interests:* Bush walking, bird watching, art and craft collecting, especially bric-a-brac featuring animals.

Addresses

Home—32 Lockyer St., Camp Hill, Brisbane, Queensland, Australia 4152.

Career

State Education Department, Brisbane, Queensland, Australia, preschool assistant, 1973-76; Brisbane City Council, library assistant, 1981-85. Support-a-Reader tutor and voluntary art assistant at local primary school. Has also worked privately as a photographic colorist. *Member:* Queensland Writers' Centre, Griffith University Alumni Association.

Awards, Honors

Shock Monday has been judged a Notable Book for the Year 2000, Children's Book Council of Australia.

Writings

Shock Monday (picture book), illustrated by David Cox, Lothian Books (Melbourne), 1999.

Contributor of poetry, graphics, and design to four editions of the literary journal *Catalyst,* 1983.

Work in Progress

A picture book manuscript about a physically disabled boy.

Sidelights

Gillian Bradshaw told *SATA:* "As a writer, I am concerned with social, health and environmental issues and hope, through my work, to make some small difference to the world. I would like to address materialism and contrast it with values that really matter in life. As a children's writer, I feel the need to entertain, so humour is an important element of my work. Writing, for me, has been a progression from love of books and exposure to children's literature as a preschool assistant, library assistant, and parent. I like to write from life, so I take a notebook with me wherever I go to jot down whatever stimulates me. I favour the picture book genre because of my training in art."

BURGAN, Michael 1960-

Personal

Born March 15, 1960, in Hartford, CT; son of Bernard and Irene (Zeppa) Burgan; married Samantha Strauss, May 6, 2000. *Education:* University of Connecticut, B.A., 1983; also attended Emerson College, 1987-88. *Politics:* Democrat. *Religion:* Unitarian-Universalist. *Hobbies and other interests:* Films, music, travel, sports.

Addresses

Home—1955 Main St., East Hartford, CT 06108. *E-mail*—Mburgan@aol.com.

Career

Weekly Reader Corp., Middleton, CT, editor, 1988-94; freelance writer, 1994—. Hartford Food System, member of board of directors, 1997—. *Member:* Society of Children's Book Writers and Illustrators, Phi Beta Kappa, Phi Kappa Phi.

Writings

Boris Bigfoot's Big Feat, HarperCollins (New York City), 1995.
The Curse of Cleo Patrick's Mummy, HarperCollins, 1996.
Zelda's Zombie Dance, HarperCollins, 1996.
(Reteller) Stephen Crane, *The Red Badge of Courage,* illustrated by Kathryn Yingling and Ed Parker, Harper-Collins, 1996.
(Reteller) Mary Wollstonecraft Shelley, *Frankenstein,* illustrated by Yingling and Parker, HarperCollins, 1996.
(Reteller) Miguel de Cervantes, *Don Quixote,* illustrated by Yingling, Lars Hokanson, and Frances Cichetti, Har-perCollins, 1996.
Tiki Doll of Doom, HarperCollins, 1997.
Chocolate Cake, Huckleberry Press (South Glastonbury, CT), 1997.
The Prize, Huckleberry Press, 1997.
The Pro Sports Halls of Fame: Basketball, two volumes, Grolier, 1997.
The Associated Press Library of Disasters, four volumes, Grolier, 1998.
American Immigration, two volumes, Grolier, 1998.
Madeleine Albright, Millbrook Press (Brookfield, CT), 1998.
Dominik Hasek, Chelsea House (Philadelphia, PA), 1999.
Maryland, Children's Press (New York City), 1999.
Argentina, Children's Press, 1999.
England, Children's Press, 1999.
The Pontiac Firebird, RiverFront Books (New York City), 1999.
The Porsche 911, RiverFront Books, 1999.
The Toyota Land Cruiser, RiverFront Books, 1999.
Belgium, Children's Press, 2000.
Sheryl Swoopes, Chelsea House, 2000.
Travel Agent, Capstone Books (Mankato, MN), 2000.
Veterinarian, Capstone Books, 2000.
U.S. Army Special Forces: Airborne Rangers, RiverFront Books, 2000.
U.S. Navy Special Forces: SEAL Teams, RiverFront Books, 2000.
U.S. Navy Special Forces: Special Boat Units, RiverFront Books, 2000.

Work in Progress

The World's Fastest Military Airplanes, publication by Capstone Books expected in 2001; *The World's Wildest Roller Coasters,* Capstone Books, 2001; *The Cold War,* four volumes, for Turner Learning/Harcourt; *John Glenn,* for Aladdin Paperbacks.

Sidelights

Michael Burgan told *SATA:* "I had originally hoped to be a teacher, but one semester of student-teaching during graduate school convinced me that I should stick to my first love, writing—if I could make a living at it. Thankfully I took a job at *Weekly Reader* and found my niche: writing social studies for children. I was able to pursue my interest in history and current events while feeling I was making a contribution as an educator (of a sort). Freelancing has enabled me to pursue a wide range of topics and also try some children's fiction. With the fiction, I get to use some of my skills as a would-be playwright and, I hope, make kids laugh."

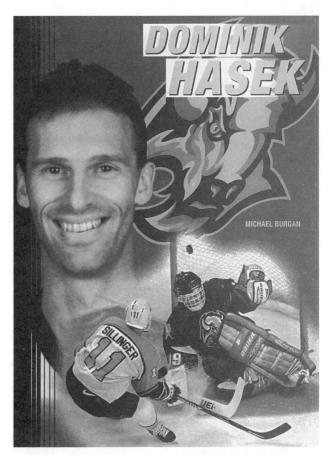

Michael Burgan has penned a biography of famous hockey goaltender Dominik Hasek, winner of the Vezina Trophy as top goalie in the National Hockey League and gold medalist in the 1998 Olympics.

For More Information See

PERIODICALS

National Geographic World, January, 1999; May, 1999; October, 1999; December, 1999; April, 2000.
School Library Journal, June, 1999, p. 140.

*   *   *

BUSBY, Cylin 1970-

Personal

First name is pronounced Sill-in; born May 1, 1970, in Hartford, CT; daughter of John R., Jr. (a police officer) and Polly A. (an obstetrician and gynecologist; maiden name, Alward) Busby. *Education:* Attended University of California, Berkeley, 1992; Hampshire College, B.A., 1993. *Politics:* Democrat. *Religion:* Roman Catholic.

Addresses

Home—528 North Orange Dr., Los Angeles, CA 90036; and 651 10th St., Brooklyn, NY 11215. *E-mail*—cylinb@hotmail.com.

Cylin Busby

Career

Random House, Inc., Knopf Books for Young Readers, New York City, editorial assistant, 1993-95; HarperCollins Publishers, New York City, associate editor, 1995-97; Simon & Schuster, New York City, editor of children's books, 1997-2000; *Teen* magazine, senior editor, 2000—. *Member:* American Library Association, Children's Book Council, Young Adult Library Services Association.

Writings

Leaves, Hampshire College (Amherst, MA), 1992.
The Chicken-Fried Rat: Tales Too Gross to Be True (for children), illustrated by Phoebe Gloeckner, HarperCollins (New York City), 1998.

Contributor to periodicals, including *Teen* magazine and *American Journal of Folklore.*

Work in Progress

The Nine Lives of Jacob Tibbs, a novel for children, due in 2000.

Sidelights

Cylin Busby told *SATA:* "I've always wanted to write, so I did the most obvious thing I could—I got a job in publishing. I've worked as a children's book editor at three of the biggest publishers in the world and enjoy both sides of publishing—both working with authors and working as an author. Having been an editor gives me more insight into how the publishing world works. I recommend it for anyone who wants to be a writer.

"My first book, *The Chicken-Fried Rat,* was born out of my love for funny urban legends and my desire to bring those stories to young readers. My second novel for young readers is a historical story about a ship's crossing from England to the new Americas in the eighteenth century. This novel has required a lot of research—something else I enjoy. You're never too old to use the library, something I hope young readers will keep in mind.

"I write to expand my world, to bring new things to people—especially to young people. Reading and writing are the best forms of travel I know—you can go anywhere and do anything through books."

For More Information See

PERIODICALS

Bulletin of the Center for Children's Books, November, 1998, p. 91.
School Library Journal, February, 1999, p. 104.

C

CAMBURN, Carol A.
See CAMBURN-BRACALENTE, Carol A.

* * *

CAMBURN-BRACALENTE, Carol A. 1962-
(Carol A. Camburn)

Personal

Born October 21, 1962, in Doylestown, PA; daughter of Joseph H., Sr. and Hilda (Novakovitz) Camburn; married James J. Bracalente, September 24, 1988. *Education:* Moore College of Art and Design, B.F.A. *Hobbies and other interests:* "My favorite hobby is owning and caring for my horse, Billy. He is my gift and a great influence in my life."

Addresses

Home and office—Quakertown, PA. *E-mail*—cacamburn@easy-pages.com.

Career

Freelance illustrator and designer, 1989—. Art director for Healthy HairCare Products (horse grooming products). *Member:* Society of Children's Book Writers and Illustrators.

Writings

ILLUSTRATOR; UNDER NAME CAROL A. CAMBURN

Amanda Agee, *The Beast Who Couldn't Say Boo,* Modern Publishing, 1996.
Lynnette Long, *One Dollar: My First Book about Money,* Barron's (Hauppauge, NY), 1998.
Laura T. Barnes, *Twist and Ernest,* Barnesyard Books, 1999.

Carol A. Camburn-Bracalente provided the heart-warming illustrations for Laura T. Barnes's true-life tale of a lonely little donkey who wins the friendship of a beautiful show horse. (From Twist and Ernest.*)*

Contributor of illustrations to equine magazines.

Work in Progress

Illustrating *Teeny Tiny Ernest,* for Barnesyard Books, due in September 2000; illustrating *Happy's Friends.*

Sidelights

Carol A. Camburn-Bracalente told *SATA:* "I grew up in rural Pennsylvania on a farm. I have always loved animals and always enjoyed drawing them. I had a very strong interest in children's illustration and animating animal characters, which represents my strongest ability—to create 'characters.' My freelance work has allowed me to work in many areas of illustration, including product packaging, coloring books, toys, and children's books.

"I was influenced at an early age by Preston Blair, who, at the time, was an artist for Walt Disney. I had purchased a Walter Foster 'how to draw' book by Preston Blair and exchanged a few notes with him through the years. He has passed away, but his kind words and influence will always remain with me."

* * *

CARRICK, Carol (Hatfield) 1935-

Personal

Born May 20, 1935, in Queens, NY; daughter of Chauncey L. and Elsa (maiden name, Schweizer) Hatfield; married Donald Carrick (an artist), March 26, 1965 (died June 26, 1989); children: Christopher, Paul. *Education:* Hofstra University, B.A., 1957.

Addresses

Home—High St., Edgartown, MA 02539.

Career

Coronet, New York City, staff artist, 1958-60; H. Allen Lightman (advertising agency), New York City, staff artist, 1960-61; freelance artist, 1961-65; writer for children, 1965—.

Awards, Honors

Society of Illustrators Award for *The Pond;* Children's Book of the Year, Child Study Association, for *Beach Bird,* 1974, for *Lost in the Storm,* 1975, for *The Blue Lobster,* 1977, for *The Foundling,* 1979, for *A Rabbit for Easter,* 1979, for *Some Friend!,* 1980, for *The Climb,* 1981, for *The Accident,* 1981, for *The Empty Squirrel,* and 1985, for *Stay Away from Simon;* Children's Book of the Year Award, Library of Congress, 1974, Pick of the List, American Bookseller, 1989 and 1990, all for *Lost in the Storm;* Outstanding Science Trade Book for Children, National Science Teachers Association and the Children's Book Council, 1975, for *The Blue Lobster,* and 1975, for *The Crocodiles Still Wait;* Children's Science Book Award Junior Honor Book, New York Academy of Sciences, 1975, and Best Children's Book of the Season selection, *Saturday Review,* 1976, both for *The Blue Lobster;* Children's Book Showcase award, Children's Book Council, 1975 and 1976, for *Lost in the Storm,* and 1978, for *The Washout;* Children's Choice award, International Reading Association and the Children's Book Council, 1975, for *The Blue Lobster,* 1979, for *Paul's Christmas Birthday,* 1982, for *The Empty Squirrel,* 1984 and 1985, for *What a Wimp!;* Children's Choices, International Reading Association and the Children's Book Council, 1975, for *Old Mother Witch,* 1978, for *The Foundling,* and 1979, for *Octopus;* Children's Choices, International Reading Association, 1976, for *The Accident,* 1978, for *Sand Tiger Shark,* and

1984, for *Patrick's Dinosaurs;* named one of the Children's Books of the Year, Child Study Association, 1980, for *The Crocodiles Still Wait,* 1981, for *Ben and the Porcupine,* 1983, for *Two Coyotes,* and 1983, for *What a Wimp!;* Children's Books of the Year, Library of Congress, 1980, for *The Climb,* 1980, for *The Crocodiles Still Wait,* and 1983, for *Patrick's Dinosaurs,* 1987, for *What Happened to Patrick's Dinosaurs?;* Best Books of the Year selection, *New York Times,* and named one of the 100 Best Books of the Year, New York Public Library, both 1980, both for *The Crocodiles Still Wait;* New York Branch of the English-Speaking Union Books-Across-the-Sea Ambassador of Honor Book, 1982, for *Ben and the Porcupine;* Best Books of the Year selection, *School Library Journal,* 1985, for *Stay Away from Simon!,* and 1986, for *What Happened to Patrick's Dinosaurs?;* Named one of 100 Titles for Reading and Sharing, New York Public Library, 1985, Best Children's Books, *Christian Science Monitor,* and Ussby Books for Retarded Children, 1985, all for *Stay Away from Simon!;* Editor's Choice and Books for Vacation Reading, *New York Times,* 1986, Pick of the Lists, American Bookseller, 1986 and 1987, Notable Book, American Library Association, 1986 and 1987, California Young Readers Medal, California Reading Association, 1989, all for *What Happened to Patrick's Dinosaurs?;* Magic Award, *Parenting* magazine, 1989, for *Big Old Bones;* Gold Medal, National Parenting Publications, 1993, Parents' Choice Honor, 1993, Blue Ribbons, *Bulletin of the Center for Children's Books,*

Carol Carrick

"And they made roads for people to drive on."

Imaginative Patrick concocts his own explanation for the disappearance of dinosaurs in Carrick's picture-book tale. (*From* What Happened to Patrick's Dinosaurs?, *illustrated by Donald Carrick.*)

1993, Editors' Choice, *Booklist,* 1993, Notable Book, American Library Association, 1994, Notable Children's Book, *School Library Journal,* 1994, Orbis Pictus Award, National Council of Teachers of English, 1994, all for *Whaling Days;* Notable Books for Children, Smithsonian, 1995, for *Valentine.*

Writings

FOR CHILDREN; ILLUSTRATED BY HUSBAND, DONALD CARRICK

The Old Barn, Bobbs-Merrill, 1966.
The Brook, Macmillan, 1967.
Swamp Spring, Macmillan, 1969.
The Pond, Macmillan, 1970.
The Dirt Road, Macmillan, 1970.
A Clearing in the Forest, Dial, 1970.
Sleep Out, Seabury, 1973.
Beach Bird, Dial, 1973.
Lost in the Storm, Seabury, 1974.
Old Mother Witch, Seabury, 1975.
The Blue Lobster: A Life Cycle, Dial, 1975.
The Accident, Seabury, 1976.
Sand Tiger Shark, Seabury, 1977.

The Highest Balloon on the Common, Greenwillow, 1977.
The Foundling, Seabury, 1977.
Octopus, Seabury, 1978.
The Washout, Seabury, 1978.
Paul's Christmas Birthday, Greenwillow, 1978.
A Rabbit for Easter, Greenwillow, 1979.
Some Friend!, Houghton/Clarion, 1979.
What a Wimp!, Clarion, 1979.
The Crocodiles Still Wait, Houghton/Clarion, 1980.
The Climb, Clarion, 1980.
Ben and the Porcupine, Clarion, 1981.
The Empty Squirrel, Greenwillow, 1981.
The Longest Float in the Parade, Greenwillow, 1982.
Two Coyotes, Clarion, 1982.
Patrick's Dinosaurs, Clarion, 1983.
Dark and Full of Secrets, Clarion, 1984.
Stay Away from Simon!, Clarion, 1985.
What Happened to Patrick's Dinosaurs?, Clarion, 1986.
The Elephant in the Dark, Clarion, 1988.
Left Behind, Clarion, 1988.
Big Old Bones: A Dinosaur Tale, Clarion, 1989.
Aladdin and the Wonderful Lamp, Scholastic, 1989.
In the Moonlight, Waiting, Clarion, 1990.

FOR CHILDREN

The Dragon of Santa Lalia, illustrated by Benjamin Levy, Bobbs-Merrill, 1971.

Norman Fools the Tooth Fairy, illustrated by Lisa McCue, Scholastic, 1992.

Whaling Days, illustrated by David Frampton, Clarion, 1993.

Two Very Little Sisters, illustrated by Erika Weihs, Clarion, 1993.

Banana Beer, illustrated by Margot Apple, Whitman, 1995.

Valentine, illustrated by Paddy Bouma, Clarion, 1995.

Melanie, illustrated by Alisher Dianov, Clarion, 1996.

Patrick's Dinosaurs on the Internet, illustrated by David Milgrim, Clarion, 1999.

Upside-Down Cake, illustrated by P. Bouma, Clarion, 1999.

Mothers Are Like That, illustrated by Paul Carrick, Clarion, 2000.

Some of Carrick's books have been published in Swedish, Finnish, Danish, German, and Japanese.

Adaptations

The Accident was produced for videocassette, Barr Films, 1985; *The Foundling,* videocassette, Grey Haven Films, 1986, and cassette, Houghton, 1990; *Patrick's Dinosaurs,* cassette, Houghton, 1987; *What Happened to Patrick's Dinosaurs?,* cassette, Houghton, 1988; *Old Mother Witch,* videocassette, Phoenix, 1989; *Sleep Out,* cassette, Houghton, 1989; *Lost in the Storm,* cassette, 1990.

Sidelights

Carol Carrick has written almost fifty books for children, many of them illustrated by her late husband, Donald. Carrick focuses on nature, the lives of animals, and the adventures and misadventures of young boys in her popular and award-winning picture books and middle-grade readers. Some of her best-known and loved titles include *Patrick's Dinosaurs* and its sequels, *The Blue Lobster* and other books about animals, and her picture books which use her own sons, Christopher and Paul, as the main characters. Since her husband's death in 1989, Carrick has continued to produce both picture books and works for middle-grade readers and has found a new family collaborator. Working with her son Paul, an illustrator, she published *Mothers Are Like That,* in 2000.

Carrick grew up in Queens, New York, in a time when that borough still had aspects of the countryside to it. With a pond nearby, Carrick discovered the world of nature through tadpoles and frogs. Her neighborhood, suburban in Carrick's youth, was still surrounded by trees and woods. Growing up, Carrick never thought of herself as a writer. She liked books, but it was the illustrations that attracted her. "I remember loving Raggedy Ann and Andy as a child," Carrick once told *SATA.* "My mother read all of them to me. When I read them now, I think they're very sentimental and sticky. What I really liked about them were the illustrations.... And in *The Little Small Red Hen* it was the pictures, not the stories, that affected me as a child."

Carrick studied art in college and then worked as a staff artist on the magazine *Coronet,* where she met her future husband, the landscape painter, Donald Carrick. The couple began a collaborative effort when publishers for whom Donald Carrick was supplying illustrations suggested that he try a children's book. Carol Carrick decided she could supply the text, though, as she once told *SATA,* "I don't have a great sense of fantasy, so I never really thought of myself as a writer." For the event, Carrick came up with the text for *The Old Barn,* the first of three dozen picture book collaborations featuring the husband and wife. Carrick studied one such old barn in Vermont and produced a simple story about nature's effects on the barn and the creatures it shelters. "That is all, and yet the mood lingers, enhancing the nobility of the barn and the effect of the atmosphere," remarked Mary Silva Cosgrave in a *Horn Book* review of this debut title.

This was the first of many titles dealing with aspects of nature. Others in the same vein include *The Brook, Swamp Spring, The Pond,* and *A Clearing in the Forest.* Reviewing *The Brook, Horn Book*'s Ethel L. Heins felt "Imagistic words ... [and] impressionistic paintings extend and complement each other," while a contributor for *Kirkus Reviews,* writing about *Swamp Spring,*

A nine-year-old boy struggles with the ramifications of his father's illness and the grief that follows his father's death in Carrick's sensitive book for young readers. (From Upside-Down Cake, *illustrated by Paddy Bouma.)*

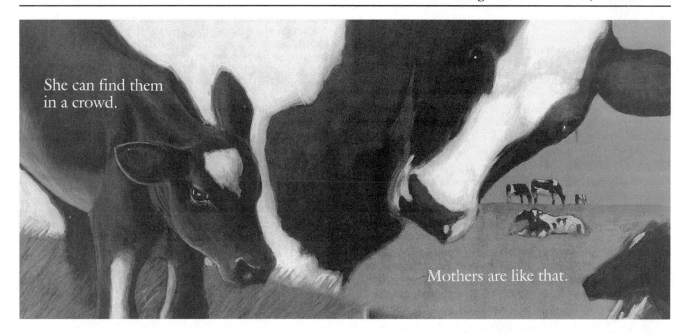

She can find them
in a crowd.

Mothers are like that.

Carrick and her son collaborated on a picture book about mothers of all species and the ways in which they care for their young. *(From* Mothers Are Like That, *written by Carol Carrick and illustrated by Paul Carrick.)*

concluded, "Evocative books are often vapid, but this one has substance."

The animals in nature also provide focus for many of the Carricks' collaborative efforts. One of her most popular titles and one that garnered many awards is *The Blue Lobster,* which details the life cycle of that crustacean. "This is not only an informative book but one that will increase awareness," wrote Roger Caras in the *New York Times Book Review.* Caras concluded, "This is a very satisfying nature book for the beginning reader." Juliet Kellogg Markowsky, writing in *School Library Journal,* claimed, "It is the measured, elegant prose and the dramatic yet realistic watercolor illustrations ... which place this above the usual 'life cycle' accounts." The Carricks continued this winning combination in other animal books, including *Sand Tiger Shark, Octopus, The Crocodiles Still Wait,* and *Two Coyotes.* In *The Crocodiles Still Wait,* Carrick looks at the life cycle of that amphibian in the age of the dinosaurs, noting how they have survived while the dinosaurs have become extinct. *Horn Book*'s Virginia Haviland praised the "animated and colorful" illustrations, further noting that the "text describes equally energetically the exotic characteristics of crocodile life."

Such musings about dinosaurs led to the writing of one of Carrick's personal favorites, *Patrick's Dinosaurs.* On a visit to the zoo, Patrick's older brother talks about dinosaurs, scaring the younger brother, until Patrick finds out they all died millions of years ago. Reviewing the title in *Publishers Weekly,* a critic remarked, "the Carricks display again their talents and the empathy with young readers that makes their adventures special." Georgess McHargue wrote in the *New York Times Book Review,* "it is ... an amusing look at the role of dinosaurs in kids' mental lives." Patrick makes a return

in *What Happened to Patrick's Dinosaurs?,* in which young Patrick becomes fascinated by the extinct creatures and develops his own explanation for their disappearance. "Carol Carrick's text masterfully understates Patrick's fanciful imagination," remarked Jacqueline Elsner in a *School Library Journal* review. Steven Kroll, writing in the *New York Times Book Review,* called this second Patrick title a "grand tribute to the powers of imagination."

Fans had to wait thirteen years for *Patrick's Dinosaurs on the Internet,* a third volume about the young boy's adventures. Looking up information on dinosaurs, Patrick falls asleep at his computer only to be awakened by a dinosaur who has come to take Patrick back to his planet for show and tell. "Patrick's latest adventure is purely entertaining fare," wrote a contributor to *Publishers Weekly.* The same writer concluded, "Young technophiles won't learn a thing about real dinos, software or outer space, but they will be entertained."

When Carrick's two sons were young, she and her husband used many of their adventures as ideas for picture books. The "Christopher" books chronicle the events of a young boy and his dog over many volumes. In *Sleep Out,* young Christopher becomes frightened while camping out, but a "wolf" turns out to be his own dog. The award-winning *Lost in the Storm* shows Christopher worried and frightened when his beloved pet becomes lost in a storm. "Once again the Carricks merge their talents and their feelings for nature and children," commented Heins in a *Horn Book* review of the work. In *The Accident,* Christopher must deal with the death of his dog, while in *The Foundling,* he initially rejects the abandoned dog his parents produce as a substitute. Another storm and its aftermath are shown in *The Washout,* and in *Ben and the Porcupine,* Christopher's new dog tangles with said beast. Reviewing that title, but also describing the "Christopher" books as a whole, a reviewer wrote in *Publishers Weekly:* "The Carricks have made young Christopher extremely popular with children who discover the boy wrestling with familiar dilemmas in gently understated stories." Other books in the series include *Dark and Full of Secrets* and *Left Behind,* in which Christopher gets lost on the subway during a school field trip. "This book is sure to generate a waiting list," noted Ruth Semrau in a *School Library Journal* review.

Over time, the Carricks worked out their own method of collaboration. As Carol Carrick once told *SATA:* "Actually, we didn't work together. Sometimes, we talked about an idea and I would say, 'Why don't we do a book about such and such?' and then he would agree or disagree. But we didn't sit side by side and work together on a project. I would show him a draft of my manuscript, because I respected his opinion. But he didn't work on a book until I sold the manuscript. Then he would make a mental time slot for the illustrations and on request from the editor, he'd make a dummy of the book."

Carrick also wrote of her own technique in an entry for *Something about the Author Autobiography Series:* "I have always needed the security of knowing my characters and setting well, either through a great deal of research or through my own experience. So it felt comfortable in my story *Sleep Out* to use my own son [Christopher] in the setting of Greenwich Village, where we lived, and at our cabin in Vermont.... I also wrote about our second son, Paul, whose character was slightly younger: *Paul's Christmas Birthday, A Rabbit for Easter, The Empty Squirrel,* and *The Highest Balloon on the Common.*"

As her sons grew older, Carrick began to write problem novels for them. "I can't really think of anything I've written that's directly related to my own childhood," Carrick once told *SATA,* "outside of the fact that I always felt like an outsider and a lot of my books like, *What a Wimp!* and *Some Friend!* are about kids who are not popular." *Stay Away from Simon!,* set in the nineteenth century, dealt with the idea of misfits. Carrick once said, "I wrote that book because I was out of ideas and it was crisis time. My sons were getting older and I really didn't know what was going on in their lives. If I had had a daughter, I probably would have gone into writing a teenage book because she would have rekindled things from my childhood. Since children's books stay in print a long time it's hard to keep them sounding contemporary. I wanted mine to have a more timeless quality so I tried setting them in an earlier period. Since I like to understand my material, I read all I could about early American life. That's how I wrote *Stay Away from Simon!,* with Simon, again, as an outsider." A contributor to *Children's Books and Their Creators* noted, "Carol's sensitivity finds its fullest expression in her books for older readers," and further remarked, *Stay Away from Simon!* "is a powerful adventure story of a retarded boy, feared and shunned, who rescues two

children lost in a snowstorm." *What a Wimp!,* dealing with a bully, was one of the Carricks' "most appealing" books, according to a contributor in *Publishers Weekly.*

Writing about certain periods of time also presented obstacles for Carrick's meticulous nature. The author once noted, "I can never get enough research. I did a book called *The Elephant in the Dark* which takes place around 1800, and I never learned all I wanted to about training elephants. There aren't a lot of journals in that period. If I wanted to start with Will getting up in the morning, I had to think, 'Well, what did they eat then? What did they wear? Did they cook in a fireplace or in a stove?' But all those little necessities of daily life gave me the ideas for the plot." For her 1999 novel, *Upside-Down Cake,* Carrick used her own experience of her husband's death from cancer to tell the story of a young boy's reactions to his father's death from the same illness. *Booklist* reviewer Grace Anne A. DeCandido noted, "The gentle messages ... are simply stated," while a contributor to *Publishers Weekly* concluded, "This well-observed story provides a mirror for those coping with grief and will also aid those who wish to understand and empathize with a grieving friend."

With her husband's death in 1989, Carrick herself had to learn the lesson to keep moving and to take life a day at a time. Since 1990, she has produced picture books and beginning novels for young readers. A boy tries to attract the Tooth Fairy in *Norman Fools the Tooth Fairy,* while Carrick tells the story of two nineteenth-century circus-performing midgets in *Two Very Little Sisters.* Her *Whaling Days* is a nonfiction treatment of the history of whaling, a book that "encourages curiosity, particularly about the natural world, in a very understated, matter-of-fact way," according to *Horn Book* contributor Elizabeth S. Watson. With *Banana Beer,* Carrick tackles the difficult problem of alcohol abuse by a parent in picture book format. Single-parenting is dealt with in *Valentine,* in which a new-born lamb helps to ease the pain of a mother's absence for a little girl. Lee Bock, writing in *School Library Journal,* called this title a "very successful effort that children will relate to and enjoy." In *Melanie,* Carrick presents an original fairy tale in which a grandfather tries to cure his granddaughter's blindness. Writing in *Booklist,* Lauren Peterson claimed that this book "is sure to attract primary-grade children."

And with *Mothers Are Like That,* Carrick seems to have come full circle in her books, once again working with a family member. This time it is her son Paul who illustrated the book about mothers of all species and the ways in which they care for their young. "The mother-son collaboration quietly praises mothers of all species," noted a contributor for *Publishers Weekly,* who concluded that the book "makes an especially apt bedtime book for parent and child to share."

Works Cited

Review of *Ben and the Porcupine, Publishers Weekly,* April 17, 1981, p. 62.

Bock, Lee, review of *Valentine, School Library Journal,* May, 1995, p. 82.

Caras, Roger, review of *The Blue Lobster, New York Times Book Review,* May 4, 1975, p. 45.

"Carrick, Carol," *Children's Books and Their Creators,* edited by Anita Silvey, Houghton Mifflin, 1995, pp. 122-23.

Carrick, Carol, entry in *Something about the Author Autobiography Series,* Volume 18, Gale, 1994.

Cosgrave, Mary Silva, review of *The Old Barn, Horn Book,* October, 1966, pp. 558-59.

DeCandido, Grace Anne A., review of *Upside-Down Cake, Booklist,* November 1, 1999, p. 528.

Elsner, Jacqueline, review of *What Happened to Patrick's Dinosaurs?, School Library Journal,* May, 1986, p. 68.

Haviland, Virginia, review of *The Crocodiles Still Wait, Horn Book,* August, 1980, p. 425.

Heins, Ethel L., review of *The Brook, Horn Book,* February, 1968, p. 53.

Heins, Ethel L., review of *Lost in the Storm, Horn Book,* April, 1975, pp. 136-37.

Kroll, Steven, review of *What Happened to Patrick's Dinosaurs?, New York Times Book Review,* April 27, 1986, p. 25.

Markowsky, Juliet Kellogg, review of *The Blue Lobster, School Library Journal,* May, 1975, p. 53.

McHargue, Georgess, "Dinosaurs Galore," *New York Times Book Review,* November 13, 1983, p. 40.

Review of *Mothers Are Like That, Publishers Weekly,* March 6, 2000, p. 109.

Review of *Patrick's Dinosaurs, Publishers Weekly,* September 16, 1983, p. 125.

Review of *Patrick's Dinosaurs on the Internet, Publishers Weekly,* September 6, 1999, p. 102.

Peterson, Lauren, review of *Melanie, Booklist,* September 15, 1996, p. 245.

Semrau, Ruth, review of *Left Behind, School Library Journal,* December, 1988, p. 83.

Review of *Swamp Spring, Kirkus Reviews,* February 1, 1969, p. 93.

Review of *Upside-Down Cake, Publishers Weekly,* September 13, 1999, p. 84.

Watson, Elizabeth S., review of *Whaling Days, Horn Book,* May-June, 1993, p. 345.

Review of *What a Wimp!, Publishers Weekly,* May 27, 1983, p. 67.

For More Information See

BOOKS

Fourth Book of Junior Authors and Illustrators, edited by Doris de Montreville and Elizabeth D. Crawford, H. W. Wilson, 1978.

PERIODICALS

Booklist, May 1, 1992, p. 1606; May 1, 1993, p. 1595; October 1, 1993, p. 347; April 14, 1995, p. 1422; December 1, 1999, p. 709.

Bulletin of the Center for Children's Books, July, 1993, p. 341; October, 1993, p. 41; April, 1994, p. 266; November, 1996, p. 92.

New York Times Book Review, August 22, 1993, p. 19.

Publishers Weekly, November 10, 1989, p. 60; February 22, 1993, p. 96; March 14, 1993, p. 31; August 23, 1993, p. 70; January 16, 1995, p. 455.

School Library Journal, October, 1989, p. 101; July, 1990, p. 320; November, 1991, p. 59; April, 1992, p. 90; May, 1993, p. 112; March, 1994, p. 213; April, 1995, p. 98; November, 1996, p. 79; September, 1999, p. 178.

*   *   *

CASTLE, Robert
See HAMILTON, Edmond

*   *   *

CHARBONNEAU, Eileen 1951-

Personal

Born April 11, 1951, in Long Island, NY; daughter of Vincent (a business owner) and Katherine (Zorovich) Charbonneau; married Edward Gullo (a news correspondent), August 19, 1972; children: Abigail, Mariah, Susannah. *Education:* State University of New York at Fredonia, B.A.; attended River Arts Film School at Woodstock, New York. *Hobbies and other interests:* Genealogy, contra-dancing, shape-note singing.

Addresses

Home—P.O. Box 20, Cold Spring, NY 10516. *E-mail*—ECharbonn@aol.com. *Agent*—Susan Yven, Susan Herner Rights Agency, P.O. Box 303, Scarsdale, NY 10583.

Career

Freelance writer, 1974—. Worked as a teacher, waitress, and department store receiver; community theater director and actress; La Leche League leader and district advisor; Girl Scout leader. *Member:* Society of Children's Book Writers and Illustrators, Young Adult Writers Network.

Awards, Honors

Golden Medallion Award, Romance Writers of America, 1989, for *The Ghosts of Stony Clove;* Phyllis A. Whitney Award; Christopher Columbus Discovery Award in Screenwriting; honorable mention, Philadelphia Writers' Conference, Juvenile Writing Category, MARA Award (2nd place), Fiction from the Heartland Competition (2nd place), Best Books citation, American Library Association, all for *In the Time of the Wolves;* Holt Medallion Award (2nd place) for *The Mound Builders' Secret;* Rita Award nominations for *The Randolph Legacy* and *Rachel LeMoyne.*

Writings

The Ghosts of Stony Clove, Orchard Books, 1988.

Eileen Charbonneau

In the Time of the Wolves, Tor Books, 1994.
The Mound Builders' Secret (Z-Fave "You-Solve-It Mystery" series), Zebra Books, 1994.
Disappearance at Harmony Festival (Z-Fave "You-Solve-It Mystery" series), Zebra Books, 1994.
Honor to the Hills, Tor Books, 1996.
Waltzing in Ragtime, Tor/Forge, 1996.
The Randolph Legacy, Tor/Forge, 1997.
Rachel LeMoyne, Forge/Doherty, 1998.
The Connor Emerald, Timeless Books, 2000.

Contributor to periodicals, including *New York Times, Newsday, Mothering, Lady's Circle, Highlights for Children, The Writer,* and *Midwifery Today;* fiction editor for a literary magazine and a state newsletter.

Work in Progress

The Codetalker, a romantic suspense novel set in New York City during the Second World War; *Five Aprils,* an historical novel set during the American Civil War.

Sidelights

New York author Eileen Charbonneau is a storyteller whose first two novels, *The Ghosts of Stony Clove* and *In the Time of the Wolves,* enthralled her readers and won widespread critical praise and numerous awards. In the years since, Charbonneau has created several more books and made a name for herself as the writer of evocative and insightful historical fiction appealing to a wide range of readers. One of her recurrent themes is the need for tolerance and understanding between people; it

is a message about which Charbonneau has strong feelings. As the author once told *SATA,* she is motivated by her own ethnicity and childhood experiences. "My family's story was the first I wanted to tell. I'm a multi-ethnic product of Irish, Slovene, French, Canadian, and Native American roots that somehow came together on the sidewalks of New York when this century was young.... Striving to understand another person's viewpoint comes naturally—chances are that view is part of me."

Charbonneau grew up on Long Island in New York, the middle child of ten. Her family lived in a small 1920s vintage three-bedroom cottage (with a single bathroom). It was a "great childhood for a future writer in the middle of that crew, believe me!" Charbonneau told *Authors and Artists for Young Adults* in an interview. "My sisters and brothers were, and are, a very diverse lot. My parents were very loving toward each other and us. We were treasured. I loved being in the middle of all that male/female energy."

Charbonneau was a keen student, and she fell in love with reading; it was one leisure time activity that was inexpensive and afforded a measure of privacy in her close living quarters. The "family library" consisted of a set of old encyclopedias and a dictionary, so young Eileen cherished her library card. She read voraciously. "The library was the place where the books lived. I started with fairy tales, every version I could get my hands on, went on to borrow my sister's comic books, then to Nancy Drew. After that, biographies fascinated me, and then the currently ongoing *everything else!*" she remarked. Charbonneau said that of all the books she read as a youngster, the one that influenced her most was Harper Lee's 1960 Pulitzer Prize-winning novel *To Kill a Mockingbird,* a powerful story about the trial of a black man in a Southern town. "I loved the characters, the big heart of that book, and its time-and-place-defying courage."

Charbonneau decided to become a writer in fourth grade when she wrote an imaginative story about a dog that made her classmates laugh and won praise from her teacher, but at first her writing was strictly for her own amusement. She attended the State University of New York, earning a bachelor of arts degree, and took courses at River Arts Film School in Woodstock, New York. In 1972 she married journalist Edward Gullo and moved to Buffalo, New York, where they started their family of three daughters.

During these years, Charbonneau continued to read and dream of becoming a writer. Because she was so busy with her family, however, the prospect of becoming an author seemed like wishful thinking. "Then a friend told me I wrote good letters and invited me to attend an adult education class about writing for publication," Charbonneau recalled in her interview. "I laugh now when I think of how I resisted her suggestion. I was too busy with diapers to handle deadlines too! But that class changed my life. I didn't think I could earn money as a writer until I got it through my head [that] writers don't have to live in ivory towers with a dozen degrees. Some were like my teacher, who was amazingly like me—a mom who had a great stay-at-home job!"

Charbonneau spent the next few years working on two novels that were never published—her "practice books." While researching one of them, she chanced upon an old legend of the Catskill Mountains. "The story fascinated me and I tried to cram it into the book I was writing, but it kept telling me it wanted a book of its own. I finally listened, and it became the center of the story I wove around it." The result was Charbonneau's first book, the young adult novel *The Ghosts of Stony Clove.*

Set in the Catskills in the early nineteenth century, the work recounts the adventures of a half-Native American, half-French teenage boy named Asher Woods. Because of his mixed parentage and his status as an indentured servant, Asher is shunned by most of the people in his small town, but he becomes friends with a young woman named Ginny Rockwell. Ginny's father has died, leaving Ginny and her mother in impoverished circumstances. Wandering in the woods one day, Asher and Ginny come upon an old house that is said to be haunted. The young people are surprised to discover that Squire Sutherland, the elderly landowner whom everyone thought was dead, is still alive. Ginny begins taking care of the old man; Asher decides to travel West to find his family, who abandoned him when he was five years old. Sutherland dies, leaving his house and land to Ginny, and when Asher returns from his quest, he and Ginny fall in love and decide to marry.

Elizabeth Mellett of *School Library Journal* wrote that *The Ghosts of Stony Clove* is "fast-paced" and "entertaining." A critic for *Horn Book* recommended the novel as "a good introduction to historical fiction," and a *Booklist* reviewer wrote that, in addition to the elements of romantic adventure, some readers may "find deeper themes of prejudice and revenge to ponder."

Charbonneau continued the saga of the Woods family in her second book, *In The Time of the Wolves.* Set in 1824, it recounts the adventures of Asher and Ginny's rebellious fifteen-year-old son, Joshua Woods. Father and son track some migrating wolves through the Catskills, and along the way Asher and Joshua learn to understand and respect each another. "Technically a sequel to *The Ghosts of Stony Clove,* this [book] stands well on its own . . . an uniquely urgent story, hard to put down or to forget," *Kliatt* reviewer Laura B. Warren wrote. Cheryl A. Chlysta of the *Voice of Youth Advocates* echoed those comments, noting that "The characterization throughout this story is well developed and believable. The historical references are accurate and a good reflection of this time period in early American history." *Booklist* reviewer Merri Monks commented, "Intrigue, excellent characterizations, the mysteries surrounding Josh's father's past, a touch of the supernatural, and the hardships of 1824 ('the year without summer') will keep readers enthralled."

Set in the Catskill Mountains in the early nineteenth century, Charbonneau's novel recounts the adventures of a half-Native American, half-French teenage boy named Asher Woods. (Cover illustration by Neil Waldman.)

Charbonneau struck out in a new direction with her next two books, interactive "You Solve-It Mysteries" for young adults. *The Mound Builders' Secret* and *Disappearance at Harmony Festival* challenge readers to solve a mystery by reading the text and searching the illustration on the book's cover for clues. In both cases, the answer can be found only after breaking the seal on the pages of the final chapter. In the *Mound Builders' Secret,* a boy named Tad visits an archeological dig. There he meets Linda, the half-Cherokee teenager who supervises the site. The excavation is desecrated, and Tad and Linda team up to find the culprit. *Disappearance at Harmony Festival* reunites the pair as they search for a missing person.

Charbonneau also wrote a third "You Solve-It Mystery" book, but the publisher closed down the series before the work could be published. She submitted it to several publishers, and Timeless Treasures agreed to publish it as a stand-alone mystery called *The Connor Emerald;* it is scheduled for publication in 2000.

Charbonneau returned to historical fiction and the adventures of the Woods family in *Honor to the Hills.* This third installment in the saga is set in 1851 and focuses on Ginny and Asher's sixteen-year-old granddaughter, Lily, who has a rebellious streak like her father, Joshua. Lily and the rest of her family are outraged by the enactment of the Fugitive Slave Law of 1850, which makes it legal for Southern bounty hunters to come North to capture both runaway slaves and free blacks. They are further enraged when Lily's older sister returns home, mute and badly burned from a deadly arsonist's fire that razed her School for Ladies and Misses of Color. Lily sets out to thwart the slave catchers who are active in the area, but complications arise when Lily falls in love with a penniless young Irish immigrant named Hugh Delaney.

Critics praised the book and lauded Charbonneau's imaginative storytelling. "This is a multi-layered story of two young people coming of age, of the Underground Railway in the turbulent years prior to the Civil War, and the diverse ethnic heritage that makes up our nation. Characters, plot, and location are described and developed so that the reader can almost see the people and their home," wrote reviewer Cynthia Beatty Brown in *Voice of Youth Advocates.* "This latest title will be best appreciated by readers who already know the Woods family, as Charbonneau skillfully weaves in familiar personalities and subtle references to the family history with a new story line involving the next generation's attempts to secure justice for their black neighbors," said a reviewer for the *Bulletin of the Center for Children's Books.* "As the [Woods] family has settled at Stony Clove, so has Charbonneau's writing skill matured, making poetry of the glances between lovers and kin, bonding spiritual elements with realistic elements in the atmospheric mountain setting," a writer for *Kirkus Reviews* observed.

Charbonneau created a new set of characters for her next novel, *Waltzing in Ragtime,* her first venture into adult fiction. The story, set in 1903, concerns twenty-three-year-old Olana Whittaker, the spoiled daughter of a lumber baron. Olana is working as a reporter for a San Francisco newspaper when she is assigned to cover the opening of Sequoia National Park. There she meets Matthew Hart, the park's long-haired forest ranger. Matthew, a staunch environmentalist, is determined to protect his park from loggers like Olana's father. Initially, she and Matthew are hostile to one another, but after she is caught in a blizzard in the Sierra Nevada Mountains and he saves her life, they begin to understand each other and fall in love. Charbonneau recounts the trials and tribulations of their romance in a story full of action, murder, love, and surprising plot twists, some of which are set around the 1906 San Francisco earthquake. "Charbonneau's mix of sexy romance and melodrama provides plenty of entertainment," wrote a *Publishers Weekly* reviewer. *Washington Post Book World* critic Bob Allen gave a similar assessment,

stating "This provocative historical romance … has an almost made-for-TV miniseries sheen to it.... Despite a certain predictability in both plot and characterization, this is a well-told, extremely entertaining tale."

Charbonneau continued historical themes in her next adult book, *The Randolph Legacy,* her personal favorite of the books she has written. Like *Waltzing in Ragtime,* it is a sprawling romantic adventure filled with larger-than-life characters, action, and adventure. The story begins in 1805 with twelve-year-old American orphan Henry Washington being severely flogged by the brutal Englishman who has impressed him into being his midshipman. Crippled by the beating, Henry draws the compassion of a Frenchman who saves his life, hides him away on the ship, and educates him. Eight years later, Henry, now a young man, meets an American Quaker missionary, Judith Mercer, on her way home from England. Although Judith is ten years older than

When Henry Washington finds out he is the third son of a wealthy Virginia landowner and tries to return to the plantation to recover his birthright, he must convince his older brothers, who see him as a rival and a fortune hunter. (Cover illustration by Thomas Doughty.)

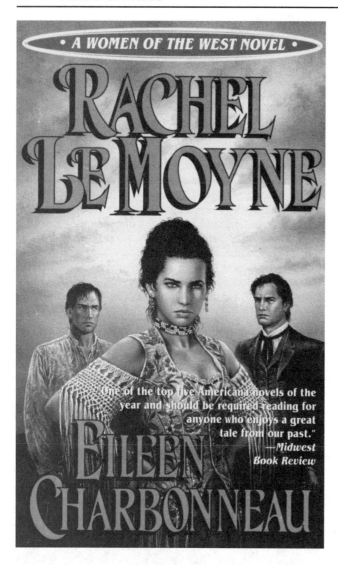

In Charbonneau's contribution to the "Women of the West" series, the spirited protagonist tries to reconcile her half-Choctaw heritage with the Presbyterian upbringing she has received while living with missionaries. (Cover illustration by Royo.)

Henry, they fall in love. Judith not only rescues Henry, she also discovers his true identity: he is actually Ethan Randolph, the third son of a wealthy Virginia landowner. The plot becomes more complicated when Henry, with Judith's help, tries to return to the Randolph plantation and recover his birthright. The women of the family are convinced that Ethan is who he claims to be, but his older brothers are not; to them, he is a rival and a fortune-hunter. In a review of *The Randolph Legacy,* a *Publishers Weekly* critic commented, "Charbonneau ... once again shows impressive command of the elements of historical romance in a tale of suffering, revenge, redemption, and, of course, love, set in post-Revolutionary America."

Charbonneau has more recently published *Rachel Le-Moyne,* one volume in Forge's "Women of the West" series. In this book, the title character attempts to reconcile her half-Choctaw blood with the Presbyterian

upbringing she has received while living with missionaries. When the Choctaw send surplus corn to the starving people in Ireland in the 1830s, Rachel goes along as an emissary. She marries an Irish firebrand named Darragh Ronan to save him from prison, and this leads to trouble when the couple return to the United States. Darragh kills a man who menaces Rachel, and the couple flee west to Oregon by wagon train. During their adventures along the way, their relationship develops and they fall in love. Charbonneau "has melded disparate historical events, real people, and fictional characters into a compelling tale of clashing cultures, religions, and classes transformed by the challenge of the American frontier," wrote Cynthia Johnson of *Library Journal.* Patty Englemann of *Booklist* hailed *Rachel LeMoyne* as "a powerful and dramatic tale of moral fortitude and love in a world ruled by ignorance and hate," but a critic for *Publishers Weekly* described the book as "predictable" although "partly redeemed by its colorful atmosphere and brave, resourceful heroine."

Having earned a reputation as the author of historical novels, Charbonneau told *Authors and Artists for Young Adults* that she is working on two new books in this genre—*The Codetalker,* a romantic suspense novel set in New York City during the Second World War, and *Five Aprils,* set during the American Civil War. She has said of her work, "An actress needs a stage, a plumber needs a broken sink. I need paper, a writing tool, and perseverance.... I have stories to tell. My hope is that they will reach further than myself and touch other hearts."

Works Cited

Allen, Bob, review of *Waltzing in Ragtime, Washington Post Book World,* October 6, 1996, p. 8.

Brown, Cynthia Beatty, review of *Honor to the Hills, Voice of Youth Advocates,* June, 1996, p. 94.

Charbonneau, Eileen, interview with *Authors and Artists for Young Adults,* November, 1999.

Chlysta, Cheryl A., review of *In the Time of the Wolves, Voice of Youth Advocates,* April, 1995, p. 20.

Englemann, Patty, review of *Rachel LeMoyne, Booklist,* May 15, 1998, p. 1593.

Review of *The Ghosts of Stony Clove, Booklist,* May 15, 1988, p. 1606.

Review of *The Ghosts of Stony Clove, Horn Book,* July, 1988, p. 501.

Review of *Honor to the Hills, Bulletin of the Center for Children's Books,* May, 1996, p. 295.

Review of *Honor to the Hills, Kirkus Reviews,* December 15, 1995, p. 1767.

Johnson, Cynthia, review of *Rachel LeMoyne, Library Journal,* May 15, 1998, p. 113.

Mellett, Elizabeth, review of *The Ghosts of Stony Clove, School Library Journal,* June, 1988, p. 115.

Monks, Merri, review of *In the Time of the Wolves, Booklist,* December 1, 1994, pp. 663-64.

Review of *Rachel LeMoyne, Publishers Weekly,* April 27, 1998, p. 46.

Review of *The Randolph Legacy, Publishers Weekly,* July 21, 1997, p. 185.

Review of *Waltzing in Ragtime, Publishers Weekly,* July 1, 1996, p. 44.

Warren, Laura B., review of *In the Time of the Wolves, Kliatt,* May, 1995, p. 6.

For More Information See

PERIODICALS

Booklist, August, 1997, p. 1876.
Chicago Sun-Times, August 14, 1988, p. 19.
Kirkus Reviews, May 1, 1988, p. 689.
Voice of Youth Advocates, October, 1988, p. 180.

*   *   *

CHEESE, Chloe 1952-

Personal

Born December 6, 1952, in London, England; daughter of Bernard (an artist and printmaker) and Sheila (an artist and illustrator; maiden name, Robinson) Cheese; married Philip Shaw (a lecturer), 1984 (divorced, 1999); children: Arthur, Florence. *Education:* Attended Cambridge Art School, 1969-72; Royal College of Art, London, M.A., 1976. *Politics:* "Labour (Socialist)." *Religion:* None.

Chloe Cheese

Addresses

Home—10 South Croxted Rd., London SE21 8BB, England. *E-mail*—chloe@benchees.demon.co.uk.

Career

Freelance illustrator. Also works as an art lecturer, including positions with Notre Dame University, Beirut, Lebanon, and with art schools and universities in London, England. *Member:* Association of Illustrators (patron).

Awards, Honors

Royal Academy Drawing Prize, 1972; Printmaking Prize, Lloyds Bank, 1981; runner-up for Mother Goose Award, 1996.

Writings

ILLUSTRATOR

Rudyard Kipling, *How the Alphabet Was Made,* Macmillan (London, England), 1983, Peter Bedrick (New York City), 1987.

Adrian Mitchell, editor, *The Orchard Book of Poems,* Orchard Books, 1993.

Michael Rosen, editor, *Walking the Bridge of Your Nose,* Kingfisher (New York City), 1995.

Amy Hest, *The Babies Are Coming,* Crown (New York City), 1997.

Roger McGough, editor, *The Kingfisher Book of Poems about Love,* Kingfisher, 1997.

Contributor of illustrations to periodicals, including *Sunday Times, Telegraph* newspapers, and the *New Yorker.*

Work in Progress

A limited-edition book about the author's childhood; illustrating a children's book about the cats of Beirut.

Sidelights

Chloe Cheese told *SATA:* "I have been a freelance illustrator since leaving the Royal College of Art. I illustrated primarily food and wine at first and came indirectly to children's books. I still work on fine art lithographic prints and paintings, which have been exhibited in London and Japan.

"My childhood was spent in a small village (Great Bardfield) in the county of Essex. My brother and I lived with my mother, who was part of a group of artists resident in the village. The artists were interested in recording the landscape and the life of the village community. I have very vivid visual memories from that time in the 1950s and 1960s—of the village people, their agricultural and craft skills, their way of life (which has almost disappeared now), and also of the houses and work of my mother's friends.

"An important period for me was, as a student, spending three months in Paris. From this time came my interest in drawing food inspired by the beautiful French *patisserie* in shop windows.

"I started illustrating children's books after reading to my small children every day. I then began to think about illustrating books for them. I found that drawing children was made easy by having Arthur and Florence living with me. I knew the way they stood, sat, and ran so well, and their physical proportions and movements at different ages. I could put this knowledge together with my past illustrating experience and my own life experiences to draw, with pleasure, for children."

*   *   *

COVILLE, Bruce 1950-
(Robyn Tallis)

Personal

Born May 16, 1950, in Syracuse, NY; son of Arthur J. (a sales engineer) and Jean (an executive secretary; maiden name, Chase) Coville; married Katherine Dietz (an illustrator), October 11, 1969; children: Orion Sean, Cara Joy. *Education:* Attended Duke University and State University of New York at Binghamton; State University of New York at Oswego, B.A., 1974. *Politics:* "Eclectic." *Religion:* Unitarian.

Addresses

Agent—Ashley Grayson, 1342 18th Street, San Pedro, CA 90732.

Career

Author and playwright. Wetzel Road Elementary, Liverpool, NY, teacher, 1974-81. Co-host and co-producer of *Upstage,* a cable program promoting local theater, 1983. Has also worked as a camp counselor, grave digger, assembly line worker, and toy maker. *Member:* Society of Children's Book Writers and Illustrators.

Awards, Honors

California Young Reader Medal, 1996-97, for *Jennifer Murdley's Toad;* Knickerbocker Award, New York State Library Association, for entire body of work, 1997; over a dozen Children's Choice awards from various states, including Arizona, Hawaii, and Nevada.

Writings

PICTURE BOOKS

The Foolish Giant, illustrated by wife, Katherine Coville, Lippincott, 1978.
Sarah's Unicorn, illustrated by K. Coville, Lippincott, 1979.
Sarah and the Dragon, illustrated by Beth Peck, Harper, 1984.

Bruce Coville

My Grandfather's House, illustrated by Henri Sorensen, BridgeWater, 1996.

JUVENILE FICTION

The Brave Little Toaster Storybook, Doubleday, 1987.
Murder in Orbit, Scholastic, 1987.
Monster of the Year, Pocket, 1989.
Goblins in the Castle, Pocket, 1992.
The Dragonslayers, Pocket, 1994.
Oddly Enough (short stories), illustrated by Michael Hussar, Harcourt, 1994.
The World's Worst Fairy Godmother, illustrated by K. Coville, Pocket, 1996.
The Lapsnatcher, illustrated by Marissa Moss, BridgeWater, 1997.
I Was a Sixth-Grade Alien, illustrated by Tony Sansevero, Pocket, 1999.
Odder Than Ever (short stories), Harcourt, 1999.
The Attack of the Two-Inch Teacher, illustrated by T. Sansevero, Pocket, 1999.
I Lost My Grandfather's Brain, illustrated by T. Sansevero, Pocket, 1999.
Peanut Butter Lover Boy, illustrated by T. Sansevero, Pocket, 2000.
The Prince of Butterflies, illustrated by John Clapp, Harcourt, 2000.
Zombies of the Science Fair, illustrated by T. Sansevero, Pocket, 2000.

YOUNG ADULT NOVELS

Space Station ICE III, Archway, 1985.
Fortune's Journey, BridgeWater, 1995.
(With Jane Yolen) *Armageddon Summer,* Harcourt, 1998.

"CHAMBER OF HORROR" SERIES; YOUNG ADULT NOVELS

Bruce Coville's Chamber of Horror: Amulet of Doom, Archway, 1983.
Bruce Coville's Chamber of Horror: Spirits and Spells, Archway, 1983.
Bruce Coville's Chamber of Horror: The Eyes of the Tarot, Archway, 1984.
Bruce Coville's Chamber of Horror: Waiting Spirits, Archway, 1985.

"A.I. GANG" SERIES

Operation Sherlock, NAL, 1986.
Robot Trouble, NAL, 1986.
Forever Begins Tomorrow, NAL, 1986.

"CAMP HAUNTED HILLS" SERIES

How I Survived My Summer Vacation, Pocket, 1988.
Some of My Best Friends Are Monsters, Pocket, 1989.
The Dinosaur That Followed Me Home, illustrated by John Pierard, Pocket, 1990.

"MY TEACHER" SERIES

My Teacher Is an Alien, Pocket, 1989.
My Teacher Fried My Brains, Pocket, 1991.
My Teacher Glows in the Dark, Pocket, 1991.
My Teacher Flunked the Planet, Pocket, 1992.

"MAGIC SHOP" SERIES

The Monster's Ring, Knopf, 1982.
Jeremy Thatcher, Dragon Hatcher, illustrated by Gary A. Lippincott, Harcourt, 1991.
Jennifer Murdley's Toad, illustrated by G. A. Lippincott, Harcourt, 1992.
The Skull of Truth, illustrated by G. A. Lippincott, Harcourt, 1997.

"NINA TANLEVEN" SERIES

The Ghost in the Third Row, Bantam, 1987.
The Ghost Wore Gray, Bantam, 1988.
Ghost in the Big Brass Bed, Bantam, 1991.

"SPACE BRAT" SERIES; CHAPTER BOOKS

Space Brat, illustrated by K. Coville, Pocket, 1992.
Blork's Evil Twin, illustrated by K. Coville, Pocket, 1993.
The Wrath of Squat, illustrated by K. Coville, Pocket, 1994.
Planet of the Dips, illustrated by K. Coville, Pocket, 1995.
The Saber-toothed Poodnoobie, illustrated by K. Coville, Pocket, 1997.

"ALIEN ADVENTURES" SERIES

Aliens Ate My Homework, illustrated by K. Coville, Pocket, 1993.
I Left My Sneakers in Dimension X, illustrated by K. Coville, Pocket, 1994.
The Search for Snout, illustrated by K. Coville, Pocket, 1995.
Aliens Stole My Body, illustrated by K. Coville, Pocket, 1998.

"UNICORN CHRONICLES" SERIES

Into the Land of the Unicorns, Scholastic, 1994.
The Song of the Wanderer, Scholastic, 1999.

COMPILER AND EDITOR

Bruce Coville's Book of Monsters, Scholastic, 1993.
Bruce Coville's Book of Aliens, Scholastic, 1994.
Bruce Coville's Book of Ghosts, illustrated by J. Pierard, Scholastic, 1994.
Bruce Coville's Book of Nightmares, Scholastic, 1995.
Bruce Coville's Book of Spine Tinglers, Scholastic, 1996.
Bruce Coville's Book of Magic, Scholastic, 1996.
Bruce Coville's Book of Monsters II, illustrated by J. Pierard, Scholastic, 1996.
Bruce Coville's Book of Aliens II, Scholastic, 1996.
Bruce Coville's Book of Ghosts II, illustrated by J. Pierard, Scholastic, 1997.
Bruce Coville's Book of Nightmares II, illustrated by J. Pierard, Scholastic, 1997.
Bruce Coville's Book of Spine Tinglers II, Scholastic, 1997.
Bruce Coville's Book of Magic II, Scholastic, 1997.

RETELLER; PICTURE BOOKS

William Shakespeare, *William Shakespeare's The Tempest,* illustrated by Ruth Sanderson, Bantam, 1993.
William Shakespeare, *William Shakespeare's A Midsummer Night's Dream,* illustrated by Dennis Nolan, Dial, 1996.
William Shakespeare, *William Shakespeare's Macbeth,* illustrated by Gary Kelley, Dial, 1997.
William Shakespeare, *William Shakespeare's Romeo and Juliet,* illustrated by D. Nolan, Dial, 1999.

OTHER

(Author of book and lyrics) *The Dragon Slayers,* music by Angela Peterson, first produced at Syracuse Musical Theater, 1981.
(Author of book and lyrics) *Out of the Blue,* music by A. Peterson, first produced at Syracuse Musical Theater, 1982.
(Author of book and lyrics with Barbara Russell) *It's Midnight: Do You Know Where Your Toys Are?,* music by A. Peterson, first produced at Syracuse Musical Theater, 1983.
(With others) *Seniority Travel Directory,* Schueler Communications, 1986.
(With others) *The Sophisticated Leisure Travel Directory,* Schueler Communications, 1986.
(Compiler and editor) *The Unicorn Treasury,* illustrated by Tim Hildebrandt, Doubleday, 1987.
The Dark Abyss (adult novel), Bantam, 1989.
Prehistoric People (nonfiction), illustrated by Michael McDermott, Doubleday, 1990.
(Compiler and editor) *Herds of Thunder, Manes of Gold: A Collection of Horse Stories and Poems,* illustrated by Ted Lewin, Doubleday, 1991.
(Compiler) *A Glory of Unicorns,* illustrated by Alix Berenzy, Scholastic, 1998.

Contributor to anthologies, including *Dragons and Dreams,* 1986, and *Read On! Two,* Books 4 and 6, 1987. Contributor to *Harper's Bookletter, Sesame Street Parent's Newsletter, Cricket,* and *Wilson Library Bulletin.*

Associate editor, *Syracuse Business* and *Syracuse Magazine,* both 1982-83; editor and columnist, *Seniority,* 1983-84. Author, under pseudonym Robyn Tallis, of two books in the "Planet Builder" series, *Night of Two New Moons,* 1985, and *Mountain of Stolen Dreams,* 1988.

Adaptations

The Monster's Ring (cassette), Recorded Books, 1992; *The Ghost Wore Gray* (cassette), Recorded Books, 1993; *Jennifer Murdley's Toad* (cassette), Listening Library, 1996; *Jeremy Thatcher, Dragon Hatcher* (cassette), Listening Library, 1996; *Aliens Ate My Homework* (cassette), Listening Library, 1998; *Into the Land of the Unicorns: The Unicorn Chronicles Book I* (cassette), Listening Library, 1998; *The Skull of Truth* (cassette), Listening Library, 1998; *My Teacher Is an Alien* (cassette), Listening Library, 1998.

Sidelights

Bruce Coville is well known as a writer of juvenile fiction and the author of children's best-sellers such as *Jeremy Thatcher, Dragon Hatcher.* His novels draw heavily on mythic creatures, such as unicorns and dragons, and science fiction traditions, such as aliens and space stations, often with a humorous twist. He has also contributed to and edited volumes of short stories and completed several musical plays for younger audiences. As he once told *SATA,* Coville cherishes memories of his childhood, noting that his early surroundings nurtured his vivid imagination: "I was raised in Phoenix, a small town in central New York. Actually, I lived well outside the town, around the corner from my grandparents' dairy farm, which was the site of my happiest childhood times. I still have fond memories of the huge barns with their mows and lofts, mysterious relics, and jostling cattle. It was a wonderful place for a child to grow up. In addition to the farm, there was a swamp behind the house, and a rambling wood beyond that, both of which were conducive to all kinds of imaginative games." It was during this period that Coville began to develop the heightened sensibility usually possessed by writers of fantasy.

Coville's father, not bookish himself, was instrumental in exposing the young Bruce to the delightful world of literature. Coville once recounted in *SATA:* "Despite this wonderful setting, much of what went on at that time went on in my head, when I was reading, or thinking and dreaming about what I had read. I was an absolute bookaholic. My father had something to do with this." Coville went on to explain: "He was a traveling salesman, a gruff but loving man, who never displayed an overwhelming interest in books. But if anyone was to ask me what was the best thing he ever did for me I could reply without hesitation that he read me *Tom Swift in the City of Gold.* Why he happened to read this to me I was never quite certain, but it changed my life. One night after supper he took me into the living room, had me sit in his lap, and opened a thick, ugly brown book (this was the *original* Tom Swift) and proceeded to open a whole new world for me. I was enthralled, listened

raptly, waited anxiously for the next night and the next, resented an intrusion, and reread the book several times later on my own. It was the only book I can ever remember him reading to me, but it changed my life. I was hooked on books."

Coville may have loved books, but like many other authors, the realization that he wanted to be a writer came very abruptly. He once told *SATA:* "I think it was sixth grade when I first realized that writing was something that I could do, and wanted to do very much. As it happened, I had spent most of that year making life miserable for my teacher by steadfastly failing to respond to the many creative devices she had to stimulate us to write. Then one day she simply (finally!) just let us write—told us that we had a certain amount of time to produce a short story of substance. Freed from writing topics imposed from without, I cut loose, and over several days found that I loved what I was doing. This may not be the first time that I knew I wanted to write, but it's the time that I remember." In addition to writing, Coville himself went on to be a teacher. He held a full-time position at Wetzel Road Elementary School, in Liverpool, New York, for seven years starting in 1974.

However, writing was always to be Coville's first love. He was introduced to the possibilities of writing for children by the woman who would later become his mother-in-law. He once explained in *SATA* that she "gave me a copy of *Winnie the Pooh* to read, and I suddenly knew that what I really wanted to write was children's books—to give to other children the joy that I got from books when I was young. This is the key to what I write now. I try with greater or lesser success, to make my stories the kinds of things that I would have enjoyed myself when I was young; to write the books I wanted to read, but never found. My writing works best when I remember the bookish child who adored reading and gear the work toward him. It falters when I forget him."

As he developed into an experienced writer, Coville worked in different genres. He created musical plays such as *The Dragon Slayers,* first produced at Syracuse Musical Theater. He contributed to anthologies of fantasy stories, such as *Dragons and Dreams.* But it was in the area of picture books, beginning with the publication of *The Foolish Giant* in 1978, that Coville made a significant mark. Illustrated by his wife, Katherine, that first tale for younger readers tells of a mild, clumsy giant who has difficulty being accepted by the ordinary people of his village until he saves them from an evil wizard. In the years since that first book, Coville has published numerous other tales for children, culminating in the appearance of several of his works on children's best-seller lists.

Many of Coville's books are jam-packed with the trappings of traditional mythic imagery: supernatural spirits, tarot cards, unicorns, prehistoric monsters, and futuristic creatures at the outer edge of the universe. He once discussed this in *SATA:* "Myth is very important to me. My picture books have firm roots in basic mythic patterns. Hopefully, the patterns do not intrude, but provide a structure and depth that enhances my work." Coville often combines imaginary creatures with present-day people to create a tale of mystery or adventure. In *The Ghost in the Third Row,* for instance, Nina discovers an actual ghost haunting the theater where she is acting in a murder drama. Nina returns with her friend Chris in *The Ghost Wore Gray,* where the two try to discover the story behind the spirit of a Confederate soldier who appears in a New York hotel. "Despite the fantasy element of a ghost, this is a mystery," notes *School Library Journal* contributor Carolyn Caywood, who adds that the tale "evokes real feeling."

Some of Coville's most popular books have been those that involve Mr. Elive's Magic Shop. In *Jeremy Thatcher, Dragon Hatcher,* young Jeremy escapes his tormenter Mary Lou only to find himself in a strange shop where he buys an unusual egg. When the egg hatches a baby dragon—that no one else but Mary Lou can see—Jeremy finds himself in the midst of adventure. "The book is filled with scenes that will bring laughter and

Action and romance are combined in Coville's tale of a resourceful teenage actress who leads a theater troupe along the Oregon Trail during the Gold Rush era. (Cover illustration by Heide Oberheide.)

near tears to readers," notes Kenneth E. Kowen in *School Library Journal.* Reviewer Kathleen Redmond writes in *Voice of Youth Advocates* that the story is a good combination of real and fantasy worlds and "is right on target." Coville returns to the magic shop in *Jennifer Murdley's Toad,* where Jennifer purchases a lonely toad hatched from a witch's mouth. In aiding her pet, Bufo, who seeks his lost love, Jennifer herself is turned into a toad and learns to appreciate her inner strengths. *School Library Journal* contributor Margaret C. Howell praises Coville's theme as "particularly well handled," adding that "the story moves well, with realistic characterizations."

Coville believes that a knowledge of mythic patterns and imagery can facilitate children's growth and social understanding. He once argued in *SATA:* "This 'making sense' is a process that generally takes a lifetime and yet, sadly, it is all too often never even begun. To utilize myth as a guide in this quest one must be familiar with its patterns and structures, a familiarity that is best gained from reading or hearing myth and its reconstructions from earliest childhood on." Coville thinks that the literature he himself writes plays a part in exposing young people to the mythological realm. "I do not expect," he explained in *SATA,* "a child to read my picture books and suddenly discover the secret of the universe. I do hope that something from my works will tuck itself away in the child's mind, ready to present itself as a piece of a puzzle on some future day when he or she is busy constructing a view of the world that will provide at least a modicum of hope and dignity."

Beyond his grounding in classic fantasy, Coville has filled many of his books with a zany, pungent humor aimed squarely at his young audience. In reviewing *Planet of the Dips, School Library Journal* critic Anne Connor referred to the book as "literary junk food" appealing to "beginning readers with a passion for weird words, stupid jokes and odd behavior." For his part, Coville defends the outrageous extremes of such stories. "There are those who want to keep children's books 'tasteful,' and ten-year-old boys are not tasteful," he told *SATA.* "One of the reasons we have this problem of reluctant readers, especially among boys, is that we're not writing to who and what we are. If you write a book that's a brilliant character study and is wonderfully tasteful and no kid ever reads it, you've failed.... There's another problem, where you publish to only the lowest common denominator, where you start with that and don't go anywhere else. If you do that, you've failed, too. To me, there's a sweet spot in between, where you start with boisterous energy that will engage, and then you take the reader somewhere else."

Coville acknowledges that he has a particular knack for fast-paced comedic storytelling, a talent borne out by the success of his four books in the "My Teacher" series, each of which sold over one million copies. But he also diversified into other types of books during the 1990s, including a series of retellings of Shakespeare's classic plays. Coville found the task of adapting *The Tempest, A Midsummer Night's Dream, Macbeth,* and other works a satisfying challenge. "I've learned little ways to squeeze in more and more of the language, but keep it accessible," he told *SATA.* "Both my editor and I are aware of the hutzpah of what we are doing. We want to be respectful of the source and of the audience. We work really hard on these books." Reviewing *William Shakespeare's Romeo and Juliet* in *Booklist,* Michael Cart calls the picture book "an accessible and entertaining introduction to one of Shakespeare's most popular works." Describing the text for *William Shakespeare's Macbeth* as being "true to the dark, brooding spirit of the play," *Booklist* contributor Hazel Rochman predicted that Coville's "dramatic narrative will keep [middle graders] reading."

Expanding further, Coville published several novels for young adults during the 1990s as well. *Fortune's Journey* combined action and romance in its tale of a resourceful teenage actress leading a theater troupe across the West during the Gold Rush era. The book received mixed reviews, with some critics praising the work strongly and others faulting the author for less-than-believable characters. "Part of it was, people complained that it was warped by a kind of contemporary mindset taking on these historical characters," Coville once told *SATA.* "But I'd done the research, and I knew there was a lot more that young women were doing back then than people now think." *Armageddon Summer* follows the story of two teenagers caught up in a religious cult with their parents. Co-written with author Jane Yolen, the novel received more consistently favorable reviews. Writing in *Booklist,* Roger Leslie praised Coville and Yolen for "explor[ing] their rich, thought-provoking theme with the perfect balance of gripping adventure and understated pathos, leavened by a dollop of humor."

Coville has remained committed to educating as well as entertaining young people. As he explained in *SATA:* "This may seem like a long-term goal and a minimal result for the work involved, but I am, after all, a teacher. This has always been our lot. We deal with a child for a year, pour our hearts and souls into his development, and then send him on his way with the scant hope that somehow, someday, some little of what we have tried to do may present itself to him when it is needed.... But this is idle speculation. The first and foremost job in writing is to tell a whacking good story. You just have to hope it might mean something before you're done."

Personal motivation and social idealism both fuel Coville's commitment to children's literature. "There are two reasons that people go into writing for children," he told *SATA.* "It's either to heal a wounded childhood, or to celebrate a happy one. It's about nine to one (in favor of) the healing to the happy. But I had a happy childhood, and I love children's books. They're delicious ... the writing is better, the stories are more interesting. I do it out of a sense of joy and excitement. But it's also a political choice. I feel that one of the ways I can have real impact is working for kids."

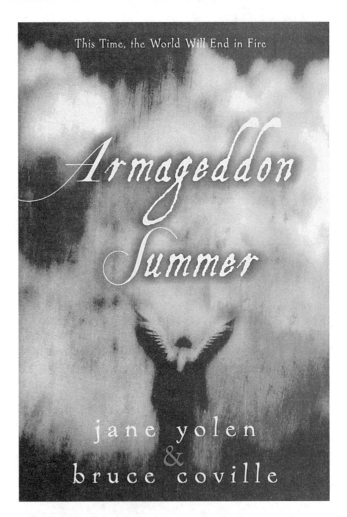

With coauthor Jane Yolen, Coville penned the story of fourteen-year-old Marina and sixteen-year-old Jed, who are caught up in a religious cult with their parents and struggle for independence from the adults' influence. (Cover photo by Kamil Vojnar.)

Works Cited

Cart, Michael, review of *William Shakespeare's Romeo and Juliet, Booklist,* December 1, 1999, p. 700.

Caywood, Carolyn, review of *The Ghost Wore Gray, School Library Journal,* September, 1988, p. 183.

Connor, Anne, review of *Planet of the Dips, School Library Journal,* December, 1995, p. 79.

Howell, Margaret C., review of *Jennifer Murdley's Toad, School Library Journal,* September, 1992, p. 250.

Kowen, Kenneth E., review of *Jeremy Thatcher, Dragon Hatcher, School Library Journal,* May, 1991, p. 91.

Leslie, Roger, review of *Armageddon Summer, Booklist,* August, 1998, p. 272.

Redmond, Kathleen, review of *Jeremy Thatcher, Dragon Hatcher, Voice of Youth Advocates,* June, 1991, p. 106.

Rochman, Hazel, review of *William Shakespeare's Macbeth, Booklist,* November 1, 1997, p. 464.

For More Information See

PERIODICALS

Booklist, November 15, 1994, p. 593; September 1, 1996, p. 133.

Bulletin of the Center for Children's Books, February, 1991, p. 133; July, 1992, p. 292; July, 1996, p. 385; January, 1998, p. 117.

Kirkus Reviews, June 15, 1994, p. 842.

Locus, November, 1991, p. 53; April, 1992, p. 45; July, 1992, p. 48.

Publishers Weekly, July 27, 1992, p. 63.

School Library Journal, December, 1984, p. 100; February, 1988, p. 72; December, 1989, p. 98; September, 1990, p. 239; January, 1992, p. 108.

Times Educational Supplement, November 20, 1987, p. 30.

Voice of Youth Advocates, October, 1989, p. 221; February, 1996, p. 369.*

Autobiography Feature

Joy Cowley

1936-

Influences

In the light of other writers' experience, it would be easy for me to have a fatalistic attitude toward my own writing and to say that this was my destiny. The stereotypical ingredients are there: the active imagination, the background of family poverty and violence, and an escape from it into the world of books. The formula is familiar but I don't believe in predestination. Nor do I believe that there is any such thing as a "bad" childhood experience. All experience carries the potential for good, and the more traumatic an experience, the greater its transcendental potential. So this is a story of a childhood rich in living. Like all accounts of early years, it is also a story of influences. Daily I carry with me the people who have shaped what I am, and however I regarded their influence at the time, I now value all as gift and would not be without any of it. In its telling, this story carries special thanks to adults everywhere who put down their burdens of busyness to make time to enjoy the company of a child. There can be no greater gift to a child, no greater investment in the future.

I was the eldest of a family of five—four girls and then, much later, a boy. Our parents suffered chronic impairment. Dad was a Scot from Ayr, who came out to New Zealand on the *Tainui* with his family in 1926. Partly blind, profoundly deaf, and with a heart condition which kept him an invalid for most of his life, he seemed to us a frail man who might at any moment roll off the edge of the bed into the black well of death. Each time he had yet another bout of rheumatic fever, we would be brought to the side of his bed to receive his last words: "Look after ye're sisters. Be a good girl for ye're mither." We all lived in preparation for his departure and yet, when death finally came, it took him by surprise, in the middle of a mouthful of breakfast after an early morning spent in the garden planting celery.

For all his sickness Dad had an outgoing personality, and I remember him as a lively and loving man, with a quick impatient mind. The frustrations wrought by his handicaps built up and regularly exploded, sometimes with shattering effect. Mum, though physically strong, suffered from schizophrenia, which worsened as she grew older. While we understood our father's illness and could predict his mood swings, our mother's sickness went unrecognised. We didn't understand her obsessions or her sudden wild fury, and we were mostly afraid of her. Our home was often a battleground but, through it all, our parents' love for each other survived. It was a romantic Hollywood type of love, passionate, possessive, self-absorbed, ill-suited to the challenges of sickness, poverty, and five children.

Dad had been born into the middle of six children. They were all very close and all noisy. My Scottish grandparents' house rocked with activity, people making things, doing things, playing instruments and singing, and always arguing with each other. Argument didn't necessarily mean conflict. It was a form of exercise which would cease as abruptly as it had begun. Laughter was equally loud. Even when they were sharing some confidence, this family shouted. Maybe my father's deafness had created the habit. Whatever, their house was never still.

When I was about four years of age, I was sitting in the washhouse next to the kitchen in my grandparents' house, playing with the shoe polish tins and brushes. In the kitchen my grandmother was cooking lunch, and I could hear the comfortable sounds of her singing, punctuated with the rattle of pots and dishes. "Oh, ye'll tak' the high-road and I'll tak' the low, and I'll be in Scotland afore ye . . . ."

My grandfather came past the washhouse door, heading her way. He was walking stealthily on his toes and, when he saw me, he put his fingers to his lips. A few seconds later the song in the kitchen was interrupted by a scream and a loud clatter. My grandfather ran back past the washhouse door, laughing, his hands over his head. Grandma ran after him, waving a saucepan and yelling, "Ye dirr-ty beast! Ye dirr-ty beast!" At the age of four I assumed that Grandad had walked into the kitchen with dirty shoes, and I was puzzled at the strength of Grandma's reaction.

Mum's family was mainly of Scandinavian descent, a quiet gentle people who called each other dear and darling and seemed to sit a lot, talking, drinking cups of tea, reading the Bible. My Swedish grandmother had a sweetness to her which we could almost taste. She hugged us, called us her "precious," using the adjective as a noun, and talked about Jesus as though he lived next door. Grandpa, her husband, was a big man who didn't much like small children, and I didn't come to know him until I was much older. Early childhood visits to my mother's family were visits to a feminine world of hugs and kisses, soft voices, and the perfume of Mum's two beautiful younger sisters, Phoebe and Beulah, who actually wore red nail polish, although Nanna would shake her head and say painting nails was worldly.

The eight in my mother's family were mainly fair: blondes or redheads with green or hazel eyes. But my mother and her oldest sister were dark and looked different from the others. When I was young, I was told it was because our grandfather's mother was Spanish. We discover now that this wasn't true. We are almost certain that our great-grandmother was Maori—which explains for me a lot of the information stored in my chromosomes.

Neither of my parents' families valued books. Dad's people were always too busy for reading. Mum's family considered that the only book to read was the Bible. Books were not a part of my preschool years but drawing was, and that was more bane than blessing for the adults round me. The writer's compulsion to capture and possess the world found early expression in scribbles on any clean surface. Pencil drawings on brown wrapping paper, clear walls, furniture, rows of tiny faces on the newspaper which was our tablecloth, figures in licked indelible pencil on the sheets and pillowcases . . . I couldn't help myself. A blank surface triggered automatic behaviour. A coin or a fingernail would scratch back new paint. A stick drew pictures in sand. A piece of broken brick made giant families on a pavement of concrete path. The word graffiti is new. The reaction to it is old. My obsession received more punishment than reward.

Much of my preschool years were spent between grandparents' houses, with the strongest early influence coming from my two grandmothers: one, a short plump Scotswoman who was seldom quiet or still, who was always knitting, sewing, playing an accordion, dancing, arguing, always rushing at life; the other, a gentle, passive Swedish woman who cried at sad stories and saw the world as something to be suffered on the way to heaven. I felt secure and loved with them both. Nanna was warm with hugs and kisses. Grandma was exciting and fun. There was

Joy Cowley

an exquisite sense of well-being curled up in Nanna's lap and feeling the movement of the hairs in the mole on her cheek as she called me her precious and her treasure. Then there was going to the afternoon picture show with Grandma, who carried brown paper bags into the darkness containing pigs trotters, doughnuts, custard squares, and chocolate frogs filled with peppermint cream. I didn't understand the films and remember only a blue and white light flickering high up in front. Going to the pictures was a wonderful secret and sticky meal which my grandma shared with me in the darkness and always with the understanding, "Ye'll no tell ye mither."

When I was four and a half, the third girl in our family was born. My Scottish grandmother, aware of my parents' difficulties, wanted to officially adopt me, and because she was someone who didn't readily take no for an answer, there was some friction between her and my mother. The effect of this was to greatly reduce the time spent with grandparents. Almost overnight, the security and status I had enjoyed was gone, and I had to learn to fit in with my own parents, whose expectations of life and children were very different.

My parents moved house often in those early days. When I turned five we were living in a farm cottage in the Oharia valley at the back of Johnsonville. It was a while before we could move back into the city so that I could start school, and here was a new change which required even greater adjustment. School. A large room of children I'd never seen before and a teacher who had her hair done in a bun at the back of her neck, just like my Swedish Nanna, and who looked about the same age. In fact she was nothing like my experience of grandmothers. There were no nice names, no fun, no comfort. She shouted at us and pulled our hair to make us sit up straight. She also had a long wooden ruler, and when we didn't know our words, we got whacked round the legs.

Now, I had been eager to begin school. Everyone had told me that when I started school I'd learn to read. But that didn't happen. All we got were letters, black marks on paper, white dusty lines on the green chalkboard. They weren't pictures. They didn't mean anything. Oh, I didn't mind the sound games—hissing sssss for snake, or blowing imaginary smoke rings with p-p-p-p-p-for pipe, but the rest wasn't much fun. Indeed, it was a nightmare. I seemed to be the slowest in the class. Eventually I'd have to guess a word and likely as not I'd get it wrong. Whack! I'd try again. Whack!

Those early school days were not all fear-ridden. The classroom was full of wonderful drawing materials which we didn't have at home, blackboards, big sheets of paper, crayons, coloured chalk, jars of thick paint. And drawing was extended into modelling with plasticene, cutting coloured paper, threading large wooden beads. As well, I discovered for the first time in my life the fun of the playground and friendship with children my own age. School would have been enjoyable but for that teacher and her letters and ruler. Some of the children called her Mrs. Hitler. I knew that wasn't her real name but had something to do with the war. There was war everywhere in those days. It leaked out of the radio with "This is the BBC London calling," it filled up the centre of the *Free Lance* and *Weekly News* with pictures of dead and missing soldiers, and was coiled along the beaches in rolls of barbed wire. War was all about blackouts and ration books and me saying that my aunties had taken me to the zoo when all the time we went to visit American soldiers in funny little houses. At school the boys drew pictures of planes like ducks dropping eggs in flight and chanted, "Heil Hitler, yah, yah, yah! What a naughty little man you are! You eat your porridge with a knife and fork. Heil Hitler, yah, yah, yah!" I thought this was funny to say but I didn't know what it had to do with our teacher.

I was one of three children still on Book One of Whitcombe and Tombes Progressive Readers. The others were all on Book Two or Book Three. Each morning I would wait with an ache in my stomach for the Book One group to be called to the front of the class where the teacher sat, her ruler tapping the chair leg. Then it would be my turn and the awfulness made me feel I was going to vomit. I wanted so much to give a right answer but I hadn't the faintest idea what the words were. Whack! went the ruler, and I would start to cry. Whack again to make me stop bawling and try again. One morning something happened. No, I didn't vomit. As the ruler descended, I wet my pants. I stood there, with everyone looking, as the hot urine ran down my legs, soaked my socks and shoes, and then made a puddle on the wooden floor. I don't remember what the teacher said, but it was angry. She grabbed me by the hair, forced me down, and rubbed my face in the puddle as

though I were a kitten. Then she sent one of the bigger boys out to get the sawdust bucket.

I don't remember what happened after that. Nor can I recall how or when I learned to read. But I do know when I became a reader. I was in Standard 1 in a different school and with a different teacher who was handing out "real" books. These were not reading texts with lists of words and sounds. They had exciting stories with pictures on every page. One of them was put on my desk. My first real book! It was the story of a duckling called Ping, and I read it, there and then, from cover to cover. I was so excited by the story I forgot I was a poor reader. I was immediately lost on the Yangtze River, far away from the classroom and my fear of words. That book was a doorway into another world, and I had entered joyfully, meeting my own expectation that I would find excitement and adventure. When the story ended, I promptly returned to the first page and began again, making a new discovery. The story was exactly the same with the second reading! It hadn't changed as spoken stories did. I had discovered the constancy of print!

It seemed to me that after *Ping,* everything changed and I became instantly an avid and accomplished reader. I know it didn't happen like that. The instant change was in my attitude to reading. It was no longer an exercise without meaning. I had found that reading accessed story. As often as I picked up a book, I could take that journey to other worlds and have safe adventures.

My appetite for story and my fascination with it became limitless. When I was nine, my father took me to join the local library. The children's section was very small but a kindly librarian directed my rapacious appetite to certain authors in the adult section: Alexander Dumas, Jules Verne, Victor Hugo, the Bronte sisters, Dickens, James Fenimore Cooper, R. M. Ballantyne, Mark Twain, R. L. Stevenson, Oscar Wilde. My parents who had been pleased with my progress were now alarmed, and my Scottish grandmother warned that so much reading would make me soft in the head.

I can still recall the smell of that small Otaki public library: sun-warmed wood, old books, and dust combining to make an incense which I breathed in through my heart to my imagination. The library was all things to me, a sanctuary, a mine of treasure, a house of maps to secret lives in secret worlds. The library became my other home.

In my parents' house there were certain restrictions, mainly because reading got in the way of household duties, and books had to go underground. Well, under something, be it a tea towel on the kitchen bench while I peeled the potatoes, or under the blankets at night read by a torch stolen from the kitchen. My father used to complain about the quality of Eveready batteries and once wrote to the manufacturer demanding a refund!

At school I developed a split focus, reading a book on my lap under the desk, with ears alert for the teacher's questions. As far as I was concerned, time without a book was time ill spent.

In my twelfth year, a family friend gave me her old bicycle, and I rode to school with a book open on the handlebars. The inevitable happened. One morning, in the middle of an engrossing story, I peddled into the back of a parked van. The bike and I both suffered some physical damage, but that was not the end of the matter. The law became involved. At a general school assembly I appeared between the headmaster and a traffic officer as an example of irresponsible road behaviour. My classmates were initially impressed, but they soon lost interest when they realised that I wasn't going to prison. As for the headmaster's threats of what would happen if I did it again, they were a waste of breath. My parents couldn't afford to have the bike repaired and I resumed walking to school—with a book in my hands.

At this stage we were living in Foxton. I was in Standard 5 and at another turning point. If I became a reader in Standard 1, I became a writer in Standard 5, quite simply because a teacher told me I was good and I believed him.

If we pause here for a moment to reflect on our schooling, we may discover that we excelled at certain subjects not so much through natural ability, but because we had a good relationship with our teacher. In the same way we may find that difficulty with a subject had a lot more to do with a difficult classroom situation than with our lack of skill. It's a sobering realisation, and one which places a huge responsibility on the teaching profession. I've put it to many people, including large groups of teachers, and each time seen a hall of nodding heads. The influence of our teachers is much greater than we realise.

Well, here I was in Standard 5, and I had a teacher who seemed to actually like children. He saw them as people. He worked on the principle of praising achievement rather than punishing error, and the effect he had on a large unruly class was dramatic. Big fourteen-year-old boys with nicotine-stained fingers became enthusiastic about poetry. "Oh young Lochinvar has come out of the west, / Through all the wide border his steed was the best" or "There was an ancient mariner and he stoppeth one of three / 'By thy long grey beard and glittering eye, wherefore stoppest thou me?'" In the afternoons, as reward for the day, we were read books in serial form: R. M. Ballantyne's *Coral Island* and Rider Haggard's *King Solomon's Mines.* Shy children who were marginal readers became addicted to the thrill of story and wrote their own, page after page. The whole class came alive.

My imagination exploded that year. There is no other word for it. The long rambling stories inspired by my favourite authors were not labelled "untidy" or "erratic." They got stamped "good work" or even "excellent." My drawing was no longer an aberration. I was introduced to watercolour paints. I learned about washes and perspective. And I discovered poetry. I realised that people could arrange words in such a way that when you read them you went cold all over and vibrated like a violin. "And ice mast-high came floating by, / as green as emerald" or "In the harbours in the Islands of the Seven Seas, / are the tiny white houses and the orange trees."

That year I borrowed a class copy of Palgrave's *Golden Treasury of Verse* and began to learn poems so that I would always have them in my head. Most of those memorised are still with me. I also began to write verse, most of it hugely sentimental, for example, "The Swagger's Song," written when I was eleven.

Trampin' down the dusty 'ighway,
Tramp, tramp, then tramp some more,
Feet ever movin', swag on me back,
Just keep on walkin' is me law.

I always foller that same ol' rule
Though it don't get me nowhere.
Sky above me, earth beneath.
Can't says I ever care.

Might stop at an 'ouse for a meal or two
But as for me bed,
It's just a hedge by the dusty road
With earth to piller me 'ead.

Don't have no money to spend,
Don't want to scrimp and save.
The yellow gorse, the wattle flowers
Is all the gold I have.

Never care 'bout being rich.
Can't says I ever will.
Been a swaggie all me life
And am a swaggie still.

In that it is easy to find an eleven-year-old strongly influenced by the poem "Meg Merrilees."

In this same year and inspired by the same teacher, I began writing and drawing for the children's page of the *Wellington Southern Cross* newspaper. They had a reward system whereby a contributor who accumulated fifty points received a book prize. The books were classics: *Treasure Island, Oliver Twist, Wuthering Heights.* I now had the beginnings of my own library. The first book to arrive was *Treasure Island.* It was beautifully bound, but I was disappointed that it had no inscription on the inside leaf. How would people know it was a prize? To this day that old copy of *Treasure Island* has the endpaper inscribed in a childish scrawl: "This book is awarded to Joy Summers for her excellent original work in the Southern Cross Children's Page." I showed it off to my teacher, who looked at the inscription and managed to say all the right things without a twitch.

I was now writing two kinds of prose and verse, the serious stuff for myself and light-hearted entertainment for the children's page, since this was usually the kind of material published. Here is a "serious poem," a twelve-year-old's view of some domestic problem. I no longer remember what caused the passionate cry.

I dreamed a dream and it was vain
As leaves strewn by the wind.
I dreamed a dream but once again
My foolish heart was blind.
Youth is blind it does not see
Beyond its wild desires.
I turn to face reality.
Hope flees. My dream, expires.

I continued to write this kind of poetry inspired by Palgrave's *Golden Treasury of Verse,* but the rhymes I sent to the children's page were usually influenced by A. A. Milne or Edward Lear and sometimes took the shape of cautionary tales. The long poem about the boy called Willie who stole money from his mother's purse and spent it on lollies was largely autobiographical, as was the ending: "Willie stammered for words. He could find no excuse. And 'twas then that Mum's hairbrush came into use."

Money, or the lack of it, was always a problem in our house. The invalid's pension never went far enough, and our poor Mum was not a good manager. My sister Joan and I found ways of helping out and in return received a portion of what we earned as pocket money. We gathered lupin seed, pine cones, mushrooms, and blackberries in season and sold them. My Scottish grandma had taught me to crochet, and I made lacy shawls which sold in the local bookshop. We went to the Foxton dump and gathered old sacks, bottles, copper, lead, aluminum, and brought them home to be sold as scrap. Some of the sacks, boiled up in the copper, became extra blankets for us on cold nights. Then I discovered a new way to make money. I was now in Standard 6 and found that many of my classmates found kissing very interesting. I drew pictures of men and women kissing, Hollywood style, and sold them for a penny each. Business was good—until some parent complained to the headmaster.

When my sisters and I were young, we viewed our parents as we did the weather. We enjoyed the sunshine and took shelter as best we could from the storms which were frequent. The table would be turned over, windows broken, furniture smashed. Neighbours would call the police and a weary constable would pedal his bicycle yet again to the Summers' house. But our parents' preoccupation with each other also gave us a freedom we might not have had in another family, and we became resourceful at an early age, building a world where parents had no entry. This, of course, was the world of story which my sisters and I inhabited almost every evening. I was the storyteller. I regurgitated my reading in varied forms, usually as long serials which continued night after night. Joan, Heather, and I would curl up in the one bed, filling the darkness with children of our own age who had extraordinary adventures from which they always emerged triumphant and unscathed. In the darkness girls like us swung on vines over jungle temples filled with giant pythons or they battled sharks and alligators with pocketknives. Bombs exploded. We escaped. Evil kings and queens locked us in dungeons. We found hidden trapdoors. These storytelling sessions went on for about five years, and in them we remade our days.

If we found affirmation in these stories, support also came to us through our church community where kindly folk placed an umbrella over our parents' poverty. There were frequent gifts from people not much better off than ourselves, boxes of good used clothing or windfall apples, potatoes, shortbread or seed cake, and occasionally the great treasure of a bag of old *Reader's Digests* or Captain Marvel comics.

The church we attended was the Foxton Presbyterian, an old wooden building which always smelled of polish and flowers. We went two or three times on a Sunday, to Sunday school, morning service, and then again on a Sunday evening. My fondness for church, like my passion for books, was considered unhealthy by my Scottish grandma, who was no doubt always alert for signs of her daughter-in-law's illness in the children. For my part I don't know why I became so concerned with religion. It seemed to satisfy a need in the way a glass of cold water satisfied on a hot day, and there were no words to describe it. It was like poetry. I absorbed it and felt good inside.

I did have difficulty though with God—or at least with the God my mother talked about. Jesus I could understand, but God was like the subject of sex—fascinating, dreadful, mysterious, and full of contradictions. My feelings about God were a mixture of attraction and fear—the same feelings that I had for my parents, although I didn't make that connection at the time. Another problem in my young religious beliefs was the way people talked about the devil. I couldn't bear to think of anyone being so hated, and I used to pray secretly, hoping Mum would never find out, that God would love the devil and be nice to him.

We were expected to read the Bible right through every year. Some years I could just make it by skipping all the laws and the begat bits. Much of it I found dull, but there were parts which were as alive as Palgrave's *Golden Treasury,* and these I read, reread, and memorized—whole psalms and chapters from the St. John gospel. I could stand on Foxton Beach in a nor'wester and recite: "The wind bloweth where it listeth and thou hearest the sound thereof but knowest not whence it cometh or whither it goeth: so it is with everyone that is born of the Spirit." I wouldn't know what the passage meant but would feel my skin turn cold and experience the wind blowing right through a great hole in my chest. That's how it was with poetry—and sometimes, that's how it was when I wrote stories.

For my secondary education I went daily from Foxton to Palmerston North Girls High School, and here I discovered the group of strong women who were to be like a family of aunts for me over the next few years. Not all of them. There were a couple of teachers who had difficulty with this clumsy untidy girl who didn't fit anywhere, but there were others like my Standard 5 teacher who saw potential under the grime of poverty and who went out of their way to help me develop that potential.

The bus ride to Palmerston each day was a long one, leaving at 7:00 a.m. and arriving back at Foxton at 5:00 p.m. This was my reading time, much of it spent on poetry. This was the space in which I engaged in my first love affair, a very real romance which lasted several years— with the poet John Keats. Even now, remembering that noise-filled bus on back-country roads brings back an ache under the ribs and a religious silence filled with the stillness of eternal words. "My heart aches and a drowsy numbness pains my sense as though of hemlock I have drunk."

There was almost no time for reading at home. My brother was born in my third form year. There were now five children. My parents' situation deteriorated. My father made a couple of suicide attempts. My mother believed that her mother-in-law was a witch who was casting evil spells on all of us. We were always in debt. At weekends and holidays, Joan and I worked. We plucked chickens at a local poultry farm, did baby-sitting, housework, gardening. The so-called tomboy of the family, I had labouring jobs, cutting firewood, painting houses, helping to mix and lay concrete. I worked at the fish-and-chip grill room. I went from door to door selling anything which could be sold— lettuce seedlings, parsley, strings of flounder, blackberries. But at the end of my fifth form year I had to break the news to my teachers that I would not be coming back to the sixth form. My parents had said I must go out to work full-time.

What happened then, I do not know. But within a few days I was called to the office to talk with a couple of my teachers. They said they could arrange a regular part-time

Cowley at home with cat and computer in Marlborough Sounds, New Zealand.

job for me, if my parents would agree. I would be the editor of the children's page of the *Palmerston North Daily Times,* work I could do after school. Of course, this meant that I would have to live in Palmerston North during the school week, but they could arrange board with the Baptist minister and his wife who lived near the school. I would earn five pounds a week, two pounds for my board and three pounds for my parents.

As you may imagine, this was heady stuff to a sixteen-year-old. I became the NFC lady—NFC meaning News for Children—and I could run the page as I wished, providing I got the copy to the print room by 5:00 p.m. on a Friday. I had a small windowless office which smelled of printer's ink, and a typewriter on a table under a yellow light bulb. I was in heaven.

Every school afternoon of my sixth form year, I played editor. What I was doing was an extension of the storytelling I did for my sisters. In the guise of a much-travelled middle-aged woman who had a badly behaved dog called Crackers. I wrote an editorial letter for each issue. Some weeks Crackers took over the typewriter instead and told tales about me. Crackers and I were very popular. I organised writing and colouring-in competitions (my drawings, of course) and ran joke and riddle and "believe it or not" columns. I published children's writing on a points system borrowed from my own days as

contributor to the *Southern Cross.* I was not adverse to publishing my own work either, although conscience didn't allow me to add names or points to my writing.

Again, I was divided between two kinds of writing, the lighthearted stuff for the children's page and my own "serious" work. Only one of my sixth form poems has survived. It deals with the struggle I was experiencing in "real" writing, that of the gap between inspiration and the words as they fell on paper. It is called "Words."

Words are very difficult
To hold in the hand.
They leap up like electric fish
Or fall away, fine as sand,
Or else they melt on the palm
Like snowflakes made of air,
And when you open your fingers
You find there is nothing there.

Once I caught a word like a blossom
And held it for most of a day.
But when I looked at it that evening,
It had gone from gold to grey.
Its perfume had disappeared,
Its petals were limply spread.
I laid it on some paper,
Thinking that it was dead.

I looked again at the paper
In the early morning hours
And oh wonder! The page had sprouted
A whole bed of golden flowers!

At the end of the year I was offered full employment with the *Manawatu Daily Times.* My parents would not consider it. Journalists were a notorious lot—free-thinkers, communists, even atheists—and I had already been too much under their influence. No, I was to have a good steady job back in my hometown. They apprenticed me to the local pharmacist, work that seemed remote from creative writing at the time. But pharmacy did teach me a certain discipline in thinking, which was to help me as a writer later on.

After I left school, I didn't write anything for four years—mainly because the influences had gone, the teachers who had encouraged me, the librarian who put aside special books, the reporters who sat on my desk and treated me as an equal. They weren't there. I had no one to write for. But that changed when I moved to Palmerston North and joined a writer's group. I went hesitantly to one of the meetings to honour a promise I had made to my sixth form English teacher, that I would continue to write stories. But in the company of other writers I surprised myself with a volcanic eruption of creative energy. It was then I discovered that if I didn't have someone to write for, there was no inspiration. Writing was an act of love.

We were a small group—Dell Adsett, Stanley Roche, Alice Glenday, Kathleen Mayson, Wendy Simons, Neva Clarke, Dorothea Joblin. Again, our meetings were like the storytelling sessions of my childhood but moved into another gear. We sold short stories to periodicals and small literary magazines, but mostly we wrote for each other, sharing in our writing the parables of our lives.

During the mid-1960s I had two short stories, "The Moth" and "The Silk," published by *Short Story International,* an American reprint magazine which found its way to a book stall in New York's Grand Central Station. Anne Hutchens, a young Doubleday editor, bought a copy and somewhere, between trains, our lives connected, and there began a long friendship with both Anne and the American readers. At that time, I was a farmer's wife, a mother of four young children, walking in gumboots down a mud-caked drive to the mailbox. The cows had been milked, the cowshed cleaned, and there were a few minutes to read paper and mail over breakfast before the house chores began. But what was this elegant cream envelope with the New York frank mark? I unfolded the sheet of paper that announced a publisher called Doubleday and read, "I like your story. Have you written a novel?"

A novel? I sat down and reread the letter to make it real. Of course I had not written a novel. How did one do that? Could I start a short story and simply keep on going? How many words would be needed?

I wrote back the simple truth. No, I had not written a novel, but I was thinking about it.

Six months later, there came another letter from Ann, "Remember that novel you were considering? Do you have anything yet to show me?"

That did it. The same day, as soon as the children were in bed for the evening, I sat at the typewriter and worked into the small hours on a longish story which could perhaps be the first chapter of a novel. Anne read it, liked it, and in a very short time I had an agreement plus half an advance royalty which I invested in household help to free me for writing.

Eighteen months later, *Nest in a Falling Tree* was published, reviews were pouring in, and Doubleday was asking for another book. I had moved from short story writer to novelist without knowing how to write a novel. I felt a fraud and was sure that it was only a matter of time before someone cried out from the crowd that the Emperor had no clothes. Still the tributes came pouring out of the mailbox while I milked cows, chopped wood for the stove, cuddled the children, cooked and cleaned and attempted to shore up a shaky marriage made all the more fragile by this sudden success. Eventually, my restless husband found happiness but with someone else, a young woman who loved him and wanted to marry him. My self-esteem lay around my ankles. He didn't want me but he wanted to keep the children. Oh, I knew that he couldn't do that. Of course, he couldn't. I ran for help. A stone-faced lawyer told me that the children did not belong to either parent until a custody hearing and then, without a doubt, the court would place the two boys with their father, the two girls with me.

These four children had been born within four-and-a-half years. They were so close that they did everything as a quartet. Whatever happened to their parents, they could not be separated from each other.

At the age of thirty I was emotionally bankrupt.

It is only when all dependency is stripped away that we discover who we are and what we have. The next year was filled with pain and the rapid growth that comes from a near-death experience. In a hospital, a gentle psychiatrist showed me the first words of his report—"No evidence of psychosis. Normal reaction to abnormal stress"—and then he sent me home to get on with living.

Living was paced in an orderly fashion. There was a day job in the dispensary of a suburban pharmacy, weekend visits from the children, and evenings spent at the typewriter in my small apartment. I was trying to finish my second novel, *Man of Straw,* an unhappy book that was obviously therapy writing, although I did not see that at the time. As well, I was writing humorous children's stories, short, easy-to-read pieces for the New Zealand Education Department's school magazines.

I had always told stories to children, my younger siblings, friends' children, and then my own, but it was not until my son Edward was having difficulty with learning to read that I began writing for children. With the help of Edward's teacher, who provided a vocabulary list and support, I wrote of a boy who did not want to read.

Edward's early-reading problems had been different from mine, although we may both have been late developing the coordination necessary to decode print. Whereas I had always been an imaginative child, Edward could not relate to fiction, and early visits to libraries netted books on trains, tractors, cars. His eyes would light up with an account of a motor-bike race, but when I read fairy tales, he would mutter, "That's not true. That's not true." His sisters and little brother adored *Charlotte's Web* and had me read it twice. Edward said, "Animals don't talk," and spent story time unrolling and tying a ball of string so that he could open cupboards and switch off his light from his bed. In fact, the only fiction work that interested Edward was Dr. Seuss's *Green Eggs and Ham.* The text meant nothing to him, but he was fascinated by the illustration of a train running on impossibly high and precarious trestles. How could a train do that?

The reading problem was compounded by Edward's sisters who could both read before they began school. He was not going to compete with them but instead focussed on occupations at which he excelled—model-making, simple machinery repairs, design drawing of planes and tractors.

The stories I wrote for Edward were, in fact, fiction. But they were based on his interests and activities, and in them he was always a hero. Edward saves the barn from burning. Edward makes a plane, flies it, and lands it in the hay paddock. Edward teaches his father to scuba dive. Edward saves his father from a shark. The stories had drama, usually, a joke or two, and a surprise ending which encouraged him to read to the last sentence. Sometimes, I indulged his interest in bathroom humour. For example, there was the story about our cat who ate a tin of baked beans and whirled around the ceiling like a deflating balloon.

Edward enjoyed stories that were meaningful to him and was soon dictating his own hero yarns which I would edit and present back to him in book form. This process had little to do with the basal texts and word drills that had shaped his concept of "reading." This was fun—although I must admit that his reading speed did not really take off until he had advanced enough to tackle *Popular Mechanics* magazines. Predictably, Edward became an aeronautical engineer.

After Edward, I worked in a similar way with other students from his school, then with children from other schools. Many of these children had been arbitrarily labelled "dyslexic." Dyslexia was the buzz word in those days. They had a frozen attitude to reading. They all did some mirror writing. But then, I guessed that if I were learning Greek, I would get many of my letters back-to-front, too. These children seemed to have no left/right confusion in the activities they enjoyed. I watched them making intricate models with small parts, cutting and pasting paper, playing ball games, and I noticed how well-coordinated they were in occupations that had their enthusiasm. On the other hand, most of them had the entrenched attitude that they were "not good readers" and were not willing to risk further failure.

My own early reading experience connected with theirs, and I realised how important it was that children see themselves as "readers" long before they actually are reading. Children needed entertaining, meaningful stories, stories that affirmed them and made them feel good about themselves. To give children dull and difficult material was a crime against their natural love of learning. How many adults would read dull and difficult material by choice?

Teachers were using my stories in the classroom, making their own books, doing their own illustrations. They wanted the stories published.

So there, in 1969, in my little apartment, I divided my writing time between the heavy gut-wrenching novel and the funny little stories that made children laugh and forget that they hated reading. It doesn't take any depth of wisdom to understand the process of personal metamorpho-sis that was going on, but at the time I was not aware of it. Like most writers, I believed that my writing had external origins.

Good things happened in the early 1970s. I met Malcolm Mason, a Wellington writer, war hero, and accountant, who had been on his own for five years. He loved me without expectation of change, and he wanted to celebrate that love. It was a little while before I could trust a relationship that was not hedged about by conditions, but Malcolm was persistent. He visited me in a car full of flowers. He sent love songs, one line at a time, in telegrams to my workplace. Whether he was in New Zealand, or travelling in Europe, he would phone every day with the same message. He genuinely loved my children. It was all too good to be true. When he asked me to marry him, it did occur to me that a man twenty-five years older than myself was not likely to leave me for a younger women, but all the same I was convinced that a love so big, so generous, so life-giving, could not last. Other people looked at the age difference and shook their heads. But it did last. For fifteen years that love filled all the corners of the universe and we flew in it, supremely powerful as lovers are. My children came back to me. Malcolm's youngest son lived with us. Days were shaped by laughter and family activity, and words flew off the typewriter. The fairy tale of happily-ever-after went on and on until 1984 when Malcolm got lymphoma.

In the days before his death, we held on to each other, laughing and crying, and Malcolm said, "Remember those buggers who said our marriage would never last? They are finally right!"

Those rich years in Wellington produced four more novels for Doubleday, a number of short stories, and an increased output in early reading stories for children. Roald Dahl bought the film rights of my first novel *Nest in a Falling Tree* to make a screenplay for his wife, actress Pat Neal, who was recovering from a stroke. We visited Roald and Pat in Great Missinden, Buckinghamshire, England, in the early days of the shooting of the movie, which was changed considerably from the novel and renamed *The Road Digger.* It was Roald who introduced a virtual nondrinker to that lethal American delight, the martini. I drank several like lemonade and was horribly ill, vomiting into the Dahl's beautiful indoor swimming pool. They laughed and Pat told me that she had once done the same thing down the front of Audrey Hepburn's dress.

The money for the film rights to the book bought us a holiday home in a remote bay of the Marlborough Sounds.

The years with Malcolm in Wellington also began a love affair with travel, trips around the Pacific, backpacking in South America, the Australian outback, India. At the same time, my spiritual journey was leading me to the mystical tradition of the Catholic church, and I became a Catholic in 1982.

During the late 1970s I was visiting a number of schools and working with teachers who urgently wanted new reading materials for their students. The New Zealand Education Department planned to revise the national reading programme, "Ready-to-Read," and they accepted some of my stories for publication, but these would not be in the schools until 1983. I phoned June Melser, a teacher friend who also had editorial experience, and asked her if she would help me to write an early-reading programme.

After some hesitation, June agreed, and we began the "Story Box" reading programme.

Who would publish the new books? New Zealand commercial educational publishers were still committed to the old basal and phonics-based reading programmes and would not understand these little story books. Certainly our stories were so carefully structured that they were, in effect, basal texts with in-built phonemic exercises, but the engineering was hidden. Story was the thing. We wanted the child to have easy and entertaining stories, illustrated and published with the quality of fine trade picture books.

It was June Melser who told me about Wendy Pye, a young woman publisher in Auckland who was publishing cookery books and trade journals but who was wanting to move into educational materials. Could we send her some of our "Story Box" stories to look at?

I went to Auckland to meet Wendy Pye and was impressed by a dynamic young woman who looked me in the eye and said, "I don't know a thing about early reading but I am going to learn." She then went on to tell me that she had found the names of New Zealand's top reading gurus and sent them the manuscripts for evaluation. The response had been very positive, she said, and she was going to raise the finances to publish a quality series, if we would entrust the stories to her.

We had found our publisher but what about illustrators? Most established New Zealand illustrators were not interested. Whoever had heard of children's books of eight and sixteen pages? It became my task to visit the art and design schools and the polytechnic colleges to find talented students who could be interested in illustrating children's books. One such student was Elizabeth Fuller, who did the wonderful illustrations for the Mrs. Wishy-Washy books and *Huggles.*

The Story Box Reading Programme of a hundred and twelve books was published in New Zealand between 1980 and 1982. It was originally intended for New Zealand schools to meet an urgent need. We had no idea that it would take off like wildfire around the world. In 1993 Wendy Pye took the books in a suitcase to the Frankfurt Book Fair and there met Americans Tom and Arlene Wright, who traded in educational books out of their San Diego garage. The Wrights had sold their second car to raise the fares for Frankfurt and were actively looking for a reading programme when they met Wendy. Twelve years later, the Wright Group was one of the biggest publishers of early reading material in the United States, and the Story Box Reading Programme, adapted for the USA, was in more than 30 percent of American classrooms.

Malcolm's death left a huge hole in my life and the lives of my grown children. We huddled together, comforting each other with warm and funny stories of this larger-than-life man who filled our hearts but was so lacking in our days, and our lives went on. Eventually I moved from Wellington to our family vacation farm in the Marlborough Sounds, where I still live today. It was there in 1989 that I was married again, to Terry Coles, a kind and gentle man who had been a good friend to Malcolm and me. Again, the marriage caused some concern amongst our acquaintances, not because of an ostensible age gap, but because Terry was a Catholic priest. The reaction was brief, and then the Church, with considerable love and some embarrassment, moved over to make room for us.

Now, in 1997, with the comfort of a good marriage and grandchildren about me, I write mainly trade books for children—picture books, early chapter books, and novels. There are still a few reading texts from time to time, but with over five hundred early reading books published, I try to place my time in writing workshops to encourage other authors.

I have never been one of those writers who say, "Oh, I just write for myself." I don't believe we honestly do that. For me, writing is always a leaning of the heart towards a reader, and an unread story, like an unsung song, is only half alive. Sometimes the intended reader has plural form, a specific group of children, perhaps. Sometimes the writing is for one person, the little boy who hates onions, or the girl who wants me to write about her dead horse. Although I have vowed that I will not write another adult novel unless I have something really worth saying, there has always been at the back of awareness a promise to myself that I would write another book for Anne, my original Doubleday editor. When Anne married Ken McCormack, Doubleday's editor-in-chief, she left to work for Knopf, but the friendship has continued for over thirty years and, if a new adult novel comes into being, it will be for that friendship.

Yet, there is more to creative writing than communication. At its best, creative writing involves some metaphysical process which taps into a cosmic voice, new and surprising to the writer. How many of us have looked at the lines we have typed and seen them for the first time? How many of us feel deeply the interconnectedness of all writing? Words are the tools of our craft, but they often originate in a wordless state outside of our sensory perception. For that reason, one can never describe the process except through metaphor.

Here are some lines which I wrote after reading Margaret Mahy's celebrated book *Memory.* I've called this piece "The Storyteller," and it describes how I feel about the stories I've received from that great army of authors who go right back to childhood reading, stories which turned my life around and gave me the tools of empowerment.

The storyteller is a thief,
stealing stars at night
and hammering them into dishes
for bread and butter days.

The storyteller is a magician,
making doors that are never
either open or shut,
and windows you can put to your eye
to see over horizons.

The storyteller is a seamstress,
stitching the ordinary things of earth
to make wondrous garments
for long and difficult journeys.

The storyteller is a liberator,
knocking down walls
with the thrust of a pen
and wrenching wide open
seed, egg, stone, brick, word,
to set truth free.

Writings

FOR CHILDREN

The Duck in the Gun, illustrated by Edward Sorel, Doubleday, 1969, illustrated by Robyn Belton, Shortland (Auckland, New Zealand), 1984.

The Silent One, illustrated by Hermann Griessle, Knopf, 1981, illustrated by Sherryl Jordan, Whitcoulls, 1981.

The Terrible Taniwha of Timberditch, Oxford University Press (Auckland), 1982.

The Fierce Little Woman and the Wicked Pirate, illustrated by Jo Davies, Shortland, 1984.

(With Mona Williams) *Two of a Kind* (stories), illustrated by Jane Amos, Blackberry Press (Upper Hutt, New Zealand), 1984.

Salmagundi, illustrated by Philip Webb, Oxford University Press, 1985.

Brith the Terrible, Shortland, 1986.

Captain Felonius, illustrated by Elizabeth Fuller, Shortland, 1986.

The Lucky Feather, illustrated by Philip Webb, Shortland, 1986.

Pawprints in the Butter, Mallinson Rendel (Wellington, New Zealand), 1991.

Bow Down Shadrach, illustrated by Robyn Belton, Hodder & Stoughton (Auckland), 1991, Wright Group (Seattle, WA), 1996.

Happy Birthday Mrs. Felonius, Omnibus (Australia), 1992.

The Day of the Rain, Mallinson Rendel, 1993.

The Screaming Mean Machine, Scholastic, 1993.

Gladly Here I Come, Penguin (Harmondsworth), 1994, Wright Group, 1996.

Beyond the River, Scholastic New Zealand, 1994.

Song of the River, Wright Group, 1994.

Write On, Scholastic New Zealand, 1994.

Guide for Young Authors, Wright Group, 1994.

The Day of the Snow, illustrated by Bob Kerr, Mallinson Rendel, 1994.

Tulevai, Scholastic New Zealand, 1995.

The Happy Hens Series, Scholastic New Zealand, 1995.

The Day of the Wind, Mallinson Rendel, 1995.

Sea Daughter, Scholastic New Zealand, 1995.

The Mouse Bride, paintings by David Christiana, Scholastic, 1995.

The Cheese Trap, Scholastic New Zealand, 1995.

Nicketty-Nacketty-Noo-Noo-Noo, Scholastic New Zealand, 1995.

Joy Cowley Answers Kids' Questions, Scholastic New Zealand, 1995.

Brave Mama Puss ("Puss Quartet"), Reed (Auckland), 1995.

Papa Puss to the Rescue ("Puss Quartet"), Reed, 1995.

Mabel and the Marvelous Meow ("Puss Quartet"), Reed, 1995.

Oscar in Danger ("Puss Quartet"), Reed, 1995.

Gracias the Thanksgiving Turkey, illustrated by Joe Cepeda, Scholastic, 1996.

Snake and Lizard, Wright Group, 1996.

Singing Down the Rain, Harper Collins, 1997.

The Bump, Scholastic New Zealand, 1997.

The Great Bamboozle, Scholastic New Zealand, 1997.

A Haunting Tale, Scholastic New Zealand, 1997.

Ticket to the Sky Dance, Penguin New Zealand, 1997.

Starbright and the Dream-Eater, Penguin New Zealand, 1998.

The Wild West Gang, Harper Collins New Zealand, 1998.

Big Moon Tortilla, Boyds Mills Press, (Honesdale, PA), 1998.

More of the Wild Wests, Harper Collins Auckland, 1999.

The Rusty, Trusty Tractor, Boyds Mills Press, 1999.

The Video Shop Sparrow, illustrated by Gavin Bishop, Mallinson Rendel (Wellington, New Zealand), 1999.

Agapanthus Hum and the Eyeglasses, illustrated by Jennifer Plecas, Philomel, 1999.

Agapanthus Hum and Major Bark, illustrated by Jennifer Plecas, Philomel, 2001.

Agapanthus Hum and the Angel Hoot, illustrated by Jennifer Plecas, Philomel, 2002.

Author of more than five hundred early reading books, including *Mrs. Wishy-Washy, The Meanies, Huggles, The Hungry Giant,* and *My Sloppy Tiger.* Most of these were published by The Wright Group (Bothell, WA).

FOR ADULTS; FICTION

Nest in a Falling Tree, Doubleday, 1967.

Man of Straw, Doubleday, 1971.

Of Men and Angels, Doubleday, 1973.

The Mandrake Root, Doubleday, 1976.

The Growing Season, Doubleday, 1979.

Heart Attack and Other Stories, Hodder & Stoughton, 1985.

Classical Music, Penguin Auckland, 1999.

OTHER

Whole Learning: Whole Child, Wright Group, 1994.

Contributor, *New Zealand Short Stories,* Vol. 3, Oxford University Press, 1975. Stories have appeared in New Zealand literary periodicals and school readers; writer of radio scripts for New Zealand Broadcasting Corporation. Several of Cowley's books have been translated into Spanish.

CUTLER, Jane 1936-

Personal

Born September 24, 1936, in Bronx, NY; daughter of Emanuel (a manufacturer) and Beatrice (a homemaker; maiden name, Drooks) Cutler; children: Franny, David, Aaron. *Education:* Northwestern University, B.A., 1958; San Francisco State University, M.A., 1982. *Hobbies and other interests:* Reading, swimming, hiking, theater, art, music.

Addresses

Agent—George Nicholson, Sterling Lord Literistic, Inc., 65 Bleecker Street, New York, NY 10012. *E-mail*—janecutler@earthlink.net.

Career

Writer, editor, and writing teacher. *Member:* Authors Guild, Authors League of America, National Organization for Women, Society of Children's Book Writers and Illustrators.

Awards, Honors

Herbert Wilner Award for short fiction, 1982; PEN prize for short fiction, 1987; *Mr. Carey's Garden* was nominated for the Show Me Readers Award, Missouri Association of School Librarians; *Rats!* was nominated for the Nene Reading List for Hawaii Schools; *Spaceman* was nominated for the William Allen White Children's Book Award and the Mark Twain Award; Best Children's Books of the Year, Bank Street College of Education, for *The Song of the Molimo;* Master List, New York Public Library, 1999, Notable Social Studies Trade Book for Young Readers, Children's Book Council, 2000, and Zena Sutherland Award for Children's Literature, 2000, nominated for the Golden Kite Award, all for *The Cello of Mr. O.*

Writings

NOVELS; FOR CHILDREN

Family Dinner, Farrar, Straus & Giroux, 1991.
No Dogs Allowed, illustrated by Tracey Campbell Pearson, Farrar, Straus & Giroux, 1992.
My Wartime Summers, Farrar, Straus & Giroux, 1994.
Rats! (sequel to *No Dogs Allowed*), illustrated by Tracey Campbell Pearson, Farrar, Straus & Giroux, 1996.
Spaceman, Dutton, 1997.
The Song of the Molimo, Farrar, Straus, 1998.
'Gator Aid (sequel to *Rats!*), illustrated by Tracey Campbell Pearson, Farrar, Straus & Giroux, 1999.
Leap, Frog!, Farrar, Straus & Giroux, 2001.

PICTURE BOOKS; FOR CHILDREN

Darcy and Gran Don't Like Babies, illustrations by Susannah Ryan, Scholastic, 1993.
Mr. Carey's Garden, illustrations by G. Brian Karas, Houghton, 1996.
The Cello of Mr. O, illustrations by Greg Couch, Dutton, 1999.
The Birthday Doll, Farrar, Straus & Giroux, 2001.

Contributor of adult short stories to periodicals, including *American Girl, Redbook, North American Review,* and the *Chicago Tribune;* edited and wrote textbooks, encyclopedias, and developed remedial reading materials for children. Also a featured author on C-Span Books.

Sidelights

Jane Cutler is the author of well-received novels and picture books about family life. In her novels *No Dogs Allowed* and its sequels, *Rats!* and *'Gator Aid,* Cutler portrays the adventures and misadventures of brothers Jason and Edward Fraser. The brothers are embroiled in a number of humorous situations, such as encountering the neighborhood bully, pretending to be a dog, taking a camping trip, making the annual school clothes shopping trip, caring for pet rats, dealing with girls and romance at school, and discovering a baby alligator in the park lake. About *No Dogs Allowed,* a *Kirkus Reviews* critic commented, "The dialogue is on target, and the brothers make an entertaining pair," whose activities would appeal to readers who have enjoyed books by such well-known authors as Beverly Cleary and Johanna Hurwitz. Jana R. Fine also commented in her review for *School Library Journal* on the realistic characters and "upbeat and lightweight" tone; and in *Publishers Weekly* a critic suggested that while the book's tone is "surprisingly funny," the "humor masks weightier matters."

Nancy Vasilakis, writing in *Horn Book,* compared the sequel *Rats!* favorably to its predecessor, noting the "convincing characterizations" and "lighthearted humor that will appeal to those children who have read through Beverly Cleary and are looking for more." Although *Booklist* reviewer Ilene Cooper found the humor a little forced, she conceded, "There are still some very funny moments." "What makes these stories so inviting," added Maggie McEwen in *School Library Journal,* "is Cutler's exceptional talent for describing events from the boys' rather literal point of view." Maintaining that some of the humor of *'Gator Aid* will elude the target audience, *Horn Book* critic Vasilakis judged this later sequel to be an "undemanding, light read with characters a notch or two above stereotypes." In *Booklist,* Stephanie Zvirin remarked on the book's "pleasant comedy," but also the "thought provoking undercurrent" about how statements can be distorted into wild rumors.

In a departure from her earlier lighthearted, humorous novels, Cutler published *My Wartime Summers,* a first-person novel set in midwestern America during World War II. In this work the main character, Ellen, matures from a young girl into a teenager over three wartime summers during which she gradually becomes aware of the war and what it means in human terms. According to a *Publishers Weekly* reviewer, "The author's use of period details is so convincing that the book reads like autobiography." "Ellen is an interesting character," added Louise L. Sherman in *School Library Journal,* judging that the author "successfully conveys the many emotions of her narrator and the other characters." However, in Sherman's view, the episodic plot structure could pose problems for readers not well versed in history.

In the novel *Spaceman,* readers meet fifth-grade student Gary. Due to his learning disabilities, Gary earned the nickname "spaceman" because he "spaces out" when under pressure. After he is transferred to a special-needs classroom, Gary improves under the tutelage of a talented teacher. "Gary is a kid misunderstood and misplaced, and his dilemma is one with which many children can identify," asserted Janice M. Del Negro in her review for the *Bulletin of the Center for Children's Books.* Instead of falling prey to the temptation to sentimentalize Gary and the other special-needs students, Cutler, in the view of a *Publishers Weekly* critic, "uses the occasion for crisp, brisk storytelling." Writing for *School Library Journal,* Janet M. Bair suggested that classroom teachers could make good use of this book to "encourage discussion and promote empathy towards those who have different learning styles." "This compelling story ... will help increase awareness and empathy," added Lauren Peterson in her *Booklist* review.

In Jane Cutler's entrancing picture book, well-intentioned gardener neighbors suggest various ways of killing the snails that are eating Mr. Carey's plants until one night he teaches them about the snails' secret beauty. (From Mr. Carey's Garden, *illustrated by G. Brian Karas.)*

For her second historical novel, *The Song of the Molimo,* Cutler chose an untried topic: the 1904 World's Fair in St. Louis. In particular, she focused on twelve-year-old Harry Jones, a fictional character, and his relationship with Ota Benga (a real historical figure) and four other African Pygmies who have been brought to the fair and put on display in the Anthropology Exhibit. Researchers believe that the Pygmies are intellectually inferior and try to prove their inferiority through their experiments. Harry, and his cousin Frederick, who is in charge of caring for the Pygmies, realize that the Pygmies deserve the same respect as other humans—an enlightened view in their prejudiced society—and plan to save their new friends. The work elicited qualified praise. Calling the novel both "informative and entertaining," Brenda Moses-Allen, writing in *Voice of Youth Advocates,* added, "Her descriptions of the Fair, its exhibits, and the mores of the people at that time are very believable." In a review for *Bulletin of the Center for Children's Book,* Elizabeth Bush found Cutler to be unrealistic in her negative portrayal of the exhibit chief McDougal. However, in Bush's view Cutler "leads readers to some interesting questions about confronting the unknown and the reliability of 'scientific evidence.'"

Cutler has written several notable picture books. In *Darcy and Gran Don't Like Babies,* Cutler shows how one grandmother dealt with the feelings of her granddaughter for the new baby in the house. *Mr. Carey's Garden* treats a more unusual topic—snails eating holes in Mr. Carey's plants. When his gardening neighbors suggest various ways of killing the snails, they are baffled at his negative response, until one night they discover the snails' secret beauty. "A succinct but beautiful lesson in tolerance and understanding" is how Judith Constantinides described this work in *School Library Journal.* So too, Stephanie Zvirin of *Booklist* called the book "quiet" yet with "meaning that carries on beyond the confines of the story." *The Cello of Mr. O* describes the response of an elderly cellist to life in a war-ravaged community. By playing his cello amidst the ravages of war, Mr. O brings hope through his music. According to Ilene Cooper of *Booklist,* Cutler manages to "overlay the everyday horrors of war with a patina of hope." "Cutler's focus on turning calamity on its head will likely have an uplifting effect on readers young and old," enthused a *Publishers Weekly* critic.

About her works, Jane Cutler told SATA, "My own books are built around my characters: thoughtful characters, idiosyncratic characters, humorous characters. It is people who interest me most, and the books reflect this. But, like every writer, I need also to concern myself with plot—there has to be a story, after all! Fortunately, my characters have busy, active lives, which are, like most lives, full of stories."

Works Cited

Bair, Janet M., review of *Spaceman, School Library Journal,* May, 1997, p. 131.

In 'Gator Aid, from Cutler's popular series about the adventures of brothers Jason and Edward Fraser, imaginative second-grader Edward is certain he has seen an alligator in the Shaw Park lake and soon the whole town is astir. (Illustrated by Tracey Campbell Pearson.)

Bush, Elizabeth, review of *The Song of the Molimo, Bulletin of the Center for Children's Books,* October, 1998, pp. 55-56.

Review of *The Cello of Mr. O, Publishers Weekly,* August, 16, 1999, p. 84.

Constantinides, Judith, review of *Mr. Carey's Garden, School Library Journal,* May, 1996, p. 91.

Cooper, Ilene, review of *The Cello of Mr. O, Booklist,* December 15, 1999, p. 782.

Cooper, Ilene, review of *Rats!, Booklist,* February 1, 1996, p. 932.

Del Negro, Janice M., review of *Spaceman, Bulletin of the Center for Children's Books,* May, 1997, p. 318.

Fine, Jana R., review of *No Dogs Allowed, School Library Journal,* December, 1992, p. 80.

McEwen, Maggie, review of *Rats!, School Library Journal,* April, 1996, p. 106.

Moses-Allen, Brenda, review of *The Song of the Molimo, Voice of Youth Advocates,* June, 1999, p. 112.

Review of *My Wartime Summers, Publishers Weekly,* August 15, 1994, p. 96.

Review of *No Dogs Allowed, Kirkus Reviews,* November 1, 1992, p. 1374.

Review of *No Dogs Allowed, Publishers Weekly,* November 9, 1992, p. 85.

Peterson, Lauren, review of *Spaceman, Booklist,* March 15, 1997, p. 1242.

Sherman, Louise L., review of *My Wartime Summers, School Library Journal,* November, 1994, p. 102.

Review of *Spaceman, Publishers Weekly,* February 24, 1997, p. 92.

Vasilakis, Nancy, review of *'Gator Aid, Horn Book,* September, 1999, p. 609.

Vasilakis, Nancy, review of *Rats!, Horn Book,* May-June, 1996, pp. 334-35.

Zvirin, Stephanie, review of *'Gator Aid, Booklist,* August, 1999, p. 2056.

Zvirin, Stephanie, review of *Mr. Carey's Garden, Booklist,* March 15, 1996, p. 1268.

For More Information See

PERIODICALS

Booklist, October 15, 1998, p. 420.
Horn Book, May-June, 1996, p. 322.
Horn Book Guide, March, 1993, p. 66.
Publishers Weekly, April 17, 1995, p. 62.

ON-LINE

Cutler's Web site is located at http://www.janecutler.com.

D

DAVIDSON, Hugh
See HAMILTON, Edmond

*   *   *

DOGYEAR, Drew
See GOREY, Edward (St. John)

*   *   *

DOWDY, Mrs. Regera
See GOREY, Edward (St. John)

*   *   *

DUNREA, Olivier (Jean-Paul Dominique) 1953-

Personal

Name was originally Clarence Miller, Jr.; surname is pronounced "DUN-ray"; born September 22, 1953, in Virginia Beach, VA; son of Clarence (a baker) and Marian (a homemaker; maiden name, Goodwin) Miller. *Education:* Attended University of Delaware, 1971-73; West Chester State College (now University), B.A., 1975; Washington State University, M.A. (theater and music), 1976. *Politics:* None. *Religion:* None. *Hobbies and other interests:* Reading, running, gardening, camping, and building stone dams.

Addresses

Home and office—214 Wendover St., Philadelphia, PA 19128.

Career

Worked variously as a waiter, secretary, and management consultant; freelance artist and actor in Philadel-

phia, PA, San Francisco, CA, and New York City, 1976-79; writer and illustrator, 1976—. Teacher of art and theater to children; leader of workshops in makeup design, watercolor illustration, mask making, movement and nonverbal communication, and model building. Has exhibited in Philadelphia, PA, and New York City. *Member:* English-Speaking Union, Philadelphia Children's Reading Round Table.

Awards, Honors

Cooper/Woods Award (travel grant), English-Speaking Union, 1980; residency grant, National Endowment for the Arts and Delaware State Arts Council, 1981-83; Outstanding Pennsylvania Children's Author, 1985; Celebrating Literacy Award, International Reading Association, 1987; *Skara Brae* was selected one of Child Study Association of America's Children's Books of the Year, 1987.

Writings

PICTURE BOOKS; SELF-ILLUSTRATED

Eddy B, Pigboy, Atheneum, 1983.
Ravena, Holiday House, 1984.
Fergus and Bridey, Holiday House, 1985.
Mogwogs on the March!, Holiday House, 1985.
Skara Brae: The Story of a Prehistoric Village, Holiday House, 1986.
Deep Down Underground, Macmillan, 1989.
Eppie M. Says ..., Macmillan, 1990.
The Broody Hen, Doubleday, 1992.
The Painter Who Loved Chickens, Farrar, Straus, 1995.
Noggin and Bobbin by the Sea, Celebration Press (Glenview, IL), 1996.
The Tale of Hilda Louise, Farrar, Straus, 1996.
The Trow-Wife's Treasure, Farrar, Straus, 1998.
Appearing Tonight! Mary Heather Elizabeth Livingstone, Farrar, Straus, 1999.
Bear Noel, Farrar, Straus, 2000.

ILLUSTRATOR

Nathan Zimelman, *The Star of Melvin,* Macmillan, 1987.

Barbara Brenner, *The Boy Who Loved To Draw: Benjamin West,* Houghton, 1998.

Joy Cowley, *The Rusty, Trusty Tractor,* Boyds Mills Press, 1999.

OTHER

The Writing Process, Stronetrow Studio, 1990.

Sidelights

Since his debut in 1983, author and illustrator Olivier Dunrea has created a steady stream of picture books, including concept books, stories of family life—modern and ancient—and stories about artists. Many of Dunrea's picture books testify to his love of animals and his interest in archaeology and folklore of the British Isles. "I don't write books or make pictures for children," Dunrea told *SATA.* "I make them for myself. It just so happens that children like what I do as much as I do!"

A middle child of four, Dunrea was born in Virginia Beach, Virginia, in 1953. He grew up in a busy household full of siblings and pets. "As a child my major fascination was with farm animals and rocks," Dunrea told *SATA.* "Most of my time was spent either taking care of livestock on our homestead or drawing them and making up stories about them. Chickens, geese and pigs are my favorites." Dunrea was the only person in his family to attend college, earning a Master of Arts degree in theater arts and music. For five years, Dunrea worked as a professional actor, singer, and dancer. In addition, he designed stage sets and costumes. Dunrea won several travel scholarships, which gave him the opportunity to visit Scotland, the Orkney Islands, and the Outer Hebrides islands, where he researched—including sketching, painting, and photographing—ancient monuments. About his first visit in 1978 Dunrea recalled for *SATA,* "It was this trip to the British Isles that would most affect my writing and artwork . . . . In the latter part of the twentieth century the world seems so very complicated—to both children and adults alike. My fascination is with the ancient past, when things were more mysterious, more magical, and more permanent. Therefore, my favorite kind of stories to write and illustrate usually center around my own characters that I've created from my imagination. They live in a prehistoric, stony setting."

In such books as *Ravena, Mogwogs on the March!, Deep Down Underground,* and *The Trow-Wife's Treasure,* Dunrea demonstrates his interest in archaeology and folklore. *Ravena* tells the story of a nonconformist banshee, a female spirit of Scottish folklore, who searches for a new home. Commentators appreciated Dunrea's pastel illustrations framed by stones. "The illustrations in subdued tones convey the atmosphere of the locale," noted a *Publishers Weekly* reviewer, and *School Library Journal* critic Hayden E. Atwood described the artwork as "superior illustrations." Yet several critics also wished for a meatier story. In the concept book *Mogwogs on the March!* Dunrea portrays a group of gnomes going on a hike. *Publishers Weekly*

The hero of Olivier Dunrea's cheerful self-illustrated picture book, **The Painter Who Loved Chickens,** *gains acclaim when he decides it is best to paint the subject he truly favors.*

reviewer Sean F. Mercier found the brightly attired gnomes "beguiling."

Deep Down Underground is also a concept book, this time one meant to teach counting by following the trail of a mole through its underground passageways. Critics praised the work for both its art and rhyming, alliterative, and onomatopoetic text. A *Publishers Weekly* reviewer pointed out the book's "unusual theme and lovely art," an appraisal similar to *Horn Book* contributor Ellen Fader's when she described the work as "out of the ordinary and intriguing." *Deep Down Underground* is a "celebration of nature, a delightful puzzle, and an invitation to look sharply at the small wonders around us," concluded Anna Biagioni Hart in *School Library Journal.* In *The Trow-Wife's Treasure,* Dunrea recounts in Scottish dialect how a farmer helps a troll find her missing child. Although *Horn Book* reviewer Nancy Vasilakis noted that the plot appears to tell a "simple story of kindness rewarded," she contended that the illustrations in "this arresting book suggest something deeper and more mystical." So too, *Booklist* critic Helen Rosenberg remarked on the "detailed and striking" illustrations and called the work a "satisfying tale, with true Scottish flavor."

With the nonfiction picture book *Skara Brae: The Story of a Prehistoric Village,* Dunrea shows young readers a glimpse of prehistoric life in Skara Brae, which was discovered in the Orkney Islands, north of Scotland. Among Dunrea's many pen-and-ink drawings are seascapes, architectural diagrams and site plans, and imagined scenes of village life. Writing in the *Bulletin of the Center for Children's Books,* Zena Sutherland praised the text as "well written and organized," adding that "graceful illustrations elaborate significantly on an

A warmhearted farmer from the mythical island of Nord Eyris unhesitatingly agrees to help a strange little troll woman find her lost baby. (From The Trow-Wife's Treasure, *written and illustrated by Dunrea.)*

inherently interesting subject." *Horn Book* critic Ann A. Flowers found that Dunrea's text "gives a clear description of the settlers' primitive way of life; the illustrations are fascinating," though she found his drawings of animals and humans "not quite convincing." "Children and adults are sure to be intrigued," Marguerite F. Raybould asserted in *School Library Journal.*

At one time during his childhood, Dunrea had fifteen dogs as companions, so it comes as no surprise that in *Fergus and Bridey,* Bridey is a special dog, Fergus's best friend. Together they set out on a series of adventures. A *Publishers Weekly* critic predicted that Fergus and Bridey are such "quaint characters" that readers would find them irresistible. In *Eppie M. Says . . . ,* Eppie does not entertain herself with a dog, but with her gullible younger brother, Ben, who believes her every word, ridiculous or not. According to John Peters in *School Library Journal,* Dunrea's "quirky [visual] details ... add to the general hilarity" of this picture book.

Dunrea illustrated several books about artists, such as Barbara Brenner's picture book biography of colonial American artist Benjamin West, *The Boy Who Loved to Draw,* and his own fictional work *The Painter Who Loved Chickens.* For the former, Dunrea created period paintings that "pay their respects to the art of the period but retain warmth and a childlike puckishness" to quote a *Publishers Weekly* reviewer. According to Carolyn Phelan in *Booklist,* Dunrea's illustrations for *The Boy Who Loved to Draw* "present clear visual expressions of the activities and emotions related in the story." *Horn Book* critic Mary M. Burns declared the work a "handsome interpretation, faithful to its subject, lively to

read, distinctively colonial in pictorial content, and cast in a well-designed format."

Because chickens were among Dunrea's favorite animals to draw as a child, the story of an artist who loves to paint chickens was a natural choice for a picture book. After halfheartedly painting other subjects, the hero of *The Painter Who Loved Chickens* finally gains acclaim by painting what he prefers—fowl. The "unassuming text straightforwardly conveys his emotion-filled, clearly delineated story," praised a *Publishers Weekly* reviewer. Describing the work as a "tribute to individual talent and dogged determination," Mary M. Burns, writing for *Horn Book,* deemed it a "unique creation." "It's a zany story, a joyful celebration of following your dreams," enthused Hazel Rochman in *Booklist.* Dunrea, like his hero, has succeeded in following his own path.

Works Cited

Atwood, Hayden E., review of *Ravena, School Library Journal,* November, 1984, p. 106.

Review of *The Boy Who Loved to Draw: Benjamin West, Publishers Weekly,* July 5, 1999, p. 70.

Burns, Mary M., review of *The Boy Who Loved to Draw: Benjamin West, Horn Book,* September, 1999, p. 622.

Burns, Mary M., review of *The Painter Who Loved Chickens, Horn Book,* July-August, 1995, pp. 448-49.

Review of *Deep Down Underground, Publishers Weekly.* September 29, 1989, p. 67.

Fader, Ellen, review of *Deep Down Underground, Horn Book,* November-December, 1989, p. 757.

Review of *Fergus and Bridey, Publishers Weekly,* March 22, 1985, p. 59.

Flowers, Ann A., review of *Skara Brae: The Story of a Prehistoric Village, Horn Book,* September-October, 1986, p. 607.

Hart, Anna Biagioni, review of *Deep Down Underground, School Library Journal,* September, 1989, p. 224.

Mercier, Sean F., review of *Mogwogs on the March!, Publishers Weekly,* December 6, 1985, p. 75.

Review of *The Painter Who Loved Chickens, Publishers Weekly,* March 13, 1995, p. 69.

Peters, John, review of *Eppie M. Says . . . , School Library Journal,* October, 1990, p. 90.

Phelan, Carolyn, review of *The Boy Who Loved to Draw: Benjamin West, Booklist,* September 15, 1999, p. 262.

Review of *Ravena, Publishers Weekly,* November 9, 1984, p. 65.

Raybould, Marguerite F., review of *Skara Brae: The Story of a Prehistoric Village, School Library Journal,* May, 1986, p. 90.

Rochman, Hazel, review of *The Painter Who Loved Chickens, Booklist,* March 1, 1995, p. 1247.

Rosenberg, Helen, review of *The Trow-Wife's Treasure, Booklist,* April 15, 1998, pp. 1450-51.

Sutherland, Zena, review of *Skara Brae, Bulletin of the Center for Children's Books,* May, 1986, p. 164.

Vasilakis, Nancy, review of *The Trow-Wife's Treasure, Horn Book,* July-August, 1998, pp. 471-72.

For More Information See

PERIODICALS

Booklist, March 15, 1999, p. 1332.
Bulletin of the Center for Children's Books, December, 1984, p. 64.
New York Times Book Review, September 15, 1985, p. 20; May 21, 1995, p. 22.

Publishers Weekly, September 14, 1990, p. 124; September 2, 1996, pp. 129-30; February 9, 1998, p. 95; March 1, 1999, p. 68; January 10, 2000, p. 70.
School Library Journal, August, 1985, p. 53; December, 1985, pp. 71-72; June, 1995, p. 80; September, 1996, p. 177; October, 1999, p. 134.*

E–F

EDGY, Wardore
See GOREY, Edward (St. John)

* * *

EVANS, Hubert Reginald 1892-1986

Personal

Born May 9, 1892, in Vankleek Hill, Ontario, Canada; died June 17, 1986; married Anna Winter, 1920 (died, 1960); children: three.

Career

Novelist, poet, and writer of children's fiction. Newspaper reporter in Toronto, Ontario, and British Columbia for four years; worked for commercial fisheries and as a fisheries officer in salmon conservation in British Columbia. *Military service:* Rocky Mountain Rangers, 1915-19; served in France and Flanders.

Writings

FOR CHILDREN, EXCEPT AS NOTED

Forest Friends: Stories of Animals, Fish, and Birds West of the Rockies, Judson Press, 1926.
The New Front Line (for adults), Macmillan, 1927.
Derry, Airedale of the Frontier, illustrated by F. C. Yohn, Dodd, 1928.
Derry's Partner, illustrated by Frank E. Schoonover, Dodd, 1929.
Derry of Totem Creek, illustrated by H. E. M. Sellen, Dodd, 1930.
The Silent Call, illustrated by Sellen, Dodd, 1930.
North to the Unknown: The Achievements and Adventures of David Thompson (nonfiction), illustrated by Ruth Collins, Dodd, 1949.
Mist on the River (for adults), Copp, 1954.
Mountain Dog, Westminster Press, 1956, published as *Son of the Salmon People,* 1981.

Whittlings (poems), illustrated by Robert Jack, Harbour Publishing, 1976.
Endings (poems), Madeira Park, 1978.
O Time in Your Flight (for adults), Madeira Park, 1979.
Mostly Coast People (poems), Madeira Park, 1982.

Also author of *Bear Stories* and *Silversides: The Life of a Sockeye Salmon;* of some two hundred stories; and of several plays for Canadian radio. Contributor to periodicals, including *Saturday Evening Post, Toronto Star Weekly, Maclean's, Canadian Magazine,* and *St. Nicholas.*

Sidelights

Hubert Reginald Evans spent most of his adult years living in and writing about the Skeena River area of British Columbia. Many of his writings were directed toward readers in their early teens, although Evans published novels for adults and also collections of verse. Evans' stories focus on life in the wilderness of the province while touching on such issues as conservation and discrimination against Native Canadians. Several of his stories, including his "Derry" books *North to the Unknown* and *Mountain Dog,* have a dog as a primary character. Evans' Newfoundlands and Airedales are depicted as the most loyal of friends, accompanying and supporting their masters on numerous adventures.

Evans served overseas during World War I, and his first novel, *The New Front Line,* is a largely autobiographical story of an ex-soldier returning home to the northern British Columbia frontier and getting married. His next three books are novels for children: *Derry, Airedale of the Frontier, Derry's Partner,* and *Derry of Totem Creek.* Set again in the North, they are episodic but fast-paced adventures loosely connected by the hero Ed Sibley and his dog, dramatizing their conflicts with the wilderness, wild animals, and assorted characters, good and evil.

In the 1920s and 1930s, Evans published two hundred stories in American and Canadian magazines, including *Saturday Night, Maclean's,* and the *Canadian Magazine.*

He also wrote sixty serials and several plays for CBC radio.

Mist on the River, published in 1954, is considered a classic. It tells the story of Gitkshan Indians whom Evans knew personally. Cy Pitt, the protagonist, is caught between the attractions of the white world as represented by Prince Rupert and Vancouver, and the tribal traditions of the Indians' inland village. His sister June chooses the white world, and her future seems more optimistic than that of their cousin Dot, who survives by prostitution. But while Cy envies June's freedom, his marriage to Miriam, daughter of the old chief, Paul, binds him to the past and the local. The conflict is dramatized in the fate of Dot's boy, Steve, who dies because his grandfather will not allow him to be treated with the medicine of the white man. The death of Paul suggests that Cy, as the new chief, may be able to preserve the best of the old and reconcile it with the best of the new. *Mist on the River* has been commended by anthropologist Harry Hawthorne for its accuracy in depicting native characters and customs.

In his next novel for children, *Mountain Dog,* Evans returns to the setting of *Mist on the River* and to a similar theme. Hal Harrigan is an Indian like Cy, but is more successful than him. Educated in Vancouver and planning to study wildlife management, he defeats the plans of an exploiter, a sawmill owner who attempts to destroy the community, and ensures the safety of both the salmon run and his people. Due to renewed interest in Evans' theme, the novel was republished in 1981 as *Son of the Salmon People.*

In *Twentieth-Century Children's Writers,* Janet E. Baker credited Evans' juvenile works for "their well-observed detail and their exciting, imaginative plots." Baker added that Evans' work compares favorably with that of Ernest Thompson Seton and Charles G. D. Roberts, well-known Canadian authors of dog stories.

In the 1970s and early 1980s, Evans published three collections of poetry and another autobiographical adult novel, *O Time in Your Flight.* The novel describes southwestern Ontario in 1899 as seen through the eyes of a boy, Gilbert Egan. It recounts such historic events as the celebration of the end of the Boer War and of New Year's Eve at the turn of the century, side by side with vivid details of everyday living and the universal joys, sorrows, dreams, and humiliations of childhood.

Works Cited

Baker, Janet E., *Twentieth-Century Children's Writers,* "Hubert (Reginald) Evans," 4th edition, St. James Press, 1995.

For More Information See

BOOKS

Dictionary of Literary Biography, Volume 92: *Canadian Writers, 1890-1920,* Gale, 1990.

PERIODICALS

Books in Canada, May, 1981, p. 40.
Canadian Children's Literature, number 21, 1981, p. 83; number 25, 1982, p. 80; number 74, 1994, p. 94; spring, 1996, p. 80.

Obituaries

PERIODICALS

Toronto Star, June 18, 1986.*

*   *   *

FALL, Andrew
See ARTHUR, Robert (Jr.)

*   *   *

FLEMING, A. A.
See ARTHUR, Robert (Jr.)

*   *   *

FORBES, Robert
See ARTHUR, Robert (Jr.)

G

GAER, Joseph 1897-1969
(Yossef Gaer)

Personal

Original name, Joseph Fishman; born March 16, 1897, in Yedinitz, Russia; immigrated to United States in 1917, naturalized citizen in 1926; died December 7, 1969, in Santa Monica, CA; son of Solomon and Naomi (Shkolnik) Fishman; married Fay Ratner, March 14, 1923; children: Elsa Gay (Mrs. Duncan R. Luce), Paul Joseph. *Education:* Attended colleges in the United States and Canada. *Politics:* Democrat. *Religion:* Jewish.

Career

University of California, Berkeley, teacher, 1930-35; U.S. Government, Washington, DC, chief field supervisor and editor-in-chief of Federal Writers Project, 1935-39, consultant to administrator of Farm Security Administration, 1939-41, special assistant to Secretary of Treasury, 1941-43; Congress of Industrial Organizations, publicity director of Political Action Committee, 1943-45; Pamphlet Press (division of Reynal & Hitchcock), founder and director, 1945-46; Boni & Gaer (later Gaer Associates Publishing Co.), New York, NY, president, 1946-49; Jewish Heritage Foundation, Beverly Hills, CA, founder and director, 1958-69. Member of American Jewish Committee, Commission of Jewish Affairs. Consultant to film producers. *Member:* International Institute of Arts and Letters (fellow), Screenwriters Guild, National Jewish Music Council (board member), Foundation for Arts, Religion and Culture.

Awards, Honors

Distinguished merit citation, National Conference of Christians and Jews, 1964; American Honorarium citation, 1966.

Writings

The Magic Flight: Jewish Tales and Legends, Frank-Maurice, 1926.
The Legend Called Meryom (novel), Morrow, 1928.
(Adapter) *The Burning Bush: Adapted Folklore Legends,* Sinai Press for Union of American Hebrew Congregations, 1929.
How the Great Religions Began (Book Find Club selection), R. M. McBride, 1929, new and revised edition, Dodd, 1935, school edition, Dodd, 1963.
(Adapter) *The Unconquered: Adapted Folklore Legends,* Sinai Press for Union of American Hebrew Congregations, 1932.
Washington: City and Capital, U.S. Government Printing Office, 1937.
Men and Trees: The Problem of Forest Conservation and the Story of the United States Forest Service, Harcourt, 1939.
Fair and Warmer: The Problem of Weather Forecasting and the Work of the United States Weather Bureau, Harcourt, 1939.
Consumers All: The Problem of Consumer Protection, Harcourt, 1940.
Toward Farm Security: The Problem of Rural Poverty and the Work of the Farm Security Administration, U.S. Government Printing Office, 1941.
(With J. L. Kaukonen and Elliott H. Moyer) *What Uncle Sam Owes You,* Funk, 1943.
The First Round: The Story of the CIO Political Action Committee, Duell, Sloan & Pearce, 1944.
Everybody's Weather (for children), Lippincott, 1944, revised edition, 1957.
Angels Could Do It Better: The Story of Dunbarton Oaks (pamphlet), American Labor Party, 1945.
Heart upon the Rock (novel; Jewish Book Guild selection), Dodd, 1950.
The Lore of the Old Testament (Book Find Club and Jewish Book Guild selection), Little, Brown, 1951.
The Lore of the New Testament (Book Find Club and Pulpit Book Club selection), Little, Brown, 1952.
Young Heroes of the Living Religions, Little, Brown, 1953.
Holidays around the World, Little, Brown, 1953.

The Adventures of Rama: The Story of the Great Hindu Epic Ramayana (for children), Little, Brown, 1954.
The Fables of India, Little, Brown, 1955.
The Wisdom of the Living Religions, Dodd, 1956.
(With Alfred Wolf) *Our Jewish Heritage,* Holt, 1957, new edition, Wilshire, 1967.
The Legend of the Wandering Jew, New American Library, 1961.
What The Great Religions Believe, Dodd, 1963.
(With Ben Siegel) *The Puritan Heritage: America's Roots in the Bible,* New American Library, 1964.

EDITOR

Our Federal Government and How It Functions, Hastings House, 1939.
Our Washington: A Comprehensive Album of the Nation's Capital in Words and Pictures, A. C. McClurg, 1939.
Our Lives: American Labor Stories, Boni & Gaer, 1948.
(And author of introduction and notes with Chester C. McCown) *The Bible for Family Reading,* Little, Brown, 1956.
(And author of introduction and notes) *The Jewish Bible for Family Reading,* Yoseloff, 1957.
The Best of Recall, Yoseloff, 1962.
The Best of Recall #2, Yoseloff, 1967.
Ambrose Gwinett Bierce: Bibliography and Biographical Data (originally published in mimeographed form, 1935), B. Franklin, 1968.
Bret Harte: Bibliography and Biographical Data (originally published in mimeographed form, 1935), B. Franklin, 1968.
Frank Norris (Benjamin Franklin Norris): Bibliography and Biographical Data (originally published in mimeographed form, 1934), Folcroft, 1969.
Bibliography of California Literature: Fiction of the Gold-Rush Period, Drama of the Gold-Rush Period, Poetry of the Gold-Rush Period (originally published in mimeographed form, 1935), B. Franklin, 1970.
Jack London: Bibliography and Biographical Data (originally published in mimeographed form, 1934), B. Franklin, 1970.
The Theatre of the Gold Rush Decade in San Francisco (originally published in mimeographed form, 1935), B. Franklin, 1970.
Bibliography of California Literature: Pre-Gold Rush Period (originally published in mimeographed form, 1935), B. Franklin, 1970.
Upton Sinclair: Bibliography and Biographical Data (originally published in mimeographed form, 1935), B. Franklin, 1971.
California in Juvenile Literature (originally published in mimeographed form, 1935), B. Franklin, 1972.
The Torah for Family Reading, J. Aronson (Northvale, NJ), 1986.

EDITOR; MIMEOGRAPHED PAMPHLETS PUBLISHED UNDER AUSPICES OF CALIFORNIA LITERARY RESEARCH PROJECT

Mary Austin: Bibliography and Biographical Data, 1934.
John M. Letts, *An Alphabetical Index to California Illustrated,* 1935.
Index: California and Its Gold Regions by Fayette Robinson, 1935.

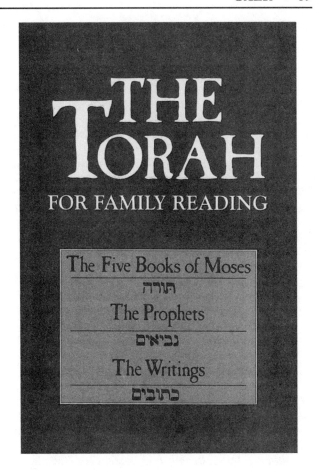

In Joseph Gaer's adaptation of the Hebrew Scriptures, the text has been made more accessible through historical background information, description, and explication as well as simplification of language.

Index: California and Oregon; or, Sights in the Gold Region and Scenes by the Way, by Theodore Taylor Johnson, 1935.
Index: California Life Illustrated, by William Taylor, 1935.
Index: Diary of a Physician in California: Being the Result of an Actual Experience, by James L. Tyson, 1935.
Index: Eldorado; or, Adventures in the Path of Empire: Comprising a Voyage to California, via Panama, by Bayard Taylor, 1935.
Index: Eldorado; or, California as Seen by a Pioneer, 1850-1900, by D. A. Shaw, 1935.
Index: Hunting for Gold: Reminiscences of Personal Experience and Research in the Early Days of the Pacific Coast from Alaska to Panama, by William Downie, 1935.
Index: Life in California During a Residence of Several Years in That Territory: Comprising a Description of the Country and the Missionary Establishments, by Alfred Robinson, 1935.
Index: Mountains and Molehills; or, Recollections of a Burnt Journal, by Frank Marryat, 1935.
Index: Personal Adventures in Upper and Lower California in 1848-1849; With the Author's Experience at the Mines, by William Redmond Ryan, 1935.
Index: Recollections and Opinions of an Old Pioneer, by Peter H. Burnett, 1935.

Index: Sixteen Months at the Gold Diggings, by Daniel B. Woods, 1935.

Index: The Annals of San Francisco: Containing a Summary of the History of the First Discovery, Settlement, Progress and Present Condition of California and With a Complete History of All the Important Events Connected with Its Great City, by Frank Soule, John H. Gihon, and James Nisbet, 1935.

Index: The Gold Regions of California: Being a Succinct Description of the Geography, History, Topography, and General Features of California: Including a Carefully Prepared Account of the Gold Regions of That Fortunate Country, Edited by George G. Foster, 1935.

Index: The Story of the Mine: As Illustrated by the Great Comstock Lode of Nevada, by Charles Howard Shaw, 1935.

Index: Three Years in California, by J. D. Borthwick, 1935.

Index: Three Years in California, by Walter Colton, 1935.

Index: What I Saw in California: Being the Journal of a Tour by the Emigrant Route and South Pass of the Rocky Mountains, Across the Continent of North America, the Great Desert Basin, and Through California in the Years 1846, 1847, by Edwin Bryant, 1935.

Contributor to _Universal Jewish Encyclopedia, Encyclopedia of Religion and Ethics, Children's Encyclopedia_, and _Book of Knowledge;_ contributor to periodicals, including _Bookman, Dial, Saturday Review_, and _New Republic._ Editor, _Recall_ (publication of the Jewish Heritage Foundation).

Sidelights

An educator, organization executive, editor, and author, Joseph Gaer began his career as a lecturer in contemporary literature at the University of California, Berkeley, in the early 1930s. In 1935 he left his teaching post to serve as editor-in-chief and chief field supervisor of the Federal Writers Project, where he remained until 1939. Gaer then acted as consultant for the Farm Security Administration. During World War II he was special assistant to U.S. secretary of the treasury and, for a time, also was publicity director of the Congress of Industrial Organizations. In 1945 he founded and directed the Pamphlet Press, a division of Reynal & Hitchcock. During the next four years, he served as president of the publishing firm of Boni & Gaer, later named Gaer Associates. In 1958 he became founder and director of the Jewish Heritage Association in Beverly Hills, California. Among Gaer's many writings are the novels _The Legend Called Meryom_ and _Heart upon the Rock_, the children's titles _Everybody's Weather_ and _The Adventures of Rama: The Story of the Great Hindu Epic Ramayana_, the history _How the Great Religions Began_, a number of commentaries on religion, and various farm economy studies. Gaer was editor of _Our Federal Government and How It Functions; Our Lives: American Labor Stories;_ New England guides to Massachusetts, Maine, and New Hampshire; and many other publications. He also contributed short stories, articles, plays, and poetry to periodicals such as the _Menorah Journal, Southwest Review, Saturday Review, New Republic,_ and _Dial._*

*   *   *

GAER, Yossef
See GAER, Joseph

*   *   *

GARTH, Will
See HAMILTON, Edmond

*   *   *

GAUTHIER, Gail 1953-

Personal

Born September 28, 1953, in Middlebury, VT; daughter of Henry (a farmer) and Shirley (an institutional cook; maiden name, Adams) Gauthier; married E. Russell Johnston III (a civil engineer), July 23, 1977; children: William Russell Johnston, Robert Gauthier Johnston. _Education:_ University of Vermont, B.S. (education). _Hobbies and other interests:_ History, education.

Addresses

Agent—c/o Publicity director, G. P. Putnam's Sons, 345 Hudson St., 14th Floor, New York, NY 10014.

Career

University of Connecticut, Storrs, CT, educational assistant, 1976-80, workshop instructor in the Division of Extended and Continuing Education, 1980-81; Middlesex Community College, Middletown, CT, instructor in the Community Services Division, 1982-83. Community volunteer, PTO member, classroom volunteer, Sunday school teacher, CE Board member, Boy Scout volunteer, all 1986—; conducts school and library presentations related to writing, 1996—.

Awards, Honors

Choice Book of 1996 selection, Cooperative Children's Book Center, 1996, and Children's Book of the Year selection, Bank Street College, both for _My Life among the Aliens; A Year with Butch and Spike_ and _Club Earth_ both named Children's Books of the Year by Bank Street College.

Writings

FOR CHILDREN

My Life among the Aliens, illustrated by Santiago Cohen, Putnam (New York City), 1996.

A Year with Butch and Spike, Putnam, 1998.

Club Earth (sequel to _My Life among the Aliens_), Putnam, 1999.

The Hero of Ticonderoga, Putnam, 2001.

Contributor to periodicals, including *Cricket*. Books have been published in four foreign countries.

Work in Progress

Children's fiction; researching the eighteenth-century history of Vermont and Massachusetts and medieval history.

Sidelights

According to a *Kirkus Reviews* contributor, Gail Gauthier's *My Life among the Aliens* "is a droll and irreverent comedy, at the center of which beats a heart of gold." Narrator Will Denis and his younger brother, Robby, meet space aliens who land in their neighborhood at the beginning of summer vacation. Initially, only the boys and their friends realize the visitors are aliens, and each chapter of the book contains a separate story about their encounters and adventures. In one chapter, human mothers intimidate some of the aliens, while in another chapter, an alien shows the children how to play with real dinosaurs. The book also features an alien-influenced talking dog and Robby's tour of the galaxy. Discussing *My Life among the Aliens* in the *School Library Journal,* Anne Connor called it "a delightful science-fiction romp in which the impossible is presented as if it were perfectly natural."

In *A Year with Butch and Spike,* cousins Butch and Spike Couture—also known as the Cootches—are the bad boys of Theodore Ervin Memorial Elementary School. Model student Jasper Gordon finds himself seated between Butch and Spike in the sixth grade classroom of Mrs. McNulty, a teacher also known as Mrs. McNutt. Mrs. McNulty assigns Jasper and another student to work with Butch and Spike and two other less-than-stellar students and to serve as good examples for the boys, but Jasper begins to admire the independent and gutsy cousins. "Gauthier does not skimp on any chance for humor, deploying satire and slapstick in turn," wrote Susan P. Bloom in a *Horn Book* review of *A Year with Butch and Spike.* Jasper begins to see that Mrs. McNulty is more than a strict disciplinarian. She belittles and humiliates her students to make them conform, telling the children that they are not allowed to think, just obey. *School Library Journal* contributor Coop Renner said McNulty "unwittingly creates the possibility for a kind of group solidarity that allows all six kids to mature." According to *Booklist* contributor Michael Cart, "Gauthier demonstrates a real talent here for humorous hyperbole and episodic classroom comedy."

Club Earth is the sequel to *My Life among the Aliens.* Will, Robby, and their parents turn their home into a vacation spot for aliens. Saliva, an alien, serves as the resort's manager, allowing only the best aliens to visit the Denis's home. When alien guest Alphonse decides to make the Denis household his permanent address, the family looks for ways to close the resort.

Gauthier once commented: "I fell into writing for children. I had been writing other types of fiction, with little success. I thought my first book, *My Life among the Aliens,* was a fluke—something that just happened. A lot of my family's experience went into the book, and I considered it a gift for my children and their friends. It was only later that I realized I had found my material.

"Writing for children gives me an opportunity to explore interests that I seem to share with them. Children are definite outsiders in a world controlled by adults, and the outsider theme is one I find myself attracted to. Using humor to attack the status quo is something I find children enjoy (I certainly did when I was in grade school), and it fits in with my outsider stories about aliens, bad boys, and girls who don't understand getting together to play with Barbie dolls.

"Children rarely write books. They don't publish them, edit them, or review them. They don't decide which books end up on bookstore or library shelves or school reading lists. Grown-ups do all that. Kids have no control over an aspect of their lives that can either bring them so much in the way of pleasure and meaning or just be another method of indoctrinating them into the adult world. My hope is that I can try to be a voice for them."

Works Cited

Bloom, Susan P., review of *A Year with Butch and Spike,* *Horn Book,* May-June, 1998, p. 342.

Cart, Michael, review of *A Year with Butch and Spike,* *Booklist,* June 1, 1998, p. 1765.

Conner, Anne, review of *My Life among the Aliens,* *School Library Journal,* June, 1996, p. 122.

Review of *My Life among the Aliens, Kirkus Reviews,* April 1, 1996, p. 529.

Renner, Coop, review of *A Year with Butch and Spike,* *School Library Journal,* June, 1998, p. 145.

For More Information See

PERIODICALS

Children's Book Review Service, July, 1996, p. 155.
Horn Book Guide, fall, 1996, p. 292.
Kirkus Reviews, March 1, 1998, p. 338.
Publishers Weekly, March 9, 1998, pp. 68-69.

*   *   *

GEWE, Raddory
See GOREY, Edward (St. John)

*   *   *

GLEESON, Libby 1950-

Personal

Born September 19, 1950, in Young, New South Wales, Australia; daughter of Norman John (a teacher) and Gwynneth (a homemaker; maiden name, Whitten) Gleeson; married Euan Tovey (a scientist); children: Amelia, Josephine, Jessica. *Education:* University of Sydney, B.A., 1973; New South Wales Department of Education, teaching certification, 1975. *Hobbies and other interests:* Family, reading, swimming, tennis, community arts.

Addresses

Home—11 Oxford St., Petersham, NSW 2049, Australia. *Agent*—Curtis Brown, P.O. Box 19, Paddington NSW 2021, Australia.

Career

Instructor in secondary school and university, 1974-86; visiting lecturer at various universities, 1985—; full-time writer, 1989—. Has also been a consultant for teaching English as a second language, 1986-90. Authors' representative on Public Lending Right Committee of Australia. *Member:* Australian Society of Authors (Chair, 1999-2000).

Awards, Honors

Angus & Robertson Award for Writers for Young Readers, 1984, highly commended, Australian Children's Book of the Year, 1985, shortlisted for New South Wales Premier's Award, 1985, South Australia Premier's Award, 1985, and Guardian Newspaper's Award for Children, all for *Eleanor, Elizabeth;* Honor Book, Australian Children's Book of the Year, 1988, and shortlisted for Victorian Premier's Award, 1988, both for *I Am Susannah;* Children's Literature Peace Prize, 1991, and International Board on Books for Young People (IBBY) Award, 1992, both for *Dodger;* Prime Minister's Multicultural Award, 1991, for *Big Dog;* Honor Book, Children's Book Council of Australia, Picture Book of the Year honor, 1993, for *Where's Mum?;* shortlisted for Australian Children's Book of the Year, 1994, for *Love Me, Love Me Not;* Children's Book of the Year award, Children's Book Council of Australia, 1997, for *Hannah Plus One; Queen of the Universe* was shortlisted for Australian Children's Book of the Year, 1998; *Hannah and the Tomorrow Room* was shortlisted for the Australian Children's Book of the Year, 2000; Winner, Bologna Ragazzi, and shortlisted, Australian Children's Book of the Year, both 2000, both for *The Great Bear.*

Writings

NOVELS; FOR YOUNG READERS

Eleanor, Elizabeth, Holiday House, 1984.
I Am Susannah, Penguin (Ringwood, Victoria), 1986, Holiday House, 1987.
One Sunday, illustrated by John Winch, HarperCollins (Pymble, New South Wales), 1988.
Dodger, Penguin, 1990, Puffin (New York City), 1993.
Skating on Sand, illustrated by Ann James, Viking (Ringwood, Victoria), 1994.
Hannah Plus One, illustrated by Ann James, Viking, 1996, Puffin, 1996.

Queen of the Universe, illustrated by David Cox, Omnibus Books (Norwood, South Australia), 1998.
Refuge, Viking, 1998.
Hannah and the Tomorrow Room, illustrated by Ann James, Viking, 1999.

PICTURE BOOKS

Big Dog, illustrated by Armin Greder, Ashton Scholastic, 1991, published as *The Great Big Scary Dog,* Tambourine Books (New York City), 1994.
Uncle David, illustrated by Armin Greder, Ashton Scholastic (Lisarow, New South Wales), 1992.
Where's Mum?, illustrated by Craig Smith, Ashton Scholastic, 1992.
Mum Goes to Work, illustrated by Penny Azar, Ashton Scholastic, 1993.
Sleeptime, Ashton Scholastic, 1993.
Hurry Up!, illustrated by Mitch Vane, SRA School Group (Santa Rosa, CA), 1994.
Walking to School, illustrated by Linda McClelland, SRA School Group, 1994.
The Princess and the Perfect Dish, illustrated by Armin Greder, Ashton Scholastic (Sydney, Australia), 1995.
The Great Bear, illustrated by Armin Greder, Scholastic, 1999.

OTHER

Love Me, Love Me Not (short stories; for children), Ashton Scholastic (Lisarow, New South Wales), 1993, Viking, 1993.
Writing Hannah, On Writing for Children, Hale and Ironmonger (Sydney, Australia), 1999.

Also author of numerous short stories, including "The Boy Who Wouldn't Get Out of Bed," "Bedtime Story," "Farewell," "In the Swim," and "Her Room." Gleeson's works have been translated into Swedish, Dutch, German, and Italian.

Sidelights

Award-winning Australian children's author Libby Gleeson grew up in rural New South Wales. During her childhood, her family moved quite often because of her father's teaching career. "There were six children and no television," Gleeson once told *Something about the Author (SATA).* "That meant family entertainment was usually reading. I read everything I could get my hands on. I think I decided then that to be a writer and to make books would be a most wonderful occupation. I didn't set out to do this straight away. I studied at the University of Sydney and became a secondary school teacher.

"After two years teaching I set out to see the world. I spent five years traveling and working in western Europe, England, and America. At the same time, I wrote constantly—determined to become a writer. I began my first novel, *Eleanor, Elizabeth,* while I was living in London. I joined a group of writers who met regularly and discussed work-in-progress. That experience helped me shape the text and develop my own critical skills. It is a novel that grew out of my bush childhood, with historical material of the last century largely taken from the childhood of my grandparents. It is fiction, not autobiography."

The story centers around a young girl named Eleanor who has just moved to a new town. In the course of the move, Eleanor discovers her grandmother's diary, written in 1895 when her grandmother was twelve. The diary helps Eleanor come to terms with her new home, and, as Connie Tyrrell Burns wrote in *School Library Journal,* "to appreciate her own concerns in the light of her grandmother's." The diary also helps save the lives of Eleanor, her brother, and a friend when they escape from a raging brush fire by finding her grandmother's secret cave.

In *I Am Susannah* it is the main character's best friend who moves away, leaving Susannah to deal with her self-involved mother, making new friends, and her first encounter with adolescent kissing games. At the same time, a mysterious woman with a supposedly tragic past, known as the "Blue Lady," moves into her best friend's old house. When Susannah, an aspiring artist, spies the Blue Lady's artistic talents, the two begin a friendship of their own. Nancy Vasilakis praised *I Am Susannah* in *Horn Book* for its "excellent characterizations and an exploration of pertinent contemporary themes."

During the early 1990s Gleeson published a handful of picture books, including *The Great Big Scary Dog,* books about work and school, and the fairy tale *The Princess and the Perfect Dish.* The first, called an "unusual and engaging book" by *School Library Journal* reviewer Lisa Dennis, is the story of how three young children, using their imaginations and some very colorful costumes, help a little girl overcome her fear of a neighborhood dog. While Ann A. Flowers noted in *Horn Book* the "satisfying conclusion" to a common childhood dilemma and Hazel Rochman of *Booklist* described the end as a "most satisfying reversal," a *Publishers Weekly* critic suggested that the advice the book offers is "poor—even contrary."

In what Gleeson called her "mum period" books, because she wrote them while her children were very young, Gleeson served up slices of daily life. These books include *Mum Goes to Work, Where's Mum?, Sleeptime, Hurry Up!,* and *Walking to School.* In 1993 *Where's Mum?,* with its imaginative response to why Mum was late to arrive at the daycare center, was named an Honor Book by the Children's Book Council of Australia.

As a response to society's pressure on girls to be overly thin, Gleeson wrote the fairy tale *The Princess and the Perfect Dish,* which is about a princess with a voracious appetite and a healthy attitude toward her body size and shape. According to *Horn Book* reviewer Karen Jameyson, a "few delicious deviations" from traditional fairytale fare make the book a "mouth-watering, entertaining, and provocative delight."

In 1993 Gleeson published a young adult novel, *Dodger,* which deals with themes of adolescent anxieties and adjustments. Mick Jamieson is a troubled student of thirteen who has faced many challenges. Since his mother's recent death, Mick has had to move from a small Australian country town to suburban Campbelltown to live with his grandmother. His father, a truck driver, is away all the time, although Mick is constantly hoping for his return. *Dodger* is also the story of Penny, a first-year teacher who sees enough in Mick to cast him as the Artful Dodger in the school production of *Oliver Twist,* despite the resistance of several other teachers. In a review for *Magpies,* Stephanie Owen Reeder noted the sensitive handling of the relationship between Mick and Penny, as well as Gleeson's portrayal of "young adolescents dealing with life in believable settings, and in a way which captures the emotions of the reader."

For emergent readers Gleeson wrote two easy-reading novels about Hannah: *Skating on Sand* and *Hannah Plus One.* In the former, six-year-old Hannah, the youngest of three siblings, insists on bringing her skates on a family vacation to the seashore in New South Wales. In *Hannah Plus One* Hannah must come to terms with her feelings about the expected arrival of a new sibling— who might turn out to be twins. Critics found much to like about each novel. "Both books begin with a passage in the first person before switching to a closely-observant third person for the remainder," explained Jameyson. "They are also written in the present tense—a form that seems to enhance their effectiveness and immediacy. And the dialogue is so authentic that you'd swear you had your ear to a cup on the wall instead of your eyes on the page." In *Magpies* Mandy Cheetham praised *Skating on Sand* for its sensitivity and humor, as well as the author's "ear for dialogue." "This funny, meticulously written story dramatises perfectly the trials of the youngest in the family," added Dennis Hamley in *School Librarian.* Irene Babsky, reviewing *Hannah Plus One* in *School Librarian,* called the work "delightful ... a real nugget of family life, not to be missed."

With *Refuge,* a novel for young readers, Gleeson focused on the plight of the refugees from East Timor (in Indonesia) who are hiding to avoid being deported from Australia. In particular, Gleeson placed the issue in the context of one family, that of Andrew and Anna, who defy their parents and hide a refugee in their home in Sydney. According to John Murray in *Magpies,* Gleeson effectively combines the issue of refugees and the action of the novel, putting into perspective the moral and legal issues of hiding refugees and delving into the characters' motives. "I can imagine readers of twelve to sixteen debating their individual positions on the matters raised in *Refuge,* wishing to learn more about the East Timorese struggle against Indonesian dominance," Murray concluded.

Gleeson's own three children have had considerable influence on her work. "I am constantly observing them and being reminded of my own experiences as a child," she once told *SATA.* "I try to bring to the reader the feelings of those real experiences so that they can identify with the characters—whether they be kids from the bush as in *Eleanor, Elizabeth,* the city as in *I am Susannah,* or suburbia as in *Dodger.*"

Works Cited

Babsky, Irene, review of *Hannah Plus One, School Librarian,* August, 1997, p. 145.

Burns, Connie Tyrrell, review of *Eleanor, Elizabeth, School Library Journal,* June, 1990, pp. 121-22.

Cheetham, Mandy, review of *Skating on Sand, Magpies,* March, 1995, p. 26.

Dennis, Lisa, review of *The Great Big Scary Dog, School Library Journal,* May, 1994, p. 94.

Flowers, Ann A., review of *The Great Big Scary Dog, Horn Book,* September-October, 1994, pp. 576-77.

Review of *The Great Big Scary Dog, Publishers Weekly,* April 11, 1994, pp. 63-64.

Hamley, Dennis, review of *Skating on Sand, School Librarian,* August, 1995, p. 108.

Jameyson, Karen, "Typical Turbulence: Writing and Raising a Family," *Horn Book,* March-April, 1997, pp. 225-27.

Murray, John, review of *Refuge, Magpies,* March, 1998, p. 38.

Reeder, Stephanie Owen, review of *Dodger, Magpies,* March, 1991, p. 4.

Rochman, Hazel, review of *The Great Big Scary Dog, Booklist,* April 1, 1994, p. 1458.

Vasilakis, Nancy, review of *I Am Susannah, Horn Book,* September, 1989, pp. 628-29.

For More Information See

BOOKS

St. James Guide to Children's Writers, fifth edition, St. James Press (Detroit), 1999, pp. 424-25.

PERIODICALS

Australian Book Review, November, 1993, p. 63; October, 1995, p. 62; February, 1998, p. 56.

Horn Book, September, 1989, p. 628; April, 1991, p. 65; July-August, 1993, pp. 443, 496.

Junior Bookshelf, December, 1996, p. 252.

Magpies, September, 1993, p. 224; March, 1994, p. 32; May, 1997, p. 30.

Publishers Weekly, April 11, 1994, p. 63.

School Library Journal, June, 1989, pp. 104-05; September, 1993, p. 208; November, 1996, p. 146; August, 1997, p. 145.

Voice of Youth Advocates, October, 1989, p. 212; August, 1990, p. 160.

GOREY, Edward (St. John) 1925-2000 (Eduard Blutig, Drew Dogyear, Mrs. Regera Dowdy, Wardore Edgy, Raddory Gewe, Roy Grewdead, Redway Grode, O. Mude, Edward Pig, E. D. Ward, Ogdred Weary, Dogear Wryde)

OBITUARY NOTICE—See index for *SATA* sketch: Born February 22, 1925, in Chicago, IL; died April 15, 2000, in Hyannis, MA. Author, illustrator, and designer. Although Gorey earned a Bachelor's degree from Harvard University in 1950, his only formal artistic training was derived from classes he attended sporadically at the Art Institute of Chicago. In 1953, he accepted a position in the art department at Doubleday Publishing Company in New York, where he worked as a staff artist and book-jacket designer. His first picture book, *The Unstrung Harp; or, Mr. Earbrass Writes a Novel,* directed primarily to adults, was published by Duell, Sloan, & Pearce that same year. In 1957, Doubleday published *The Doubtful Guest,* the first of Gorey's works considered appropriate for children. Two more such efforts, *The Object Lesson* and *The Bug Book,* followed in each of the two subsequent years. Late in 1959, Edmund Wilson offered a favorable assessment of Gorey's artistry in the *New Yorker,* prompting more widespread attention to Gorey's works and helping to usher in four decades of very prolific and often critically acclaimed activity for the artist. Gorey's books for children and adults are distinguished primarily by their subject matter, although in most instances the distinction is subtle: his tales for the young are generally regarded as nonsense fiction in the style of nineteenth-century author/illustrators Edward Lear and Heinrich Hoffmann, while his stories for adults are more pointed and satiric. Among young people and students of children's fiction, Gorey is esteemed primarily for his skill as an illustrator. He collaborated successfully with a number of well-known authors of juvenile literature, providing pictures for stories by Lear, John Ciardi, Florence Parry Heide, and John Bellairs, among others. Gorey's own picture books featuring turn-of-the-century settings reveal his art at its finest: intricate pen and ink sketches with cross-hatched backgrounds and characters in the period costume that Gorey found "more interesting to draw." His gothic-style illustrations, commonly praised for their evocation of mood, are also admired for their depth of detail—most notably, the furniture and patterned wallpaper that distinguish interior scenes. Several of Gorey's works, including *The Monster Den, The Dong with a Luminous Nose,* and *The Shrinking of Treehorn,* were named to the *New York Times* list of Best Illustrated Children's Books for their respective years of publication. Gorey is also respected for his work in other media. In 1978, he received an Antoinette Perry (or "Tony") Award for his costume and set designs for the Broadway show *Dracula.*

OBITUARIES AND OTHER SOURCES:

BOOKS

Children's Literature Review, Volume 36, Gale, 1995.

PERIODICALS

Dance Magazine, July, 2000, p. 12.
Detroit Free Press, April 18, 2000.
Newsweek, May 1, 2000, p. 72.
New York Times, April 17, 2000.

GREWDEAD, Roy
See GOREY, Edward (St. John)

*   *   *

GRODE, Redway
See GOREY, Edward (St. John)

H

HAMILTON, Edmond 1904-1977
(Alexander Blade, Robert Castle, Hugh Davidson, Will Garth, Brett Sterling, Robert Wentworth)

Personal

Born October 21, 1904, in Youngstown, OH; died February 1, 1977, in Lancaster, PA; son of Scott B. and Maude (Whinery) Hamilton; married Leigh Brackett (a science-fiction writer), December 31, 1946 (died March 18, 1978). *Education:* Attended Westminster College, New Wilmington, PA, 1919-21.

Career

Freelance writer, primarily of science fiction, 1926-77, including staff writer position for *Superman* comics, 1940s. *Member:* Authors Guild of America.

Awards, Honors

Guest of honor, Twenty-second World Science Fiction Convention, 1964; elected to First Fandom Science Fiction Hall of Fame, 1967.

Writings

The Metal Giants, Swanson, 1932.
The Horror on the Asteroid, Ian Allan, 1936.
Murder in the Clinic, Utopian, 1945.
Tiger Girl, Utopian, 1945.
The Monsters of Juntonheim, Pemberton, 1950.
Tharkol, Lord of the Unknown, Pemberton, 1950.
City at World's End, Fell, 1951.
The Star of Life, Torquil Press, 1959.
The Sun Smasher (bound with *Starhaven,* by Ivar Jorgenson), Ace Books, 1959.
The Haunted Stars, Torquil Press, 1960.
Battle for the Stars, Torquil Press, 1961.
(Contributor) Larry Shaw, editor, *Great Science-Fiction Adventures,* Lancer Books, 1963.

The Valley of Creation, Lancer Books, 1964.
Fugitive of the Stars (bound with *Land beyond the Map,* by Kenneth Bulmer), Ace Books, 1965.
Doomstar, Belmont-Tower, 1966.
The Harpers of Titan (bound with *Dr. Cyclops,* by Henry Kuttner and *Too Late for Eternity,* by Bruce Walton), Popular Library, 1967.
A Yank at Valhalla, Ace Books, 1973.
What's It Like out There? (short story collection), Ace Books, 1974.
(Editor) *The Best of Leigh Brackett,* Doubleday, 1977.
The Best of Edmond Hamilton, edited and introduced by wife, Leigh Brackett, Ballantine, 1977.
The Lake of Life, R. Weinberg (Chicago), 1978.

"JOHN GORDON" SERIES

The Star Kings, Fell, 1949.
Beyond the Moon, Signet, 1950.
Return to the Stars, Lancer, 1970.

"INTERSTELLAR PATROL" SERIES

Outside the Universe, Ace, 1964.
Crashing Suns, Ace, 1965.

"STARWOLF" SERIES

The Weapon from Beyond, Ace, 1967.
The Closed Worlds, Ace, 1968.
World of the Starwolves, Ace, 1968.

"CAPTAIN FUTURE" SERIES

(Under pseudonym Brett Sterling) *Danger Planet,* Popular Library, 1967.
Calling Captain Future, Popular Library, 1967.
Galaxy Mission, Popular Library, 1967.
Captain Future and the Space Emperor, Popular Library, 1967.
Outlaw World, Popular Library, 1968.
The Magician of Mars, Popular Library, 1968.
Quest beyond the Stars, Popular Library, 1968.
Outlaws of the Moon, Popular Library, 1969.
The Comet Kings, Popular Library, 1969.
Planets in Peril, Popular Library, 1969.
Captain Future's Challenge, Popular Library, 1969.

Also author of scripts, including *Black Terror* (comic strip), 1941-45. Contributor of more than four hundred short stories to science-fiction publications.

Sidelights

"Out of the twenties into the early thirties came [Edmond] Hamilton," wrote Donald A. Wolheim, "and a sudden spark that was momentarily to light up the greatest concept of the world of science-fiction ideas: the galactic civilization.... A civilization of intelligent beings, in contact with each other, trading with each other, banded together in some sort of Federation of the Stars to assist, to enlighten, to defend." As a young author of science fiction, Hamilton primarily wrote for the "pulp" publications of the period. His most noted stories centered on the exploits of the Interstellar Patrol, "a patrol ship of the stars traveling many hundreds of times the speed of light," Wolheim explained. "And crewed by one being each of a dozen or two dozen intelligent cooperating civilized worlds."

Within this realm, Hamilton helped to introduce many innovative and widely imitated concepts. The notion that Earth is controlled by aliens from outer space has been credited to Hamilton, as has the idea of programming robots to perform specific tasks. *Weird Tales* and *Amazing Stories* were the first to create the idea of galactic civilization. Hamilton was also one of the first science-fiction writers to explore the concept of devolution, a kind of evolution in reverse, in which cosmic radiation causes higher life forms to regress with each successive generation until, finally, they reach their lowest and most primitive state. Hamilton was also the creator of what is now termed "space opera." He wrote many such stories for publications including *Air Wonder Stories, Amazing, Startling,* and *Thriller Wonder Stories.* Hamilton was so well-known for space operas that his absence was conspicuous in *Planet Stories,* regarded as the epitome of the genre.

Hamilton's best-known character was Captain Future, who was Curt Newton, also known as the Wizard of Science and the Man of Tomorrow. He saved the solar system time and again with the help of Grag the robot, Otho the android, and Simon Wright, a brain in a box. A magazine called *Captain Future,* published quarterly from 1940 to 1944, contained a short novel of Captain Future's adventures in each issue. Hamilton wrote most of these novels, along with some later Captain Future stories in *Startling Stories.*

Hamilton wrote hundreds of stories during his lifetime. His later writings, according to Wolheim, proved Hamilton to be "a far more sophisticated, far more able and skilled a story-teller than the youth who pounded out those tales of the Patrol." Chad Oliver described Hamilton's early work in *Twentieth-Century Science-Fiction Writers* as showing "the defects of the genre he pioneered. The action was fast and furious and sometimes absurd. The characterization was minimal and the dialogue was ghastly. But Hamilton was fond of the Big Idea, and he could communicate the excitement of

sweeping concepts.... His stories had verve and feeling, and they were alive." Wolheim wrote that Hamilton's style is "marked by endless exclamation points, a gosh-wow-golly type of writing, our side against theirs plotting, a last-minute rush to the lever that alone would save or destroy the day, and a bang leaving everyone breathless." Hamilton's later works, beginning with *City at World's End,* are more refined and less melodramatic. The characters are more believable, and there is more subtlety in the stories. Although this marked the end of a lot of the excitement present in earlier works, there is still an element of adventure, but it is tempered with realism. Although the quality of his work improved, Wolheim suggested that Hamilton could not "hope to surpass that concept which for one moment pushed the borders of science fiction ahead."

Works Cited

Oliver, Chad, *Twentieth-Century Science-Fiction Writers,* "Edmond Hamilton," 3rd edition, St. James Press, 1991.
Wolheim, Donald A., *The Universe Makers,* Harper, 1971.

For More Information See

BOOKS

Contemporary Literary Criticism, Volume I, Gale, 1973.
Dictionary of Literary Biography, Volume 8: *Twentieth-Century American Science-Fiction Writers,* Gale, 1981.
Moskowitz, Samuel, *Seekers of Tomorrow,* World Publishing, 1966.

PERIODICALS

Analog, December, 1950; August, 1951; November, 1959; November, 1960; June, 1962; September, 1965; August, 1977.
Galaxy, April, 1963.
Luna Monthly, August, 1969.
Magazine of Fantasy & Science Fiction, November, 1977; October, 1989.
New Worlds, June, 1969.
New York Times Book Review, November 10, 1974.
Publishers Weekly, March 14, 1977.
Science Fiction Review, January, 1971.*

*   *   *

HAND, Elizabeth 1957-

Personal

Born March 29, 1957, in San Diego, CA; daughter of Edward (an attorney) and Alice Ann (a social worker; maiden name, Silverthorn) Hand; children: Callie Anne Silverthorn. *Education:* Catholic University of America, B.A., 1984. *Religion:* Roman Catholic.

Addresses

Home—P.O. Box 133, Lincolnville, ME 04849. *Agent*—Martha Millard Literary Agency, 204 Park Ave., Madison, NJ 07940.

Career

National Air and Space Museum, Smithsonian Institution, archival researcher, 1979-86; National Air and Space Museum's Archival Videodisc Program, co-founder; writer.

Awards, Honors

James Tiptree, Jr. Award, 1995, for *Waking the Moon;* Nebula Award, Science Fiction and Fantasy Writers of America, and World Fantasy Award, World Fantasy Convention, both 1995, both for best novella "Last Summer at Mars Hill."

Writings

Winterlong (science fiction novel), Bantam, 1990.
Aestival Tide, Bantam, 1991.
Icarus Descending, Bantam, 1993.
Waking the Moon, HarperPrism (New York City), 1995.
Glimmering: A Novel, HarperPrism, 1997.
Last Summer at Mars Hill (short story collection), Harper-Prism, 1998.
Black Light, HarperCollins, 1999.

Also author of *12 Monkeys.* Critic for *Washington Post, Detroit Metro Times,* and *San Francisco Eye.* Contributor of stories to books, including *Year's Best Horror Stories XVII,* edited by Karl E. Wagner, DAW (New York), 1989, *Full Spectrum 2,* Doubleday (New York City), 1989, and *Year's Best Horror 2,* edited by Ramsey Campbell, Carrol and Graf (New York City), 1991. Contributor to the series "X-Files" and "Millennium," based on the television shows.

Sidelights

Elizabeth Hand emerged on the science-fiction scene as a novelist after publishing only three short works. Her first published short story was "Prince of Flowers," which appeared in *Twilight Zone.* It is a fantasy story about a woman, Helen, who works in a museum in Washington, D.C. Her job is to open new crates and inventory the strange objects and papers received by the museum. Among the items she takes home to liven up her apartment is a "spirit puppet," an Indonesian item that had been packed for nearly a century. This story was included in Karl Edward Wagner's *Year's Best Horror Stories XVII.*

Hand's next story, "On the Town Route," was published a year later in *Pulphouse.* It concerns a woman who travels with an ice cream truck vendor through an impoverished area of Virginia. There she sees the poor, ignorant people who buy (or sometimes accept for free) his ice cream. Some of them even seem to be dependent on his visits for any food at all. One night they accidentally hit one of the girls with the truck, believing her to be dead until her blind mother revives her and takes her home.

Hand's third short story, "The Boy in the Tree," was published shortly before her first novel and is noticeably more akin to science fiction than the previous stories. "The Boy in the Tree" is set in the future at a research facility that treats psychopaths. The central figure of the story is an empath, a person trained to treat patients by making a mental connection with them after tasting a bit of their blood. The relationships between the empaths are strange, characterized by vampiric kissing to see into the psychopathic minds treated by the other empaths.

Winterlong, Hand's first novel, was published in 1990. The book describes a future Earth where biological weapons have destroyed much of the world's population. Wendy and Raphael, twins who have been separated since birth, travel across the nightmarish landscape, facing danger from mutated cannibalistic children and deadly exotic plants. As the twins reunite, they enact the legend of the Final Ascension, which will decide the future of humankind. D. Douglas Fratz wrote in *Twentieth-Century Science-Fiction Writers,* "There are some marvelous characters here, but none seems to act on his or her own volition; all feel driven by unseen forces." Sherry Hoy, reviewing *Winterlong* in *Voice of Youth Advocates,* stated that Hand "weaves a tale that is achingly haunting and disquieting, surreal yet compelling.

In the novel *Black Light,* published in 1999, Hand tells the story of high-school senior Charlotte Moylan and her godfather, filmmaker Axel Kern. The notorious Kern arrives in Charlotte's hometown of Kamensic to host a Halloween party replete with drugs and dark and perverse characters, including various members of the Benandanti and the Malandanti, who are, as a critic for *Kirkus Reviews* explained, "two opposing groups of magicians . . . [that] struggle to control human destiny." After experiencing unsettling visions and meeting the strange Professor Warnick, Charlotte learns that her godfather is deeply involved in a dangerous conspiracy. Jackie Cassada praised Hand's "lucid style" in *Library Journal,* and a reviewer for *Publishers Weekly* declared that the book "should strongly appeal to aficionados of sophisticated horror."

Works Cited

Review of *Black Light, Kirkus Reviews,* March 15, 1999, p. 418.

Review of *Black Light, Publishers Weekly,* March 8, 1999, p. 51.

Cassada, Jackie, review of *Black Light, Library Journal,* April 15, 1999, p. 148.

Fratz, D. Douglas, "Elizabeth Hand," *Twentieth-Century Science-Fiction Writers,* 3rd edition, St. James Press, 1991.

Hoy, Sherry, review of *Winterlong, Voice of Youth Advocates,* April, 1991, p. 43.

PERIODICALS

Analog, February, 1991, p. 176; April, 1993, p. 160;
　　February, 1994, p. 159; December, 1995, p. 181.
Locus, October, 1992, p. 35; February, 1995, p. 17.
Magazine of Fantasy and Science Fiction, October, 1995,
　　p. 43.
New York Times Book Review, December 9, 1990, p. 32;
　　September 12, 1993, p. 36; September 10, 1995, p. 46.
Washington Post Book World, October 28, 1990, p. 10;
　　October 25, 1992, p. 9; September 26, 1993, p. 11;
　　August 13, 1995, p. 9; June 8, 1997, p. 7.*

*　　*　　*

HARRIS, David 1942-

Personal

Born February 19, 1942, in Pt. Pirie, South Australia;
son of Francis William (an electrician) and Queenie
Anna Rose (a teacher; maiden name, Lyne) Harris;
married second wife, Christine (a writer), July 6, 1989;
children: Sue, Paul, Andrew, Sam, Jenny. *Education:*
Adelaide University, B.A. (teaching diploma), 1963.
Hobbies and other interests: "I enjoy watching the sun
rise and the moon set at the same time, swimming in the
dark, climbing hills, and eating mocha torte."

Addresses

Agent—Jenny Darling and Associates, P.O. Box 235,
Richmond, VR 3121, Australia; *E-mail*—davidbooks@
dove.net.au.

Career

Has worked variously as a writer and teacher. *Member:*
Australian Society of Authors, Royal Geographical
Society, South Australian Writers Centre, Ekidnas Chil-
dren's Writers Group.

Awards, Honors

Runner-up, Christina Stead Award for biography, 1994;
visiting fellowship in history, University of New England; Virgiliana Medal, Italian Encyclopedic Institute;
shortlisted for the New South Wales Premier's Literary
Award, 1999.

Writings

FOR CHILDREN

The Carclew Ghost and Other Stories, McGraw-Hill, 1976.
A Man Called Possum, Penguin, 1998.

"CLIFFHANGERS" SERIES; FOR CHILDREN

Devil's Island, Penguin, 1999.
Fortress, Penguin, 1999.
Dead Silence, Penguin, 1999.
Firebug, Penguin, 1999.

David Harris

NONFICTION; FOR ADULTS

*Black Horse Odyssey: Search for the Lost City of Rome in
　　China,* Wakefield Press (Kent Town, South Australia),
　　1992.
No Bed of Roses: Memoirs of a Madam, Wakefield Press,
　　1993.
*What A Line! The Story of the People Who Made the Hoist
　　an Australian Icon,* Hills Industries, 1996.
High Tide: Australians Doing Business in Asia, Wakefield
　　Press, 1997.
The Bucks and Hens Book, Transworld, 1998.

OTHER

Also author of thirty children's television scripts and
two feature documentary scripts. Contributor of over
three hundred reviews and feature articles to major
Australian newspapers. Writer of technical works for
international aid programs and public relations and
speech writing for the South Australia Department of
Health and Welfare. Co-editor of *Coasting* (1988), the
Eyre Peninsula regional arts anthology. Author of
textbooks on writing fiction and biography.

Work in Progress

Three novels and one biography.

Sidelights

Australian author and educator David Harris is a prolific writer of articles and books in many genres, including history, biography, travel, business, textbooks, cultural studies, and juvenile novels. "I love writing all kinds of things because the work takes me on journeys of discovery," he wrote on his website. "I've written in a plane above the Black Sea, a room in Istanbul with a huge bear staring at me through the window, a slum in Bombay, a mountain top on the Silk Road, a Chinese train, a Fijian beach, and here at home with the door open onto the garden."

Since Harris enjoys adventure in his own life, it is not surprising that he should write adventurous novels. *The Carclew Ghost and Other Stories* is a collection of short stories for reluctant readers about a ghost in a house named Carclew, while *A Man Called Possum* is an adaptation for juvenile readers of a book by Max Jones about a mysterious hermit who survived on the banks of the Murray River.

With Harris's "Cliffhangers" series of juvenile novels for Penguin, Australia, readers follow teenage boy protagonists on fast-paced adventures. For example, in the novel *Devil's Island*, Luke battles a raging sea in a kayak and then finds himself on the infamous Devil's Island. There he must use his wits to survive life-threatening obstacles and the evil intentions of a mad scientist. Robert Holden, in his review of *Devil's Island* and *Fortress* for the *Australian Book Review*, noted Harris's debt to classic boys' adventure stories, such as *Treasure Island* and *Robinson Crusoe*. Holden wrote, "The narrative structure is certainly from the Indiana Jones school of white-knuckle adventure which sweeps us headlong into action. Plausibility and character development may be sacrificed to action and adventure but at least the sheer entertainment level never falters.... The fact that David Harris can take such a simple plot and still manage to instill tension and dramatic energy is a tribute to his storytelling skills." In *Fortress*, Harris recounts the adventures of Matt as he and a diverse group of others protest against activities at a nearby uranium plant. Holden judged this novel to be less successful than the series debut because the plot is not as taut and many characters are stereotypical. Nevertheless, he judged that the "book's exploits could entertain and satisfy younger readers."

Works Cited

David Harris's homepage, http://davidbooks.mtx.net.

Holden, Robert, "Roller Coaster Ride," *Australian Book Review*, April, 1999, pp. 40-41.

HARRIS, John (Wyndham Parkes Lucas) Beynon 1903-1969 (John Beynon, Johnson Harris, Lucas Parkes, John Wyndham)

Personal

Born July 10, 1903, in Knowle, Warwickshire, England; died March 11, 1969; son of George Beynon (a barrister) and Gertrude (Parkes) Harris; married Grace Wilson, 1936. *Education:* Educated at Bedales School in Hampshire. *Hobbies and other interests:* Leatherworking, bookbinding.

Career

Writer. Worked in advertising and farming. *Military service:* Royal Signal Corps, served in World War II.

Writings

SCIENCE-FICTION NOVELS

(Under pseudonym John Beynon) *The Secret People*, Newnes, 1935, Lancer Books, 1967.

(Under pseudonym John Beynon) *Foul Play Suspected*, Newnes, 1936.

(Under pseudonym Johnson Harris) *Live in Time*, Utopian, 1946.

Sleepers of Mars, Coronet, 1973.

UNDER PSEUDONYM JOHN WYNDHAM; SCIENCE-FICTION NOVELS

Planet Plane, Newnes, 1936, published as *Stowaways to Mars*, Fawcett, 1972.

The Day of the Triffids, Doubleday, 1951.

Out of the Deeps, Ballantine, 1953, published as *The Kraken Wakes*, M. Joseph, 1953, abridgment by G. C. Thornley published under same title, Longmans, Green, 1959, abridgment by S. S. Moody published under same title, Longmans, Green, 1961.

Re-birth, Ballantine, 1955, published as *The Chrysalids*, M. Joseph, 1955.

Village of the Damned, Ballantine, 1957, published as *The Midwich Cuckoos*, M. Joseph, 1957.

(And under pseudonym Lucas Parkes) *The Outward Urge*, Ballantine, 1959.

The Trouble with Lichen, Ballantine, 1960.

The Infinite Moment, Ballantine, 1961.

The John Wyndham Omnibus (contains *The Day of the Triffids*, *The Kraken Wakes*, and *The Chrysalids*), Simon & Schuster, 1966.

Chocky, Ballantine, 1968.

Web, M. Joseph (London), 1979.

COLLECTIONS OF SHORT STORIES

Jizzle, Dobson, 1954.

The Seeds of Time, M. Joseph, 1956.

Tales of Gooseflesh and Laughter, Ballantine, 1956.

Consider Her Ways, and Others, M. Joseph, 1961.

The Best of John Wyndham, Sphere Books, 1973.

Wanderers of Time, Coronet, 1973.

The Man from Beyond and Other Stories, M. Joseph, 1975.

Work represented in anthologies, including *The Year's Best Science Fiction,* edited by Harry Harrison and Brian Aldiss, Severn House, 1977; and *The Zeitgist Machine,* edited by Damien Broderick, Angus & Robertson, 1977. Contributor to periodicals, including *Wonder Stories.*

Adaptations

The Chrysalis was adapted to audio in 1985.

Sidelights

John Harris wrote his best-known novel, *The Day of the Triffids,* under the pseudonym John Wyndham, the persona whom Julius Kagarlitsky of *Twentieth-Century Science-Fiction Writers* called "the truest disciple of H. G. Wells in English literature." In fact, Harris credited *The Time Machine* and *War of the Worlds* as the two science-fiction novels that most influenced him. In his own novels, Harris applies Wells' technique of building the story around a single premise, and then considering the many ways in which the central event or idea impacts people and places. Wells' influence on Harris is also evident in the fact that the premise is usually connected to a catastrophe of some kind. In contrast, Harris opposed the Jules Verne approach to science fiction, which focuses on technical details for their own sake. Harris introduced only the technical elements necessary to lend realism to the story.

The Day of the Triffids is a novel in which the human race, blinded during a meteor shower, is threatened by carnivorous plants. It depicts the dissolution of social order, a recurring theme in Harris's work. In other novels, this social breakdown is followed by collectivism. In *The Chrysalids,* for example, a nuclear war all but destroys Earth, leaving only a few surviving communities that remain isolated from each other for centuries. As time passes, mutations make the survivors more and more hideous. Their communities take on a restrictive nature, rejecting anything that is different. Convinced that their present states represent perfection, they attempt to control further change. Progress eventually wins, however, as the children begin to form a collective "self" that hates cruelty and vows to rebuild a better world.

In *The Midwich Cuckoos,* aliens choose several places on Earth, including the small town of Midwich, and put all the inhabitants to sleep. Soon after, it becomes clear that the aliens have impregnated the women, and the human-alien hybrids will rule humankind. Because of the intellectual and spiritual superiority of the aliens, the humans quickly submit to their will. Much of their strength lies in their telepathic ability, which enables them to rule as a collective force without giving up their individual identities. H. H. Holmes, in the *New York Herald Tribune Book Review,* declared the novel to be "inescapably readable."

Works Cited

Holmes, H. H., review of *The Midwich Cuckoos, New York Herald Tribune Book Review,* March 16, 1958, p. 12.

Kagarlitsky, Julius, *Twentieth-Century Science-Fiction Writers,* "John Wyndham," 3rd edition, St. James Press, 1991.

For More Information See

PERIODICALS

New Statesman, September 28, 1957; March 7, 1975.

New York Herald Tribune Book Review, August 19, 1951; December 27, 1953; March 16, 1958.

New York Times, July 22, 1951.

Observer, March 28, 1965; April 7, 1968.

Spectator, September 7, 1951; September 27, 1957.

Time, March 10, 1958.

Times Literary Supplement, August 31, 1951; August 14, 1953; April 25, 1968; May 23, 1975.

Voice Literary Supplement, July, 1985.

Washington Post Book World, March 24, 1968.

Obituaries

PERIODICALS

New York Times, March 12, 1969.*

*   *   *

HARRIS, Johnson
See HARRIS, John (Wyndham Parkes Lucas) Beynon

*   *   *

HEIDE, Florence Parry 1919-
(Alex B. Allen, Jamie McDonald)

Personal

Surname is pronounced "*high*-dee"; born February 27, 1919, in Pittsburgh, PA; daughter of David W. (a banker) and Florence (an actress, columnist, and drama critic) Parry; married Donald C. Heide (an attorney), November 27, 1943; children: Christen, Roxanne, Judith, David, Parry. *Education:* Attended Wilson College; University of California, Los Angeles, B.A., 1939. *Politics:* Republican. *Religion:* Protestant.

Addresses

Home—6910 Third Ave., Kenosha, WI 53143. *Agent*—Curtis Brown, 10 Astor Pl., New York, NY 10003.

Career

Writer. Before World War II worked variously at Radio-Keith-Orpheum (RKO), and at advertising and public relations agencies, all in New York City, and as public

Florence Parry Heide

relations director of the Pittsburgh Playhouse, Pittsburgh, PA. *Member:* International Board on Books for Young People, American Society of Composers, Authors, and Publishers (ASCAP), Authors Guild, Authors League of America, Society of Children's Book Writers and Illustrators, Council for Wisconsin Writers, Children's Reading Round Table.

Awards, Honors

Children's Book of the Year award, Child Study Association of America, 1970, for *Sound of Sunshine, Sound of Rain,* and 1972, for *My Castle;* American Institute of Graphic Arts selection as one of the fifty best books of the year, 1971, Children's Book Show selection, American Institute of Graphic Arts, 1971-72, Best Illustrated Children's Book citation, *New York Times,* 1971, Children's Book Showcase selection, 1972, Jugendbuch Preis for best children's book in Germany, 1977, graphic arts prize from Bologna Book Fair, 1977, Notable Book citation, American Library Association (ALA), and Best of the Best Books 1966-78 citation, *School Library Journal,* 1978, all for *The Shrinking of Treehorn;* second prize for juvenile fiction, Council for Wisconsin Writers, and Golden Kite honor book, Society for Children's Book Writers and Illustrators, both 1976, both for *Growing Anyway Up;* Golden Archer Award, 1976; Notable Book citation, American Library Association (ALA), 1978, for *Banana Twist,*

1981, for *Treehorn's Treasure,* 1982, for *Time's Up!;* Litt.D. from Carthage College, 1979; Charlie May Simon Award, 1980, for *Banana Twist;* first prize, Council for Wisconsin Writers, 1982, for *Treehorn's Treasure;* honorable mention, Council for Wisconsin Writers, 1982, for *Time's Up!;* Notable Book citation, ALA, Best Book citation, *School Library Journal,* and Editors' Choice award, *Booklist,* all 1990, all for *The Day of Ahmed's Secret;* first prize, Council for Wisconsin Writers, 1990, and Charlotte Award, New York State, 1991, both for *The Day of Ahmed's Secret;* Outstanding Children's Book Award, New Hampshire Writers and Publishers Project, 1992, Notable Children's Trade Book in the Field of Social Studies, 1992, Editors' Choice award, *Booklist,* 1992, Best Books of 1992 list, *Parent's* magazine, Children's Book of Distinction, *Hungry Mind Review,* 1993, and Rhode Island Children's Book Award master list, 1993, all for *Sami and the Time of the Troubles.*

Writings

FOR CHILDREN

Benjamin Budge and Barnaby Ball, illustrated by Sally Mathews, Four Winds, 1967.

(Under pseudonym Jamie McDonald, with Anne and Walter Theiss and others) *Hannibal,* illustrated by Anne and Walter Theiss, Funk, 1968.

Maximilian Becomes Famous, illustrated by Ed Renfro, McCall, 1970.

Alphabet Zoop, illustrated by Mathews, McCall, 1970.

Giants Are Very Brave People, illustrated by Charles Robinson, Parents' Magazine Press, 1970.

The Little One, illustrated by Ken Longtemps, Lion, 1970.

Sound of Sunshine, Sound of Rain, illustrated by Longtemps, Parents' Magazine Press, 1970.

The Key, illustrated by Ati Forberg, Atheneum, 1971.

Look! Look! A Story Book, illustrated by Carol Nicklaus, McCall, 1971.

The Shrinking of Treehorn (also see below), illustrated by Edward Gorey, Holiday House, 1971.

Some Things Are Scary, Scholastic Book Services, 1971.

Who Needs Me?, illustrated by Mathews, Augsburg, 1971.

My Castle, illustrated by Symeon Shimin, McGraw, 1972.

(With brother, David Fisher Parry) *No Roads for the Wind* (textbook), Macmillan, 1974.

God and Me, illustrated by Ted Smith, Concordia, 1975.

When the Sad One Comes to Stay (novel), Lippincott, 1975.

You and Me, illustrated by Smith, Concordia, 1975.

Growing Anyway Up, Lippincott, 1975.

Banana Twist, Holiday House, 1978.

Changes, illustrated by Kathy Counts, Concordia, 1978.

Secret Dreamer, Secret Dreams, Lippincott, 1978.

Who Taught Me? Was It You, God?, illustrated by Terry Whittle, Concordia, 1978.

By the Time You Count to Ten, illustrated by Pam Erickson, Concordia, 1979.

Treehorn's Treasure (also see below), illustrated by Gorey, Holiday House, 1981.

The Problem with Pulcifer, illustrated by Judy Glasser, Lippincott, 1982.

The Wendy Puzzle, Holiday House, 1982.

Time's Up!, illustrated by Marylin Hafner, Holiday House, 1982.

Banana Blitz, Holiday House, 1983.

I Am, Concordia, 1983.

The Adventures of Treehorn (includes *The Shrinking of Treehorn* and *Treehorn's Treasure*), Dell, 1983.

Treehorn's Wish (also see below), illustrated by Gorey, Holiday House, 1984.

Time Flies!, illustrated by Hafner, Holiday House, 1984.

Tales for the Perfect Child, illustrated by Victoria Chess, Lothrop, 1985.

Treehorn Times Three (contains *The Shrinking of Treehorn, Treehorn's Treasure, and Treehorn's Wish*), Dell, 1992.

Grim and Ghastly Goings-On (poems), illustrated by Chess, Lothrop, 1992.

The Bigness Contest, illustrated by Victoria Chess, Little, Brown, 1994.

(With daughters, Judith Heide Gilliland and Roxanne Heide Pierce) *It's about Time!: Poems,* illustrated by Cathryn Falwell, Clarion, 1999.

WITH SYLVIA WORTH VAN CLIEF; FOR CHILDREN

Maximilian, illustrated by Renfro, Funk, 1967.

The Day It Snowed in Summer, illustrated by Longtemps, Funk, 1968.

How Big Am I?, illustrated by George Suyeoka, Follett, 1968.

It Never Is Dark, illustrated by Don Almquist, Follett, 1968.

Sebastian (includes songs by Van Clief), illustrated by Betty Fraser, Funk, 1968.

That's What Friends Are For, illustrated by Brinton Turkle, Four Winds, 1968.

The New Neighbor, illustrated by Jerry Warshaw, Follett, 1970.

(Lyricist) *Songs to Sing about Things You Think About,* illustrated by Rosalie Schmidt, Day, 1971.

(Lyricist) *Christmas Bells and Snowflakes* (songbook), Southern Music, 1971.

(Lyricist) *Holidays! Holidays!* (songbook), Southern Music, 1971.

The Mystery of the Missing Suitcase, illustrated by Seymour Fleishman, Albert Whitman, 1972.

The Mystery of the Silver Tag, illustrated by Fleishman, Albert Whitman, 1972.

The Hidden Box Mystery, illustrated by Fleishman, Albert Whitman, 1973.

Mystery at MacAdoo Zoo, illustrated by Fleishman, Albert Whitman, 1973.

Mystery of the Whispering Voice, illustrated by Fleishman, Albert Whitman, 1974.

Who Can? (primer), Macmillan, 1974.

Lost and Found (primer), Macmillan, 1974.

Hats and Bears (primer), Macmillan, 1974.

Fables You Shouldn't Pay Any Attention To, illustrated by Chess, Lippincott, 1978.

WITH DAUGHTER ROXANNE HEIDE PIERCE; FOR CHILDREN

Lost! (textbook), Holt, 1973.

I See America Smiling (textbook), Holt, 1973.

Tell about Someone You Love (textbook), Macmillan, 1974.

Mystery of the Melting Snowman, illustrated by Fleishman, Albert Whitman, 1974.

Mystery of the Vanishing Visitor, illustrated by Fleishman, Albert Whitman, 1975.

Mystery of the Lonely Lantern, illustrated by Fleishman, Albert Whitman, 1976.

Mystery at Keyhole Carnival, illustrated by Fleishman, Albert Whitman, 1977.

Brillstone Break-In, illustrated by Joe Krush, Albert Whitman, 1977.

Mystery of the Midnight Message, illustrated by Fleishman, Albert Whitman, 1977.

Face at Brillstone Window, illustrated by Krush, Albert Whitman, 1978.

Fear at Brillstone, illustrated by Krush, Albert Whitman, 1978.

Mystery at Southport Cinema, illustrated by Fleishman, Albert Whitman, 1978.

I Love Every-People, illustrated by John Sandford, Concordia, 1978.

Body in the Brillstone Garage, illustrated by Krush, Albert Whitman, 1979.

Mystery of the Mummy's Mask, illustrated by Fleishman, Albert Whitman, 1979.

Mystery of the Forgotten Island, illustrated by Fleishman, Albert Whitman, 1979.

A Monster Is Coming! A Monster Is Coming!, illustrated by Rachi Farrow, F. Watts, 1980.

Black Magic at Brillstone, illustrated by Krush, Albert Whitman, 1982.

Time Bomb at Brillstone, illustrated by Krush, Albert Whitman, 1982.

Mystery on Danger Road, illustrated by Fleishman, Albert Whitman, 1983.

Timothy Twinge, illustrated by Barbara Lehman, Lothrop, 1993.

Oh Grow Up!: Poems to Help You Survive Your Parents, Chores, School, and Other Afflictions, illustrated by Nadine Bernard Westcott, Orchard Books, 1996.

Tio Armando, illustrated by Ann Grifalconi, Lothrop, 1998.

WITH DAUGHTER JUDITH HEIDE GILLILAND; FOR CHILDREN

The Day of Ahmed's Secret, illustrated by Ted Lewin, Lothrop, 1990.

Sami and the Time of the Troubles, illustrated by Lewin, Clarion, 1992.

The House of Wisdom, illustrated by Mary Grandpre, DK Ink, 1999.

UNDER PSEUDONYM ALEX B. ALLEN; FOR CHILDREN

(With Van Clief) *Basketball Toss Up,* illustrated by Kevin Royt, Albert Whitman, 1972.

(With Van Clief) *No Place for Baseball,* illustrated by Royt, Albert Whitman, 1973.

(With son, David Heide) *Danger on Broken Arrow Trail,* illustrated by Michael Norman, Albert Whitman, 1974.

(With Van Clief) *Fifth Down,* illustrated by Dan Siculan, Albert Whitman, 1974.

(With D. Heide) *The Tennis Menace,* illustrated by Timothy Jones, Albert Whitman, 1975.

Adaptations

It Never Is Dark (filmstrip with cassette or record), BFA Educational Media, 1975; *Sound of Sunshine, Sound of Rain,* an animated short film, was produced by Filmfair in 1984 and nominated for an Academy Award from the Academy of Motion Picture Arts and Sciences.

Sidelights

Florence Parry Heide "has an antic sense of humor that refuses to be cowed," Jane Yolen once wrote of the American author of children's books in the *New York Times Book Review.* "She absolutely insists on coming at things sideways." In picture books, chapter books, novels for young adults, mysteries, and poetry collections, Heide blends tongue-in-cheek humor to detail the adventures of the incredible shrinking boy, Treehorn, in her most popular series of books, featuring illustrations by Edward Gorey. She maintains the same sort of humor in writings about other youngsters, Jonah and Noah among them, in books such as *Banana Twist* and *Time Flies!.* She spoofs fables and advice to children in other easy readers and opens the door to madcap mayhem in the anti-cautionary *Tales for the Perfect Child.* But Heide also has a serious side, and in novels and stories such as *When the Sad One Comes to Stay, Tio Armando, Secret Dreamer, Secret Dreams,* and *Sound of Sunshine, Sound of Rain,* she tackles such difficult themes as

In modern-day Beirut, ten-year-old Sami goes through the typical activities of children everywhere, while coping with the bombing and fighting in his war-ravaged city. (From Sami and the Time of the Troubles, *cowritten by Heide and Judith Heide Gilliland and illustrated by Ted Lewin.)*

alienation, death of a relative, blindness, and mental disability.

Heide has written scores of novels in collaboration, first with Sylvia Worth Van Clief, and then with three of her children, David, Roxanne, and Judith. Such collaborative efforts have spawned the well-loved mystery series for reluctant readers, "The Spotlight Detective Club" and "Brillstone Apartments," as well as award-winning picture books which focus on life in the Middle East, *The Day of Ahmed's Secret, Sami and the Time of the Troubles,* and *The House of Wisdom.*

A self-proclaimed "late-bloomer," Heide did not begin writing children's books until after her five children had started school. Once started, she quickly established a prolific and award-winning career. In the course of her more than three decades of writing, she has published over eighty titles. Well-known for her ability to find humor in parent-child struggles, Heide is often praised by critics for her whimsical imagination and her exuberant, if sometimes irreverent, wit, as well as her strong characterizations and her keen perception of the colorful but often difficult and confusing life of a child.

Heide's account of her own childhood, like many of her books, is marked with a strong sense of love, hope, and comedy, as well as the insecurities involved in adapting to circumstances beyond her control. Her mother, a successful actress, gave up her career to marry and raise children. When Florence was not quite three years old, her father, a banker, died. Her mother, faced with the immediate need to support her family, left her two children temporarily with her parents, and moved to Pittsburgh, where she established a photography studio and became a regular columnist and drama critic for the *Pittsburgh Press.*

When Heide's mother was financially able, she brought her children to live with her in Pittsburgh. Missing the constant companionship of the bustling home of her grandparents and competing for time with her mother's two demanding careers, Florence was initially lonely and shy. Her memories of life in Pittsburgh include the anxious moments of a very sensitive adolescent, as well as many good times with friends and family. But throughout her childhood, Heide maintained her belief in the power of a cheerful spirit, a strength she attributes largely to her mother, who so courageously faced the unexpected disaster of her husband's death. The young girl's ability to confront difficult situations with a loving disposition and a sense of humor figures prominently in Heide's later writings.

After receiving her bachelor's degree in English at the University of California, Los Angeles, Heide worked for a few years in New York and Pittsburgh in advertising. She then met and married Donald Heide, settling happily into family life. Heide noted in an essay for *Something about the Author Autobiography Series* (*SAAS*), "Even as a child, I always knew what I wanted to be when I grew up—a mother. I'd meet the right person, I'd have

children, I'd live happily ever after. And I did, and I am."

But as her children went off to school, Heide began to seek another vehicle for her energy. Her first attempt at a career was a joint venture into the hot fudge sauce business with her friend, Sylvia Worth Van Clief. The two women began daily experiments with hot fudge recipes, but, since neither of them enjoyed kitchen work, the project was short-lived. Heide and Van Clief then turned to writing songs—Heide writing lyrics, Van Clief writing the music—but they could not find buyers for their work. When they began to write children's songs, however, they immediately found a market, and Heide settled upon what felt like a natural career: "Writing for children was an unexpected delight: I could reach my child-self (never long away or far from me) and I could reach the selves of other children like me . . . . Ideas flew into my head. I couldn't write fast enough to accommodate them. I wrote, and I wrote, and I wrote."

One of Heide's most popular and acclaimed works is the 1971 picture book *The Shrinking of Treehorn.* Treehorn is a very serious and competent boy who wakes up one morning to discover that he is shrinking. In dangling sleeves and dangerously long pants, he reports the strange phenomenon to his mother, father, principal, and teacher. The familiar adult reaction to children's announcements ("Think of that," his mother responds. "I just don't know why this cake isn't rising the way it should." "We don't shrink in this class," his teacher admonishes), are both funny and painful. "That, indeed," remarked Caroline C. Hunt in a *Children's Literature* discussion of the book, "is a frequent problem of the child in the (adult) world: not to be noticed, not to be taken seriously." The inflexible structure of the adult world is accentuated by illustrator Edward Gorey's two-dimensional, ordered, geometric line drawings, which interact as a "brilliant fugue with Heide's witty text," according to *Horn Book* contributor Gertrude Herman. The reviewer concluded that *The Shrinking of Treehorn* demonstrates the apparent adult dictum that "wonders may occur, but they are not allowed to disturb this universe." Margery Fisher, reviewing the title in *Growing Point,* called its story a "classic example of the deplorable lack of imagination and observation in grown-ups which constantly amazes the young."

Two "Treehorn" sequels continue to juxtapose youthful wonder with the rigidity of adult order. In *Treehorn's Treasure,* no one pays any attention to the boy when he discovers a money tree in the backyard, and in *Treehorn's Wish,* his parents have forgotten his birthday and refuse to take any hints to rectify matters. Hunt observed that the "sequels explore the same idea of marginalization through different central metaphors," but felt that "the alternative metaphors have less immediate appeal than that of size alone."

Size rears its head again in Heide's 1994 *The Bigness Contest* in which Beasley the hippopotamus despairs that he is too large, until an aunt assures him that hippos are meant to be big. This aunt holds a bigness contest to

The caravans came. The dust rose and the sun burned, and still they came.

Young Ishaq, living in Baghdad in the ninth century, is fascinated by the House of Wisdom, where the smartest men from all over the world congregate to learn and converse. (From The House of Wisdom, *cowritten by Heide and Judith Heide Gilliland and illustrated by Mary Grandpre.)*

bolster Beasley's spirits, and he is sure to win, until a huge cousin emerges from the water to take the title. Not to worry, for Beasley finds a second contest where he is certain to claim first prize—a laziness contest. "Beasley is a lovable character with a sincere heart," observed Lynn Cockett in a *School Library Journal* review. *Booklist*'s Hazel Rochman concluded, "Silly humor can do a lot for self-image."

More inflexible adults trouble Noah, the main character in Heide's humorous books *Time's Up!* and *Time Flies!*. The young boy has his hands full adapting to life in a new neighborhood and dealing with the thought of a new brother or sister on the way. His mother, busy with her dissertation, leaves him to the care of his father, an efficiency fanatic who times him at his chores. With parents who seem to make life more difficult for him, Noah finds the strength within himself and in people around him to adapt to his circumstances. Reviewing *Time Flies!* in *Bulletin of the Center for Children's Books,* Zena Sutherland noted, "Heide's at her best when she writes with a light, wry touch, and in this book that's maintained throughout."

Parents are similarly unhelpful in Heide's 1982 book, *The Problem with Pulcifer,* in which a boy who prefers reading to television becomes a subject of concern among his parents, teachers, and a psychiatrist. "A very funny book that is written with acidulated exaggeration but that has a strong unstated message," a reviewer for the *Bulletin of the Center for Children's Books* summarized. And Jonah, in *Banana Twist* and *Banana Blitz,* is a boy who wants to escape adult supervision altogether, applying for admission to a boarding school that promises a television set and refrigerator in every dorm room. His parents, on the other hand, are health food fanatics who think television is the devil's doing. At his new school, he hopes to satisfy his twin desires for non-stop television and banana splits. A reviewer for *Booklist* called *Banana Twist* a "laugh-filled story."

But while adults are always in nominal control, the Pulcifers, Jonahs, and Noahs of Heide's books are by no means powerless. In a playful spoof on the struggle between parents and children, Heide's 1985 collection of stories *Tales for the Perfect Child* presents a series of manipulative, willful, and often deceitful children who manage to get their own way in spite of their less calculating parents' authority. Sutherland, writing in *Bulletin of the Center for Children's Books,* felt that "the bland, sly humor" of the seven gathered stores "is Heide at her best," and "the fact that her protagonists prevail over fate and mothers will undoubtedly win readers." More anti-cautionary advice is served up in *Fables You Shouldn't Pay Any Attention To,* "[s]even brief morality spoofs glorifying greed, laziness, dishonesty, etc. in which the evil doer is always rewarded and the do-gooder suffers," as Laura Geringer described the book in *School Library Journal.* Yolen, writing in the *New York Times Book Review,* called the collection "offbeat, silly, and outrageous." And teaming up in 1996 with her daughter, Roxanne Heide Pierce, Heide provides advice for young readers in *Oh, Grow Up! Poems to Help You Survive Parents, Chores, School, and Other Afflictions,* and with this one, the title tells it all. A reviewer for *Publishers Weekly* dubbed this a "droll collection" that is "always full of fun."

Heide employs humor also in the service of dealing with childhood fears. In *Grim and Ghastly Goings-On* she uses poems to "indulge kids' delicious fear of monsters," according to *Booklist*'s Rochman. "Another winner," declared Nancy Menaldi-Scanlan in a *School Library Journal* review of this poetry collection. *Timothy Twinge* is also a rhyming story, dealing with every childhood fear imaginable, from monsters to aliens, the last of which do come at night, but quiet Timothy's fears. Jacqueline Elsner, writing in *School Library Journal,* praised the book for allowing Timothy "to solve his problems without parental involvement." Heide and her daughter also employ rhyme in *It's about Time!,* an "inviting collection," according to Robin L. Gibson in *School Library Journal,* whose "overall tone is light and humorous."

Additionally, Heide has written numerous books for adolescents that directly confront pain and alienation. In her first novel, *When the Sad One Comes to Stay,* Sara— a young girl whose ambitious and rather insensitive mother has taken her away from her home with her kindhearted father—receives comfort and friendship from an eccentric old woman named Crazy Maisie. When a choice must be made between her mother and Crazy Maisie, Sara casts her lot with her mother—and with probable loneliness as well. Focusing on different manifestations of realities that are beyond one's control, Heide wrote her 1970 story about a blind boy, *Sound of Sunshine, Sound of Rain,* in order to help her readers understand what it would be like to be blind. In her 1978 book, *Secret Dreamer, Secret Dreams,* Heide explores the consciousness of a mentally handicapped young woman who cannot communicate with anyone. These works do not offer happy or resolved endings, but are commended by critics for their sensitive characterizations and realistic perspectives. Selma K. Richardson, writing in *St. James Guide to Children's Writers,* commented on the quality of these books, claiming "Keenly sensitive characterization and tight prose distinguish Heide's first-person narratives for emerging adolescents."

Such sensitivity to theme and subject also appears in books for younger readers. In the 1998 *Tio Armando,* Heide and her daughter Roxanne tackle the difficult topic of death when a beloved relative passes away. A contributor for *Kirkus Reviews* called the picture book a "graceful chronicle of the last year in a beloved greatuncle's life," and further applauded the "unusually wellcrafted" prose.

Among her many other works, Heide has written two mystery series: one featuring the Spotlight Detective Club, and the other set at Brillstone Apartments. Heide began writing mysteries in order to draw in reluctant readers with easy, intriguing, and fast-paced plots. The first mysteries were written with her friend and partner, Van Clief. When Van Clief died, Heide's daughter Roxanne collaborated with her mother on the mystery series and several other projects. One of Heide's sons, David, and her other daughter, Judith Gilliland, have also co-authored books with her. In a *School Library Journal* review of *Body in the Brillstone Garage,* Robert E. Unsworth noted that there was "enough action to keep even reluctant readers turning pages."

Teaming up with daughter Judith, who had spent five years in the Middle East, Heide has produced awardwinning books set in that region. In the picture book *The Day of Ahmed's Secret,* a young Egyptian boy describes his daily life in Cairo and waits to share with his family in the evening a surprise—he is now able to write his name. Mary Lou Burket, reviewing the book in *Five Owls,* called it a "seamless evocation of a day of work for a boy in modern Cairo" that "has been sensitively written." Set in war-torn Lebanon, *Sami and the Time of the Troubles* is another picture book, this time following the daily life of a boy living in troubled and dangerous times. "While the physical and emotional desolation of Sami's world is painfully felt," noted *Horn Book*'s Ellen Fader, "children will be left with a sense of hope that

Sami and the other young people of the city will be able to make a difference and stop the war." A further picture book for older readers dealing with the Mid-East is *The House of Wisdom,* set in Iraq during the ninth century. Ishaq, the son of a translator, roams the world searching for books of learning to bring back to his Caliph's library, the House of Wisdom, in Baghdad. "[T]he narrative transports readers to the Islamic Empire, at a time of dramatic academic and cultural growth," observed a reviewer for *Publishers Weekly.*

Whether writing of shrinking boys or wandering scholars, Heide's "particular strength lies in her delineation of character," as Richardson noted. Her underlying message—whether presented in humorous or dramatic form—is one of personal responsibility and empowerment. Heide commented in *SAAS* that she wrote *When the Sad One Comes to Stay,* "because I wanted you younger readers (yes, you) to understand that although you may feel you have no choices, that the decisions are made for you by the GrownUps: where you live and who you live with, how late you stay up, where you go to school, whether you're rich or poor—everything's

Heide's collection of poems centers on various subjects related to time. (From It's about Time!, *written by Heide, Judith Heide Gilliland, and Roxanne Heide Pierce and illustrated by Cathryn Falwell.)*

decided by THEM! All but the most important thing: what kind of person you're going to be. And this is a choice you make each day."

Works Cited

Review of *Banana Twist, Booklist,* February 15, 1982, p. 762.

Burket, Mary Lou, *The Day of Ahmed's Secret, Five Owls,* October, 1995, pp. 21-22.

Cockett, Lynn, review of *The Bigness Contest, School Library Journal,* May, 1994, p. 95.

Elsner, Jacqueline, review of *Timothy Twinge, School Library Journal,* November, 1993, p. 82.

Fader, Ellen, review or *Sami and the Time of the Troubles, Horn Book,* July-August, 1992, pp. 445-46.

Fisher, Margery, review of *The Shrinking of Treehorn, Growing Point,* November, 1989, p. 5260.

Geringer, Laura, review of *Fables You Shouldn't Pay Any Attention To, School Library Journal,* February, 1979, p. 56.

Gibson, Robin L., review of *It's about Time!, School Library Journal,* May, 1999, p. 107.

Heide, Florence Parry, *The Shrinking of Treehorn,* Holiday House, 1971.

Heide, Florence Parry, essay in *Something about the Author Autobiography Series,* Volume 6, Gale, 1988, pp. 141-59.

Herman, Gertrude, "A Picture Is Worth Several Hundred Words," *Horn Book,* January, 1989, p. 104.

Review of *The House of Wisdom, Publishers Weekly,* August 23, 1999, p. 58.

Hunt, Caroline C., "Dwarf, Small World, Shrinking Child: Three Version of Miniature," *Children's Literature,* Vol. 23, 1995, pp. 127-35.

Menaldi-Scanlan, Nancy, review of *Grim and Ghastly Goings On, School Library Journal,* October, 1992, p. 88.

Review of *Oh, Grow Up!: Poems to Help You Survive Parents, Chores, School, and Other Afflictions, Publishers Weekly,* February 5, 1996, p. 90.

Review of *The Problem with Pulcifer, Bulletin of the Center for Children's Books,* October, 1982.

Richardson, Selma K., "Heide, Florence Parry," *St. James Guide to Children's Writers,* 5th edition, edited by Sara Pendergast and Tom Pendergast, St. James, 1999, pp. 489-92.

Rochman, Hazel, review of *The Bigness Contest, Booklist,* March 15, 1994, p. 1372.

Rochman, Hazel, review of *Grim and Ghastly Goings On, Booklist,* September 15, 1992, p. 144.

Sutherland, Zena, review of *Tales for the Perfect Child, Bulletin of the Center for Children's Books,* November, 1985, p. 48.

Sutherland, Zena, review of *Time Flies!, Bulletin of the Center for Children's Books,* December, 1984, p. 66.

Review of *Tio Armando, Kirkus Reviews,* March 1, 1998, p. 339.

Unsworth, Robert E., review of *Body in the Brillstone Garage, School Library Journal,* November, 1980, p. 47.

Yolen, Jane, "By Aesop and Others," *New York Times Book Review,* April 30, 1978, p. 46.

For More Information See

BOOKS

Authors of Books for Young People, 3rd edition, Scarecrow Press, 1990.

Children's Books and Their Creators, edited by Anita Silvey, Houghton Mifflin, 1995.

PERIODICALS

Booklist, April 1, 1992, p. 1449; March 1, 1996, p. 1185; March 15, 1999, p. 1344; September 15, 1999, p. 261.

Bulletin of the Center for Children's Books, January, 1984; May, 1992, p. 239; July, 1994, p. 359; March, 1996, p. 229; April, 1999, p. 381.

Horn Book, April, 1976, p. 155; February, 1982, p. 42; December, 1990, p. 739.

New York Times Book Review, March 5, 1972, p. 8; November 16, 1975, p. 52; October 18, 1981, p. 49; February 16, 1986, p. 22; June 2, 1996, p. 25.

Publishers Weekly, July 27, 1992, p. 64; March 14, 1994, p. 72; April 26, 1999, p. 85.

School Library Journal, January, 1985, p. 75; October, 1985, p. 155; August, 1990; December, 1990; April, 1996, p. 126; May, 1998, p. 116; January, 2000, p. 132.*

—Sketch by J. Sydney Jones

*   *   *

HEMPHILL, Kris (Harrison) 1963-

Personal

Born February 24, 1963, in North Kingstown, RI; daughter of Robert Glen (a naval officer) and Shirley Ann (a homemaker; maiden name, Nichols) Harrison; married Meredith Scott Hemphill (a lawyer), August 10, 1991; children: Kevin, Brian, Rachel. *Education:* Virginia Polytechnic Institute and State University, B.S.; George Washington University, M.B.A. *Religion:* Protestant.

Addresses

Home—2770 Red Oak Cir., Bethlehem, PA 18017. *E-mail*—Hemphill@fast.net.

Career

Signet Bank, Alexandria, VA, commercial loan officer, 1985-89; MCI Telecommunications, Washington, DC, worked in finance, 1989-93; writer.

Writings

A Secret Party in Boston Harbor, illustrated by Daniel Van Pelt and John F. Martin, Silver Moon Press (New York City), 1998.

For More Information See

PERIODICALS

School Library Journal, December, 1998, p. 84.

*   *   *

HOWARD, Paul 1967-

Personal

Born April 1, 1967, in Stevenage, England; son of Edward (an engineer) and Una (a civil servant; maiden name, Tyrrell) Howard; married Alison Millar (a documentary film director), June 17, 1994; children: Samuel. *Education:* Attended Hertfordshire College of Art and Design, 1985-86; Leicester Polytechnic, B.A. (with first class honors), 1989. *Religion:* Roman Catholic. *Hobbies and other interests:* Family activities, swimming, running, reading, socializing, cinema.

Addresses

Home—122A Durham Rd., Wimbledon, London SW20 0DG, England. *Office*—Room 1Q, 2 Michael Rd., Fulham, London SW6 2RD, England.

Career

British Aerospace, Stevenage, England, business apprentice, 1983-85; Natural History Museum, London, England, worked in exhibitions and maintenance, 1989-90; illustrator, London, 1990—. Walker Books, held an editorial position. *Member:* National Trust.

Awards, Honors

Primary English Award, c. 1996, for *A Year in the City.*

Writings

ILLUSTRATOR

Jan Morrow, *School for Witches,* Longman, 1991.
Audrey Randall and Terry Cash, *The Fireworks Display,* Longman, 1991.
Sheila Mallinson and Bob Seberry, *Dizzy, the Cat Burglar,* Longman, 1991.
Ann Sawyer, *Peter and His Mouse Friends,* Longman, 1991.
Catherine Storr, *Finn's Animal,* Heinemann, 1992.
Kathy Henderson, *Jim's Winter,* Walker Books (London, England), 1992.
Susan Hill, *Friends Next Door,* Walker Books, 1992.
Hill, *A Very Special Birthday,* Walker Books, 1992.
Lisa Bruce, *Jazeera's Journey,* Methuen (London), 1993.
Gillian Cross, *The Tree House,* Methuen, 1993.
Amy Hest, *Rosie's Fishing Trip,* Candlewick Press, (Cambridge, MA), 1994.
Jan Mark, *Taking the Cat's Way Home,* Walker Books, 1994.
Bruce, *Nani's Holiday,* Methuen, 1994.
Gillian Cross, *What Will Emily Do?,* Methuen, 1994.

Martin Waddell, *John Joe and the Big Hen,* Candlewick Press, 1995.
Bruce, *Jazeera in the Sun,* Methuen, 1995.
Helen Cresswell, *A Game of Catch,* Hodder & Stoughton (London), 1995.
Dick King-Smith, *The Invisible Dog,* Viking (London), 1995.
Penelope Lively, *Staying with Grandpa,* Viking, 1995.
Rita Phillips Mitchell, *One for Me, One for You,* Walker Books, 1995.
King-Smith, *Treasure Trove,* Viking, 1996.
Henderson, *A Year in the City,* Candlewick Press, 1996.
Anne Fine, *Care of Henry,* Walker Books, 1996.
Lucy Daniels, *Hamster Hotel,* Hodder & Stoughton, 1996.
Daniels, *Puppy Puzzle,* Hodder & Stoughton, 1996.
Daniels, *Kitten Crowd,* Hodder & Stoughton, 1996.
Daniels, *Rabbit Race,* Hodder & Stoughton, 1996.
Gene Kemp, *Dog's Journey,* Collins (London), 1996.
Alison Morgan, *Granny and the Hedgehog,* Red Fox (London), 1996.
Jenny Nimmo, *The Witch's Tears,* Collins, 1996.
Richard Brown, *Atul's Christmas Hamster,* Cambridge University Press (Cambridge, England), 1996.
Phyllis Arkle, *The Village Dinosaur,* Puffin, 1996.
Daniels, *Chick Challenge,* Hodder & Stoughton, 1997.
Daniels, *Guinea-Pig Gang,* Hodder & Stoughton, 1997.
Daniels, *Mouse Magic,* Hodder & Stoughton, 1997.

Paul Howard

Daniels, *Pony Parade,* Hodder & Stoughton, 1997.
Daniels, *Gerbil Genius,* Hodder & Stoughton, 1998.
Daniels, *Lamb Lessons,* Hodder & Stoughton, 1998.
Daniels, *Duckling Diary,* Hodder & Stoughton, 1998.
Daniels, *Doggy Dare,* Hodder & Stoughton, 1998.
Daniels, *Cat Crazy,* Hodder & Stoughton, 1998.
Daniels, *Pet's Party,* Hodder & Stoughton, 1998.
Allan Ahlberg, *Mockingbird,* Candlewick Press, 1998.
Michael Rosen, editor, *Classic Poetry: An Illustrated Collection,* Candlewick Press, 1998.
Mark, *Lady Long Legs,* Walker Books, 1998.
Kemp, *The Wishing Tower,* Collins, 1998.
Joan Lingard, *Tom and the Tree House,* Hodder & Stoughton, 1998.
Ahlberg, *The Bravest Ever Bear,* Candlewick Press, 1999.
Daniels, *Hedgehog Home,* Hodder & Stoughton, 1999.
Daniels, *Donkey Derby,* Hodder & Stoughton, 1999.
Daniels, *Frog Friends,* Hodder & Stoughton, 1999.
Daniels, *Bunny Bonanza,* Hodder & Stoughton, 1999.
Daniels, *Ferret Fun,* Hodder & Stoughton, 1999.
Daniels, *Rat Riddle,* Hodder & Stoughton, 1999.
Daniels, *Foal Frolics,* Hodder & Stoughton, 1999.
Daniels, *Cat's Cradle,* Hodder & Stoughton, 1999.
Rita Phillips Mitchell, *There's More to a Banana,* Walker Books, 1999.
Lingard, *The Egg Thieves,* Hodder & Stoughton, 1999.
Nimmo, *Esmeralda and the Children Next Door,* Houghton (Boston, MA), 2000.
Lingard, *River Eyes,* Hodder & Stoughton, 2000.

Work in Progress

Illustrating *The Owl Who Was Afraid of the Dark,* by Jill Tomlinson, *One Shiny Dollar,* by Geraldine McCaugheran, and *Full Full Full of Love,* by Trish Cooke; research for a picture book.

Sidelights

Paul Howard told *SATA:* "Illustrating children's books is a privilege. I am extremely lucky. I fell into the children's book world when an old friend gave me the job of illustrating some children's educational books. From then on, I was hooked. I never realized how much variety there was within children's books until then.

"I try to treat every story with an appropriate illustrative 'style,' rather than stamp everything I do with the same look. I enjoy the challenge of this and, although obviously restricted by my own stylistic limitations, I love the variety.

"When in the early stages, I love sorting out the pace of a story, finding its peaks, and working this through until I am satisfied. A book is a tactile object, and you do not know if it works unless you continuously keep a check by dummying rough pencil sketches into a book, just to feel the pace in the turn of each page.

"*Classic Poetry* is a portfolio of my work. It captures all sides of me. I am a stickler for research and immersed myself in the poetry completely. It was a gift project. My ultimate aim was to give young people (and adults, for that matter) an extra dimension to the poems alone. It was a daunting prospect with such powerful words, but if my pictures give an extra hint at the meaning of the poems and a flavor of the period in which they were written, then for that, in itself, I can feel proud.

"I find American illustration for children quite fascinating in that it seems to be either photo-realist or amazingly creative and wild. I love Lane Smith's work, and William Joyce's, and the humor of Mark Buehner.

"For anyone wishing to illustrate children's books, I would say that if you believe you are talented enough and keep at it, you will find a way through somehow. Enjoy it and it will show through, and someone will discover your talents."

*   *   *

HUNTER, Anne B. 1966-

Personal

Born March 24, 1966, in Lake Worth, FL; daughter of R. M. (an architect) and Gloria S. (a housewife) Hunter; married Andrew Knafel (an organic farmer), November 6, 1999. *Education:* Earlham College, B.F.A.

Addresses

Home—Shaftsbury, VT.

Career

Illustrator, artist, author, 1991—.

Writings

SELF-ILLUSTRATED; PUBLISHED BY HOUGHTON MIFFLIN

Possum's Harvest Moon, 1996.
Possum and the Peeper, 1998.
What's under the Log?, 1999.
What's in the Pond?, 1999.
What's in the Meadow?, 2000.
What's in the Tide Pool?, 2000.

ILLUSTRATOR

Vivian Sathre, *On Grandpa's Farm,* Houghton Mifflin, 1997.
Jane Yolen, *Nocturne,* Harcourt Brace, 1997.
Julie Larios, *Have You Ever Done That?,* Front Street Books, 2000.

Sidelights

With the publication in 1996 of her first self-illustrated picture book, *Possum's Harvest Moon,* Anne B. Hunter was hailed by critics as a promising new voice in children's literature. In the simple story, Possum is inspired by the sight of the brilliantly glowing harvest moon to have a party for his friends. *Bulletin of the Center for Children's Books* contributor Lisa Mahoney, who focused on Hunter's quietly poetic narrative, stated

Anne B. Hunter

that the author adds "readaloud interest through alliteration ... unobtrusive rhyme ... and attention to detail." The story took a backseat with some reviewers, however, to Hunter's illustrations. Using pen and ink and watercolors, Hunter produced a look that *Publishers Weekly* interviewer Julie Yates Walton characterized as "evocative of the classic books [Hunter] admires most." In an interview with Walton, Hunter herself stated, "When I was a child I was more inclined to the reassuring and the more traditional," mentioning Maurice Sendak, Garth Williams, Chris Van Allsburg, and Barry Moser as significant influences on her style of picture book illustration. "Possum's secret world is beautifully rendered in subtle earth tones and exquisitely detailed pen-and-ink line work," enthused Lauren Peterson in *Booklist*. Other reviewers were similarly enthusiastic about Hunter's debut effort and contended that *Possum's Harvest Moon* would work equally well as a bedtime story and as a supplementary text on the seasons. The book is "a merry illumination of the moonglowing, green-growing, bug-buzzing profusion of a seasonal last hurrah," according to a reviewer in *Publishers Weekly.*

Possum's Harvest Moon was followed by *Possum and the Peeper,* a related title that met with similar accolades from critics. In this story, Possum is awakened from his winter hibernation by a rude and persistent noisemaker and sets out to discover who it is. He shortly meets several of his friends, all of whom are equally disgruntled by being woken in this way. A reviewer for *Publishers Weekly* noted that while Hunter effectively used a pen-and-ink cross-hatch style to reflect the night world in *Possum's Harvest Moon,* in *Possum and the Peeper* Hunter "washes the pages with watercolors in a cool palette of avocado greens and shimmering yellows." Again, critics pinpointed the strength of Hunter's

book in a simple story well told accompanied by appealing, kid-friendly illustrations. *Possum and the Peeper* is "perfect for both lap sharing and reading aloud," claimed Helen Rosenberg in *Booklist.*

After the publication of her first book, Hunter was invited to illustrate several picture book written by others, including established children's book author Jane Yolen. In Yolen's *Nocturne,* a poem about the night that "lulls readers into repose and soothing visions," according to a reviewer for *Publishers Weekly,* Hunter's pen-and-ink and watercolor illustrations provide a thread of a story line to the impressionistic text. While Yolen's poem is beautifully written, *Booklist* reviewer Lauren Peterson allowed, "it is Hunter's exquisite artwork that sets this apart from the scores of other similar picture books." Hunter's illustrations were also credited with supplying gaps in the poetic narrative of Vivian Sathre's picture book, *On Grandpa's Farm.* "Together, artist and author convincingly capture the stillness in the country air, and the unhurried pace of a summer day," remarked a reviewer in *Publishers Weekly.*

In her *Publishers Weekly* interview with Walton, which was conducted shortly after the publication of her first book, Hunter stated: "I feel very fortunate. There are a lot of wonderful books that, because they don't sell right off, get put aside and are passed over. Taste and what people buy don't necessarily have a lot to do with what's really good. If my book hadn't sold—sure, I wouldn't be as happy. But I would just keep doing what I am doing. I'm not out to create something that's just going to sell. It's important to be true to your individual view, because then you do your best work."

Works Cited

Mahoney, Lisa, review of *Possum's Harvest Moon, Bulletin of the Center for Children's Books,* October, 1996, pp. 64-65.

Review of *Nocturne, Publishers Weekly,* October 13, 1997, p. 74.

Peterson, Lauren, review of *Nocturne, Booklist,* October 1, 1997, p. 339.

Peterson, Lauren, review of *Possum's Harvest Moon, Booklist,* September 1, 1996, p. 127.

Review of *On Grandpa's Farm, Publishers Weekly,* September 15, 1997, p. 76.

Review of *Possum and the Peeper, Publishers Weekly,* February 23, 1998, p. 76.

Review of *Possum's Harvest Moon, Publishers Weekly,* June 24, 1996, p. 58.

Rosenberg, Helen, review of *Possum and the Peeper, Booklist,* June 1, 1998, p. 1779.

Walton, Julie Yates, interview with Anne B. Hunter, *Publishers Weekly,* December 16, 1996, p. 32.

For More Information See

PERIODICALS

Children's Playmate, September, 1997, p. 16.
Horn Book, September-October, 1996, p. 579.
Publishers Weekly, November 8, 1999, p. 71.*

J

JOCELYN, Marthe 1956-

Personal

Born February 24, 1956, in Toronto, Canada; daughter of Gordon (a teacher) and Joy (a social worker; maiden name, Martyn) Jocelyn; married Tom Slaughter; children: Hannah May Jocelyn, Nell Marie Jocelyn.

Addresses

Home and office—552 Broadway, New York, NY 10012. *Agent*—Ethan Ellenberg, 548 Broadway, New York, NY 10012. *E-mail*—JessTom4HN@aol.com.

Career

Jesse Design (toy and children's clothing design and manufacture) owner and designer, 1983-98; author.

Writings

The Invisible Day (chapter book), illustrated by Abby Carter, Dutton, 1997.
The Invisible Harry (chapter book), illustrated by Abby Carter, Dutton, 1998.
(And illustrator) *Hannah and the Seven Dresses* (picture book), Dutton, 1999.
Hannah's Collections (picture book), Dutton, 2000.
Earthly Astonishments (middle-grade novel), Dutton, 2000.

Also co-author of a play, *The Time Players,* with Holly Shepard.

Sidelights

Marthe Jocelyn told *SATA:* "I started to write seriously when I was nearly forty. Before that, I was running my own toy-design company and raising two daughters.

"When the children were little, I made picture books just for them, about them. When my older daughter was about nine, she started to ask when she'd be allowed to walk to school alone. That got me thinking about the limits for young children in big cities. I was inspired to write *The Invisible Day,* about a girl who becomes invisible in New York and has a sudden chance for unguarded adventure. The sequel, *The Invisible Harry,* was written the following year, in response to my younger daughter's unfulfilled wish of having a dog.

Marthe Jocelyn

"When I was a child, I liked to read books about ordinary children who stumbled across enchantment. Many of those stories were quite old-fashioned; it was fun for me to set the same world-skewing magic in contemporary New York.

"After two chapter books, I was ready to present my editor with the rough dummy for a picture book, called *Hannah and the Seven Dresses.* Because I never trained as an artist, I was not confident of my illustration skills. The brilliant art director, Sara Reynolds, was familiar with some of my toy designs. She suggested that I try to replicate the feeling of my toys by using fabric collage for the pictures. The end result is a unique book, of which I am very proud. I have recently completed a companion volume, called *Hannah's Collections.*

"I also have a middle grade novel called *Earthly Astonishments,* and it is the most difficult I have written so far. It is set in 1884 and takes place mostly in Coney Island, New York. I loved doing the research, and find myself still reading book after useful book, long after my own book is done! I guess I'll have to find another story to tell, to use up all the tidbits.

"Sometimes it is hard to get started on something new; I find myself circling, like a seagull, getting up the right speed to swoop in and attack the prize."

Jocelyn is noted for her engaging female protagonists and humorous depiction of contemporary urban life. In her first book, *The Invisible Day,* fifth-grader Billie Stoner's problem is her mother, who hovers over her constantly in order to protect her from the dangers of living in New York City. Billie's mother can even watch over her daughter at school, because she is the school librarian. Then, one day, on a school outing in Central Park, Billie spies an abandoned make-up bag and stashes it secretively in her backpack. When she tries some of the powder the next day, it magically renders her invisible, and Billie is off on a series of adventures around school and then in the city. Billie's "first-person narrative gives the book a chatty, comfortable tone," observed Lucy Rafael in a *School Library Journal* review. The highlight of the book for *Quill & Quire* contributor Teresa Toten, however, is Jocelyn's depiction of the city: "Jocelyn gives a wonderful kid's-eye account of Soho and Greenwich Village, conveying the wonder of the streets when an adult is not hovering." A reviewer for *Publishers Weekly* concurred: "The fun of this whimsical, high-spirited novel comes in following Billie's great adventure and tasting her freedom from scrutiny."

When Billie is ready to become visible again, she seeks out the help of teenage super-scientist Jody, who invented the invisible make-up, and its antidote, and is reunited with her family at the end of *The Invisible Day.* Jody takes a more central role in Jocelyn's sequel, *The Invisible Harry,* when she and Billie agree that her invisible powder may be the answer to Billie's longing for a dog (and her mother's adamant refusal to allow it). What Billie didn't consider, however, is that an invisible

Hannah can't decide which of her beautiful dresses to wear on her birthday, so the inventive little girl decides to wear them all in Jocelyn's playful picture book illustrated with fabric collages. (From Hannah and the Seven Dresses, *written and illustrated by Jocelyn.)*

dog still barks and urinates at will, thus making the puppy she adopts, though invisible, much more difficult to hide. In the end, Billie's decision to find the dog a proper home allows her to exercise her better qualities. "Billie's constructive handling of her problems and her amusingly perceptive comments about the people in her world add depth to the story," remarked Maggie McEwen in *School Library Journal.*

Jocelyn's first self-illustrated picture book, *Hannah and the Seven Dresses,* bears some of the same strengths as her earlier chapter books in its whimsical story line and engaging female lead. Here, Hannah possesses seven beautiful dresses, and solves the problem of having to decide which of them to wear by assigning each dress its own day. Hannah's toy elephant does the same in the background of each fabric-collage illustration. This part of the story reinforces concepts such as color recognition and the days of the week for the preschool audience, reviewers noted. When Hannah's birthday falls on a Tuesday, however, her Tuesday dress doesn't seem special enough for the occasion, nor do any of the others, so the inventive little girl decides to wear all of her lovely dresses at once. This presents problems of its own, but nothing that Hannah can't handle. *"Hannah and the Seven Dresses* is an amusing, colourful book with a simple and satisfying story—just about the hardest kind to create," averred *Quill & Quire* contributor Loris Lesynski.

Works Cited

Review of *The Invisible Day, Publishers Weekly,* October 27, 1997, p. 76.

Lesynski, Loris, review of *Hannah and the Seven Dresses, Quill & Quire,* March, 1999, p. 68.

McEwen, Maggie, review of *The Invisible Harry, School Library Journal,* December, 1998, p. 126.

Rafael, Lucy, review of *The Invisible Day, School Library Journal,* March, 1998, p. 182.

Toten, Teresa, review of *The Invisible Day, Quill & Quire,* January, 1998, p. 38.

For More Information See

PERIODICALS

Booklist, November 15, 1998, p. 590.
Kirkus Reviews, December 15, 1999.
School Library Journal, July, 1999, p. 74.

*   *   *

JOHNSTON, Lynn (Beverley) 1947-

Personal

Full name, Lynn Beverley Johnston; born May 28, 1947, in Collingwood, Ontario, Canada; daughter of Mervyn (a jeweler) and Ursula (an artisan; maiden name, Bainbridge) Ridgway; married first husband (a cameraman), c. 1975 (divorced); married John Roderick Johnston (a dentist and pilot), February 15, 1977; children: (first marriage) Aaron Michael; (second marriage) Katherine Elizabeth. *Education:* Attended Vancouver School of Art, 1964-67. *Religion:* Unitarian-Universalist. *Hobbies and other interests:* Travel, doll collecting, playing the accordion.

Addresses

Home—North Bay, Ontario. *Office*—c/o Andrews McMeel Publishing, 4520 Main St., Kansas City, MO 64111.

Career

Animation apprentice at Canawest Films; McMaster University, Hamilton, Ontario, worked as a medical artist, 1968-73; freelance commercial artist and writer, 1973—; author and illustrator of "For Better or for Worse" cartoon strip syndicated by Universal Press Syndicate, 1979—. President, Lynn Johnston Productions, Inc.

Lynn Johnston

Awards, Honors

Reuben Award, National Cartoonists Society, 1986, for outstanding cartoonist of the year; named member of the Order of Canada, 1992; National Cartoonists Society Category Award for best comic strip; Pulitzer Prize nomination; Quill Award, National Association of Writing Instrument Distributors; Inkpot Award, San Diego Comics Convention; EDI Award; four honorary degrees.

Writings

SELF-ILLUSTRATED CARTOON BOOKS

David! We're Pregnant!, Potlatch Publications, 1973, published as *David! We're Pregnant!: 101 Cartoons for Expecting Parents,* Meadowbrook, 1977, revised edition, 1992.

Hi, Mom! Hi, Dad!: The First Twelve Months of Parenthood, P. M. A. Books, 1975, revised edition, Meadowbrook, 1977.

Do They Ever Grow Up?, Meadowbrook, 1978, published as *Do They Ever Grow Up?: 101 Cartoons about the Terrible Twos and Beyond,* 1983.

"FOR BETTER OR FOR WORSE" COMIC COLLECTIONS

I've Got the One-More-Washload Blues, Andrews & McMeel, 1981.

Is This "One of Those Days," Daddy?, Andrews & McMeel, 1982.

It Must Be Nice to Be Little, Andrews & McMeel, 1983.

More Than a Month of Sundays: A For Better or for Worse Sunday Collection, Andrews & McMeel, 1983.

Elly Patterson grapples with a new job, two adolescent children, and pregnancy in this collection of comic strips from Lynn Johnston's popular syndicated cartoon "For Better or for Worse." (From What, Me Pregnant?, *written and illustrated by Johnston.)*

Our Sunday Best: A For Better or for Worse Sunday Collection, Andrews & McMeel, 1984.

Just One More Hug, Andrews & McMeel, 1984.

The Last Straw, Andrews & McMeel, 1985.

Keep the Home Fries Burning, Andrews & McMeel, 1986.

It's All Downhill from Here, Andrews & McMeel, 1987.

Pushing 40, Andrews & McMeel, 1988.

A Look Inside—For Better or for Worse: The Tenth Anniversary Collection, Andrews & McMeel, 1989.

It All Comes Out in the Wash (contains reprints from previous books), Tor Books, 1990.

If This Is a Lecture, How Long Will It Be?, Andrews & McMeel, 1990.

For Better or for Worse: Another Day, Another Lecture (contains reprints from previous books), Tor Books, 1991.

What, Me Pregnant?, Andrews & McMeel, 1991.

For Better or for Worse: You Can Play in the Barn, But You Can't Get Dirty (contains reprints from previous books), Tor Books, 1992.

For Better or for Worse: You Never Know What's around the Corner (contains reprints from previous books), Tor Books, 1992.

Things Are Looking Up, Andrews & McMeel, 1992.

For Better or for Worse: It's a Pig-Eat-Chicken World (contains reprints from previous books), Tor Books, 1993.

For Better or for Worse: Shhh—Mom's Working! (contains reprints from previous books), Tor Books, 1993.

But, I Read the Destructions!: For Better or for Worse, T. Doherty Associates, 1993.

"There Goes My Baby!": A For Better or for Worse Collection, Andrews & McMeel, 1993.

It's the Thought That Counts—: For Better or for Worse Fifteenth Anniversary Collection, Andrews & McMeel, 1994.

Starting from Scratch, Andrews & McMeel, 1995.

Love Just Screws Everything Up, Andrews & McMeel, 1996.

Remembering Farley: A Tribute to the Life of Our Favorite Cartoon Dog, Andrews & McMeel, 1996.

Growing Like a Weed: A For Better or for Worse Collection, Andrews McMeel, 1997.

Middle Age Spread: A For Better or for Worse Collection, Andrews & McMeel, 1998.

The Lives behind the Lines: 20 Years of For Better or for Worse, Andrews McMeel, 1999.

Sunshine & Shadow: A For Better or for Worse Collection, Andrews McMeel, 1999.

The Big 5-0: A For Better or for Worse Collection, Andrews McMeel, 2000.

Isn't He Beautiful?, Andrews McMeel, 2000.

Isn't She Beautiful?, Andrews McMeel, 2000.

ILLUSTRATOR

Bruce Lansky, editor, *The Best Baby Name Book in the Whole Wide World,* Meadowbrook Press, 1979.

Vicki Lansky, *The Taming of the C.A.N.D.Y. Monster,* revised edition, Book Peddlers, 1988.

Vicki Lansky, *Practical Parenting Tips for the First Five Years,* revised and enlarged edition, Meadowbrook Press, 1992.

OTHER

Has also contributed one story and a cover illustration to *Canadian Children's Annual.*

Sidelights

A precious, tiny baby and the family dog are sharing a moment. They are both on the floor, happily munching on the canine's food. When a parent discovers them, they look up from their feast with smiles, and dog food, on their faces. This scene of family disarray comes courtesy of Lynn Johnston, the creator of the "For Better or for Worse" comic strip, where this tableau graced the cover of her book, *Things Are Looking Up.* When it comes to chronicling the problems and phobias of the typical North American family, no one does it like Johnston. Her drawings of the fictional—but believable—Patterson family are seen in hundreds of newspapers in the United States and Canada, and "For Better or for Worse" has consistently been voted as one of the top five strips in reader polls.

"For Better or for Worse" developed out of many of Johnston's real life situations and concerns. The strip is populated by the Patterson family: two parents, two children, and a family dog. In this slice-of-life strip, there is a harried mother named Elly, and her nice and slightly bumbling husband, John. Elly was named after one of Johnston's friends, who died in high school from a tumor. Her friend Elly also wore her hair in the same way that Elly Patterson now does.

There are more similarities, too. Both the Johnstons and the Pattersons are Canadian. Johnston is married to Rod, who, like his fictional counterpart John, is a tall, affable dentist who is also a pilot and model railroader. The two Patterson children, Michael and Elizabeth, are near in age to the Johnston children, Aaron and Katie, whose middle names have become the first names of the cartoon characters. The Johnstons even had an English sheep dog named Farley (who passed away). The Johnstons later owned a black spaniel named Willie, now deceased. Finally, Elly's brother Phil is a trumpet player just like Johnston's brother, Alan Philip Ridgway.

And there are yet more subtle, more emotional similarities. Johnston herself has admitted that both she and Elly want to be rescuers. They both feel motivated to try to fix everyone and everything in their family. Rod Johnston admitted to Jeanne Malmgren in the *St. Petersburg Times Floridian* that "their insecurities are similar. They both worry about saying the wrong thing and offending somebody. Lynn also overworks like Elly. She gets exhausted, trying to please everybody all the time. And the losing weight thing. They both do that."

Johnston's emotional closeness to her characters has made them very real to her. Rod has said: "You can ask her what Elly's wearing today, and she'll tell you. If you ask about their house, she'll describe the sun room at the back and the driveway and all the junk in the garage."

Middle Age SPREAD

In her collection of "For Better or for Worse" comics, Johnston explores the balancing act that middle-aged women face as they care for aging parents and the demands of children, home, and career.

At a certain point, though, the parallels end. "I find that somehow the characters develop their personalities independently of me," Johnston told Janice Dineen in the *Toronto Star*. Husband Rod has also noted the differences, telling Malmgren that Lynn has more polish than her fictional character, and that she "is much more of a businessperson. And she's more in charge of our family than Elly is." Johnston's children "both look very, very different from the characters in the strip, and their lives are very different," Johnston commented in an interview for *Authors and Artists for Young Adults*. Her son once said: "'I don't want Michael to wear glasses, I

want him to be as separate from me as he can be,' and so Elizabeth got the glasses, which was great for my daughter who does not wear glasses."

The addition of daughter April also signals a departure for Johnston. While she grappled with her feelings of wanting another baby, she worked out this issue on paper instead of in reality. "I brought the baby into the strip," Johnston remarked to Dineen, "because for a while I really wanted another baby. I thought about adopting but instead, in the end, I made my baby up."

April is a very unique character in the strip, since she is the only one who is totally fictional and not based on one of Johnston's family members. "I can have a lot more fun with her and reveal a lot more about her private life because in reality she doesn't exist, so it's not as though I'm opening up a closet that no one has a right to see in," Johnston once related.

The suburban and slightly idyllic life of the Patterson family is somewhat removed from Johnston's own beginnings. Johnston, a self-described angry child, used drawing and art as an outlet for her emotions. "I drew lots when I was mad," she recalled in a *People* article by Ned Geeslin. "It helped me vent my anger. I was really an angry girl, even in elementary school. I wanted to be grown up. I'd fantasize and draw a picture of what I'd look like when I was old and what my husband would look like."

Sometimes this tendency for fantasizing would land her in difficulties in school, like the time where she doodled all over her math exam. "It was often hard for me to take anything seriously and even though I enjoyed school, there were times, especially during math class, when I would rather draw than take part," she told *Authors and Artists for Young Adults*. But things weren't always so dire—"I remember (on the math exam) ... getting an 'A' for the doodles and a 'D' for the exam," Johnston quipped.

The child of a watchmaker and a self-taught calligrapher and illustrator, one of Johnston's early memories was of her mother correcting her posture. "My mum was a real stickler for posture," Johnston said to Malmgren. "She made me walk around with a book on my head and stand against the wall to make sure my shoulders were back." As an adult, her rebellion against this teaching comes out in her work—Elly Patterson has an almost perpetual slouch. "So whenever I draw that slouch," she added, "it's almost a direct way of getting back at my mother."

Her parents' artistic sensibilities were to greatly influence Johnston in her later career. "My mother had tremendous talent when it came to painting and craft work. She was always making hooked rugs and all that sort of thing, but she was a calligrapher for my grandfather who was a stamp dealer." She spent a lot of time with her father, who was one of the greatest influences on her artistic talent. "My dad was a closet cartoonist. More than drawing cartoons, he appreciated cartoons. We would pour over these illustrations one at a time and he would point out the drawings and what made them funny. He just loved comics; he loved cartoons."

More than simply appreciate cartoons and movies, Johnston's father would encourage her to analyze the humor in them, see how timing and setting played an important part in the humor of a piece. This was great training for the work Johnston would later do in her strip, where timing was essential. "He wouldn't just take you to a movie. He would talk about the comedy as it was timed and as it was set up and how difficult it was to set up these pratfalls. So comedy for me was not just a matter of sitting down and enjoying it, it was a matter of analyzing it as well. That went for both cartoons in the paper and cartoon behavior on live film."

For a short while, Johnston was enrolled in the Vancouver School of Art. She quit, however, and took jobs in animation and illustration. Marrying a cameraman named Doug, she moved to Ontario because of the better job opportunities. But Johnston found herself missing the mountains of British Columbia. Still, the move proved to be the right decision when she found a job in the city of Hamilton. "I got a wonderful job as a medical artist for McMaster University.... They trained me to do medical illustration. I did first year medical school and went to all the anatomy courses and did dissection and everything with the medical students," she once said. "It was a great time of learning and a whole new career and I loved it." Soon, her son Aaron was born. Unfortunately, Johnston and her husband soon separated and Doug moved back to Vancouver.

After her divorce, Johnston started to do freelance work out of her home and soon found her business booming. Oddly enough, it was her obstetrician who started a chain of events that would eventually lead to her being offered a contract for a comic strip. Knowing that she was a comic artist, he challenged her to come up with some cartoons to be put on the ceiling above his examining tables. "I was the type of person that liked a challenge, and if somebody I admired gave me a challenge, I went through that open door. That challenge was enough to make me do eighty drawings for him." With the help of friends, she found a publisher for the illustrations, eventually completing enough material for three books.

Submissions editors at Universal Press Syndicate had seen Johnston's first book, *David! We're Pregnant!,* and they were impressed with the quality and humor in her drawings. They were searching for a comic strip that could compete with the family-oriented "Blondie" and "Hi and Lois" and thought Johnston might be a shoo-in for that position. She was contacted and asked if she could produce in a four-frame format.

Johnston was both excited and nervous about the proposition. She had never written in a daily format, but was willing to give it a try. Shortly after Universal Press's offer, she sent them samples of a strip she had developed based loosely on her own family life. To her surprise, they accepted her submissions and offered her a daily, syndicated strip. She received a one-year development contract with which she was allowed to work on her strip for a year before it was published. After the year, she was offered a twenty-year contract.

"When I got the contract, I was totally blown out of the water," she told Malmgren. "It was the opportunity of a lifetime, but at the same time, it was terrifying. I never thought I would be able to come up with funny gags 200 or 300 times a year." She turned to Cathy Guisewite, the creator of the very successful "Cathy" comic strip, for some friendly advice. Guisewite suggested that before doing the art she should write all the dialogue down as if she were doing script. "I had a tremendously good relationship with her on the phone," Johnston once remarked. "she gave me lots of hints on how she worked and then I went from there."

Over 150 papers signed on to carry "For Better or for Worse," even before the strip began to officially run. "It's hard to sell a new feature to papers, and many new cartoonists only start with about fifty papers, and maybe they never get past that," the cartoonist said. "I know now some young people who are struggling and they cannot seem to get past their fifty papers. So for me to start with 150 was quite an exciting thing. But then it was one of the first of the family strips that was not done by a man and also was done in a contemporary style. So I was breaking new ground in a way.... I was very fortunate."

As her comic career was developing, another story had been brewing as well. A few years before, while driving along with her young son, she happened to spot a small plane flying overhead. She loved flying and small aircraft, so on a whim she drove to the airport to see the plane land. "An old acquaintance jumped out of the plane and walked over and we had a conversation. He invited me to fly with him to the next airport for a hamburger," she told *Authors and Artists for Young Adults.* Shortly afterward, the two realized that they were pretty compatible, except for one thing. He wanted to move north, and she wanted to stay in southern Canada. Overlooking this slight obstacle she and Rod Johnston were married in 1976. He adopted her son and they had a daughter of their own shortly afterward.

Rod's graduation from dental school and their move to the north coincided with Johnston's proposal from Universal Press Syndicate. She found herself working on packing boxes in an effort to land the job with Universal. Shortly afterward, they moved to northern Manitoba, where Rod became a flying dentist. Lynn was offered a twenty-year contract with Universal.

Johnston cites some of her husband's qualities as being helpful to her career. "We [cartoonists] are very difficult people to live with," she once remarked. "In order to maintain a career that's based on fantasy, you have to live with someone who is very down to earth, who is very reassuring." Rod has provided her with this stability, as well as something else equally essential. "He's also very funny. He's one of the funniest people I know."

The move to northern Canada proved to be fortuitous in many ways. First, Johnston got to have a remarkable adventure and meet new and different people. Second, it helped ease her adjustment to the fame she was getting. "It was good for me because the publicity was something that I didn't know how to handle. I'm a frustrated actor as it probably shows in the work that I do. And so if I had more access to the city, I probably would have

been a bigger jerk than I was. It was a very good thing that I lived in isolation for six years and I learned how to handle the publicity and not be such a ham."

Johnston works almost every day. In the studio of the big log house they own in northern Ontario, where they moved after Manitoba, she produces her strip. "I like to sit in a corner with my feet up and a cup of coffee and a couple of pads of paper and I like to just write before I do anything." It takes her about one or two days to write the dialogue for one week of her comic strip, a task that is especially trying for her. "There's a fine line between what makes something funny and what makes something just barely amusing. I think it takes a sort of acting ability to be able to set up a scene, get the expressions and then bring it to a punch line. All in four frames. It's a knack that's taken me a long time to develop," she confided to Malmgren. Johnston feels that over the course of a week, one or two strips will be significantly funny, while the rest just build the story line.

After the writing process, she sets to work creating the art. "I waste almost no paper. I draw it in pencil, then I go over it with India ink pens. Then the art goes to her assistant who puts the grey tones onto the art by computer. Coloring is also done electronically. "You have to be the characters as you are drawing," Johnston told Dineen. "You have to feel what the character is feeling. Even the dog: as he stretches, I feel that." In this way, her feelings of being a frustrated actor have

The Lives behind the Lines ... *contains selections from two decades of Johnston's syndicated comic strip about the problems and phobias of a typical North-American family.*

benefited her drawing. In her career, Johnston has drawn more than five thousand "For Better or for Worse" sketches. "It's like writing little sitcoms all the time and I'm playing all the roles and controlling all the camera angles," she told Dineen.

Johnston's early comics were very simple sketches of the Pattersons. Their two children were tiny, and they acquired a small spaniel puppy also, who was the inspiration for Farley, who had been part of the family before her remarriage to Rod. They dealt with the normal grind of a family growing up together—parents and kids fighting, exhaustion and mess, and so on. But as the Patterson family has grown and grown up, Johnston has tackled more complex and controversial issues in her strip.

At one point, Elly has to deal with the problem of her friend, who gave birth to a baby with six fingers on both hands. Later on, the Pattersons discover their own feelings on race relations as an Asian family moves into the house across the street. In a 1992 story line, Mike Patterson finds out that his friend, Gordon, is being abused by his father. Johnston admitted that the strip was taken from an incident that had happened to a friend of her daughter. She told John Przybys in the *Las Vegas Review-Journal:* "It was an experience I had and it bothered me. And, sometimes, when experiences bother you, you know how you tend to dream about them? For me, the dreaming came out on paper."

Johnston tackled another difficult topic in a 1993 strip series. In it, family friend Lawrence Poirier admits to his family that he is gay. Unfortunately, his parents react badly, denying the news and eventually kicking him out of the house. This topic choice was partly inspired by Johnston's brother-in-law, Ralph, who is gay. Ralph revealed his feelings to the family years before, but the admission of his homosexuality changed her family forever. "What happens when you hear this news is you change," Johnston told John Tanasychuk of the *Detroit Free Press.* "You change because your point of view is shattered. You think one thing about the person and then this comes along. You realize that they haven't changed. It's you."

Johnston was a catalyst for family healing when this situation happened. By writing a series of strips about a gay character, the cartoonist hoped to reach her readers with this same sort of information and sharing she had discovered. However, because of the controversial topic, forty papers took alternate material and nineteen cancelled the strip outright. About this reaction, Johnston commented to Tanasychuk, "It surprises me in today's environment that people would want to [keep] something like that out of a newspaper. I think that the readers should be able to decide for themselves whether they want to read it."

Johnston received more than three thousand letters after the strips were published, two thirds of which praised her for having the courage to address the issue. However, there was also a significant amount of vicious, negative comments on the strip that could only be described as "hate mail." "What happens when something like this hits the paper," Johnston once stated, "is that the very angry people and generally very religious people unite first because they are used to crusading against something that they feel is threatening to their beliefs. The very angry, angry letters came first, the very angry response, and then, as soon as the angry response was visible, the thinking, caring people and especially people who work with families ... started to write."

"I took a chance. I knew there would be some controversy," Johnston concluded. "And I didn't intend it to be quite as overwhelming as it was. Nonetheless it's a subject that horrifies, terrifies people. They're so afraid of it and so unwilling to learn about it, and that's why it's taking so long for acceptance and understanding to happen." Johnston turned all the letters over to the sociology department of her local university, where they were sorted and studied. "People were outraged that I would allow this word to enter their home. That it would be something that they would see on the comics page.... It was a really amazing situation. Not something I would want to engineer again." She later added, however, that a "great deal of good was done despite the emotional roller coaster ride we all endured!"

In general, Johnston receives a lot of positive feedback from her more controversial strips. "If I do something of a serious nature, I'll get one letter against and 20 letters for," she told Przybys. "People are really comfortable reading about (serious) stuff as long as I'm careful to treat it with dignity and in a light way, because it *is* an entertainment medium and people do read comics for fun." The problem with confronting a controversial issue is that other special interest groups have sometimes requested that Johnston give equal time to their causes: A "lot of people want me to go further: 'Oh gosh, if she's willing to talk about child abuse, let's have her champion the abortion issue.' It's dangerous, when you do realistic things, turning the strip into a soapbox and people wanting you to champion their cause. You can't do that."

Asked whether she would enter into such a controversial area again, Johnston answered: "I often find myself writing and being surprised by the twists or the conversation that has just shown up. So I don't know what's going to happen. I certainly don't plan on shying away from controversy, but I don't intend to cause such concern for editors again. It was a difficult time for them because they were damned if they did and damned if they didn't." She feels that pretty much any topic is fair game as long as it fits her strip. "I don't think I betrayed the style of work that I do."

The cartoonist's willingness to take on just about any issue in her strip is sometimes bemoaned by her family because they realize that she will agonize for weeks until the story has run. With her children, Johnston knows that she can't use anything too personal from their lives. "I think the fact that neither of my kids reads my work is not an insult. It's a compliment in that they trust me, they know that they don't have to read it and watch over my shoulder to make sure that I'm not invading their privacy."

However, with her husband sometimes the issue is a little different. There was once a strip that ran where John breaks a foot by having a huge frozen turkey fall on it. Although this didn't really happen to him, he could not live it down. "I took tremendous abuse for that," he told Malmgren. "Everywhere I went, people were asking 'Where's the cast?'" On the other hand, Johnston finds that her husband is "probably my very best editor," as she related to *Authors and Artists for Young Adults*. He has provided essential editing advice and suggestions on what works and what is funny. "At one point though, he was saying 'Gosh, John always ends up a bit of a buffoon and I don't like that.' I was impressed by that, and yet at the same time, he said 'But if it's funny, it's awfully hard not to let it go.' ... So I try not to make John look like a twit, I try to give them equal twit billing."

Johnston has won numerous awards and accolades throughout her career. In 1986, she won the prestigious Reuben Award for outstanding cartoonist of the year from the National Cartoonists Society, making her the first female and the youngest person ever to win. At the time, Johnston felt a little cowed by winning the award. "I felt at the time that it was too much, too soon. I really felt that I hadn't earned it yet," she once confessed. "I was afraid of the statue. It's a huge, heavy thing. I brought it home and hid it. I didn't want to look at it because I didn't feel that I could live up to it."

The award literally changed her life. "The morning after I got home from the award ceremony, I walked into my studio and everything looked different, just the whole room had a different meaning to it. It was terrifying. And the one person I knew who would understand was Charles M. Schulz, so I sat down and started to write him a letter. As I was sealing the letter in the envelope, the phone rang. It was [Schulz], and he said, 'Hi, when you walked into your studio this morning, did everything look different?'" That moment not only helped Johnston get over her fear, but she knew she had found a good friend in the creator of the famous "Peanuts" comic strip.

Johnston has cited the camaraderie among her fellow cartoonists as one of the benefits of her career. "There are times when you feel drained. The deadlines get you down and you can't think of anything. You feel pressured ... and it's great to call each other. We're very supportive of each other. Even though there is competition for space in magazines and on comic pages, there's a tremendous amount of camaraderie." She was heartened by the strong backing she received from other cartoonists when the backlash from her Lawrence story was becoming evident.

Johnston also admits she likes to visit her fellow cartoonists and peek into their studios. "The first thing you want to do is see the studio because it's sort of a shrine," she once said. "It's one of those jobs that requires almost no equipment. I mean, many of us don't even have anything as expensive as a word processor. It's all pens and paper, which are very easy to obtain. The rest all comes from you. So there's a certain magic to that corner and that old wooden drafting table. You want to stand in that place that's so full of fantasy."

In comic strip popularity polls held by many newspapers in the early 1990s, Johnston's "For Better or for Worse" consistently placed in the top five, and, even more consistently, the top two spots. Johnston's strip was picked number one by readers of such newspapers as the *Detroit Free Press, The Oregonian,* the *Toronto Star,* the *L.A. Life Daily News,* the Denver *Rocky Mountain News,* the Norfolk *Virginian Pilot,* the *Cincinnati Enquirer,* and the Monterrey County, California, *Herald.*

But these statistics aren't surprising, considering the almost universal appeal of Johnston's work. She is barraged by fan mail from people who claim that the cartoonist is drawing from their experience. "I'm ... surprised by how many people read the strip then tell me, 'My daughter said that exact thing,' or 'That happened to me yesterday,'" Johnston admitted to Dineen. One woman who was confined to a body cast wrote to tell Johnston that although things were going poorly, she had laughed at one of Johnston's strips. Johnston was so touched that she sent the original of the strip to the woman.

When asked about the reasons for the popularity of her strips, Johnston replied, "I think because people can identify with it, and I try to be very true to life. I enjoy what I do and I think it shows. The letters I get tend to tell me that people trust me and want to confide in me. They feel that I'm talking about their family and that it's the truth."

Johnston readily admits that she loves her job, telling Dineen, "I wouldn't trade it for anything. It keeps me in touch with people and their lives. I get to make people laugh." She knows that her cartooning is not only a profession, but a means of self-expression. "This is my way of communicating. Some people use music or dance or literature. I use cartooning." Her husband has mused that perhaps, with the Patterson family aging in the strip, Johnston will eventually write her way out of a job. But she disagrees, believing that there will always be a story line for her fictional family. In the final analysis, the strip is more than just work for Johnston. "I research a lot of my feelings through the strip. My personal philosophy comes out in it. The strip is what I do best."

Works Cited

Dineen, Janice, "Better Than Ever," *Toronto Star,* October 9, 1992.

Geeslin, Ned, "For Better or Worse, Canadian Cartoonist Lynn Johnston Draws Her Inspiration from Reality," *People,* September 15, 1986.

Johnston, Lynn, interview with Nancy E. Rampson for *Authors and Artists for Young Adults,* May 26, 1993.

Malmgren, Jeanne, "It's Getting 'Better,'" *St. Petersburg Times Floridian,* February 1, 1989.

Przybys, John, "Getting Serious," *Las Vegas Review-Journal,* May 31, 1992.

Tanasychuk, John, "Gay Teen Comes Out in For Better or for Worse," *Detroit Free Press,* March 17, 1993.

For More Information See

PERIODICALS

Chatelaine, February, 1987; June, 1989.
Detroit Free Press, August 8, 1993, pp. 1J, 4J.
Los Angeles Times Book Review, November 26, 1989; September 13, 1992.
Variety, January 1, 1986.

—*Sketch by Nancy E. Rampson*

* * *

JOYCE, Bill
See JOYCE, William

* * *

JOYCE, William 1957-
(Bill Joyce)

Personal

Born December 11, 1957; married; wife's name, Elizabeth; children: Mary Katherine, Jack. *Education:* Graduated from Southern Methodist University.

Addresses

Home and office—3302 Centenary Blvd., Shreveport, LA 71104.

Career

Screenwriter, author, and illustrator. Continuing cover artist for the *New Yorker* magazine. Producer, co-screenwriter, and set designer for film *Buddy,* Columbia Pictures, 1997. Executive producer of animated children's television show *Rolie Polie Olie,* Disney Channel, 1998—. National Center for Children's Illustrated Literature, board member, 1999—.

Awards, Honors

Best Book Award, *School Library Journal,* 1985, for *George Shrinks;* Redbook Award, 1987, and Christopher Award (best illustration), 1988, both for *Humphrey's Bear;* Best Illustrated Award, *New York Times,* 1989, for *Nicholas Cricket;* Parents' Choice Award, 1991, for *A Day with Wilbur Robinson;* Silver Medal, Society of Illustrators, and Reading Magic Award, both 1992, both for *Bently and Egg;* Gold award, Society of Illustrators, 1993, for *Santa Calls;* Emmy Award nomination, Outstanding Special Class—Animated Program, National Academy of Television Arts and Sciences, and

Certificate of Merit, San Francisco International Film Festival, and Gemini Award for Best Writing in a Children's of Youth Program, Academy of Canadian Cinema and Television, and Award of Excellence, Alliance for Children's Television, all 1999, all for animated television show *Rolie Polie Olie.*

Writings

AUTHOR AND ILLUSTRATOR

George Shrinks, Harper, 1985, special miniature edition, 1985.
Dinosaur Bob and His Adventures with the Family Lazardo, Harper, 1988.
A Day with Wilbur Robinson, HarperCollins, 1990.
Bently and Egg, HarperCollins, 1992.
Santa Calls, HarperCollins, 1993.
The Leaf Men and the Brave Good Bugs, HarperCollins, 1996.
Buddy (middle-grade novel), HarperCollins, 1997.
The World of William Joyce Scrapbook, HarperCollins, 1997.
Dinosaur Bob (board book), HarperCollins, 1998.
Life with Bob (board book), HarperCollins, 1998.
Baseball Bob (board book), HarperCollins, 1999.
Rolie Polie Olie, HarperCollins, 1999.
Snowie Rolie, HarperCollins, 2000.

ILLUSTRATOR

Catherine and James Gray, *Tammy and the Gigantic Fish,* Harper, 1983.
(Under name Bill Joyce) Marianna Mayer, *My First Book of Nursery Tales: Five Mother Goose Stories,* Random House, 1983.
Bethany Roberts, *Waiting-for-Spring Stories,* Harper, 1984.
Elizabeth Winthrop, *Shoes,* Harper, 1986.
Jan Wahl, *Humphrey's Bear,* Holt, 1987.
Joyce Maxner, *Nicholas Cricket,* Harper, 1989.
Stephen Manes, *Some of the Adventures of Rhode Island Red,* HarperCollins, 1990.

Also contributor of illustrations to periodicals, including cover art for the *New Yorker.*

OTHER

(With Caroline Thompson) *Buddy* (screenplay), Columbia Pictures, 1997.

Adaptations

A Day with Wilbur Robinson has been optioned as a feature-length animated film by Walt Disney Feature Animation; *Dinosaur Bob* has been optioned as a full-length motion picture by Walt Disney Feature Animation; *Santa Calls* has also been optioned for film.

Work in Progress

Producing and designing a feature length animated motion picture based on *Nicholas Cricket* for Warner Brothers Feature Animation.

Sidelights

Author-illustrator William Joyce has a dream: to be remembered for "a significant contribution to the cause of global silliness," as he told Sally Lodge in a *Publishers Weekly* interview. In books such as *Dinosaur Bob and His Adventures with the Family Lazardo, A Day with Wilbur Robinson, Bently and Egg, The Leaf Men and the Brave Good Bugs, Buddy,* and *Rolie Polie Olie* Joyce presents characters and settings that are colorful, magical and slightly wacky. Joyce's cast of players includes such unique characters as a baseball-playing dinosaur, a frog who can sing and paint, a little boy who wakes up one morning to find himself becoming very, very small, an aging socialite who keeps a menagerie which includes three hundred St. Bernards and two gorillas on her New York estate, and a billiard-ball shaped robot who loves doing the rumba in his underwear. Drawing on a wide range of influences, ranging from artists Maxfield Parrish, Maurice Sendak, and N. C. Wyeth to Technicolor movies, Joyce imbues his illustrations with vivid colors and painstaking detail. In Joyce's world, it is perfectly normal for a city family to adopt a friendly dinosaur or a "dull day" at a friend's house to include entertainment by jazz-playing frogs and a robot butler. Malcolm Jones, Jr., writing in *Newsweek,* summed up the author's appeal by noting that "looniness is Joyce's briar patch.... Reading Joyce is like hanging out with that slightly raffish uncle who came to town a couple of times a year, the one who drank martinis ... and always kept a few cherry bombs in the bottom of his suitcase. He was the guy who taught you that fun is the most important thing you can have."

Joyce became interested in drawing and storytelling at an early age. "I loved to draw and I loved to make things up," Joyce once told *Something about the Author (SATA).* "I always took play a little more seriously ... and I always liked to be the guy who got into the story part of the adventure." He received his first artistic kudos for a pictorial rendition of a dog and cat; soon after this success, Joyce moved on to bigger subjects, such as rampaging dinosaurs lopping off the heads and arms of cavemen. Joyce notes that, when sketching these later works, he "always ran out of red crayon and red pen faster than anything because of all the gore and blood."

Joyce wrote his first successful story while still in grade school. "Billy's Booger" chronicles the adventures of a young boy who "sneezes up" a talkative—and very smart—booger. Over the years, Billy's jovial, diminutive, "green and sort of slimy" pal has become a popular part of the author's school visits. Joyce observes in his interview: "Pandemonium ensues when I start drawing him.... [Billy's Booger] appeals to that sense of grotesque kids seem to love." Joyce's story of Billy and his pal—and the trouble that story got him into at school—will form the basis of an upcoming picture book.

While he enjoyed reading and watching movies and television, Joyce had ambivalent feelings about school—with the exception of art classes. "I hated [school] and loved it.... I hated getting up in the morning. I hated having to go there every day. I hated having to study. I hated having to sit there and learn mathematics.... I liked the social aspect of school—I mean I had a blast—but I hated the tyranny of learning," he recalled in *SATA.* A self-admitted daydreamer, Joyce spent a lot of time imagining himself as a secret agent, until he realized that "secret agents sometimes get killed *and* kiss girls."

Joyce eventually decided to study filmmaking and illustration at Southern Methodist University. Part of his decision was based on a long-term fascination with movie imagery. "I got into movies," he told *SATA.* "There were extraordinary things like Oz, Robin Hood, King Kong.... I was completely swept away.... Picture books and movies have a lot in common in that they both tell their stories visually in color, movement, and composition. Often, when I'm working on my books, it plays as a movie in my head."

Joyce began sending samples of his work to publishers before his graduation from college; within a short time, he received a number of contracts for his illustrations. While happy to gain the practical experience, Joyce eventually found himself becoming a bit frustrated. He notes in his interview: "I began to enjoy it less and less as it went on. I began to work more and more of my own stories into [the assignments]."

Joyce wrote his first self-illustrated book in 1985. *George Shrinks* tells the story of a little boy who wakes up one day to find that he has shrunk several sizes. Instead of panicking, George uses a number of ingenious tricks to get his daily chores done, including feeding his goldfish by diving into their bowl and saddling his baby brother to take out the trash. Writing in the *New York Times Book Review,* Ralph Keyes called the story "a thoroughly charming piece of work." He added that the book's minimalist prose is "a perfect foil for Mr. Joyce's whimsical, perceptive illustrations." John Cech, reviewing this debut book in *Washington Post Book World,* noted that "Joyce gives this well-worn fantasy situation new wrinkles through illustrations that are generous in their sense of humor, character and clever pace." Cech went on to observe that these elements "hold the reader in the spell of young George's adventures."

Joyce introduced one of his most popular characters in the follow-up to *George Shrinks,* entitled *Dinosaur Bob and His Adventures with the Family Lazardo.* Bob the dinosaur meets the Lazardos during their annual safari in Africa. The entire family is so taken by the gentle giant that they invite him to live with them in beautiful Pimlico Hills. Once he is happily settled in his new home, the good-natured dinosaur's baseball-playing skills make him popular with the entire neighborhood; unfortunately, his enthusiasm for chasing cars eventually gets him into trouble with the local police. After a series of adventures-on-the-lam, Bob is reunited with his adopted family and all is well. In a review of *Dinosaur Bob* for the *New York Times Book Review,* Mordecai Richler declared that Bob is "the most adorable of dinos." Richler went on to note that Joyce "managed the illustrations with considerable panache. His artwork makes it clear why Bob is such a hit with the Lazardos." A *Time* reviewer concurred, noting: "William Joyce's plot and pictures provide laughter, thrills, and most important, a happy ending." Several reviewers drew attention to Joyce's apparent love of Deco camp. A *Publishers Weekly* contributor noted the "illustrational style reminiscent of 1920s magazine advertising," while Michael Dirda commented in *Washington Post Book World,* "Not quite tongue-in-cheek, the story nonetheless offers up a number of little touches of Depression-era culture." Included among these are homages to Raymond Chandler, F. Scott Fitzgerald, and Bob the dinosaur himself, who "acts rather like a more benign King Kong, as he travels down the Nile." *Dinosaur Bob* has inspired two board book spin-offs, *Life with Bob* and *Baseball Bob.*

Joyce added to his repertoire of unique characters in *A Day with Wilbur Robinson,* which was based on some of the more unusual goings-on in his family. An eye-popping adventure full of music, magic, and mystery, *Wilbur Robinson* centers on a boy's day-long visit with his friend's unorthodox family. Action is the name of the game at the Robinson abode, where Uncle Art regales listeners with tales about his escapades in outer space and giant goldfish mingle with dog-riding frogs. In his commentary on *Wilbur Robinson* for the *New York Times Book Review,* David Leavitt wrote: "Painted in such a realistic way, the bizarre events in the pictures seem appealingly plausible.... This is a charming, new-fangled, old-fashioned book." Michael Cart, reviewing the book in the *Los Angeles Times Book Review,* announced "Joyce is arguably the most original talent working in the children's-book field today. Who else could have created a family as endearingly wacky as the Robinson's?"

The drawings in *Bently and Egg* marked a departure for Joyce. Instead of his usual palette of bold colors, Joyce utilizes soft watercolor pastels reminiscent of Beatrix Potter's "Peter Rabbit" tales to tell the story of the frog Bently Hopperton and his efforts to save a duck friend's egg. Whether guarding the egg or sailing in a balloon, Bently's ingenuity never fails him. Jones, writing in *Newsweek,* found the high-spirited adventures of Joyce's amphibious protagonist highly enjoyable, calling the book "every bit as zestful as its predecessors.... Bently is never at a loss. Jubilantly resourceful, he has a swell time being a hero." *Horn Book*'s Nancy Vasilakis hailed the "playful language" as "full-bodied and musical," explaining that it is "a pleasure to read aloud." Cathy Collison praised the gentle, soft illustrations, writing in the *Detroit Free Press* that the artwork is "on the Caldecott Medal level."

Joyce's next book, *Santa Calls,* is "an extravagant homage to Hollywood as much as to the holidays," according to Roger Sutton in *Bulletin of the Center for Children's Books.* Art Atchinson Aimesworth and his adoring little sister Esther live with their aunt and uncle, who run a Wild West show. Art is too busy dreaming of

invention, adventure, and heroism to be nice or even pay attention to Esther—until the day Santa sends a mysterious message to their Texas home asking them to come north. When Esther is seized by the Queen of the Dark during their travels, Art insists *he* will rescue her alone—and does, in a madcap adventure reminiscent of Hollywood serials. "Joyce combines fast-paced narrative with his witty, infectious illustrations, which ... look like a child's Technicolor dreams," Michael Anderson remarked in the *New York Times Book Review.* "The whole book has a 1930s feel," Ilene Cooper explained in *Booklist,* "from the stylized art to the very nature of the adventure, with its overtones of Saturday movie serials." As Jane Marino concluded in *School Library Journal, Santa Calls* is "a tour de force that should not be missed."

Joyce's next book, *The Leaf Men and the Brave Good Bugs,* had its genesis in a story the artist told his young daughter. As he related to Lodge in *Publishers Weekly,* he had just returned home after caring for a terminally ill friend. "I was sad and she could tell. She asked me to tell her a story, which is something she almost never asks and something I almost never do. And *The Leaf Men* tumbled out of my mouth, pretty much fully formed. Months later I realized that the story was about loss and how memories of people you've lost who are dear to you can keep them alive."

The Leaf Men and the Brave Good Bugs tells of the battle for both the life of an elderly woman and the health of her garden. When the woman takes ill, she is confined to bed and unable to tend her garden. Her rosebush grows sickly at the same time, and the insects in the garden decide to summon the mysterious Leaf Men to help them battle the evil Spider Queen and restore the garden. While a *Reading Time* contributor noted that "there are multiple layers to this complex story," other critics found that Joyce's "characteristically offbeat and occasionally eerie illustrations carry the day," as a *Publishers Weekly* writer stated. In a *Booklist* review, Susan Dove Lempke praised the artist's unique perspective which presents characters "depicted in lush green, enticing paintings filled with fascinating detail."

Although very busy with writing and illustrating books, Joyce has found time to do work in motion pictures as well. He was one of several illustrators who contributed designs to the Disney computer-animated film *Toy Story,* and he co-wrote and co-produced the 1997 film *Buddy,* a real life story about Gertrude Lintz, an eccentric socialite who attempted to raise a gorilla on her New York estate in the 1930s. *Buddy* was also turned into a chapter book. "I came across Mrs. Lintz's life by accident while researching something else," Joyce told Lodge. "I was thrilled, since it blends my three big enthusiasms: the 1930s, King Kong and eccentric households." Lintz raised the gorilla named Buddy only to discover the animal was not made for city living. Joyce adapted his tale from this actual situation.

In the book, Buddy sports ties, eats at a formal table, and shops at Bergdorf's. Gertie raises him from infancy and takes him with her everywhere she goes. But on a trip to the World's Fair in 1933, she finally realizes that Buddy cannot deal with the close quarters of even the most sumptuous of hotels. He makes a bid for freedom on the African Safari ride at the Fair, and this finally lets Gertie know that her charge is ready for a change of life. She decides to sacrifice her feelings and finds the perfect environment for him at the Philadelphia Zoo. Carol Ann Wilson, writing in *School Library Journal,* remarked, "Youngsters will empathize with Gertie, who must wistfully temper her childlike enthusiasm when faced with reality." Wilson also drew attention to Joyce's "sepia-toned drawings" which "serve as visual vignettes of the period." *Booklist'*s Cooper noted that the "whole book has the deco feel of the 1930s in which the events took place."

Joyce has also completed full-length screenplays for *A Day with Wilbur Robinson* and *Santa Calls,* and hopes for productions some time in the future. Also in the works are a series of holiday specials for Fox Television. Joyce also continues his career as a children's book writer and illustrator. As he told Lodge, "No matter what happens, I know I always have three or four books in the works to come home to." One of those books was the 1998 *The World of William Joyce Scrapbook,* an assemblage of "interesting tidbits and artistic insights," according to *Booklist'*s Cooper, that "will be of particular interest to budding artists."

In 1999 Joyce issued a picture book titled *Rolie Polie Olie.* Based on an Emmy Award winning television program of the same name that Joyce produced, the book tells the tale of a round robot living on a planet where everything, but everything is round. For the projects, Joyce and his friends collaborated with three hundred animators on several continents to develop computerized animation over the internet to tell the story of his intergalactic robots. In the book, after a day of adventures with his family, including mom, dad, sister Zowie, and dog Spot, Olie is too excited to go to bed. Dancing in his underpants and having fun with chores have taken their toll. Michael Cart, writing in *Booklist,* called the book "a sweet, spirited story, told in verse." The characters are all spherical, with bodies reminiscent of billiard balls, while computer-generated backgrounds add a sort of three-dimensional, science fiction look to the enterprise.

Joyce says that many of his story and character ideas come "out of nowhere." "I'll see something that will trigger a series of thoughts or I'll just have some odd phrase words at the back of my mind," he told *SATA.* "At some point, something strikes my fancy from my past, and ends up being in a book." Joyce often turns to his family for inspiration; in fact, he notes that developing characters is often a family affair: "Elizabeth [his wife] actually posed for a lot of my characters.... My nephews would pose for me, my dad would pose for me, whoever's around. I'll say 'Stand here, put on this cap, do this.'" Joyce's works appeal to both young and old. "They strike a playful chord that grownups remember from their own childhoods," Joyce told *SATA.* "[The

books] ... harken back to the sort of shared popular culture that we all grew up with on television—Flash Gordon from the thirties, the Stooges from the forties, Bugs Bunny from the fifties. Growing up watching television, you would see this constant barrage of cool stuff ... it's become a sort of shared sensibility." Jones voiced the sentiment of a legion of the author-illustrators fans in *Newsweek:* "Once you enter Joyce's world, you'll never want to leave."

Works Cited

Anderson, Michael, review of *Santa Calls, New York Times Book Review,* December 19, 1993, p. 16.

Cart, Michael, "Picture Windows to the World," *Los Angeles Times Book Review,* November 25, 1990, pp. 24-25.

Cart, Michael, review of *Rolie Polie Olie, Booklist,* November 1, 1999.

Cech, John, "A Palette of Picture Books," *Washington Post Book World,* November 10, 1985, pp. 19, 22.

Collison, Cathy, review of *Bently and Egg, Detroit Free Press,* March 18, 1992.

Cooper, Ilene, review of *Buddy, Booklist,* August, 1997, p. 1901.

Cooper, Ilene, review of *Santa Calls, Booklist,* August, 1993, p. 2060.

Cooper, Ilene, review of *The World of William Joyce Scrapbook, Booklist,* January 1, 1998, p. 805.

Review of *Dinosaur Bob and His Adventures with the Family Lazardo, Publishers Weekly,* June 24, 1988, p. 111.

Review of *Dinosaur Bob and His Adventures with the Family Lazardo, Time,* December 12, 1988, p. 87.

Dirda, Michael, review of *Dinosaur Bob and His Adventures with the Family Lazardo, Washington Post Book World,* October 9, 1988, pp. 10-11.

Jones, Malcolm, Jr., "Make Room for Bently," *Newsweek,* March 16, 1992, p. 72.

Keyes, Ralph, review of *George Shrinks, New York Times Book Review,* December 29, 1985, p. 23.

Review of *The Leaf Men and the Brave Good Bugs, Publishers Weekly,* July 15, 1996, p. 73.

Review of *The Leaf Men and the Brave Good Bugs, Reading Time,* May, 1997, p. 22.

Leavitt, David, "Can I Go Over to Wilbur's?," *New York Times Book Review,* November 11, 1990, p. 29.

Lempke, Susan Dove, review of *The Leaf Men and the Brave Good Bugs, Booklist,* October 1, 1996, pp. 358-59.

Lodge, Sally, "William Joyce Goes Hollywood—Sort Of," *Publishers Weekly,* September 16, 1996, pp. 28-29.

Marino, Jane, review of *Santa Calls, School Library Journal,* October, 1993, pp. 44-45.

Richler, Mordecai, review of *Dinosaur Bob, New York Times Book Review,* November 13, 1988, p. 60.

Sutton, Roger, review of *Santa Calls, Bulletin of the Center for Children's Books,* October, 1993, pp. 48-49.

Vasilakis, Nancy, review of *Bently and Egg, Horn Book,* March-April, 1992, pp. 191-92.

Wilson, Carol Ann, review of *Buddy, School Library Journal,* August, 1997, p. 136.

For More Information See

BOOKS

Children's Books and Their Creators, edited by Anita Silvey, Houghton, 1995.

Children's Literature Review, Volume 26, Gale, 1992.

Sixth Book of Junior Authors and Illustrators, Wilson, 1989.

St. James Guide to Children's Writers, 5th edition, St. James Press, 1999.

PERIODICALS

Bulletin of the Center for Children's Books, September, 1997, p. 165; February, 1998, p. 208.

Magpies, March, 1997, p. 29; July, 1997, p. 30.

Publishers Weekly, February 1, 1999, p. 86; September 6, 1999, p. 101.

School Library Journal, January, 1997, p. 37; February, 1998, p. 100.

Southern Living, December, 1996, p. 102.

Variety, June 9, 1997, p. 69.

*   *   *

JUDAH, Aaron 1923-

Personal

Born October 19, 1923, in Bombay, India; son of Joseph (a fund secretary) and Kate Judah; married October 19, 1978; children: Daniel. *Education:* Attended Lawrence College, India, 1942-43. *Politics:* "All party sympathy." *Religion:* "Jewish agnostic."

Addresses

Home—35 Drayton Grove, London W13 OLD, England.

Career

Worked as bridge-boy on Cunard ship, 1943-44; draftsman in munitions factory in London, England, 1945-46; trainee physiotherapist, 1946-49; physiotherapist in London, Norway, Israel, India, Australia, France, and Spain, 1949-72; part-time physiotherapist and writer, 1972—. *Member:* Chartered Society of Physiotherapists (London).

Writings

FOR CHILDREN

Tommy with the Hole in His Shoe, Faber, 1957.

The Adventures of Henrietta Hen, Faber, 1958.

Tales of Teddy Bear, Faber, 1958.

Basil Chimpy Isn't Bright, Faber, 1959.

Miss Hare and Mr. Tortoise, Faber, 1959.

The Pot of Gold, and Two Other Tales, Faber, 1959, Barnes, 1960.

Anna Anaconda: The Swallowing Wonder, Faber, 1960.

Basil Chimpy's Comic Light, Faber, 1960.

God and Mr. Sourpuss, Barnes, 1960.

Henrietta in the Snow, Faber, 1960.

Henrietta in Love, Faber, 1961.

(Self-illustrated) *The Proud Duck,* Faber, 1961.

The Elf's New House, Faber, 1962.

The Careless Cuckoos, Faber, 1963.

(Self-illustrated) *Ex-King Max Forever!,* Faber, 1963.

(Self-illustrated) *The Fabulous Haircut,* Faber, 1964.

On the Feast of Stephen, Faber, 1965.

NOVELS

Clown of Bombay, Faber, 1963, Dial, 1968.

Clown on Fire, Macdonald, 1965, Dial, 1967.

Cobweb Pennant, Dent, 1968.

Lillian's Dam, Dent, 1970.

Sidelights

In his writings for children, Aaron Judah employs a range of experience and emotion. The people and animals in his tales are balanced between wonder and reality, fear and joy, harshness and tenderness, humor and sadness. His animal characters live in animal and human worlds, and frequently represent virtues and vices. For example, foxes are wily, camels are selfish, owls are well-educated, hedgehogs are kind, and pandas are wise. According to numerous critics, Judah illustrates a variety of morals in his children's stories in a simple and direct manner. The language of his children's stories is straightforward, and his tone is described by Myles McDowell in *Twentieth-Century Children's Writers* as "lyrical without being coy or whimsical." McDowell added, "The tone is central to the success of these tales. The words leap from the page demanding to be read aloud." McDowell deemed *Miss Hare and Mr. Tortoise* a perfect example of the best of Judah's children's writing. The book is a love story containing fear, humor, wonder, and tenderness.

Sensitivity and humor are Judah's keys to success in his adult novels *Clown of Bombay* and *Clown on Fire.* The main character in these works, a rebellious teenager by the name of Joe Hosea, is the grandson of a clown. In the *New York Times Book Review,* Joseph Hitrec wrote of *Clown on Fire:* "Hosea ... did his pubescent best to pick clean the adult world as it confronted him in India during the last war. Joe's verve and glee in his galloping disengagement from society had a purity so close to moral it joined him to the elite of fictional teen-age rebels from Huck Finn to Kim and Holden Caulfield. Joe's frontal assault on the mysteries of existence at a preposterous prep-school in the Himalayas was a tonic of zaniness and truth: It proved Aaron Judah to be a comic writer of considerable gifts."

Judah once commented: "A few decades ago the complaint of the serious novelist was that the majority of the reading public read 'trash.' But readers they were, and there was always the hope of catching their interest with some inspired phrase and eventually uplifting their literary tastes. The flight from 'trash' was then no more rare than spiritual enlightenment. Now that challenge no longer exists. The novelist doesn't try to write a second novel better than his first; he must write better than his first; he must write better than television.

"In my own home the television—even this impoverished black and white affair—is singing, laughing, weeping, whispering, yelling, shooting, killing, raping, and looting its way into the house for over fifty hours a week. The horrendous end results of television on the young mind has been the storm center of national scandals, yet not for one precious minute has its mouth been stopped up. For the 1970s, at least, the battle is lost, and many excellent writers have given up trying to write better than television. Instead, they write *for* it.

"Another and more insidious evil particular to 'the box' is its readaptation of the classics to the myopic demands of the viewers. A much-voiced argument of the television buffs is that sales of a great novel (unabridged!) always increases after its depiction on television. One wonders what the 'imbecilified' hordes of buyers get out of the real thing."

Works Cited

Hitrec, Joseph, review of *Clown on Fire, New York Times Book Review,* June 11, 1967.

McDowell, Myles, "Aaron Judah," *Twentieth-Century Children's Writers,* 4th edition, St. James Press, 1995.

For More Information See

PERIODICALS

Christian Science Monitor, June 29, 1967; June 25, 1968.
New York Times Book Review, May 12, 1968.
Saturday Review, June 3, 1967.
Time, May 19, 1967.
Times Literary Supplement, November 11, 1965; February 12, 1970.*

K

Welwyn Wilton Katz

1948-

The book was red, bound in black, and slim, easy for six-year-old hands to hold. A girl—her name was Jane—was on the cover. She had long tidy blond curls and pretty features, perfect skin and a dress you could never imagine playing in. Her dog Spot sat at her feet, looking up at her with tongue-lolling adoration, waiting for her to notice him. She didn't. She didn't look at Spot, and she didn't look over her shoulder to where her brother Dick was doing boy-things with a baseball. All her concentration was on the book she held open in her hands. Her book, too, was red, bound in black, and easy to hold. Another Jane was on the cover. That second Jane, too, had blond curls framing a perfect face, a spotless dress no one could ever run or skip in, a devoted dog at her feet, and a brother playing baseball in the background. That Jane, too, held a book, and on its cover, tiny but clear, was the identical tableau of Dick, Spot, and Jane once again. And once again, that third Jane held a book with herself on its cover. So it went, on and on, without any ending, if only someone had eyes wide enough to see.

This was magic, pure and simple. It was my first awareness of that otherworld that can be observed in even the simplest things within our own world. I have spent the rest of my life catching glimpses of the otherworld within our own, and now and then creating it in my own books, and sometimes, uneasily, dwelling in it in my mind. But never afterward did the message of its existence come through more clearly to me than on the cover of that Dick-and-Jane "reader."

And nowhere else was that magical otherworld so carefully stomped out and denied than in the words that were printed in large type behind that wondrous cover. *Look, Jane. Look at Dick. See Dick run. See Spot run. See Dick and Spot run. Look, Jane, look.*

Betrayal. Magic on the cover, and trivia inside.

Every day our Grade One teacher stood over us with a long pointer, commanding each of us in turn to read these and other stultifying sentences aloud, then rearranging us in rows, from the best reader to the worst. I got to sit in the coveted front left desk, but it meant nothing to me. From the moment I learned the meaning of those black marks on the page, I hated smug-faced Dick and panting Spot, and I hated even more prim little Jane with her docile perfection. And when I held the book open and looked again at its cover, there was a blackness at the heart of the magic. Because this was me, Welwyn, holding open that book, not one of that infinite progression of Janes; this was an ordinary little six-year-old covered with freckles and cursed with red hair that my mother cut in half-inch-long, ruler-straight bangs. By holding Jane's book open in my freckled hands I was spoiling something wondrous and strange, because I was not Jane, you see. No matter how hard I tried I could not imagine myself part of the infinite sequence of unvarying Janes; no matter what, I knew I could not be on the cover of a book being held by a larger, invisible Jane, and that book held by another and progressively larger other. By being who I was I broke the pattern, that lovely, repetitive chain that had no ending and forced me to be its beginning, stuck in the real world of *See Spot run*! while infinity went on without me.

For two years I hated to read. My mother could read anything to me, from fable to storybook, and she would, whenever my two younger sisters and my baby brother gave her a chance, and I would sit spellbound. But take a book into my own two hands by choice and read it myself, I would not. My baffled mother consulted my teacher, who assured her that I was the best reader in the class, and that she was as flummoxed as my mother. I, too, didn't understand it. The world of story was magical to me, but I still would not read on my own unless I had to.

One-year-old Welwyn Wilton Katz with her father.

One day when I was eight my mother consulted the librarian of the local bookmobile, and when she came home she was carrying a very thick book called *The Castle of Adventure* by Enid Blyton. For three nights running she read this thrilling novel to me. On the fourth night she began as usual, but then, right in the middle of the most exciting part, she stopped. "This book is too long," she said. (It wasn't; it was only because the type was large that the book was thick, but I didn't know that.) "I'm too busy to read it all to you. We'll never get it done before it has to go back to the library."

"But Mom!" I protested tearfully. "You have to read it. It's too exciting to stop!"

"Then you read it," she said.

And so I did. And when I had finished that one, I read another and another and another. From that time to this the pleasure of holding an as-yet unread book in my own two hands has been one of the greatest in my life. But if there is magic on the cover, I only hope for it in the book. I never let myself forget Dick and Spot and the revolting Jane, and the way the glimpse of wonder on the cover was dashed to pieces by the mundane words inside. I will never forget the treachery I felt by not being Jane, and so interrupting infinity.

If I had been older, I might have seen a different darkness in the magic of Jane's cover. I might have seen it a terrible fate to stand forever on that cover with her book open and never able to turn the page. When I became a writer myself, and wrote *The Third Magic,* I was very careful indeed not to doom my heroine Morgan to an endless cycle of repeating, identical events. But at six years of age the grandeur of that vast unbroken chain of repeating Janes seemed part of a world much superior to the one I was in, and I would have given a great deal to be blond and pretty and a link in that magical chain, instead of being who I was in a world where people did not go on forever, but instead grew old and died.

I had two parents, neither of whom were much older than forty at the time. My mother had left home at seventeen to enter nursing school. She says she skipped classes and usually stayed out long past her curfew and was always being told off by her superiors, but I have a feeling she must have been a good nurse, once she finally graduated. I never knew anyone calmer in a crisis, or more comforting to be with, if you were sick. My father was one of those untaught geniuses who was always inventing something or building something, and in the end he got the Order of the British Empire for his contribution to the development of radar. My mother gave up nursing when her four children came along, and she looked after us, and cooked and cleaned and washed and ironed and did the shopping by hand because she didn't drive, and gardened and canned her produce and squished great big horrid white tomato worms, and the only time I ever saw her squeamish was over a snake that she found in the garden. She is probably the most courageous, determined, stubborn woman I know, and the only person I could never successfully lie to in my whole life.

My father was away a lot, and he didn't *read* me stories, but he *told* me the stories of the explorers as if he'd been there with them. I remember vividly lying in the big double bed in what had been the den of our tiny East London, Ontario, house until one too many children came along, while Dad used the globe my daughter now owns and traced the journey of the explorers as he remembered it from his history classes in school. My favourite explorer was Balboa, who had first discovered the Pacific Ocean. I tried to imagine how it must have felt to look on a body of water so huge, so unknown, so terrifyingly challenging, just when you thought you'd crossed the biggest ocean in the world. Dad was a born teacher, but lack of formal education prevented him from becoming one, and so he and a friend of his began an electronics factory just down the street. Eventually he made himself a wealthy man from it. But I never forgot Balboa, and sometimes, when Dad was annoyed with me or one of the rest of us, I'd sidle up to him and ask him to explain incorporation or how the gasoline engine worked, and that would be the end of his anger. He ended up leaving us twenty years later and moving with a new wife, Peggy, to his own otherworld of Cornwall where he'd discovered his ancestors had come from, and there he lived in a castle, or so its turreted and crenelated tower implied to all of us. But that was a long time after my requests for explanations of engines and incorporation, and a long, long time after I was eight and my sister Roberta (whom we all called Robbie) was seven, and she and I would walk down to the factory from our house a few blocks away and go importantly into my father's office to ask for our Christmas shopping money.

Dad would give us two dollars between us, a fortune by any account, and we would then, the two of us, go cash-fisted down to McKerlie's hardware store and buy our Christmas presents for the whole family. My other sister Beverly, three years younger than me, who remains Bevvie to us all though she is now an important lawyer in Canada's Department of Justice, was not allowed to do this, of course. Bevvie looked like an angel and could be counted on to do the worst possible thing, in the worst place, at the worst time. I remember how she sold my baby brother Robert into slavery, and how worshipfully he trotted along beside her to his new owner, a local boy who thought he'd get to keep Robert for life. Bevvie proudly came home and announced to our mother she'd actually got a whole quarter for Robert, and she was utterly bewildered when no one else seemed to think it was a bargain. And then there was the snowman, a perfect likeness of a hated teacher, right in front of his classroom window. A rebel from the beginning, our Bevvie. She had her own way of entering the otherworld—a path she made for herself out of effrontery and instinct and the most unique combination of intelligence, self-centredness, and aesthetics I have ever known.

I never understood Robbie. As a child she seemed so quiet, so biddable; a dreamy, thoughtful worrier we called the peacemaker of the family. When she was little, you could always get Robbie to do anything you wanted. On one of our Christmas shopping expeditions to McKerlie's I actually nagged her all the way home into telling me what she had bought me—a beautiful blue piggy bank. And then, of course, I was furious with her. Poor bewildered Robbie, who'd only done what I nagged her to do, and then had to bear the brunt of my fury for spoiling the surprise. I suppose all her daydreams meant that she, too, had a path to the otherworld, but if so, she never spoke of it.

I should have had an inkling of her future when I was just about twelve and baby-sitting the others and suddenly got an anonymous phone call that there was a bomb on our doorstep. The person hung up at once. I looked out. Yes, there was a large bundle on the doorstep. There was a ticking noise, too. I dithered about what to do. I could call our parents, or the police—yes—but what if it went off while I did? Okay, so get the others to safety first. I woke Robbie, Bevvie, and Robert and made them all go down to the basement and kneel under a table. Then, of course, I couldn't get to the telephone. We waited. Nothing happened. Suddenly Robbie said, "I can't stand this any more," and this ten-year-old kid escaped my quickest grab, ran up the stairs to the front door, opened it, picked up the

From left, sister Robbie, mother Anne Wilton, baby brother Robert, Welwyn (aged nine), and sister Bevvie.

package, tore over to the curb, and threw it down there. She only just got back when it exploded. I will never forget running after her up the stairs and then standing at the front door, helpless and without courage, watching her run, saving our lives. I often think of that these days, now that she is a high-powered, tough business woman with a Ph.D. in English literature that somehow turned out to be the right qualification for being vice-president of the Toronto Stock Exchange and, later, president of the Canadian Securities Institute.

My brother, Robert Junior, was eight years younger than me and I was in love with him from the moment he was born. He had beautiful sandy curls I envied and the biggest, most beautiful eyes ever unfairly given to a boy. Robert never had a shorter pet name, but he had a long one. He used to watch Casey Jones on television, an old show about a trainman; and he was passionate about trains, so we called him Robert Neil Wilton Junior Casey Jones. Robert was only sixteen when he went with my father on the first Western trade expedition to what was then called Red China. He tells me of standing in (what else?) the train station of what was then called Shanghai, he and my father somehow separated from the rest of the trade group, and of the pin-drop silence there, two white people alone and stared at by a sea of Chinese faces who had never seen white people before.

Robert is a pharmaceutical representative these days and is always coming to my rescue. When I was pregnant with my only child, I suffered for three months from the most unromantic malady possible: itchy feet. Most people laughed; but just you try three months of unrelenting itch, so bad that you can't even sleep. I was supposed to be on bed-rest and all I could do was pace the floors all night and all day. Not one doctor among all my specialists figured out what was wrong, but Robert did—Vitamin B deficiency, brought on because my baby was using all of my own supply. I have never ceased to be grateful for that, or for the million-and-one other favours he has done me over the years.

It might seem odd that in one family two of the children were named Robert and Roberta, but my father (Robert Wilton Senior) was determined that at least one kid—preferably a boy—would be named after him. When my baby brother came along, the last of all of us, my father immediately named him after himself. It didn't matter that it might be confusing to have a Roberta and a Robert Junior and a Robert Senior in the same family. Names were very important to my father.

I was named after the company my father began when I was born—Welwyn Electric, it was called. Dad named me that because his company was associated with a company of the same name whose headquarters were in Welwyn Garden City in England. At first, I hated that name. It still has its disadvantages—I'm always having to spell it or pronounce it for someone—but it's a name I'm sure no other woman in the world has, and the Electric part of it, though not actually on my birth certificate, seems to have the right feel.

I want to be Electric. Electricity, as everyone sensible knows, is magical. How many grownups hold a baby in their arms and go to a light switch and flick it, and then point triumphantly to where, halfway across the room, a light has turned on? And then the baby, wonderingly,

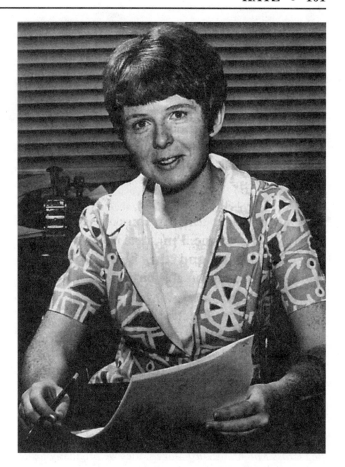

Welwyn Wilton Katz at eighteen, finishing high school.

touches the switch, and the light goes off. On. Off. On. Off. Magic. Don't tell me about electrons and closed circuits and heated filaments and all that nonsense. If you could tell me what an electron is, what it really is, I might change my mind. But not even the physicists seem to know. Is it a particle, or not? Even Einstein wasn't sure. To me electricity is yet another glimpse of that otherworld that lies within our own the same way infinity lies within it on the cover of books like Dick and Jane and in three-way mirrors and in the regularity of sunrise and moonset. I like it, now, that I was named after Welwyn Electric.

About thirty years ago my father became fascinated by genealogy, and he has researched the Wilton name back to the sixteenth century, and using byways and a few impressive feats of logic, actually managed to connect us to Hugh Courtenay, Earl of Devon and Baron of Okehampton, who died in 1344. But we Wiltons, Dad always says proudly, we Wiltons survived what earls and barons did not, we outlived civil war and plague and the rapacity of the nobility and being wiped out by warfare, and we did it because we kept our heads down—translated, we were basically poor farming folk or even serfs and so we didn't attract the wrong people's attention, or do anything worth opposing. I don't know that he can say that about this generation of Wiltons, or even that he would want to.

Until I was nine we lived in the east end of London, Ontario, an industrial area of the city wound with train tracks and factories, barbed wire fences we wouldn't let stop us, and one beautiful ancient oak tree at the end of the street. I ate its bitter acorns while reading books in its shade, and chewed tar balls when they redid the roads, and watched with fascination the horses with their incredible bladders patiently plodding from house to house dragging carts full of bread and milk, knives and scissors and sharpening wheels, and one tinkling, rattling, ironmongery of a wagon whose driver had to whip up his horse to make it move at all, the whole time yelling "Junky, Junky, JOE!" at the top of his lungs. This was my world, when I was nine, in 1957.

I wish now I had known the last time Geordie would deliver the milk by horse and cart, the last time I'd see "Junky Junky Joe," the last time I would taste the licorice and gum flavour of tar from the road, the last time I picked up a telephone receiver to hear the operator say, "Number, please," the last time my mother would put a note in the milk-box for "three loaves of bread, cinnamon buns, and a jelly roll, if they're fresh." I didn't pay enough attention to these ordinary everyday features of a life that seemed utterly predictable, and so I didn't know that it was a dying life and not predictable at all, because it was about to be changed forever. What I did pay attention to was *Peter Pan*, the "Swallows and Amazons" books, Jack and his amazing parrot Kiki in Enid Blyton's "Adventure" series, *Veronica* (and others) *at the Wells* (a whole series of books about British girls who became ballet dancers), countless stories, like *Toby Tyler*, of boys (they were always boys) running away to join the circus, *The Story of Una and the Red Cross Knight*, the *Just Mary* stories we originally heard on radio, before we became the first house in London, Ontario, to have a television.

I learned to bake and wash dishes and change diapers before I was nine, took a couple of years of ballet lessons and one abortive year of tap dancing. Summer holidays and Saturdays were heaven. While I was still only eight I got alone on and off buses to and from the YWCA where I swam and played games and read their stocks of Nancy Drews and Hardy Boys, and then wandered a block over to the children's library, where I read some more. I became the official "reader aloud to the sick" in our family, and kitchen drawer tidier *par excellence*. I avoided the downstairs with its spooky furnace room full of arms of pipes and a big red oil-drum and the immortal remains of old coal, and kept my sisters awake at night imagining bathrobe ghosts and warning of terrible dangers under the floorboards.

Once I woke at night and discovered that my parents had disappeared. I looked for them all through the house, but they were gone—every child's greatest nightmare. But there were three young siblings to be looked after. I did my duty and phoned the operator, who phoned the police. Being a well-taught child, naturally I knew my exact address. The police arrived very quickly, siren going, turning lamp alight. My parents were next door, having a quiet summer drink with the neighbours. They had left all the windows open so they could hear if we awoke. They had checked on us virtually every hour. And there they were, stuck with explaining to the police that they had not abandoned their children. I still think, however, that I did the right thing. After all, I was the eldest. I had responsibilities. *I* wasn't afraid, oh no, but just imagine if Robbie or Bevvie or Robert were to wake and find our parents were

gone. So I did my duty. I'm not quite sure why it wasn't appreciated more.

All these activities, mundane and otherwise, had to change. I knew this. I had a destiny, and it was to be the leader of the runaway expedition that would consist of myself and my two sisters (Robert was too young). After all, if so many storybook characters could run away and have such wonderful adventures, then we could—and should—too. Clearly it was my duty, as eldest, to organize the expedition. And so, while my chocolate chip cookies burned in the oven, and even while I brought the whole neighbourhood of kids in to eat all the cakes and cookies my mother had slaved over for a party she was having the next day, at the back of my mind I was always planning the escape route my sisters and I would take when we ran away. London, Ontario, was situated on the Thames River, which eventually found its way to other rivers which flowed into the Great Lakes. And so, I reasoned, if we followed water long enough we would eventually get to the Atlantic Ocean. Then all we had to do was follow the coast, and eventually we would end up in Florida.

Florida was good, because we could live on free oranges there and never get cold. But of course we would need a few provisions on the journey. For months, whenever my mother baked, I would sternly eye my two sisters, making sure that for every delicious tidbit they ate they would put two away for the journey. Eventually, of course, the smell in the closet where I hid all these goodies from my parents' eagle eyes drew my mother's attention.

Eric, who persuaded Welwyn to teach mathematics.

The plan was laid bare. I could no longer even remember much of why I'd made it in the first place. The stale tarts and crumbling cookies and mouldy cinnamon buns were thrown away, I was soundly spanked, and the Florida journey was over before it began.

I did succeed, or so I was told, in running away from home, even though I didn't think of it as that. I was barely nine, and my best friend Paul and I were looking to find the place where a huge airplane had just crashed somewhere in East London. We were miles away from the actual site and going in entirely the wrong direction when my father, hastily summoned from work by my terrified mother, found us. In his eyes, this was clearly running away and dangerous to boot, and once again I was spanked. I never did see the burned jet.

Magic. Adventure. I was always looking for it, trying to make it happen. When we moved, just after I was nine, to a brand-new house on the edge of a ravine that led to bluffs overlooking the Medway River with woods everywhere, and the name of the place turned out to be Dead Horse Canyon—well! I immediately knew what I had to do. With the first book of Arthur Ransome's famous "Swallows and Amazons" series in one hand and a notebook in the other, I sat on the bluff overlooking the river, snaking its way through Dead Horse Canyon towards the Thames, and I made a list. Kettle, saucepan, tea, matches, I wrote; tent, blankets, pillow. It was all the things Susan Walker of the sailing ship *Swallow* wrote in her list when she and her siblings first got permission to sail over and set up camp on Wild Cat Island in the middle of an unnamed lake in England's beautiful Lake District. There was no lake in the view before *me,* and no island. Even a very small sailboat would quickly go aground in the beaver-dammed shallows below me. But it was water, and there was wilderness around it. It was the closest I could get to the sailing, camping, child-affirming world of the Swallows and Amazons I loved.

Why were the twelve Ransome books so good? I believe it was because they accessed the otherworld of a childhood that was real and believable yet free of adult restraint. I wanted that world. I wanted to be in it. I didn't want to be in the mundane world it seemed to me everyone else was in. And so I made lists of my future camping trips (which I was not, sadly, to make until I was an adult), and planned my future sailing expeditions (though I never stepped on a sailboat's deck until I was in my twenties). I concentrated on the future while it seemed to me that everyone else lived happily in the moment. I couldn't see how they could be so happy that way, because once the moment was gone, it was gone, never to be repeated. The Dick and Jane book with infinity on its cover promised more to life than that. And so I schemed and planned for the future while others lived from day to day. I knew, I simply knew, that there was another world where the future was unlimited and magic could hold a person spellbound, caught up in a chain of forever.

I remember one night when I was eight, lying beside Bevvie who was bubbling away contentedly in the dark, that I heard a song come on the radio in the living room next door. It was a very popular song at the time, but it seemed that until that moment I had never actually heard it. It was a song that began by instructing the listener to enjoy him/herself, because it was later than he/she thought. It

then went on, to my horrified ears, to warn the listener that the years go by as quickly as a wink, that the end was coming, that you'd better get all your living in now, at once, before it was all too late.

My mother was ironing, out in the living room. I remember vividly the lovely hot linen smell. At the same time she was singing along with the radio. She was actually singing that song! Didn't she know, couldn't she understand, that it was her own death-knell she was singing? She was old, old, old, forty-two at least, and that song was telling her how little time she had left, and there she was, wasting that little time ironing and happily singing along with the song that was giving her this dire warning. I wanted to leap out of bed and yell at her that the song had been written for *her,* and for Dad too, down in the workroom hammering on some piece of woodwork, and equally old. I wasn't old yet, so for a while I was exempt, but not them, no, not them. They were going to die soon and leave me and my sisters and baby brother all alone. I cried that night, silently, so as not to wake Bevvie, because the loneliness of my own future was so huge and so terrible, and also because Mom didn't *know,* she *didn't* understand, she *couldn't* see the horrible irony of her singing that song when it was prophesying her own doom.

For days afterward I went around turning off the radio whenever that song came on and treating my parents with the respectful reverence one generally reserves for people on their deathbeds. It wore off eventually. After all, neither of them did die. In fact, it is now forty years later and they are still (respectively) ironing and singing along with the radio and doing carpentry in the workroom. But I have never once ceased to be aware that the finite world is what they, and in fact most people I know, live in. And I, increasingly aware of the finite world's unsatisfactory nature, never ceased to look for ways to the infinite.

To long for the magic of the otherworld in concepts like infinity is not to wish to be immortal. Many people believe that their souls *are* immortal. I'm not sure what I think about that, but over the years I have come to be sure that one moment at a time is all our *bodies* have—a lifetime of "nows." And that is enough, ample even, if only we can search each moment for the extra truth and magic it holds, and savour that magic in our memories. My deepest fear is that just before the moment of my death I will look back and see too many wasted moments.

And so, paradoxically, I have spent far too many of my waking moments planning for the future, even *living* for the future. This is the height of folly for someone who believes in squeezing moments like oranges. I don't pretend to understand it in myself, but the urge to think out and plan and shape the future is a strong one in me. I have used it to my advantage in my writing, and certainly in the planning, of my books. But the worst mistakes I've made in my personal life have been the result of thinking too hard about alternative futures for myself, and imagining I could control them. I don't believe I've ever made a really bad blunder by simply following my feelings.

And so, when I sat down on that bluff over looking the Medway River and planned my first camping trip there, a camping trip which never took place because I lived in a real world where parents had something to say about anything a nine-year-old did, I was making the mistake of thinking that just because a character in a book could do

The author with Patsy Aldana (left), publisher of Groundwood Books, and Margaret K. McElderry at the Bologna Children's Book Fair.

something, I was capable of it as well. Was I right to make the list? Even now, I don't know. It showed belief in the otherworld, and my access to it. And it showed that no matter how I planned for it and organized for it and begged for it, that sometimes the otherworld is not within my reach.

High school days. I had friends, for the first time in my life. They were mostly from the school band where I played flute—Valerie and Lee and Pauline, Liz and Shirley, Chris and Darrell. School dances where Darrell and I fox-trotted and tangoed while everyone else did Chubby Checker's "twist." Oh, it was fun. Darrell never kissed me once, and I didn't mind a bit. We were dancing friends, and music friends, and someone I could rant at in letters from the summer camp I hated. I could always rely on him to send just the right response (a razor blade, once, when I'd rebelled at shaving my legs). I never had more fun on a dance floor than I did with Darrell (at least not until I met Peter Bangarth, my current partner and future one, I believe forever).

There was the band trip to North Bay by train in the dead of winter, the free day spent there tobogganing in minus-thirty-degree temperatures, with me, Shirley, and Val all sitting bum-naked in the three adjacent sinks in the foyer of the women's washroom, thawing out our anatomy with as much hot water as the inadequate taps provided. There were slumber parties where Shirley put itching powder in our bras and Charlene taught us things about our bodies our mothers never wanted us to know. There was also homework, a great deal of homework. I always had to achieve; I pushed myself to be the best. My mother didn't care when I came home with the highest marks in my class, and in my grade, and eventually in my entire city; she was just glad I wasn't getting below a B. In Mom's eyes there was lots more to life than pushing yourself to be the best,

and I don't know now that I disagree with her. Dad, on the other hand, always was proud of my successes in school, and unlike many other male chauvinists of his day (which he somehow was, also), he always encouraged me to be the best I could be, and never imagined that I was limited to traditional female occupations. I graduated from high school *summa cum laude,* was the valedictorian of the graduating class, accepted two of the six scholarships I was offered, and then off I went to university, with the firm idea in my head that I would become a biochemist.

That firm idea had come about halfway through my graduating year when I was taking all the wrong subjects for biochemistry in university. I remember the guidance counsellor sitting me down and telling me firmly, "Welwyn, there is no way, no way at all you can drop French and Spanish and pick up physics and geometry this late in the year and expect to pass."

No way? Just watch me, I thought.

He did, while I got the highest final marks in both subjects.

But in university my firm ideas about biochemistry began to waver. First, I found I didn't much like chemistry. And then there was math, that I was actually astonishingly good in. It was really only because I had an astonishingly good teacher, but I didn't know that. They didn't either, I guess, because at the end of my first year they asked me to join the honours math program. Well, I had taken computer science too, and was good at that as well. So I decided to take a combined honours in computer science and math and not to close any doors on the biochemistry side. It meant a heavy course load in second year, and for the first time in my life, I rebelled at it all. I didn't like anything I was taking, I was within a nose of being grown up and I still didn't know what I wanted to be when I got there, I hated going from class to class, the only girl in a sea of boys, all of whom made me nervous because they were nervous of me. I didn't have any friends again; I was living at home and never joined a sorority or a club; in short, I hated university and my life in it and to the great astonishment of everyone, including myself, I actually failed a course and lost my scholarship.

Eric put me back on track. He was a decent, funny, highly organized person who knew exactly what he was going to do with his life and—as far as I can now discover—did it all exactly as he planned. We got engaged when I was in third year at university, and he persuaded me to graduate and become a math teacher as he intended to do. By this time, that was just about all I was qualified to do, having taken such a hodgepodge of courses. There was one course, just one course, in my whole university career that I liked—no, loved. It was a course I took in my third year only because I needed an "arts" credit to graduate. It was, of course, English literature.

I sometimes wonder now how different my life would have been had I discovered English in my first year at university instead of my last. Had I done so, I am sure I would have dropped all my silly chemistries and physics and maths and done what I am meant to do, which is to study literature, and produce it. I grieve for the loss I suffered by having found that course too late. On the other hand, if I had found it early, I would certainly have gone on to do a Ph.D. in English literature, and maybe I would have spent my life reading and analyzing other people's fiction instead of producing my own. Who knows?

But that course, that vital English course, was a worm in my heart for the first four years of my teaching of mathematics at a local secondary school. And then, oh fatal day, I came across the Narnia books, which the bookseller assured me were "not just for children," and then I discovered Tolkien's great *Lord of the Rings,* and that was that. From then on I knew that I had to find and read more books "like Tolkien."

Unfortunately for me, there weren't any, or at least, hardly any. After I'd read David Lindsay and the Perelandra series of C. S. Lewis and then in desperation gone on to children's fantasy such as E. Nesbit's and Edward Eager's, I was finished. No fantasy left to read. None. What was the matter with the market? Why weren't people writing the books I wanted to read?

Well, they were, hundreds of them inspired by Tolkien and wanting what I wanted, books that didn't exist and so had to be written by themselves. But of course all of that writing took time to finish, and then lots more time to reach a publisher, and then more time still to reach the marketplace. And for all that time those hundreds of new authors, such as Terry Brooks, didn't know other people were writing the same kind of book they were. Neither did I, when I decided to start writing my own fantasy novel. Even if I had, I don't think I would have simply waited until those new Tolkien-type books finally came out. Something very important had reawakened in me when I read *Lord of the Rings.* I wanted to create my own fantasy otherworld, not just visit someone else's.

So, four years after becoming a math teacher, and while still earning my living by teaching math, I began writing my *magnum opus.* I called it *The Pledge-Readers.* It had four—count'em—four completely different sentient peoples living on one geographically amazing world that I spent much of my spare time making maps for. I had no idea then how hard it is to write about alien peoples who are not merely humans in disguise. C. J. Cherryh and Larry Niven are the only two writers I've discovered in the last twenty-five years who can do it believably. And one of *my* four sentient peoples was even a group of water-dwellers! But what did I know? I'd not written so much as a single piece of fiction since I'd been in high school and got 96 percent on a story I wrote for a twelfth-grade final exam, and I was undertaking my own *Lord of the Rings* with blithe and probably very lucky ignorance.

I had what I thought of as a plot—my one major hero had to travel all over this huge invented world I'd called Karusad, and somehow discover the most honourable and wise person of each of the four separate sentient peoples and get them all together at the most horrible place on Karusad (a place that was really quite remarkably like Mordor in *Lord of the Rings),* and then these representatives of each of the four peoples of Karusad would together read an ancient document and so save the world from the evil of my Sauron-like villain. I *thought* that was the plot. What it was, of course, was the final scene of what must be written first—a very large book with enough events to get my hero *believably* across all of this huge world and involved *believably* with all four of the sentient peoples. And the events had to be sufficiently interesting that the reader wouldn't be bored by the hero's travelling time. And

the events had to cause *believable* ways for my hero to discover the most honourable of each of the four alien peoples.

I didn't know a thing about characterization, about event-caused character change, about character-caused events, or really, even, about thematic resolution. And so for the last three years of my seven-year high school math teaching career I followed my maps and allowed the setting to help me make up the events as I went along.

At the end of those three years the story was six hundred foolscap, pencil-written pages in length and still wasn't more than a third finished. I knew that at that rate the book never would be finished, because teaching had become more time-consuming and demanding the more I did of it. It's a mystery to me why that happened. I hadn't devoted much of myself to math or to my students at first, because it turned out that I didn't marry Eric after all, and he'd been pretty much my entire motivation for teaching math in the first place. But then, round about the time I first started writing, the students became fascinating individuals to me, and I spent more and more time inventing ways to make their understanding of math clearer. I created extra questions, millions of them, I think. Over the last three years of my teaching career I became known as the "handout queen" of South Secondary School. And so there was less and less time and energy to spend on the book.

I'd been best friends with a masters student in psychology named Albert Katz for about three years, starting when I began teaching. One day, over a game of cards, he asked me to marry him. I was actually winning the hand, and my first reaction was, "Darn, why did he have to go and ask me now?" My second was more ominous. My best friend had asked me to marry him. If I said no, because I didn't really believe in marriage, I would lose my best friend. If I said I'd have to think about it, it would ruin his trust in whatever answer I finally gave him. If I said yes, I'd be taking a chance on ruining our friendship. It all flashed through my mind very quickly. Could I live happily without my best friend? No. And so I said yes. And so we got married, and we remained best friends—with more separateness than is usual for the falling-in-love kind of marriage, and therefore much less difference to our relationship than there might have been. For four years we remained best friends while I supported Albert as he got first his masters and then his Ph.D. He got a job as an academic at the University of Western Ontario and then returned the favour, as best friends do, by offering to support *me* while I took a leave of absence from my teaching for a couple of years to finish my book.

I was in heaven. I sat at my desk and wrote for a year straight, seven days a week most weeks, eight to ten hours a day. I have never been in a state of such prolonged happiness in all my life since. A year of that, and I had finished the book. More important, I was hooked on writing.

I persuaded myself that I needed that second year's leave of absence to type the book, fixing it up as I typed, and send it out to publishers. Seven hundred and fifty pages of typed text later, I did so. While I was waiting for the publishers' replies, I continued to write. I had created some children in one important scene in *The Pledge-Readers,* and for some reason those children remained with me. I cared about them more than a lot of the more important

Tintagel, Cornwall, the legendary birthplace of King Arthur and the setting for **The Third Magic.**

characters in the book. I decided, while I was waiting to hear from the publishers, that I would write a whole book with a child as a main character.

It was a short book—only eighty-seven pages long. I called it *Sam Brownlee and the Ramble-Gimble Cake.* I never sent it to a publisher, but I had a marvellous time writing it. I kept at it, while the rejection slips for *The Pledge-Readers* began to pour in. When I finished *Sam Brownlee* I started a new book. I had learned a lot about writing from what I now see as my apprenticeship with *The Pledge-Readers* and *Sam Brownlee.* I still believed that "story" was more important than "literary stuff," but I had seen how hard it was to create enough events to get my characters to where I needed them to be, unless the characters cooperated by needing to do things to get them there as well.

I began *The Prophecy of Tau Ridoo.* There were four main characters in the book instead of four sentient peoples, and they were all human children, and there were flaws in the fantasy world I created, but I never once made up a map for it. And the events happened not strictly because I needed something to happen to pass the time, but because my characters did things to cause those events to happen. And they did them for their own reasons. I had, as I said earlier, learned a lot from my mistakes with *The Pledge-Readers.*

By the time I had finished *The Prophecy of Tau Ridoo,* my second year's leave of absence was over, but I still wasn't a published writer. After two years I had learned that some publishers take nine months just to reject your book. Not every publisher in the world had seen *The Pledge-Readers,* but enough had rejected it that I had bad feelings about it. I sat down and reread it, and I could see that it needed to be scrapped completely, except for the basic plot and characters, and the whole thing rewritten. This was not a minor project. The board of education wouldn't let me take any more leave. It was either quit my job completely, or return to teaching.

It was a harder decision than it ought to have been. I had been brought up in a family and a world where you were paid if you worked hard, and if you weren't paid, you weren't worth much. It was difficult to cast aside that world-view, without knowing for certain whether I would ever be able to make my living as a writer. I had worked hard for two full years without earning a single penny. But Albert, still my best friend, convinced me to make the right decision: the *write* decision. And since then, except for some supply teaching and night school and one short-lived stint as an English teacher at a private school, I have been a full-time writer, with all that goes along with it.

I spent another couple of years on the rewrite of *The Pledge-Readers,* changing its title to *The Mirana Pledge.* It was a much better book when I was done. I sent it to every science fiction and fantasy publisher in the English-speaking world. In the meantime, I sent out *The Prophecy of Tau Ridoo.* I started with Margaret K. McElderry, who was then at Atheneum, because she had published all the children's fantasies I had marked as my favourites in my new massive reading of children's literature. She wrote me a very kind letter of rejection. Then I sent *Prophecy* to someone else, and someone else again. I began writing a sequel to *Prophecy,* and then, after finishing that, another sequel. I still had no good news about publishing, but I couldn't stop writing now—I was addicted.

I was in the middle of the third book in the *Prophecy* series, writing away at my desk in the basement of the house Albert and I were living in at the time, when I heard the heartrending *THUD* of a heavy object being dropped on the front doorsill upstairs. I knew what it was. I sat there, pencil in hand, my heart beating very hard. I had to breathe a dozen or so long breaths before I had the courage to climb the stairs and open the front door, where the mail was waiting for me. Yes, it was my book—the big one, *The Mirana Pledge* that I had taken over four years to write, and another two to rewrite. It had been nine months at Del Rey/Ballantine, the last publisher in the world to have it still under consideration. And now, here it was, back.

They don't send it back to you if they are going to publish it.

I opened the box. There was a personal letter there from Lester del Rey. It told me how much he had enjoyed *The Mirana Pledge,* and how he had almost decided to publish it. But he had just taken a chance on a big book by one newcomer to the fantasy world, Terry Brooks, and he didn't feel he could take on a second. And so *Sword of Shannara* was published, and *The Mirana Pledge* was not.

I knew it never would be, now. The last publisher had rejected it. Six years of effort, six years of my life were gone, my book stillborn.

I went back down to the basement. I sat at my desk. I cried. And then, I got up, put away the box with *The Mirana Pledge* in it, and went back to my desk. Still crying, I picked up my pencil. And then I went on writing the third book in the *Prophecy* series. That was when I knew for sure that I would be a writer, a published writer, one day. It was because I picked up my pencil and went on, you see. I could not have done that if I wasn't sure, in my heart, that one day, one of my books would not be stillborn.

I have not to this day ever reread *The Mirana Pledge,* but I have not burned it, or thrown it away. It is a part of me, as I am of it. I don't regret that book that started me writing and did so much of what was necessary to turn me into a real writer. I think of those six years it took me to write and rewrite *The Mirana Pledge* in the same way a doctor must think of her six years at university learning her specialty. I taught myself; that was the only difference. But I mourn the book, as I mourn the deaths of all those I love.

Shortly after that, to my astonished delight, *The Prophecy of Tau Ridoo* was finally accepted by a small Canadian publisher who also bought, sight unseen, the two sequels. He actually published *The Prophecy of Tau Ridoo* about a month before I gave birth to Meredith, but he ran out of money before he could publish the other two in the sequence. By then, however, I had already written, and had accepted—by Margaret K. McElderry of all people! *Witchery Hill,* a story about a couple of children caught up

A ring of ancient standing stones near Lumphanan, Scotland, where the final scene of Come Like Shadows *takes place. Her research led Katz to believe that the real Macbeth died here.*

in the real witchcraft that still is practised on the Channel Island of Guernsey. I went to Guernsey to do the research for that, and happened upon many of the things that ended up in the book, including an actual book of magic spells called *Le Petit Albert,* and the legend that if you once got hold of it, you could never get rid of it. Children are always enthralled when I tell them that there really is a Trepied tomb on Guernsey, as there is in the book, and that it was indeed used by local witches for their sabbats. It was at Trepied that I first began to believe that places are not just geography, but history too, sponges for everything that has ever happened there. And if evil has happened at a place, as had happened at Trepied, I seem to be able to feel it. That went into *Witchery Hill* as well.

My next published book was *Sun God, Moon Witch,* about a girl and her cousin trying to prevent a local developer's plan to destroy an ancient circle of standing stones—something like Stonehenge. Throughout the book they find out that the stone circle means even more than they think. That book was the product of an old story my father had told me as a child about how on his father's farm in the west of Canada their well went dry, and how my grandfather had hired a dowser (water-witcher) to use a forked stick to find the right place to dig a new one. My father was a skeptic, aged ten or so, but not only did they find water exactly where the dowser said they would, they found it exactly as far down as the man had said it would be. I combined dowsing and my love of standing stones to write this book, which in the end almost caused me to stop writing altogether.

I actually wrote it before *Witchery Hill,* and sent it to lots of publishers, who rejected it. Then, the year Albert and I were on sabbatical with our baby Meredith, and I hadn't been doing any writing at all because Meredith didn't sleep for more than a few hours at a time for the first eighteen months of her life, when (on pain of threatened death) she finally began to sleep through the night, I began to consider writing again. We were living in Berkeley where I knew no one, and Albert had a decent job to go to and people to talk to, and I didn't have anyone and I was lonely and desperate to write. But I knew I couldn't take on anything new, because I was so tired. So I pulled out *Sun God, Moon Witch,* which I thought must need some rewriting. I reread it, saw what was wrong with it right away (or so I thought), and began to rewrite it. I was three-quarters of the way through the book, and excited as anything about it, sure that it was the very best book I'd ever done, when I got a phone call from Groundwood Books in Canada. They had had the *original* version of the book for over a year, and suddenly they'd decided they wanted to publish it. Well, now I was in a quandary. I told them I was rewriting it, and told them how, and they said it sounded good to them, and to finish it fast, and they would publish it in the fall. So I worked like a fiend and sent it to them by their deadline, proudly sure that this was the best writing I'd ever done.

They read it, told me it was no good, that it couldn't even be salvaged by rewriting, to throw it in the trash.

They told me they liked the original version, the one I now loathed, much better.

When something like this happens, it strikes at the very core of what it is to be a writer. A writer writes alone, each word, each sentence, each piece of dialog, each event, the product of a decision that only the writer can make. Writers *must* rely on their judgement, or they are paralyzed. And these professional publishers of mine, who had already published *Witchery Hill* in Canada, had told me that they thought my book, that I thought was great, was good only for the trash can. They had made me question my own judgement. I decided to stop writing.

We got home from Berkeley, and I set up the computer in my old office, but I never used it. My publishers knew what they had done to me by this time, and they kept phoning me, telling me I was a good writer, that I mustn't stop writing, offering to apply the already paid advance to my next book, and so on. But I couldn't, I *couldn't,* be a writer, if I couldn't be sure I was making the correct decisions about what I was writing.

Then, one day, I entered the office just to clean away the cobwebs. There was the computer, black-screened. There was the keyboard, cloth-covered. There was my chair, that I hadn't sat in for months. Did it feel the same? It did. Would the computer still turn on, after all this time? It would. Hours later I looked up, and I found that I had written five pages of a new book, one I hadn't planned or even dreamed of, and the writing was good, oh, it was so good. (It was so good that even when the book was finally finished, four years and about forty drafts later, those five pages had never changed—though they ended up the first five pages of Chapter Two, instead of Chapter One.) And I knew then that whatever was the truth of *Sun God, Moon Witch,* I was a writer, and it was time for me to get back to it.

I rewrote *Sun God, Moon Witch,* a completely different book than the second version, or the first. I never reread either of those two versions. It was the third version that was published; but I didn't throw either of the other two into the trash. They were part of me. To throw either of them away would have been to throw myself away.

After that I went back to the book I had those five pages for already. I had never written an entire book to fit with the vision begun by five previously written pages, but this was what I had to do here. Those five pages, set at Tintagel in Cornwall where King Arthur had supposedly been born, were simply too good to waste. And so I spent months plotting, and thinking, and replotting, and reading myth and ancient Celtic poetry, then drawing time lines of events, and thinking through who was who and where each of them were at various times and in various worlds, and making a map (yes, another map—but this time, the map was made to *fit* the events, not to *create* them). Then I began to write.

It was a hard book, a very hard book, and even as I wrote I knew it would be one I would have to rewrite and rewrite to make it worthy of those five pages I had written in a blur that first day in my office so long ago. Finally, a first draft was done. It was actually about draft fifteen, and I knew there was still lots wrong with it, but it was close enough to being readable to send to my publishers to get their help on the further rewrites. And so, finally, I sent out *The Third Magic,* and the long battle for publication of what is certainly one of my most powerful and magical books began.

I knew the publishers would take a few months to come back to me with their suggested revisions, and I was very tired and glad to think I was in for a holiday until then.

But a contest with a huge prize was announced just then—the International Fiction Contest for the best manuscript for children aged eleven and up. By this time I really wanted to win a contest, and especially one that had a prize of $13,000 and a trip to Italy, with publication in five languages thrown in as an added incentive. I had a manuscript for children of roughly the right age group *The Third Magic*. But unfortunately, the manuscript could not be one that a publisher had seen, and I'd just sent *The Third Magic* to both my publishers. And so I was faced with a decision. Either I wouldn't enter the contest, or in five months (the contest deadline) I would have to write a whole new book, tired as I was.

False Face was the answer. I had never written a book in five months before, and never any book when I was so tired, and with so few original ideas left after the complexities and difficulties of *The Third Magic*. But I began, doggedly, looking for an idea. My by-now three-year-old daughter Meredith and I went to our local Museum of Archaeology, and she saw an Iroquois False Face mask staring at her out of a display case and she screamed. The rest is history. Plotting was magical, writing was the way it so seldom is, as if all I had to do was sit there and take dictation from a little voice in my head. I finished the book in three months, put it away, rewrote it, put it away, put the finishing touches on it, and sent it to the contest by the deadline.

And I won.

With *False Face* I became a recognized major writer in my own country and others. As well as the International Fiction Contest, *False Face* won the Mark and Greta Ebel Award and was short-listed for every major award in Canada. *School Library Journal* in the United States gave it a starred review and named it a Best Book of the Year, and

Celebrating Katz's winning the Ruth Schwartz Award for Out of the Dark. *From left: Meredith Katz, age 12, Peter Bangarth, Welwyn Katz, and Aurora Bangarth, age 12.*

the book was included in the American Booksellers Association "Picks of the Lists." It became a Junior Library Guild selection, chosen as an outstanding book for older readers. It was nominated for the South Carolina Young Adult Book Award. Clearly as a writer I was on my way.

I have written five books since. *The Third Magic* aged me terribly, in battle after battle with my publishers that resulted in a stack of drafts that reached from floor to ceiling, but when it was finally published it won for me Canada's highest literary prize, the Governor General's Award. Next came *Whalesinger,* set in Point Reyes, California, which was the only place where I felt completely at peace the entire year we were on sabbatical in Berkeley. It was a place where Sir Francis Drake was supposed to have spent some seven weeks during his circumnavigation of the globe, and a place where grey whales came very close to land. It was a place that didn't belong where it was—a peninsula that over many centuries of many earthquakes had moved six hundred miles north of its birthplace, bringing the geology and plants and animals and birds of Southern California with it to Northern California.

I felt the alienness of Point Reyes very keenly. That alienness, and its fundamental loneliness, were the bonds that I had with it, for I knew that I didn't belong in Berkeley or California and maybe not even with the man who had for years been my best friend. I felt so lonely that year, except for my baby Meredith; so without solidity, so dangerously still and waiting—just as Point Reyes sat, waiting for the next earthquake that would move it somewhere away from where it was. Nothing that Albert did could lessen this feeling. Later, while I was writing *Whalesinger,* I saw a baby orca whale born at the Vancouver Aquarium. It was one of the most joyous experiences of my life, and that feeling went into *Whalesinger;* and then, a few weeks later, that baby orca died. I mourned it as if it had been my own child. Then I miscarried my own real baby; a second time, and this one was one that Albert had refused to believe I even carried. He would not mourn what he did not believe in, and so I lost my best friend altogether, because what he could not believe in denied my own grief.

I had never believed in the falling-in-love kind of love and so it was only true to life's ironies that just at that time when I was most vulnerable I would meet and fall in love with Doug Bale, the reporter who interviewed me about winning the Governor-General's Award for *The Third Magic*. It was fitting that I did this during the last six weeks of writing my book *Whalesinger,* the part of the book where my hero discovered he needed to learn forgiveness.

Come Like Shadows began a year later, a book about the curse on the play *Macbeth* and for which Doug and I spent a summer in Scotland following the thousand-year-old footsteps of the real man Macbeth, who was not at all as Shakespeare portrayed him. Doug and I had a grand time doing this, and despite many arguments he saw me through yet two more books *Time Ghost,* which has I think the neatest time travel mechanism I've ever seen in any book; and finally, my favourite, *Out of the Dark,* about modern Ben and his love of the Vikings and his need to learn from them how to leave the past behind and make a home for himself in the real world, where there is magic enough for anyone.

There is also heartbreak in the real world, and Doug and I came to learn that no matter how much we loved each other, we couldn't live together without chipping away and eventually mortally wounding the essence of what each of us was.

Two years have passed since then, and I have gone through a long illness and a long period of remembering what I once was and what I must be again. I am now back at work on my next book, *Ghost Gambit,* a sequel to *Time Ghost,* another novel about the mysteries of time.

All of my books are about time. All of them are about how the past intrudes endlessly on the present. All of them are about a little girl, aged six, standing holding a red book bound in black and learning for the first time about infinity, and magic, and the need to find it in everyday life, and the all-too-real possibility of betrayal.

That little girl grew up, and married, and had a baby who grew to be a best-friend daughter, and a best-friend husband who was lost, and another marriage and another separation, and—finally—another togetherness with someone who, this time, makes her feel as if the magic in everyday life will not go away.

But nothing is ever finished. The past will keep on happening. The little girl who has grown up will keep on writing, and she will be in my present and in my future, and I will keep on looking for her kind of magic in everyday things.

An infinity of faces reflected in a three-way mirror, and no way, no way at all, to tell where they all began. If that isn't magic, what is?

Writings

FICTION

The Prophecy of Tau Ridoo, illustrated by Michelle Desbarats, Tree Frog Press, 1982.

Witchery Hill, Atheneum, 1984.

Sun God, Moon Witch, Douglas & McIntyre, 1986.

False Face, Douglas & McIntyre, 1987, McElderry, 1988.

The Third Magic, Douglas & McIntyre, 1988, McElderry, 1989.

Whalesinger, McElderry, 1990.

Come Like Shadows, Viking, 1993.

Time Ghost, McElderry, 1995.

Out of the Dark, Douglas & McIntyre, 1995, McElderry, 1996.

KEST, Kristin 1967-

Personal

Born November 12, 1967, in Hershey, PA; daughter of Michael C., Jr. and Carol L. (a factory worker and beekeeper; maiden name, Paul; present surname, Spangler) Tushup; companion of Sandra Slonaker (a teacher). *Education:* Attended Pennsylvania School of the Arts. *Politics:* Independent. *Religion:* Atheist.

Addresses

Home and office—1542 West Philadelphia St., York, PA 17404. *Agent*—Harriet Kasak, HK Portfolio, Inc., 666 Greenwich St., Suite 860, New York, NY 10014.

Career

Illustrator and fine artist, 1991—. York Craftsman's Guild, teacher of stained glass classes. Illustrations represented in annual shows, Society of Illustrators, 1993, 1998, 1999, and 2000.

Writings

ILLUSTRATOR

Sneed B. Collard III, *Do They Scare You? Creepy Creatures,* Charlesbridge Publishing (Watertown, MA), 1992, revised edition published as *Creepy Creatures,* 1997.

George S. Fichter, *Butterflies and Moths,* Western Publishing (New York City), 1993.

Fichter, *Bees, Wasps, and Ants,* Western Publishing, 1993.

Robert Michael Pyle, *Insects,* Houghton (Boston, MA), 1993.

Alvin Silverstein, Virginia B. Silverstein, and Robert A. Silverstein, *Eagles, Hawks, and Owls,* Western Publishing, 1994.

Fichter, *Endangered Animals: 140 Species in Full Color,* Western Publishing, 1995.

Judith Janda Presnall, *Animal Skeletons,* F. Watts (New York City), 1995.

Deborah Merrians, *I Can Read about Spiders,* Troll Communications (Mahwah, NJ), 1997.

Alden Kelley, *A Tree Is a Home,* Creative Teaching Press, 1997.

Kathy Kranking, *The Bug Book,* Golden Books (New York City), 1997.

Barbara Gaines Winkleman, *Flying Squirrel at Acorn Place,* Soundprints (Norwalk, CT), 1998.

Kristin Kest

Merrians, *I Can Read about Insects,* Troll Communications, 1999.

Laura Gates Galvin, *Bumblebee at Apple Tree Lane,* Soundprints, 2000.

Madeleine Dunphy, *The Peregrine's Journey: A Story of Migration,* Millbrook Press (Brookfield, CT), 2000.

Sidelights

Kristin Kest told *SATA:* "Growing up in a big family of scientists and artists, it's easy to see how I started an illustration career in natural history. Bugs, bones, shells, birds, and occasionally small, furry critters were brought home (by me) so I could study and draw them. My mom didn't like it much, but she tolerated it 'in the name of art.'

"Art school was brief and painful, but I did hook up with fellow artist and now fellow illustrator, Mark Zug. Mark taught me what I needed to know about being a great artist. Since I met him in 1985, Mark's influence has been a major part of my work. Together we studied the art of Maxfield Parrish, N. C. Wyeth, Frank Frazetta, and many others. One of my favorite illustrators, Walter Linsenmaier, had a great impact on me, actually propelled me into insect art in particular. Other favorites

of mine have included J. Lansdowne, John Dawson, Robert Bateman, and Velasquez.

"Most people ask me how I can create on demand: 'Don't you have to wait for your muse?' The general belief is that the hand of god touches the artist and she/he makes a mad dash to the studio and frantically brush-jousts with a canvas, hopefully capturing the rapture and the moment of the fleeting idea. Not me. I sit down at my studio table early in the morning, and I work. I've trained my muse to come to me. I have to, but I love what I do. It's what gets me out of bed in the morning—along with a zillion other things I like to do!

"After I quit the art school, it took me an additional four years on my own, working to create a professional portfolio. It was ready in 1992, and it immediately landed me the first two of my books for Golden Books (Western Publishing). I was twenty-four years old. Perhaps I didn't need an art degree to become an illustrator, but it's not what I would tell young people who want a career in art. In fact, I am currently attending York College of Pennsylvania to get a degree in fine art and a minor in biology.

"Eventually I hope to illustrate *and* write my own books and expand my fine art options in painting, sculpture, and stained glass. I don't ever intend to retire. I can't. I've got too much to do!"

*   *   *

KHAN, Rukhsana 1962-

Personal

First name is pronounced "ruk-SA-na"; born March 13, 1962, in Lahore, Pakistan; emigrated to Canada in 1965; daughter of Muhammad Anwar (a tool and dye maker) and Iftikhar Shahzadi (a homemaker) Khan; married Irfan Haseeb Alli (a production manager), March 31, 1979; children: four. *Education:* Seneca College of Applied Arts and Technology, earned degree as a biological-chemical technician; currently attends University of Toronto. *Religion:* Islam.

Addresses

c/o Stoddart Kids, Stoddart Publishing Co. Ltd., 34 Lesmill Rd., North York, Ontario M3B 2T6, Canada. *E-mail*—irruali@idirect.com.

Career

Writer and storyteller. *Member:* Canadian Society of Children's Authors, Illustrators, and Performers, Storytellers of Canada, Storytelling School of Toronto.

Awards, Honors

Honorary Januscz Korczak International Literature Award, Polish Section of International Board on Books for Young People, 1998, for *The Roses in My Carpets;*

Writers' Reserve grant, Ontario Arts Council, 1998; Artists in Education grant, 1998-99; shortlisted, Red Maple Award, Ontario Library Association, 2000, for *Dahling If You Luv Me Would You Please, Please Smile.*

Writings

Bedtime Ba-a-a-lk (picture book), illustrated by Kristi Frost, Stoddart Kids, 1998.

The Roses in My Carpets (picture book), illustrated by Ronald Himler, Stoddart Kids, 1998.

Dahling If You Luv Me Would You Please, Please Smile (novel), Stoddart Kids, 1999.

Muslim Child (short stories), Napoleon, 1999.

The Kite Thief (picture book), Scholastic Canada, 2000.

Contributor of short stories to magazines, including *Message International;* contributor of songs to *Adam's World* children's videos, produced by Sound Vision.

Sidelights

"Growing up Muslim in North America was very difficult," Rukhsana Khan told *SATA.* "I'd cringe with the release of each mega-blockbuster depicting Muslims as merciless bumbling terrorists or ignorant taxi drivers. As a writer, I wanted to change that, addressing that stereotype and show us for what we truly were. I started writing seriously for publication around the time the Salman Rushdie controversy started. I was absolutely furious at the book *Satanic Verses,* though I had no wish to kill Mr. Rushdie. With the *fatwa,* once again we Muslims looked like a bunch of barbaric idiots. Why couldn't someone stand up and speak on the issues, explaining exactly what was so offensive about the book and why it was hate literature? I kept ranting to my husband, 'Why doesn't someone write something to respond to this? Why doesn't someone *do* something?' My husband turned the question back on me. If I had such a problem with it, why didn't *I* do something about it? So I decided I would.

"I attended conferences and seminars on writing. I took courses and read books. Lots of books. Tons of books.

"In particular I went to one children's writing conference in Boston because the best in the children's writing field were going to be there. I went with trepidation because one of the speakers would be a Western woman who'd written a book about a Muslim character. This was a case where this white lady had gotten the culture all wrong. It was clear, almost from the beginning of the book, that a 'white feminist' had imposed her sensibilities on a girl who wouldn't have been exposed to them within the scope of the novel. There was some merit in the book, but unfortunately the book did perpetuate a lot of the prevalent Muslim stereotypes that so upset me.

"When I got to the conference, I found out that she'd written a sequel. I couldn't believe it. She hadn't left well enough alone. I actually forked out some of my hard earned money and bought it. In the sequel this

Rukhsana Khan

writer had undone all the good she'd done in the first book. She'd reverted the entire story back to stereotype.

"Perhaps I'm naive. My husband tells me often enough that I am. Perhaps I really did think I could change the world. But at that moment, what I really was up against fully hit me. Here I was, a dowdy old housewife, with quaint old-fashioned principles, trying to show this big amorphous blob of Western society that they'd pegged us 'Moslems' all wrong. How could I, without even a complete university education (as all the alumni of the conference boasted), how could I even aspire to such a lofty goal? Who did I think I was?

"It was too much. I felt as though I'd been climbing a cliff ten miles high, having only reached ten feet above the ground, when some force or another decided to up the ante and add another mile of cliff to be climbed. To say the task seemed daunting is an understatement.

"So I did something I can do. I cried. (So much for the spunky heroine.)

"I had the crazy idea of confronting this woman, right in the lecture she was to give the next day, and taking her to task for the damage she'd done.

"A wise friend advised me not to confront the lady, but to take her aside, tell her politely how and why her book had so offended me, and start with the positives. So I did.

"It is extremely hard, at least for me, to be calm, cool, and rational when something has hurt me this deeply. I started that way, honest I did. Saying how I thought the descriptions were beautiful and she had really captured the feel of the land. I spoke of how well she had dealt with the tricky subject of polygamy (in the first book; she reverted to stereotype in the second) and then I began explaining, or trying to explain, through the flowing tears, how much she had reinforced the stereotypes that I was trying so hard to reform.

"She defended her work. She said she had given it to several friends of hers from the culture and they'd found nothing wrong with it. I tried to tell her that they would have been too in awe of her to honestly criticize. I tried to explain the inaccuracies regarding Islam, etc., etc.

"For every point I made, rather than listening, she countered with her own. Soon the tears dried. Anger replaced hurt. I thought to myself, she's not interested in my grievances. She's not interested that she made mistakes. She's only interested in herself.

"A curious thing happened. I stopped crying and I listened more carefully. She talked about how important it was to get the names of everything right. How much research she'd done. She'd even made sure she'd spelt the name of the string cot they used to sleep on right. I said, yes, but these were all superficial things. She'd got them right, but she'd got the thought processes wrong. They wouldn't think like that.

"And while she spouted platitudes and good wishes for my future as a writer, I nodded but didn't really listen. I watched her. Trying to calm me. Trying to soothe me like a weepy toddler, and I hardened my resolve.

When a little girl conjures up a flock of sheep to aid in her efforts to go to sleep, she meets resistance from them on every front. (From Bedtime Ba-a-a-lk, *written by Khan and illustrated by Kristi Frost.)*

"Well, I thought to myself, I have no control over what other people write. It's a free country and it's a good thing it is. I rely on that freedom too. I wouldn't have it any other way.

"And then another thought came into my head.

"This lady thought she was so good. As a writer, I thought she was okay. The first book was written fairly well, but I couldn't even get through the second. And I thought, her level of writing isn't so far above mine. It's attainable. I could write like that, or better, I hoped. There were many spots in the story where the narrative had lost focus. I wouldn't have done that.

"And then I invited her to the amateur readings that night. I was determined to read my best story there, and suddenly I wanted her to hear it.

"Surprisingly, that night I wasn't nervous. Not at all. I got up when it was my turn, and I read to the small group gathered there. Not one missed word, not one stumble. The whole story flowed.

"Afterward, there was a pause, and then applause. And I watched to see what she would do. If she came up to congratulate me, that meant my piece wasn't very good and she could afford to be gracious. If she ignored me, it meant it was good.

"She ignored me. Didn't say another word to me for the rest of the conference.

"I came home, perhaps a handhold higher on that cliff I'm climbing, resolved to make it to the top.

"What I realized is that people, including Salman Rushdie, will write all kinds of garbage about Islam. In order to fight them, I'll have to be better.

"I'm working on it.

"It helped that two weeks after I got back, my editor told me she was publishing that story. And about two years later, it won an international literary award."

In her first picture book, *Bedtime Ba-a-a-lk,* Khan provides a twist on the usual scenario of a reluctant child counting sheep in order to be lulled to sleep. Here, a little girl conjures up a flock of sheep to aid in her efforts to go to sleep, meeting resistance from them on every front. First they require her to imagine more light on the far side of the fence so they can see what they are jumping into, then they get bored by the activity they have performed so many times before and demand entertainment instead. When the girl imagines a carnival for them, however, the sheep are so entranced they forget to jump at all. So the girl uses her imagination once again to make the recalcitrant flock disappear and a more compliant one appear in its place. *Quill & Quire* reviewer Patty Lawlor praised the author's sonorous text: "*Bedtime Ba-a-a-lk* opens almost poetically with lyrical language, phrasing and pacing, immediately creating an effective sleepytime mood." A reviewer for

For a young boy living in a refugee camp in Afghanistan, the craft of weaving is the only beautiful, hopeful thing he sees in his grim world. (From The Roses in My Carpets, *written by Khan and illustrated by Ronald Himler.)*

Kirkus Reviews praised the illustrations and text both for their "light touch": "A little bit of dream manipulation goes a long way in this lullaby tale," the reviewer stated.

Khan's second picture book strikes a decidedly different tone. *The Roses in My Carpets* tells the story of a day in the life of a young boy who lives in a refugee camp in Afghanistan with his mother and younger sister. Khan follows the boy as he rises early in the morning after a recurrent nightmare, prays at the mosque, eats, goes to school, prays again, then practices the craft of weaving. Learning to weave is the highlight of the boy's day, being the only beautiful thing he sees in the grim world of the camp and offering him hope that he will one day be able to support his family on his earnings from the work. "Khan hints at the boy's powerful emotions in spare prose, and handles her difficult subject matter sensitively," commented a reviewer in *Publishers Weekly.* While at his weaving lesson, the boy learns his sister has been hit by a truck, though she will recover. That night he has a nightmare similar to the earlier ones, but this time he and his mother and sister take refuge on a bed of roses the size of the carpet he is learning to weave. *Booklist* reviewer Linda Perkins noted that while children will likely need supplemental information on the Islamic religion and the war in Afghanistan, "still,

this is a rare and welcome glimpse into a culture children usually don't see."

Works Cited

Review of *Bedtime Ba-a-a-lk, Kirkus Reviews,* June 15, 1998, p. 896.
Lawlor, Patty, review of *Bedtime Ba-a-a-lk, Quill & Quire,* March, 1998, pp. 71-72.
Perkins, Linda, review of *The Roses in My Carpets, Booklist,* November 15, 1998, p. 596.
Review of *The Roses in My Carpets, Publishers Weekly,* October 5, 1998, p. 90.

For More Information See

PERIODICALS

School Library Journal, November, 1998, pp. 87-88.*

* * *

KURLAND, Michael (Joseph) 1938-
(Jennifer Plum)

Personal

Born March 1, 1938, in New York, NY; son of Jack (a manufacturer) and Stephanie (a dress designer; maiden name, Yacht) Kurland; married Rebecca Jacobson, 1976. *Education:* Attended Hiram College, 1955-56, University of Maryland, 1959-60, and Columbia University, 1963-64; also studied in Germany, 1960-61. *Politics:* Whig. *Religion:* Secular humanist. *Hobbies and other interests:* Politics, bear baiting, barn storming, lighter-than-air craft, carnivals, vaudeville, science fiction incunabula.

Addresses

Home—New York, NY. *Agent*—Richard Curtis Associates, 340 East 66th St., New York, NY 10021.

Career

Full-time writer, 1963—. High school English teacher, Ojai, CA, 1968; managing editor, *Crawdaddy* magazine, 1969; editor, Pennyfarthing Press, San Francisco and Berkley, CA, 1976—. Occasional director of plays for Squirrel Hill Theatre, 1972—. *Military service:* U.S. Army Intelligence, 1958-61. *Member:* Authors Guild, Authors League of America, Mystery Writers of America, Science Fiction Writers of America, Institute for Twenty-first Century Studies, Computer Press Association.

Awards, Honors

Edgar Scroll, Mystery Writers of America, 1971, for *A Plague of Spies,* 1979, for *The Infernal Device;* American Book Award nomination, 1979, for *The Infernal Device.*

Writings

NOVELS

(With Chester Anderson) *Ten Years to Doomsday,* Pyramid, 1964.

Mission: Third Force, Pyramid, 1967.

Mission: Tank War, Pyramid, 1968.

Mission: Police Action, Pyramid, 1969.

A Plague of Spies, Pyramid, 1969.

The Unicorn Girl, Pyramid, 1969.

Transmission Error, Pyramid, 1971.

(Under pseudonym Jennifer Plum) *The Secret of Benjamin Square,* Lancer Books, 1972.

The Whenabouts of Burr, DAW Books, 1975.

Pluribus, Doubleday, 1975.

Tomorrow Knight, DAW Books, 1976.

The Princes of Earth, T. Nelson, 1978.

The Infernal Device, New American Library, 1978.

(With S. W. Barton) *The Last President,* Morrow, 1980.

Death by Gaslight, New American Library, 1982.

Gashopper, Doubleday, 1987.

Ten Little Wizards, Berkley, 1987.

Star Griffin, Doubleday, 1987.

Perchance, New American Library, 1988.

A Study in Sorcery, Ace, 1989.

Button Bright, Berkley, 1989.

Too Soon Dead, St. Martin's, 1997.

The Girls in the High-heeled Shoes, St. Martin's, 1998.

NONFICTION

The Spymaster's Handbook, Facts on File, 1988.

World Espionage: A Historical Encyclopedia, Facts on File, 1993.

A Gallery of Rogues: Portraits in True Crime, Prentice-Hall, 1994.

How to Solve a Murder: The Forensic Handbook, Macmillan, 1995.

How to Try a Murder: The Armchair Lawyer's Handbook, Macmillan, 1997.

Editor with H. Beam Piper, *First Cycle* (Ace Books, 1982). Author of editorials for *National Examiner,* 1966, and of "Impropa-Ganda" column in *Berkley Barb,* 1967. Contributor to *Worlds of Tomorrow.*

Sidelights

During a career that has spanned more than three decades, author Michael Kurland has written over a dozen novels—in thriller, science fiction, and fantasy genres—as well as a handful of nonfiction works on crime and espionage. In his early novel *The Whenabouts of Burr,* Kurland takes readers on a trip through time and parallel times to check out the authenticity of the U.S. Constitution, a story that *Publishers Weekly* critic Barbara A. Bannon called "clever, funny, unpredictable." In the "intriguing story" *Pluribus,* to quote Sally C. Estes and Elinor Walker of *Booklist,* Kurland speeds forward in time to an era seventy-three years after a mutated virus has killed most life on Earth. With *The Princes of Earth* Kurland has created an even more distant future when the galaxy is a confederation of planets—human and nonhuman. Main character Adam

Starting with a fictional murder, mystery writer Michael Kurland explains the use of forensics techniques for solving crimes. (Cover illustration by Michael J. Freeland.)

Warrington leaves his planet to attend a university on Mars, becoming involved in a series of adventures. Several critics praised the work for its characters and plot. Writing in *Booklist* Sally C. Estes and Stephanie Zvirin called Adam an "appealing character" and the plot both "farfetched" yet "entertaining." Judging the characters to be well drawn, *School Library Journal* critic Susan Cain added, "There is enough action to maintain interest." Set at the end of the twenty-second century, *Star Griffin* follows courier Peter Lyons through mystery and intrigue when someone tries to steal the secure case he is delivering. According to Genevieve Stuttaford in *Publishers Weekly,* the novel is a "light, engaging story that draws together its many elements in a series of clever, pleasing surprises."

In 1979 Kurland won an Edgar scroll from the Mystery Writers of America for *The Infernal Device,* in which sleuth Sherlock Holmes and his nemesis, Professor James Moriarty, team up to prevent war from erupting between Russia and Great Britain. "Kurland's writing is tight and the plot moves well," wrote Barbara A. Bannon in *Publishers Weekly,* "but the resolution is a bit too smooth to allow for the expected suspense." Kurland again uses previously created characters, this time author Randall Garrett's Lord Darly, in *Ten Little Wizards.* In this fantasy exists an alternate universe reminiscent of medieval England and full of magic, a characteristic to which Jan E. V. W. Hanson attributed the "tale's charm" in a review for *Voice of Youth Advocates.* Maintaining that "detail and characterization are convincing," Hanson continued, "the fast pace and clever plot will entertain." "An agreeable interlude," concluded Roland Green in *Booklist.*

In *Perchance,* another sci-fi novel of multiple universes, Delbit Quint, apprenticed to a mad scientist, blips from universe to universe, encountering adventure and misadventure. *Kliatt* reviewer Bette D. Ammon and *Publishers Weekly* critic Penny Kaganoff both felt that Kurland created "likable characters." According to Ammon, Kurland "writes well, using a challenging vocabulary and thought-provoking historical concepts." Kaganoff also complimented Kurland for his "smooth storytelling and piquant entwining of social injustices and personal decency." As in *Perchance,* in *The Last President* Kurland changes history, this time the administration of

Kurland's mystery, set in the middle of the Great Depression, follows a society columnist in his attempt to solve the murder of a man who offered him incriminating pictures of famous people. (Cover illustration by Cathie Bleck.)

U.S. President Richard Nixon after the Watergate break in. *New York Times Book Review* critic Newgate Callendar praised the work, calling it "hard to put down."

Depression-era New York City is the setting of Kurland's mysteries *Too Soon Dead* and *The Girls in the High-heeled Shoes,* both featuring newspaper reporter Alexander Brass and his sidekick, Morgan DeWitt. In the former, the sleuths investigate the mystery of a newspaper reporter who was killed while pursuing a hot story. In the second novel, Brass and DeWitt solve the murder of Two-Headed Mary, a woman with many identities. A *Publishers Weekly* critic commented on the "bright, funny dialogue" of *Too Soon Dead,* adding that Kurland has created a "thoroughly engaging showcase for a likable bunch of characters."

Kurland has also written nonfiction about espionage and crime, including such titles as *The Spymaster's Handbook, World Espionage, Gallery of Rogues,* and *How to Solve a Murder.* In *The Spymaster's Handbook* he explains the basics and tools of intelligence operations and describes real twentieth-century spies. Though commentator Susan Ackler in *Voice of Youth Advocates* expressed some reservations about the age-appropriateness of Kurland's writing style and humor, she noted that "there is an excellent section with chapters on famous spies."

Works Cited

Ackler, Susan, review of *The Spymaster's Handbook, Voice of Youth Advocates,* April, 1989, pp. 59-60.

Ammon, Bette D., review of *Perchance, Kliatt,* April, 1989, p. 24.

Bannon, Barbara A., review of *The Infernal Device, Publishers Weekly,* November 13, 1978, p. 61.

Bannon, Barbara A., review of *The Whenabouts of Burr, Publishers Weekly,* June 2, 1975, p. 56.

Cain, Susan, review of *The Princes of Earth, School Library Journal,* November, 1978, p. 76.

Callendar, Newgate, review of *The Last President, New York Times Book Review,* August 31, 1980, p. 17.

Estes, Sally C., and Elinor Walker, review of *Pluribus, Booklist,* p. 1109.

Estes, Sally C., and Stephanie Zvirin, review of *The Princes of Earth, Booklist,* April 1, 1978, p. 1249.

Green, Roland, review of *Ten Little Wizards, Booklist,* February 1, 1988, p. 907.

Hanson, Jan E. V. W., review of *Ten Little Wizards, Voice of Youth Advocates,* October, 1988, p. 194.

Kaganoff, Penny, review of *Perchance, Publishers Weekly,* November 11, 1988, p. 50.

Stuttaford, Genevieve, review of *Star Griffin, Publishers Weekly,* February 6, 1987, p. 88.

Review of *Too Soon Dead, Publishers Weekly,* January 27, 1997, pp. 80-81.

For More Information See

PERIODICALS

Kirkus Reviews, January 15, 1997, p. 99; July 1, 1998, p. 934.

Library Journal, January, 1994, p. 108.

Publishers Weekly, March 21, 1980, pp. 54-55; November 29, 1993, p. 60; June 22, 1998, p. 88.

School Library Journal, January, 1989, p. 108.*

L

LIFTON, Betty Jean

Personal

Born in New York, NY; adopted daughter of Oscar and Hilda Kirschner; married Robert Jay Lifton (a professor of psychiatry and a writer), March 1, 1952; children: Kenneth Jay, Karen, Natasha. *Education:* Barnard College, B.A., 1948.

Addresses

Home—300 Central Park West, New York, NY 10024.

Career

Children's author, playwright, journalist, biographer, and psychologist.

Awards, Honors

New York Herald Tribune award, 1960, for *Kap the Kappa,* and 1970, for *Return to Hiroshima;* National Book Award nomination, 1973, for *Children of Vietnam.*

Writings

FOR CHILDREN

A Dog's Guide to Tokyo, photographs by E. Hosoe, Norton, 1969.
(With Thomas C. Fox) *Children of Vietnam,* Atheneum, 1972.
(Editor) *Contemporary Children's Theater* (includes play adaptation of *Kap the Kappa*), Avon, 1974.

FOR CHILDREN; FICTION

Joji and the Dragon, illustrated by Eiichi Mitsui, Morrow, 1957.
Mogo the Mynah, illustrated by Anne Scott, Morrow, 1958.
Joji and the Fog, illustrated by E. Mitsui, Morrow, 1959.
Kap the Kappa, illustrated by E. Mitsui, Morrow, 1960.
The Dwarf Pine Tree, illustrated by Fuku Akino, Atheneum, 1963.

Joji and the Amanojaku, illustrated by E. Mitsui, Norton, 1965.
The Cock and the Ghost Cat, illustrated by F. Akino, Atheneum, 1965.
The Rice-Cake Rabbit, illustrated by E. Mitsui, Norton, 1966.
The Many Lives of Chio and Goro, illustrated by Yasuo Segawa, Norton, 1966.
Taka-Chan and I: A Dog's Journey to Japan, by Runcible, photographs by Eikoh Hosoe, Norton, 1967.
Kap and the Wicked Monkey, illustrated by E. Mitsui, Norton, 1968.
The Secret Seller, illustrated by Etienne Delessert, Norton, 1968.
The One-Legged Ghost, illustrated by F. Akino, Atheneum, 1968.
The Mud Snail Son, illustrated by F. Akino, Atheneum, 1971.
The Silver Crane, illustrated by Laszlo Kubinyi, Seabury, 1971.
Good Night, Orange Monster, illustrated by Cyndy Szekeres, Atheneum, 1972.
Jaguar, My Twin, illustrated by Ann Leggett, Atheneum, 1976.
I'm Still Me (novel), Knopf, 1981.
Tell Me a Real Adoption Story, illustrated by Claire A. Nivola, Knopf, 1994.

FOR ADULTS

Moon Walk (play), music and lyrics by the Open Window, produced on Broadway at City Center, New York City, 1970.
Return to Hiroshima, photographs by E. Hosoe, Atheneum, 1970.
Twice Born: Memoirs of an Adopted Daughter, McGraw Hill, 1975, Penguin, 1977.
Lost and Found: The Adoption Experience, Dial, 1979.
A Place Called Hiroshima (sequel to *Return to Hiroshima*), photographs by E. Hosoe, Kodansha, 1985.
The King of Children: A Biography of Janusz Korczak, Farrar, Straus, 1988, reprinted with introduction by Elie Wiesel, St. Martin's, 1997.

Journey of the Adopted Self: A Quest for Wholeness, Basic, 1994.

Has also written psychological books on adoption.

Sidelights

Betty Jean Lifton has blended several interests to create a body of work that reaches both children and adults. In her children's stories and picture books, she frequently deals with Asian themes, reflecting the years she spent in both Japan and Hong King during the 1950s and early 1960s. In picture books, she details the doings of Joji, a peace-loving scarecrow who must eternally be helped out of difficult situations, or of Kap, a river elf with a turtle's back and a monkey's face whose mischievous antics fill two volumes and also a play for children. There are ghosts and samurai populating these picture books, all "characterized by humor, an economy of words, vivid characterizations, well-structured narratives drawn from Japanese folktales without diluting the cultural source, and handsomely imaginative and colorful brush and ink illustrations," according to Christian H. Moe, writing in *St. James Guide to Children's Writers.* Several nonfiction works also have resulted from

In Betty Jean Lifton's sequel to her **Return to Hiroshima,** *she further chronicles the destruction of the city by the atomic bomb and the profound effect the devastation had on survivors.*

Lifton's interests in Asia, including the award-winning *Return to Hiroshima* and *Children of Vietnam.*

Additionally, Lifton, an adopted child, has concerned herself with the condition of orphaned and adopted children. In books for young readers as well as for adults, she has examined aspects of adoption, from looking for one's biological parents to a biography of a Polish doctor and educator who gave his life in the Second World War to be with his orphan charges. In the picture book *Tell Me a Real Adoption Story,* Lifton presents the subject of open adoption, and in her teen novel, *I'm Still Me,* she tells the story of a high school junior who attempts to track down her biological mother.

Lifton and her psychiatrist husband lived in Tokyo from 1952 to 1954. From 1954 to 1956 they lived in Hong Kong, and in 1960, they again returned to Japan for a two-year stay, residing in Tokyo, Kyoto, and Hiroshima. Lifton's interest in Asian culture, art, folkcrafts, and legends was developed during those years. Her first book was published in 1957, setting the tone for more than a dozen to follow. *Joji and the Dragon* tells the story of the scarecrow Joji who is taken on as a friend by the very crows he is supposed to scare off. His master decides to get rid of him and bring in a dragon instead. But the helpful crows manage to frighten the dragon away, and Joji is restored to his rightful position, guarding the rice paddy. Moe noted that Lifton's debut picture book deals with "oriental themes" such as "non-violence and the eternal recurrence of nature" which are staples of such Japanese folktales and legends as the Joji stories. In *Joji and the Amanojaku,* Joji is captured by the frightful demon of the title, only to be once again rescued by the friendly crows. "Joji," Moe wrote, "a lively espouser of non-violence, is appealing to the very young." Writing in *Horn Book,* Ethel L. Heins claimed the book was "fast-moving," with "carefully chosen words and effective brush drawings."

With the character Kap, Lifton adapts another Japanese legend, this time of a prankish river elf, who is half turtle and half monkey. In *Kap the Kappa,* the elf leaves his river home and attempts to pass himself off as a human, adopted by a fisherman. But his mischievous nature finally reveals him to all, and he decides to return to the river, to his true parents, understanding that he cannot become human. Moe called Kap "an inspired creation." Lifton again presents the trickster in *Kap and the Wicked Monkey,* in which the river elf and the monkey in question, Saru, try to outdo one another in tricks. The kappas, however, must keep water in the shallow depression on top of their heads, or else they will perish. Kap almost dies trying to best Saru, but a beautiful white crane rescues Kap at the last moment. Zena Sutherland, writing in *Bulletin of the Center for Children's Books,* noted that the "story has action and humor."

In *The Dwarf Pine Tree,* an evergreen undergoes a painful transformation to become beautiful enough to save the life of a princess that it has grown to love before fading away to become a tree spirit. Moe called this picture book a "minor masterpiece," reflecting the "gentle spirit of Buddha." Animals also make appearances in these picture books. *The Cock and the Ghost Cat* presents a rooster who saves its master from an attack by a morphed giant ghost cat in this "distinguished book," according to *Booklist* reviewer Ruth P. Bull. Writing in the *New York Times Book Review,* Al Hine called the book a "superb reworking of old Japanese spook material." A rabbit, famous for his rice-cakes, wants desperately to become a samurai in *The Rice-Cake Rabbit.* The humor "borders on poignancy," according to Priscilla L. Moulton in a *Horn Book* review.

A farmer and his wife are reborn as a fox and chicken respectively in *The Many Lives of Chio and Goro,* while a dog named Runcible takes readers on a tour of Japan in *Taka-Chan and I,* an "utterly charming" book, according to Hal Borland writing in the *New York Times Book Review.* An umbrella becomes honored as a god in *The One-Legged Ghost,* and a childless couple is blessed with a mud snail in response to their wish for a child in *The Mud Snail Son.* Such devoted parents are they, that after years of careful nurturing and sacrifice, the snail turns into a handsome young son. Paul Heins called this book a "smoothly told tale" in a *Horn Book* review, and further noted that the "sensitivity of the tale is perfectly reflected in the illustrations."

Lifton also made use of her Asian experiences in nonfiction books that garnered awards and critical praise. In *Return to Hiroshima,* she chronicles the destruction of that city by the atomic bomb and its effects on the survivors. Her 1985 sequel, *A Place Called Hiroshima,* further records the changes to that city in the fifteen years since her previous book. Lifton's text produces a "memento mori of great beauty, power, and commitment to peace and disarmament," commented *Booklist* critic Ray Olson in a review of the latter title. In *Children of Vietnam,* Lifton, collaborating with Thomas C. Fox, gathered the recollections of youthful victims of the war—including an eyewitness account of the My Lai massacre. A *Publishers Weekly* reviewer remarked that Lifton's interviews with these children "reveal with stark simplicity the cruel idiocy of war." Writing in *Booklist,* Elinor Walker called the book "a telling commentary on the Vietnam War." *Children of Vietnam* was nominated for the National Book Award.

Other books from Lifton reflect her interest in adoption. For adults and young adults she has written several nonfiction titles, including *Twice Born: Memoirs of an Adopted Daughter,* "a parable about the search for identity," according to Julia Whedon, writing in the *New York Times Book Review.* Her 1979 *Lost and Found: The Adoption Experience,* continues in the same vein with Lifton arguing for open adoption and describing her own arduous struggles to find her biological mother. In 1994, Lifton continued this discourse on adoption with *Journey of the Adopted Self: A Quest for Wholeness,* blending interviews with adoptees with her own experience as an adopted child to describe the cumulative closed adoption process, a policy that Lifton claims forces trauma on adoptees. According to Lifton and

Blending interviews with adoptees with her own experience as an adopted child, Lifton describes the cumulative closed adoption process, a policy that Lifton believes forces trauma on adoptees. (Cover photo by Sally S. Fine.)

others, the tangle of emotional pain and confusion that many adoptees suffer could be alleviated if birth records were open and the adopted children could discover their roots. Genevieve Stuttaford, reviewing the book in *Publishers Weekly,* acknowledged that Lifton had written before on the subject of open adoption, but termed this a "more profound investigation of the trauma." Stuttaford pointed out that Lifton omitted the role of the father in much of the debate and paid little attention to cases in which the birth mother is unfit to raise a child, but concluded that it was an "eloquent book."

Written specifically for younger readers on the subject of adoption are Lifton's novel, *I'm Still Me,* and her picture book, *Tell Me a Real Adoption Story.* In the former title, Lori, a high school junior, is inspired by a history assignment to explore her roots and to finally search for her biological parents. Along the way she tries to deal with feelings of abandonment and her guilt at keeping the search a secret from her adoptive parents, whom she loves. Finally finding her birth mother, Lori discovers ambivalent feelings for this woman who put her up for adoption. Reviewing the novel in *Bulletin of the Center for Children's Books,* Sutherland noted that there had been many such books of a child's search for birth parents, but that *I'm Still Me* "treats the subject with far more depth and sensitivity than the others." With *Tell Me a Real Adoption Story,* a little adopted girl is frightened by the made-up tales of adoption her mother gives her, wanting instead her own story. Only when her mother tells her this real story, does the little girl feel relieved. Written in dialogue form, the book presents frequently asked questions from adopted children. *Booklist*'s Stephanie Zvirin pointed out, "Parents and children can use the book as a model for working out their own discussion."

Additionally, in *The King of Children,* Lifton has written a biography of Janusz Korczak, a little-known Holocaust figure. In a way, such a project was a blending of interests for Lifton, dealing both with the plight of children and adoption, for Korczak, a Polish Jew, was an early espouser of children's rights. A doctor, children's book writer, and educator, Korczak ran an orphanage in pre-World War II Warsaw that allowed children a voice in the decision-making process. When the Nazis began rounding up the Warsaw Jews and shipping them to certain death at the Treblinka concentration camp, Korczak—who had the possibility of escape—stayed with the two hundred children in his orphanage and died with them in the gas chambers. A contributor for *Kirkus Reviews* claimed the book was "[a]n important and affecting addition ... to the history of the Nazi horror—and of the struggle for the establishment of children's rights." Writing in the *New York Times Book Review,* Geoffrey Wolff felt the book "displays the biographer's story-telling skill, her ability to ... move the emotions as well as the tale."

According to many critics, Lifton brings this same emotive skill to all her work, whether it be a retold folktale from Japan or the account of a troubled adopted child. Working from her dual interests in Asian cultures and in the subject of adoption, Lifton has created both fiction and nonfiction for readers old and young which open doors and provoke discussion.

Works Cited

Borland, Hal, review of *Taka-Chan and I, New York Times Book Review,* November 5, 1967, p. 68.

Bull, Ruth P., review of *The Cock and the Ghost Cat, Booklist,* October 1, 1965, p. 55.

Review of *Children of Vietnam, Publishers Weekly,* November 27, 1972, p. 40.

Heins, Ethel L., review of *Joji and the Amanojaku, Horn Book,* June, 1965, p. 269.

Heins, Paul, review of *The Mud Snail Son, Horn Book,* August, 1971, p. 380.

Hine, Al, review of *The Cock and the Ghost Cat, New York Times Book Review,* November 7, 1965, p. 55.

Review of *The King of the Children, Kirkus Reviews,* February 15, 1988, p. 264.

Moe, Christian H., "Lifton, Betty Jean," *St. James Guide to Children's Writers,* 5th edition, edited by Sara Pendergast and Tom Pendergast, St. James Press, 1999, pp. 650-51.

Moulton, Priscilla L., review of *The Rice-Cake Rabbit, Horn Book,* April, 1966, p. 191.

Olson, Ray, review of *A Place Called Hiroshima, Booklist,* October 1, 1985, p. 188.

Stuttaford, Genevieve, review of *Journey of the Adopted Self, Publishers Weekly,* February 21, 1994, p. 242.

Sutherland, Zena, review of *I'm Still Me, Bulletin of the Center for Children's Books,* April, 1981, p. 155.

Sutherland, Zena, review of *Kap and the Wicked Monkey, Bulletin of the Center for Children's Books,* July, 1968, p. 162.

Walker, Elinor, review of *Children of Vietnam, Booklist,* February 15, 1973, p. 569.

Whedon, Julia, review of *Twice Born, New York Times Book Review,* November 2, 1975, pp. 38-39.

Wolff, Geoffrey, "A Saint's Life in Warsaw," *New York Times Book Review,* July 31, 1988, p. 16.

Zvirin, Stephanie, review of *Tell Me a Real Adoption Story, Booklist,* June 1 & 15, 1994, p. 1841.

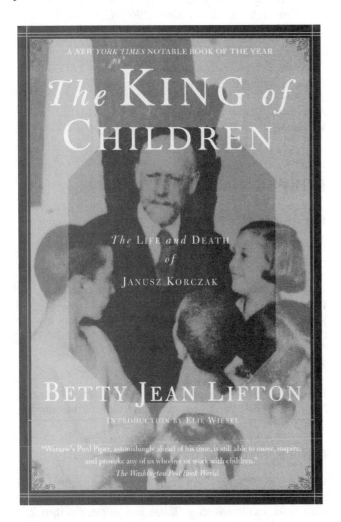

Lifton's compelling biography narrates the life story of the Polish doctor and early espouser of children's rights who gave his life during the Holocaust rather than abandon the children he cared for in his orphanage.

For More Information See

BOOKS

Authors of Books for Young People, 3rd edition, Scarecrow, 1990.
Third Book of Junior Authors, H. W. Wilson, 1972.

PERIODICALS

Booklist, November 1, 1968, p. 314; April 15, 1994, p. 1490.
Bulletin of the Center for Children's Books, October, 1965, p. 35; April, 1968, p. 130; September, 1970, p. 14; December, 1970, p. 62; May, 1972, p. 142; June, 1973, p. 158.
Horn Book, July-August, 1994, p. 442.
Library Journal, August, 1988, p. 157; March 1, 1994, p. 105.
New Republic, June 6, 1988, pp. 44-49.
New York Review of Books, September 29, 1988, pp. 7-10.
New York Times Book Review, November 19, 1968, p. 67; May 2, 1971, p. 45; February 1, 1981, p. 35; May 1, 1994, p. 21; August 24, 1997, p. 24.
People Weekly, August 26, 1985, p. 22.
Publishers Weekly, January 29, 1979, p. 107; June 21, 1985, p. 86; July 12, 1985, p. 32.
School Library Journal, October 10, 1976, pp. 108-09; November, 1985, p. 98; July, 1994, p. 79.

* * *

LIONNI, Leo(nard) 1910-1999

OBITUARY NOTICE—See index for *SATA* sketch: Born May 5, 1910, in the Netherlands; died of complications from Parkinson's disease, October 12, 1999, in Siena, Italy. Graphic designer, art director, artist, and author of books for children. Lionni earned a Ph.D. in economics from the University of Genoa in 1935, but worked as a freelance designer until moving to the United States in response to the rise of fascism in Italy. He became art director for the Philadelphia advertising agency N. W. Ayer & Sons in 1939. There he made a name for himself by commissioning artwork from celebrated fine artists such as Fernand Leger, Willem de Kooning, and Alexander Calder in pursuit of ad copy for clients such as Ford Motor Company, General Electric, and *Ladies Home Journal.* In 1961, Lionni returned to Italy, where he had spent much of his youth, and remained there until his death, concentrating on his brass and iron sculptures and on writing books for children. His first such work, *Little Blue and Little Yellow,* which remains one of his best known, was conceived as a means of entertaining his grandchildren during a long train ride. In the story, which was illustrated with pieces of paper torn from a handy magazine, Little Blue and Little Yellow have a variety of adventures, culminating in a game of hide-and-seek in which they lose each other, only to be reunited behind a tree where they hug, becoming Little Green. A *New York Times* Best Illustrated Book, *Little Blue and Little Yellow* is now considered a classic of children's literature, offering a story that is both a basic lesson in color mixing and an insightful look at integration, individuality, family acceptance, and the

personal changes friendship brings. Commentators have appreciated Lionni's ability to make his viewers more aware of the natural world through his illustrations and the thoughtfulness and subtlety of his texts, while children usually relate to Lionni's imaginative cut-outs, finger paintings, construction paper scraps, and other media for their similarity to kindergarten art. Lionni received Caldecott Honor Book citations for *Inch by Inch* in 1961, *Swimmy* in 1964, *Frederick* in 1968, and *Alexander and the Wind-up Mouse* in 1970. In addition to a number of other awards for individual titles, Lionni was given a Recognition of Merit Award by the George G. Stone Center for Children's Books for his body of work in 1976, and received a gold medal from the American Institute of Graphic Arts in 1984. Lionni's last picture book, *An Extraordinary Egg,* was published in 1994. Three years later, the author published his memoirs, *Between Worlds: The Autobiography of Leo Lionni.*

OBITUARIES AND OTHER SOURCES:

BOOKS

Dictionary of Literary Biography, Volume 61: *American Writers for Children since 1960,* Gale, 1987.
St. James Guide to Children's Writers, St. James Press, 1999.

PERIODICALS

Chicago Tribune, October 18, 1999, sec. 2, p. 6.
Los Angeles Times, October 18, 1999, p. A18.
New York Times, October 17, 1999, p. A51.
Washington Post, October 18, 1999, p. B6.

* * *

LOEPER, John J(oseph) 1929-

Personal

Born July 9, 1929, in Ashland, PA; son of Peter H. (in retail business) and Mary M. Loeper; married Jane Knawa, June 13, 1959. *Education:* College of New Jersey, B.S. and M.A.; also attended University of Pennsylvania, Rutgers University, and Pennsylvania State University. *Politics:* Republican. *Religion:* Roman Catholic.

Addresses

Home—25204 Pelican Creek Circle, #103, Bonita Springs, FL 34134. *Agent*—Marian Reiner, 20 Cedar St., #102, New Rochelle, NY 10801-5248.

Career

Worked as teacher, guidance counselor, and school administrator in New Jersey and Pennsylvania. Artist, with work exhibited in galleries and museums throughout the United States and at a solo show, New York City, 1986; art appears on book covers and in advertising promotions. New Hope-Solebury School District, president of school board, 1969-72; New Hope-Solebury

Free Library, president. *Member:* Hatboro Historical Society (president and founder), New Hope Historical Society (vice president), Historical Archaeological Review Board, Collier County, FL.

Awards, Honors

American Educators Medal, Freedoms Foundation, 1965; named Knight of Order of the Holy Sepulchre by Pope John Paul II, 1995; Hands across the Sea, English Speaking Union.

Writings

Men of Ideas, illustrated by James McCrea and Ruth McCrea, Atheneum (New York City), 1970.
Going to School in 1776, Atheneum, 1973.
The Flying Machine: A Stagecoach Journey in 1774, Atheneum, 1976.
The Golden Dragon: By Clipper Ship around the Horn, Atheneum, 1978.
The Shop on High Street: The Toys and Games of Early America, Atheneum, 1978.
Mr. Marley's Main Street Confectionery: A History of Sweets and Treats, Atheneum, 1979.
Galloping Gertrude: By Motorcar in 1908, Atheneum, 1980.
By Hook and Ladder: The Story of Fire Fighting in America, Atheneum, 1981.
Away We Go! On Bicycles in 1898, Atheneum, 1982.
The House on Spruce Street, self-illustrated, Atheneum, 1982.

Going to School in 1876, Atheneum, 1984.
Crusade for Kindness: Henry Bergh and the ASPCA, Atheneum, 1991.
Meet the Dudleys in Colonial Times, Marshall Cavendish (Tarrytown, NY), 1999.
Meet the Allens in Whaling Days, Marshall Cavendish, 1999.
Meet the Drakes on the Kentucky Frontier, Marshall Cavendish, 1999.
Meet the Wards on the Oregon Trail, Marshall Cavendish, 1999.
Meet the Webbers of Philadelphia, Marshall Cavendish, 1999.

Contributor to reading books and social studies textbooks. Contributor of articles and poems to professional journals, popular magazines, and newspapers.

Sidelights

John J. Loeper told *SATA:* "I have written several books for young readers. One, *Going to School in 1776,* has celebrated its twenty-eighth year in print. My books deal with Americana. In 1997, Benchmark Books (Marshall Cavendish) requested a series on the American family. One of them, *Meet the Dudleys in Colonial Times,* is based on the family of John Dudley, who came to Guilford, Connecticut, around 1670. Other books deal with families from Kentucky, California, Nantucket, and Philadelphia. All are based on actual families."

M–N

MACKALL, Dandi D(aley) 1949-

Personal

Born March 24, 1949, in Kansas City, MO; daughter of F. R. (a physician) and Helen (a nurse; maiden name, Eberhart) Daley; married Joseph S. Mackall (a professor and writer); children: Jennifer, Katy, Dan. *Education:* University of Missouri—Columbia, B.A., 1971; University of Central Oklahoma, M.A., 1989; also attended Institute of Biblical Studies, Arrowhead, CA, Trinity Evangelical Divinity School, and Southern Nazarene University. *Politics:* Independent. *Religion:* Christian.

Addresses

Home and office—1254 Tupelo Lane, West Salem, OH 44287. *E-mail*—dmackall@ashland.edu. *Agent*—Elizabeth Frost Knappman, New England Publishing Associates, Inc., P.O. Box 5, Chester, CT 06412.

Career

Freelance manuscript reviewer and editor, 1978-86; University of Central Oklahoma, Edmond, lecturer in writing for the children's literature market, 1986-89; freelance writer and public speaker, 1989—. Southwest Community College, Creston, IA, instructor, 1984-86; Southern Nazarene University, instructor, 1986-89; Ashland University, instructor, 1990-94; Institute of Children's Literature, instructor. Speaker at more than seventy-five "young authors" programs; guest on television and radio programs. *Member:* Society of Children's Book Writers and Illustrators (religious coordinator, 1990-94).

Writings

The Blessing Is in the Doing, Broadman (Nashville, TN), 1983.
A Spiritual Handbook for Women, Prentice-Hall (Englewood Cliffs, NJ), 1984.
Remembering..., Tyndale (Wheaton, IL), 1985.

When the Answer Is No, Broadman, 1985.
(Contributor) *Christmas Programs for Organizations,* Standard Publishing (Cincinnati, OH), 1986.
The Best Christmas Ever, Standard Publishing, 1986.
A Secret Birthday Gift, Standard Publishing, 1987.
A Super Friend, Standard Publishing, 1987.
Me First, Standard Publishing, 1987.
Splitting Up: When Your Friend Gets a Divorce, Harold Shaw (Wheaton), 1988.
Allyson J. Cat, Standard Publishing, 1989.
Just One of Me, Harold Shaw, 1989.
Allyson J. Cat Coloring Book, with cassette, Standard Publishing, 1989.
The Christmas Gifts That Didn't Need Wrapping, illustrated by Mathers, Augsburg-Fortress (Minneapolis, MN), 1990.
It's Only Ali Cat, Standard Publishing, 1990.
An Ali Cat Christmas, illustrated by Kathryn Hutton, Standard Publishing, 1991.
Kay's Birthday Surprise, illustrated by Dawn Mathers, Augsburg-Fortress, 1991.
Kids Are Still Saying the Darndest Things, Prima Publishing (Rocklin, CA), 1993.
A Gaggle of Galloping Ghosts, Hanna Barbera, 1995.
No Biz like Show Biz, Hanna Barbera, 1995.
Millionaire Astro, Hanna Barbera, 1995.
Home Sweet Jellystone, Hanna Barbera, 1995.
Kids Say the Greatest Things about God: A Kid's-Eye View of Life's Biggest Subject, Tyndale, 1995.
Seasons, Landoll's, 1995.
Baby Animals, Landoll's, 1995.
Secret Night, Landoll's, 1995.
Who's a Goblin?, Landoll's, 1995.
The Halloween Secret, Landoll's, 1995.
Circus Counting, Landoll's, 1995.
ABC's of Lunch, Landoll's, 1995.
Things That Go, Landoll's, 1995.
Bugs and Butterflies, Landoll's, 1995.
Under the Water, Landoll's, 1995.
Santa's Toy Shop, Landoll's, 1995.
Scooby Doo and Scrappy in 1.2.3, Hanna Barbera, 1996.
Pebbles and Bamm Bamm in a Colorful Game, Hanna Barbera, 1996.

Dandi D. Mackall

Jetsons in Shapes, Hanna Barbera, 1996.

Yogi and Boo Boo ABC's, Hanna Barbera, 1996.

Kindred Sisters: New Testament Women Speak to Us Today; A Book of Meditation and Reflection, Augsburg, 1996.

Picture Me at Walt Disney World's 25th Anniversary, Disney, 1997.

Chicken Soup for the Kid's Soul, Batgirl, 1998.

Problem Solving, Ferguson (Chicago, IL), 1998.

Teamwork Skills, Ferguson, 1998.

Self-Development, Ferguson, 1998.

Easter Adventure, Concordia, 1998.

(Compiler) *Why I Believe in God: And Other Reflections by Children,* Prima Publishing, 1999.

Portrait of Lies, created by Terry Brown, Tommy Nelson (Nashville), 2000.

Off to Bethlehem!, HarperCollins (New York City), 2000.

No, No Noah!, Broadman, 2000.

The Big-Mouth Lion, Broadman, 2000.

Mary's Donkey, Broadman, 2000.

Moses, Pharaoh, and the Snake, Broadman, 2000.

Silent Dreams, Eerdmans, 2001.

Other books include the pop-up books *Daniel and the Lion's Den, Noah's Ark,* and *Jonah and the Whale,* all 1995; *The Princess and the Pea* and *Town and Country*

Mouse; titles in the "My First Book" series include *My First Book of Words, My First Book of Numbers, My First Book of Toys, My First Book of Shapes, My First Book of Colors,* and *My First Book of Time.* Author of a humor column, published in an Iowa newspaper, 1984-86. Contributor to magazines around the world, including *Guidepost, Moody Monthly, Christianity Today, Power for Living, Christian Parenting,* and *Today's Christian Woman.* Creator of text for greeting cards.

"CINNAMON LAKE" MYSTERY SERIES

The Secret Society of the Left Hand, illustrated by Kay Salem, Concordia (St. Louis, MO), 1996.

The Case of the Disappearing Dirt, illustrated by Salem, Concordia, 1996.

The Cinnamon Lake Meow Mystery, illustrated by Salem, Concordia, 1997.

Don't Bug Me Molly!, illustrated by Salem, Concordia, 1997.

Of Spies and Spider Webs, illustrated by Salem, Concordia, 1997.

The Cinnamon Lake-ness Monster, illustrated by Salem, Concordia, 1997.

Soup Kitchen Suspicion, illustrated by Salem, Concordia, 1998.

The Presidential Mystery, illustrated by Salem, Concordia, 1999.

"HORSEFEATHERS!" SERIES; YOUNG ADULT NOVELS

Horsefeathers!, Concordia, 2000.
Horse Cents, Concordia, 2000.
A Horse of a Different Color, Concordia, 2000.
Horse Whispers in the Air, Concordia, 2000.
Horse Angels, Concordia, 2000.
Home Is Where Your Horse Is, Concordia, 2000.

"KIDS SAY" SERIES

(Compiler) *Kids Say the Cutest Things about Mom!,* Trade Life Books (Tulsa, OK), 1996.
(Compiler) *Kids Say the Cutest Things about Dad!,* Trade Life Books, 1997.
Kids Say the Cutest Things about Love, Trade Life Books, 1998.
Why I Believe in God: And Other Reflections by Children, Prima, 2000.
What Kids Know about Angels, Source Books, 2001.
101 Things Kids Wonder, Source Books, 2001.
101 Commandments . . . of Children, Source Books, 2001.

"LITTLE BLESSINGS" PICTURE BOOKS

Blessings Everywhere, illustrated by Elena Kucharik, Tyndale, 2000.
God Makes Nighttime Too!, illustrated by Kucharik, Tyndale, 2000.
Rain or Shine, illustrated by Kucharik, Tyndale, 2000.
Birthday Blessings, illustrated by Kucharik, Tyndale, 2001.

"PICTURE ME" SERIES

Picture Me as Goldilocks, illustrated by Wendy Rasmussen, Picture Me Books (Akron, OH), 1997.
Picture Me as Jack and the Beanstalk, illustrated by Rasmussen, Picture Me Books, 1997.
Picture Me as Little Red Riding Hood, illustrated by Rasmussen, Picture Me Books, 1997.
Picture Me with Jonah, Picture Me Books, 1997.
Picture Me with Noah, Picture Me Books, 1997.
Picture Me with Moses, Picture Me Books, 1997.
Picture Me with Jesus, Picture Me Books, 1997.

"PUZZLE CLUB" MYSTERY SERIES

The Puzzle Club Christmas Mystery, illustrated by Mike Young Productions, Concordia, 1997.
The Puzzle Club Activity Book, Concordia, 1997.
The Puzzle Club Picture Book, Concordia, 1997.
The Mystery of Great Price, Concordia, 1997.
The Puzzle Club Case of the Kidnapped Kid, Concordia, 1998.
The Puzzle Club Poison-Pen Mystery, Concordia, 1998.
The Puzzle Club Musical Mystery, Concordia, 1998.
The Puzzle Club Meets the Jigsaw Kids, Concordia, 1999.

Author of other books in the series, including *The Counterfeit Caper, The Case of the Missing Memory,* and *The Petnapping Mystery,* published by Concordia between 1997 and 2000.

"READY, SET, READ!" BEGINNING READER SERIES

God Made Me, illustrated by Michelle Neavill, Augsburg-Fortress, 1992.
Jesus Loves Me, illustrated by Kathy Rogers, Augsburg-Fortress, 1994.
So I Can Read, illustrated by Deborah A. Kirkeeide, Augsburg-Fortress, 1994.

Work in Progress

Silent Dreams for Eerdmans (Grand Rapids, MI) expected in 2001; *101 Ways to Talk to God* for Source Books, due in 2001.

Sidelights

Dandi D. Mackall told *SATA:* "I love to write! I even love to rewrite and revise. When I was a ten-year-old tomboy, I won my first contest with fifty words on 'why I want to be bat boy for the Kansas City A's.' But the team wouldn't let a girl be bat boy—my first taste of rejection!

Mackall's uplifting story portrays a girl who sets up her own stable and revels in her intense bond with horses.

"I've amassed drawerfuls of rejections since, but along the way I've hung in there and have seen just over two hundred of my books into print. Last year over one million copies of my works were sold in the United States, with several titles translated into fourteen languages. Three titles in the 'Puzzle Club' mystery series were animated and shown on national television.

"Although I began writing books for grownups—humor, how-to's, inspirationals—when my children were born, I added children's books to the mix. Beginning with board books and baby books when my children were infants, I progressed through picture books and chapter books, middle-grade fiction and nonfiction, never dropping an age group, but simply adding another one. Finally, with our teens all in high school, I've started a new series of young adult fiction, 'Horsefeathers!' I grew up with horses, backyard horses—the kind you keep as friends in your own backyard. It's been great to draw on my earlier horse-loving days to build my main character in the series, a teenaged, female horse whisperer.

"I'm blessed with a husband who is also a writer and understands why the beds aren't made and there's nothing on the table at dinner time, and I'm blessed with children who offer encouragement and a never-ending supply of stories. I believe that God has stories already created for us if we're listening and looking and willing to work like crazy to make those stories the best they can be. I suppose that's really why I write."

For More Information See

PERIODICALS

Booklist, November 1, 1993, p. 500.
Voice of Youth Advocates, August, 1998, pp. 223-24.

*   *   *

MARCELLINO, Fred 1939-

Personal

Born October 25, 1939, in New York, NY; son of Fred (an electrical contractor) and Angela (a homemaker; maiden name, Giambalvo) Marcellino; married Jean Cunningham (an art director), June 30, 1969; children: Nico. *Education:* Attended Cooper Union; Yale University, B.F.A., 1962. *Hobbies and other interests:* Ballet, film, music, theater, and gardening.

Addresses

Home—333 East 30th St., Apt. 16J, New York, NY 10016. *Office*—432 Park Ave. S., New York, NY 10016.

Career

Graphic artist and illustrator. Worked variously as designer of record album covers and book dust jackets; illustrator of books for children and middle readers. *EXHIBITIONS:* "Best Picture Books," Donnell Library, New York City, 1991; "The Art of Children's Book Illustration," Montclair Art Museum, New Jersey, 1991; "The Original Art," Society of Illustrators, 1991.

Awards, Honors

Fulbright fellow, 1963; Best Cover Design, American Book Awards, 1980, 1982, and 1983; Off-the-Cuff (Cuffies) Award for most promising new artist, *Publishers Weekly,* and Randolph Caldecott Honor Book citation, American Library Association (ALA), both 1990, both for *Puss in Boots;* Notable Children's Book citation, ALA, for *The Story of Little Babaji* and *Ouch!: A Tale from Grimm.*

Writings

I, Crocodile, edited by Michael di Capua, HarperCollins, 1999.

ILLUSTRATOR

Tor Seidler, *A Rat's Tale,* Farrar, Straus, 1986.
Charles Perrault, *Puss in Boots,* translated by Malcolm Arthur, Farrar, Straus, 1990.
Hans Christian Andersen, *The Steadfast Tin Soldier,* retold by Tor Seidler, HarperCollins, 1992.
Tor Seidler, *The Wainscott Weasel,* HarperCollins, 1993.
Edward Lear, *The Pelican Chorus and Other Nonsense,* HarperCollins, 1995.
Helen Bannerman, *The Story of Little Babaji,* HarperCollins, 1996.
Brothers Grimm, *Ouch!: A Tale from Grimm,* retold by Natalie Babbitt, HarperCollins, 1998.
E. B. White, *Trumpet of the Swan,* HarperCollins, 2000.

Sidelights

Award-winning children's author and illustrator Fred Marcellino developed an interest in art as a young boy. Refining his creative abilities in high school and college, he turned his talents into a career, eventually becoming a designer of record album covers and book dust jackets. Marcellino first broke into print when he produced the black and white illustrations for *A Rat's Tale,* Tor Seidler's 1986 novel for middle readers; he created his first full-color picture book in 1990. That work, a retelling of Charles Perrault's seventeenth-century classic folktale *Puss in Boots,* won Marcellino widespread critical acclaim as well as a prestigious Randolph Caldecott Honor Book citation for excellence in children's book illustration. Marcellino continued to illustrate others' stories until 1999, when his first self-illustrated story, *I, Crocodile,* appeared to rave reviews.

Marcellino considers his own pursuit of a career in art to be closely tied to his sister's involvement in the craft. He believes that if he alone had dabbled in art, he might have been urged by his parents to channel his energies into different areas. "In school I certainly was encouraged to pursue art, and it was very much a part of my early identity being the kid who could draw," Marcellino once recalled in an interview with *Something about the Author (SATA).* "It gave me a special feeling—it drew a lot of attention to myself and was also what I enjoyed doing."

Marcellino remembers that comic book and cartoon art most influenced him in his childhood, and that he had very few books. "I thought Walt Disney characters were just wonderful and adored the funnies," he recounted. "It wasn't until I was in high school that I discovered the world of painting and sculpture, but my taste was very uninformed—a young person's taste." The first "serious artists" Marcellino admired were nineteenth-century painters like Dutch expressionist Vincent van Gogh and French post-impressionist Paul Gauguin. "These experiences coincided with the first few times I went to museums by myself," the artist conceded. "I always went to museums as a kid, but I was sort of dragged there. When you go by yourself, it's a different experience."

Unlike many artists, Marcellino received extensive training in high school. "I had a very unusual art department—for a New York City school—at Bayside High School," the designer surmised. "Philip Frankle, the head of the art department in my school, modeled classes after those of his mentor, Leon Friend, who was a very famous teacher during the 1930s and 1940s. My education at Bayside was very unusual and extremely intense for a high school, especially a public school art department. Mr. Frankle was quite an inspiration. I don't think I would have then gone on to Cooper Union if it wasn't for his advice. It's probably one of the smartest things I ever did."

While at Cooper, Marcellino became involved with a theater group, designing stage sets. He also spent one summer vacation as the scenic designer for a friend's theater troupe at Princeton University. "That was an adventure; I don't think I've ever worked so hard in my life," the artist commented. Next, Marcellino moved on to Yale University and eventually went to Italy on a Fulbright fellowship. During college, he considered a career in architecture, but opted to study painting and sculpture. "At one point I became terribly snobbish about the idea of being a painter and anything less than that wasn't enough," he noted. "I had a very singular kind of attitude toward fine arts. I changed afterward when I tried to really figure out who I was and where my abilities really lie."

After college, some of Marcellino's first assignments were spot illustrations for *New York* magazine. He also began to design record album covers. Stints in preparing promotional materials and advertisements followed. When he moved into the arena of book jackets and covers, Marcellino found his career "really took off." He once told *SATA,* "That's when I really discovered more or less who I was and what I wanted to do."

Marcellino's first venture in illustrating an entire book came with Tor Seidler's 1986 middle reader novel, *A Rat's Tale.* The fantasy describes a community of rats who live in the wharf district of Manhattan, a borough of New York, and explores the complexities of human existence through the personification of rodents as it follows the coming-of-age adventures of Montague Mad-Rat the Younger. Paralleling human society, the rat community has its variant forms of bigotry and prejudice. For example, Montague and his family are viewed as lower class because they work with their paws, live in sewers, and sometimes associate with people. But when the rat race needs fifty thousand dollars to bribe the human who is slowly poisoning the community, the rodents find that only the diligent craftsmanship of the Mad-Rat family can save them in time. During the desperate quest for survival, Montague meets and eventually befriends his estranged uncle, Montague Mad-Rat the Elder, whose odd behavior once made the younger rat curse the family name. Through this experience, the nephew learns to believe in himself and eventually wins the heart of a beautiful she-rat.

Using black and white illustrations, Marcellino sought to capture and enhance the humor found in Seidler's story. For example, when a young, aristocratic rodent in *A Rat's Tale* discovers that his tail has been contaminated with poison, Marcellino presents the ill rat resting in a fancy high-heeled slipper—his neatly bandaged tail protruding from the shoe's opening at the toe. A rat doctor, or rather a ratitioner, is shown holding a human wristwatch, which is nearly as large as he is, as he takes the youth's pulse. In another drawing, the artist features Montague's love interest, Isabel Moberly-Rat, relaxing in a bubble bath in an empty ham can. Her mother sits on the edge of the tub, a towel over her shoulder and deep concern on her face, as she quizzes her young daughter about her newfound friendship with the lower-class Montague.

"What I liked about the world Seidler created in the book was that it was highly illustratable," Marcellino once told *SATA.* "The basic situations just cried out for pictures. Sometimes you read a book and you don't want it visualized for you—the images would be better left to your imagination. But in *A Rat's Tale,* the situations with the rats in New York City entice the reader to want to see what it looks like." Marcellino explained that the book's humorous text was his "way into the illustration to a great extent."

Marcellino confessed that he and Seidler did not work closely together when producing *A Rat's Tale.* They essentially operated through Farrar, Straus and Giroux editor Michael di Capua, although Seidler and the artist conversed frequently. "It seemed to work out very well," Marcellino admitted. "I think an author needs, or rather has to be, distant from the text. He has to trust the illustrator and be able to accept his vision of it—be somewhat open-minded about it." The artist added, "With *A Rat's Tale,* I believe there were times when Tor wanted to say that he didn't imagine an illustration done in a certain way, but he held back. And in the end, I think he was glad that he didn't speak out as the book turned into something he couldn't have imagined, but something he was very pleased with."

Various critics were also charmed by the message and illustrations in *A Rat's Tale*. Marcellino's art is said to add significantly to the warmth and depth of the book. "The quiet, gray pencil illustrations," according to reviewer Ann A. Flowers in *Horn Book*, "bring out the humorous aspects of the story ... and the book design is elegantly simple."

Despite the success of *A Rat's Tale*, Marcellino had yet to realize his ultimate ambition of illustrating a full-color children's book. "I've always wanted to do a book," explained Marcellino to *SATA* once. "I chose *Puss in Boots* because the level of humor in it really attracted me as did the extraordinary possibilities for illustration." Marcellino acknowledged that the challenge of designing a book that has been told and illustrated many times is a good way to introduce oneself in the competitive field of children's book illustration. "It puts you in a position where everyone who looks at the book will measure you against the past and the way other people have done the book," the artist observed.

Marcellino's illustrations capture the subtle richness of Tor Seidler's tale of weasel Bagley Brown, Jr., who wrestles with an inferiority complex because of the unparalleled fame of his deceased father and his unrequited love for a beautiful fish. (From The Wainscott Weasel.*)*

Marcellino's version of the 1697 fairy tale, dedicated to his son, Nico, was translated by Malcolm Arthur. It colorfully presents the adventures of a spirited cat named Puss who, up until his master's death, had lived a relatively quiet life chasing rats and mice. When the master's three sons divide his property, the two eldest receive a mill and a donkey, respectively. The youngest son inherits the only remaining possession—the faithful feline. Soon, Puss's new owner begins to fear that without the money or resources similar to those left to his brothers, he will perish. Devising a plan to help his young master, Puss dons a pair of knee-high boots and leaves his little village. He then captures a rabbit and presents it to the king on behalf of his owner.

Continuing to kill wild game for the king's supper, the clever cat attempts to impress the royal leader further by creating a new identity for his owner—that of rich nobleman Marquis of Carabas. Puss even forces a group of peasants to tell the king that the lands they harvest belong to the marquis. The feline also tricks the real land baron, an ogre, into surrendering his castle and property. Impressed by the marquis's apparent wealth, the king suggests a marriage between his daughter, a beautiful princess, and Puss's owner. In the end, Puss becomes a nobleman and leads a life of luxury.

Marcellino acknowledged the influence of nineteenth-century French illustrator Paul-Gustave Dore's work on his own drawings for the story, and he paid tribute to the earlier illustrations in subtle ways when he used a similar concept or adaptation. For example, Marcellino saluted Dore in a drawing that depicts Puss as he scares the peasants who, as a result, lie to the king about the ownership of the fields they harvest. "Dore did a wonderful illustration with a circle of peasants bowing down to Puss, which I thought was a brilliant idea," Marcellino recalled. "I couldn't just reproduce it, so I decided to take a different point of view—a very, very *low* point of view which I found very funny—to see the peasants' rear ends sticking up in the air, while preserving Dore's idea of the circle."

Some critics have pointed out the unconventionality of Marcellino's approach to the *Puss in Boots* design, particularly in his placement of the book's title and credits on the back cover. As Marcellino designed the cover, he found that the image of Puss became larger and larger in each of his drafts. His editor at Farrar, Straus and Giroux finally suggested leaving the title and credits off the front cover entirely. "It's the kind of solution only a brilliant editor would ever suggest," Marcellino once told *SATA*. "It's something every designer would like to do—totally unconventional, yet perfectly sensible. However, I'll never be able to do it again; it would completely lose impact the second time around."

A number of critics hailed Marcellino's work in *Puss in Boots* for its originality and brilliant execution. Charles Simic, writing in the *New York Times Book Review*, called the artist's illustrations "fine" and "witty and skillful." Simic noted that Marcellino is "faithful to the

In his pastel illustrations for Tor Seidler's retelling of Hans Christian Andersen's The Steadfast Tin Soldier, *Marcellino aligns the reader's perspective with the tin soldier's, adding emotional depth and interest to the poignant story.*

period, to its costumes, interiors and even cuisine." In a *Washington Post Book World* review, Perry Nodelman also praised Marcellino's "richly detailed" illustrations, asserting that the book is "an impressive debut." The reviewer continued, "These sly, beautiful pictures evoke the ambiguous nature of fairy tales in a way that should please and repay the close attention of both art specialists and children." Marcellino's *Puss in Boots* was also lauded by various groups associated with children's literature. In addition to a Caldecott Honor Book distinction, the illustrated book earned the artist the *Publishers Weekly* Off-the-Cuff (Cuffies) Award as a most promising new artist.

To decide which settings and style of clothing to use in *Puss in Boots,* Marcellino researched the original tale and its time period. As he began work on the story, he tried to present the legend in a fairly accurate historical context while maintaining accessibility to the modern young reader. After a careful study of late seventeenth-

century costuming, for instance, Marcellino opted for a highly stylized and simplified version for his illustrations.

The artist relied on this same research ethic while preparing the illustrations for Tor Seidler's recounting of nineteenth-century Danish storyteller Hans Christian Andersen's *The Steadfast Tin Soldier.* Deducing that the Andersen classic should be set in Copenhagen in the 1850s or 1860s, Marcellino ventured to Denmark to study the city. Despite his extensive research, Marcellino admitted that the presentation would still be his interpretation of the period and place. "It isn't really historically correct," he judged, "but it isn't really wrong, either."

The tale of *The Steadfast Tin Soldier* follows a one-legged tin soldier, so made because his creator ran out of tin before he was finished. Taken to a new home with his twenty-four brothers, the soldier develops an instant affection for his new neighbor, a little lady dancer constructed out of paper and owned by the same family as the tin men. While the soldier dreams of asking the dancer to be his wife, he falls victim to misfortune when he is dropped and lost by his young owner. Soon two neighborhood boys find the soldier amid a rainstorm and set him afloat in a paper boat down a gutter. Chased by a water-rat and later swallowed by a fish, the soldier is finally returned home after the fish is caught and sold to his owner's cook. His reunion is short-lived, however, as another boy places the soldier in the stove to melt. The dancer meets her end at his side after the wind catches her and blows her into the flames as well.

To accompany a story "charged with both romance and heroism," according to a reviewer in *Publishers Weekly,* Marcellino created "masterful pastel illustrations," featuring "alternating perspectives [that] achieve striking visual effect." *Horn Book* reviewer Ellen Fader similarly noted that Marcellino's tendency to align the reader's perspective with the tin soldier's "gives the story a decidedly dramatic appeal." The story is set during the Christmas holidays, corresponding to the original release of the story in 1838, and Marcellino's "pastel tones sparkle with the formal drama of the holiday," Fader continued.

In his interview for *SATA,* Marcellino once asserted that the transition from dust jack design to children's book illustration was easy for him. "I don't think about drawing for children—about what they understand or what they want to see," the artist rendered. "It's the child in me that is in my mind. I don't think I've lost touch with my childhood. Being a child is a part of one's life so I trust myself and assume that if I like it, other adults and children will like it too. I just trust in my own

The story of a self-satisfied crocodile stolen by Napolean's army from the shores of the Nile and deposited in a fountain in the Tuileries, Marcellino's self-illustrated **I, Crocodile** *is a sly commentary on worldly power.*

feelings." Being a father, however, has given him some perspective on what kids like. "I think you can read a child a telephone book, and if it is *you* reading to him, he will love it," the artist concluded. Marcellino further claimed that books like *Puss in Boots* are created for both children and adults and that people of varying ages can derive many different things from the story. "I enjoy what many call children's books, and I think a lot of adults like such books too and buy them for themselves, not for children. Maybe they say a book is for a child as an excuse to buy it for themselves. I would really like to design an illustrated book that didn't have to pretend it was only for children." Some critics contend that Marcellino achieved this aim in his first self-illustrated story, *I, Crocodile,* but first came several illustration projects for other authors.

Garnering comparisons to E. B. White's timeless children's classic, *Charlotte's Web,* Tor Seidler's *The Wainscott Weasel,* with illustrations by Marcellino, goes one step further toward accomplishing the illustrator's ambition to create a book for adult as well as child audiences. In the story of Bagley Brown, Jr., a handsome weasel with an inferiority complex due to the unparalleled stature of his now-deceased father and his unrequited love for a beautiful fish named Bridget, Seidler creates an "animal society [that] is wonderfully amusing and consistent, with entertainingly uneasy relationships between predators and their possible prey," remarked a reviewer for *Kirkus Reviews.* Seidler's characters come to life in Marcellino's black-and-white illustrations, "one of the book's high points," according to Janice Del Negro in *Booklist. Bulletin of the Center for Children's Books* reviewer Roger Sutton compared *The Wainscott Weasel* to E. B. White's classic animal stories and described Marcellino's illustrations as having "an appealingly soft texture but a careful and clever composition that gives them life and humor." In a *Five Owls* review, Stephen Fraser dubbed *The Wainscott Weasel* "a rollicking adventure, a comedy, a love story, and most assuredly a book that will live on in children's memories."

For his next project, Marcellino returned to the realm of classic children's literature, a treasure trove he would return to again and again. In *The Pelican Chorus and Other Nonsense,* the illustrator re-presents three stories by nineteenth-century author Edward Lear, perhaps best known for his "Owl and the Pussycat" rhyme. In addition to that story, this volume contains the little-known tale of "The Pelican Chorus," a send-up of Victorian manners and mores, and "The New Vestments," a version of the traditional folktale "The Emperor's New Clothes." Marcellino's "wildly comic illustrations" ably complement the original poems' epoch and mood, according to a reviewer in *Horn Book. Booklist* reviewer Lauren Peterson stated that the illustrations are "painted so realistically that their absurdity seems totally plausible." Reviewers seemed to suggest that in Marcellino, Lear had found an illustrator whose "exuberant joy," as Kathleen Whalin put it in *School Library Journal,* matches the author's "fine word play." A reviewer for *Publishers Weekly* likewise considered the book ample evidence that Marcellino's artistry was a fine match for Lear's; this critic concluded that *The Pelican Chorus and Other Nonsense* is "a must have for fans of Lear—and of Marcellino."

Marcellino next produced a new version of Helen Bannerman's 1899 classic book for children, *Little Black Sambo,* a story beloved by children for a century but one whose racist language and illustrations ruined the effort for many. Marcellino sets *The Story of Little Babaji* in India, where Bannerman lived for many years, and changes the names of the characters to the more respectful Papaji, Mamaji, and Little Babaji. "Otherwise, the text is the same, and it is a joy to read aloud those simple sentences with their satisfying repetition and rhythm," exclaimed Hazel Rochman in *Booklist.* Marcellino's illustrations infuse the successive confrontations between Little Babaji and the tigers with humor: "The tigers are by turns haughty, intimidating, and immensely silly in their exaggerated preening and posturing," remarked a reviewer for *Publishers Weekly.* A reviewer for *Kirkus Reviews* likewise approved of Marcellino's take on the original rendition: "this remake combines a star illustrator and a story with proven appeal: You can't beat it."

Marcellino's next illustration project, *Ouch!: A Tale from Grimm,* accompanies Natalie Babbitt's retelling of a Brothers Grimm tale, "The Devil with the Three Golden Hairs." In the story, which Marcellino sets in the Middle Ages, a low-born infant is predicted to become the husband of the princess, and when the prediction reaches the king's ears, he does everything in his power to prevent it. First he tricks the boy's parents into giving the child to him, then the king puts him in a box and sets him afloat on the river, expecting that will be the end of the boy. A number of years later, however, the child returns as the miller's adopted son. The king's final trick is to send the young man to the devil with the request of three golden hairs, an impossible task which he is able to accomplish thanks to the unexpected help he receives from the devil's grandmother. "Marcellino's own tricks of light and shadow, expressive portraiture, full-bodied palette, and varied format make this brilliantly designed book a visually piquant feast as well as a verbally fleet feat," contended Betsy Hearne in *Bulletin of the Center for Children's Books.* As in his earlier illustrations for older stories, Marcellino's art work strives to emphasize the humorous aspects of the text, a factor commented upon by Kate McClelland in *School Library Journal:* "With comic perspectives and sly expressions, Marcellino introduces a farcical cast—from the king to the Devil's grandmother." And like critics of Marcellino's earlier works, Hearne noted the "intergenerational" appeal of *Ouch!:* "Read it to everybody you can find. Show them the pictures. Such artistry is a little bit of heaven on earth."

"There are few picture-book artists as gifted or versatile as Fred Marcellino," remarked Selma G. Lanes in *Parents' Choice,* explaining the level of interest elicited by the appearance of Marcellino's first solo publication. In the story of a self-satisfied crocodile stolen by

Napoleon's army from the shores of the Nile and deposited in a fountain in the Tuileries, Marcellino's *I, Crocodile* is a sly commentary on worldly power, and the author's "piece de resistance," according to a *Publishers Weekly* reviewer. The tone of the crocodile's first-person narrative was compared to that of A. Wolf in Jon Scieszka's *The True Story of the Three Little Pigs,* and *Booklist* reviewer Ilene Cooper contended that Marcellino's irresistible protagonist "can get as much out of an eye roll as Groucho Marx." When the French tire of the novelty, the crocodile is slated for the dinner table, but instead slips away into the sewers, from which he intermittently emerges to consume an unwary passer-by. "He's such an engaging sort that readers will surely forgive him," a critic predicted in *Kirkus Reviews,* adding that "a crocodile must eat, after all." The contributor to *Publishers Weekly* went on to say, "Although its plump pickle-shaped body, chubby legs and devastatingly polite manner don't seem threatening, this is one stolen artifact that literally bites back." Perhaps especially pleasing to Marcellino, a reviewer for *Horn Book* claimed "this is one publication with appeal to many different audiences."

When asked to describe his work, Marcellino once told *SATA* that he found his style difficult to characterize. "There is certainly a very traditional look about what I do. But I think one of the things that is different about the appearance of my work is that it has a cinematic quality—modern in the sense that the objects are cut off, or seen from nontraditional viewpoints. It's all a result of trying to wed pictures and words. *Style* for me is a result, not a premise. When you solve all the problems you're faced with in an original manner, you end up with a style."

Works Cited

Cooper, Ilene, review of *I, Crocodile, Booklist,* October 15, 1999, p. 456.

Del Negro, Janice, review of *The Wainscott Weasel, Booklist,* November 1, 1993, p. 519.

Fader, Ellen, review of *The Steadfast Tin Soldier, Horn Book,* March-April, 1993, p. 192A.

Flowers, Ann A., review of *A Rat's Tale, Horn Book,* March-April, 1987, pp. 212-13.

Fraser, Stephen, review of *The Wainscott Weasel, Five Owls,* January-February, 1994, pp. 62-63.

Hearne, Betsy, review of *Ouch!: A Tale from Grimm, Bulletin of the Center for Children's Books,* January, 1999, pp. 159-60.

Review of *I, Crocodile, Horn Book,* January, 2000, p. 67.

Review of *I, Crocodile, Kirkus Reviews,* October, 1999, p. 1647.

Review of *I, Crocodile, Publishers Weekly,* September 27, 1999, p. 103.

Lanes, Selma G., review of *I, Crocodile,* "Parents' Choice," *Amazon,* www.amazon.com/(May 22, 2000).

Marcellino, Fred, telephone interview for *Something about the Author,* conducted by Kathleen J. Edgar, June 11, 1991.

McClelland, Kate, review of *Ouch!: A Tale from Grimm, School Library Journal,* December, 1998, p. 100.

Nodelman, Perry, "The Cat's Pajamas," *Washington Post Book World,* November 4, 1990, p. 19.

Review of *The Pelican Chorus and Other Nonsense, Horn Book,* September-October, 1995, pp. 615-16.

Review of *The Pelican Chorus and Other Nonsense, Publishers Weekly,* May 15, 1995, p. 71.

Peterson, Lauren, review of *The Pelican Chorus and Other Nonsense, Booklist,* September 1, 1995, p. 79.

Rochman, Hazel, review of *The Story of Little Babaji, Booklist,* September 1, 1996, p. 126.

Simic, Charles, "Cats Watch Over Us," *New York Times Book Review,* November 11, 1990, p. 30.

Review of *The Steadfast Tin Soldier, Publishers Weekly,* November 9, 1992, p. 81.

Review of *The Story of Little Babaji, Kirkus Reviews,* July 15, 1996, p. 1044.

Review of *The Story of Little Babaji, Publishers Weekly,* August 5, 1996, p. 441.

Sutton, Roger, review of *The Wainscott Weasel, Bulletin of the Center for Children's Books,* November, 1993, p. 99.

Review of *The Wainscott Weasel, Kirkus Reviews,* September 1, 1993, p. 1151.

Whalin, Kathleen, review of *The Pelican Chorus and Other Nonsense, School Library Journal,* July, 1996, p. 73.

For More Information See

PERIODICALS

Booklist, November 15, 1998, p. 582.

Bulletin of the Center for Children's Books, September, 1995, pp. 19-20; September, 1996, pp. 5-6.

Horn Book, January, 1999, p. 73.

Kirkus Reviews, October 1, 1986; November 1, 1998.

New Statesman, November 27, 1987.

New York Times Book Review, January 25, 1987; March 14, 1999, p. 31.

Publishers Weekly, August 31, 1990; September 20, 1993, p. 73; November 29, 1999, pp. 41, 56.

School Library Journal, October, 1996, p. 84.

Washington Post Book World, January 11, 1987.*

*   *   *

MARCIANO, John Bemelmans

Personal

Son of Barbara Bemelmans; grandson of Ludwig Bemelmans (a writer and illustrator).

Career

Writer and illustrator.

Writings

(With Ludwig Bemelmans) *Madeline in America and Other Holiday Tales* (contains "Madeline in America," "The Count and the Cobbler," "Bemelmans' Christmas Memory," and "Sunshine"), Scholastic Inc. (New York City), 1999.

Enhancing his grandfather's original text and sketches with his own artwork, John Bemelmans Marciano has collected three holiday stories by Ludwig Bemelmans, including one about the inimitable Madeline. (From Madeline in America and Other Holiday Tales.*)*

Bemelmans: The Life and Art of Madeline's Creator, edited by C. Hennessy, illustrated by Ludwig Bemelmans, Viking (New York City), 1999.

For More Information See

PERIODICALS

Oakland Press, January 12, 2000, p. D-3.*

*   *   *

MARTIN, George R(aymond) R(ichard) 1948-

Personal

Born September 20, 1948, in Bayonne, NJ; son of Raymond Collins (a longshoreman) and Margaret (Brady) Martin (employed by a lingerie manufacturer); married Gale Burnick, November 15, 1975 (divorced, 1979). *Education:* Northwestern University, B.S.J. (summa cum laude), 1970, M.S.J., 1971. *Religion:* None.

Addresses

Home—102 San Salvador, Santa Fe, NM 87501. *Agent*—Pimlico Literary Agency, 155 East 77th St., Suite 1A, New York, NY 10021.

Career

Freelance writer and editor, 1979—. Volunteers in Service to America (VISTA), Washington, DC, communications coordinator for Cook County Legal Assistance Foundation, Chicago, IL (in fulfillment of alternative service as a conscientious objector to military service), 1972-74; Continental Chess Association, Mount Vernon, New York, tournament director in Chicago, 1973-75; Clarke College, Dubuque, IA, instructor in journalism, 1976-79. *Member:* Science Fiction and Fantasy Writers of America (South-Central vice president, 1996—), Writers Guild of America (West).

Awards, Honors

World Science Fiction Society, Hugo Award, 1974, for "A Song for Lya"; Hugo Award nominations, 1974, for "With Morning Comes Mistfall," 1976, for "Storms of Windhaven," and 1978, for *Dying of the Light;* Nebula Award nominations, 1974, for "With Morning Comes Mistfall," 1975, for "A Song for Lya," 1976, for "Storms of Windhaven," and 1978, for "The Stone City"; fellow of Bread Loaf Writers Conference, 1977; two Hugo Awards, 1979, for "The Sandkings" and "The Way of Cross and Dragon"; Nebula Awards, Science Fiction Writers of America, 1979, for "The Sandkings" and 1985, for "Portraits of His Children;" *Locus* Awards, 1981, 1982 (received two awards), and 1984; Daikon Award, Japan, for best short fiction in translation, for "Nightflyers"; Balrog Award, 1983, for *The Armageddon Rag;* finalist for Writers Guild Award, 1986;

George R. R. Martin

Gigamesh Award, Spain, 1987, for *Songs the Dead Men Sing;* Daedelus Award, 1987, for *Wild Cards;* Bram Stoker Award, 1987, for "The Pear-Shaped Man"; World Fantasy Award, 1988, for "The Skin Trade."

Writings

NOVELS

Dying of the Light, Simon & Schuster, 1978.
(With Lisa Tuttle) *Windhaven,* Timescape, 1981.
Fevre Dream, Poseidon Press, 1982.
The Armageddon Rag, Poseidon Press, 1983.

SHORT STORY COLLECTIONS

A Song for Lya and Other Stories, Avon, 1976.
Songs of Stars and Shadows, Pocket Books, 1977.
The Sandkings, Timescape, 1981.
Songs the Dead Men Sing, illustrated by Paul Sonju, Dark Harvest, 1983.
Nightflyers, Bluejay Books, 1985.
Tuf Voyaging, Baen Books, 1986.
Portraits of His Children, illustrated by Ron Lindahn and Val Lakey Lindahn, Dark Harvest, 1987.
The Pear-Shaped Man, Pulphouse, 1991.

"WILD CARDS" SERIES; EDITOR

Wild Cards: A Mosaic Novel, Bantam, 1986.
Aces High, Bantam, 1987.
Jokers Wild: A Wild Cards Mosaic Novel, Bantam, 1987.
Aces Abroad: A Wild Cards Mosaic Novel, Bantam, 1988.
Down and Dirty: A Wild Cards Mosaic Novel, Bantam, 1988.
(With Melinda M. Snodgrass) *Ace in the Hole: A Wild Cards Mosaic Novel,* Bantam, 1990.
(With Melinda M. Snodgrass) John J. Miller, *Dead Man's Hand: A Wild Card Novel,* Bantam, 1990.
(With Melinda M. Snodgrass) *One-Eyed Jacks: A Wild Cards Mosaic Novel,* Bantam, 1991.
(With Melinda M. Snodgrass) *Jokertown Shuffle: A Wild Cards Mosaic Novel,* Bantam, 1991.
(With Melinda M. Snodgrass) *Double Solitaire: A Wild Cards Mosaic Novel,* Bantam, 1992.
(With Melinda M. Snodgrass) *Dealer's Choice: A Wild Cards Mosaic Novel,* Bantam, 1992.
(With Melinda M. Snodgrass) *Card Sharks: A Wild Cards Mosaic Novel,* Baen Books, 1993.
(With Melinda M. Snodgrass) *Marked Cards: A Wild Cards Mosaic Novel,* Baen Books, 1994.

"SONG OF ICE AND FIRE" SERIES

A Game of Thrones, Bantam, 1996.
A Clash of Kings, Bantam, 1999.

EDITOR

New Voices in Science Fiction: Stories by Campbell Award Nominees, Macmillan, 1977.
New Voices I: Spellbinding Original Stories by the Next Generation of Science Fiction Greats: The Campbell Award Nominees, Harcourt, 1978.
New Voices II: Spellbinding Original Stories by the Next Generation of Science Fiction Greats: The Campbell Award Nominees, Harcourt, 1979.

New Voices III: Spellbinding Original Stories by the Next Generation of Science Fiction Greats: The Campbell Award Nominees, Berkley Publishing, 1980.

New Voices IV: Spellbinding Original Stories by the Next Generation of Science Fiction Greats: The Campbell Award Nominees, Berkley Publishing, 1981.

(With Isaac Asimov and Martin H. Greenberg) *The Science Fiction Weight-Loss Book,* Crown, 1983.

The John W. Campbell Awards, Volume V, Bluejay Books, 1984.

(With Paul Mikol) *Night Visions 3,* Dark Harvest, 1986, published as *Night Visions: All Original Stories,* Century, 1987, published as *Night Visions: The Hellbound Heart,* Berkley Publishing, 1988.

OTHER

(With Pat Broderick, Neal McPheeters, and Doug Moench) *Sandkings* (graphic novel; based on Martin's short story), DC Graphics, 1987.

Television writings include five episodes for the series *The Twilight Zone,* 1986, and thirteen episodes for the series *Beauty and the Beast,* 1987-90. Contributor to science fiction magazines, including *Analog* and *Science Fiction and Science Fact,* and anthologies. Martin's work has been translated into French, German, Spanish, Italian, Swedish, Dutch, Japanese, Portuguese, Croatian, Russian, Polish, Hungarian, Finnish, and Esperanto.

Adaptations

"Remembering Melody" was adapted for an episode of HBO's *The Hitchhiker,* 1984; "Nightflyers" was adapted for a feature film, Vista Films, 1987; "The Sandkings" was adapted for the premiere episode of Showtime's *Outer Limits,* 1995.

Work in Progress

More titles in the "Song of Ice and Fire" series.

Sidelights

In a field where prolific production is the norm, science fiction and fantasy writer George R. R. Martin has earned an auspicious reputation with a surprisingly small number of works, winning two Nebula awards and three Hugo awards, the most prestigious awards given for science fiction, among his many honors. His novella "The Sandkings" won both the Hugo and Nebula awards in 1979 and was adapted for television; an early horror novel, *The Armageddon Rag,* has achieved cult status; and his short story collections have remained popular over the years. Martin also has edited Bantam's "Wild Cards" series, fifteen novels written by teams of some of science fiction's most popular authors.

Martin's small output is explained in part by the ten years he spent writing for the television and movie industry instead of producing books. For much of the 1980s, Martin worked in Hollywood writing and producing shows such as *Beauty and the Beast* and the remake of *The Twilight Zone,* and writing movie scripts and developing pilots for television series that were never produced. Martin told Michael Levy in a *Publishers Weekly* profile, "I was paid very well, but as a writer I just can't stand spending a year of my life on a project and then nobody sees it except four guys in some office in Burbank." So in the mid-1990s Martin returned to his first love, writing books, and began working on a new fantasy series, "Song of Ice and Fire," projected to be six novels, and considered by Martin to be his *magnum opus.* The series, inspired by the English War of the Roses, was launched in 1996 with *A Game of Thrones,* a novel which Levy called "virtuosic," and continued with the *A Clash of Kings* in 1999. Martin's comeback to the world of sci-fi and fantasy has been welcomed by a fan base eager for more of his imaginary journeys.

Martin was born on September 20, 1948, one of three children of Raymond and Margaret Martin. Growing up in Bayonne, New Jersey, in a solidly working class environment, Martin needed fantasy worlds. "My father was a longshoreman," Martin told Levy, "My mother worked at Maidenform. I grew up in a federal housing project, and we didn't even own a car." As a child, therefore, Martin built "wonderful dreamcastles in my imagination," and this fanciful dream life still influences his fiction. He calls his fascination with the imaginary "a love of the romantic vision," and it was cultivated partly by the reading he did as a youngster, including the works of Robert A. Heinlein, Andre Norton, H. P. Lovecraft, J. R. R. Tolkein, and superhero comics, which he collected. His first "publication" was a letter to the editor of *Fantastic Four* when he was a preteen. The enterprising Martin sold monster stories to neighborhood kids for pennies, the price of which included a dramatic reading by the young author.

Martin went to college at Northwestern University in Evanston, Illinois, where he studied journalism and graduated *summa cum laude* in 1970. That year, at age twenty-one, he sold his first short story, "The Hero," to *Galaxy* magazine; it was published in February 1971. Martin earned his masters degree in journalism, also at Northwestern, in 1971. After graduation, during the final stages of the Vietnam War, he enlisted as a conscientious objector and performed alternate service with VISTA from 1972 to 1974, attached to the Cook County Legal Assistance Foundation.

Martin continued to sell stories during this time, many of them published in *Analog,* whose editor, Ben Bova, was interested in science fiction with edgy, sexy plot lines as well as sociological and anthropological insights. Martin earned both Hugo and Nebula Award nominations for the 1974 story "With Morning Comes Mistfall," the "first story to separate Martin from the scores of other short story writers," according to Don D'Ammassa in *Twentieth-Century Science-Fiction Writers.* In it Martin creates a mysterious world populated by the Wraiths who prey on unsuspecting travelers. In "A Song for Lya," a telepath and an empath travel to a world where converts to a new religion are committing suicide. This story won Martin his first Hugo and also earned a Nebula nomination.

Martin married in 1975 and took a teaching position at Clarke College in Iowa as an instructor in journalism. During these years Martin began work on his first novel, *Dying of the Light,* an interplanetary adventure story with a strong love interest between Earthman Dirk t'Larien and Gwen, who is committed to another elsewhere. On the dying planet of Worlorn, aliens hunt the few remaining inhabitants, and Dirk lends a touch of knightly morality to the proceedings. *Kliatt*'s E. Barbara Boutner, reviewing this book (which had been serialized in *Analog*) thought it was a "fine novel," and one that attempted to "explore grander themes of duty, courage and loyalty." A reviewer for *Publishers Weekly* wrote that Martin's debut novel had "more of the tone of swords-and-sorcery—or, indeed, of Arthurian legend—than of conventional SF." Likewise, Rosemary Herbert, reviewing the novel in *Library Journal,* said, "This tale of both male and female heroism is a refreshing addition to the corpus of science fiction."

In 1978 Martin became writer-in-residence at Clarke College and decided to write full time. Despite the turmoil of a divorce, he produced both novels and short story collections through the early 1980s. *Windhaven,* co-written with Lisa Tuttle, appeared in 1981. It is set on a distant planet whose low gravity enables the inhabitants, descendants of survivors from a stranded starship, to strap wings to their arms and fly. The Flyers live in a structured society, but Maris of Lesser Amberly refuses to give up her wings to a male, and her rebellion against tradition sets off a revolution that changes the entire planet. Roland Green, reviewing the novel for *Booklist,* thought that the collaboration between Martin and Tuttle was successful, producing "excellent characterization, superb prose with a poetic flavor, numerous powerful scenes, and a rich and well-developed background."

Martin also published two well-received collections of short stories, *A Song for Lya and Other Stories* and *Songs of Stars and Shadows.* Reviewing the latter collection in *Booklist,* Dan Miller observed that the stories were "heavily laden with melancholy and pessimism by one of science fiction's brightest young talents." A third collection of short stories, *The Sandkings,* including an award-winning story of that name, was published in 1981. The title story features rich and ruthless Simon Kress who plays godlike games with the intelligent alien bugs he breeds. Martin told David Bischoff of *Omni* that he wanted to see if he could use "the symbols and traditional tropes and images and furniture [of science fiction] to accomplish the goal of scaring the reader, the main thing that drives horror." Critics' responses suggested that he was successful; a reviewer for the *Washington Post Book World* called *The Sandkings* a "terror tour-de-force." Martin utilized his newfound talent for horror in his next two novels.

In Martin's next novel, *Fevre Dream,* Joshua York, a very sallow and strange young man, offers Abner Mash the chance to captain a new luxury steamboat on the condition that he ask no questions about the happenings on board. Marsh eventually figures out that York and his traveling companions are vampires. York then explains

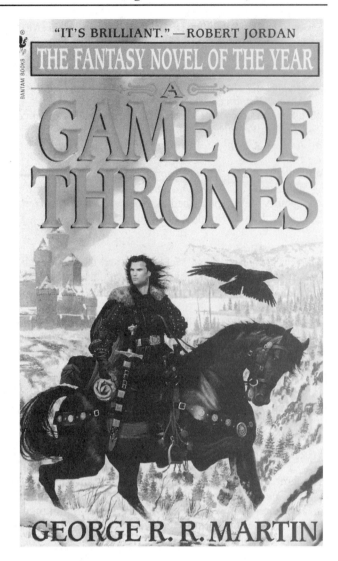

Set in the mythical Seven Kingdoms where the seasons are chimerical, Martin's novel follows protagonist Lord Stark of Winterfell, the king's councilor, as he battles the numerous enemies of the throne. (Cover illustration by Stephen Youll.)

to Marsh that he is a "good" vampire; he has discovered a substitute for blood and is determined to deliver it to all the vampires of the world. However, a rival vampire, Damon Julian, wants no part of the ersatz product, and in the end, Marsh and York must face Julian. A *Kirkus Reviews* critic said that Martin's vampire novel was "firmly grounded in the Twain-worthy steamboat setting" and "abundantly creepy," while Martha Jones of *Library Journal* made note of the author's "fine hand for description [and] creative interpretation of vampire legends."

Martin's next novel again departed from science fiction. *The Armageddon Rag* blends supernatural themes with the world of rock music; "one of the most original, inventive, and best written horror novels of all time," according to D'Ammassa. In the novel, Martin examines the optimistic and enthusiastic generation who attended college in the late 1960s. At the center of the story is a writer, Sandy Blair, who is investigating the ritual murder of rock promoter Jamie Lynch. The trail leads him across America and back in time to the murder of the lead singer of the anarchistic rock group, Nazgul, which had also been promoted by Lynch. Blair meets former members of the group and becomes the public relations man for their comeback. He discovers almost too late that he is a pawn in a "carefully orchestrated game of madness," according to *Booklist*'s Martin A. Brady. "Martin masterfully evokes the aura of tuned-in, turned-on, idealistic youth," Brady commented. Barbara A. Brannon of *Publishers Weekly* called the book "a hallucinatory story by a master of chilling suspense," and *Analog*'s Tom Easton said it was "a cracking good story."

For the next thirteen years, Martin put aside novel writing, although he produced notable collections of short stories such as *Songs the Dead Men Sing, Nightflyers, Tuf Voyaging,* and *Portraits of His Children.* He maintained a busy schedule editing Bantam's "Wild Cards" series and other collections. His focus, however, was in Hollywood, where he wrote scripts for

In his second title about the Seven Kingdoms, Martin introduces a myriad of new characters to his fantasy epic inspired by the English War of the Roses. (Cover illustration by Stephen Youll.)

television series, including *The Twilight Zone,* for which he wrote five scripts, and *Beauty and the Beast,* for which he wrote thirteen episodes. He also wrote numerous unproduced teleplays and screenplays, as well as a pilot for ABC, "Doorways," that was never produced. By the mid-1990s, Martin had had enough of Hollywood and wanted to return to his first love, writing novels.

Martin's agents recommended that he focus on one genre, suggesting that his fans were having difficulty in identifying him as sci-fi or horror. "[S]o my decision then to do a high fantasy book was partly motivated by the Imp of the Perverse in me refusing to be typecast," Martin told Levy of *Publishers Weekly.* He had enjoyed fantasy since he was young, but thought that most fantasy was just "warmed-over Tolkein," as he told Levy. He wanted to create a series that blended a strong historical background with elements of fantasy, but did not overdo the element of magic. To Martin, nothing kills magic more quickly than making it seem commonplace, so he vowed to keep magic magical by using it economically and sparingly. Inspired in part by the War of the Roses, Martin originally planned "Song of Ice and Fire" as a three-book series. He began work on the first novel, *A Game of Thrones,* but when he had written over a thousand pages and was nowhere near the end of the first book, he realized that he would have to make the series much longer. After reshuffling the stories and titles, he decided that he could tell the story in six books.

A Game of Thrones, published in 1996, is set in the mythical Seven Kingdoms where the seasons are chimerical: winter may last for decades in this land; summer may be equally long. It is a land of sword and sorcery, with kings, queens, knights, and lords all vying for the throne. Lord Stark of Winterfell, the protagonist, is the king's councilor, and he needs abundant heroism to battle the enemies of the throne. This first novel since his Hollywood hiatus was welcomed by reviewers and hungry Martin fans. A critic in *Publishers Weekly* declared that Martin "makes a triumphant return ... with this extraordinarily rich new novel." *Booklist*'s Green remarked that "Martin reach[ed] a new plateau" with the novel, and a contributor in *Kirkus Reviews* called *A Game of Thrones* a "vast, rich saga, with splendid characters and an intricate plot flawlessly articulated."

Martin decided to take his time with "Song of Ice and Fire" so that he could develop character and plot beyond the confines of teleplays. He took two years to write the second volume, *A Clash of Kings,* published in 1999. "In the sequel ... Martin skillfully limns the complicated, bitter politics of an inbred aristocracy," wrote Roberta Johnson in a *Booklist* review. Johnson continued, praising Martin's "dark, crisp plotting." Many new characters were introduced in this lengthy installment, including Princess Arya Stark, who battles the forces of darkness to regain her late father's throne, the amoral Queen Cersei, the dwarf Tyrion Lannister, and Prince Brandon, among hundreds of others. A reviewer for *Publishers Weekly* called the entire series "a truly epic

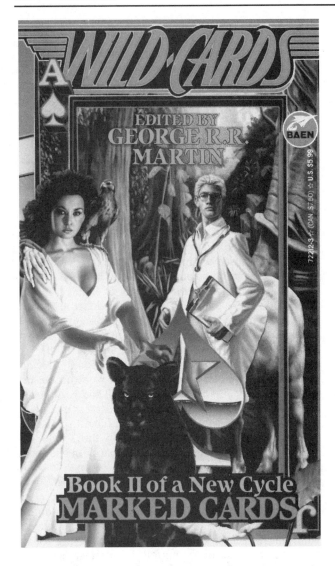

Hannah Davis, the reporter who is the protagonist of Martin's suspenseful novel, uncovers a conspiracy to annihilate those with the wild card virus. (Cover illustration by Barclay Shaw.)

fantasy ... [Martin] provides a banquet for fantasy lovers with large appetites."

One of the problems with epics is the enormous cast of characters—Martin provides a twenty-eight-page list of them. In fact, a writer for *Kirkus Reviews* said that despite the "flawless plotting" and "fully realized characters," the novel's drawbacks included "the impossibility of remembering ... who's who or what's been going on." However, *Library Journal*'s Jackie Cassada commented, "Martin has created a rich world filled with characters whose desire for love and power drive them to extremes of nobility and betrayal."

In his interview with Levy, Martin summed up his desires for "Song of Ice and Fire," which he believes will attract new readers to fantasy. "I hope readers will appreciate my handling of magic, the strong attention to language, characterization, and historical detail, the effort to make the book less predictable.... I want to

provide a journey we haven't taken before, take the readers to new places, show them things that they will remember the rest of their lives." Martin's childhood need for an imaginary place apart from his everyday reality has happily transformed itself into a writing career that has traveled from science fiction to horror to fantasy. His next stop is anybody's guess.

Works Cited

Bischoff, David, "The New 'Outer Limits'," *Omni,* April, 1995, pp. 34-41.

Boutner, E. Barbara, review of *Dying of the Light, Kliatt,* spring, 1979, p. 18.

Brady, Martin A., review of *The Armageddon Rag, Booklist,* September 1, 1983, p. 4.

Brannon, Barbara A., review of *The Armageddon Rag, Publishers Weekly,* October 14, 1983, p. 44.

Cassada, Jackie, review of *A Clash of Kings, Library Journal,* January, 1999, p. 165.

Review of *A Clash of Kings, Kirkus Reviews,* December 1, 1998, p. 1701.

Review of *A Clash of Kings, Publishers Weekly,* December 21, 1998, p. 59.

D'Ammassa, Don, "Martin, George R(aymond) R(ichard)," *Twentieth-Century Science-Fiction Writers,* 3rd edition, St. James Press, 1991, pp. 530-32.

Review of *Dying of the Light, Publishers Weekly,* September 5, 1977, p. 68,

Easton, Tom, review of *The Armageddon Rag, Analog,* March, 1984, pp. 165-66.

Review of *Fevre Dream, Kirkus Reviews,* August 1, 1982, p. 895.

Review of *A Game of Thrones, Kirkus Reviews,* July 1, 1996, p. 936.

Review of *A Game of Thrones, Publishers Weekly,* June 10, 1991, p. 90.

Green, Roland, review of *Windhaven, Booklist,* June 15, 1981, p. 1334.

Green, Roland, review of *A Game of Thrones, Booklist,* August, 1996, p. 1889.

Herbert, Rosemary, review of *Dying of the Light, Library Journal,* October 15, 1977, p. 2185.

Johnson, Roberta, review of *A Clash of Kings, Booklist,* January 1 and 15, 1999, p. 842.

Jones, Martha, review of *Fevre Dreams, Library Journal,* September 15, 1982, p. 1770.

Levy, Michael, "George R. R. Martin: Dreamer of Fantastic Worlds," *Publishers Weekly,* August 26, 1996, pp. 70-71.

Miller, Dan, review of *Songs of Stars and Shadows, Booklist,* October 1, 1977, p. 269.

Review of *The Sandkings, Washington Post Book World,* December 27, 1981, p. 12.

For More Information See

BOOKS

St. James Guide to Horror, Ghost, and Gothic Writers, St. James Press (Detroit, MI), 1998.

PERIODICALS

Booklist, May 15, 1986, p. 1361; March 15, 1993, p. 1301.

Kliatt, July, 1993, p. 18; July, 1994, p. 16; November, 1995, p. 17.
Library Journal, February 15, 1990, p. 215; August, 1990, p. 147.
New York Times, January 12, 1986.
Publishers Weekly, August 20, 1982, p. 59; November 30, 1984, p. 88; January 10, 1986, p. 75; June 12, 1987, p. 75; April 22, 1988, p. 76.
School Library Journal, February, 1983, p. 95.
Washington Post Book World, December 22, 1985, p. 8; July 28, 1996, p. 8.*

—Sketch by J. Sydney Jones

*   *   *

MASOFF, Joy 1951-

Personal

Born September 26, 1951, in Brooklyn, NY; daughter of Edward and Dora (Galperin) Masoff; married Lou Scolnik (a designer), September 17, 1978; children: Alexander James, Tish. *Education:* Pratt Institute, B.F.A., 1973.

Addresses

Home—14 Five Ponds Dr., Waccabuc, NY 10597.
Office—Masoff Scolnik Design, 39 Fields Lane, North Salem, NY 10560. *E-mail*—Joy@webfields.com.

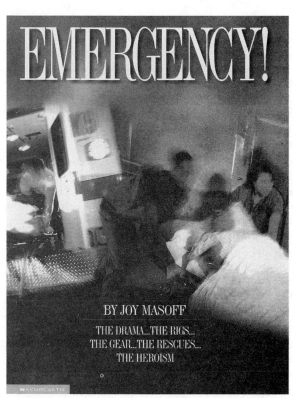

Based on numerous interviews and on-site observations, Joy Masoff's informative book for young readers discusses the personnel, equipment, and procedures involved in emergency medical treatment.

Agent—Michael Congdon, Don Congdon Associates, 156 Fifth Ave., New York, NY 10010.

Career

Reader's Digest Association, Pleasantville, NY, art director, 1978-85; Masoff Scolnik Design, North Salem, NY, co-owner, 1985—.

Awards, Honors

Quick Pick for Reluctant Young Readers, American Library Association, 1999, for *Fire!;* Notable Social Studies Trade Book, The Book Council/National Council for Social Studies, for *Emergency!*

Writings

Fire!, photographs by Jack Resnicki and Barry D. Smith, Scholastic Inc. (New York City), 1998.
Emergency!, Scholastic Inc., 1999.
Oh, Yuck! The Encyclopedia of Everything Nasty, illustrated by Terry Sirrell, Workman Publishing (New York City), 2000.
The Chronicle of America, Volume I: *Colonial Times, 1600-1700,* Volume II: *The American Revolution, 1700-1800,* Scholastic Inc., 2000.

Writer and designer of videotape viewer's guides, including "Walter Cronkite Remembers the 20th Century," "The Living Edens," "Mysteries of the Bible," and "Ancient Mysteries."

Work in Progress

A girls' sports series and internet website.

Sidelights

Joy Masoff told *SATA:* "Sadly, all too often, my 'real' job intrudes on the one I love most—writing for kids aged eight to twelve. Maybe it's the nine years I spent as a scout leader. Maybe it's all the hours I've spent as a soccer, softball, sailing, and basketball mom. Or maybe it's just that in my heart I'm still a ten-year-old, full of a sense of invincibility and the inextinguishable feeling that I can do *anything* I set my mind to. I love seeing the world through younger eyes.

"At any rate, I have a tremendous respect for children. They are bright, curious, clever, and deserving of far more than they usually get. In my books, which I like to think of as 'coffee table books' for kids, I try to mix great photography with lively text—always a little 'hip' and humorous, always visually exciting. That's my challenge, and my joy!"

For More Information See

PERIODICALS

Booklist, January 1, 1999, p. 868.
Bulletin of the Center for Children's Books, April, 1998, p. 289; February, 1999, p. 209.

Horn Book, March-April, 1998, p. 236; March, 1999, p. 227.
Publishers Weekly, December 21, 1998, p. 68.
School Library Journal, March, 1998, pp. 198-99.

* * *

MAYFIELD, Katherine 1958-

Personal

Born April 22, 1958, in St. Louis, MO; daughter of William Allen and Jeroldine (Marquart) Mayfield. *Education:* Loretto Heights College, B.A.; also attended Webster University. *Hobbies and other interests:* Nature, psychology, philosophy, parapsychology.

Addresses

Home—Northampton, MA. *E-mail*—kmayfield1@aol.com.

Career

Pianist for Amherst Ballet and Five College Dance Department in Massachusetts; actress, including appearances in "The Unbelievable Truth" and the television series *Guiding Light;* conducts workshops for actors.

Katherine Mayfield

Writings

Smart Actors, Foolish Choices: A Self-Help Guide to Coping with the Emotional Stresses of the Business, Back Stage Books (New York City), 1996.
Acting A to Z: The Young Person's Guide to a Stage or Screen Career, Back Stage Books, 1998.

Contributor to periodicals, including *Stage Directions, Dance Spirit,* and *Dance Teacher Now.*

Work in Progress

The Dancer's Ultimate Career Guide; Arny the Actor Saves the Day; research on "New Age" topics and parapsychology.

Sidelights

Katherine Mayfield told *SATA:* "I've always loved books, ever since I learned how to read. When I read books, I learn about people and places, ideas and possibilities that I never would have learned otherwise. Books allow you to pick and choose what you want to learn—whether you want to learn about life while reading a mystery or a biography, or while reading about nature or geography or space travel. Books can open up a whole new view of life for those who love them.

"What I love about writing is that I can take an idea, or something I've discovered, and offer it through a book to anyone who wants to learn about it. Each person can choose whether he or she agrees with the author; each person can choose whether to make use of the information. I like the fact that I can put my ideas out there in the world for people to use or not use as they see fit.

"What I wanted to accomplish in writing my books was to offer actors of every age the opportunity to look at the profession of acting from a new perspective. For young actors, *Acting A to Z* explains the acting business clearly and simply, with practical information that's useful in helping them make a career decision. It offers information that actors don't find in the usual media representations of 'show business,' and I hope that it will help young people to discover some truths about the acting business and eliminate some of the illusions surrounding ideas of what it's like to be a professional actor.

"With *Smart Actors, Foolish Choices,* I wanted to offer all actors a new way to see their choice to be an actor, along with new ideas for overcoming some of the emotional stresses involved in pursuing a career. Writing is personally fulfilling for me, both when I'm in the process of working on a book and when I find that others are helped by insights which I can provide. This, I believe, is the best way to approach a career in any field: if it's something you love to do and it helps other people, then it's worthwhile."

For More Information See

PERIODICALS

Kliatt, May, 1999, p. 36.
Voice of Youth Advocates, June, 1999, p. 130.

ON-LINE

Search www.actingbiz.com for articles by the author.

*   *   *

McCULLEN, Andrew
See ARTHUR, Robert (Jr.)

*   *   *

McDONALD, Jamie
See HEIDE, Florence Parry

*   *   *

MEYER, Carolyn (Mae) 1935-

Personal

Born June 8, 1935, in Lewistown, PA; daughter of H. Victor (in business) and Sara (maiden name, Knepp) Meyer; married Joseph Smrcka, June 4, 1960 (divorced, 1973); married E. A. Mares (an author and educator), May 30, 1987; children: Alan, John, Christopher, one daughter. *Education:* Bucknell University, B.A. (cum laude), 1957. *Politics:* Liberal. *Religion:* Episcopalian.

Addresses

Home—Denton, TX. *Office*—1120 N. Locust St., Denton, TX 76201. *Agent*—Amy Berkower, Writers House Inc., 21 W. 26th St., New York, NY 10010.

Career

Worked as a secretary, late 1950s; freelance writer, 1963—. Institute of Children's Literature, instructor, 1973-79; Bucknell University, Alpha Lambda Delta Lecturer, 1974, guest lecturer in children's literature, 1976-78. Presenter at workshops in high schools and colleges. *Member:* Authors Guild, Phi Beta Kappa.

Awards, Honors

Notable Book citation, American Library Association (ALA), 1971, for *The Bread Book,* 1976, for *Amish People,* and 1979, for *C. C. Poindexter;* Children's Book Showcase award, Children's Book Council, 1977, for *Amish People;* Best Books citation, *New York Times,* 1977, for *Eskimos: Growing Up in a Changing Culture;* Best Book for Young Adults citation, ALA, 1979, for *C. C. Poindexter,* 1980, for *The Center: From a Troubled Past to a New Life,* 1985, for *The Mystery of the Ancient Maya,* 1986, for *Voices of South Africa* and *Denny's Tapes,* 1992, for *Where the Broken Heart Still Beats,*

Carolyn Meyer

1993, for *White Lilacs;* YASD Best Books citation, *Voice of Youth Advocates,* 1988, for *Denny's Tapes* and *Voices of South Africa;* Author of the Year Award, Pennsylvania School Librarians Association, 1990.

Writings

NONFICTION FOR YOUNG PEOPLE

Miss Patch's Learn-to-Sew Book, illustrated by Mary Suzuki, Harcourt, 1969.
(Self-illustrated) *Stitch by Stitch: Needlework for Beginners,* Harcourt, 1970.
The Bread Book: All about Bread and How to Make It, illustrated by Trina Schart Hyman, Harcourt, 1971.
Yarn: The Things It Makes and How to Make Them, illustrated by Jennifer Perrott, Harcourt, 1972.
Saw, Hammer, and Paint: Woodworking and Finishing for Beginners, illustrated by Toni Martignoni, Morrow, 1973.
Christmas Crafts: Things to Make the 24 Days before Christmas, illustrated by Anita Lobel, Harper, 1974.
Milk, Butter, and Cheese: The Story of Dairy Products, illustrated by Giulio Maestro, Morrow, 1974.
The Needlework Book of Bible Stories, illustrated by Janet McCaffery, Harcourt, 1975.
People Who Make Things: How American Craftsmen Live and Work, Atheneum, 1975.
Rock Tumbling: From Stones to Gems to Jewelry, photographs by Jerome Wexler, Morrow, 1975.

Amish People: Plain Living in a Complex World, photographs by Michael Ramsey, Gerald Dodds, and the author, Atheneum, 1976.

Coconut: The Tree of Life, illustrated by Lynne Cherry, Morrow, 1976.

Lots and Lots of Candy, illustrated by Laura Jean Allen, Harcourt, 1976.

Eskimos: Growing Up in a Changing Culture, photographs by John McDougal, Atheneum, 1977.

Being Beautiful: The Story of Cosmetics from Ancient Art to Modern Science, illustrated by Marika, Morrow, 1977.

Mask Magic, illustrated by Melanie Gaines Arwin, Harcourt, 1978.

The Center: From a Troubled Past to a New Life, Atheneum, 1980.

Rock Band: Big Men in a Great Big Town, Atheneum, 1980.

(With Charles Gallenkamp) *The Mystery of the Ancient Maya,* Atheneum, 1985, revised edition, Simon & Schuster, 1995.

Voices of South Africa: Growing Up in a Troubled Land, Harcourt, 1986.

Voices of Northern Ireland: Growing Up in a Troubled Land, Harcourt, 1987.

A Voice from Japan: An Outsider Looks In, Harcourt, 1988.

Multicultural Sing and Learn: Folk Songs and Monthly Activities, Good Apple, 1994.

In a Different Light: Growing Up in a Yup'ik Eskimo Village in Alaska, photographs by John McDonald, Simon & Schuster, 1996.

FICTION FOR YOUNG PEOPLE

C. C. Poindexter, Atheneum, 1979.

Eulalia's Island, Atheneum, 1982.

The Summer I Learned about Life, Atheneum, 1983.

The Luck of Texas McCoy, Atheneum, 1984.

Elliott & Win, Atheneum, 1986.

Denny's Tapes, McElderry, 1987.

Wild Rover, McElderry, 1989.

Killing the Kudu, McElderry, 1990.

Japan—How Do Hands Make Peace? Earth Inspectors No. 10, McGraw, 1990.

Where the Broken Heart Still Beats: The Story of Cynthia Ann Parker, Harcourt, 1992.

White Lilacs, Harcourt, 1993.

Rio Grande Stories, Harcourt, 1994.

Drummers of Jericho, Harcourt, 1995.

Gideon's People, Harcourt, 1996.

Jubilee Journey, Harcourt, 1997.

Mary, Bloody Mary, Harcourt, 1999.

Isabel I, Scholastic, 2000.

Anastasia, the Last Grand Duchess, Scholastic, 2000.

"HOTLINE" SERIES; NOVELS FOR YOUNG ADULTS

Because of Lissa, Bantam, 1990.

The Problem with Sidney, Bantam, 1990.

Gillian's Choice, Bantam, 1991.

The Two Faces of Adam, Bantam, 1991.

OTHER

McCall's (magazine), author of columns "Cheers and Jeers," 1967-68, and "Chiefly for Children," 1968-72,

and of multi-part series on crafts and women, and consulting editor for "Right Now" section, 1972. Contributor of articles and book reviews to periodicals, including *Family Circle, Redbook, Golf Digest, Los Angeles Times, Accent on Leisure, Town and Country, Publishers Weekly,* and *Americana.*

Sidelights

The author of over fifty books for young readers, Carolyn Meyer has achieved notable success in both nonfiction and fiction. She has written numerous well-received books based on her encounters with Eskimos, members of Amish religious groups, rock 'n' roll bands, and the peoples of South Africa, Northern Ireland, and Japan. Additionally, she has also produced a score of young adult novels, including award-winners such as *C. C. Poindexter, Denny's Tapes, Where the Broken Heart Still Beats,* and *White Lilacs.* Meyer is also the author of the Bantam "Hotline" series about high schoolers who staff a counseling hotline and confront such strong issues as teen suicide and drug abuse.

As Meyer noted in *Something about the Author Autobiography Series* (*SAAS*), she grew up bookish and shy. "Status in the classroom wasn't my problem," she recalled. "Status on the playground was another matter. I couldn't do ANYTHING, like catching a ball or hitting it, or running fast enough to beat anybody anywhere.... Most of the time I managed to bring an excuse from my mother so I wouldn't have to go out at recess."

But Meyer also developed a way with words and a strong imagination. "Being an only child, a homely child, and an intelligent child, I learned to live a rich inner life," she wrote in *SAAS.* "It was probably an excellent way for any writer to begin." By the time she was in high school, Meyer served as editor of the school newspaper and yearbook. She also held a series of summer jobs in which she wrote advertisements for radio and graduated with hopes of becoming a radio scriptwriter. Meyer went on to Bucknell University—where she majored in English and received high grades—but found upon graduation in 1957 that there were few good jobs available for a woman with a college degree. Unsure how to proceed with her career, she accepted the conventional advice of the day, spending a few years as a secretary before becoming a wife and mother.

Meyer still kept writing, though. First, she tried without success to publish a novel and to sell short stories to the prestigious *New Yorker.* Eventually, she found her first story published in a secretarial magazine. The tale was printed in shorthand, and no one in her family could read it but her. Finally, Meyer wrote her first book—a how-to volume for young girls called *Miss Patch's Learn-to-Sew Book.* Meyer went on to write several more craft books. Then, "as my children became older," she wrote in *SAAS,* "I became less interested in 'how to do it' and more interested in the people who did it." *People Who Make Things: How American Craftsmen Live and Work* became her first effort in researching a book by going beyond the library and out into the wider world. Newly divorced and trying to establish a sense of independence, Meyer traveled throughout the United States, talking to potters, weavers, woodworkers, blacksmiths, and glass-blowers.

Meyer soon worked out a similar formula for her own happiness: she built her life around being a writer and wrote books inspired by her experience of life. One day while visiting her mother in her old hometown of Lewistown, Pennsylvania, Meyer passed an Amish family—one of many in the general area—riding in their horse-drawn buggy. Members of Amish religious groups typically shun much of the technology that has been invented since the original Amish congregations were founded in Germany and Switzerland centuries ago. Meyer, who as a German American is distantly related to the Amish, realized that she had grown up in their presence without ever trying to get to know them. Her curiosity sparked a second journalistic book—*Amish People: Plain Living in a Complex World.* Writing in the *New York Times Book Review,* Edward Hoagland called Meyer's book "an excellent introduction to Amishism."

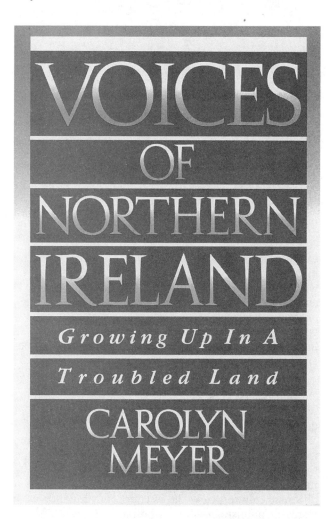

Through interviews with both Protestants and Catholics in Northern Ireland, Meyer fashioned an informative book about the difficulty of living in a country damaged by constant conflict.

Soon thereafter she encountered a white woman who had married into an Eskimo family in Alaska, and the two worked together to describe the woman's new way of life for the book *Eskimos: Growing Up in a Changing Culture.*

Meyer also found that her life and the people she met could form the basis of novels. Her first published novel, *C. C. Poindexter,* is somewhat autobiographical. C. C., a fifteen-year-old girl who is six-foot-one and getting taller, tries to find a sense of direction for her life while watching her parents struggle through the aftermath of divorce. As Meyer noted in her autobiography, "It's really the story of a misfit—C. C.'s height is what separates her from others—and I had plenty of personal experience in that area." This debut novel earned Meyer a "Best Books for Young Adults" citation from the American Library Association and convinced her that her writing could go in nonfiction and fiction directions, both of which she has continued to follow.

One of Meyer's sons helped inspire her second novel. One summer Meyer took her children with her to the Caribbean island of St. Lucia. There, as she researched a fairly conventional book about coconuts, her son had a more eye-opening experience when he became friends with a black family that lived permanently on the island. Meyer adapted her son's adventure for *Eulalia's Island,* in which thirteen-year-old Sam, a morose boy from Pennsylvania, goes along on a family vacation to the Caribbean, meets fourteen-year-old island native Eulalia, and gains a new appreciation of life and himself.

Meanwhile Meyer, who had spent a dozen years living as a housewife in suburban Connecticut, looked around for a new place to live as part of her new life as a professional writer. She finally settled in New Mexico, and then later, with her second husband, moved to Texas. In the years since Meyer went west, many of her young adult novels—including *The Luck of Texas McCoy, Elliott & Win,* and *Wild Rover*—have been set in the region and have been inspired by people she met there. The title character of *Texas McCoy* is a sixteen-year-old girl who inherits a New Mexico ranch and battles successfully to keep it running. "Meyer writes with storytelling flair," said Trev Jones in *School Library Journal,* "and young readers will sense immediately the importance of Texas' inheritance to her."

Elliott & Win tells the story of fourteen-year-old Win who hopes to receive some adult guidance in a Big Brother sort of program, but when he is paired with opera-loving Elliott, he is disappointed. Disappointment soon turns to distrust when a buddy tells Win that Elliott is probably homosexual; however, Win eventually comes to appreciate his new friend. David Gale, writing in *School Library Journal,* called this a "well-crafted story of human concerns."

Another award-winning fiction title from Meyer is the 1987 *Denny's Tapes,* in which the seventeen-year-old boy of the title, the child of a black father and white mother, is caught in the middle of a new marriage. When his mother remarries, Denny finds himself falling in love with his new white stepsister. Thrown out of the house, he drives cross-country in search of his father and his roots. *Booklist*'s Hazel Rochman felt that teens would be interested in "the gritty details of Denny's journey," and "moved by the search for a father which is also a struggle for identity."

Never one to shy away from difficult subjects, Meyer deals with physical disability in *Killing the Kudu.* Eighteen-year-old Alex, a paraplegic, learns to deal with his life, coming to terms with the cousin who caused his disability and finding his first love. Dislocation is the theme of *Where the Broken Heart Still Beats,* a fictionalized account of Cynthia Ann Parker, kidnapped as a child by Comanches and reunited with her biological family twenty-five years later. But once forcibly rejoined with her white relatives, Cynthia feels lost and longs for her Indian life. The only friend she finds in her new life is her adolescent cousin, Lucy, who narrates the tale. Betsy Hearne, writing in *Bulletin of the Center for Children's Books,* dubbed this a "thoughtful and thought-provoking book," while Ann W. Moore called it a "fascinating look at the Comanche and their captives" in a *School Library Journal* review.

More Texas history is served up in the novels *White Lilacs* and *Jubilee Journey,* both of which deal with race relations in a small town. In the first of these companion volumes, the year is 1921 and twelve-year-old Rose Lee watches as her black community is threatened by the whites in the town of Dillon. The white townspeople, wanting to create a park out of a stretch of land where blacks have settled, try to move them to a miserable tract of land outside of town. "Perfectly evoking time and place, Meyer carefully layers detail upon detail," noted Cindy Darling Codell in a *School Library Journal* review of the novel. "Thoughtful readers will hope for an encore," Codell concluded. In 1997, Meyer continued the story in *Jubilee Journey.* This time, many years have passed and Rose Lee's granddaughter and great-grandchildren come south to Dillon from their northern home. Emily Rose, one of these great-grandchildren and one who has always felt comfortable in her enlightened Connecticut community, learns some new and painful truths about the history of her family and about the history of race relations in America.

With the 1999 *Mary, Bloody Mary,* Meyer made a larger historical leap, back into the sixteenth century, to provide a "riveting slice of fictional royal history" which "paints a sympathetic portrait of Henry VIII's oldest daughter, before she earns the title Bloody Mary," according to a reviewer for *Publishers Weekly.* More such historical fiction followed, including *Isabel I,* the story of the Queen of Spain's early years, and *Anastasia, the Last Grand Duchess,* an account of the daughter of the last emperor of Russia.

In addition to such stand-alone novels, Meyer has also written a four-volume series for Bantam, "Hotline," about a group of high school kids operating an emergency phone service. Teen suicide is dealt with in the first

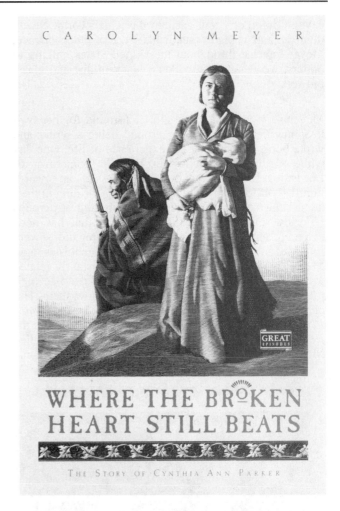

Dislocation is the theme of Meyer's historical novel, a fictionalized account of Cynthia Ann Parker, kidnapped as a child by Comanches in 1836 and reunited with her biological family twenty-five years later. (Cover illustration by Mark Summers.)

of these, *Because of Lissa,* in which the phone service is inaugurated as a response to Lissa's death. "YAs will welcome this book, as it offers a solution with sensitivity and understanding," commented Linda Zoppa in a *School Library Journal* review. Subsequent volumes continue with the adventures and encounters of this hotline group, dealing with sex, runaways, and alcohol and drug abuse.

Despite her success as a novelist, Meyer has continued with her journalistic books. "I enjoy writing fiction, but the lure of nonfiction remains strong," she noted in *SAAS.* "Sometimes I think the two kinds of writing come from different parts of the brain—one from the imaginative, childlike side, the other from the intellectual, rational, disciplined adult half." Her ability to explain different cultures drew the attention of an editor at the Harcourt publishing house, who brought her a challenging project: travel to South Africa—scene of great racial tension between an oppressed black majority and the ruling white minority—and gather material for a book that would show young people what it was like to grow up there. The book became *Voices of South Africa: Growing Up in a Troubled Land.*

At first Meyer had little notion of how to approach her assignment, except for the hunch that calling herself a "journalist" while visiting the country "would make me immediately suspect." Then an obliging white South African whom she met while visiting her travel agent gave her a list of people she could contact. Starting from there and billing herself simply as a children's author, Meyer toured South Africa and spoke to as many different kinds of people as she could, although she found that white people were sometimes defensive, children were sometimes afraid to speak freely in the presence of their teachers, and black people were difficult for any white writer to meet. Despite such obstacles, as Cathi MacRae wrote in *Wilson Library Bulletin,* "Meyer still manages to offer an engrossing personal account of one American's effort to understand. She smoothly combines travelogue, conversations, and historical background." "I tried to be fair," Meyer wrote in *SAAS.* "Being fair usually offends everyone. Whites thought I didn't understand, blacks thought I was much too soft on whites. I was in a no-win situation, like

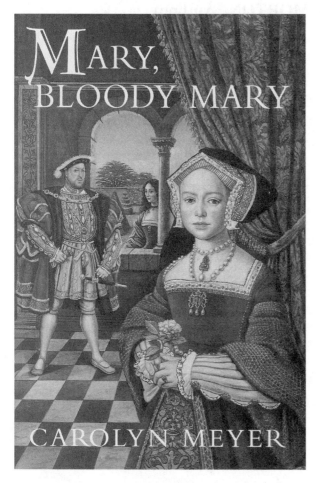

Recounting in first-person narration the childhood of Mary Tudor, daughter of Henry VIII, Meyer lends a personal voice to the difficult experiences of the young girl who would become one of England's most disliked queens. (Cover illustration by Teresa Fasolino.)

nearly everyone there." A writer for *Kirkus Reviews* called the work a "brilliant study" and declared: "Readers who seek understanding, rather than easy answers, will find it here."

Meyer repeated the formula for *Voices of South Africa* to create additional books in the same format. A visit to Northern Ireland resulted in *Voices of Northern Ireland: Growing Up in a Troubled Land,* a record of her journey and of the interviews she conducted with Protestants and Catholics alike. *Horn Book*'s Ethel R. Twichell commented, "Meyer is a shrewd observer and appears to have had the gift of encouraging the young to talk to her."

A visit to Japan, however, was much different than the other journeys. In English-speaking countries, Meyer noted in *SAAS,* "I could usually find people to talk to, to spend time with. In Japan, however, I was up against a language barrier.... Beyond language lay the culture barrier." In Japan, Meyer explained, "there are even [social customs] for what may be worn into the toilet. I was never quite sure what was expected of me, never confident of the polite thing to do in all kinds of circumstances." Acknowledging the barriers, Meyer titled her study *A Voice from Japan: An Outsider Looks In.* Despite such difficulties, however, Rosie Peasley, writing in *School Library Journal,* felt readers would keep "turning pages happily" because of "[f]ascinating details about Japanese homes, bedding, food, education, and customs."

Meyer has also written of cultures far afield in the Americas. Her 1977 *Eskimos: Growing Up in a Changing Culture* provided a vivid introduction to a vanishing way of life. Almost twenty years later, Meyer returned to the fictionalized Yup'ik village of that book to take a look at what changes the years had wrought for the next generation in the book, *In a Different Light: Growing Up in a Yup'ik Eskimo Village in Alaska.* *Booklist* reviewer Chris Sherman remarked, "[Meyer] provides a vivid and thoughtful portrait of a culture in transition."

Whether writing about distant cultures, gawky adolescents, or teenagers at risk, Meyer "eschews the easy plotline and delves into the uncomfortable realities of our world," according to M. Jean Greenlaw and Elizabeth D. Schafer writing in the *St. James Guide to Young Adult Writers.* "[O]ne awaits her new works with a sense of anticipation," those authors concluded.

Works Cited

Codell, Cindy Darling, review of *White Lilacs, School Library Journal,* October, 1993, p. 152.

Gale, David, review of *Elliott & Win, School Library Journal,* March, 1986, p. 178.

Greenlaw, M. Jean, and Elizabeth D. Schafer, "Meyer, Carolyn (Mae)," *St. James Guide to Young Adult Writers,* 2nd edition, edited by Tom Pendergast and Sara Pendergast, St. James, 1999, pp. 585-87.

Hearne, Betsy, review of *Where the Broken Heart Still Beats, Bulletin of the Center for Children's Books,* November, 1992, pp. 117-18.

Hoagland, Edward, review of *Amish People, New York Times Book Review,* May 9, 1976, p. 14.

Jones, Trev, review of *The Luck of Texas McCoy, School Library Journal,* February, 1985, p. 86.

MacRae, Cathi, "The Young Adult Perplex," *Wilson Library Bulletin,* December, 1988, p. 92.

Review of *Mary, Bloody Mary, Publishers Weekly,* September 27, 1999, p. 106.

Meyer, Carolyn, *Something about the Author Autobiography Series,* Volume 9, Gale, 1990.

Moore, Ann W., review of *Where the Broken Heart Still Beats, School Library Journal,* September, 1992, pp. 278-79.

Peasley, Rosie, review of *A Voice from Japan, School Library Journal,* November, 1988, p. 138.

Rochman, Hazel, review of *Denny's Tapes, Booklist,* November 1, 1987, pp. 466-67.

Sherman, Chris, review of *In a Different Light, Booklist,* May 1, 1996, p. 1496.

Twichell, Ethel R., review of *Voices of Northern Ireland, Horn Book,* January-February, 1988, p. 87.

Review of *Voices of South Africa, Kirkus Reviews,* September 1, 1986, p. 1377.

Zoppa, Linda, review of *Because of Lissa, School Library Journal,* January, 1991, p. 114.

For More Information See

BOOKS

Authors and Artists for Young Adults, Volume 16, Gale, 1995.

Authors of Books for Young People, 3rd edition, Scarecrow, 1990.

Fifth Book of Junior Authors and Illustrators, H. W. Wilson, 1983.

PERIODICALS

Booklist, November 15, 1990, p. 655; October 1, 1994, p. 328; June 1, 1995, p. 1753; March 15, 1996, p. 1282; September 1, 1997, p. 126.

Bulletin of the Center for Children's Books, April, 1978, p. 131; November, 1978, p. 48; December, 1979, p. 75; October, 1984, p. 32; May, 1986, p. 174; November, 1986, p. 55; November, 1987, p. 52; November, 1988, p. 80; January, 1991, pp. 125-26; September, 1994, p. 19; April, 1995, p. 282; May, 1996, p. 309; September, 1997, p. 19.

Horn Book, August, 1975, p. 391; August, 1976, p. 415; February, 1978, p. 61; December, 1978, p. 646; October, 1982, p. 520; May, 1987, p. 358; September-October, 1996, p. 622.

Kirkus Reviews, January 1, 1986, p. 215; September 1, 1987, p. 1323; October 1, 1992, p. 1258; July 15, 1993, p. 937; June 15, 1994, p. 849; April 15, 1996, p. 604.

New York Times Book Review, December 18, 1977, p. 23; January 20, 1980, p. 30; July 16, 1995, p. 27.

Publishers Weekly, May 30, 1994, p. 57; May 8, 1995, p. 296.

School Library Journal, September, 1982, p. 141; November, 1990, p. 50; July, 1991, p. 88; September, 1995, pp. 219, 227; June, 1996, p. 162; January, 1998, p. 114; October, 1999, p. 154.

Voice of Youth Advocates, February, 1991, p. 354; April, 1993, p. 27; June, 1995, p. 96; June, 1996, p. 98; August, 1996, p. 150.*

*   *   *

MORTON, Anthony
See ARTHUR, Robert (Jr.)

*   *   *

MUDE, O.
See GOREY, Edward (St. John)

*   *   *

MYSTERIOUS TRAVELER, The
See ARTHUR, Robert (Jr.)

*   *   *

NORMAN, Jay
See ARTHUR, Robert (Jr.)

O

OPIE, Iona 1923-

Personal

Born October 13, 1923, in Colchester, England; daughter of Sir Robert George (a pathologist) and Olive (maiden name, Cant) Archibald; married Peter Opie (an author and folklorist), September 2, 1943 (died, February 5, 1982); children: James, Robert, Letitia. *Education:* Attended schools in England; Oxford University, M.A., 1962. *Politics:* Conservative. *Religion:* Church of England.

Addresses

Home and office—Mells House, West Liss, Hampshire GU33 6JQ, England.

Career

Author. *Military service:* Women's Auxiliary Air Force, Meteorological Section, 1941-43; became sergeant.

Awards, Honors

Coote Lake Research Medal (joint winner with husband, Peter Opie), 1960; European Prize of the City of Caorle (Italy; joint winner), 1964; Chicago Folklore Prize (joint winner with Peter Opie), 1970; Children's Books of the Year selection, Child Study Association of America, 1973, for *The Oxford Book of Children's Verse,* and 1974, for *The Classic Fairy Tales; D.Litt., Southampton University, 1987; Children's Picture Book Award, *Redbook,* 1988, and Notable Book, American Library Association, both for *Tail Feathers from Mother Goose;* Nottingham University, D.Litt, 1991; May Hill Arbuthnot Lecturer, 1991; Picture Book Award, Parents Choice, and Reading Magic Award, both 1992, both for *I Saw Esau,* with illustrations by Maurice Sendak; Surrey University, D.Univ., 1997.

Writings

(Editor) *Ditties for the Nursery,* illustrated by Monica Walker, Oxford University Press, 1954.
(With son, Robert Opie and Brian Alderson) *The Treasures of Childhood: Books, Toys, and Games from the Opie Collection,* Pavillion, Little, Brown, 1989.

Iona Opie

(With Moira Tatem) *A Dictionary of Superstitions,* Oxford University Press, 1989.

The People in the Playground, Oxford University Press, 1993.

(Editor) *My Very First Mother Goose,* illustrated by Rosemary Wells, Walker, Candlewick, 1996.

(Editor) *Here Comes Mother Goose,* illustrated by Wells, Walker, Candlewick, 1999.

COMPILER; BOARD BOOKS

Little Boy Blue and Other Rhymes, illustrated by Rosemary Wells, Walker, Candlewick, 1997.

Humpty Dumpty and Other Rhymes, illustrated by Wells, Walker, Candlewick, 1997.

Wee Willie Winkie and Other Rhymes, illustrated by Wells, Walker, Candlewick, 1997.

Pussy-Cat Pussy-Cat and Other Rhymes, illustrated by Wells, Walker Candlewick, 1997.

WITH HUSBAND, PETER OPIE

(Compiler) *I Saw Esau,* Williams & Norgate, 1947, new edition illustrated by Maurice Sendak, Walker, 1992.

(Editor) *The Oxford Dictionary of Nursery Rhymes,* Clarendon, 1951, new edition published by Oxford University Press, 1997.

(Compiler) *The Oxford Nursery Rhyme Book,* illustrated by Joan Hassall and others, Clarendon, 1955.

Christmas Party Games, Oxford University Press, 1957.

The Lore and Language of Schoolchildren, Clarendon, 1959.

(Compiler) *The Puffin Book of Nursery Rhymes,* illustrated by Pauline Baynes, Penguin, 1963, published as *A Family Book of Nursery Rhymes,* Oxford University Press, 1964.

Children's Games in Street and Playground: Chasing, Catching, Seeking, Hunting, Racing, Dueling, Exerting, Daring, Guessing, Acting, Pretending, Clarendon, 1969.

(Editor) *Three Centuries of Poetry and Nursery Rhymes for Children* (exhibition catalogue), Oxford University Press, 1973, J. G. Schiller, 1977.

(Editor) *The Oxford Book of Children's Verse,* Oxford University Press, 1973.

(Compiler) *The Classic Fairy Tales,* Oxford University Press, 1974.

A Nursery Companion, Oxford University Press, 1980.

(Compiler) *The Oxford Book of Narrative Verse,* Oxford University Press, 1983.

The Singing Game, Oxford University Press, 1985.

(Editor) *Tail Feathers from Mother Goose: The Opie Rhyme Book,* Little, Brown, 1988.

(Editor) *Babies: An Unsentimental Anthology,* illustrated by Bob Graham, Murray, 1990.

Children's Games with Things: Marbles, Fivestones, Throwing and Catching, Gambling, Hopscotch, Chucking and Pitching, Ball-Bouncing, Skipping, Tops and Tipcat, Oxford University Press, 1997.

Contributor to reference works, including *Encyclopaedia Britannica* and *New Cambridge Bibliography of English Literature.*

The Opie Collection of Children's Literature and the Opie papers are housed in the Bodleian Library at the University of Oxford.

Adaptations

The Lore and Language of Schoolchildren, British Broadcasting Corporation (BBC), 1960.

Sidelights

With her husband, Peter, Iona Opie was a pioneer in the study of children's games, nursery rhymes, fairy tales, and language with such respected volumes as *The Oxford Dictionary of Nursery Rhymes, The Classic Fairy Tales, The Lore and Language of Schoolchildren,* and *Children's Games in Street and Playground.* Together the pair studied the derivation of nursery rhymes and children's games. Throughout their life together, the Opies collected over twenty thousand children's books, many of them from before 1800, and assembled a representative collection of children's toys and games.

Upon the death of her husband in 1982, Iona Opie has carried on this scholarly tradition with *The Singing Game* and *Children's Games with Things,* which rounded out the research the couple did in over forty years of collaboration. Additionally, Iona Opie has culled her vast collection to produce two large volumes of nursery rhymes illustrated by Rosemary Wells, *My Very First Mother Goose* and *Here Comes Mother Goose,* as well as several board books adapted from these two volumes. As Robert Protherough noted in *Twentieth-Century Children's Writers,* the Opies have made "an outstanding contribution to our understanding of writing for children and can claim a major share in establishing it as a legitimate field for scholarship."

Iona was born in Colchester, England, and was raised primarily by her mother. "My parents met when my father took part in a tennis tournament, and at the mere sight of him, my mother fell in love," Opie once told *SATA.* "When he went back to Africa, they'd known each other three weeks; she waited for him devotedly for seven years, through the entire first World War." The two were later married, but Opie's father was largely absent. "My father was a director of the Wellcome Research Laboratories in Khartoum, Africa, so most of his time was spent there. I worshiped him from afar and grew up wanting to become a plant pathologist, because he was a pathologist, studying tropical diseases. When my sister and I were young, he'd turn up occasionally, a complete stranger, and his arrivals disrupted the even tenor of our lives. My mother looked after us with the utmost care; my father thought we were pampered."

At age six, Iona attended prep school and made her first book, "all of twelve pages about spiders, with pictures and a plaited woolen thread for binding," Opie once recalled for *SATA.* "It was hung up on the notice board. The school was run on the Dalton system which meant that we had control over our own work. A week's assignment was done anytime we chose during the week. I'm sure that later helped me be more organized."

A voracious reader as a child, Opie once told *SATA* that she was known as "a bookworm (which I thought a horrid word). Consuming book after book, I loved both the pictures and the story, loved everything down to the smell of the pages. My tastes were by no means literary: I didn't read anything highfallutin', couldn't boast of having read Horace or Dickens at age seventeen. My mother was not literary in the least; most of her books were about antique furniture or gardening. She despised novels for being a waste of time and read only the very popular ones, necessary for dinner party discussion." An early book-buying proclivity would become a fixture of her life. "When I was about fourteen I began buying antiquarian books ... mostly poetry in leather or half-leather, and limited editions. My mother was tolerant, and did not press her own conviction that secondhand books harbor germs."

During the Second World War, Opie, affected by the death of a friend, joined the services to help out in the war effort. "I joined the Meteorological Section and was happily, permanently, in the ranks," Opie told *SATA*. "I rose to being a sergeant. We'd do hourly observations and send our material off on the teleprinter which was connected to all the other stations; then we'd receive material from the whole network, all over Britain. I'd set about making my map, plotting the information. The map was then taken to the forecaster who would draw in the isobars and interpret the weather information to the pilots."

She met her future husband and collaborator as a result, fittingly enough, of looking for a book to read. A friend gave her *I Want to Be a Success* by Peter Opie. Reading the book, she was attracted to its author, and soon the two started a communication that grew into romance and eventually, in 1943, to marriage. Later, children came on the scene, and Opie left the service when her husband took on an editorial position at a publishing house which had moved its offices to the country to avoid the London bombings.

It was there, with time on their hands, that the Opies embarked upon a collaborative project which was to occupy almost all their time for nearly the next forty years. Iona described to Jonathan Cott in *Pipers at the Gates of Dawn* how they became interested in nursery rhymes: "One day, Peter and I were walking alongside a cornfield, and we took a ladybird onto ... I forget whose finger it was. But we recited the rhyme— 'Ladybird, ladybird, / Fly away home, / Your house is on fire / And your children all gone'—and we wondered where the verse came from, how old was it? We got bitten by these questions." They soon went to London's Kensington Public Library and then on to the British Museum to try to track down sources of the old rhyme. The most recent book with information about the ladybird rhyme in the library was J. O. Halliwell's *Nursery Rhymes of England,* published in 1842. The Opies decided that there must be room for a new book

on the origins of nursery rhymes. Shortly thereafter, the couple began work on *The Oxford Dictionary of Nursery Rhymes,* which would be more than seven years in the making.

A literary prize and large printing of one of Peter Opie's titles, *The Case of Being a Young Man,* allowed the couple to pursue their writing and research full time. The first fruit of their labor appeared as *I Saw Esau,* published in 1947. The book is an accumulation of nearly two hundred traditional rhymes familiar to the young, including counting rhymes, insulting rhymes, and even praising rhymes. The Opies not only compiled all these rhymes, but also traced their derivations, both arcane and obvious. "The book presents artful texts, mainly old, irrefutable evidence," noted Philip Morrison in a *Scientific American* review of the 1992 edition, with illustrations by Maurice Sendak. Morrison further commented, "In the word-song, you hear the origin of poetry, the catch of the sound dominant over mere aptness or reason. In the jest and wordplay, you glimpse the rise of wit and humor."

The Oxford Dictionary of Nursery Rhymes, a work of unprecedented scholarship in the field, was published in 1951. In it, the Opies compiled over five hundred rhymes, songs, nonsense jingles, and lullabies which have been traditionally handed down to the young, generation after generation. Each of these includes information such as earliest known publication, origin, and the illustrations that have accompanied it over the years. *The Oxford Nursery Rhyme Book* followed in 1955, and four years later *The Lore and Language of Schoolchildren,* based on contributions from five thou-

Here am I, Little Jumping Joan;
When nobody's with me, I'm all alone.

An anthology of more than sixty Mother Goose rhymes, **My Very First Mother Goose *has been noted for the whimsical humor of Opie's text and Rosemary Wells's illustrations.***

sand schoolchildren, was published. Iona Opie once described the questionnaires which they used in classrooms to _SATA:_ "Our questionnaires were very informal, wide open, and we never included 'yes' or 'no' questions. The idea was not that the children spelt words right or made nice sentences; they were just allowed to let rip, describing what they thought was especially good or silly or describing any games they played with a ball, etc. If they mentioned a game without fully describing it, we'd write back to that particular child, asking to know more about this game that, perhaps, we'd never heard of before. There were always several children in a class from whom I could quote in the book."

The Opies began their own collection of books shortly after they married. Amid the Opies' ever-increasing myriad of books, there were numerous first editions and association copies. Soon the collection grew to such an extent that it all but pushed the family of five out of their country home.

In 1969, the Opies published _Children's Games in Street and Playground,_ based on a survey of ten thousand children. Later, Iona researched children's games by going to the playground every week for twelve years. "I never minded talking to the children, but I was a bit scared of the grown-ups," Opie told Cott. "For me there's been excitement in communicating with the children and discovering that what they're doing now connects back with the past. It's hard not to feel the extra life and wonderful battiness of the children; they can get drunk on nothing." Describing her research methods to Cott, Opie explained: "I sort of moon about, I'm a sort of typical village idiot, really; I never even know how to play marbles, I can't always follow the game and I have to get the children to explain. And they love explaining, they know more than I do. Playtime is the one time when children are the 'superiors.' Adults sometimes ask us why we used the word 'people' in our book on children's games, 'You need six people to play a game,' for example. But that's what they themselves say. We never like to make fun of children, because this isn't what we'd want to have done to us."

The Opies' book on games included everything from hand-clapping to skipping, and was followed up in 1985 with _The Singing Game,_ "as fine as anything [the Opies] have ever done," according to Ray Olson in _Booklist._ The volume includes a "historical overview that demonstrates the ancient and medieval roots" of 133 games, explained Olson.

Other Opie collaborative efforts include _The Oxford Book of Children's Verse_ and _The Classic Fairy Tales._ "Peter and I lived together more than most married couples," Opie once told _SATA._ "We lived together and worked together; we were together all day long every day, except when once a fortnight, he went up to his library, The London Library, and I went up to mine, The British Library. His death was a total loss to me, except that I've always felt he was still here. When I want to talk to him, I talk to him. I knew his mind so well that when he had to leave _The Singing Game_ half written I

A companion volume to **My Very First Mother Goose,** **Here Comes Mother Goose** _assembles sixty more rhyming favorites with the same joyful flair. (Edited by Opie and illustrated by Rosemary Wells.)_

just went on writing in the genuine Opie style, feeling I'd inherited the family firm."

Following Peter's death, over twenty thousand volumes of the Opies' children's books went to the Bodleian Library, Oxford, purchased in part through a fund raised by the Prince of Wales. Meanwhile, Iona Opie has continued researching and recording. She has published _The Treasures of Childhood,_ with her son, Robert, and author Brian Alderson, and _A Dictionary of Superstitions,_ with Moira Tatem. Reviewing the latter title, a contributor for _Wilson Library Bulletin_ commented, "This dictionary stands as testimony to humans' ability to freight with portentous meaning nearly every everyday object or experience." Mary Ellen Quinn noted in a _Booklist_ review, "Opie and Tatem's thoroughly researched _Dictionary of Superstitions_ will appeal to scholars and other readers."

Opie has also gone forward with the scholarly work of research that she began with her husband, publishing in 1993 _The People in the Playground,_ a reworking of diary material gathered in the late 1970s as she observed kids on the playgrounds in British schools. "This interesting log reveals play to be an avenue of escape from childhood's pervasive fears and anxieties," noted a reviewer for _Publishers Weekly._ In ways, the volume offers a natural complement to the earlier _The Lore and Language of Schoolchildren_ and _Children's Games in Street and Playground._ More directly connected to that later work and with *The Singing Game,* was Opie's 1997 *Children's Games with Things,* "an essential addition to the reference collection of any library interested in the lives of children," according to John Murray in a *Magpies* review. Here Opie examines the implements of children's games, from marbles to tops and balls. The history of such games covers over two thousand years.

Opie has also continued publication of nursery rhymes culled from the still large Opie collection. Enlisting the artistic energy of writer-illustrator Rosemary Wells, Opie has brought out *My Very First Mother Goose,* and in 1999, *Here Comes Mother Goose,* both large illustrated compendiums of nursery rhymes for children. Reviewing this first of these, Nancy Willard wrote in the *New York Times Book Review,* "It would be hard to imagine a more perfect introduction to mystery, laughter and poetry." The book includes numerous rhymes, from "Jack and Jill" to "Humpty Dumpty." "This is a joyful book," Willard further noted, "in which the cow jumps over the moon and the children are all full of high jinks but protected by the magic words of a blessing." *Booklist*'s Hazel Rochman remarked that *My Very First Mother Goose,* is ideal for "reading aloud and chanting, and singing to the very youngest child," while a contributor for *Publishers Weekly* called it an "exuberant anthology."

Sixty more rhyming favorites, including "Old King Cole," "Old Mother Hubbard," and "Dusty Bill from Vinegar Hill," among others, are collected—again with illustrations from Wells—in *Here Comes Mother Goose.* A reviewer for *Publishers Weekly* commented that this "beguiling companion to *My Very First Mother Goose* abounds with wit and charm," going on to add, "there is no one like Opie for authoritative presentation of traditional verse." In a *Booklist* review, Rochman called the second collection "a splendid, large-size companion volume," while *Horn Book* critic Martha V. Parravano claimed the second anthology "is even more successful than the first." Parravano concluded, "So here comes Mother Goose—and, to those who welcome this book into their lives, many, many hours of shared reading pleasure." Additionally, Opie and Wells have also teamed up for several board books of individual nursery rhymes culled from the larger collections, including *Humpty Dumpty and Other Rhymes, Little Boy Blue and Other Rhymes, Wee Willie Winkie and Other Rhymes,* and *Pussy-Cat Pussy-Cat and Other Rhymes.*

For Opie, there are no regrets that she did not follow her youthful dream of becoming a plant pathologist like her father, or that her working life with husband Peter allowed for little socializing. Her life has been devoted to the gathering and explication of childhood games, songs, rhymes, and verses. "There shouldn't be any such thing as regrets," Opie once told *SATA.* "Life is just how it shapes itself. There came a moment ... when I was mowing the lawn, when I suddenly had a blinding flash of realization that it had all been worthwhile."

Works Cited

Cott, Jonathan, *Pipers at the Gates of Dawn,* Random House, 1983.

Review of *A Dictionary of Superstitions, Wilson Library Bulletin,* February, 1990, p. 111.

Review of *Here Comes Mother Goose, Publishers Weekly,* November 1, 1999, p. 56.

Morrison, Philip, review of *I Saw Esau, Scientific American,* October, 1992, p. 126.

Murray, John, review of *Children's Games with Things, Magpies,* March, 1998, p. 21.

Review of *My Very First Mother Goose, Publishers Weekly,* August 5, 1996, p. 442.

Olson, Ray, review of *The Singing Game, Booklist,* October 1, 1985, pp. 183-84.

Parravano, Martha V., review of *Here Comes Mother Goose, Horn Book,* November-December, 1999, p. 749.

Review of *The People in the Playground, Publishers Weekly,* May 10, 1993, p. 61.

Protherough, Robert, "Opie, Iona and Peter," *Twentieth-Century Children's Writers,* 4th edition, St. James Press, 1995.

Quinn, Mary Ellen, review of *A Dictionary of Superstitions, Booklist,* December 1, 1989, pp. 76-77.

Rochman, Hazel, review of *Here Comes Mother Goose, Booklist,* October 1, 1999, p. 354.

Rochman, Hazel, review of *My Very First Mother Goose, Booklist,* September 1, 1996, p. 127.

Willard, Nancy, review of *My Very First Mother Goose, New York Times Book Review,* November 10, 1996, p. 38.

For More Information See

BOOKS

Children and Their Books: A Celebration of the Work of Iona and Peter Opie, edited by Gillian Avery and Julia Briggs, Oxford University Press, 1990.

PERIODICALS

Booklist, March 1, 1998, p. 1141.

Christian Science Monitor, December 4, 1969.

Horn Book, February, 1970; July-August, 1990, p. 475; November-December, 1996, p. 752; September-October, 1998, p. 602.

New York Review of Books, July 23, 1970.

New York Times Book Review, November 13, 1988, p. 41; April 22, 1990, p. 26; May 17, 1992, p. 23; January 16, 2000, p. 27.

New Yorker, November 23, 1992, p. 75.

Publishers Weekly, July 29, 1988, p. 134; May 25, 1992, p. 55; September 30, 1996, pp. 41-42; October 4, 1999, p. 73.

School Library Journal, February, 1990, p. 14; March, 1990, p. 156; October, 1996, p. 116; December, 1996, p. 31; December, 1997, p. 98; October, 1999, p. 141.

Times Educational Supplement, October 10, 1969; April 23, 1999.

OPIE, Peter (Mason) 1918-1982

Personal

Born November 25, 1918, in Cairo, Egypt; died February 5, 1982, in West Liss, Hampshire, England; son of Philip Adams (a surgeon) and Margaret (maiden name, Collett-Mason) Opie; married Iona Archibald, September 2, 1943; children: James, Robert, Letitia. *Education:* Attended Eton.

Career

Author and folklorist. *Military service:* Royal Fusiliers, Royal Sussex Regiment, 1939-41; became lieutenant. *Member:* Folklore Society (president, 1963-64), British Association for the Advancement of Science (president of anthropology section, 1962-63).

Awards, Honors

Chosen Book Competition (joint winner), 1944; Silver Medal, Royal Society of Arts, 1953; Coote Lake Research Medal (joint winner with wife, Iona Opie), 1960; M.A., Oxford University, 1962; European Prize of the City of Caorle (Italy; joint winner), 1964; Chicago Folklore Prize (joint winner with Iona Opie), 1970; Children's Books of the Year, Child Study Association of America, 1973, for *The Oxford Book of Children's Verse,* and 1974, for *The Classic Fairy Tales.*

Writings

I Want to Be a Success (autobiography), Michael Joseph, 1939.
Having Held the Nettle, Torchstream, 1945.
The Case of Being a Young Man, Wells Gardner, Darton, 1946.

WITH WIFE, IONA OPIE

(Compiler) *I Saw Esau,* Williams & Norgate, 1947, new edition illustrated by Maurice Sendak, Candlewick, 1992.
(Editor) *The Oxford Dictionary of Nursery Rhymes,* Clarendon, 1951, new edition published by Oxford University Press, 1977.
(Compiler) *The Oxford Nursery Rhyme Book,* illustrated by Joan Hassall and others, Clarendon, 1955.
Christmas Party Games, Oxford University Press (New York City), 1957.
The Lore and Language of Schoolchildren, Clarendon, 1959.
(Compiler) *The Puffin Book of Nursery Rhymes,* illustrated by Pauline Baynes, Penguin, 1963, published as *A Family Book of Nursery Rhymes,* Oxford University Press, 1964.
Children's Games in Street and Playground: Chasing, Catching, Seeking, Hunting, Racing, Duelling, Exerting, Daring, Guessing, Acting, Pretending, Clarendon, 1969.
(Editor) *Three Centuries of Poetry and Nursery Rhymes for Children* (exhibition catalogue), Oxford University Press, 1973, J. G. Schiller, 1977.

(Editor) *The Oxford Book of Children's Verse,* Oxford University Press, 1973.
(Compiler) *The Classic Fairy Tales,* Oxford University Press, 1974.
A Nursery Companion, Oxford University Press, 1980.
(Compiler) *The Oxford Book of Narrative Verse,* Oxford University Press, 1983.
The Singing Game, Oxford University Press, 1985.
Children's Games with Things: Marbles, Fivestones, Throwing and Catching, Gambling, Hopscotch, Chucking and Pitching, Ball-Bouncing, Skipping, Tops and Tipcat, Oxford University Press, 1997.

Contributor to reference works, including *Encyclopaedia Britannica* and *New Cambridge Bibliography of English Literature.*

The Opie Collection of Children's Literature and the Opie papers are housed at the Bodleian Library at the University of Oxford.

Adaptations

(Also host) *The Lore and Language of Schoolchildren,* British Broadcasting Corporation (BBC), 1960.

Sidelights

Peter Opie collaborated for nearly forty years with his wife Iona, helping to pioneer the study and publication of nursery rhymes, children's games, and fairy tales. Together they produced revered volumes in the fledgling field of child folklore studies, including *The Oxford Dictionary of Nursery Rhymes, The Classic Fairy Tales, The Lore and Language of Schoolchildren, Children's Games in Street and Playground,* and *The Singing Game.* The pair collected over twenty thousand children's books, many of them from before 1800, and a representative collection of children's toys and games to aid in their research. Philip Morrison, reviewing an updated version of the Opies' first collaborative title, *I Saw Esau,* remarked, "For nearly four decades the Opies acted as intrepid ethnographers among the great tribe of children—watching, listening, sometimes advancing in giant steps, along the mean streets and open greens of Britain and beyond. In volume after volume, they assembled and annotated the folklore and folkways that pass from child to child in the old and vigorous culture all of us shared for years before we were compelled to depart."

Born in Cairo, Egypt, Peter Opie grew up in various places in England, forming an early love for books, citing some of his favorites as *Winnie the Pooh* and Cowper's *John Gilpin.* At age seven, Opie's parents departed for India and left their son behind in Sherborne under the care of distant relatives. From this point on, the young boy grew to depend on his own resources. When he was eight years old, Opie contributed his first piece of writing for publication: a story of a tiger shoot for his prep school magazine. He had an early propensity for collecting—books, toys, whatever.

Then at age thirteen, he enrolled at Eton. After graduation, his mother wanted him to go on to Cambridge, but he wanted to become a writer, so she made a bargain with him. If he could write a book and get the work published, Opie would not have to attend college. He wrote a youthful autobiography about his visits to India and his years at Eton, *I Want to Be a Success,* and it was published. Opie entered on the career of a professional writer, barely out of his teens.

With the outbreak of the Second World War in 1939, Opie joined the Royal Fusiliers and was then commissioned into the Royal Sussex Regiment, but an accident during training derailed his military career in 1941. He subsequently returned to writing and lived for a time with his mother in a London flat. It was during the early years of the war that he received a fan letter from a young woman, Iona Archibald, who had read his autobiography and felt a kindred spirit. The two met and ultimately married in 1943. Opie wrote two more books on his own, *Having Held the Nettle,* and *The Case of Being a Young Man,* but his work for the rest of his life involved his researches undertaken with his wife in the origins of folklore, in particular nursery rhymes and children's lore and games.

The couple's first book, *I Saw Esau,* published originally in 1947, "initiated [the Opies'] lifelong research into children's games and verses," according to *School Library Journal* reviewer Shirley Wilton in a review of the 1992 reprint of that first title, with illustrations by Maurice Sendak. Presented in this debut volume was an initial sampling of short rhymes, chants, and riddles that the Opies had collected. "It is the voices of children echoing over the generations with the same banter, the same gross humor, and the same defiance of adult authority that gives the collection its universal quality," Wilton further noted, dubbing the book "a delight for all ages."

I Saw Esau is divided under headings such as "Insults," "Teasing," "Nonsense," and "Reality." For insults, the couple discovered: "Tommy Johnson is no good, / Chop him up for firewood; / When he's dead, boil his head, / Make it into gingerbread." The title verse is "a small drama of love and grammar," according to Morrison: "I saw Esau kissing Kate, / The fact is we all three saw; / For I saw him, / And he saw me, / And she saw I saw Esau." Reviewing the 1992 edition in *Books for Keeps,* Robert Hull called it "a lovely, funny book." Susan Toepfer, reviewing the reprinted work in *People Weekly,* declared that "these rhymes explode with spunk and life." A contributor for *Publishers Weekly* praised the new edition and the work of the Opies: "Because the Opies' particular genius lay in mapping the verbal turf of children themselves ... the rhymes they collected portray not only the playfulness of childhood but its occasional crudeness and cruelty as well."

In 1951, the couple published their long-awaited *The Oxford Dictionary of Nursery Rhymes,* a work of unprecedented scholarship in the field. An overnight success, the dictionary helped establish the point,

Peter Opie's I Saw Esau *is an accumulation of nearly two hundred traditional rhymes familiar to the young, with information about the derivations, both arcane and obvious, of the verse. (Illustrated by Maurice Sendak.)*

according to Leonard Marcus writing in the *New York Times Book Review,* "that 'childish' things, when viewed dispassionately, might yield important clues to the elaborate workings of collective memory, to the very means by which a culture sustains itself over the generations." This volume contains over five hundred examples of nursery rhymes, along with nonsense rhymes, lullabies, and songs. The Opies present the earliest known version of each verse, a discussion of its origins, and a comparison with similar verses from countries around the world.

The Oxford Nursery Rhyme Book followed in 1955, and four years later *The Lore and Language of Schoolchildren,* based on contributions from five thousand schoolchildren, was published. In 1969, the Opies published *Children's Games in Street and Playground,* based on a survey of ten thousand children, a furtherance of the work begun in *The Lore and Language of Schoolchildren.*

The Opies also began their own collection of books and children's toys and games shortly after they married, helping them with their folklore studies. Peter recalled to Jonathan Cott in *Pipers at the Gates of Dawn,* "It began with nursery rhymes, but we were always looking to the future, and we realized that no one could be a proper research worker unless he possessed the books himself. So we went around to the antiquarian bookshops. We realized we'd probably someday work on fairy tales, and that, in turn, would lead to something else." That first nursery rhyme book was an 1820 edition of *The Cheerful Warbler* and set the couple on a path that led to a collection of over twenty thousand children's books, comics, and chapbooks, which included a large number of eighteenth-century volumes.

Amid the Opies' ever-increasing myriad of books, there were numerous first editions and association copies. Peter described to Cott holding "in one's hand something that the author held in *his* hand" as "wonderful," but he said he didn't "care for ideas like magic. That it makes you tingle, yes. And even buying a first edition of an author whom you like is an expression of love, much like buying a ring for a lady: it's an expression of your affection and respect. And if I read an eighteenth-century book, I like to do so in an eighteenth-century edition, because this is how one gets close, you see."

The Opies published many other volumes of verses and fairy tales, including *The Oxford Book of Children's Verse,* a collection of over three hundred poems spanning five hundred years of British and American literature, and *The Classic Fairy Tales,* which presents twenty-four of the all-time favorites such as "Sleeping Beauty," "Little Red Riding Hood," and "Snow White." Both of these volumes provide background information, and *The Classic Fairy Tales* gives the stories as they first appeared in English. For the fairy tales, these early forms are often the most brutal or violent. In addition to the stories, the Opies provide a discussion of how such tales have changed over the generations. With "Cinderella," for example, they show how the slipper changed over time from red velvet with pearl braiding to glass.

Though Opie died in 1982 of a heart attack, his work has been carried on by his wife, Iona. More than half-done at the time of his death, *The Singing Game* was published in 1985 and continued the work begun in *The Lore and Language of Schoolchildren* and *Children's Games in Street and Playground.* In this volume, the Opies collected over one hundred fifty singing games that "draw upon history, anthropology, archaeology, literature, popular culture, and art," according to Alison Lurie writing in the *New York Review of Books.* Such verses and songs have survived for generations and may, as the Opies point out in the book, have originated in ritual seasonal dances and festivals, in courtship formalities, or even in magical rites. "This book includes the authentic tunes for most of the games," Lurie further pointed out, "transcribed in all cases from tapes made in the field, and many attractive illustrations .... Also remarkable is the Opies' lively, unassuming style, and their general good humor toward other scholars in their field."

Upon Opie's death, the Opie book collection was moved to Oxford University's Bodleian Library, while the toy collections have been maintained at the Opies' Mells House in Hampshire. Both in the groundbreaking work he and his wife did in children's verses and games, and in the collection of books, toys, and games, Peter Opie's work lives on.

Works Cited

Cott, Jonathan, *Pipers at the Gates of Dawn,* Random House, 1983.

Hull, Robert, review of *I Saw Esau, Books for Keeps,* March, 1996, p. 28.

Review of *I Saw Esau, Publishers Weekly,* May 25, 1992, p. 55.

Lurie, Alison, "Life's Greatest Hits," *New York Review of Books,* October 24, 1985, pp. 35-36.

Marcus, Leonard, "Play's the Thing," *New York Times Book Review,* April 22, 1990, p. 26.

Morrison, Philip, review of *I Saw Esau, Scientific American,* October, 1992, p. 126.

Opie, Peter, and Iona Opie, *I Saw Esau,* Candlewick, 1992.

Toepfer, Susan, review of *I Saw Esau, People Weekly,* August 10, 1992, p. 33.

Wilton, Shirley, review of *I Saw Esau, School Library Journal,* June, 1992, p. 110.

For More Information See

BOOKS

Children and Their Books: A Celebration of the Work of Iona and Peter Opie, edited by Gillian Avery and Julia Briggs, Oxford University Press, 1990.

PERIODICALS

Booklist, October 1, 1985, pp. 183-84; June 15, 1992, pp. 1848-49.

Bulletin of the Center for Children's Books, October, 1988, p. 49.

Carlton Miscellany, spring, 1970.

Growing Point, January, 1991, p. 5462.

Horizon, winter, 1971.

Horn Book, February, 1970; March-April, 1981, p. 208; July-August, 1990, pp. 475-76; January-February, 1992, p. 754.

Independent, June 28, 1989; November 22, 1989.

The Independent Magazine, October 28, 1989, p. 60.

Library Journal, January 15, 1970.

London Times, October 4, 1969.

New Statesman and Society, March 19, 1993, p. 38.

New York Review of Books, July 23, 1970.

New Yorker, April 4, 1983, p. 47; January 9, 1984, p. 109.

Observer, October 19, 1969.

Publishers Weekly, July 29, 1988, p. 134.

School Library Journal, February, 1990, p. 14; March, 1990, p. 156.

Times Educational Supplement, October 10, 1969.

Washington Post, December 13, 1974.

Wilson Library Bulletin, March, 1990, p. 15.

P

PACK, Robert 1929-

Personal

Born May 19, 1929, in New York, NY; married Isabelle Miller, 1950 (marriage ended); married Patricia Powell, 1961; children: Erik, Pamela, Kevin. *Education:* Dartmouth College, B.A., 1951; Columbia University, M.A., 1953.

Addresses

Home—Montana. *Agent*—David R. Godine Publishers, 9 Lewis St., Lincoln, MA 01773-3817.

Career

Barnard College, New York City, associate in poetry, 1957-64; Middlebury College, Middlebury, VT, professor of English, 1964-70, Abernathy Professor, 1970-78, Bread Loaf Writers Conference, staff member, 1963-72, director, 1973-94; writer.

Awards, Honors

Fulbright fellowship, 1956-57; National Institute of Arts and Letters award for creative work in literature, American Academy Award in literature, both 1957; Borestone Mountain Poetry Award, first prize, 1964; National Council for the Arts award.

Writings

POETRY

The Irony of Joy, Scribner (New York City), 1955.
A Stranger's Privilege, Macmillan (New York City), 1959.
Guarded by Women, Random House (New York City), 1963.
Selected Poems, Chatto & Windus (London), 1964.
Home from the Cemetery, Rutgers University Press (New Brunswick, NJ), 1969.
Nothing but Light, Rutgers University Press, 1972.
Keeping Watch, Rutgers University Press, 1976.

Waking to My Name: New and Selected Poems, Johns Hopkins University Press (Baltimore, MD), 1980.
Faces in a Single Tree: A Cycle of Monologues, David R. Godine (Boston, MA), 1984.
Clayfeld Rejoices, Clayfeld Laments: A Sequence of Poems, David R. Godine, 1987.
Before It Vanishes: A Packet for Professor Pagels, David R. Godine, 1990.
Fathering the Map: New and Selected Later Poems, University of Chicago Press (Chicago, IL), 1993.
Poems for a Small Planet, University Press of New England (Hanover, NH), 1993.
Minding the Sun, University of Chicago Press, 1996.
Rounding It Out: A Cycle of Sonnetelles, University of Chicago Press, 1999.

CRITICISM

Wallace Stevens: An Approach to His Poetry and Thought, Rutgers University Press, 1958.
Affirming Limits: Essays on Morality, Choice, and Poetic Form, University of Massachusetts Press (Amherst, MA), 1985.
The Long View: Essays on the Discipline of Hope and Poetic Craft, University of Massachusetts Press, 1991.

EDITOR

(With Donald Hall and Louis Simpson) *New Poems of England and America,* Meridian, 1957, second edition (with Hall), 1962.
(And translator with Marjorie Lelash) *Mozart's Librettos,* Meridian, 1961.
(With Tom Driver) *An Anthology of Modern Religious Poetry,* Macmillan, 1963.
(With Driver) *Poems of Doubt and Belief* (anthology), Macmillan, 1964.
(And author of introduction) *The Selected Letters of John Keats,* New American Library (New York City), 1974.
(With Sydney Lea and Jay Parini) *The Bread Loaf Anthology of Contemporary American Poetry,* University Press of New England (Hanover, NH), 1985.
(With Jay Parini) *The Bread Loaf Anthology of Contemporary American Short Stories,* University Press of New England, 1987.

(With Jay Parini) *The Bread Loaf Anthology of Contemporary American Essays,* University Press of New England, 1989.

(With Jay Parini) *Writers on Writing,* University Press of New England, 1991.

(With Jay Parini) *American Identities: Contemporary Multicultural Voices,* University Press of New England, 1994.

(With Jay Parini) *Introspections: American Poets on One of Their Own Poems,* University Press of New England, 1994.

(With Jay Parini) *Touchstones: American Poets on a Favorite Poem,* University Press of New England, 1994.

FOR CHILDREN

The Forgotten Secret, Macmillan, 1959.
Then What Did You Do?, Macmillan, 1961.
How to Catch a Crocodile, Knopf, 1964.
The Octopus Who Wanted to Juggle, Galileo Press, 1990.

OTHER

(Translator, with Marjorie Lelash) *Three Mozart Libretti: Complete in Italian and English,* Dover Publications (New York City), 1993.

Also author of *Inheritance,* 1992; former poetry editor, *Discovery.*

Sidelights

Robert Pack is an American poet who is known for addressing serious themes and issues, but in a manner that is provocative yet ingratiating. Burton Kendle, writing in *Contemporary Poets,* affirmed, "From his earliest works . . ., Robert Pack's poetry has celebrated man's organic relationship to all levels of creation." Kendle described Pack's poetry as "serious poetry that is still magically lighthearted."

Kendle deemed the poem "Grieving on a Grand Scale" a "representative work" by the poet. Here, a lover's death is fantasized, and the repercussions that nature's degeneration might hold for individuals are pondered. Poems like "Prayer for Prayer" and the title work in *Fathering the Map,* meanwhile, reduce the immense magnitude of Christian faith to simple needs and hopes.

Among Pack's many verse volumes are *Faces in a Single Tree,* which includes compelling monologues on domestic interaction; *Clayfeld Rejoices, Clayfeld Laments,* which includes verses charting an artist's intellectual and emotional development; *Inheritance,* a collection of interrelated poems, structured in five-line stanzas, considering the evolution of humanity; *Before It Vanishes,* which includes further speculation on the origin, and purpose, of humanity; and the aforementioned *Fathering the Map,* wherein Pack revels in the relationship between human beings and nature. Notable in *Fathering the Map* is "Wild Turkey in Paradise," wherein the narrator notes the manner in which untended apple trees affect the surroundings. Kendle ranked this poem with Pack's best work.

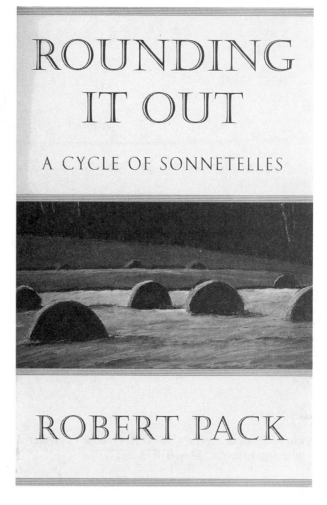

Poet Robert Pack's collection of poems reflecting natural rhythms and cycles is divided into four sections representing morning, midday, evening, and night. (Cover illustration by Cynthia Price.)

Minding the Sun, another of Pack's poetry collections, serves as further evidence of his keen appreciation of nature and his capacity for considering the vastness of the cosmos. A reviewer for *Publishers Weekly* observed that the poems in this volume "are generally intelligent, deft and provocative."

In a review for the *New Republic,* Harold Bloom wrote: "Robert Pack's *Keeping Watch* has the quiet wisdom, sanity and good workmanship we rightly expect from him. 'Maxims in Limbo' compares poorly to the Stevens of 'Like Decorations,' which it invokes, but every other poem in the book is movingly closer to home. *Nothing but Light,* Pack's previous book, was better, but even this latest volume continues to show Pack's strength as an almost unique celebrant of married love and fatherhood." *Nothing but Light* also drew praise from Louis Coxe, who, writing in the *New Republic,* claimed that Pack "has great resources as a poet, both of language and technique. . . . Indeed, I think Pack's command of the medium is altogether remarkable." Nevertheless, Coxe warned that Pack "has perhaps reached the stage when he must subside into silence or the increasingly trivial. I believe he has far too much talent and potential to do either. But while we may well and properly enjoy some poems in this book, we may also feel that we want, expect and feel the promise of, more and finer."

Reviewing Pack's *Before It Vanishes* for the *New York Times Book Review,* Liz Rosenberg wrote: "Robert Pack occupies a position of importance among poets, though not primarily as a poet. For many years he has directed the famous Bread Loaf Writers Conference in Vermont, and his work has been widely and warmly praised. Still, it remains relatively unknown. Mr. Pack's poems possess a gentle, nearly antique quality. He has written tenderly about rural Vermont and about family life, and now ... he tackles the universe."

Works Cited

Bloom, Harold, review of *Keeping Watch, New Republic,* November 20, 1976.

Coxe, Lowis, review of *Nothing but Light, New Republic,* February 3, 1973.

Kendle, Burton, *Contemporary Poets,* "Robert Pack," 6th edition, St. James Press (Detroit), 1996.

Review of *Minding the Sun, Publishers Weekly,* April 29, 1996, p. 64.

Rosenberg, Liz, review of *Before It Vanishes, New York Times Book Review,* May 6, 1990.

For More Information See

BOOKS

Bain, David Haward, and Sydney Landon Plum, editors, *At an Elevation: On the Poetry of Robert Pack,* Middlebury College Press (Middlebury, VT), 1994.

Contemporary Literary Criticism, Volume 13, Gale (Detroit), 1980.

Dictionary of Literary Biography, Volume 5: *American Poets since World War II,* Gale, 1980.

PERIODICALS

Antioch Review, fall, 1969.

Bloomsbury Review, September, 1994, p. 20.

Booklist, May 15, 1993, p. 1670; September 15, 1993, p. 119.

Choice, June, 1996, p. 1647.

Hudson Review, summer, 1994, p. 313.

Kliatt, July, 1996, p. 25.

Library Journal, June 1, 1993, p. 128; October 1, 1994, p. 78; May 1, 1996, p. 98; January, 1998, p. 100.

Massachusetts Review, winter, 1982.

Nation, March 30, 1970.

New York Times Book Review, January 27, 1985.

Poetry, February, 1995, p. 289.

Publishers Weekly, January 22, 1996, p. 65; December 1, 1997, p. 41.

Saturday Review, January 17, 1970.

Sewanee Review, October, 1992, p. 669.

Times Literary Supplement, January 29, 1993, p. 9.

Virginia Quarterly Review, summer, 1996, p. 101.

Wilson Library Bulletin, February, 1995, p. 78.*

PARKES, Lucas
See HARRIS, John (Wyndham Parkes Lucas) Beynon

*   *   *

PETERSEN, P(eter) J(ames) 1941-

Personal

Born October 23, 1941, in Santa Rosa, CA; son of Carl Eric (a farmer) and Alice (a farmer; maiden name, Winters) Petersen; married Miriam Braun (a nurse), July 6, 1963; children: Karen, Carla. *Education:* Stanford University, A.B., 1962; San Francisco State College (now University), M.A., 1964; University of New Mexico, Ph.D., 1972. *Hobbies and other interests:* Reading, hiking, bicycling, kayaking, scuba diving.

Addresses

Home—1243 Pueblo Ct., Redding, CA 96001. *Agent*—Ruth Cohen, Inc., P.O. Box 7626, Menlo Park, CA 94025.

Career

Author and educator. Shasta College, Redding, CA, instructor of English, 1964-2000. *Member:* Society of Children's Book Writers and Illustrators.

Awards, Honors

Fellowship, National Endowment for the Humanities, 1976-77; Dorothy Canfield Fisher Award nomination, 1981, for *Would You Settle for Improbable?;* Best Books for Young Adults citations, American Library Association, 1982, for *Would You Settle for Improbable?,* and 1983, for *Nobody Else Can Walk It for You;* American Bookseller Pick of the Lists designation, 1992, for *Liars;* OMAR Award, 1996, for *The Sub;* Honor Book, West Virginia Children's Book Award organization, 1997-1998, for *I Hate Company; White Water* was nominated for the Young Hoosier Book Award, the Children's Crown Award, the Sequoyah Children's Book Award, the Black-Eyed Susan Book Award, 1999, the Golden Sower Award, 1999, and the South Carolina Children's Book Award, 1999; William Allen White Award, 2000, for *White Water;* Nevada Young Readers' Award nomination, 2001, for *Can You Keep a Secret?*

Writings

Would You Settle for Improbable?, Delacorte, 1981.

Nobody Else Can Walk It for You, Delacorte, 1982.

The Boll Weevil Express, Delacorte, 1983.

Here's to the Sophomores (sequel to *Would You Settle for Improbable?*), Delacorte, 1984.

Corky and the Brothers Cool, Delacorte, 1985.

Going for the Big One, Delacorte, 1986.

Good-bye to Good Ol' Charlie, Delacorte, 1987.

P. J. Petersen

The Freshman Detective Blues, Delacorte, 1987.

How Can You Hijack a Cave? Delacorte, 1988.

(With Betsy James) *The Fireplug Is First Base,* illustrated by Betsy James, Dutton, 1990.

Liars, Simon & Schuster, 1992.

The Sub, illustrated by Meredith Johnson, Dutton, 1993.

I Want Answers and a Parachute, illustrated by Anna DiVito, Simon & Schuster, 1993.

The Amazing Magic Show, illustrated by Renee Williams-Andriani, Simon & Schuster, 1994.

Some Days, Other Days (picture book), illustrated by Diane de Groat, Scribner's, 1994.

White Water, Simon & Schuster, 1997.

Can You Keep a Secret?, illustrated by Meredith Johnson, Dutton, 1997.

My Worst Friend, illustrated by Meredith Johnson, 1998.

"I HATE ... " SERIES; PRIMARY-GRADE FICTION; PUBLISHED BY DUTTON

I Hate Camping, illustrated by Frank Remkiewicz, 1991.

I Hate Company, illustrated by Betsy James, 1994.

I Hate Weddings, illustrated by Lynne Cravath, 2000.

Adaptations

Would You Settle for Improbable? was adapted into a feature film.

Sidelights

A prolific and popular author of contemporary fiction for children and young people, Petersen is recognized for writing fast-paced, appealing books with serious themes that he lightens with optimism and humor. Setting several of his works in small towns (mostly fictional) in his native California, the author characteristically creates genre fiction—mysteries, thrillers, survival stories, school stories, romances, and works that blend genres—that is considered notable for its believable situations, realistic characterizations, and sensitive, insightful treatment of the issues faced by the young. Petersen is often praised for his understanding of both young people and human nature. He consistently addresses relationships in his books—between siblings, between friends, between parents and children, between townspeople, and between teenage members of the opposite sex. Several of Petersen's young protagonists, both boys and girls, must learn to deal with their parents' divorces or remarriages. His characters, who often start out unsure of themselves, encounter life-and-death situations, such as escaping from a violent criminal or trying to get back to shore on a white-water raft with an injured parent. Petersen also addresses more subtle issues, such as standing up for or learning to be yourself, dealing with discrimination, and deciding how to treat a classmate with cancer.

Throughout his works, Petersen stresses trust, friendship, discretion, honesty, and authenticity. At the end of his stories, his protagonists have proven themselves and have learned that, despite its complexity, life goes on. Petersen favors simple, lively narratives that are written primarily through dialogue, often spoken by his main characters. Although some observers have noted that the author's works are occasionally predictable and contrived, most reviewers consider Petersen an author of well-crafted books that are both thoughtful and entertaining. Writing in *St. James Guide to Young Adult Writers,* Carol Doxey concluded that Petersen is in "the top bracket of twentieth century young adult authors.... It is apparent that P. J. Petersen enjoys writing for young adults. He handles difficult ethical problems that young people confront with ease and intelligence. He doesn't preach, but subtly portrays possible solutions to problems encountered by young adults in their ever-changing world. His realistic, exciting stories ... filled with emotion, human relationships, and the good and evil that fill the world of today, all deal with how young people can and do survive, as they seek and usually find the answers they need."

Born in Santa Rosa, California, Petersen grew up on a prune farm about six miles from the nearest town, Geyersville. "Because actual travel was impossible," the author wrote in *Sixth Book of Junior Authors and Illustrators,* "I settled for traveling through books—reading about people whose lives were different than mine." His main source for books was the Geyersville Public Library, where the three shelves of children's books were replaced every two or three months with new titles from the bookmobile. Petersen noted, "I generally read every volume on the shelves." As a child, Petersen read everything he could find, including the Western adventure novels of Zane Grey and the Nancy Drew mystery series by Carolyn Keene. However, his favorite book was *Tom Sawyer* by Mark Twain; he recalled, "The picture of Injun Joe trapped in the cave still sends chills through me." Petersen also listened to dramatic radio programs such as *The Whistler, The Fat Man,* and *Suspense,* which he later credited with influencing his writing, especially in his use of dialogue. While he worked on his family's farm, Petersen related the stories that he read to his younger brother, though he often changed the endings. He also made up his own stories and, as he noted, "was delighted to find that my brother couldn't always tell the difference between my creations and 'real' ones." At the age of eight, Petersen decided to become a writer. Many of his earliest works were written in emulation of the plays he heard on the radio. However, at the time, small-town farm boys were expected to become farmers or mechanics, not writers; Petersen stated, "I never changed my mind about writing, but after a while I quit announcing my plans."

As a high school student, Petersen discovered authors such as John Steinbeck, Agatha Christie, Tennessee Williams, Willa Cather, and James Thurber; he also read Superman comic books and *Mad* magazine. In high school, Petersen began to write seriously, focusing on short stories as a preparation for writing novels. He received his first rejection slip at sixteen. After attending Stanford University, Petersen moved to what he called "a tiny room in a run-down section of San Francisco" and began to work on his first novel, which he finished in a year. Petersen recalled, "I thought it was nearly perfect, but none of the publishers agreed." After receiving six rejection slips, he shoved the novel into a drawer. He once told *SATA:* "After that painful experience, I avoided similar disappointments by never finishing anything. I spent years writing the first halves of novels." He added in *Sixth Book of Junior Authors and Illustrators,* "Without realizing it, I had come to believe what I had been told as a child. Boys from Geyersville don't become writers." Disenchanted with the idea of becoming a novelist, Petersen decided to become a teacher. He moved to San Francisco to attend San Francisco State College in order to earn his master's degree. In 1963, he married Marian Braun, a nurse; they have two daughters, Karen and Carla. After receiving his master's degree in 1964, Petersen became an instructor at Shasta College in Redding, California. He received his Ph.D. from the University of New Mexico in 1972 and was awarded a fellowship from the National Endowment for the Humanities in 1976.

In the summer of 1978, Petersen attended his twenty-year high school reunion. After returning home, he decided to give writing a final try. His daughter Karen, then in junior high, began to share the books that she was reading with her father. Petersen once told *SATA,* "Seeing how excited she was about reading, I decided to write a book for her. If I couldn't interest a publisher (and I was understandably pessimistic), I intended to give her the manuscript—a present from a loving

father." Petersen began working on the book, which eventually became his first published novel, *Would You Settle for Improbable?* As he once told *SATA,* he felt "a quiet satisfaction growing inside me. By luck, I had stumbled into the kind of writing that was right for me." Petersen added in *Sixth Book of Junior Authors and Illustrators* that writing "was suddenly fun again. I was laughing at the jokes, wincing at the painful parts. It was like the old days, when I was out in the prune orchard telling stories to my brothers. I had finally discovered where I belonged."

Petersen once told *SATA,* "My novels deal with the difficult ethical problems that young people face . . . . Although I try to avoid preaching, my own preferences can be seen in the approach to life taken by my central characters—the ones who keep trusting and hoping and caring, even though they're often hurt and disappointed." He has said that his first published novel, *Would You Settle for Improbable?,* "involves the difficulty of changing destructive patterns." In this work, ninth-grader Michael Parker and his friends—whose journal entries make up the core of the story—attempt to change the antisocial behavior of Arnold Norberg, a former resident

When eighth-grader Sam discovers he has the power to tell when someone is lying, his previously quiet life in small-town Alder Creek becomes very complicated.

Young Jimmy doesn't want to get out of bed, uncertain whether today will be a good day or a bad day, in Petersen's accurate portrayal of childhood dilemmas. (From Some Days, Other Days, *illustrated by Diane de Groat.*)

of juvenile hall who has entered their junior high. Although Arnold is shunned initially, he gains the respect of his classmates when he attempts to divert the principal's anger after a prank is committed. Even when Arnold steals a car and runs away with the class's money, a solid core of friends awaits his return. Zena Sutherland of *Bulletin of the Center for Children's Books* called *Would You Settle for Improbable?* "an effective first novel," while a critic in the *Horn Book* considered it "a finely crafted novel, at once funny and touching" that included "a memorable cast of characters." *Would You Settle for Improbable?* was later turned into a feature film.

The sequel to *Would You Settle for Improbable?, Here's to the Sophomores,* finds the characters in high school. In this book, Michael breaks his leg, gets expelled from school, and lands in a lunchroom brawl, only to be saved by his secret sweetheart Margaret. He also helps his friend Warren, a boy whose parents are divorcing. A nonconformist, Warren leads a protest against the issue of mandatory attendance at assemblies, a situation that leads to the suspension of nearly fifty students. Arnold Norberg also reappears in the story, reformed from his life of crime. Although humorous, the novel stresses standing by one's convictions despite peer pressure; in

addition, Petersen depicts the problems faced by both white and Chicano students as they attempt to accept one another. Noting the novel's "fast action, snappy dialogue, and authentic atmosphere," a critic in *Horn Book* called *Here's to the Sophomores* a "thoughtful novel on accepting differences and standing up for one's beliefs." *School Library Journal* reviewer Kathleen W. Craver concluded, "The integration conflicts ring true and the dilemma of an adolescent who chooses not to conform to a peer group would be good book talk material." Petersen once told *SATA* that the novel "involves the characters who appeared in the first book. I had left them at their junior high school graduation. What, I wondered, would have happened to them in high school? How would the change of surroundings effect each of these people? I finally decided to write about their first two weeks of high school. By stopping at that point I could leave it up to the readers to decide how things would go after that."

One of Petersen's most well-received early books is *Nobody Else Can Walk It for You,* which the author has noted "concerns responses to violence." In this work, eighteen-year-old Laura and seven younger adolescents from the YMCA confront three menacing motorcyclists while on a backpacking trip. The hoodlums assault the boys and make passes at the girls. In order to escape, the children perform individual acts of daring. Finally, Laura and Irene, an older woman, lead the group up a mountain where the cyclists cannot follow on their bikes. The group must face Brian, the psychotic leader of the bikers, before they can finally reach safety. Writing in *School Library Journal,* George Gleason noted, "Transcription of teenage dialogue is deliciously accurate, and several characters are outstanding.... You cheer the courageous actions of several." Sally Estes of *Booklist* added, "The story is a cliff-hanger from page one."

In 1991, Petersen began producing his popular series of "I Hate ..." stories. These works—*I Hate Camping, I Hate Company,* and *I Hate Weddings*—are humorous chapter books for early readers that feature Dan, a boy whose parents are divorced. In *I Hate Camping,* Dan's mother sends him on an overnight camping trip with her boyfriend Mike and his two children. The campers go through a variety of experiences and emotions before coming to an understanding of each other. Carolyn Jenks, writing in *School Library Journal,* predicted that readers just beginning chapter books "will identify with these people and will laugh at and with them," while Chris Sherman of *Booklist* concluded that Petersen has created "a satisfying story with plenty of action." In *I Hate Company,* Dan is not pleased with the long-term invitation that his mother extends to her old friend Kay, a recent divorcee, and her son Jimmy. Kay is looking for a job, so Dan tries to help her in order to speed up the process and regain his privacy. Inadvertently, he wins Kay a position; when she and her son leave, Dan finds that he misses them—a little. A critic in *Kirkus Reviews* stated, "The young narrator's voice sounds authentic, but his take on the world just doesn't ring true." However, Chris Sherman of *Booklist* noted, "Children who've had to put up with annoying houseguests will sympathize with Dan." In *I Hate Weddings,* Dan is invited to attend his father's marriage to Joan, a woman with children. Dan wonders where he is going to fit in; although his best efforts backfire, they serve to break the ice between the two families. *Booklist* critic Karen Simonetti concluded that the book is "guaranteed to have young readers giggling and nodding their heads in empathy."

Another of Petersen's most popular books for primary graders is *The Sub.* In this work, two best friends, James and Ray, trade identities to fool their substitute teacher. James soon gets tired of the prank, especially when he gets blamed for Ray's misconduct and messy desk. After Ray sprains his ankle and the wrong sets of parents are called, James confesses to the prank. He is made to pick up litter during recess by the teacher, who has been aware of the joke all along and gains James's respect through her patience and humor. Writing in *Booklist,* Kay Weisman noted, "Realistic characters and believable, humorous situations are Petersen's strengths." Mary Lou Budd, writing in *School Library Journal,* concluded that older readers as well as younger ones will enjoy the book, saying, "[S]tudents will be eager to read this one."

My Worst Friend is a book for primary graders in which one of the protagonists, Sara Trent, has cancer. Sara and Jenny Jones have shared a competitive relationship since nursery school. When Sara becomes ill with a malignant brain tumor, Jenny feels lost without her competitor. After Sara returns to school, Jenny feels obliged to be nice to her, even when Sara is at her most acerbic. At the end of the story, Jenny learns that Sara needs to be treated normally, without pity. In a *Booklist* review, Weisman said, "Although the pair's behavior may seem somewhat over the top, it is refreshing to find a story about friendship that isn't cloyingly sweet." A critic in *Horn Book* called *My Worst Friend* "a story notable both for its dead-on middle-grade dialogue as well as for its unsentimental look at a serious subject." Writing in *Bulletin of the Center for Children's Books,* Deborah Stevenson stated, "Petersen is deft at conveying the elaborateness of Sara's nastiness and the warring of Jenny's accumulated resentment with her newfound pity."

White Water is among Petersen's most highly regarded stories for middle graders. In this work, Greg's father, who wants him to become more assertive, takes the boy and his younger half-brother James on a white-water rafting trip. When his father is bitten by a rattlesnake, Greg has to take him downstream for a full day in order to get help. Greg and James overturn the raft, meet a bear, and have other terrifying experiences before they reach their destination. Once home, Greg goes through an earthquake that hits his San Francisco home, but he has learned enough about himself to realize that he can keep his cool during an emergency. John Peters of *Booklist* stated, "This white-water rafting adventure skims along at a breathless clip." Calling *White Water* "a pulse-pounding adventure," a critic in *Kirkus Reviews* declared, "The book is a thrill ride."

Works Cited

Budd, Mary Lou, review of *The Sub, School Library Journal,* July, 1993, pp. 86-87.

Craver, Kathleen W., review of *Here's to the Sophomores, School Library Journal,* April, 1984, p. 127.

Doxey, Carol, "P. J. Petersen," *St. James Guide to Young Adult Writers,* edited by Tom Pendergast and Sara Pendergast, 2nd edition, St. James Press, 1999, pp. 685-87.

Estes, Sally, review of *Nobody Else Can Walk It for You, Booklist,* April, 1982, p. 1014.

Gleason, George, review of *Nobody Else Can Walk It for You, School Library Journal,* May, 1982, pp. 73-74.

Review of *Here's to the Sophomores, Horn Book,* June, 1984, p. 341.

Review of *I Hate Company, Kirkus Reviews,* October 15, 1994, p. 1414.

Jenks, Carolyn, review of *I Hate Camping, School Library Journal,* May, 1991, p. 82.

Review of *My Worst Friend, Horn Book,* 1999.

When Greg's father is bitten by a rattlesnake during their white-water rafting trip, normally unassertive Greg must be courageous and resourceful to commandeer their trip downstream. (Cover illustration by Greg Harlin.)

Peters, John, review of *White Water, Booklist,* June 1, 1997, p. 1705.

Petersen, P. J., essay in *Sixth Book of Junior Authors and Illustrators,* edited by Sally Holmes Holtze, Wilson, 1989, pp. 221-23.

Sherman, Chris, review of *I Hate Camping, Booklist,* June 15, 1991, pp. 1967-68.

Sherman, Chris, review of *I Hate Company, Booklist,* November 1, 1994, p. 500.

Simonetti, Karen, review of *I Hate Weddings, Booklist,* March 1, 2000.

Stevenson, Deborah, review of *My Worst Friend, Bulletin of the Center for Children's Books,* October, 1998, p. 70.

Sutherland, Zena, review of *Would You Settle for Improbable?, Bulletin of the Center for Children's Books,* October, 1981, p. 35.

Weisman, Kay, review of *My Worst Friend, Booklist,* October 15, 1998, p. 422.

Weisman, Kay, review of *The Sub, Booklist,* June 1 and 15, 1993, p. 1836.

Review of *White Water, Kirkus Reviews,* May 15, 1997, p. 805.

Review of *Would You Settle for Improbable?, Horn Book,* February, 1982, p. 55.

For More Information See

BOOKS

Major Authors and Illustrators for Children and Young Adults, Gale, 1993, pp. 1866-67.

Petersen, P. J., essay in *Speaking for Ourselves, Too,* edited by Donald R. Gallo, National Council of Teachers of English, 1993.

PERIODICALS

Booklist, October 1, 1993, p. 345.

Bulletin of the Center for Children's Books, September, 1993, p. 21.

Kirkus Reviews, November 1, 1993, p. 1396; October 15, 1997, p. 1586.

School Library Journal, January, 1998, p. 90.

*   *   *

PIG, Edward
See GOREY, Edward (St. John)

*   *   *

PLUM, Jennifer
See KURLAND, Michael (Joseph)

*   *   *

POWELL, Randy 1956-

Personal

Born on August 26, 1956, in Seattle, WA; son of Ray and Marilyn Powell; married, wife's name, Judy (a nurse), 1983; children: Eli, Drew. *Education:* University of Washington, B.A. (English, history, and communications), 1981; M.A. (education), 1984.

Career

Writer, 1988—. Teacher, alternative school for junior high and high school dropouts, 1984-88; Boeing Company, Everett, WA, technical writer, 1989—.

Awards, Honors

Best Books for Young Adults citation, American Library Association, and Pen West Award for Children's Literature, 1993, both for *Is Kissing A Girl Who Smokes Like Licking an Ashtray?;* Best Books for Young Adults citation and "Quick Picks" for Young Adults selection, both American Library Association, both for *Dean Duffy;* Junior Literary Guild selection, 1999, and Best Books for Young Adults citation, American Library Association, both for *Tribute to Another Dead Rock Star.* Powell's novels have also received nominations for several state reading awards.

Writings

My Underrated Year, Farrar, Straus and Giroux, 1988.
Is Kissing A Girl Who Smokes Like Licking an Ashtray?, Farrar, Straus and Giroux, 1992.
Dean Duffy, Farrar, Straus and Giroux, 1995.
The Whistling Toilets, Farrar, Straus and Giroux, 1996.
Tribute to Another Dead Rock Star, Farrar, Straus and Giroux, 1999.

Powell's works have been translated into Greek, French, Slovenian, Polish, and German.

Adaptations

All of Powell's novels have been adapted for audiocassette by Books on Tape; *Tribute to Another Dead Rock Star* has been optioned for a movie by All Media/Showtime.

Work in Progress

Long May You Run, a young adult novel about a father-son relationship, to be published by Farrar, Straus and Giroux, expected 2001.

Sidelights

"I was about nineteen the summer I wrote my first novel," author Randy Powell told *Authors and Artists for Young Adults* in an interview, "and it was about a kid who was nineteen who had no idea what he was doing or where he was going. That novel was never published, but I've been writing about characters like him ever since." Powell's searching, struggling, and often very humorous characters include Roger Ottosen in *My Underrated Year,* who is trying to choose between football and tennis; Biff Schmurr in *Is Kissing a Girl Who Smokes Like Licking an Ashtray?,* who has a definite confidence problem; Dean Duffy in the novel *Dean Duffy,* who is trying to decide if he should make baseball his whole life; Stan in *The Whistling Toilets,* who wonders why he does not have the drive to succeed in tennis; and Grady in *Tribute to Another Dead Rock Star,* who is trying to make some sense of his life after the death of his rock-star mom. Each of Powell's characters is caught at a fragile moment when he is trying to decide on the direction his life should take. Powell's coming-of-age novels are particularly life-like and are often open-ended, leaving the resolution up to the reader.

Sports are often a part of Powell's novels. His protagonists play football, baseball, and tennis, but for Powell, sports is the vehicle though which he examines mature themes. "After my first YA novel, I thought I might be an author of what critics like to call 'character-driven sports books,'" Powell told *Authors and Artists for Young Adults,* "but I found writing sports scenes over and over can be very dull for me. I like to grow in my work, to find surprises." He now writes about family relationships, love, fitting in and bailing out, and dealing with neglect and rejection. As a critic for *Publishers Weekly* wrote in a review of *Tribute to Another Dead Rock Star,* "Through sharply defined characters and lively, often humorous dialogue, Powell allows readers to comfortably examine some serious issues." This is true of all of his work.

Powell grew up in Seattle, Washington. He was an active child, not one to stay inside and read. "I was obsessed with sports growing up, both organized and unorganized," Powell said in his interview. "If I wasn't playing some sport, I was fantasizing about one. I played Little League football, basketball, and baseball, and the high point of my very young career was when our Little League football team won the all-city championship in Seattle and I was given the game ball by my team. I was eleven years old then, and it was definitely a moment of glory. Somehow over the years, I managed to lose that ball, and I've been looking for it ever since."

By high school he had given up football to concentrate on tennis, a sport he still plays when his busy schedule allows time. His change of focus encompassed not only sports, but also his enjoyment of words. "I liked books well enough. There was *The Catcher in the Rye* and *Catch-22,* and short stories by Woody Allen published in the *New Yorker.* I really threw myself into each novel, identifying not only with the main character, but also with the writer. I started to write, to see if I could do things like the author I was reading at the time." Powell began to write short stories and to type them in the school typing room during lunch. His early efforts earned only rejections slips when he sent them to publications such as the *New Yorker,* but he was not discouraged by this. "The rejection letters all began with 'Dear Author.' I thought, this is great. They're calling me an author."

After graduating from high school, Powell attended the University of Washington, earning a bachelor's degree

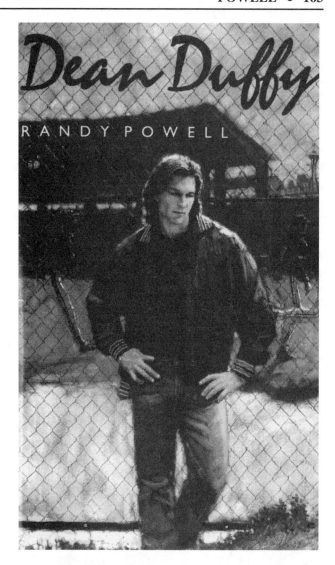

When the eighteen-year-old protagonist of Randy Powell's novel must give up his dreams of a baseball career because of injuries, he tries to put his life in order and re-evaluate his plans for the future. (Cover illustration by Todd Doney.)

in English, history, and communications, followed by a master's degree in education. While in college he continued to write, eventually building his confidence to attempt a novel. After obtaining his master's degree, he taught at an alternative school for junior high and high school dropouts. "It was demanding work," Powell told *Authors and Artists for Young Adults.* "I loved the kids, working with them, relating to them, but it takes all your creativity being a teacher."

During his four years as a teacher, Powell became interested in writing for young adults. Reading Robert Cormier's *The Chocolate War* revealed to him the possibilities of the genre. "I realized I had found a home here," he said. Increasingly he was developing his own voice instead of merely copying writers he admired. "Rather than aiming at a certain market, I just tried writing from inside, to find the old powerful impressions and memories of my own childhood." His first attempt at a young adult story, "Tennis Isn't Fun Anymore," was rejected, but helpful criticism encouraged him to try again with more focus on the YA audience. Plucking a personal memory from his life and blending it with fictional components, he created a tale about a high school sophomore whose dreams of making the varsity football team and being number one on the tennis team are jeopardized by a brother and sister with exceptional athletic ability. He worked on the story in the early morning and at night until he had a finished manuscript which he sent to several publishers.

"I was in the teachers' lounge at school the day I got a call from Margaret Ferguson at Farrar, Straus and Giroux to tell me they wanted to take on my first novel," Powell recalled. "I was so happy I just took the afternoon off and went and played pinball." The novel was *My Underrated Year.* In the work, high school sophomore Roger Ottosen thinks he has achieved success: He believes he has earned a spot on the varsity

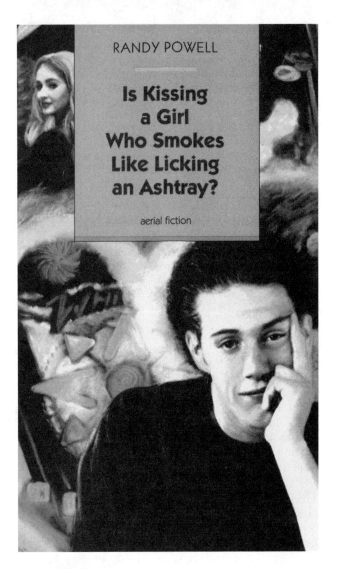

Nerdy Biff and wisecracking Heidi are encouraged to spend time together by their relatives and discover an unlikely, but intimate, friendship. (Cover illustration by Hilary Mosberg.)

football team, and also thinks he is assured of the first position on the tennis team. Then the twins come to town. Paul Mountain is a strong, powerful running back who beats out Roger for a starting spot. Mary Mountain, a tennis whiz who decides to try out for the boys' team, threatens Roger's claim to top seed by trouncing his main competitor.

Roger should despise both Mountains, but he is falling in love with Mary Jo. He grows despondent and almost quits playing football, but a friend convinces him to continue, if only for the junior varsity team. Roger is afraid to play tennis with Mary Jo, wary of both her skill and his ability to effectively compete against his love interest. By the end of the book, Roger is rewarded for his tenacity. He earns a position on the varsity as a punt returner and wins the award as "Most Underrated" at the end-of-season banquet. He works through his concerns about Mary Jo, and finds that his training and concentration have paid off when he defeats her in a tennis match. Their growing friendship suffers a setback from this, but is not destroyed.

Powell's first book was generally well received. Writing in *School Library Journal,* Gerry Larson stated, "Roger's candid narration humorously and poignantly exposes the fragile ego of the teenage athlete.... Adolescent anxiety, jealousy, insecurity, and an all-consuming passion for sports make Roger an appealing and believable character." Larson also applauded Powell's handling of sports scenes, commenting, "Teen readers will empathize with the emotional roller coaster of high-school sports and friendships."

The story includes a subplot about Roger's relationship with his new stepfather. It is he who encourages Roger to go to the sports banquet where he is honored. A critic for *Publishers Weekly* observed that the "most involving aspect of the non-sports scenes can be found in the relationship between Roger and his mother and her new husband ... many of these scenes are genuinely moving." *Horn Book*'s Nancy Vasilakis praised both the "well-crafted sports scenes [that] succeed in raising the reader's adrenaline level," and the problems with personal relationships Roger faces that give the novel "added weight" and for which "the author wisely offers no easy answers." Vasilakis concluded, "The complex, ambiguous relationships set down in the novel, combined with its exciting sports setting, make engrossing reading and mark a fine debut for a new writer of young adult fiction."

After this positive reception, Powell immediately produced his second novel, but, like many novelists, his ambition to surpass his first book almost worked against him. "I was writing about a guy who loves baseball, for whom baseball is a sort of god," Powell remarked. "And then injuries diminish his abilities, threatening any chance for college scholarships." The book was sprawling, filled with incident and character. Powell's editor rejected it but encouraged him to rewrite it and refine the plot. Powell wrote another draft of the book, focusing on a shorter time frame, and produced a manuscript that was accepted by Farrar, Straus, and Giroux. That work, *Dean Duffy,* would be delayed for publication, though, after an experimental writing project proved equally successful.

When Powell's son was born, "I took a paternity leave," he explained, "and during that time wrote a book that had nothing whatever to do with sports. I wanted to try to write a book from an outline and so had sketched in about fifty scenes, but by scene two when Biff meets Heidi, I just threw away the outline and followed my main characters around." His exercise in writing became the novel *Is Kissing a Girl Who Smokes Like Licking an Ashtray?,* and his editors liked the book so much that they published it before *Dean Duffy.* That was the end of Powell's interest in writing character-driven sports books. "By then I had grown bored with writing sports scenes, anyway," Powell related. "I no longer concentrate on those. Sports may be in the books, but not as the centerpiece."

Is Kissing a Girl Who Smokes is "a funny and tender tale of an unlikely friendship," according to Roger Sutton, writing in *Bulletin of the Center for Children's Books.* Biff, a senior in high school, is a nerd: "a wild-haired recovering pinball addict who looks like he's 14, and is yet to have his first date," as Barbara Flottmeier described him in *Voice of Youth Advocates.* He has a crush on Tommie but can only follow her around school and occasionally manage to say "Hi." When Heidi, a tough-mouthed, wisecracking, cigarette-smoking teenager comes to town, Biff's world is turned upside down. Heidi is younger than Biff, but more experienced and older in every other way. She has been suspended from her school and is staying with relatives, friends of Biff's older sister. Biff is encouraged to spend time with Heidi. Although unwilling at first, Biff is quickly attracted to his opposite, as Heidi is to him. His streak of common sense resounds in her; her wild abandon and mood swings amaze him.

Flottmeier wrote, "These two impossible opposites find enough things to talk about, fight about, and laugh about in two days to feel the beginnings of a sweet friendship and, perhaps, even love.... It's a warm, funny, poignant romance with true-to-life dialogue and an almost believable plot." A reviewer for *Publishers Weekly* commented that Powell's "delightfully goofy novel starts looping around like a pocket full of jumping beans" with the entrance of Heidi, and concluded, "Funny and poignant, with a fresh, wry viewpoint and impeccable characterizations, this novel is a joy to read." A contributor to *Kirkus Reviews* called the book an "engaging, readable story featuring razor-sharp dialogue, nicely articulated chemistry between the characters, and a happy ending." His second publication earned Powell an American Library Association Best Book for Young Adults citation.

Dean Duffy, Powell's second completed manuscript, was finally published in 1995. Powell had focused the work on the summer and fall of Dean's eighteenth year, after he has graduated from high school and is trying to figure

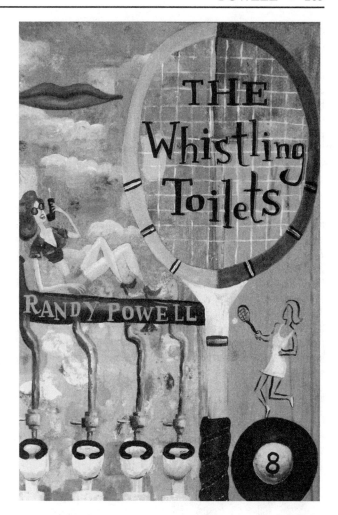

Junior tennis superstar Ginny Forrester, having a career crisis, is aided by an old childhood friend, who helps her regain her confidence even as she assists him in rediscovering his ambition. (Cover illustration by Josh Gosfield.)

out what to do with his life. A baseball career seems unlikely because an injury has curtailed his pitching, and his batting during the last two years of high school has been pathetic. His dreams of baseball greatness, nurtured since Little League days, are gone. Instead, he must put his life in order and re-evaluate his hopes for the future.

During the summer after graduation Dean house-sits and, for the first time in his life, begins to feel like a loser. He then becomes involved with a high-school dropout who is a single mother and tries to take stock of himself. Encountering several old baseball buddies, he starts to think about the game again. When a former coach finagles him a "trial" scholarship at a private school, Dean must truly confront his demons and decide how much baseball is worth to him. At the end of the novel, Dean is handed a pen to sign the offer, but readers must decide for themselves what he does.

Joel Shoemaker, writing in *School Library Journal,* thought the ending was "delightfully ambiguous," and that *Dean Duffy* "has stronger subplots and more likable characters than Powell's earlier YA novels." In *Bulletin of the Center for Children's Books,* Roger Sutton observed, "Powell's writing is easy and fresh, and while there's perhaps a bit too much preaching delivered via conversation, it's done with an offhand air, and Dean himself is such a darned nice guy you can't help wanting to give him some advice." Sutton also commented positively on Powell's open ending, observing that "readers will have a ball figuring out which way the wind is blowing." *Booklist*'s Jeanne Triner remarked that the "first-person narrative is straightforward and smoothly written.... [Dean] could serve as a good role model for boys driven by their interest in sports." Triner also noted, "There are several strong female characters, who make this an enjoyable read for girls as well." *Horn Book*'s Maeve Visser Knoth said, "[Powell] includes enough play-by-play details to satisfy fans of the genre, but he has also created a strong, well-developed character struggling with serious issues." A reviewer for *Publishers Weekly* called the novel a "nifty coming-of-age tale," and drew attention to the "ambiguous yet upbeat ending [which] provides a fitting climax." The same reviewer concluded, "With his effortless writing,

Utilizing the grunge counterculture of Seattle, Powell examines the human costs of the rock-and-roll life as personified by the son of a deceased rock star. (Cover illustration by Josh Gosfield.)

Powell creates a recognizable world and peoples it with characters who are remarkably sympathetic and complex." *Dean Duffy* garnered another American Library Association Best Book for Young Adults citation for Powell.

Sports play a secondary role in Powell's fourth novel, *The Whistling Toilets,* in which junior tennis superstar Ginny Forrester is having a career crisis. Sent home from the tennis circuit to reorient herself, she is coached by her old childhood friend, Stan Claxton. Once a promising tennis player himself, Stan already feels obsolete at sixteen. As he sees it, his one positive achievement is coaching disadvantaged kids at a recreation center. Stan grabs at the chance to coach Ginny, and together they prepare for her comeback at a local tennis tournament. Stan is attracted to Ginny and badly wants to help restore the confidence she mysteriously lost on the junior circuit. He slowly uncovers the guilty secret plaguing Ginny: her tennis coach on the circuit made sexual advances to her, and she was complicit in the incident. Stan helps her put the incident behind her, while Ginny helps Stan rediscover his ambition and worth. There are many subplots, including one about Ginny's wealthy rival and another involving Stan's two goofball friends who are as attracted to Ginny as Stan is. (The eponymous toilets are an inside joke that Stan ultimately shares with Ginny.)

Janice M. Del Negro wrote in *Bulletin of the Center for Children's Books,* "Stan is romantically confused yet ironically aware," and observed that a "sense of humor and a distinct voice carry the reader ... toward a satisfying denouement with quirky but determined motivation." *Booklist*'s Jean Franklin stated, "Powell's fourth book has a lot to offer: an authentic setting; lively, well-drawn characters with ... goofy charm; and great dialogue that rings true." A critic for *Kirkus Reviews* declared, "If this sounds like just another romance with a sports setting, it's not. It's something of a love story, in which two really likable and interesting characters share a profound friendship that transcends infatuation and leads them to a better understanding of themselves and each other...." A contributor to *Publishers Weekly* echoed the sentiment, noting, "Readers need not be sports enthusiasts to feel the energy and catch the humor of this narrative ... especially because the verbal matches between teens prove to be more exciting than on-the-court battles."

A native of the Seattle area, Powell finds it a natural setting for his books. For most of them, the setting is secondary, but for *Tribute to Another Dead Rock Star,* Powell focused on the musical reputation of Seattle and the musicians, like Jimi Hendrix and Kurt Cobain of Nirvana, who worked and died there. Utilizing the grunge counter-culture of Seattle, Powell examines the human costs of the rock-and-roll life as personified by the son of a deceased rock star.

Fifteen-year-old Grady Grennan is invited to Seattle to speak at a concert honoring his dead mother. She was famous hard-rocker Debbie Grennan, who died of an overdose of drugs and alcohol three years earlier. The trip gives Grady the chance to examine his unhappy life. Abandoned by his mother when he was seven, he has been shuttled around all his life. Now his grandmother, with whom he has been living, has remarried and is preparing for a long journey across America with her new husband. Grady must make new living arrangements and is faced with hard choices. He must also decide how he really feels about his mother and what he will say about her at the concert.

In Seattle, Grady stays with his mother's old boyfriend, Mitch; Mitch's new wife, Vickie; his retarded thirteen-year-old half-brother, Louie; and the rest of their family. Mitch and Vickie are Christians, and Vickie wants to help Grady find the right path. Louie is a cruel reminder of Debbie's excesses: mentally disabled, Louie is lovable but developmentally stuck at five years old. Grady and Vickie lock horns from the moment he steps in the door, but as he gets to know them, Grady begins to understand the workings of the family, as well as his troubled relationship with his dead mother. Grady and Vickie argue over family, love, and faith, and in so doing unlock reservoirs within each other.

Well-received by critics, *Tribute to Another Dead Rock Star* has also been optioned for a film. A reviewer for *Publishers Weekly* commented, "Powell poses some provocative questions in this unglamorized, introspective look at the fringes of the rock-star scene." Jack Forman remarked in *School Library Journal* that Grady's "low-key first-person narrative is alternately sarcastic and self-reflective, and his touching, ambivalent remembrances of his flamboyant mother are skillfully intertwined with his candid account of his fitful, turbulent, and ultimately successful search for a family he's always missed." A critic for *Horn Book* also had plaudits for the novel, saying, "The smoothly written novel depicts a real teen with unusual parentage, and eloquently portrays the complexities and affections of family life."

"All of my characters tend to be people struggling with their own identity," Powell explained. "They're trying to find the purpose of life—or even if there is a purpose. Trying to figure out if things are a matter of free will or are pre-destined. They are struggling between having the courage to move on, to change, to grow, versus just playing it safe or staying in place. But beyond that, I don't really plan any message with my books. I'm not so much concerned with the effect of my books, but that I enjoy the writing. I need to please myself first to make a book work. That's why I don't concentrate on sports books anymore. There are only so many ways you can write play-by-play. It gets boring. I don't want to preach in my books. My characters are usually going through a dilemma in their lives, and as often as not I will leave the solution open at the end. I like to let the readers try to figure out what the character should or will do."

Powell, who rises at four o'clock in the morning to write before going off to his technical writing job, is a tireless reviser. "My books go through a first draft before I even know where they are going. I don't like to write from outline, so I end up throwing a lot of stuff away. The second and third drafts focus the story more." This professionalism has its rewards. The film option for *Tribute to Another Dead Rock Star* may help him achieve his ultimate dream of becoming a full-time writer of fiction.

Powell is bothered by people asking him when he is going to write an adult book, "as if books for a young adult audience are not really books. But writing for middle grade readers and young teenagers is what I *want* to do. I wouldn't trade them for an adult audience. I put my heart and soul into it. I find that audience much more gratifying. I want to connect with that audience."

Works Cited

Review of *Dean Duffy, Publishers Weekly,* April 17, 1995, p. 62.

Del Negro, Janice M., review of *The Whistling Toilets, Bulletin of the Center for Children's Books,* November, 1996, p. 110.

Flottmeier, Barbara, review of *Is Kissing a Girl Who Smokes Like Licking an Ashtray?, Voice of Youth Advocates,* August, 1992, p. 169.

Forman, Jack, review of *Tribute to Another Dead Rock Star, School Library Journal,* March, 1999, p. 130.

Franklin, Jean, review of *The Whistling Toilets, Booklist,* September 15, 1996, p. 233.

Review of *Is Kissing a Girl Who Smokes Like Licking an Ashtray?, Kirkus Reviews,* June 15, 1992, p. 784.

Review of *Is Kissing a Girl Who Smokes Like Licking an Ashtray?, Publishers Weekly,* June 22, 1992, p. 64.

Knoth, Maeve Visser, review of *Dean Duffy, Horn Book,* July-August, 1995, p. 468.

Larson, Gerry, review of *My Underrated Year, School Library Journal,* December, 1988, p. 122.

Review of *My Underrated Year, Publishers Weekly,* September 9, 1988, p. 138.

Powell, Randy, interview with *Authors and Artists for Young Adults,* conducted November 2, 1999.

Shoemaker, Joel, review of *Dean Duffy, School Library Journal,* May, 1995, p. 122.

Sutton, Roger, review of *Is Kissing a Girl Who Smokes Like Licking an Ashtray?, Bulletin of the Center for Children's Books,* June, 1992, p. 275.

Sutton, Roger, review of *Dean Duffy, Bulletin of the Center for Children's Books,* July, 1995, p. 395.

Review of *Tribute to Another Dead Rock Star, Publishers Weekly,* April 12, 1999, p. 76.

Review of *Tribute to Another Dead Rock Star, Horn Book,* May-June, 1999, p. 337.

Triner, Jeanne, review of *Dean Duffy, Booklist,* April 15, 1995, p. 1493.

Vasilakis, Nancy, review of *My Underrated Year, Horn Book,* January-February, 1989, p. 81.

Review of *The Whistling Toilets, Kirkus Reviews,* July 1, 1996, p. 972.

Review of *The Whistling Toilets, Publishers Weekly,* July 29, 1996, p. 89.

For More Information See

BOOKS

St. James Guide to Young Adult Writers, 2nd edition, edited by Tom Pendergast and Sara Pendergast, St. James Press, 1999.

PERIODICALS

Booklist, November 1, 1988, p. 471; June 1, 1992, p. 1760; March 1, 1999, p. 1203.
Kirkus Reviews, January 15, 1999, p. 150.
Kliatt, May, 1994, p. 12; November, 1995, p. 48; May, 1998, p. 16.
School Library Journal, October, 1995, p. 91; October, 1996, p. 148.
Voice of Youth Advocates, February, 1989, p. 288; August, 1995, p. 164; June, 2000, pp. 93-97.

ON-LINE

Randy Powell's Web site is located at http://www.randypowell.com.

—*Sketch by J. Sydney Jones*

* * *

PRELUTSKY, Jack 1940-

Personal

Born September 8, 1940, in Brooklyn, NY; son of Charles (an electrician) and Dorothea (a housewife; maiden name, Weiss) Prelutsky; married wife, Carolynn, 1979. *Education:* Attended Hunter College (now of the City University of New York); has studied voice at several music schools. *Hobbies and other interests:* Making plastic and metal sculptures, bicycling, inventing word games, collecting books and model frogs.

Addresses

Home—Olympia, WA. *Agent*—c/o Greenwillow Books, 1350 Avenue of the Americas, New York, NY 10019.

Career

Poet and singer. Has worked as a cab driver, busboy, actor, photographer, furniture mover, potter, sculptor, day laborer, waiter, carpenter, clerk, bookseller, and door-to-door salesman.

Awards, Honors

Children's Book Showcase, Children's Book Council, 1977, and Best of the Best Books, *School Library Journal,* 1979, both for *Nightmares: Poems to Trouble Your Sleep;* Children's Choice, International Reading Association/Children's Book Council, 1978, for *The Mean Old Mean Hyena;* Outstanding Books of the Year selection, *New York Times,* 1980, for *The Headless Horseman Rides Tonight;* Best Books selection, *School Library Journal,* 1980, for *The Headless Horseman Rides Tonight,* 1981, for *The Wild Baby,* 1983, for *The*

Random House Book of Poetry for Children and *The Wild Baby Goes to Sea,* and 1986, for *Read-Aloud Rhymes for the Very Young;* Children's Reviewers' Choice, *Booklist,* 1980, for *The Headless Horseman Rides Tonight;* Children's Book of the Year, Child Study Association, and Book of the Year, Library of Congress, 1983, both for *The Random House Book of Poetry for Children;* Parents' Choice Award, Parents' Choice Foundation, and Garden State Children's Book Award, New Jersey Library Association, both 1986, both for *The New Kid on the Block;* Notable Children's Recording, American Library Association, 1987, for *The New Kid on the Block;* Notable Book, Association for Library Services to Children, and Editor's Choice, *Booklist,* both 1990, both for *Something Big Has Been Here.*

Writings

(Translator) Rudolf Neumann, *The Bad Bear,* illustrated by Eva Johanna Rubin, Macmillan, 1967.
(Translator) Heinrich Hoffman, *The Mountain Bounder,* Macmillan, 1967.
A Gopher in the Garden and Other Animal Poems (also see below), illustrated by Robert Leydenfrost, Macmillan, 1967.
(Translator) *No End of Nonsense: Humorous Verses,* illustrated by Wilfried Blecher, Macmillan, 1968.
Lazy Blackbird and Other Verses, illustrated by Janosch, Macmillan, 1969.
(Translator) *Three Saxon Nobles and Other Verses,* illustrated by Rubin, Macmillan, 1969.
(Translator) James Kruess, *The Proud Wooden Drummer,* illustrated by Rubin, Doubleday, 1969.
The Terrible Tiger, illustrated by Arnold Lobel, Macmillan, 1970.
Toucans Two and Other Poems (also see below), illustrated by Jose Aruego, Macmillan, 1970 (published in England as *Zoo Doings and Other Poems,* Hamish Hamilton, 1971).
Circus!, illustrated by Lobel, Macmillan, 1974.
The Pack Rat's Day and Other Poems (also see below), illustrated by Margaret Bloy Graham, Macmillan, 1974.
Nightmares: Poems to Trouble Your Sleep, illustrated by Lobel, Greenwillow, 1976.
It's Halloween, illustrated by Marylin Hafner, Greenwillow, 1977.
The Snopp on the Sidewalk and Other Poems, illustrated by Byron Barton, Greenwillow, 1977.
The Mean Old Mean Hyena, illustrated by Lobel, Greenwillow, 1978.
The Queen of Eene (also see below), illustrated by Victoria Chess, Greenwillow, 1978.
Rolling Harvey down the Hill (also see below), illustrated by Chess, Greenwillow, 1980.
The Headless Horseman Rides Tonight: More Poems to Trouble Your Sleep, illustrated by Lobel, Greenwillow, 1980.
Rainy, Rainy Saturday, illustrated by Hafner, Greenwillow, 1980.
(Adapter) Barbro Lindgren, *The Wild Baby,* illustrated by Eva Eriksson, Greenwillow, 1981.
It's Christmas, illustrated by Hafner, Greenwillow, 1981.

The Sheriff of Rottenshot: Poems, illustrated by Chess, Greenwillow, 1982.

Kermit's Garden of Verses, illustrated by Bruce McNally, Random House, 1982.

It's Thanksgiving, illustrated by Hafner, Greenwillow, 1982.

The Baby Uggs Are Hatching, illustrated by James Stevenson, Greenwillow, 1982.

Zoo Doings: Animal Poems (includes *A Gopher in the Garden and Other Animal Poems, Toucans Two and Other Poems,* and *The Pack Rat's Day and Other Poems*), illustrated by Paul O. Zelinsky, Greenwillow, 1983.

It's Valentine's Day, illustrated by Yossi Abolafia, Greenwillow, 1983.

(Adapter) Lindgren, *The Wild Baby Goes to Sea,* illustrated by Eriksson, Greenwillow, 1983.

(Compiler and editor) *The Random House Book of Poetry for Children,* illustrated by Lobel, Random House, 1983.

It's Snowing! It's Snowing!, illustrated by Jeanne Titherington, Greenwillow, 1984.

What I Did Last Summer, illustrated by Abolafia, Greenwillow, 1984.

The New Kid on the Block, illustrated by Stevenson, Greenwillow, 1984.

My Parents Think I'm Sleeping, illustrated by Abolafia, Greenwillow, 1985.

Ride a Purple Pelican, illustrated by Garth Williams, Greenwillow, 1986.

(Adapter) Rose Lagercrantz and Samuel Lagercrantz, *Brave Little Pete of Geranium Street,* illustrated by Eriksson, Greenwillow, 1986.

(Compiler and editor) *Read-Aloud Rhymes for the Very Young,* illustrated by Marc Brown, Knopf, 1986.

(Adapter) Lindgren, *The Wild Baby Gets a Puppy,* illustrated by Eriksson, Greenwillow, 1988.

Tyrannosaurus Was a Beast: Dinosaur Poems, illustrated by Lobel, Greenwillow, 1988.

(Collector and editor) *Poems of A. Nonny Mouse,* illustrated by Henrik Drescher, Knopf, 1989.

Beneath a Blue Umbrella, illustrated by Williams, Greenwillow, 1990.

Something Big Has Been Here, illustrated by Stevenson, Greenwillow, 1990.

(Compiler and editor) *For Laughing Out Loud: Poems to Tickle Your Funny Bone,* illustrated by Marjorie Priceman, Knopf, 1991.

Twickham Tweer (from *The Sheriff of Rottenshot*), illustrated by Eldon Doty, DLM, 1991.

There'll Be a Slight Delay: And Other Poems for Grown-Ups, illustrated by Jack Ziegler, Morrow, 1991.

Sweet and Silly Muppet Poems, illustrated by Joe Ewers, Western, 1992.

The Dragons Are Singing Tonight, illustrated by Peter Sis, Greenwillow, 1993.

(Compiler and editor) *A. Nonny Mouse Writes Again!,* illustrated by Priceman, Knopf, 1993.

(Translator) Stefania Maria De Kennessey, *Jumping Jacks: Six Humorous Songs,* Hildegard Publishing, 1994.

(Compiler and editor) *For Laughing Out Louder: More Poems to Tickle Your Funnybone,* illustrated by Priceman, Knopf, 1995.

Monday's Troll, illustrated by Sis, Greenwillow, 1996.

A Pizza the Size of the Sun, illustrated by Stevenson, Greenwillow, 1996.

(Compiler and editor) *Beauty of the Beast: Poems from the Animal Kingdom,* illustrated by Mielo So, Knopf, 1997.

(Compiler and editor) *Dinosaur Dinner (with a Slice of Alligator Pie): Favorite Poems by Dennis Lee,* illustrated by Debbie Tilley, Knopf, 1997.

(Compiler and editor) *Imagine That: The Poems of Never-Was,* illustrated by Kevin Hawkes, Random House, 1998.

(With Dr. Seuss) *Hooray for Diffendoofer Day!,* illustrated by Lane Smith, Knopf, 1998.

(Compiler and editor) *The Twentieth-Century Children's Poetry Treasury,* illustrated by So, Knopf, 1999.

The Gargoyle on the Roof, illustrated by Sis, Greenwillow, 1999.

Dog Days: Rhymes Around the Year, illustrated by Dyanna Wolcott, Knopf, 1999.

Awful Ogre's Awful Day, illustrated by Zelinsky, Greenwillow, 2000.

It's Raining Pigs and Noodles, illustrated by Stevenson, Greenwillow, 2000.

The Frogs Wore Red Suspenders, HarperCollins, in press.

Archives of Prelutsky's work are kept in the University of Southern Mississippi's De Grummond Collection and the University of Minnesota's Kerlan Collection.

Adaptations

People, Animals and Other Monsters (record; cassette; includes poems from *The Snopp on the Sidewalk, The Queen of Eene, Rolling Harvey Down the Hill, The Pack Rat's Day, A Gopher in the Garden,* and *Toucans Two and Other Poems*), Caedmon, 1982.

Nightmares and *The Headless Horseman Rides Again: Poems to Trouble Your Sleep* (record), Caedmon, 1983.

It's Thanksgiving (cassette), Listening Library, 1985.

The New Kid on the Block (cassette), Listening Library, 1986.

It's Halloween (cassette), Scholastic, 1987.

It's Christmas (cassette), Scholastic, 1987.

Ride a Purple Pelican (cassette), Listening Library, 1988.

Read-Aloud Rhymes for the Very Young (cassette), Knopf, 1988.

It's Valentine's Day (cassette), Scholastic, 1988.

Something Big Has Been Here (cassette), Listening Library, 1991.

The New Kid on the Block (animated computer program), Random House, 1993.

An audio recording has also been produced for *Rainy, Rainy Saturday* (cassette), Random House, and *A Pizza the Size of the Sun* (cassette; read by the author), Listening Library. Prelutsky's poems have been included in *Graveyard Tales* (record), NAPPS.

Sidelights

"For poetic creativity, accuracy, and appeal, there is no match for Jack Prelutsky," wrote a contributor to *Children's Books and Their Creators.* Prelutsky has written, translated, and edited over seventy books of poetry for young readers. Known for an irreverent style, Prelutsky blends strong rhythms, a classical sense of meter, zany alliteration, and engaging word play to come up with verses celebrating the grosser or spookier or sometimes simply the sillier side of human behavior in brief poems that have won the hearts of young readers. Teaming up with illustrator James Stevenson, Prelutsky has created several books that have become minor classics of the genre, including the award-winning and perennial favorites *The New Kid on the Block, Something Big Has Been Here,* and *A Pizza the Size of the Sun.* Prelutsky has also explored the world of ghosts, goblins, spooks, and monsters in a bevy of books, many illustrated by Arnold Lobel, including *The Terrible Tiger, Nightmares: Poems to Trouble Your Sleep, The Headless Horseman Rides Tonight: More Poems to Trouble Your Sleep,* and *Tyrannosaurus Was a Beast.* Prelutsky has written about childhood concerns, as well, from going to sleep at night to the non-adventures of summer vacation, and has chronicled holidays in several volumes of witty verse. Additionally, Prelutsky has translated volumes of children's verse and stories from German and Swedish, and has been a busy editor, compiling numerous collections of humorous and nonsense poetry from around the world.

Born in Brooklyn, New York, Prelutsky was a gifted and restless child whose intelligence made it difficult for him to conform to the undemanding expectations of public school. His overactive mind also made it hard for his mother and teachers to manage him. "In those days," Prelutsky recalled to Allen Raymond in *Early Years,* "schools and parents didn't have the knowledge, the machinery or the experience to handle kids like me." However, it soon became clear that this boy with behavior problems also had a rare talent: a magnificent singing voice.

At the age of ten, Prelutsky's abilities were already recognized by many people. Some considered him a prodigy and paid the boy to sing at weddings and other special occasions. The Choir Master of New York's Metropolitan Opera considered the boy so gifted that he willingly gave Prelutsky free singing lessons. As a teenager, the promising opera student attended the High School of Music and Art in New York City, where he also studied piano. He graduated from the school in 1958.

It seemed like Prelutsky was on his way to an operatic career. But then one day his determination was shattered when he heard the world renowned Luciano Pavarotti perform. After that, Prelutsky abandoned the idea of becoming a famous opera singer. "I knew I could never compete with him.... I didn't have the fire in the belly," he commented in *Early Years.* Prelutsky experimented with numerous other professions. He became an excellent photographer, good enough to earn a living and even exhibit some of his work, but not—in his opinion—the best. He also worked at manual labor jobs, and during the 1950s and 60s, became an itinerant folk singer, potter, and sculptor.

Prelutsky had always felt that he was meant to be an artist, but he was not sure if being a folk singer was what he wanted to be for the rest of his life. One day he decided to try drawing and soon came up with a couple dozen imaginary creatures for which he created short poems. Encouraged by a friend, he submitted these to a publisher who was vastly uninterested in his art. With a second publisher, Macmillan, and its children's editor, Susan Hirschman, however, Prelutsky found an appreciative audience. Hirschman was very interested, but in his poetry, not in the art. After his first meeting with Hirschman, Prelutsky was convinced he had found a career in which he could be the best because he resolved to approach his verse in a way that would excite children.

He remembered that when he was a boy poetry seemed terribly dull with no relevance to the real world. His childhood friends, Raymond reported, "used to think poets had to be either boring,... siss[ies,] or dead." But in his introduction to *The Random House Book of Poetry for Children* the author asserts that children do not have a natural aversion to verse. "For very young children, responding to poetry is as natural as breathing. Even before they can speak, most babies delight in the playful cadences of nursery rhymes and the soothing rhythms of lullabies.... Poetry is as delightful and surprising as being tickled or catching a snowflake on a mitten.... But then something happens to this early love affair with poetry. At some point during their school careers, many children seem to lose their interest and enthusiasm for poetry and their easygoing pleasure in its sounds and images. They begin to find poetry boring and irrelevant, too difficult or too dull to bother with."

Critics rarely fault Prelutsky for being too dull to bother with. From his first offering, *A Gopher in the Garden and Other Animal Poems,* it was clear to reviewers that he was an original. A *Kirkus Reviews* contributor described those early verses: "From epigram to extended, entangled word-play, from tyrannosaur ... to the multilingual mynah bird ... a collection to capture the most difficult audience." These nonsense rhymes delighted kids and reviewers alike. Virginia Haviland, writing in *Horn Book,* noted, "[Prelutsky] sustains the fun without a letdown in easy, delightful rhymes and rhythms, and with words that call for reading aloud and chanting in response by young listeners." In Prelutsky's early years of writing, he also translated verse on a regular basis. In his own early collections, he focused on animals and on nonsense, not particularly in that order.

His first collaboration with illustrator Lobel was *The Terrible Tiger,* "a perfect book to read aloud to your child," according to a reviewer for *Publishers Weekly.* The tiger in question has an appetite that will not be sated by any amount of grocers, bakers, or farmers.

Finally a tailor, swallowed in a gulp, makes a reappearance to chastise the beast. In subsequent books, Prelutsky wrote of toucans, zebras, and pack rats, all with a light tone in humorous jingles and bouncy rhythms. Teaming up again with Lobel, he earned an American Library Association (ALA) Notable Book award for *Nightmares: Poems to Trouble Your Sleep,* an "ogre's gallery [that] makes other monster poems turn pale," according to a contributor for *Kirkus Reviews. Horn Book*'s Paul Heins called the collection a "series of twelve tongue-in-cheek poems about the gruesome subjects of folklore and superstition." *The Snopp on the Sidewalk, and Other Poems* contains a menagerie of imaginary beings, including the critter of the title, as well as the raging gibber and harmless meath. Prelutsky teamed up with Lobel again for a sequel to *Nightmares,* the 1980 *The Headless Horseman Rides Tonight,* and again in 1988 for *Tyrannosaurus Was a Beast.*

More beasts are served up in *The Dragons Are Singing Tonight* and *Monday's Troll,* both with illustrations from Peter Sis. In the former title, the two "outdo themselves with this fanciful series of poems about dragons," according to a critic in *Publishers Weekly.* Here is Prelutsky on a dragon's identity crisis: "I'm tired of being a dragon / Ferocious and brimming with flame, / The cause of unspeakable terror / When anyone mentions my name." *Horn Book*'s Mary M. Burns declared, "This book is irresistible." Sis and Prelutsky also teamed up on the 1996 *Monday's Troll,* a book about more ogres and mythical meanies. "Prelutsky is up to his usual hilarious no good in this new collection of witchy, wizardly, ogreish poems," noted Ann A. Flowers in *Horn Book.* In a lengthy review in *Bulletin of the Center for Children's Books,* Deborah Stevenson concluded, "Overall, the merit of this volume lies in its demonstration of the worth of craftsmanship. Prelutsky and Sis are thankfully not content to coast along on their nice, juicy, monstrous topic, but instead continually invest every idea, every phrase, every image with a serious and creative attention that enhances rather than detracting from the entertainment quotient." A further joint effort from Prelutsky and Sis is the 1999 *The Gargoyle on the Roof,* "another winner from a pair of seasoned collaborators, and fans can only hope they keep them coming," as a reviewer for *Publishers Weekly* commented.

Another rewarding collaborative effort for Prelutsky has been with the illustrator Stevenson. In several award-winning titles, the two have created large volumes that address more than one single issue, as most of Prelutsky's other books do. Critics note that the topics of such books as *The New Kid on the Block* and *Something Big Has Been Here* generally tend toward the gross, an important factor in making them among Prelutsky's most popular all-time titles. Reviewing *The New Kid on the Block,* a collection of over one hundred nonsense and silly verses, a contributor for *Kirkus Reviews* noted that Prelutsky is "a natural rhymester" and has "a keen sense of what tickles kids. His rhymes are infectious, his verses ineradicable." The same reviewer further noted that the collaborative effort with Stevenson was the coup that made the book: "both have an offhand drollery that

knows no age distinctions." "Undeniably a winner," is how Betsy Hearne described this effort in *Booklist.* Included in this volume were meanies and monsters, along with humorous wordplay and driving rhythms. Judy Greenfield, writing in *School Library Journal,* felt "Prelutsky's new collection ... will convert to poetry lovers many elementary readers, who will laugh knowingly at his outrageous exaggerations." Greenfield pointed joyously to lines such as: "Homework! Oh, homework! / I hate you! You stink! / I wish I could wash you / away in the sink...."

Another omnibus collaborative volume of silliness and irreverence is served up in *Something Big Has Been Here,* a book that provides "a wealth of funny new verse," according to *Booklist*'s Bill Ott. The fun continues in *A Pizza the Size of the Sun,* which earned the duo the appellation of "Poetry's bad boys," from a contributor to *Publishers Weekly.*

Prelutsky has also worked with material from deceased authors. At the time of his death, Theodor Geisel—better known to his legion of fans as Dr. Seuss—left bits and pieces of several projects lying around in his office. One of those bits turned into the 1998 *Hooray for Diffendoofer Day!,* which Prelutsky, working with artist Lane Smith, crafted from the sketches Geisel left behind. The Diffendoofer School is the sort every student wishes he or she attended. Here teachers teach kids how to think, not just how to take tests, and the school librarian insists the kids talk louder. "The completed text, which adds a whimsical story that celebrates individuality, is ... faithful to the Seussian spirit," noted *Booklist* contributor Michael Cart.

In addition to creating his own work, Prelutsky has also edited and compiled numerous volumes of verse, from folk poems to humorous rhymes from around the world. He often adds his own poems to such collections, as in *Poems of A. Nonny Mouse* and its sequel, *A. Nonny Mouse Writes Again!,* in which anonymous poems from around the world are credited to the rodent of the title. He also gathers poems dealing with imaginary subjects and animals, as in *Imagine That: Poems of Never-Was* and *Beauty of the Beast: Poems from the Animal Kingdom.* Additionally, Prelutsky has also put together several anthologies, such as the 1999 *The Twentieth-Century Children's Poetry Treasury,* a collection of two hundred verses. *Booklist*'s Hazel Rochman noted, "Teachers and librarians will want to use this millennial volume with Prelutsky's *The Random House Book of Poetry for Children* (1983) to introduce our best children's poets and encourage children to write about their immediate experience."

Every year, Prelutsky spends a few weeks traveling and visiting schools, where he tells stories, performs songs, and recites poetry. He remarks in *Children's Literature in Education:* "Until I started visiting schools, I tended to work in a sort of vacuum, never really knowing how my books were received by the only really important audience—the children. Book reviews are, of course, important.... [But] it's the children that really matter."

In his work, critics cite Prelutsky for refusing to talk down to children, nor turning them off to verse by creating lifeless, uninteresting poetry. The key, he discovered early on, was to write verses that children could relate to while also presenting them in an interesting manner. Regarding the content of his verses, *Dictionary of Literary Biography* contributor Anita Trout commented, "Prelutsky's poetry features animals and fantastic beasts which behave in inventive ways. He also writes of people and problems familiar to youngsters: dealing with the neighborhood bully, going to school, and being afraid of the dark. Writing in traditional poetic forms, he employs puns, alliteration, and word play in ways which have caused him to be ranked among the masters of contemporary verse for children." Trout concluded, "Contemporary poets such as Jack Prelutsky restore the fun and fascination in the study of the English language and its rhythmic patterns."

Works Cited

Burns, Mary M., review of *The Dragons Are Singing Tonight, Horn Book,* September-October, 1993, p. 615.

Cart, Michael, review of *Hooray for Diffendoofer Day!, Booklist,* May 1, 1999, p. 1532.

Review of *The Dragons Are Singing Tonight, Publishers Weekly,* October 11, 1993, p. 88.

Flowers, Ann A., review of *Monday's Troll, Horn Book,* May-June, 1996, p. 345.

Review of *The Gargoyle on the Roof, Publishers Weekly,* July 5, 1999, p. 71.

Review of *A Gopher in the Garden, Kirkus Reviews,* July 15, 1967, p. 805.

Greenfield, Judy, review of *The New Kid on the Block, School Library Journal,* November, 1984, p. 127.

Haviland, Virginia, review of *A Gopher in the Garden, Horn Book,* December, 1967, p. 744.

Hearne, Betsy, review of *The New Kid on the Block, Booklist,* October 15, 1984, p. 310.

Heins, Paul, review of *Nightmares, Horn Book,* October, 1976, pp. 513-14.

Miles, Betty, editor, "When Writers Visit Schools: A Symposium," *Children's Literature in Education,* Volume 11, number 3, 1980, pp. 133, 135-136.

Review of *The New Kid on the Block, Kirkus Reviews,* September 1, 1984, p. J-76.

Review of *Nightmares, Kirkus Reviews,* June 15, 1976, p. 690.

Ott, Bill, review of *Something Big Has Been Here, Booklist,* March 15, 1991, p. 1488.

Review of *A Pizza the Size of the Sun, Publishers Weekly,* June 24, 1996, p. 61.

Prelutsky, Jack, "Introduction," *The Random House Book of Poetry for Children,* Random House, 1983, pp. 18-19.

"Prelutsky, Jack," *Children's Books and Their Creators,* edited by Anita Silvey, Houghton Mifflin, 1995, pp. 536-37.

Prelutsky, Jack, *The Dragons Are Singing Tonight,* Greenwillow, 1993.

Prelutsky, Jack, *The New Kid on the Block,* Greenwillow, 1984.

Raymond, Allen, "Jack Prelutsky ... Man of Many Talents," *Early Years,* November-December, 1986, pp. 38, 40-42.

Rochman, Hazel, review of *The Twentieth-Century Children's Poetry Treasury, Booklist,* December 15, 1999, p. 783.

Stevenson, Deborah, review of *Monday's Troll, Bulletin of the Center for Children's Books,* March, 1996, pp. 217-18.

Review of *The Terrible Tiger, Publishers Weekly,* March 2, 1970, p. 82.

Trout, Anita, "Jack Prelutsky," *Dictionary of Literary Biography,* Volume 61: *American Writers for Children since 1960: Poets, Illustrators, and Nonfiction Authors,* Gale, 1987, pp. 242-47.

For More Information See

BOOKS

Children's Literature Review, Volume 13, Gale, 1987.

Fifth Book of Junior Authors and Illustrators, edited by Sally Holmes Holtze, H. W. Wilson, 1983.

Potts, Cheryl, *Poetry Fun by the Ton with Jack Prelutsky,* Alleyside, 1995.

Shaw, John Mackay, *Childhood in Poetry,* Gale, 1967.

St. James Guide to Children's Writers, 5th edition, edited by Sara Pendergast and Tom Pendergast, St. James, 1999, pp. 866-68.

Through the Eyes of a Child: An Introduction to Children's Literature, edited by Donna E. Norton, Merrill, 1983, pp. 322-23.

PERIODICALS

Booklist, September 15, 1996, p. 241; March 15, 1997, p. 1253; April 1, 1997, p. 1335; November 15, 1997, p. 552; October 15, 1998, p. 425; October 1, 1999, p. 355; November 1, 1999, p. 536.

Horn Book, August, 1970; April, 1971; August, 1974; December, 1974; October, 1977; April, 1978; June, 1978, October, 1980; October, 1982; September-October, 1984; January-February, 1986; January-February, 1987; September-October, 1988; January-February, 1990; September-October, 1996, p. 605; July-August, 1998, p. 479.

New York Times Book Review, June 2, 1996, p. 25; November 16, 1997, p. 36; May 31, 1998, p. 40; November 21, 1999, p. 46; January 16, 2000, p. 27.

Publishers Weekly, February 9, 1998, p. 24; February 16, 1998, p. 21; July 13, 1998, p. 77; August 23, 1999, p. 57; October 4, 1999, p. 72; February 7, 2000, p. 41.

School Library Journal, September, 1996, p. 219; April, 1997, p. 41; January, 1998, p. 104; June, 1998, p. 121; November, 1998, p. 108; October, 1999, p. 141; December, 1999, p. 125.*

R

RATLIFF, Thomas M. 1948-
(Carroll Thomas, a joint pseudonym)

Personal

Born March 31, 1948, in St. Louis, MO; son of Grover Buford (a minister) and Caroline Emily (a teacher; maiden name, Morse) Ratliff; divorced, 1985; children: Christian Thomas. *Education:* Attended Tunxis Community College, 1987-88; Central Connecticut State University, B.S.Ed., 1991, M.S., 1994. *Politics:* "Unspecified." *Religion:* "Deist."

Addresses

Home—25 Broad St., Plainville, CT 06062. *E-mail*—tomrat@worldnet.att.net.

Thomas M. Ratliff and Carole B. Shmurak, who write under the joint pseudonym Carroll Thomas.

Career

Bolton Center School, Bolton, CT, teacher of history and English, 1998-99; Northwestern High School, Winsted, CT, teacher of history and English, 1999—. Central Connecticut State University, adjunct instructor, 1993—; Teikyo Post University, adjunct instructor, 1998—. *Military service:* U.S. Navy, 1967-70; served in Vietnam.

Writings

(With Carole B. Shmurak, under joint pseudonym Carroll Thomas) *Matty's War* (juvenile novel), Smith & Kraus (Lyme, NH), 1999.

Contributor to *Middle School Journal* and *Research in Middle Level Education*.

Work in Progress

Blue Creek Farm, another novel featuring Matty Trescott, with Shmurak, under pseudonym Carroll Thomas.

Sidelights

Thomas M. Ratliff told *SATA:* "*Matty's War* was a collaborative effort, in that each of us brought different knowledge and interests. We found, by brainstorming together and editing each other's work, we could achieve a credible voice and a unity of characters. For me, having someone to write with provides lots of motivation, as well as a sounding board for ideas. Writing about Matty's life (in two books now) has been very rewarding. She is a real character to me, and I think of her as a part of my family."

ROBINSON, Spider 1948-
(B. D. Wyatt)

Personal

Born November 24, 1948, in New York, NY; son of Charles Vincent (a salesman) and Evelyn (a secretary; maiden name, Meade) Robinson; married Jeanne Rubbicco (a dancer, dance teacher, and writer), July, 1975; children: Luanna Mountainborne. *Education:* State University of New York at Stony Brook, B.A., 1972; attended State University of New York College at Plattsburgh and Le Moyne College. *Politics:* "None whatever." *Religion:* "Pantheist/Humanist."

"Subversive, dangerous, iconoclastic, cantankerous. Puns, palindromes, puzzlers, posers, pranks, and poetry. A three ring circus of ideas—I loved it!"   —John Varley

Spider Robinson created the colorful Callahan's Place, a neighborhood tavern frequented by time travelers, aliens, and others, all united by Callahan's Law: Shared pain is lessened, shared joy is increased (and bad puns are always appreciated). (Cover illustration by James Warhola.)

Addresses

Home and office—Tottering-on-the-Brink, 1663 Henry St., Halifax, Nova Scotia, Canada B3H 3K4. *Agent*—Kirby McCauley, 425 Park Ave. S., New York, NY 10016.

Career

Long Island Commercial Review, Syosset, NY, realty editor, 1972-73; science fiction writer, 1973—. Contributing editor, *Galaxy,* 1974-77; book reviewer, *Destinies,* 1977-79, and *Analog,* 1978-80. Chairman of the board of directors, Dance Advance Association. *Member:* Writers Federation of Nova Scotia (chairman, executive council).

Awards, Honors

John W. Campbell Award, 1974, for short story "The Guy with the Eyes"; *Locus* (magazine) Award, 1976, for best critic, and 1977, for best novella, "Stardance"; Hugo Award, World Science Fiction Convention, 1976, for best novella, "By Any Other Name," 1977, for best novella, "Stardance," and 1983, for best short story, "Melancholy Elephants"; Nebula Award, Science Fiction Writers of America, 1977, for best novella, "Stardance"; E. E. Smith Memorial Award, 1977; Pat Terry Memorial Award, 1977.

Writings

Telempath, Berkley, 1976.
Callahan's Crosstime Saloon (story collection), R. Enslow, 1977.
(With wife, Jeanne Robinson) *Stardance,* Dial, 1979.
Antinomy (story collection), Dell, 1980.
(Editor) *The Best of All Possible Worlds* (anthology), Ace Books, 1980.
Time Travelers Strictly Cash (story collection), Ace Books, 1981.
Mindkiller, Holt, Rinehart and Winston, 1982.
Melancholy Elephants and Others (story collection), Penguin (Toronto), 1984, Tor Books (New York), 1985.
Night of Power, Baen, 1985.
Callahan's Secret, Berkley, 1986.
Time Pressure, Ace Books, 1987.
Callahan and Company (omnibus), Phantasia Press, 1987.
Callahan's Lady, Ace Books, 1989.
True Minds (collection), Pulphouse, 1990.
Kill the Editor, Pulphouse Publishing, 1991.
(With Jeanne Robinson) *Starseed,* Ace Books, 1991.
Lady Slings the Booze, Ace Books, 1992.
The Callahan Touch, Ace Books, 1993.
Off the Wall at Callahan's, Tor Books, 1994.
(With Jeanne Robinson) *Starmind,* Ace Books, 1995.
Callahan's Legacy, Tor Books, 1996.
Deathkiller (compilation of *Time Pressure* and *Mindkiller*), Baen, 1996.
The Callahan Chronicals (omnibus), Tor Books, 1997.
The Star Dancers (combined reprint of *Stardance* and *Starseed*), Baen, 1997.
Lifehouse, Baen, 1997.

SPIDER ROBINSON

"Nobody's perfect. But Spider comes pretty damned close."—Ben Bova

CALLAHAN'S CROSSTIME SALOON

When a three-legged alien lizard-cyborg plots to destroy the world, the characters of Robinson's novel rescue earth from evil by their love for one another and their close-knit community spirit. (Cover illustration by James Warhola.)

User Friendly (collection), Baen, 1998.
Callahan's Key, Bantam, 2000.
The Free Lunch, Tor Books, 2000.

Also contributor to *Chrysalis 4,* Kensington, 1979, and *New Voices 2,* Harcourt, 1979. Work appears in anthologies, including *Analog Annual,* edited by Ben Bova, Pyramid Publications, 1976, and *The Best of Galaxy,* Volume III, edited by Jim Baen, Award Books, 1976. Author of "Galaxy Bookshelf" column, *Galaxy,* 1974-77. Contributor of short stories and novellas, sometimes under pseudonym B. D. Wyatt, to *Analog, Fantastic, Vertex, Cosmos, Galaxy,* and other magazines.

Adaptations

Callahan's Crosstime Saloon has been adapted as a role-playing game, Games Ltd., 1992, and a CD-ROM game, Legend Entertainment/Take Two, 1997.

Work in Progress

By Any Other Name, a short story collection, for Baen.

Sidelights

Book review editor Max Wyman of the *Vancouver Sun* once summarized the effect that the prolific science fiction author Spider Robinson has had on his readers in these words: "He articulated a simple slogan of social belief that has become the watchword mantra for a substantial chunk of the Internet generation." Indeed, looking back on Robinson's early writings, it is apparent that the writer has a knack for predicting quirky emerging technological devices and trends, such as the virtual reality gadgets and games in *Mindkiller,* for example. However, while the award-winning writer's plots and characters often involve a strong element of the fantastic, he is also a rationalist who has an unshakeable faith in the power of the human mind to create a better world, and even to rescue it from our own potentially cataclysmic mistakes. Robinson's fiction is humanistic and bubbling with optimism; reviewer Shannon Rupp of the Vancouver-based "alternate weekly" *Georgia Strait* has described it as "Prozac-on-the-page."

According to Max Wyman, Spider Robinson is not religious. In fact, he told Wyman that "the only kind of church I'd duck into to get out of the rain is the kind where everyone's a little vague about the prophet's name, but they preserve the important stuff he had to say." Robinson lists his religion as pantheism (a vague set of beliefs which hold that God is the transcendent reality of which the material world and humanity are only manifestations). That being the case, he feels there is no grand divine plan for the future; whatever will be depends on what humanity makes of it. As Robinson explained in a 1996 keynote address to the annual conference of RadCon (a non-profit, Washington-state-based organization that promotes interest in science and science fiction literature), "Cynicism is a clever way of justifying ... selfishness, so that you can live with yourself." He added, "As for myself, I was already a cynic when the sixties began.... Hope came slowly to me ... so I've written cheery, basically optimistic science fiction stories in which responsible individuals solve great problems by applying their attention and intelligence to them."

Although Robinson now lives in Halifax, Nova Scotia, a small port city on Canada's east coast, he was born in 1948 in the Bronx, New York. His parents, Evelyn and Charles Vincent Robinson did *not* name him Spider—he legally changed his name in the 1970s. "Spider" was a nickname given to him by college friends for his love for the work of blues musician "Spider" John Koerner. However, as *Georgia Strait* book reviewer Shannon Rupp has pointed out, "at six-foot-one and one hundred and twenty-eight pounds, [Robinson] leaves no doubt as to how he got his moniker."

Being "a freak reading prodigy as a child," as Robinson described himself in his keynote speech, he read widely.

"My mother placed almost no constraints on my reading, so I was a cynic at six," he quipped. In those bygone days, cynicism—even among adults—was not the pervasive theme in society that it became during the latter decades of the twentieth century. Robinson recalled how back in his childhood "movies and books seemed to end with the assumption that Virtue Would Triumph and Love Would Conquer All, even if they took satirical potshots at society along the way. It was possible to shock your teachers by quoting [the eccentric nineteenth-century American journalist and satirist] Ambrose Bierce. Only the very rich entered marriage planning for the divorce. We did not feel a need to train our children that any adult who smiled at them was a potential rapist."

When Robinson was a teenager in the 1960s, U.S. involvement in Vietnam was at its peak, the anti-war movement was in full swing, and many young people were venting a growing disillusionment with the materialism of the American society and with the ways of the so-called "Establishment." For better or worse, the ill-focused idealism of the Woodstock hippy generation left an indelible mark on all aspects of American life—politics, the arts, entertainment, self-identity, and social mores. Robinson offered his evaluation of the era in his keynote speech: "A whole generation was somehow capriciously inoculated with massive conflicting overdoses of cynicism and hope, just as it was entering puberty," he said. Robinson continued, "The recommended tools for changing the world were prayer, sex, new drugs, rock and roll, and public rioting."

Robinson concluded, in his address, that in the final analysis, the sunny optimism of the Baby Boom generation gradually eroded and gave way to a graying disillusionment and to the stark realization that "protest led you to jail or hospital, new drugs led to the Manson Family or the Funny Farm, sex led to herpes and trichomoniasis and AIDS, prayer led to Jonestown, and rock-and-roll stopped leading to anything and blundered off into disco. And what did it matter, when any moment ICBMs and nuclear winter would fall?" Robinson went on to chide his own generation for not applying "rational thought plus learning" in its headlong rush to make the world a better place. He contended that what was spawned was merely cynical despair, which actually became the "very hallmark of intelligence." Yet, even as many of his contemporaries were succumbing to this despair, Spider Robinson began preaching a message of renewed hope when he began writing in the early seventies.

Robinson met his future wife, Jeanne Rubbicco, a dancer and choreographer and, later, a lay-ordained Buddhist monk and coauthor, in 1974 while they were living on a commune in the Canadian Maritime province of Nova Scotia. They were married on July 19, 1975, in a triple wedding with two other couples from the commune. Their daughter, Luanna Mountainborne, was born there, before the family moved to Vancouver, on Canada's west coast, in the late 1980s.

Robinson's first book was the high-tech sci-fi novel *Telempath,* which was published in 1976. That book, which Melanie Belviso, writing in the *St. James Guide to Young Adult Writers,* described as being "crisply written," garnered wide critical praise and served notice that Robinson was a young writer to watch. It is an imaginative tale about a young, black street killer named Isham. "[He] is programmed to kill the man responsible for ending the world as we know it," Belviso explained. "When he fails to make the kill and then discovers that his father was the man who destroyed society, Isham snaps. Fleeing from his friends and murdering his father, [he] becomes the only human who can communicate with the telepathic 'Muskies,' gaseous creatures with whom the surviving humans are at war."

Robinson's 1982 book *Mindkiller,* set in the late twentieth century, is about addicts, or "wireheads," suffering from pleasure abuse. They are addicted to a technological device that electronically stimulates their

Robinson's novel is a combination of two of his previously published stories, linking the tales of characters who battle global mind control in a futuristic Nova Scotia. (Cover illustration by David Lee Anderson.)

brain with various types of ecstatic, carnal sensations. In reviewing *Mindkiller,* Gerald Jonas of the *New York Times Book Review* proclaimed, "I'd nominate Spider Robinson, on the basis of this book, as the new Robert Heinlein." In the prequel to *Mindkiller,* entitled *Time Pressure,* Sam Meade, a sci-fi reader, and his friend, Snaker O'Malley, a sci-fi writer, encounter Rachel, a female time-traveler from the future. Her mission is to gather facts about the past and to make copies of people's minds. Sam and Snaker must decide whether to stop Rachel from her invasive charge. *Lifehouse,* which appeared in 1997, is the sequel to *Mindkiller.* A bald, naked time traveler from the past arrives on Halloween, presenting to those he meets an opportunity to change history. *Vancouver Sun* reviewer Tom Sandborn pronounced *Lifehouse* to be "fast and funny."

In 1977, a year after the publication of his first novel, Robinson introduced his signature Callahan's bar stories with a collection of stories titled *Callahan's Crosstime Saloon.* The phenomenal popularity of these novels and short stories among sci-fi enthusiasts is evidenced by the presence of Internet sites and news and chat groups dedicated to an ongoing dialogue about the themes the stories present and about their author. In 1997, there were about 460 Web sites devoted to discussions of aspects of Robinson's life and work. For his part, the author admits that he finds the fascination with his fiction astounding, especially in light of how his first story set at Callahan's Place was created. Working as a night watchman in 1977, Robinson was bored and began writing short stories to fill the long, empty hours. According to Max Wyman, Robinson wrote about where he would rather be: in "the ideal bar."

In a review of the 1996 novel *Callahan's Legacy,* Scott Fitzgerald Gray of the *Vancouver Sun* praised Spider Robinson's stories as being tales "of laughter and tears, of gentle reminders of mortality and the sound of glasses shattered in the tavern's fireplace in a toast of life, memory, and any of the elusive human bonds that tie the two together." Gray went on to describe the stories as "*Cheers* meets the *X-Files,* sort of." Callahan's Bar is located on Long Island and hosts as zany a cast of characters as one encounters in science fiction, including patron Jake Stonebender, who acts as narrator; Mike Callahan, owner and bartender; Doc, a speaker of a twisted language; Fast Eddie, a monkey-faced piano man; an alien; a telekinetic; a time-traveler; and the world's oldest woman. In the end, this bizarre potpourri of quirky characters is steadfast in its dedication to saving the world and remarkable in preserving unity and defeating evil's destructive aims.

By 1999, Robinson had published ten more books set at Callahan's Place, or at its successor Mary's Place. Reviewers and fans have consistently described these books as being both compassionate and funny; they have also noted how Spider Robinson's prose is loaded with wild, intentional puns. David Streitfeld of the *Washington Post Book World* pointed out in a review of Robinson's 1987 omnibus *Callahan and Company* that the author has used as many as ten puns in one sentence.

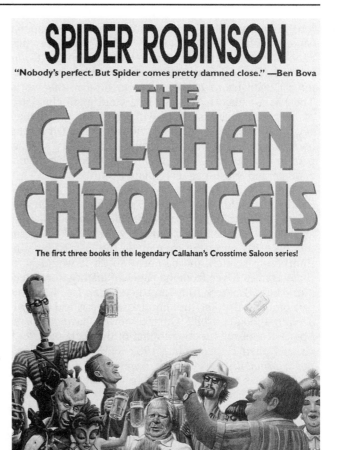

Robinson's omnibus edition includes his first three books about Callahan's Long Island bar peopled with often bizarre, but always caring, characters. (Cover illustration by James Warhola.)

Robinson himself has stressed that his stories should not be treated as a part of a series. Rather, he wants each story to stand alone. Nevertheless, characters do recur. In *Callahan's Secret,* Robinson tells four stories; the plots involve telepathic power and aliens. *Callahan and Company* conjures up new images of delightfully surreal characters, including a deprogrammed alien robot who has a love affair with Callahan's eccentric daughter; a talking dog named Ralph von Wau Wau; the Cheerful Charlies, who require a service fee of twenty-five dollars if they are successful in amusing you; a space-traveling salesman who gets around in a sleigh driven by eight flying reindeer; and a vampire. Once again, the patrons join forces to save the world. *The Callahan Touch* introduces Mary's Place, Jake Stonebender's new bar, built because Callahan's Place was destroyed by a nuclear bomb. Many of the former patrons of Callahan's gather at Mary's Place, including Lucky Duck, a new character, who drops in accidentally by crashing through the bar's skylight. There is also a suicidal scientist, a rebellious Irish fairy, and an old, haunted computer. Mike Callahan drops by to say "hello," and Jake must choose between true love and business profit. *Callahan's Legacy* is again set in Mary's Place. An alien three-legged lizard cyborg plots to destroy the world. There is a cameo by Nikola Tesla; old main characters make appearances, such as Mike and Mary Callahan; and characters that were previously relegated to the background come to the forefront as Mary's Place patrons rescue earth from evil through their love for one another and close-knit community spirit.

Scott Fitzgerald Gray praised *Callahan's Legacy* as effective in exploring "our pains and joys, our sadness and our will to be." He admiringly described Robinson this way: "If one were ever given the task of creating [him] from scratch, the best way to do it would be to snatch James Joyce from the pages of history, force-feed him Marx Brothers films and good jazz for the better part of a decade, then turn him loose on a world badly in need of a look at itself." Other reviewers have compared Spider Robinson's writing to that of the acclaimed sci-fi writer Robert Heinlein. In a 1982 review of Robinson's novel *Mindkiller, New York Times Book Review* critic Gerald Jonas wrote that "Like Mr. Heinlein in his prime, Mr. Robinson writes in a crisp, tightly controlled prose about a future that is recognizably descended from today's world yet provocatively altered." However, Robinson has disagreed with such assessments; he modestly insisted in his conversation with the *Vancouver Sun*'s Max Wyman that he's not "fit to unzip Robert's pencil case." To be presented as having talent comparable to Heinlein's is a great honor to Robinson, who recalled that the first book he read with no pictures when he was six was written by Heinlein.

The "Lady Sally's House" books, which are adult oriented, feature story lines that grew out of the Callahan's Place stories. They are set in a utopian bordello in Brooklyn run by Mike Callahan's time-traveling wife. The females working there are called "artists," and even the Callahans's daughter Mary also works there part time. In *Callahan's Lady,* the narrator who is a young prostitute, downcast after having been stabbed by her pimp, is rescued and welcomed by Lady Sally. A *Kirkus Review* assessment of the book called it "very Heinlein-ish—a conscious tribute." *Lady Slings the Booze,* the sequel to *Callahan's Lady,* features narrator Joe Quigley, a private investigator with a sixth sense, who rescues the brothel as well as his soul. Reviewer Michelle Sagara of *Quill & Quire* also compared Robinson to Heinlein, writing that the plot is one that "the modern Heinlein would approve of."

Robinson has co-authored the "Stardance" books with his wife, Jeanne. He wrote the first *Stardance* book back in 1979 to make some fast money to pay for a trip home to New York and Boston to show off their infant daughter. Robinson needed to write a story that did not require a lot of research, so he centered the plot around the topic of dance, asking his dancer wife to advise him as a technical consultant. The tale that later became *Stardance* was initially a novella for *Analog* magazine.

Jeanne served well as "technical advisor," and then she went beyond technical constructive criticism to suggestions relating to character and plot development. "Despite the obvious harmony of their relationship, it's hard to believe these two could collaborate on anything—on the surface they seem to be polar opposites. Jeanne's high energy fills the room; she's warm and animated . . . Spider's cool: he has a keen sense of irony and a cynical wit. But if you ask them, they're not opposites, they're perfect complements—a yin/yang of a team," wrote Shannon Rupp in *Georgia Strait.* She continued, "[Robinson] argued with [Jeanne], until he realized her unerring character judgements were as applicable to fictional people as to real ones, decided compromise was wise, and invited her to pull up a chair."

Stardance protagonist Shara Drummond is inspired by Jeanne. After discovering weightless dance, Shara performs in space for some aliens and sacrifices her life for the art. Her sister and boyfriend join with these aliens to help other Earthlings become stardancers with a material, Symbiote, found on the planet Titan. Stardancers can live without having to breathe or eat. They have telepathic power and are able to travel freely in space without the protection of space gear and equipment. The Starseed Foundation, where potential stardancers go to master stardancing, is set up on an asteroid. Stardancers must give up all worldly possessions before entering their training. Those Earthlings remaining in the realm of gravity become jealous and try to destroy the stardancer lifestyle. In *Starseed,* published in 1991, an aging dancer crippled with arthritis, Morgan McLeod, hopes to become a stardancer so she might continue her art unimpeded by her physical limitations. When McLeod is close to transcending her humanness to master stardancing, religiously and politically motivated humans on Earth attempt to destroy Top Step, the home of master stardancers. *Starmind,* released four years later, deals with the struggle between a husband and wife as their talents and interests compete and collide. Writer Rhea Paixao reluctantly moves with her husband, composer Rand Porter, to the luxurious Shimizu Hotel in High Earth Orbit, when he is honored with a prestigious new post. Rhea's unhappiness leads to a rift in the marriage, and she has an affair with an employee from the hotel. While that story line moves forward, another simultaneously unfolds: Earth's elite again are bent on destroying the stardancer lifestyle. With the help of telepathic non-stardancers, the stardancers find a way to bring the benefits and abilities of stardancing to all Earthlings, and their destruction is avoided.

In real life, Jeanne Robinson has actually danced in zero-gravity, even creating a dance production, called *Higher Ground,* that featured film of weightless dance. NASA invited her to join the Civilians in Space program after the 1980 performance of *Higher Ground* at the World Science Fiction Convention in Boston. Unfortunately, that dream evaporated with the Challenger explosion.

Unlike many other sci-fi writers, Spider Robinson is optimistic about the future. He predicts that if humans can learn to realize their power to resolve problems and conflicts through love and reason, life can be renewed and improved. Essentially, humans can enter into a new stage of evolution. Robinson once stated: "Many sci-fi writers have eloquently indicted mankind. I intend to spend my life presenting the case for the defense. I believe that shared pain is lessened, shared joy increased; I further maintain that to be a specific formula for saving the world. I find doom-crying (like all forms of despair) to be a cop-out, a personal irresponsibility the world can no longer afford." He summed up his keynote speech with words from Robert Heinlein: "the last item to come fluttering from Pandora's Box was Hope."

Works Cited

Belviso, Melanie, "Spider Robinson," *St. James Guide to Young Adults Writers,* St. James Press, 1999, pp. 724-25.

Review of *Callahan's Lady, Kirkus Reviews,* April 1, 1989, p. 509.

Gray, Scott Fitzgerald, review of *Callahan's Legacy, Vancouver Sun,* September 28, 1996.

Jonas, Gerald, review of *Mindkiller, New York Times Book Review,* August 29, 1982, p. 10.

Robinson, Spider, "Pandora's Last Gift," keynote address given at RadCon conference, 1996, located at http://psg.com/~ted/spider/srPandora.html.

Rupp, Shannon, review of *Starmind, Georgia Strait,* August 4-11, 1995, pp. 35-36.

Sagara, Michelle, review of *Lady Slings the Booze, Quill and Quire,* November 1992, p. 25.

Sandborn, Tom, review of *Lifehouse, Vancouver Sun,* July 12, 1997.

Streitfeld, David, "The Bar's My Destination," *Washington Post Book World,* May 29, 1988, p. 8.

Wyman, Max, "Spider Robinson," *Vancouver Sun,* August 16, 1997.

For More Information See

PERIODICALS

Algol, winter, 1977-78.

Analog, March, 1977; March, 1981; December, 1981; April, 1988; November, 1988; December, 1989; July, 1991; April, 1992; June, 1993.

Best Sellers, June, 1979.

Booklist, September 15, 1992; October 15, 1993.

Fourth Estate, June 16, 1976.

Library Journal, May 15, 1981; September 15, 1982; October 15, 1987; May 15, 1989; September 15, 1991; October 15, 1992; September 15, 1993; June 15, 1995.

Maclean's, May 14, 1979.

Magazine of Fantasy and Science Fiction, October, 1979.

New York Times Book Review, February 7, 1988.

Publishers Weekly, July 2, 1982; August 28, 1987; April 7, 1989; August 30, 1991; September 21, 1992; September 13, 1993; February 14, 1994; May 15, 1995; April 26, 1996; September 16, 1996.

School Library Journal, October, 1982.

Village Voice, September 17, 1979.

Washington Post Book World, August 29, 1982.

ON-LINE

Spider Robinson's Web site is located at http://psg.com/~ted/spider/index.html.

*   *   *

ROMANO, Melora A. 1966-

Personal

Born March 9, 1966, in Rockville Centre, NY. *Education:* Attended American Academy of Dramatic Arts for two years.

Career

Freelance writer. *Member:* Society of Children's Book Writers and Illustrators.

Writings

Meow, What Now?, illustrated by Sara Christian, Seedling Publications (Columbus, OH), 1998.

Melora A. Romano

Contributor of poems, songs, and educational materials to magazines, including *Holidays and Seasonal Celebrations, Read America!, Birth to Three Parenting, Lollipops, Joyful Child Journal, Nature Friend, Turtle, Humpty Dumpty, Jack and Jill,* and *The Friend.*

Work in Progress

Sleepy Time Barn, about a barn full of animals who don't want their owner to wake them up early in the morning.

Sidelights

Melora A. Romano told *SATA:* "I began writing approximately seven years ago, with small, simple rhymes for adults and children. Family members encouraged me to pursue it, so I took a course at the Institute of Children's Literature and received my diploma on my birthday, March 9, 1995. Since then I have been published in over a dozen magazines, and *Meow, What Now?* was published in 1998. I have published rhymes, songs, poems, and classroom activities accompanied by stories. I love to write for young children the most because they're the most difficult to write for and the most impressionable. It gives me great pleasure and reward to know that I have touched the heart and spirit of a young child. I also hope to publish stories that teach children about morals, self-esteem, and kindness. It is a privilege to be able to reach out to youngsters, and I intend to do it for as long as I am able."

S–T

SALKEY, (Felix) Andrew (Alexander) 1928-1995

Personal

Born January 30, 1928, in Colon, Panama; died April 28, 1995, in Massachusetts, from congestive heart failure; son of Andrew Alexander (a businessman) and Linda (Marshall) Salkey; married Patricia Verden, February 22, 1957; children: Eliot Andrew, Jason Alexander. *Education:* Attended St. George's College, Kingston, Jamaica, and Munro College, St. Elizabeth, Jamaica; University of London, B.A., 1955. *Hobbies and other interests:* Collecting contemporary paintings by unestablished painters and classical and contemporary editions of novels, books of poetry, and literary criticism.

Career

Writer and broadcast journalist. British Broadcasting Corporation (BBC-Radio), London, England, interviewer, scriptwriter, and editor of literary program, 1952-56; Comprehensive School, London, assistant master of English literature and language, 1957-59; freelance writer and general reviewer of books and plays, 1956-76; Hampshire College, Amherst, MA, professor of writing, 1976-95. Narrator in film *Reggae,* 1978.

Awards, Honors

Thomas Helmore poetry prize, 1955, for long poem, "Jamaica Symphony"; Guggenheim Fellowship, 1960, for novel *A Quality of Violence,* and for folklore project; Sri Chinmoy Poetry Award, 1977; Casa de las Americas Poetry Prize, 1979, for *In the Hills Where Her Dreams Live: Poems for Chile, 1973-1978;* D.Litt., Franklin Pierce College, 1981.

Writings

FOR CHILDREN

Hurricane, illustrated by William Papas, Oxford University Press (London), 1964, Oxford University Press (New York City), 1979.

Earthquake, illustrated by William Papas, Oxford University Press (London), 1965, Roy (New York City), 1969.

The Shark Hunters (reader), illustrated by Peter Kesteven, Nelson (London), 1966.

Drought (novel), illustrated by William Papas, Oxford University Press (London), 1966.

Riot (novel), illustrated by William Papas, Oxford University Press (London), 1967.

(Editor) *Caribbean Prose: Anthology for Secondary Schools,* Evans, 1967.

Jonah Simpson, illustrated by Gerry Craig, Oxford University Press (London), 1969, Roy, 1970.

Joey Tyson, Bogle-L'Ouverture (London), 1974.

The River That Disappeared, Bogle-L'Ouverture, 1979.

Danny Jones, Bogle-L'Ouverture, 1983.

The One: The Story of How the People of Guyana Avenge the Murder of Their Pasero with Help from Anancy and Sister Buxton (novel), Bogle-L'Ouverture, 1985.

Brother Anancy and Other Stories, Longman, 1994.

Some of Salkey's juvenile novels have been translated into French, German, Dutch, Finnish, and Swedish.

FOR ADULTS

A Quality of Violence (novel), Hutchinson (London), 1959.

Escape to an Autumn Pavement, Hutchinson, 1960.

West Indian Stories (anthology), Elek, 1965.

The Late Emancipation of Jerry Stover, Hutchinson, 1968.

The Adventures of Catullus Kelly, Hutchinson, 1969.

Havana Journal (nonfiction), Penguin, 1971.

Georgetown Journal: A Caribbean Writer's Journey from London via Port of Spain to Georgetown, Guayana, 1970, New Beacon Books (London), 1972.

Anancy's Score (short stories), Bogle-L'Ouverture, 1973.

Caribbean Essays: An Anthology, Evans Brothers, 1973.

Come Home, Malcolm Heartland, Hutchinson, 1976.

Anancy, Traveller (short stories), Bogle-L'Ouverture, 1988.

In the Border Country and Other Stories, Bogle-L'Ouverture, 1998.

EDITOR

West Indian Stories, Faber (London), 1960.
(Editor of Caribbean section) *Young Commonwealth Poets '65,* Heinemann (London), 1965.
(And author of introduction) *Stories from the Caribbean,* Elek (London), 1965, published as *Island Voices: Stories from the West Indies,* Liveright (New York City), 1970.
(And author of introduction) *Breaklight: An Anthology of Caribbean Poetry,* Hamish Hamilton, 1971, published as *Breaklight: The Poetry of the Caribbean,* Doubleday, 1972.
(With others) *Savacou 3-4,* two volumes, Caribbean Artists Movement (Kingston, Jamaica), 1972.
Caribbean Essays: An Anthology, Evans (London), 1973.
(And author of introduction) *Writing in Cuba since the Revolution: An Anthology of Poems, Short Stories, and Essays,* Bogle-L'Ouverture, 1977.

POETRY

Jamaica, Hutchinson, 1973, second edition, 1983.
Land, Readers and Writers (London), 1976.
In the Hills Where Her Dreams Live: Poems for Chile, 1973-78, Casa de las Americas (Havana), 1979, enlarged edition published as *In the Hills Where Her Dreams Live: Poems for Chile, 1973-1980,* Black Scholar Press (Sausalito, CA), 1981.
Away, Allison and Busby (London), 1980.

OTHER

Author of introduction to *Dread Beat and Blood* by Linton Kwesi Johnson, Bogle-L'Ouverture, 1975, and *Walter Rodney: Poetic Tributes,* Bogle-L'Ouverture, 1985. Contributor of over thirty radio plays and features to British Broadcasting Corporation, over twelve radio plays and features to radio stations in Belgium, Germany, and Switzerland, and over one hundred short stories, essays, features, and articles to newspapers and magazines in England, Europe, and Africa.

Sidelights

Although Andrew Salkey is perhaps better known for his novels and poetry for adults, he is also the author of a handful of juvenile novels. As with his adult works, Salkey's novels for children were inspired by his experiences growing up in Jamaica. Salkey was born in Colon, Panama, to Jamaican parents and then raised in Jamaica. Eventually he left Jamaica for England, where he studied at London University, earning a bachelor of arts degree in 1955. While a teacher of English literature and language at a school in London during the 1960s, Salkey began writing works for children. "I came to write children's novels by accident," Salkey once told *SATA;* "I think I'd better say by good fortune. I was asked by an old Jamaican friend to try my hand at it. He was working in educational publishing, and said that there were very few books for children written by Jamaican writers; that was 1961."

Salkey took his friend's invitation seriously, writing eight juvenile novels and editing an educational anthology of works by Caribbean writers over the next twelve years. Salkey remarked to *SATA,* "The material for my children's novels comes from all sorts of sources: from my own childhood experiences in Jamaica; from remembering the things that happened to my elementary and secondary school friends; from casual observations of children when I became an adult; and from my own imagination and will to make up the lives of girls and boys who never existed before I thought them up."

In *Earthquake* Salkey recounts the adventures of three Jamaican children, Ricky, Doug, and Polly, who spend the summer with their grandparents. One of the adventures in this "meandering story," to quote a *Kirkus Reviews* critic, is an earthquake. Earthquakes are also an aspect of another Salkey novel for children, *Jonah Simpson,* which revolves around a mystery set at a Jamaican cay, a low-lying island. Although one *Kirkus Reviews* critic remarked that the adult characters in this novel are "skillfully realized," he found the juvenile characters to be less well drawn. He also concluded that the overall tone of the novel was "overpowering" for juvenile readers because it is so introspective.

Salkey told *SATA* this about his creative process: "I tend to write in a fairly straight line, from beginning to middle to end, although in fits and starts, and I don"t mind going back over certain parts of the composition, re-writing and re-casting them, again and again, until they fit together with the other parts and help the whole story to shape up nicely. I like my writing to entertain me, if I can manage it; I like it to turn me on to write more and more, and to write well. Finally, I suppose the most important feature of my work as a writer is the matter of a central place I always give persons and personal relationships in my storytelling. I simply couldn't make a narrative move without them."

Works Cited

Review of *Earthquake, Kirkus Reviews,* May 1, 1969, p. 506.
Review of *Jonah Simpson, Kirkus Reviews,* March 15, 1970, p. 330.

For More Information See

BOOKS

Contemporary Novelists, sixth edition, St. James Press (Detroit, MI), 1996.
Dictionary of Literary Biography, Volume 125: *Twentieth-Century Caribbean and Black African Writers, Second Series,* Gale (Detroit, MI), 1993.
James, Louis, editor, *The Islands in Between: Essays on West Indian Literature,* Oxford University Press (London), 1968, pp. 100-08.
Twentieth-Century Children's Writers, fourth edition, St. James Press, 1995.

PERIODICALS

Choice, October, 1972, p. 976; March, 1995, p. 1059.

Contemporary Literature, summer, 1998, p. 212.
Jamaica Journal, June, 1968, pp. 46-54; November, 1986-January, 1987, pp. 39-43.
Library Journal, March 15, 1970.
Los Angeles Times, January 9, 1981.
New Statesman and Society, November 11, 1994, p. 41.
New York Times Book Review, September 6, 1970, p. 22.
Publishers Weekly, March 9, 1970, p. 79.
Times (London), May 1, 1995, p. 19.
Times Literary Supplement, February 20, 1969, p. 192; October 16, 1969; July 20, 1973; January 9, 1981.
World Literature Today, summer, 1979; autumn, 1980; spring, 1981; summer, 1981, summer, 1983; spring, 1993, p. 429; autumn, 1998, pp. 882-83.*

* * *

SAXON, Andrew
See ARTHUR, Robert (Jr.)

* * *

SCHINDLER, S(teven) D. 1952-

Personal

Born September 27, 1952, in Kenosha, WI; son of Edwin C. and Bettie L. (Pfefferkorn) Schindler; married. *Education:* Graduated with a degree in biology from the University of Pennsylvania. *Politics:* "Green." *Religion:* Christian. *Hobbies and other interests:* Playing the piano, recorder, and harpsichord, tennis, squash, and gardening. Also an amateur naturalist who enjoys wildflower propagation and creating ponds to attract amphibians like frogs and toads.

Addresses

Home—Philadelphia, PA. *Office*—c/o Amy Parsons, Children's Publicity, Orchard Books, 95 Madison Ave., New York, NY 10016. *Agent*—Publishers' Graphics Inc., 251 Greenwood Ave., Bethel, CT 06801.

Career

Illustrator.

Awards, Honors

Parents' Choice Award for Illustration, Parents' Choice Foundation, 1982, for *The First Tulips in Holland;* best book selection, *School Library Journal,* 1985, for *Every Living Thing,* and 1995, for *If You Should Hear a Honey Guide;* Smithsonian Award for outstanding natural history title, 1995, for *If You Should Hear a Honey Guide;* California Young Reader Medal, 1996-97, for *Don't Fidget a Feather!;* Best Children's Book of the Year—age five to eight category, Bank Street College, 1998, for *Creepy Riddles;* Notable Children's Book, American Library Association, 1999, for *How Santa Got His Job.*

Writings

ILLUSTRATOR

G. C. Skipper, *The Ghost in the Church,* Children's Press, 1976.
Susan Saunders, *Fish Fry,* Viking, 1982.
Phyllis Krasilovsky, *The First Tulips in Holland,* Doubleday, 1982.
Morrell Gipson, reteller, *Favorite Nursery Tales,* Doubleday, 1983.
Leon Garfield, *Fair's Fair,* Doubleday, 1983.
Deborah Perlberg, *Wembley Fraggle Gets the Story,* Holt, 1984.
Cynthia Rylant, *Every Living Thing,* Bradbury, 1985, Aladdin, 1988.
Elizabeth Bolton, *The Tree House Detective Club,* Troll, 1985.
Laurence Santrey, *Moon,* Troll, 1985.
Virginia Haviland, reteller, *Favorite Fairy Tales Told around the World,* Little, Brown, 1985.
Eric Suben, editor, *The Golden Goose and Other Tales of Good Fortune,* Golden, 1986.
Cynthia Rylant, *Children of Christmas: Stories for the Season,* Orchard, 1987.
Ursula K. Le Guin, *Catwings,* Orchard, 1988.
Margery Williams, *The Velveteen Rabbit,* adapted by David Eastman, Troll, 1988.
Ursula K. Le Guin, *Catwings Return,* Orchard, 1988.
Steven Kroll, *Oh, What a Thanksgiving!,* Scholastic, 1988.
(And text) *My First Bird Book,* Random House, 1989.
Bobbi Katz, *The Creepy, Crawly Book,* Random House, 1989.
Deborah Hautzig, *The Pied Piper of Hamelin,* Random House, 1989.
Melvin Berger, *As Old As the Hills,* F. Watts, 1989.
Morgan Matthews, *The Big Race,* Troll, 1989.
William H. Hooks, *The Three Little Pigs and the Fox,* Macmillan, 1989, Simon & Schuster, 1997.
Mary Blount Christian, *Penrod's Party,* Macmillan, 1990.
Mark Twain, *The Prince and the Pauper,* retold by Raymond James, Troll, 1990.
Carollyn James, *Digging Up the Past: The Story of an Archaeological Adventure,* F. Watts, 1990.
Joanne Oppenheim, *Could It Be?,* Bantam, 1990, Gareth Stevens, 1998.
Jonathan Swift, *Gulliver's Travels,* retold by Raymond James, Troll, 1990.
Megan McDonald, *Is This a House for Hermit Crab?,* Orchard, 1990.
Janet Craig, *Wonders of the Rain Forest,* Troll, 1990.
Betsy Rossen Elliot and J. Stephen Lang, *The Illustrated Book of Bible Trivia,* Tyndale, 1991.
Evan Levine, *Not the Piano, Mrs. Medley!,* Orchard, 1991.
Joanne Oppenheim, *Eency Weency Spider,* Bantam, 1991, Gareth Stevens, 1997.
Mary Blount Christian, *Penrod's Picture,* Macmillan, 1991.
The Twelve Days of Christmas, music copying and calligraphy by Christina Davidson, HarperCollins, 1991.
Megan McDonald, *Whoo-oo Is It?,* Orchard, 1992.
Erica Silverman, *Big Pumpkin,* Macmillan, 1992.
Susanne Santoro Whayne, *Night Creatures,* Simon & Schuster, 1992.

Elizabeth Jaykus, editor, *For Dad,* Peter Pauper, 1992.

Christina Anello, editor, *For Grandma,* Peter Pauper, 1992.

Jennifer Habel, editor, *For Mom,* Peter Pauper, 1992.

Rita Freedman, editor, *For My Daughter,* Peter Pauper, 1992.

Walter Retan, compiler, *Piggies, Piggies, Piggies,* Simon & Schuster, 1993.

Dawn Langley Simmons, *The Great White Owl of Sissinghurst,* Margaret K. McElderry, 1993.

Noah Lukas, *The Stinky Book,* Random House, 1993.

Constance C. Greene, *Odds on Oliver,* Viking, 1993.

Noah Lukas, *Tiny Trolls' 1,2,3,* Random House, 1993.

Noah Lukas, *Tiny Trolls' A,B,C,* Random House, 1993.

Leah Komaido, *Great Aunt Ida and Her Great Dane, Doc,* Doubleday, 1994.

Joanne Oppenheim, *Floratorium,* Bantam, 1994.

William Kennedy, *Charlie Marlarkie and the Singing Moose,* Viking, 1994.

Erica Silverman, *Don't Fidget a Feather!,* Macmillan, 1994.

Tres Seymour, *I Love My Buzzard,* Orchard, 1994.

Rose Wyler, *Spooky Tricks,* HarperCollins, 1994.

Patricia Brennan Demuth, *Those Amazing Ants,* Macmillan, 1994.

Ursula K. Le Guin, *Wonderful Alexander and the Catwings,* Orchard, 1994.

Jeff Sheppard, *Full Moon Birthday,* Atheneum, 1995.

April Pulley Sayre, *If You Should Hear a Honey Guide,* Houghton Mifflin, 1995.

Mary DeBall Kwitz, *Little Vampire and the Midnight Bear,* Dial, 1995.

Tres Seymour, *The Smash-Up Crash-Up Derby,* Orchard, 1995.

Tony Johnston, *The Ghost of Nicholas Greebe,* Dial, 1996.

Lucille Recht Penna, *Landing at Plymouth,* David McKay, 1996.

Candace Fleming, *Madame LaGrande and Her So High, to the Sky, Uproarious Pompadour,* Knopf, 1996.

Lucille Recht Penner, *The Pilgrims at Plymouth,* Random House, 1996.

Crescent Dragonwagon, *Bat in the Dining Room,* Cavendish, 1997.

Stuart J. Murphy, *Betcha!,* HarperCollins, 1997.

Arthur Dorros, *A Tree Is Growing,* Scholastic, 1997.

Megan McDonald, *Tundra Mouse: A Storyknife Tale,* Orchard, 1997.

Carolyn White, *Whuppity Stoorie: A Scottish Folktale,* Putnam, 1997.

Janet Craig, *Wonders of the Rain Forest,* Troll, 1997.

Cynthia DeFelice, *Clever Crow,* Atheneum, 1998.

Katy Hall and Lisa Eisenberg, *Creepy Riddles,* Dial, 1998.

Caron Lee Cohen, *How Many Fish?,* HarperCollins, 1998.

Stephen Krensky, *How Santa Got His Job,* Simon & Schuster, 1998.

Virginia Walters, *Are We There Yet, Daddy?,* Viking, 1999.

Candace Fleming, *A Big Cheese for the White House: The True Tale of a Tremendous Cheddar,* DK, 1999.

Harriet Ziefert, *First Night,* Putnam, 1999.

Verla Kay, *Gold Fever,* Putnam, 1999.

Ursula K. Le Guin, *Jane On Her Own: A Catwings Tale,* Orchard, 1999.

Marilyn Singer, *Josie to the Rescue,* Scholastic, 1999.

David Greenberg, *Whatever Happened to Humpty Dumpty?: and Other Surprising Sequels to Mother Goose Rhymes,* Little, Brown, 1999.

Verla Kay, *Covered Wagons, Bumpy Trails,* Putnam, 2000.

M. C. Helldorfer, *Hog Music,* Viking, 2000.

Nancy Antle, *Sam's Wild West Christmas,* Dial, 2000.

Kenneth Oppel, *Sunwing,* Simon & Schuster, 2000.

Irma Joyce, *Never Talk to Strangers,* Golden, 2000.

Rosemary and Stephen Vincent Benet, *Johnny Appleseed,* Margaret K. McElderry, 2001.

"EINSTEIN ANDERSON, SCIENCE DETECTIVE" SERIES; WRITTEN BY SEYMOUR SIMON

Einstein Anderson Science Sleuth, Viking Penguin, 1980, reprinted as *The Howling Dog and Other Cases,* Morrow, 1997.

Einstein Anderson Shocks His Friends, Viking Penguin, 1980, reprinted as *The Halloween Horror and Other Cases,* Morrow, 1997.

Einstein Anderson Makes up for Lost Time, Viking Penguin, 1981, reprinted as *The Gigantic Ants and Other Cases,* Morrow, 1997.

Einstein Anderson Tells a Comet's Tale, Viking Penguin, 1981, reprinted as *The Time Machine and Other Cases,* Morrow, 1997.

The On-Line Spaceman and Other Cases, Morrow, 1997.

Einstein Anderson Goes to Bat, Viking Penguin, 1982, reprinted as *Wings of Darkness and Other Cases,* Morrow, 1998.

Einstein Anderson Lights up the Sky, Viking Penguin, 1982, reprinted as *The Mysterious Lights and Other Cases,* Morrow, 1998.

Einstein Anderson Sees Through the Invisible Man, Viking Penguin, 1982, reprinted as *The Invisible Man and Other Cases,* Morrow, 1998.

"LOTTERY LUCK" SERIES; WRITTEN BY JUDY DELTON

Winning Ticket, Hyperion, 1995.

Prize-Winning Private Eyes, Hyperion, 1995.

Ten's a Crowd, Hyperion, 1995.

Moving Up, Hyperion, 1995.

Ship Ahoy!, Hyperion, 1995.

Next Stop, the White House!, Hyperion, 1995.

Royal Escapade, Hyperion, 1995.

Cabin Surprise, Hyperion, 1995.

Work in Progress

Cod: A Biography of the Fish That Changed the World, written by Mark Kurlansky, for Putnam.

Sidelights

Accomplished in many media and diverse styles, S. D. Schindler has illustrated over one hundred books since 1976. Schindler once said in an interview for *Something about the Author* (*SATA*): "I began drawing and coloring at an early age. My first award was when I was four; I won a red wagon at a coloring contest at a summer playground program. My favorite kinds of pictures were of animals. I had a total fascination with animals and their habitats. I loved going out looking for animals to bring home as pets as much as I loved drawing. I would

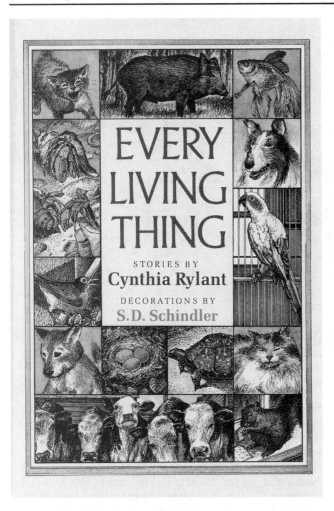

S. D. Schindler provided the small pen-and-ink illustrations for Cynthia Rylant's collection of stories expressing the positive influence animals have on people.

bring home rabbits, snakes, polliwogs, rats, mice, and even a bat once. I have an older brother and we would do coloring or drawing together. He was more advanced and was certainly a stimulus. We continued to draw together until he was in junior high school, then he stopped drawing."

Schindler once related to *SATA* that he is self-taught. Even though he never took art courses, he was known as the class artist throughout school, and he took care of the class bulletin boards and posters in grade school. Like other young children, Schindler liked to copy cartoons and characters, especially from *Mad* magazine and Disney films. His parents acknowledged his talent, but also encouraged him to work towards a technical degree because of the difficulty of making a living in the art field. During junior high school, Schindler began giving his drawings as presents; then in high school, he decided to set up at a local outdoor art exhibit to sell his botanical drawings. Schindler was so successful that he continued to set up at art exhibits to earn money for college. When he began college, he entered as a pre-med major. "The first two years I goofed off and did a lot of

drawing. I didn't really care too much for the biology courses, which was a surprise," Schindler recalled. "I guess they were too microscopic/molecular and I disliked organic chemistry. I realized in my junior year in college that I wanted to be an artist." After graduation, Schindler decided to go to New York City in search of a job in the art field. When no jobs developed, he returned to selling his artwork at outdoor exhibits. An agent visiting an exhibit noticed some pieces of Schindler's work that related to children and got him involved in textbook illustration for two years. Another agent approached him about illustrating a children's story, launching his career as a children's book illustrator.

Since then, Schindler has built a reputation as an illustrator accomplished in a variety of styles and media and known for his balanced vision. The artist typically works on five to six projects at a time, jumping from one style to the next without carrying over the previous style of work. The illustrator once told *SATA* that the style called for in any book "depends on the feel of the story," which he determines by reading "the text over and over until [he's] sure of its tone, then the pictures appear." Schindler often finds that after he draws the characters, he finds them in real life. He related, for example, that while working on *Not the Piano, Mrs. Medley!,* he went to the New Jersey shore to take photographs for his research on the book and, while there, found a woman that matched the image of the character, Mrs. Medley. The artist's work is also known for the humor it lends. Schindler once asserted: "Visual humor is so easy; I never have to think of ways to achieve it." Critics often commend Schindler for his attention to detail as well. The detail is inspired by "the appeal of diversity. I've always enjoyed observing the details and what they mean. And in drawing or painting them I enjoy combining them to achieve a whole," commented Schindler. When asked how long it takes to complete a particular book, Schindler explains that it depends on how detailed the characters and background are and the type of medium he uses. On the average, he finds it takes four weeks of work, working eight to ten hours per day, to finish a book.

In 1982, Schindler's illustrations for *The First Tulips in Holland* received the Parents' Choice Award for Illustration from the Parents' Choice Foundation. Written by Phyllis Krasilovsky, *The First Tulips in Holland* tells Krasilovsky's version of how tulips, originally a Middle Eastern flower, first came to Holland in the seventeenth century. Krasilovsky imagines a Dutch merchant who, after visiting Persia, returns with some flower bulbs for his daughter, Katrina. Katrina plants the flower bulbs in a pot in her window. When the tulips bloom, they receive much public attention and the merchant is offered huge sums of money for the tulips. He refuses the offers, instead giving the flower bulbs to Katrina as a dowry when she marries a young florist. The florist eventually builds them into a Holland trademark for everyone to enjoy. Schindler's artwork in *The First Tulips in Holland* received much praise by critics. "Brilliantly colored illustrations that echo Dutch paintings spill out to the edges of nearly every page," hailed

In 1801 the residents of Cheshire, Massachusetts produce a huge wheel of their famous cheese for President Thomas Jefferson, a true incident recreated in Schindler's amusing illustrations for Candace Fleming's **A Big Cheese for the White House.**

Joyce Maynard in *New York Times Book Review.* Schindler's work is "reminiscent of the Dutch masters" according to *School Library Journal* reviewer Eva Elisabeth Von Ancken, who also praised Schindler's sense of detail. A contributor to *Booklist* described Schindler's work as a "visual feast," while a *Publishers Weekly* critic called the artist's renderings "marvelous paintings." Commenting on the accurate detail of architecture, costume, and rendering of tulips, a *Bulletin of the Center for Children's Books* contributor claimed "the book is lovely to look at."

Schindler also illustrated one of his favorite author's books, Cynthia Rylant's *Every Living Thing.* This collection of short stories expresses the positive influence animals have on people. One story shows how getting a hermit crab as a pet helps a young orphaned child relate to his old aunt who has become his new caretaker. Another story demonstrates how a turtle assists a learning impaired child develop a friendship. Schindler's artwork is represented as "decorations" because small pen and ink renderings of the featured animal of each story are the book's only illustrations. His skill is nonetheless evident, as a *Publishers Weekly* contributor noted that the drawings "adorn as well as illustrate" the tales in the book. "Finely detailed" described *School Library Journal* critic Ruth S. Vose, who also stated that the drawings beginning each short story "express its tone" as well.

In 1988, Schindler illustrated the popular Ursula K. Le Guin book *Catwings.* The story follows four winged kittens who are encouraged by their mother to flee the dangerous city for the safety of the countryside. Writing in *New York Times Book Review,* Crescent Dragonwagon pointed out that Le Guin's story and Schindler's "marvelous ink and watercolor illustrations, especially the kitten closeups: personable, enchanting, believable" captivate the reader. "Fine illustrations show the delightfully furry and winged cats to perfection. Every cat lover will wish for one of his or her own," asserted Ann A. Flowers in her *Horn Book* review. Schindler went on to illustrate a series of sequels to the book, including *Catwings Return, Wonderful Alexander and the Catwings,* and *Jane on Her Own: A Catwings Tale.*

The 1990s were a productive period for the illustrator. In *I Love My Buzzard,* one of Schindler's favorites as he told *SATA,* Tres Seymour tells a rhyming story of a young boy who brings home unusual pets, including a buzzard, warthog, squid, and some slugs. When his mother cannot take the surprises anymore and leaves, the boy realizes he must find new homes for his pets. "Schindler adds considerably to the merriment with artfully detailed depictions of the irrepressible collector, his righteously indignant mom, and the realistic yet delightfully expressive creatures he's harboring," noted a contributor to *Kirkus Reviews.* His contribution to April Pulley Sayre's *If You Should Hear a Honey Guide,* a 1995 Smithsonian Award winner, also earned praise from critics. According to *Booklist* reviewer Julie Corsaro, "The realistically detailed mixed-media paintings are executed in earth tones that suggest the almost colorless terrain of the region." Schindler was likewise complimented for his work on Candace Fleming's *Madame LaGrande and Her So High, to the Sky, Uproarious Pompadour* by *Booklist*'s Kay Weisman, who noted that his "fanciful illustrations match the delightful silliness of the text."

Schindler's resume of illustration credits continued to grow during the rest of the decade. Highlights of his prolific output include *Tundra Mouse,* a story by Megan McDonald based on a native Alaskan narrative that incorporates traditional knife-drawn symbols along with pictures and text. "The illustrations, on warm brown paper, look like scratch board art and ingeniously echo the scratches of the storyknife," wrote Susan Dove Lempke in *Booklist,* while a *Kirkus Reviews* critic praised Schindler for creating "an uncommon blend of folkways and natural history." Another well-received project was *Don't Fidget a Feather!* by Erica Silverman, a fable of competition and sacrifice that went on to receive the California Young Reader Medal for 1996-97. "Schindler's delicate pastel illustrations lend a soft quality to the humor and warmth of Silverman's tale of friendship," observed Linda Ward-Callaghan in *Booklist.*

Though many critics maintain that some of Schindler's best work appears in the animal-centered stories he has illustrated, the artist also demonstrated his knack for grotesquely amusing monsters with his pictures for Katy Hall and Lisa Eisenberg's *Creepy Riddles.* In a review of the book, a *Horn Book* contributor cited Schindler's "detailed color illustrations that are spooky enough to produce a shiver, yet amusing enough to scare up a smile." His work on *How Santa Got His Job* brought out the whimsical, understated quality of Stephen Krensky's story. "Schindler knows exactly how to make his artwork play off the humor," wrote Ilene Cooper in *Booklist.* Also notable was *A Big Cheese for the White House,* a story by Candace Fleming based on an actual historical incident during Thomas Jefferson's presidency. Calling the book "as pleasing to look at as it is delightful to read," a *Horn Book* critic paid compliment to Schindler's "droll, elegantly limned pen, ink and watercolor illustrations." He once again showed his expertise in bringing historical themes to life with *Gold Fever,* a tale of California mining country by Verla Kay. A *Horn Book* contributor reviewed the book favorably and noted that "Schindler's colored-pencil drawings on rough textured paper aptly convey" the landscape and the arduous and dirty work of searching for gold.

For all his successes, Schindler acknowledges that illustrating is not an easy career to establish. He points out that even though his style has not changed since his graduation from college, when he first went to New York City, no one was interested in his work. Interest in Schindler's work began when an agent started representing him. "Art directors do not have to look for illustrators for children's books," he once told *SATA,* adding, "It is easier to get work once you have been published." Schindler advised young readers interested in a career as an illustrator to "be sure of yourself" and "draw, draw, draw."

Works Cited

Review of *A Big Cheese for the White House, Horn Book,* 1999.

Cooper, Ilene, review of *How Santa Got His Job, Booklist,* September 1, 1998.

Corsaro, Julie, review of *If You Should Hear a Honey Guide, Booklist,* September 1, 1995.

Review of *Creepy Riddles, Horn Book,* 1999.

Dragonwagon, Crescent, review of *Catwings, New York Times Book Review,* November 13, 1988.

Review of *Every Living Thing, Publishers Weekly,* September 20, 1985, p. 108.

Review of *The First Tulips in Holland, Booklist,* May 15, 1982, p. 1258.

Review of *The First Tulips in Holland, Bulletin of the Center for Children's Books,* June, 1982, pp. 190-91.

Review of *The First Tulips in Holland, Publishers Weekly,* April 23, 1982.

Flowers, Ann A., review of *Catwings, Horn Book,* November-December, 1988, p. 781.

Review of *Gold Fever, Horn Book,* 1999.

Review of *I Love My Buzzard, Kirkus Reviews,* March 15, 1994.

Lempke, Susan Dove, review of *Tundra Mouse, Booklist,* January 1, 1998.

Maynard, Joyce, review of *The First Tulips in Holland, New York Times Book Review,* April 25, 1982, p. 38.

Schindler, S. D., interview for *Something about the Author,* conducted by Pamela S. Dear, May 26, 1993.

Review of *Tundra Mouse, Kirkus Reviews,* August 1, 1997.

Von Ancken, Eva Elisabeth, review of *The First Tulips in Holland, School Library Journal,* March, 1982, p. 136.

Vose, Ruth S., review of *Every Living Thing, School Library Journal,* December, 1985, p. 106.

Ward-Callaghan, Linda, review of *Don't Fidget a Feather!, Booklist,* November 15, 1994.

Weisman, Kay, review of *Madame LaGrande and Her So High, to the Sky, Uproarious Pompadour, Booklist,* July 19, 1996.

For More Information See

PERIODICALS

Horn Book, March-April, 1989, pp. 205-06.
New York Times Book Review, November 12, 1989, p. 27.
Publishers Weekly, July 5, 1985, p. 67.
School Library Journal, October, 1991, p. 22.

*   *   *

SCHRECENGOST, Maity
See SCHRECENGOST, S. Maitland

*   *   *

SCHRECENGOST, S. Maitland 1938-
(Maity Schrecengost)

Personal

Surname is pronounced *Shreck*-en-gost; born June 8, 1938, in Scottdale, PA; daughter of Albert Warren and Leona (James) Shirer; married Thomas E. Schrecengost, June 11, 1960; children: Lynda D., Thomas Warren. *Education:* Allegheny College, B.A., 1960; Nova Southeastern University, M.A., 1994. *Religion:* Christian. *Hobbies and other interests:* Canoeing, birdwatching, crewel embroidery, reading, travel.

Addresses

Home—807 136th St. E., Bradenton, FL 34202.

Career

Elementary schoolteacher in Murrysville, PA, 1960-62, and Mercersburg, PA, 1980-86; Manatee County School Board, Bradenton, FL, elementary schoolteacher, 1986-2000. Presenter of writing education and research workshops; also works as writing consultant. *Member:* Society of Children's Book Writers and Illustrators, Florida Reading Association, Manatee Writers Guild.

Awards, Honors

Carolynn Washbon Award, Florida Historical Society, 1998, for *Tasso of Tarpon Springs;* Patrick D. Smith Prize for Florida Literature, Florida Historical Society, 2000, for *Panther Girl.*

Writings

UNDER NAME MAITY SCHRECENGOST

Write to Be Read, Highsmith Press (Fort Atkinson, WI), 1992.
Let Them Write! (videotape for teacher training), Title I Media Productions, 1994.
Research to Write, Highsmith Press, 1994.

S. Maitland Schrecengost

Researching People, with teacher's guide, Highsmith Press, 1996.
Researching Events, with teacher's guide, Highsmith Press, 1998.
Tasso of Tarpon Springs (juvenile novel), with teacher's guide, illustrated by Rose Stock, Maupin House (Gainesville, FL), 1998.
Panther Girl (juvenile novel), with teacher's guide, illustrated by Sal Salazar, Maupin House, 1999.

Contributor to periodicals, including *Aglow.*

Work in Progress

Help Kids Supercharge Their Writing: Mini-Lessons for Teachers; historical fiction about the Ringling circus and the Florida railroads; research on circus history and on pirates in Florida.

Sidelights

S. Maitland Schrecengost told *SATA:* "I was born in 1938 in Scottdale, a small town in southwestern Pennsylvania, the youngest of my parents' four children. It was there, at our small public library, that I fell in love with books. They became my best friends. I began scribbling at an early age, penning my 'last will and testament' at the age of ten. My 'studio' was the roof outside my bedroom window, through which I escaped to avoid detection at dishwashing time.

"Throughout my young adult years, while an at-home mom for our two children, I continued to write, with an occasional publishing success. When I resumed teaching, I became one of a core of teacher consultants for the Pennsylvania Department of Education writing project. As such, I became aware of the need for books to introduce children to the craft of writing. This resulted in the publication of *Write to Be Read, Research to Write, Researching People,* and *Researching Events.*

"As a fourth-grade teacher in Florida, I also recognized the lack of historical fiction about Florida for young readers. Thus was born *Tasso of Tarpon Springs,* the story of an immigrant Greek boy who stows away to become part of the developing sponge industry in Florida, and *Panther Girl,* the story of a Florida pioneer girl in 1843 and her friendship with a Seminole Indian boy.

"Writing for children is a wonderful and terrible responsibility. Children deserve our best. Above all else, they deserve truth. In an era of 'political correctness' and 'revisionist history,' I am ever cognizant of the importance of careful research and accurate portrayal of the historical period represented in my books."

SCHULZ, Charles M(onroe) 1922-2000

Personal

Born November 26, 1922, in Minneapolis, MN; died of heart attack, February 13, 2000, in Santa Rosa, CA; son of Carl (a barber) and Dena (Halverson) Schulz; married Joyce Halverson, April 18, 1949 (divorced, 1972); married Jean Clyde, 1973; children: (first marriage) Meredith, Charles Monroe, Craig, Amy, Jill. *Education:* Studied cartooning in an art school after graduation in 1940 from public high school in St. Paul, MN.

Career

Cartoonist and illustrator. Art instructor at Art Instruction Schools, Inc. (correspondence school), Minneapolis, MN; cartoonist, *St. Paul Pioneer Press* and *Saturday Evening Post*, 1948-49; creator of syndicated comic strip, "Peanuts," 1950-2000. *Military Service:* U.S. Army, 1943-45, served with Twentieth Armored Division in Europe; became staff sergeant.

Awards, Honors

Reuben Award as outstanding cartoonist of the year, National Cartoonists' Society, 1955 and 1964; Yale Humor Award as outstanding humorist of the year, 1956; School Bell Award, National Education Association, 1960; L.H.D., Anderson College, 1963; Peabody Award and Emmy Award, both 1966, both for CBS-TV cartoon special, *A Charlie Brown Christmas;* D.H.L., St. Mary's College of California, 1969; Charles M. Schulz Award, United Feature Syndicate, 1980, for his contribution in the field of cartooning; Ordre des arts et des lettres (France), 1990; named one of the top twenty-five newspaper people of the 20th Century, *Editor & Publisher,* 1999; Lifetime Achievement Award, National Cartoonists' Society, 2000.

Writings

CARTOON BOOKS, MANY COLLECTED FROM NEWSPAPER WORK

Peanuts, Rinehart, 1952.
More Peanuts (also see below), Rinehart, 1954.
Good Grief, More Peanuts! (also see below), Rinehart, 1956.
Good Ol' Charlie Brown (also see below), Rinehart, 1957.
Snoopy (also see below), Rinehart, 1958.
Young Pillars, Warner Press, 1958.
But We Love You, Charlie Brown (also see below), Rinehart, 1959.
Peanuts Revisited: Favorites Old and New, Rinehart, 1959.
You're Out of Your Mind, Charlie Brown (also see below), Rinehart, 1959.
"Teenager" Is Not a Disease, Warner, 1961.
Happiness Is a Warm Puppy, Determined Productions, 1962, enlarged edition, 1979.
Security Is a Thumb and a Blanket, Determined Productions, 1963, reprinted, 1983.
Christmas Is Together-Time, Determined Productions, 1964.

Charles M. Schulz

I Need All the Friends I Can Get, Determined Productions, 1964, reprinted, 1981.
What Was Bugging Ol' Pharaoh?, Warner, 1964.
A Charlie Brown Christmas (adapted from the television production; also see below), World Publishing, 1965.
Love Is Walking Hand in Hand, Determined Productions, 1965.
Charlie Brown's All-Stars (adapted from the television production; also see below), World Publishing, 1966.
Home Is on Top of a Doghouse, Determined Productions, 1966, reprinted, 1982.
Charlie Brown's Reflections, Hallmark, 1967.
Happiness Is a Sad Song, Determined Productions, 1967.
It's the Great Pumpkin, Charlie Brown (adapted from the television production; also see below), World Publishing, 1967.
Teenagers, Unite!, Bantam, 1967.
"He's Your Dog, Charlie Brown!" (adapted from the television production; also see below), World Publishing, 1968.
Suppertime!, Determined Productions, 1968.
You're in Love, Charlie Brown (adapted from the television production; also see below), World Publishing, 1968.
Charlie Brown's Yearbook (includes *"He's Your Dog, Charlie Brown!,"* *It's the Great Pumpkin, Charlie Brown, You're in Love, Charlie Brown,* and *Charlie Brown's All-Stars*), World Publishing, 1969.
Peanuts School Year Date Book, 1969-1970, Determined Productions, 1969.
For Five Cents, Determined Productions, 1970.
It Was a Short Summer, Charlie Brown (adapted from the television production; also see below), World Publishing, 1970.

It Really Doesn't Take Much to Make a Dad Happy,
Determined Productions, 1970.

Peanuts Date Book 1972, Determined Productions, 1970.

It's Fun to Lie Here and Listen to the Sounds of the Night,
Determined Productions, 1970.

The World According to Lucy, Hallmark, 1970.

Winning May Not Be Everything, But Losing Isn't Anything!, Determined Productions, 1970.

Play It Again, Charlie Brown (adapted from the television
production; also see below), World Publishing, 1971.

You're Elected, Charlie Brown (also see below), World
Publishing, 1972.

Snoopy's Secret Life, Hallmark, 1972.

The Peanuts Philosophers, Hallmark, 1972.

Love a la Peanuts, Hallmark, 1972.

It's Good to Have a Friend, Hallmark, 1972.

A Charlie Brown Thanksgiving, Random House, 1974.

There's No Time for Love, Charlie Brown (adapted from
the television production; also see below), Random
House, 1974.

It's a Mystery, Charlie Brown, Random House, 1975.

Be My Valentine, Charlie Brown, Random House, 1976.

It's the Easter Beagle, Charlie Brown (adapted from the
television production; also see below), Random House,
1976.

You're a Good Sport, Charlie Brown, Random House,
1976.

Hooray for You, Charlie Brown, Random House, 1977.

It's Another Holiday, Charlie Brown, Random House,
1977.

Summers Fly, Winters Walk (also see below), Volume III,
Holt, 1977, Volume III, Fawcett, 1980.

It's Arbor Day, Charlie Brown (adapted from the television
production; also see below), Random House, 1977.

The Loves of Snoopy, Hodder and Stoughton, 1978.

Lucy Rules OK?, Hodder and Stoughton, 1978.

The Misfortunes of Charlie Brown, Hodder and Stoughton,
1978.

Snoopy and His Friends, Hodder and Stoughton, 1978.

What a Nightmare, Charlie Brown, Random House, 1978.

It's Your First Kiss, Charlie Brown (adapted from the
television production; also see below), Random House,
1978.

Bon Voyage, Charlie Brown, and Don't Come Back!
(adapted from the film production; also see below),
Random House, 1980.

You're Not Elected, Charlie Brown, Scholastic, 1980.

Life Is a Circus, Charlie Brown (adapted from the
television production; also see below), Random House,
1981.

She's a Good Skate, Charlie Brown (adapted from the
television production; also see below), Random House,
1981.

Someday You'll Find Her, Charlie Brown, Random House,
1982.

It's Magic, Charlie Brown, Random House, 1982.

Is This Good-Bye, Charlie Brown?, Random House, 1984.

Snoopy's Getting Married, Charlie Brown, Random House,
1986.

Happy New Year, Charlie Brown, Random House, 1986.

Dogs Don't Eat Dessert, Topper, 1987.

You're on the Wrong Foot Again, Charlie Brown, Topper,
1987.

By Supper Possessed, Topper, 1988.

Sally, School Is My World, Sparkler, 1988.

Talk Is Cheep, Charlie Brown, Topper, 1988.

Snoopy, My Greatest Adventures, Sparkler, 1988.

Schroeder, Music Is My Life, Sparkler, 1988.

It Doesn't Take Much to Attract a Crowd, Topper, 1989.

Brothers and Sisters, It's All Relative: A Peanuts Book,
Topper, 1989.

*An Educated Slice: Starring Snoopy As the World Famous
Golfer,* Topper, 1990.

Don't Be Sad, Flying Ace, Topper, 1990.

Could You Be More Pacific?, Topper, 1991.

Around the World in 45 years: Charlie Brown's Anniversary Celebration, Andrews and McMeel, 1994.

Being A Dog Is a Full-time Job: A Peanuts Collection,
Andrews and McMeel, 1994.

*Make Way for the King of the Jungle: A Peanuts
Collection,* Andrews and McMeel, 1995.

Pop! Goes the Beagle, HarperFestival, 1996.

Life's Answers (and Much, Much More), Collins, 1996.

Bah, Humbug!, Collins, 1996.

Snoopy's Christmas Tree, HarperFestival, 1996.

Your Dog Plays Hockey?, HarperFestival, 1996.

Friends for Life, Collins, 1996.

Way Beyond Therapy, Collins, 1996.

Trick or Treat, Great Pumpkin, HarperFestival, 1996.

Kick the Ball, Marcie!, HarperFestival, 1996.

Love Isn't Easy, Collins, 1996.

Dogs Are from Jupiter, Cats Are from the Moon, Collins,
1996.

Happy Birthday! (And One to Glow On), Collins, 1996.

It's Christmas!, Collins, 1996.

Somebody Loves You, Collins, 1996.

Me, Stressed Out?, Collins, 1996.

I Love You!, Collins, 1996.

Season's Greetings!, Collins, 1996.

See You Later, Litigator!, Collins, 1996.

Birthdays Are No Piece of Cake, Collins, 1996.

Snoopy, Not Your Average Dog, Collins, 1996.

You Can Count on Me, Collins, 1996.

'Tis the Season to Be Crabby, Collins, 1996.

Have Another Cookie (It'll Make You Feel Better), Collins,
1996.

Sally's Christmas Miracle, HarperFestival, 1996.

Insights from the Outfield, Collins, 1997.

Life Is Like a Ten-speed Bicycle, Collins, 1997.

Love Is in the Air, Collins, 1997.

You're Divine, Valentine!, Collins, 1997.

Born Crabby, HarperCollins, 1997.

Charlie Brown: Not Your Average Blockhead, HarperCollins, 1997.

Happy Valentine's Day, Sweet Babboo!, HarperFestival,
1997.

Aaugh! A Dog Ate My Book Report!, HarperCollins, 1998.

Lucy, Not Just Another Pretty Face, HarperHorizon, 1998.

My Best Friend, My Blanket, HarperHorizon, 1998.

You're Our New Mascot, Chuck!, HarperCollins, 1998.

You Have a Brother Named Spike?, HarperCollins, 1998.

Lighten Up, It's Christmas, HarperHorizon, 1998.

Punt, Pass, and Peanuts, HarperHorizon, 1998.

The Round-headed Kid and Me, HarperHorizon, 1998.

Sally's Christmas Play, HarperHorizon, 1998.

Beware of the Snoring Ghost!, HarperCollins, 1998.

Bon Voyage!, HarperCollins, 1998.
Everyone Gets Gold Stars But Me!, HarperCollins, 1998.
A Flying Ace Needs Lots of Root Beer, HarperHorizon, 1998.
The Doctor Is In(sane), HarperHorizon, 1998.
Happy New Year!, HarperHorizon, 1998.
You're the Tops, Pops!, HarperCollins, 1998.
Have Fun at Beanbag Camp!, HarperHorizon, 1998.
I've Been Traded for a Pizza?, HarperHorizon, 1998.
Leaf It to Sally Brown, HarperHorizon, 1998.
Travels with My Cactus, HarperHorizon, 1998.
Our Lines Must Be Crossed, HarperHorizon, 1998.
Shall We Dance, Charlie Brown?, HarperHorizon, 1999.
Now That's Profound, Charlie Brown, HarperPerennial, 1999.
I Told You So, You Blockhead!, HarperPerennial, 1999.
The World Is Filled with Mondays, HarperPerennial, 1999.
Dogs Are Worth It, HarperPerennial, 1999.
Good Grief! Gardening Is Hard Work!, HarperHorizon, 1999.
Calling All Cookies!, HarperHorizon, 1999.
It's Baseball Season, Again!, HarperHorizon, 1999.

Also author of *Snoopy on Wheels*, 1983; *Snoopy and the Twelve Days of Christmas*, 1984; *Peanuts at School*, 1986; and *If Beagles Could Fly*, 1990.

PUBLISHED BY HOLT

Go Fly a Kite, Charlie Brown (also see below), 1960.
Peanuts Every Sunday (also see below), 1961.
It's a Dog's Life, Charlie Brown (also see below), 1962.
Snoopy Come Home (also see below), 1962.
You Can't Win, Charlie Brown (also see below), 1962.
You Can Do It, Charlie Brown (also see below), 1963.
As You Like It, Charlie Brown (also see below), 1964.
We're Right Behind You, Charlie Brown (also see below), 1964.
There's a Vulture Outside, 1965.
Sunday's Fun Day, Charlie Brown (also see below), 1965.
You Need Help, Charlie Brown (also see below), 1965.
Snoopy and the Red Baron, 1966.
The Unsinkable Charlie Brown (also see below), 1966.
What's Wrong with Being Crabby?, 1966, reprinted, 1992.
Who's the Funny-looking Kid with the Big Nose?, 1966.
You're Something Else, Charlie Brown: A New Peanuts Book (also see below), 1967.
It's a Long Way to Tipperary, 1967.
You'll Flip, Charlie Brown (also see below), 1967.
Peanuts Treasury, foreword by Johnny Hart, 1968.
You're You, Charlie Brown: A New Peanuts Book (also see below), 1968.
A Boy Named Charlie Brown (adapted from the film production; also see below), 1969.
You've Had It, Charlie Brown: A New Peanuts Book (also see below), 1969.
Snoopy and His Sopwith Camel, 1969.
Peanuts Classics, 1970.
Snoopy and "It Was a Dark and Stormy Night," 1970.
You're Out of Sight, Charlie Brown: A New Peanuts Book (also see below), 1970.
You've Come a Long Way, Charlie Brown: A New Peanuts Book (also see below), 1971.

"Ha Ha, Herman," Charlie Brown: A New Peanuts Book (also see below), 1972.
Snoopy's Grand Slam, 1972.
The "Snoopy, Come Home" Movie Book (adapted from the film production; also see below), 1972.
Thompson Is in Trouble, Charlie Brown: A New Peanuts Book (also see below), 1973.
You're the Guest of Honor, Charlie Brown: A New Peanuts Book (also see below), 1973.
The Snoopy Festival, 1974.
Win a Few, Lose a Few, Charlie Brown: A New Peanuts Book (also see below), 1974.
Speak Softly, and Carry a Beagle: A New Peanuts Book (also see below), 1975.
Peanuts Jubilee: My Life and Art with Charlie Brown and Others, 1975.
Don't Hassle Me with Your Sighs, Chuck, 1976.
"I Never Promised You an Apple Orchard": The Collected Writings of Snoopy, Being a Compendium of His Puns, Correspondence, Cautionary Tales, Witticisms, Titles Original and Borrowed, with Critical Commentary by His Friends, and, Published for the First Time in Its Entirety, the Novel "Toodleoo, Caribou!," a Tale of the Frozen North, 1976.
Always Stick Up for the Underbird: Cartoons from "Good Grief, More Peanuts!," and "Good Ol' Charlie Brown," 1977.
It's Great to Be a Superstar: Cartoons from "You're Out of Sight, Charlie Brown," and "You've Come a Long Way, Charlie Brown," 1977.
How Long, Great Pumpkin, How Long?: Cartoons from "You're the Guest of Honor, Charlie Brown," and "Win a Few, Lose a Few, Charlie Brown," 1977.
It's Hard Work Being Bitter: Cartoons from "Thompson Is in Trouble, Charlie Brown," and "You're the Guest of Honor, Charlie Brown," 1977.
There Goes the Shutout: Cartoons from "More Peanuts" and "Good Grief, More Peanuts!," 1977.
My Anxieties Have Anxieties: Cartoons from "You're You, Charlie Brown," and "You've Had It, Charlie Brown," 1977.
Sandlot Peanuts, introduction by Joe Garagiola, 1977.
A Smile Makes a Lousy Umbrella: Cartoons from "You're Something Else, Charlie Brown," and "You're You, Charlie Brown," 1977.
Stop Snowing on My Secretary: Cartoons from "You've Come a Long Way, Charlie Brown," and "Ha Ha, Herman, Charlie Brown," 1977.
The Beagle Has Landed (also see below), 1978.
Race for Your Life, Charlie Brown (adapted from the television production; also see below), 1978.
Snoopy's Tennis Book: Featuring Snoopy at Wimbledon and Snoopy's Tournament Tips, introduction by Billie Jean King, 1979.
And a Woodstock in a Birch Tree (also see below), 1979.
Here Comes the April Fool! (also see below), 1980.
Things I Learned After It Was Too Late (and Other Minor Truths), 1981.
Dr. Beagle and Mr. Hyde (also see below), 1981.
You're Weird, Sir! (also see below), 1982.
Classroom Peanuts, 1982.
Kiss Her, You Blockhead! (also see below), 1983.

A **Peanuts** *strip with perennially naive Charlie Brown and feisty Lucy in the 1950s.* (*From* Peanuts: A Golden Celebration.)

And the Beagles and the Bunnies Shall Lie Down Together: The Theology in Peanuts, 1984.

Things I've Had to Learn Over and Over and Over: (Plus a Few Minor Discoveries), 1984.

I'm Not Your Sweet Babboo! (also see below), 1984.

Big League Peanuts, 1985.

You Don't Look 35, Charlie Brown!, 1985.

The Way of the Fussbudget Is Not Easy, 1986.

Duck, Here Comes Another Day!, 1994.

Snoopy's Love Book, 1994.

The Cheshire Beagle, 1994.

Nothing Echoes Like an Empty Mailbox (contains selections from *And a Woodstock in a Birch Tree* and *Here Comes the April Fool*), 1995.

Sarcasm Does Not Become You, Ma'am (contains selections from *Kiss Her, You Blockhead!* and *I'm Not Your Sweet Babboo!*), 1995.

I Heard a D Minus Call Me (contains selections from *Dr. Beagle and Mr. Hyde* and *You're Weird, Sir!*), 1995.

Also author of *Fly, You Stupid Kite, Fly, A Kiss on the Nose Turns Anger Aside, The Mad Punter Strikes Again, Thank Goodness for People, What Makes Musicians So Sarcastic?,* and *What Makes You Think You're So Happy?.*

PUBLISHED BY FAWCETT

Good Ol' Snoopy (contains selections from *Snoopy*), 1958.

Wonderful World of Peanuts (contains selections from *More Peanuts*), 1963.

Hey, Peanuts! (contains selections from *More Peanuts*), 1963.

Good Grief, Charlie Brown! (contains selections from *Good Grief, More Peanuts!*), 1963.

For the Love of Peanuts (contains selections from *Good Grief, More Peanuts!*), 1963.

Fun with Peanuts (contains selections from *Good Ol' Charlie Brown*), 1964.

Here Comes Charlie Brown (contains selections from *Good Ol' Charlie Brown*), 1964.

Very Funny, Charlie Brown! (contains selections from *You're Out of Your Mind, Charlie Brown!*), 1965.

What Next, Charlie Brown? (contains selections from *You're Out of Your Mind, Charlie Brown!*), 1965.

Here Comes Snoopy (contains selections from *Snoopy*), 1966.

We're On Your Side, Charlie Brown (contains selections from *But We Love You, Charlie Brown*), 1966.

You Are Too Much, Charlie Brown (contains selections from *But We Love You, Charlie Brown*), 1966.

You're a Winner, Charlie Brown (contains selections from *Go Fly a Kite, Charlie Brown*), 1967.

Let's Face It, Charlie Brown (contains selections from *Go Fly a Kite, Charlie Brown*), 1967.

Who Do You Think You Are, Charlie Brown? (contains selections from *Peanuts Every Sunday*), 1968.

You're My Hero, Charlie Brown (contains selections from *Peanuts Every Sunday*), 1968.

This Is Your Life, Charlie Brown (contains selections from *It's a Dog's Life, Charlie Brown*), 1968.

Slide, Charlie Brown, Slide (contains selections from *It's a Dog's Life, Charlie Brown*), 1968.

All This and Snoopy, Too (contains selections from *You Can't Win, Charlie Brown*), 1969.

Here's to You, Charlie Brown (contains selections from *You Can't Win, Charlie Brown*), 1969.

Nobody's Perfect, Charlie Brown (contains selections from *You Can Do It, Charlie Brown*), 1969.

You're a Brave Man, Charlie Brown (contains selections from *You Can Do It, Charlie Brown*), 1969.

Peanuts for Everybody (contains selections from *We're Right Behind You, Charlie Brown*), 1970.

You've Done It Again, Charlie Brown (contains selections from *We're Right Behind You, Charlie Brown*), 1970.

We Love You, Snoopy (contains selections from *Snoopy, Come Home*), 1970.

It's for You, Snoopy (contains selections from *Sunday's Fun Day, Charlie Brown*), 1971.

Have It Your Way, Charlie Brown (contains selections from *Sunday's Fun Day, Charlie Brown*), 1971.

You're Not for Real, Snoopy (contains selections from *You Need Help, Charlie Brown*), 1971.

You're a Pal, Snoopy (contains selections from *You Need Help, Charlie Brown*), 1972.

What Now, Charlie Brown? (contains selections from *The Unsinkable Charlie Brown*), 1972.

You're Something Special, Snoopy! (contains selections from *The Unsinkable Charlie Brown*), 1972.

You've Got a Friend, Charlie Brown (contains selections from *You'll Flip, Charlie Brown*), 1972.

Who Was That Dog I Saw You with, Charlie Brown? (contains selections from *You're You, Charlie Brown*), 1973.

There's No One Like You, Snoopy (contains selections from *You're You, Charlie Brown*), 1973.

It's All Yours, Snoopy (contains selections from *You've Come a Long Way, Charlie Brown*), 1975.

Peanuts Double, Volume I, 1976, Volume II, 1978.

Watch Out, Charlie Brown (contains selections from *You're Out of Sight, Charlie Brown*), 1977.

You've Got to Be You, Snoopy (contains selections from *You've Come a Long Way, Charlie Brown*), 1978.

You're on Your Own, Snoopy (contains selections from *"Ha Ha, Herman," Charlie Brown*), 1978.

You Can't Win Them All, Charlie Brown (contains selections from *"Ha Ha, Herman," Charlie Brown*), 1978.

It's Your Turn, Snoopy (contains selections from *You're the Guest of Honor, Charlie Brown*), 1978.

You Asked for It, Charlie Brown (contains selections from *You're the Guest of Honor, Charlie Brown*), 1978.

It's Show Time, Snoopy (contains selections from *Speak Softly, and Carry a Beagle*), 1978.

You've Got to Be Kidding, Snoopy, 1978.

They're Playing Your Song, Charlie Brown, 1978.

You're So Smart, Snoopy (contains selections from *You're Out of Sight, Charlie Brown*), 1978.

Charlie Brown and Snoopy (contains selections from *As You Like It, Charlie Brown*), 1978.

You're the Greatest, Charlie Brown (contains selections from *As You Like It, Charlie Brown*), 1978.

Try It Again, Charlie Brown (contains selections from *You're Something Else, Charlie Brown*), 1978.

Your Choice, Snoopy (contains selections from *You're Something Else, Charlie Brown*), 1978.

Take It Easy, Charlie Brown (contains selections from *You'll Flip, Charlie Brown*), 1978.

You've Got It Made, Snoopy (contains selections from *You've Had It, Charlie Brown*), 1978.

Don't Give Up, Charlie Brown (contains selections from *You've Had It, Charlie Brown*), 1978.

That's Life, Snoopy (contains selections from *Thompson Is in Trouble, Charlie Brown*), 1978.

You've Come a Long Way, Snoopy (contains selections from *Thompson Is in Trouble, Charlie Brown*), 1979.

Play Ball, Snoopy (contains selections from *Win a Few, Lose a Few, Charlie Brown*), 1979.

Let's Hear It for Dinner, Snoopy, 1979.

Keep Up the Good Work, Charlie Brown, 1979.

Think Thinner, Snoopy, 1979.

Stay with It, Snoopy (contains selections from *Summers Fly, Winters Walk,* Volume III), 1980.

Sing for Your Supper, Snoopy, 1981.

Snoopy, Top Dog (contains selections from *The Beagle Has Landed*), 1981.

You're Our Kind of Dog, Snoopy (contains selections from *And a Woodstock in a Birch Tree*), 1981.

Also author of *Love and Kisses, Snoopy.*

"SNOOPY'S FACTS AND FUN BOOK" SERIES

Snoopy's Facts and Fun Book about Boats, Random House, 1979.

Snoopy's Facts and Fun Book about Houses, Random House, 1979.

Snoopy's Facts and Fun Book about Planes, Random House, 1979.

Snoopy's Facts and Fun Book about Seasons, Random House, 1979.

Snoopy's Facts and Fun Book about Farms, Random House, 1980.

Snoopy's Facts and Fun Book about Nature, Random House, 1980.

Snoopy's Facts and Fun Book about Seashores, Random House, 1980.

Snoopy's Facts and Fun Book about Trucks, Random House, 1980.

OTHER

Peanuts Project Book, Determined Productions, 1963.

(With Kenneth F. Hall) *Two by Fours: A Sort of Serious Book about Small Children,* Warner Press, 1965.

(Contributor) Jeffrey H. Loria and others, *What's It All About, Charlie Brown?: Peanuts Kids Look at America Today,* Holt, 1968.

(Contributor) Robert L. Short, *The Parables of Peanuts,* Harper, 1968.

(With Lee Mendelson) *Charlie Brown and Charlie Schulz: In Celebration of the Twentieth Anniversary of Peanuts,* World Publishing, 1970.

(Author of foreword) Morrie Turner, *Nipper,* Westminster, 1970.

(With Kathryn Wentzel Lumley) *Snoopy's Secret Code Book* (spelling and pronunciation guide), Holt, 1971.

The Charlie Brown Dictionary, Random House, 1973.

Peanuts Jubilee: My Life and Art with Charlie Brown and Others, Holt, 1975.

Charlie Brown's Super Book of Things to Do and Collect: Based on the Charles M. Schulz Characters, Random House, 1975.

Charlie Brown's Super Book of Questions and Answers about All Kinds of Animals from Snails to People!, Random House, 1976.

Charlie Brown's Second Super Book of Questions and Answers: About the Earth and Space from Plants to Planets!, Random House, 1977.

A **Peanuts** *strip from the 1960s, featuring the philosophizing Snoopy. (From* Peanuts: A Golden Celebration.*)*

Charlie Brown's Third Super Book of Questions and Answers: About All Kinds of Boats and Planes, Cars and Trains, and Other Things That Move!, Random House, 1978.

Charlie Brown's Fourth Super Book of Questions and Answers: About All Kinds of People and How They Live!, Random House, 1979.

(With Mendelson) *Happy Birthday, Charlie Brown,* Random House, 1979.

(With R. Smith Kiliper) *Charlie Brown, Snoopy and Me: And All the Other Peanuts Characters,* Doubleday, 1980.

Charlie Brown's 'Cyclopedia: Super Questions and Answers and Amazing Facts, Volumes 1-15, Random House, 1980-81.

Charlie Brown's Fifth Super Book of Questions and Answers: About All Kinds of Things and How They Work!, Random House, 1981.

I Take My Religion Seriously, Warner (Anderson, IN), 1989.

Snoopy Around the World, photographs by Alberto Rizzo, Abrams (New York City), 1990.

Why, Charlie Brown, Why?: A Story About What Happens When a Friend Is Very Ill, Topper, 1990.

Peanuts: A Golden Celebration, the Art and the Story of the World's Best Loved Comic Strip, HarperCollins, 1999.

TELEPLAYS; TWENTY-SIX MINUTE ANIMATED CARTOONS

A Charlie Brown Christmas, CBS-TV, 1965.
Charlie Brown's All Stars, CBS-TV, 1966.
It's the Great Pumpkin, Charlie Brown, CBS-TV, 1966.
You're in Love, Charlie Brown, CBS-TV, 1967.
He's Your Dog, Charlie Brown!, CBS-TV, 1968.
It Was a Short Summer, Charlie Brown, CBS-TV, 1969.
Play It Again, Charlie Brown, CBS-TV, 1971.
It's the Easter Beagle, Charlie Brown, CBS-TV, 1972.
You're Elected, Charlie Brown, CBS-TV, 1972.
There's No Time for Love, Charlie Brown, CBS-TV, 1973.
Race for Your Life, Charlie Brown, CBS-TV, 1976.
It's Arbor Day, Charlie Brown, CBS-TV, 1976.
It's Your First Kiss, Charlie Brown, CBS-TV, 1978.
Life Is a Circus, Charlie Brown, CBS-TV, 1981.
She's a Good Skate, Charlie Brown, CBS-TV, 1981.
Why, Charlie Brown, Why?, CBS-TV, 1990.

Also writer of screenplays for feature length animated films, *A Boy Named Charlie Brown,* National General Pictures, 1969, *Snoopy, Come Home,* National General Pictures, 1972, and *Bon Voyage, Charlie Brown, and Don't Come Back!,* 1980.

ILLUSTRATOR

Art Linkletter, *Kids Say the Darndest Things,* Prentice-Hall, 1957.

Linkletter, *Kids Still Say the Darndest Things,* Geis, 1961.

Bill Adler, compiler, *Dear President Johnson,* Morrow, 1964.

Fritz Ridenour, editor, *I'm a Good Man, But ...,* Regal, 1969.

June Dutton, *Peanuts Cookbook,* Determined Productions, 1969.

Dutton, *Peanuts Lunch Bag Cookbook,* Determined Productions, 1970.

All I Want for Christmas Is ...: Open Letters to Santa, Hallmark, 1972.

Evelyn Shaw, *The Snoopy Doghouse Cookbook,* Determined Productions, 1979.

Tubby Book Featuring Snoopy, Simon and Schuster, 1980.

Monica Bayley, *The Snoopy Omnibus of Fun Facts from the Snoopy Fun Fact Calendars,* Determined Productions, 1982.

J. C. Suarez, editor and designer, *The Snoopy Collection,* introduction by Nancy Smart, photographs by Don Hamerman, Stewart, Tabori and Chang, 1982.

Dutton, *Snoopy and the Gang Out West,* Determined Productions, 1982.

Charlie Brown's Encyclopedia of Energy: Based on the Charles M. Schulz Characters: Where We've Been, Where We're Going, and How We're Getting There, Random House, 1982.

Terry Flanagan, designer, *Through the Seasons with Snoopy: Based on the Charles M. Schulz Characters,* Random House, 1983.

Flanagan, *Snoopy on Wheels,* Random House, 1983.

Nancy Hall, *Snoopy's ABC's,* background illustrations by Art and Kim Ellis, Golden, 1987.

Hall, *Snoopy's Book of Shapes,* background illustrations by Art and Kim Ellis, Golden, 1987.

Hall, *Snoopy's 1, 2, 3,* background illustrations by Art and Kim Ellis, Golden, 1987.

Harry Coe Verr, *Let's Fly a Kite, Charlie Brown!: A Book About the Seasons,* background illustrations by Art and Kim Ellis, Golden, 1987.

Justine Korman, *Snoopy's A Little Help from My Friend,* background illustrations by Art and Kim Ellis, Golden, 1987.

*A **1970s** Peanuts commentary on book banning. (From* Peanuts: A Golden Celebration.*)*

Hall, *Snoopy's Book of Colors,* background illustrations by Art and Kim Ellis, Golden, 1987.

Hall, *Snoopy's Book of Opposites,* background illustrations by Art and Kim Ellis, Golden, 1987.

Norman Simone, *Come Back, Snoopy,* background illustrations by Art and Kim Ellis, Golden, 1987.

Abraham J. Twerski, *When Do the Good Things Start?,* Topper, 1988.

Margo Lundell, *Where's Woodstock?,* background illustrations by Art and Kim Ellis, Golden, 1988.

Korman, *It's How You Play the Game,* background illustrations by Art and Kim Ellis, Golden, 1988.

Marci McGill, *Snoopy, the World's Greatest Author,* background illustrations by Art and Kim Ellis, Golden, 1988.

Korman, *Snoopy's Two-Minute Stories,* background illustrations by Art and Kim Ellis, Western (Racine, WI), 1988.

Lundell, *Charlie Brown's Two-Minute Stories,* background illustrations by Art and Kim Ellis, Western, 1988.

Diane Damm, *A Charlie Brown Christmas,* background illustrations by Art and Kim Ellis, Golden, 1988.

Linda Williams Aber, *Get in Shape, Snoopy!,* background illustrations by Art and Kim Ellis, Western, 1989.

Aber, *You're a Star, Snoopy!,* background illustrations by Art and Kim Ellis, Western, 1990.

Robert L. Short, *Short Meditations on the Bible and Peanuts,* Westminster/John Knox Press (Louisville, KY), 1990.

Twerski, *Waking Up Just in Time: A Therapist Shows How to Use the Twelve-Steps Approach to Life's Ups and Downs,* Topper, 1990.

Mischief on Daisy Hill: Featuring the Daisy Hill Puppies, Determined Productions, 1993.

Dr. Snoopy's Advice to Pet Owners, Andrews and McMeel (Kansas City, MO), 1993.

Earth, Water, and Air: Based on the Characters of Charles M. Schulz, Derrydale, 1994.

Creatures, Large and Small: Based on the Characters of Charles M. Schulz, Derrydale, 1994.

How Things Work: Based on the Characters of Charles M. Schulz, Derrydale, 1994.

Land and Space: Based on the Characters of Charles M. Schulz, Derrydale, 1994.

People and Customs of the World, Derrydale, 1994.

Twerski, *I Didn't Ask to Be in This Family: Sibling Relationships and How They Shape Adult Behavior and Relationships,* Holt, 1996.

Sidelights

In his retirement letter to the public printed in part in *Variety,* Charles M. Schulz maintains that the only thing he "really ever wanted to be was a cartoonist and I feel very blessed to be able to do what I love for almost fifty years." A great admirer of Roy Crane, George Herriman, Al Capp, and Milt Caniff in his youth, he had a hard time selling his own comic strip at first; United Feature Syndicate finally bought it in 1950 and named it "Peanuts." Preferring to name the strip "Li'l Folks," Schulz always disliked his comic being called "Peanuts," a title that endured for nearly five decades. "Peanuts" started in eight newspapers and brought a

ninety dollars a month income; by the time of Schulz's retirement, he had written over eighteen thousand strips and had an estimated income of over "one million a week from comic-strip syndication money plus royalties from his books, toys, movies, and commercial endorsements," as noted in an *Entertainment Weekly* article. Schulz is the only cartoonist ever to have won the Reuben Award (the cartoonist's equivalent of the Oscar, designed by and named after Rube Goldberg) twice, in 1955 and again in 1964. Additionally, the National Cartoonists' Society also bestowed a posthumous Lifetime Achievement Award to the "Peanuts" creator in 2000. At the time of Schulz's death, Charlie Brown and his friends reached over 335 million readers daily.

"Peanuts" has in fact become one of the most popular comic strips of all time. As Lee Mendelson points out in his biography of Schulz, "Charlie Brown has become the symbol of mid century America ... because [he is] a basic reflection of his time," the "Mr. Anxious" of the age. Commenting on the universality of the appeal of Charlie Brown, the perpetual loser, Schulz says in *Peanuts Jubilee:* "Readers are generally sympathetic toward a lead character who is rather gentle, sometimes put upon, and not always the brightest person. Perhaps this is the kind of person who is easiest to love. Charlie Brown has to be the one who suffers because he is a caricature of the average person. Most of us are much more acquainted with losing than we are with winning. Winning is great, but it isn't funny."

Nonetheless, Schulz contended that there really is no specific "philosophy" behind the strip. Unlike many cartoonists, Schulz did all the work for the strip himself because, as John Tebbel says in a *Saturday Review* article, "'Peanuts' is so much a projection of the Schulz personality that it is inconceivable that anyone else could do it.... In the hierarchy of immortal comic strips such as 'Blondie,' 'Little Orphan Annie,' 'Andy Gump,' 'L'il Abner,' and 'Krazy Kat,' Schulz has created something unique, more successful than all the others, but paradoxically more fragile. Perhaps it is because the strip is so personal that it elicits an unprecedented identification and affection from its vast readership." Schulz draws material for the strip from his own childhood memories and from his experiences in raising five children. The popularity of the strip "cuts across every kind of classification," writes Tebbel, "for all kinds of special reasons. Schroeder, the Beethoven-loving character who is usually seen playing the piano when he isn't playing baseball, appeals to people who had never heard of Beethoven before. The little tyrant Lucy is seen by the small fry as a deliciously contrary girl.... Linus, with his security blanket, seems to speak to everyone who would like to have a blanket of his own in troubled times. And Snoopy, the beagle who has Van Goghs hanging in his doghouse and a World War I aviator's helmet on his head, is the kind of fantasy dog everyone would like to own."

Schulz added an extra dimension to Charlie Brown with his introduction to television in 1965. "Peanuts" subsidiaries, licensed by Schulz's Creative Associates, Inc.,

A **Peanuts** *strip from the 1980s on educational television.* (*From* Peanuts: A Golden Celebration.)

manufacture everything from clothing, toys, stationery, and cosmetics to furniture, lunch boxes, and Charlie Brown baseballs. Tebbel notes that Charlie Brown and his friends have even "emerged as modern evangelists" in Robert L. Short's two books, *The Gospel According to Peanuts* and *The Parables of Peanuts.* Snoopy has also been adopted by NASA as a promotional device, and, notes Tebbel, "Snoopy emblems are now worn by more than 800 members of the manned space flight team as rewards for outstanding work." The ubiquitous beagle even made international history as the official name of the LEM (Lunar Excursion Module) of the Apollo 10 manned flight to the moon in 1969. Great Pumpkin sightings are reported almost as often as UFOs, and Schroeder and his toy piano have been immortalized in the stained glass window of the Westminster Presbyterian Church in Buffalo, New York, along with Bach, Martin Luther, Duke Ellington, and Dr. Albert Schweitzer. And all because, as Tebbel concludes, "everyone sees something different, and something of himself, in Charlie Brown and his friends. He's everybody's boy."

In a telephone interview with the author on March 13, 1981, at his home in Santa Rosa, California, the author was asked, "You've become a tremendous success by doing something that you love doing. Are there ever times in spite of that when you still feel like Charlie Brown?"

Schulz: "I never said I felt like Charlie Brown. It's like any other job—you go to work every day and try to do the best you can. I always worry that perhaps I'll hit some kind of a slump and never get out of it. Yesterday I sat here all day and I really only came up with one pretty good idea, but then I started off this morning all right, and I'm always trying to make the strip better. But this whole business about my being like Charlie Brown, that's just talk."

Interviewer: "You've described the early interest in the funnies that you shared with your father, and you collected comic books at one time. Do you still have any of that early collection?"

Schulz: "No. I wish I did. I had the very first comic magazine which was ever published, and I can still remember the day I bought it. I was in downtown St. Paul with my mother and I came across this copy of *Famous Funnies* and I was delighted; here was a whole magazine with sixty-four pages of color comics in it. I couldn't believe it. I had that magazine for years, and now I don't have the slightest idea what happened to it . . . ."

Interviewer: "Leo Rosten describes humor as the 'affectionate communication of insight.' Do you think that's a good definition?"

Schulz: "Yes, I guess so. I think you just have to see things the way you as an individual see them and hope that you have a unique approach. The comic strip medium, of course, is not one that gets the critical attention that other forms of literature do. We're way down on the totem pole as far as being considered sophisticated goes. Nobody ever reviews comic strips. I guess that's a good definition of humor. I think the Hyman Kaplan pieces are some of the greatest humor ever written . . . ."

Interviewer: "You've written a bit about your own children. Did they take an active interest in the strip as youngsters?"

Schulz: "They always liked the strip, and this was very important to me and very gratifying. I would have been quite disappointed if they had felt that it wasn't really worthwhile or it wasn't funny, or it was just silly or trite; but they always read all the books, and I guess the most flattering thing of all is that they would frequently ask for some of the originals themselves. If you were to visit them, you'd find that they have originals hanging on their walls. They were always asking for drawings for their friends, and they still do. This was very important to me."

Interviewer: "When they were very young, did you ever feel a great concern about their growing up in the affluence that your work had provided for them?"

Schulz: "I don't think about affluence as much as other people do. No. I never think of myself as being affluent."

Interviewer: "You get a tremendous amount of mail. Does the majority of it come from children or adults?"

Schulz: "We get a lot of mail from adults, but there's no doubt that the greater percentage comes from children. Of course, teachers have writing projects; they're always encouraging their classes to write, and they will frequently have these class projects where everybody has to write a letter to a so-called celebrity. Actually it's very annoying. There are a couple of other annoying aspects to the mail. One is that a lot of people write and don't include a legible return address, so you can't answer them. Some don't include a return address at all. Then others have no comprehension of the time element of mailing things; a student will write saying that he has a theme due Friday and has to write to somebody and would I respond right away, and I'll get the letter maybe a month after the theme was due. They just don't have any comprehension. I'm also astounded at the number of people who cannot spell the word Snoopy, who say, "Snoppy is my favorite character." How anyone can spell Snoopy Snoppy is beyond me. Yesterday I got a letter from a doctor who three times referred to Snoppy. One would hesitate to go to a doctor who can't spell Snoopy."

Interviewer: "How much of your mail comes from other countries?"

Schulz: "It's impossible to say how much, but we get a lot from Japan. Japanese children write very nice, neat, polite letters. I would say of all of the countries, if we had to name one we get the most mail from, it would be Japan. Japanese have liked the strip for twenty-five years. I think they admire things from the United States, and the strip has been very popular there."

Interviewer: "Do people ever send you their ideas for the strip?"

Schulz: "Not really, no. When I first started, it would happen a little bit, but apparently people know that I don't use them. One of the most peculiar things is the notion that when something becomes popular, it should then be used to educate. That, of course, is fatal; the quickest way to kill something would suddenly to use it to educate. For example, if Peppermint Patty falls asleep in class, people write saying that we should do something to educate children to keep them from falling asleep in class. That of course, would immediately kill your whole idea. If you taught her how to stay awake, then you'd have to think of something else. People just have no comprehension of the difficulties of drawing a strip day after day, building up characters and themes and all of these things. It's very difficult and it's hard to sustain."

Interviewer: "There have been various attempts to interpret the strip from a theological or psychological point of view. How do you feel about this?"

Schulz: "Again, this is distorted. The only books that were written about the theological implications were written by Robert Short, and he was not really talking about what my strip was saying. What he was talking about was the ability to gather thoughts from all forms of literature that can lead to some sort of spiritual implications. Robert Short is quite a student of different forms of literature. He's very high on Kafka and Kierkegaard and Bonhoeffer. He realized that I had some things in there that other comic strips didn't have, so he wrote a thesis on the "Peanuts" strip. But he's the only one that's ever been given permission to do this. Since then we've had all sorts of people who have wanted to write a book about math or psychology or languages or anything you can think of, using the strip as the basis, but I always thought that we were very lucky to get away with it on the Robert Short books, and I didn't want to risk it on anything else. Besides, again, it could become very boring for people to see the strip being used for everything else by other people. I don't want other people using my strip that much, so we put a stop to that a long time ago."

Interviewer: "Have you ever sent a strip off and then wished that you had done it some other way?"

Schulz: "Not a particular script, but frequently something will work out very well and then you wish that you had been more careful with it from the beginning. One example would be Schroeder's playing the piano and another would be the Linus blanket thing. I think actually Charlie Brown was the first one to have a blanket. Then one thing led to another and I got some more ideas and I ended up giving the blanket to Linus. I think even the business with Schroeder playing the piano actually started with Charlie Brown singing a very light passage from Beethoven's Ninth Symphony, and that gave me the idea to use some more musical notes in the script, which I then gave to Schroeder. You don't always know how these things are going to work out; you might say you wish you had planned it a little more carefully, but you never know.

"One of the good things, of course, about a comic strip is that it goes from day to day and you don't have to plan it like you would a novel—everything doesn't have to come out easily at the end. Yesterday's strip doesn't mean anything; the only thing that matters is the piece in the paper today."

Interviewer: "You've said too that you don't expect to please everybody every day."

Schulz: "It would be fatal to try. It's wrong to worry about using something that may be directed too much to tennis players or baseball fans or musicians. I think people who are avid tennis players will appreciate it if you treat their sport with respect and authenticity. If a psychiatrist sees something in your comic strip which maybe only he understands, then he'll appreciate it all the more. But if you try to worry about whether everybody is going to understand it, you'll have a strip that is so bland that no one is going to care anything about it."

Interviewer: "Are you ever tempted to solve a problem for a 'Peanuts' character, to make something too easy?"

Schulz: "It's always tempting and it is invariably a mistake. What is tempting, of course, is to attract attention by doing so. I could work up something that would be quite sensational if Charlie Brown was finally able to kick the football, and it would get a lot of attention that November, and I'm sure we'd get some write-ups in different newspapers and magazines. But it would be like blowing your savings account, spending all your money, and then you wouldn't have anything left; it would be a big mistake . . . ."

Interviewer: "For the TV specials, you audition many children to find voices for the cartoon characters. Is it difficult to make those choices?"

Schulz: "Almost impossible. The difficulty in working with the children is that they find it very hard to read the lines the way they are written. Now and then it will come out very well and we get a real good voice. There is a certain pattern to these children's voices. There are a lot of Charlie Brown voices and a lot of Linus voices. We discovered quite early on that Lucy voices tend to shriek and become annoying, which is why we don't have Lucy in the animated cartoons very much. But we've had some good Peppermint Patty voices, and the last girl that we had for Marcie was a real marvel, but she's growing up now and I think she's lost her voice . . . ."

Interviewer: "Of all the awards you've won, is there one that has meant the most to you?"

Schulz: "I suppose the very first Reuben Award, which I won from the National Cartoonists' Society back in 1955, would have been the most exciting of all because I had only been drawing the strip for four or five years; I wanted so much to be accepted, I wanted it to be a good strip, it was my life's ambition, and then to be chosen totally out of the blue by these cartoonists themselves as the outstanding cartoonist of the year really was a tremendous thrill. I suppose that was the highlight. Winning that first Emmy, too, in 1966 for "A Charlie Brown Christmas" was very exciting . . . ."

Interviewer: "Do you get any personal appeals for advice or help from aspiring cartoonists?"

Schulz: "Now and then we do, which I find a little bit annoying, because I can't run a correspondence school. And I'm always a little mystified at people thinking that they can get opinions from others, that once you have something, you owe it to everyone else to give them advice. Plus the fact that your advice is really not necessary. If people really want to do something, they

should just go ahead and do it; they don't have to be told whether or not they're good enough. If you have to be told, then maybe you shouldn't be doing it in the first place."

Schulz continued to write, draw, and letter "Peanuts" entirely on his own into the 1990s, taking his only official vacation break for five weeks in 1997. Beyond the familiar themes he explored in his strip, he also ventured into broader issues, particularly with his 1990 animated special and book *Why, Charlie Brown, Why?* Dealing with childhood leukemia, *Why, Charlie Brown, Why?* won praise for its truthful depiction of the treatment and aftermath of the disease. "This hopeful, but honest, book could well help children to a greater understanding of a difficult subject," writes a reviewer in *Books for Keeps.* Schulz continued to receive honors, including recognition by France's Ordre des arts et des lettres in 1990 and a star on the Hollywood Walk of Fame in 1996.

A landmark in popular culture was reached in December 1999, when Schulz announced his retirement from "Peanuts" after being diagnosed with colon cancer. He included a farewell message in his final daily strip, which appeared January 3, 2000, expressing gratitude "for the loyalty of our editors and the wonderful support and love expressed to me by fans of the comic strip," and concluding with, "Charlie Brown, Snoopy, Linus, Lucy . . . how can I ever forget them . . . ." Schulz's decision to end his strip as it approached its fiftieth anniversary brought forth regrets and tributes from many sources. Longtime friend Cathy Guisewhite, creator of the comic "Cathy," tells *Newsweek* that "a comic strip like mine would never have existed if Charles Schulz hadn't paved the way. He broke new ground, doing a comic strip that dealt with real emotions, and characters people identified with."

Schulz died in his sleep at home in Santa Rosa on February 12, 2000, only hours before the publication of his final original Sunday strip. The timing underscored how much his life and his work were intertwined and elicited another wave of fond remembrances. "For 50 years, 'Peanuts' has shown us the way," says "Doonesbury" creator Garry Trudeau. "There is not a cartoonist alive who is not indebted to him, and all of us will miss his gentle and wholly original talent." Sergio Aragones, veteran cartoonist with *Mad* magazine, remarks that "in a couple of centuries, when people talk about American artists, he'll be one of the very few remembered. And when they talk about comic strips, his will be the only one ever mentioned."

Schulz's legacy showed no signs of fading away at the start of the new century. At the time of his retirement, "Peanuts" appeared in twenty-six hundred newspapers in seventy-five countries and twenty-one languages. According to *Editor & Publisher,* some ninety percent of them decided to continue on with reruns of the strip. Plans proceeded for the establishment of the Charles M. Schulz Museum, a twenty-two-thousand-square-foot facility to be attached to Santa Rosa's Redwood Empire

A 1990s **Peanuts** *offering with a put-down for Sally from Mr. Manners, Snoopy. (From* Peanuts: A Golden Celebration.*)*

Ice Arena, a "Peanuts"-themed property opened in 1968. When completed, the museum will display "Peanuts" original artwork and memorabilia in a permanent gallery, as well as offer a ninety-nine-seat theater and a research center.

Looking back, critics found considerable significance and enduring social relevance in Schulz's body of work. Summing up the broad appeal of "Peanuts," James Poniewozik writes in *Time* that "Most of us will lose more often than we win. That's the joke of Peanuts. Schulz made it funny with characters who faced a Sisyphean suburban world of kite-eating trees and yanked-away footballs with resilience and curiosity. Sincere as a pumpkin patch, his lifework is a reminder that self-awareness and a refined sense of irony do not mean affectlessness, that being a loser does not mean being defeated."

Works Cited

"For United Media, Happiness Is a Warm Response to Reruns," *Editor & Publisher,* January 10, 2000, p. 33.

"Good Grief: Why Did We Love Charles Schulz and His Unforgettable Peanuts Gang? Got a Nickel?," *Entertainment Weekly,* February 25, 2000, p. 28.

Mendelson, Lee, and Charles M. Schulz, *Charlie Brown and Charles Schulz: In Celebration of the Twentieth Anniversary of Peanuts,* World Publishing, 1970.

Obituary of Charles Schulz, *Variety,* February 21, 2000, p. 56.

Poniewozik, James, "The Good and the Grief: Charles Schulz's 'Peanuts,'" *Time,* December 27, 1999, p. 146.

Schulz, Charles M., interview with Jean W. Ross, March 13, 1981.

Schulz, Charles M., *Peanuts Jubilee: My Life and Art with Charlie Brown and Others,* Holt, 1985.

"So Long, Snoopy & Co.", *Newsweek,* January 1, 2000, p. 18.

Tebbel, John, article in *Saturday Review,* April 12, 1969.

Review of *Why, Charlie Brown, Why?, Books for Keeps,* September, 1991, p. 11.

For More Information See

BOOKS

Johnson, Rheta Grimsley, *Good Grief: The Story of Charles M. Schulz,* Pharos, 1989.

Mascola, Marilyn, *Charles Schulz, Great Cartoonist,* Rourke Enterprises, 1989.

Schulz, Monte, and Jody Millward, *The Peanuts Trivia and Reference Book,* Holt, 1986.

Trimboli, Giovanni, editor, *Charles M. Schulz: 40 Years of Life and Art,* preface by Umberto Eco, Pharos, 1990.

PERIODICALS

Art in America, March-April, 1976.
Booklist, November 1, 1974; December 15, 1999, p. 750.
Christian Science Monitor, November 29, 1968; November 11, 1970.
Detroit Free Press, February 14, 2000, p. A1.
Life, March 17, 1967.
New Republic, December 7, 1974.
New Yorker, March 18, 1967.
New York Times, May 26, 1969; June 2, 1971.
New York Times Book Review, March 12, 1967; December 7, 1975; December 11, 1977; October 26, 1980.
People Weekly, February 28, 2000, p. 52; March 6, 2000, p. 72.
Saturday Evening Post, January 12, 1957; April 25, 1964.
Saturday Review, April 12, 1969.
Time, March 3, 1957; April 9, 1965; January 5, 1970.
Washington Post, April 4, 1970.
Washington Post Book World, September 16, 1979.

Obituaries

PERIODICALS

People, February 28, 2000, p. 72.
TV Guide, March 11, 2000, p. 42.
USA Today, February 14, 2000, p. D1.*

SHMURAK, Carole B. 1944-
(Carroll Thomas, a joint pseudonym)

Personal

Born April 19, 1944, in New York, NY; daughter of Jesse L. (a pharmacist) and Bess (a secretary; maiden name, Lichtenstein) Bernstein; married Steven H. Shmurak (a psychologist), July 31, 1967; children: Jill Susannah. *Education:* Mount Holyoke College, B.A., 1965; Harvard University, M.A., 1966; Indiana University—Bloomington, Ph.D., 1974. *Politics:* Independent. *Religion:* None. *Hobbies and other interests:* Reading and writing mysteries.

Addresses

Home—15 Candlewood Lane, Farmington, CT 06032. *Office*—Central Connecticut State University, New Britain, CT 06050. *E-mail*—cshmurak@aol.com and shmurak@ccsu.edu.

Career

Science teacher at schools in New York City, 1967-71; head of science department at private school in Farmington, CT, 1974-89; Central Connecticut State University, New Britain, professor of education, 1989—. *Member:* American Educational Research Association, American Educational Studies Association, Phi Beta Kappa.

Awards, Honors

Critics Choice Award, American Educational Studies Association, c. 1998, for *Voices of Hope.*

Writings

Voices of Hope: Adolescent Girls at Single Sex and Coeducational Schools (adult nonfiction), Peter Lang (New York City), 1998.
(With Thomas M. Ratliff, under joint pseudonym Carroll Thomas) *Matty's War* (juvenile novel), Smith & Kraus (Lyme, NH), 1999.

Contributor to periodicals, including *Middle School Journal, High School Journal,* and *History of Education Quarterly.*

Work in Progress

Blue Creek Farm, another novel featuring Matty Trescott, with Ratliff, under pseudonym Carroll Thomas; research on single-gender classes in coeducational public schools.

Sidelights

Carole B. Shmurak told *SATA:* "When I got the idea for *Matty's War,* I knew that Tom Ratliff was the ideal collaborator; his knowledge of history is encyclopedic. The collaboration has been wonderful, as we feel free to try out ideas, offer criticism, and edit each other's writing. And, as our characters develop, new ideas for related books keep emerging!"

* * *

SIMON, Gabriel 1972-

Personal

Born July 8, 1972, in San Francisco, CA; son of Gerald E. (a physician) and Karolyn W. (a community activist) Simon; married, wife's name Sarah E. (a teacher), May 9, 1998. *Education:* California State University, Sacramento, B.A., 1995, teaching credential, 1996, and graduate study. *Politics:* Democrat. *Religion:* None.

Addresses

Home and office—4913 Hidden Meadow Way, Antelope, CA 95843. *E-mail*—ogfrog@pacbell.net.

Career

Dry Creek Joint Elementary School District, second-grade teacher, grade-level leader, and site technology coordinator, 1996—. Presenter of in-service workshops. Big Brothers/Big Sisters, volunteer big brother, 1999—.

Gabriel Simon

Writings

Og and His Frogs, illustrated by Dianne Finch, Peartree Books (Clearwater, FL), 1998.

Work in Progress

Og's Food Fight Delight; research on "technology implementation and literacy."

Sidelights

Gabriel Simon told *SATA:* "Writing is an escape for me, and a form of expression. As an elementary schoolteacher, I wanted to write stories which included interesting characters and catchy rhymes. My literary hero is Dr. Seuss, for his ability to play with words and project a love of language.

"I am extremely supportive of early literacy, and I am passionate about working with children. I have visited numerous schools for author visits, and I enjoy sharing my ideas and enthusiasm with students of all ages.

"My character, Og, was created to support a message of appreciating differences. Even though Og seems odd at first, when his classmates learn he has something special to share, they learn to appreciate him and his uniqueness.

"Getting my first book published was enormously enlightening, because I learned a great deal about the book industry. I am excited about the prospect of publishing more books."

*   *   *

SLEATOR, William (Warner III) 1945-

Personal

Surname is pronounced "*slay*-tir"; born February 13, 1945, in Havre de Grace, MD; son of William Warner, Jr. (a physiologist and professor) and Esther (a physician; maiden name, Kaplan) Sleator. *Education:* Harvard University, B.A., 1967; studied musical composition in London, England, 1967-68. *Politics:* Independent.

Addresses

Home—77 Worcester St., Boston, MA 02118. *Agent*—Sheldon Fogelman, 10 East 40th St., New York, NY 10016. *E-mail*—WSleator@aol.com.

Career

Author, composer, and musician. Royal Ballet School, London, England, accompanist, 1967-68; Rambert School, London, accompanist, 1967-68; Boston Ballet Company, Boston, MA, rehearsal pianist, 1974-83; freelance writer, 1983—.

Awards, Honors

Fellowship, Bread Loaf Writers' Conference, 1969; *Boston Globe-Horn Book* Award (illustration honor), Caldecott Medal Honor Book, American Library Association (ALA), Honor List citation, *Horn Book,* all 1971, American Book Award for Best Paperback Picture Book, 1981, all for *The Angry Moon;* Children's Book of the Year Award, Child Study Association of America, 1972, and Notable Book citation, ALA, both for *Blackbriar;* Best Books for Young Adults citation, ALA, 1974, for *House of Stairs,* 1984, for *Interstellar Pig,* 1985, for *Singularity,* and 1987, for *The Boy Who Reversed Himself;* Children's Choice Award, International Reading Association and Children's Book Council, 1979, and CRABbery (Children Raving about Books) Award honor book, Maryland Library System, 1980, both for *Into the Dream;* Notable Book citation, ALA, Honor List citation, *Horn Book,* both 1984, both for *Interstellar Pig;* Best Book of the Year Award, *School Library Journal,* 1981, for *The Green Futures of Tycho,* 1983, for *Fingers,* and 1984, for *Interstellar Pig;* Golden Pen Award, Spokane Washington Public Library, 1984 and 1985, both for "the author who gives the most reading pleasure"; Junior Literary Guild selection, 1985, for *Singularity;* Notable Book selection, ALA, Best Book for Young Adults designation, ALA, both 1993, both for *Oddballs.*

Writings

FOR CHILDREN AND YOUNG ADULTS, EXCEPT AS NOTED

(Reteller) *The Angry Moon,* illustrated by Blair Lent, Little, Brown, 1970.

Blackbriar, illustrated by Lent, Dutton, 1972.

Run, Dutton, 1973.

House of Stairs, Dutton, 1974.

Among the Dolls, illustrated by Trina Schart Hyman, Dutton, 1975.

(With William H. Redd) *Take Charge: A Personal Guide to Behavior Modification* (adult nonfiction), Random House, 1977.

Into the Dream, illustrated by Ruth Sanderson, Dutton, 1979.

Once, Said Darlene, illustrated by Steven Kellogg, Dutton, 1979.

The Green Futures of Tycho, Dutton, 1981.

That's Silly (easy reader), illustrated by Lawrence DiFiori, Dutton, 1981.

Fingers, Atheneum, 1983.

Interstellar Pig, Dutton, 1984.

Singularity, Dutton, 1985.

The Boy Who Reversed Himself, Dutton, 1986.

The Duplicate, Dutton, 1988.

Strange Attractors, Dutton, 1990.

The Spirit House, Dutton, 1991.

Oddballs: Stories (semi-fictionalized autobiography), Dutton, 1993.

Others See Us, Dutton, 1993.

Dangerous Wishes (sequel to *The Spirit House*), Dutton, 1995.

The Night the Heads Came, Dutton, 1996.

The Beasties, Dutton, 1997.

The Boxes, Dutton, 1998.
Rewind, Dutton, 1999.
Boltzmon!, Dutton, 1999.

Also contributor of short stories to the collections *Am I Blue? Coming Out from the Silence,* edited by Marion Dane Bauer, and *Things That Go Bump in the Night,* edited by Jane Yolen and Martin H. Greenberg. Composer, with Blair Lent, of musical score for animated film *Why the Sun and Moon Live in the Sky,* 1972. Composer of scores for professional ballets and amateur films and plays.

Adaptations

The Angry Moon was released on audiocassette by Read-Along-House; *Interstellar Pig* was released on audiocassette by Listening Library, 1987.

Work in Progress

Collaboration with composer Wes York on the opera *The Escape Artist.*

Sidelights

A popular and prolific writer of fiction for children and young adults, Sleator is regarded as a particularly original and imaginative author whose works use the genres of fantasy, mystery, and science fiction to explore personal relationships and growth. Sleator incorporates current scientific theories, suspense, and the supernatural in his books, which challenge readers to take active roles in the stories while allowing them to resonate with the feelings and experiences of his characters. Depicting boys and girls who are often reluctant heroes, Sleator takes his characters from their everyday lives into confrontations with unusual, even unnerving situations. His protagonists encounter alien beings, doppelgangers, ESP, telepathy, telekinesis, black holes, evil spirits, malevolent dolls, weird scientific experiments, time travel into the past and the future, and other strange phenomena. In addition, the characters must learn to deal with their brothers and sisters—sibling rivalry is a consistent theme—as well as with their parents and peers. Through their physical and emotional journeys, the young people in Sleator's stories discover strength and confidence within themselves while developing a greater understanding of life in general. Characteristically, Sleator appears to end his books with the situations resolved and his characters secure; however, he is fond of including surprising twists, hinting that perhaps things are not quite so rosy as readers may think.

As a writer, Sleator is often credited for setting a tone which is often referred to as darkly humorous. Although many of his books are scary, he often laces the suspense with tongue-in-cheek humor. The author is praised as a skilled creator of plot and character as well as for his ability to blend the real and the surreal. In addition, Sleator is lauded for his insight into human nature, especially in the area of family relationships, and for creating fully realized worlds in haunting, thought-

provoking page-turners. Although his works are often considered demanding and disturbing and his use of ambiguous endings is sometimes questioned, Sleator is generally considered a talented author of rich, fascinating books that appeal to young readers on several levels. Writing in *Children's Books and Their Creators,* Peter D. Sieruta noted, "Sleator has continued to show growth as a writer, and his skillful translation of scientific theories into entertaining fiction has resulted in an important body of work." *School Library Journal* contributor David Gale commented on the author's "singular talent for writing astonishing science fiction novels," while in *Horn Book,* Roger Sutton dubbed him "the master of the juvenile creepy-crawly." Writing in *English Journal,* Margaret L. Daggett stated, "Sleator succeeds with adolescents because he blends enough scientific realities with supernatural possibilities to tantalize the mind and the imagination. Readers feel refreshed after the intellectual and emotional challenges in Sleator's novels . . . . He sets us in a reality and helps us stretch our imaginations."

Born in Havre de Grace, Maryland, Sleator is the eldest son of William Warner Sleator, Jr., a physiologist and professor, and Esther Kaplan Sleator, a physician. Sleator and his siblings—two brothers, Daniel and Tycho, and a sister, Vicky—grew up in University City, Missouri, a predominantly Jewish suburb of St. Louis where the family moved after the author's father was hired by the University of St. Louis. "My parents,"

William Sleator

Sleator told *Authors & Artists for Young Adults (AAYA),* "always encouraged us to be whoever we were." Sleator began studying the piano at the age of six. At around the same time, he wrote his first story. "From that point on," he wrote in his biographical sketch for *The Scoop,* "I was always writing or composing something. And almost from the very beginning, I was fascinated by the grotesque and the macabre." For example, one of his first musical compositions was called "Guillotines in the Springtime." Sleator once said: "I suppose it came from the kind of stories, mostly science fiction, I read as a kid." As a small boy, he wrote a story, "The Haunted Easter Egg," for a school assignment about Easter. Sleator recalled that his parents "thought it was great. Of course, that was before they realized that I was going into this bizarre career without any security, but they encouraged me at the time."

In addition to science fiction and comic books, Sleator began reading works about the physical sciences. He said: "Everybody in my family is a scientist except me. I always liked science but was never good enough to be a real scientist; I was the dumbest person in the advanced class. Still, I learned a lot. I prefer science fiction that has some basis in reality; psychological stories, time-travel stories, but especially stories about people." In high school, Sleator continued writing poems and stories and composing music; he also learned to play the cello. He wrote in *The Scoop,* "When the school orchestra played one of my compositions at an assembly, everybody thought I was a genius. I did nothing to correct this impression." However, as Sleator remembered: "I wasn't a complete nerd. I rebelled with drugs, sex—all the things every kid goes through. My parents weren't happy about it, but they were looser about it than most."

After high school, Sleator attended Harvard University, where he intended to study musical composition. However, he felt that the nature of the music program was too restrictive, so he become an English major. Sleator continued to write music for student plays and films while at Harvard. After receiving his bachelor's degree in 1967, he moved to London, England, where he studied musical composition for a year while working as a pianist at the Royal Ballet School and the Rambert School. During this period, Sleator lived in the middle of a forest in an ancient cottage that had once been a pest house for people with smallpox. He shared the cottage with his landlady, a sixty-ish woman who tried to treat Sleator as a son. This experience became the subject of his first book for young people, *Blackbriar.* Before its publication, Sleator collaborated with his friend, illustrator Blair Lent, on the picture book *The Angry Moon.* A retelling of a Tlingit Indian legend, the story describes how a girl, Lapwinsa, is taken away by the moon after she laughs at it. Her friend, the boy Lupan, rescues her by making a ladder out of arrows and climbing into the sky. A reviewer in *Publishers Weekly* noted that "books like *The Angry Moon* appear only once in a blue moon." The critic stated that Blair Lent "has topped himself with this one, perhaps because William Sleator gave him such a strong story to illustrate." Writing in *School Library Journal,* Ann D. Schweibish added that *The Angry Moon* is a "highly successful adaptation and visualization" of the traditional tale.

In *Blackbriar,* which, like *The Angry Moon,* is also illustrated by Blair Lent, Sleator describes how Danny, a teenage boy, struggles for independence from his middle-aged guardian, Philippa, with whom he shares a haunted, isolated cottage in the English countryside. Danny and Philippa are shunned by the locals because of the perception that they are linked to Satanism. After Philippa and her cat are kidnapped, Danny and his friend Lark search for her. In the process, Danny discovers himself and learns the secret of the cottage, which served as a pesthouse during a seventeenth-century plague. A critic in *Kirkus Reviews* advised, "Bolt the cellar door, watch your cat closely for personality changes, and follow him—vicariously." Ashley Darlington Grayson, writing in *Fantasy Review,* stated that Danny "fails to earn any reader respect because he is thick as a post." However, Paul Heins of *Horn Book* noted that "the effectiveness of the story lies in its characterization and in its narrative skill."

In 1974, Sleator began working as the rehearsal pianist for the Boston Ballet while continuing to write fiction. With the dancers, he toured the United States and Europe and wrote three ballets performed by the company. *House of Stairs,* a book published the same year that Sleator joined the Boston Ballet, is considered among his best. A young adult novel set in a huge room that contains a labyrinthine maze of stairways leading nowhere, the story outlines how five orphaned sixteen-year-olds learn to survive in a world without walls, ceilings, or floors. The young people, who eat only if they perform dance-like rituals in front of a machine, eventually realize that they are part of a stimulus/response experiment in which food is dispensed when the subjects display hostile behavior to each other. When two of the protagonists refuse to perform the cruel acts that are required to obtain food, the scientists end the experiment. Compared by critics to such works as *Brave New World* and *Lord of the Flies, House of Stairs* is generally regarded as an exceptional study of human behavior as well as an exciting story. Called "brilliant, bone-chilling," by a reviewer in *Publishers Weekly,* the novel is dubbed "[f]orceful sci fi based on Skinnerian precepts that will have readers hanging by the skin of their teeth" by *School Library Journal* reviewer Pamela D. Pollack. Writing in her *Thursday's Child: Trends and Patterns in Contemporary Children's Literature,* Sheila A. Egoff concluded that the story is "one of the most brutal in science fiction, all the more sickeningly compelling because of its finely controlled, stark writing." Sleator told *AAYA,* "In *House of Stairs,* the kids who refused to become conditioned by hate were being human in the end, as opposed to trained animals. I always stress that. I'm not saying to be nice to other people because it's good; I'm saying, think about how other people feel because it's practical. I'm not making any moralistic, goody-goody kind of point. You will get along better with people if you are able to understand them." Sleator has also written other stories for young people that explore behavior; in addition, he is the author of *Take Charge: A Personal Guide to Behavior Modification,* an informational book for adults on which he collaborated with William H. Redd.

Sleator considers *The Green Futures of Tycho,* a story for middle graders, to be a watershed book in his career. He named the title character, the youngest of four children who is tormented by his siblings, after his youngest brother. While working in his family's garden, eleven-year-old Tycho finds a strange silver egg that was planted by aliens thousands of years before. The egg, a time-travel device, allows Tycho to go into both the past and the future. At first, Tycho uses his abilities to tease his brothers and sister. He then meets his adult self in the future and finds that the figure is becoming more and more evil and manipulative. For example, the adult Tycho uses his knowledge of the future dishonestly and also wreaks destruction on his siblings. At the end of the story, Tycho's love for his family leads him to reject his powerful but vile grownup persona; he risks death to bury the egg back in the past. In a *School Library Journal* review Pollack noted, "Sleator's expert blend of future and horror fiction is unusually stark, dark, and intriguing." Writing in *Horn Book,* Paul Heins added that though "the combination of logic and horror gives the telling a Poe-like quality ... the moral significance" of the happenings becomes clear. Sleator once said: "I really got in touch with my weirdness in [*The Green Futures of Tycho*]. That was the first book into which I was able to inject humor, and I feel humor is important. Even in a basically serious, or even a scary piece, there must be comic relief to reduce the tension. Humor is also very attractive to kids."

In 1983, Sleator left his job as an accompanist for the Boston Ballet to become a full-time author. *Interstellar Pig,* a young adult novel published the following year, is regarded by critics as one of his most popular books. In this work, sixteen-year-old Barney faces a boring summer at the beach with his doltish parents. He is intrigued when an interesting trio of strangers—Joe, Manny, and Zena—moves in next door and invites him to join them in playing a role-playing board game called Interstellar Pig. The object of the game is to possess The Piggy, a card named for a pink symbol that is an integral part of the game. However, Barney's neighbors turn out to be hostile aliens masquerading as humans, and the game turns real—and deadly. It places Barney in a life-and-death struggle for survival; at the end of the story, Barney saves both himself and planet Earth by using his head. Writing in *School Library Journal,* Trev Jones stated, "Sleator's science fiction story is compelling on first reading—but stellar on the second." *New York Times Book Review* critic Rosalie Byard called *Interstellar Pig* "a riveting adventure that should satisfy readers in the 12- to 14-year-old range, especially any who happen to be hooked on strategy games." Writing in *Junior Bookshelf,* Marcus Crouch called the novel a "remarkable story" that is "surprisingly readable," adding that "the curious details of the game get right into the reader's system." Sleator told *AAYA,* "*Interstellar Pig* is my funniest book. There were a lot of opportunities for humor in it."

Sleator currently spends half the year in Boston, Massachusetts, and the other half in Bangkok, Thailand. He once told *Something about the Author (SATA),* "I feel more at home in Thailand than in practically any other place I can think of. Partly this is because Thailand is so exotic that it feels almost like being on another planet. (Don't ask me why THAT should make me feel at home.) I also like Thai people because they turn almost any situation into an occasion to have fun, and because they are so pleasant and polite that you never know what is *really* going on in their minds, so they are a mysterious puzzle to try to figure out."

The Spirit House, a young adult novel that incorporates Thai beliefs, is considered a stylistic departure from Sleator's other works. In this story, fifteen-year-old Julie meets Bia, an exchange student from Thailand, when he comes to stay with her family. Julie's younger brother Dominic builds Bia a "spirit house," or a traditional household shrine, in the backyard to make him feel at home. However, Bia is convinced that the house is inhabited by a vengeful spirit. Julie leaves offerings for the spirit, who appears to grant her wishes. However, Julie's health begins to decline, and things begin to go badly for her, her family, and Bia. At the end of the story, Julie goes to Thailand with a jade carving containing the spirit in order to restore it to its rightful place. All appears to be well until Julie loses the carving. Calling *The Spirit House* "both scary and convincing," *Bulletin of the Center for Children's Books* reviewer Roger Sutton commented that "all of the events of the story are entirely possible, if unremittingly frightening." In a *Book World—The Washington Post* review, S. P. Somtow added that *The Spirit House* is a book "that provides no easy answers ... and the ending packs a satisfying punch." Writing in *Kirkus Reviews,* a contributor commented, "Best ... is the logical explanation of seemingly supernatural events: the reader suspends belief only to have it systematically restored. That's a feast—and a treat."

Dangerous Wishes, the sequel to *The Spirit House,* features Julie's younger brother, fourteen-year-old Dominic. After three years of bad luck have passed for Dom and his family, he and his parents travel to Bangkok for an extended stay. When everything goes awry, Dom suspects that the cause may be the jade carving that his sister tried, but failed, to deliver three years earlier. Dom and Kik, a Thai boy, try to find the charm and take it to its temple. In the process, the boys are pursued by a malevolent creature from the spirit world. They barely escape, but are able to restore the recovered charm to its rightful place. However, the question remains: will the bad luck end? Writing in *Bulletin of the Center for Children's Books,* Roger Sutton stated that "narrative coincidences that would be trite in realistic fiction here have an otherworldly eeriness that makes them convincing." *Booklist* critic Merri Monks concluded by calling the story "fast-moving." A reviewer in *Horn Book* concluded by calling *Dangerous Wishes* "Vintage Sleator." Sleator told *SATA,* "I recently built a Thai-style farmhouse in the northeast of Thailand, twelve kilometers from the Cambodian border, very close to the Khmer Rouge headquarters. I am the only westerner around for seventy kilometers, so everyone knows me and I rather enjoy it—though of course none of them speak English so they can't read my books. But it is a wonderful place to write and I have a writing room with a beautiful view of checkerboard rice fields, brilliantly green in the rainy season . . . . We also have a wonderful lush tropical garden. If I could, I would live there all year!"

With *Oddballs,* Sleator created a collection of ten short autobiographical and semi-autobiographical vignettes about his childhood and adolescence. The stories show four creative, talented children growing up in a household run by free-thinking parents who provide minimal supervision. The book is credited for depicting how, through all of their sibling rivalry and joke-playing, the Sleator children developed individuality, confidence, and independence. Writing in *Kirkus Reviews,* a critic favorably commented on Sleator's "splendid sense of comic timing" and "vivid characterizations." Betsy Hearne, writing in *Bulletin of the Center for Children's Books,* added that "Sleator evidently thrived without pause on his permissive parents' steady encouragement to violate social taboos." Writing in *School Library Journal,* contributor Michael Cart predicted, that while "serious" readers will take the book as "a kind of 'Portrait of the Artist as a Young Oddball,'" the majority will "simply relax and enjoy the wacky humor." Sleator, who dedicated *Oddballs* "To my family: Please forgive me!," noted on the flap copy, "I changed the names of everyone outside the immediate family, of course. But as far as I'm concerned, it's all in all a pretty accurate picture of what life was like. My mother, of course, might not entirely agree."

Regarding his writing, Sleator told *AAYA,* "At the beginning, I was copying other things, but with each book, I've learned to tap deeper into my subconscious. The more books I write, the more they represent who I really am . . . . Also, my style has improved; I'm a better writer, but that goes up and down . . . . " He added, "I try to make my books exciting. I also provide incentives in the sense of giving kids a more active role in the story . . . . My goal is to entertain my audience and to get them to read. I want kids to find out that reading is the best entertainment there is. If, at the same time, I'm also imparting some scientific knowledge, then that's good, too. I'd like kids to see that science is not just boring formulas. Some of the facts to be learned about the universe are very weird." Sleator also noted, "In any idea for a book, I want to see how I can explore the personal relations that would manifest from that idea." Writing in *Fifth Book of Junior Authors and Illustrators,* Sleator concluded, "I still consider myself one of the luckiest people in the world to be able to write for young people."

Works Cited

Review of *The Angry Moon, Publishers Weekly,* November 23, 1970, p. 39.

Review of *Blackbriar, Kirkus Reviews,* April 15, 1972, p. 486.

Byard, Rosalie, review of *Interstellar Pig, New York Times Book Review,* September 23, 1984, p. 47.

Cart, Michael, review of *Oddballs, School Library Journal,* August, 1993, p. 189.

Crouch, Marcus, review of *Interstellar Pig, Junior Bookshelf,* June, 1987, p. 137.

Daggett, Margaret L., "Recommended: William Sleator," *English Journal,* March, 1987, pp. 93-94.

Review of *Dangerous Wishes, Horn Book,* March, 1996, p. 200.

Egoff, Sheila A., "Science Fiction," *Thursday's Child: Trends and Patterns in Contemporary Children's Literature,* American Library Association, 1981, p. 142.

Gale, David, review of *Singularity, School Library Journal,* August, 1985, p. 82.

Grayson, Ashley Darlington, "Two by Sleator," *Fantasy Review,* December, 1986, pp. 41-42.

Hearne, Betsy, review of *Oddballs, Bulletin of the Center for Children's Books,* May, 1993, pp. 295-96.

Heins, Paul, review of *Blackbriar, Horn Book,* August, 1972, p. 378.

Heins, Paul, review of *The Green Futures of Tycho, Horn Book,* August, 1981, p. 426.

Review of *House of Stairs, Publishers Weekly,* May 6, 1974, p. 68.

Jones, Trev, review of *Interstellar Pig, School Library Journal,* September, 1984, p. 134.

Monks, Merri, review of *Dangerous Wishes, Booklist,* August, 1995, p. 1942.

Review of *Oddballs, Kirkus Reviews,* February 1, 1993, p. 154.

Pollack, Pamela D., review of *The Green Futures of Tycho, School Library Journal,* April, 1981, p. 133.

Pollack, Pamela D., review of *House of Stairs, School Library Journal,* March, 1974, p. 120.

Schweibish, Ann D., review of *The Angry Moon, School Library Journal,* February, 1971, p. 50.

Sieruta, Peter D., "Sleator, William," *Children's Books and Their Creators,* edited by Anita Silvey, Houghton Mifflin, 1995, pp. 605-06.

Sleator, William, essay in *Fifth Book of Junior Authors and Illustrators,* edited by Sally Holmes Holtze, Wilson, 1983, pp. 295-96.

Sleator, William, interview with Dieter Miller, *Authors & Artists for Young Adults,* Volume 5, Gale, 1991, pp. 207-15.

Sleator, William, foreword to and jacket copy for *Oddballs,* Dutton, 1993.

Sleator, William, essay in *The Scoop:* http://www.friend.ly.net/scoop/biographies/.

Somtow, S. P., "Something Weird in the Neighborhood," *Book World—The Washington Post,* December 1, 1991, p. 25.

Review of *The Spirit House, Kirkus Reviews,* October 15, 1991, p. 1350.

Sutton, Roger, review of *The Boxes, Horn Book,* May-June, 1998, p. 349.

Sutton, Roger, review of *Dangerous Wishes, Bulletin of the Center for Children's Books,* October, 1995, p. 70.

Sutton, Roger, review of *The Spirit House, Bulletin of the Center for Children's Books,* October, 1991, p. 30.

For More Information See

BOOKS

Davis, James E., and Hazel K. Davis, *Presenting William Sleator,* Twayne, 1992.

Drew, Bernard A., *The 100 Most Popular Young Adult Authors: Biographical Sketches and Bibliographies,* Libraries Unlimited, 1996, pp. 448-50.

Lerner, Fred, *A Teacher's Guide to the Bantam Starfire Novels of William Sleator,* Bantam, 1990.

Meet the Authors and Illustrators: 60 Creators of Favorite Children's Books Talk about Their Work, edited by Deborah Kovacs, Scholastic, 1993.

Roginski, Jim, *Behind the Covers: Interviews with Authors and Illustrators of Books for Children and Young Adults,* Libraries Unlimited, 1985.

St. James Guide to Young Adult Writers, edited by Tom Pendergast and Sara Pendergast, 2nd edition, St. James, 1999, pp. 763-65.

PERIODICALS

Booklist, October 1, 1997, p. 333; June 1 and 15, 1998, p. 769.

Horn Book, January-February, 1994, p. 75.

New York Times Book Review, April 24, 1994.

Publishers Weekly, July 12, 1999, p. 93.

Voice of Youth Advocates, February, 1994, p. 386.

*   *   *

SMITH, Pauline C.
See ARTHUR, Robert (Jr.)

*   *   *

STEARMAN, Kaye 1951-

Personal

Born April 9, 1951, in Sydney, Australia; daughter of Roy (an engineer) and Mary (a housewife; maiden name, Hill) Stearman. *Education:* University of Sydney, B.Econ. (honours), 1973; School of Oriental and African Studies, University of London, M.A. (area studies), 1979. *Politics:* "Left-wing."

Addresses

Home—Flat 2, 26 Upper Tollington Park, London, N4 3EL, England.

Career

Author. Teacher of young people and adults, London, England, 1975-79; worked in non-governmental organizations in human rights and development, 1981-87, including Amnesty International, 1987-88; Minority Rights Group, 1988-92; Healthlink Worldwide, 1993-99; CARE International, 1999—, all based in London.

Writings

(With Keith D. Suter) *Aboriginal Australians,* revised and updated edition, Minority Rights Group (London, England), 1988.

(With Rachel Warner) *Homeland,* Wayland (Hove, England), 1993.

(With Cheryl Law) *Justice,* Wayland, 1993.

Freedom of Expression, Wayland, 1993.

(With Nikki van der Gaag) *Gender Issues,* Wayland, 1995, Raintree Steck-Vaughn (Austin, TX), 1997.

Homelessness, Wayland, 1998, Raintree Steck-Vaughn, 1999.

Women's Rights: Changing Attitudes, 1900-2000, Wayland, 1999, Raintree Steck-Vaughn, 1999.

Slavery Today, Raintree Steck-Vaughn, 1999.

Work in Progress

Two books for readers age nine to eleven years old, *Why Are They on the Streets?* and *Why Do People Gamble?,* for Wayland/Hodder Headline, due in 2000.

Sidelights

Kaye Stearman has contributed a number of books for young adults to several Wayland series on human rights and global issues. These works introduce young people to serious social problems confronting humanity at the end of the twentieth century, including homelessness,

Kaye Stearman

slavery, gender inequality, freedom of expression, and child labor, among others. The works in both series, including those written solely by and co-authored by Stearman, have garnered positive critical attention for clearly presenting complex social problems and for providing a variety of viewpoints on possible solutions, pertinent statistics, and outstanding quotes. Sarah Mears, a reviewer for *School Librarian,* praised Stearman's treatise on *Freedom of Expression* as "very up to date." The book covers the variety of ways people speak out about injustice, the use and misuse of the media, and the importance of having the freedom to express differences of opinion. Stearman's effort was reviewed alongside another book in the series, and both were judged to be lacking in bias and respectful of their subjects. "This is an important and challenging new series," Mears concluded.

In *Gender Issues,* Stearman and co-author Nikki van der Gaag cover topics such as equal opportunity in employment and education, women's rights under the law, and how gender roles are changing worldwide. All the while, the duo take into consideration cultural differences, sexual orientation, the availability of such resources as family planning, childcare, and other relevant social structures. Again, this work was reviewed alongside another from the series, and though *Books for Keeps* reviewer Steve Rosson expressed some dissatisfaction with the prose style of each, he proclaimed both "very worthy, immensely detailed and thoroughly researched tomes." *Voice of Youth Advocates* reviewer Sandra Lee, on the other hand, offered only praise for the book. "The authors succeed in presenting facts and personal stories from people around the world without loading the book with opinion or lessons," Lee contended, adding that the style of presentation encourages student discussion, further investigation, and activism. In Stearman's book on *Homelessness,* the author again takes a global approach to a social problem experienced differently in the United States, India, and South Africa, for example. The author researches homelessness according to many causes, including poverty, war, natural disaster, and the breakdown of the family.

Works Cited

Lee, Sandra, review of *Gender Issues, Voice of Youth Advocates,* June, 1997, p. 138.
Mears, Sarah, review of *Freedom of Expression, School Librarian,* May, 1994, p. 77.
Rosson, Steve, review of *Gender Issues, Books for Keeps,* May, 1996, p. 23.

For More Information See

PERIODICALS

Booklist, September 1, 1999, p. 77.
School Librarian, August, 1996, p. 126.

*   *   *

STERLING, Brett
See HAMILTON, Edmond

*   *   *

TALLIS, Robyn
See COVILLE, Bruce

*   *   *

THOMAS, Carroll (joint pseudonym)
See RATLIFF, Thomas M.

*   *   *

THOMAS, Carroll (joint pseudonym)
See SHMURAK, Carole B.

W

WALGREN, Judy 1963-

Personal

Born March 5, 1963, in Iowa City, IA; daughter of Ken (an internist) and Kay (a recruiter) Walgren. *Education:* Attended Pepperdine University; University of Texas at Austin, B.A., 1986.

Addresses

Home—Dallas, TX. *E-mail*—nabari5005@aol.com.

Career

Odessa American, Odessa, TX, photojournalist, 1987; *Dallas Morning News,* Dallas, TX, photojournalist, 1987-99; freelance photojournalist, 1999—. *Member:* National Press Photographers Association.

Awards, Honors

Shared Pulitzer Prize for international reporting, 1994, for photographs of violent human rights abuses against women all over the world; Award of Excellence, Robert F. Kennedy Foundation; World Hunger Award; Barbara Jordan Award, for reporting on people with disabilities; Associated Press award for a series on immigrants and refugees in Dallas; Headliners Award for work in Southern Sudan; award from Texas Council against Violence for work with abused women; Dallas Press Club awards.

Writings

(Author and photographer) *The Lost Boys of Natinga: A School for Sudan's Young Refugees,* Houghton (Boston, MA), 1998.

Contributor to periodicals, including *People* and *Texas Monthly.*

Work in Progress

A book on African elders from nomadic tribes, telling the histories of their tribes from their perspectives, rather than the colonial perspective, with Francesca Marciano; photographs for a book on child labor.

Through text and photographs, Judy Walgren has described the refugee camp named Natinga, in which the Sudanese People's Liberation Army protects and educates boys from many different tribes of war-torn Sudan. (From The Lost Boys of Natinga.)

For More Information See

PERIODICALS

Booklist, August, 1998, p. 1990.
Bulletin of the Center for Children's Books, September, 1998, pp. 37-38.*

*   *   *

WALSH, Mary Caswell 1949-

Personal

Born January 19, 1949, in the United States; daughter of Dwight Allen (a microwave physicist) and Helen (an artist and writer; maiden name, Rayburn) Caswell; married Matthew B. Walsh (a music director), August 5, 1972; children: Teresa H., Elizabeth M. *Politics:* Democrat. *Religion:* Roman Catholic. *Hobbies and other interests:* Irish harp, singing with Cathedral of the Holy Name Gallery Singers.

Addresses

Home—1631 North New England, Chicago, IL 60707. *Office*—1103 Westgate, Oak Park, IL. *E-mail*—stellarsky@earthlink.net. *Agent*—Etta Wilson, March Media, 1114 Oman Dr., Brentwood, TN 37027.

Career

Marin General Hospital, Greenbrae, CA, family therapist and clinical coordinator of aftercare services at Adolescent Recovery Center, 1987-92; Sobriety High, San Rafael, CA, family therapist and clinical coordinator, 1992-94; Catholic Charities, Chicago, IL, psychotherapist, 1995—; private practice of psychotherapy in Chicago, IL, 1995—, and Oak Park, IL, 1998—. West Suburban Hospital, chaplain intern, 1995-97. University of San Francisco, assistant to the vice president of university relations, 1987-88. San Francisco Girls Chorus Auction, event coordinator, 1990-92; Monastery of the Holy Cross, oblate and member of foundation council, 1998—. *Member:* American Association of Marriage and Family Therapists, Illinois Associate of Marriage and Family Therapists.

Awards, Honors

Swig scholar at Hebrew University of Jerusalem, 1988; Golden Bell state and county awards, 1993.

Writings

The Art of Tradition: A Christian Guide to Building a Family, illustrated by mother, Helen Caswell, Living the Good News (Denver, CO), 1997.
(Reteller) *Saint Francis Celebrates Christmas,* illustrated by H. Caswell, Loyola University Press (Chicago, IL), 1998.

Mary Caswell Walsh

Work in Progress

Welcome Yule, Paschal Mission, The Strength of Tradition, and *The Joy of Tradition* for Liturgical Training Publications; *The Healing Way* for Ave Maria Press; three children's novels, *St. Francis and the Fierce World of Gubbio, The Miracle of Chartres,* and *St. Luke and the Legend of the First Icon;* two adult books, *A Family for Others* and *The Motherhood of God.*

Sidelights

Mary Caswell Walsh told *SATA:* "I have worked for over twenty years as a psychotherapist with families in crisis. Aware of the power of spiritual traditions to help families both face crisis and avoid problems, I began writing books for families and children, aimed at helping people access the rich spiritual resources available."

*   *   *

WARD, E. D.
See GOREY, Edward (St. John)

*   *   *

WEARY, Ogdred
See GOREY, Edward (St. John)

WENTWORTH, Robert
See HAMILTON, Edmond

*   *   *

WEST, Andrew
See ARTHUR, Robert (Jr.)

*   *   *

WEST, John
See ARTHUR, Robert (Jr.)

*   *   *

WILLIAMS, Mark
See ARTHUR, Robert (Jr.)

*   *   *

WOLFE, Gene (Rodman) 1931-

Personal

Born May 7, 1931, in Brooklyn, NY; son of Roy Emerson (a salesman) and Mary Olivia (Ayers) Wolfe; married Rosemary Frances Dietsch, November 3, 1956; children: Roy II, Madeleine, Therese, Matthew. *Education:* Attended Texas A&M University, 1949-52; University of Houston, B.S.M.E., 1956. *Religion:* Roman Catholic.

Addresses

Home—P.O. Box 69, Barrington, IL 60011. *Agent*—Virginia Kidd, Box 278, Milford, PA 18337.

Career

Writer. Project engineer with Procter & Gamble, 1956-72; *Plant Engineering Magazine,* Barrington, IL, senior editor, 1972-84. *Military service:* U.S. Army, 1952-54; received Combat Infantry badge. *Member:* Science Fiction Writers of America.

Awards, Honors

Nebula Award, Science Fiction Writers of America, 1973, for novella *The Death of Doctor Island;* Chicago Foundation for Literature Award, 1977, for *Peace;* Rhysling Award, 1978, for poem "The Computer Iterates the Greater Trumps"; Nebula Award nomination, 1979, for novella *Seven American Nights,* and 1993, for *Nightside the Long Sun;* Illinois Arts Council award, 1981, for short story "In Looking-Glass Castle"; World Fantasy Award, 1981, for *The Shadow of the Torturer,* 1989, for collection *Storeys from the Old Hotel,* and 1996, for Lifetime Achievement; Nebula Award and *Locus* Award, both 1982, both for *The Claw*

of the Conciliator; British Science Fiction Award, 1982; British Fantasy Award, 1983; *Locus* Award, 1983, for *The Sword of the Lictor;* John W. Campbell Memorial Award, Science Fiction Research Association, 1984, for *The Citadel of the Autarch.*

Writings

SCIENCE FICTION AND FANTASY

Operation ARES, Berkley Publishing (New York), 1970.
The Fifth Head of Cerberus (three novellas), Scribner (New York), 1972, reprinted, Orb, 1994.
(With Ursula K. LeGuin and James Tiptree, Jr.) *The New Atlantis and Other Novellas of Science Fiction,* edited by Robert L. Silverberg, Hawthorn (New York), 1975.
The Devil in a Forest (juvenile), Follett, 1976, reprinted, Orb, 1996.
The Island of Doctor Death and Other Stories, Pocket Books (New York), 1980, reprinted, Orb, 1997.
Gene Wolfe's Book of Days (short stories), Doubleday (New York), 1981.
The Wolfe Archipelago (short stories), Ziesing Bros. (Willimantic, CT), 1983.
Plan(e)t Engineering, New England Science Fiction Association, 1984.
Free Live Free, Ziesing Bros., 1984, new edition, Tor Books (New York), 1985.
Soldier of the Mist, Tor Books, 1986.
There Are Doors, Tor Books, 1988.
Storeys from the Old Hotel (short stories), Kerosina, 1988, reprinted, Orb, 1995.
Endangered Species (short stories), Tor Books, 1989.
Seven American Nights (bound with *Sailing to Byzantium,* by Robert L. Silverberg), Tor Books, 1989.
Soldier of Arete (sequel to *Soldier of the Mist*), St. Martin's (New York), 1989.
Pandora by Holly Hollander, Tor Books, 1990.
Castleview, Tor Books, 1991.
Castle of Days, Tor Books, 1992, reprinted, Orb, 1995.
Strange Travelers (short stories), Tor Books, 2000.

"BOOK OF THE NEW SUN" SERIES

The Shadow of the Torturer, Simon & Schuster (New York), 1980.
The Claw of the Conciliator, Simon & Schuster, 1981.
The Sword of the Lictor, Simon & Schuster, 1982.
The Citadel of the Autarch, Simon & Schuster, 1983.
The Urth of the New Sun, Tor Books, 1987.
Shadow & Claw (contains *The Shadow of the Torturer* and *The Claw of the Conciliator*), Orb, 1994.
Sword and Citadel, (contains *The Sword of the Lictor* and *The Citadel of the Autarch*), Orb, 1994.

"BOOK OF THE LONG SUN" SERIES

Nightside the Long Sun, Tor Books, 1993.
Lake of the Long Sun, Tor Books, 1993, reprinted, Doherty, 1994.
Calde of the Long Sun, Tor Books, 1994.
Exodus from the Long Sun, Tor Books, 1995.

"BOOK OF THE SHORT SUN" TRILOGY

On Blue's Waters, Tor Books, 1999.

OTHER

Peace (novel), Harper (New York), 1975, reprinted, Tor, 1995.
The Castle of the Otter (essays), Ziesing Bros., 1982.
Bibliomen, Cheap Street (New Castle, Virginia), 1984.
Empires of Foliage and Flower, Cheap Street, 1987.
For Rosemary (poetry), Kerosina, 1988.

Contributor of stories to anthologies, including awards anthologies *Best SF: 70,* 1970, *Nebula Award Stories 9, The Best SF of the Year #3,* and *Best SF: 73,* all 1974. Contributor of short stories to *Omni, New Yorker, Isaac Asimov's Science Fiction Magazine,* and other publications.

Work in Progress

Two projected titles in the "Book of the Short Sun" trilogy: *In Green's Jungle* and *Return to the Whorl.*

Sidelights

"With the publication of his tetralogy *The Book of the New Sun,* Gene Wolfe has entered the ranks of the major contemporary writers of science fiction," Pamela Sargent asserted in *Twentieth-Century Science Fiction Writers.* The series takes place far in the future in a society reminiscent of medieval Europe in its social structure where long-forgotten technologies appear magical. When Severian, an apprentice torturer, is exiled from his guild for aiding the suicide of a prisoner he loves, a journey of discovery is inaugurated that culminates in Severian's elevation to Autarch, ruler of Urth. "The far-future world of Urth through which Wolfe's characters move is a world of beauty and horror, one in which humanity's great accomplishments are not only past, but also nearly forgotten, and in which the lack of resources makes the knowledge that remains nearly useless," noted Sargent. Severian, however, possesses perfect recall, making his retrospective narration rich with detail and meaning. As Thomas D. Clareson said in his *Dictionary of Literary Biography* essay, Severian's account is "a rich tapestry rivaling any imaginary world portrayed in contemporary science fiction"; he called the series of books "one of the high accomplishments of modern science fiction."

Critics have particularly admired the realism with which Wolfe presents his imaginary society. *London Tribune* contributor Martin Hillman, for example, declared that "in the evocation of the world, and the unsettling technologies, creatures, and behavioural rules within it," Wolfe's tetralogy "is streets ahead of most tales featuring sword-bearing heroes." "Wolfe is not only deft at creating a whole and strange new world," Tom Hutchinson of the London *Times* claimed, "he also, disturbingly, makes us understand a different way of thinking."

Wolfe was born in Brooklyn, New York, and his family moved from town to town during the Great Depression: Logan, Ohio; Des Moines, Iowa; and Dallas and Houston, Texas. (His short story "Houston, 1943" is partly autobiographical.) Wolfe first fell in love with

Gene Wolfe's collection of extremely varied works of short fiction, which was first published as a limited British edition, also includes some of his original poetry.

reading while at Poe School, a Houston elementary school named for writer Edgar Allan Poe. His mother read a variety of material to him, from crime novels to classics like *Alice in Wonderland,* and he enjoyed comics such as *Famous Funnies* and *Captain Marvel.* "Someone . . . once said that there was a sentence that could be inserted into the autobiography of every author who ever lived: 'I had a mother who read to me,'" Wolfe wrote in his essay for *Contemporary Authors Autobiography Series* (*CAAS*). "I am no exception." After hurting his leg in a bicycle accident, Wolfe was forced to accept rides to school from his mother for a few weeks. He wrote in *CAAS* that it was then his life changed. It was on one of these trips that Wolfe noticed a book with a futuristic cover lying open on the car seat. His mother told him she was not interested in the work, and he could have it to read. It was *The Book of Pocket Science Fiction,* and the first science-fiction story Wolfe read was "Microcosmic God" by Theodore Sturgeon.

His love for science fiction set Wolfe apart from most of his high-school peers, and it was a "lonely time" for him. He had two friends with whom he developed "close friendships based largely on the books and magazines we loaned or gave each other." In *CAAS,* he wrote that, in addition to his mother, father, and a number of other important people in his life, he later recreated these two friends as characters in his novels.

Wolfe excelled in English and math in high school. He took a Latin class and was drawn to ancient history. (*Washington Post Book World* critic James Gunn has commented on Wolfe's use of Latin and Greek character names and terminology in his stories.) Wolfe studied mechanical engineering at Texas A&M University, then an all-male military school, and in 1952 he was drafted to serve overseas in the Korean War.

After Wolfe returned from Korea, he attended the University of Houston, graduating in 1956. He then began working as an engineer and married Rosemary Dietsch, a childhood playmate. In 1957, Wolfe and his new wife were in need of money. Having read that Gold Medal Books paid two-thousand dollars for an original paperback novel, Wolfe began writing. But he did not sell a paperback to Gold Medal, or any written work to

Wolfe's series "The Book of the New Sun" tells the story of Severian, who relates his difficulty in maintaining his own principles despite his apprenticeship to the Torturer's Guild.

any publisher, for the next eight years. Finally, in 1965, Wolfe's story "The Dead Man" was bought by *Sir!* (which he described as a "lesser skin magazine") for eighty dollars.

A second tale, "Mountains Like Mice," published in Frederik Pohl's *If,* cemented Wolfe's desire to write. From then on, although he worked primarily as an engineer, his writing career began to grow. He joined the Science Fiction Writers of America, and his stories were published regularly in *Orbit.* Damon Knight, *Orbit*'s editor (whom Wolfe calls "the greatest influence on my career"), convinced the author to develop one short work entitled "The Laughter Outside at Night" into a longer tale; this he did, and *Operation Ares* became Wolfe's first novel.

After publishing *The Fifth Head of Cerberus,* his second novel, Wolfe quit his engineering job and become an editor at a technical magazine. The work was well received by critics and sold in Great Britain, France, Germany, Italy, and Sweden. Shortly afterward, Wolfe began the story that evolved into "The Book of the New Sun," his most successful series of books. He sold it to Pocket Books' new science fiction and fantasy division, an enterprise that became the "leading science-fiction program in the world" within a year of its start, according to Wolfe.

"The Book of the New Sun" tetralogy takes place in the far future on a planet named Urth. The original volumes include *The Shadow of the Torturer, The Claw of the Conciliator, The Sword of the Lictor,* and *The Citadel of the Autarch;* Wolfe later added a one-volume sequel, *The Urth of the New Sun.* The first four titles were described by Wolfe in *CAAS* as "the autobiography of the Autarch Severian, who began life as an orphaned apprentice in the Order of the Seekers for Truth and Penitence (known unofficially as the torturers guild), was exiled for showing mercy, and rose to the throne of the Commonwealth, a peculiar monarchy occupying the South America of a world remote in time from our own."

In the *Washington Post Book World,* James Gunn called *The Shadow of the Torturer,* which Wolfe considers his most successful novel, "an engrossing narrative and perhaps a book in which wisdom can be found." Other reviewers had similar praise for the series. *Los Angeles Times Book Review* critic David N. Samuelson wrote, "'Book of the New Sun' is a monumental achievement in the oft-despised genre of science fantasy. Well written, vividly imaged, symbolically united and internally consistent, it has the dubious distinction of dwarfing what mediocre competition there is." *Magazine of Fantasy and Science Fiction* book critic Algis Budrys wrote, "Gene Wolfe is, I think, without peer at his own kind of story, and has a particular gift for the depiction of cataclysmic events through the eyes of a naive central character." Budrys continued, "Some people write a series of four books and call it a tetralogy, but Wolfe is clearly writing one book with four aspects . . . he's one of our very best."

In the sequel, *The Urth of the New Sun,* Severian attempts to revive Urth's dying sun. The novel was hailed as another triumph. Colin Greenland, writing in the *Times Literary Supplement,* stated, "If this book is less brilliant than its predecessor, the flaw is one that is hard to spot with the unaided eye." "Wolfe employs a richness of language unmatched in science fiction," Fred Lerner wrote in *Voice of Youth Advocates,* "and his imagination is equally unfettered by the traditions of the genre."

Wolfe's stories are notable for, among other things, their fully realized fictional worlds. "Gene Wolfe has few equals at representing the textures of a world, whether our own, that of antiquity, or imagined near- to far-future ones," wrote *Los Angeles Times Book Review* contributor James Sallis. "The overlap of cultures, language that rolls and shapes the world on various tongues, layers of physical detail down to the very way clothing feels against skin: it's all there." Although some critics occasionally referred to Wolfe's work as fantasy, most fans, and Wolfe himself, considered his writing pure science fiction. When asked about the difference between science fiction and fantasy, Wolfe told interviewer Brendan Baber, "Plausibility really. Science fiction is what you can make people believe; fantasy is what people have to suspend disbelief for . . . . So it's all a matter of plausibility. Do people think, 'The future might be like this?' If so, it's science fiction. If they think, 'This could never happen,' that's fantasy."

Although Wolfe became famous for his novels, his literary reputation is also bolstered by his short fiction, notably the collections *Storeys from the Old Hotel*—a highly accessible gathering of imaginative fiction—and *Endangered Species*—a somewhat more challenging volume of philosophically inclined tales. *Gene Wolfe's Book of Days* was republished in a volume entitled *Castle of Days* that also includes the essay collection *The Castle of the Otter* as well as previously unpublished fiction and nonfiction. Clareson contended in his *Dictionary of Literary Biography* essay that Wolfe is "a major figure whose stories and novels must be considered among the most important science fiction published in the 1970s." "Gene Wolfe is a writer for the thinking reader," Sargent similarly stated; "he will reward anyone searching for intelligence, crafted prose, involving stories, and atmospheric detail. He is the heir of many literary traditions—pulp stories, fantasy, adventure stories of all kinds, and serious literature—and he makes use of all of them," she continued. "His work can be read with pleasure many times; new discoveries are made with each reading, and the stories linger in one's mind."

Soldier of the Mist is innovative in its account of Latro, a soldier of ancient Greece whose memory is wiped clean every time he sleeps—payment for having seen the gods; Latro's condition necessitates the keeping of a journal in which he records each day's events—with each new day he must read the journal and relearn his life. Guided by his text and various gods, Latro journeys to regain his memory. Wolfe continues Latro's story in

Set in the far future on the planet Urth, Wolfe's novel continues the tale of the stalwart Severian, who eventually becomes monarch of the Commonwealth in the South America of Urth.

Soldier of Arete, in which Latro becomes embroiled in the political and military rivalry between Greece and Sparta. John Calvin Batchelor observed in the *Washington Post Book World* that *Soldier of the Mist,* while difficult reading, is "a work of consequence." The author "is a master of science fiction," Batchelor concluded, "and for the best of all reasons, vaulting ambition."

In 1993, Wolfe released *Nightside the Long Sun,* the first of a new four-volume epic called "The Book of the Long Sun" (and sometimes referred to as "Starcrosser's Planetfall"). *Lake of the Long Sun, Calde of the Long Sun,* and *Exodus from the Long Sun* followed. The action takes place inside the Whorl, a massive cylindrical starship whose inhabitants have long forgotten what mission, if any, the ship is on. Lit by a central "long sun," the culture of the vast ship is a cross between modern science and medieval superstition. The main character, Patera Silk, is a schoolmaster and priest who has a vision of the Outsider, a god who transcends the Whorl, that changes his life. While attempting to ransom his parish house from unsavory creditors, Silk uncovers the starting truth about the Whorl. Of the "Long Sun"

NEW SELECTED STORIES

"Today quite possibly the most important writer in the SF field."
-The Encyclopedia of Science Fiction

GENE WOLFE

STRANGE TRAVELERS

This anthology brings together sixteen of Wolfe's imaginative, typically unclassifiable tales.

series, *New York Times Book Review* critic Gerald Jonas wrote, "Mr. Wolfe loves his characters, and it is not possible to accompany them on their long and strange journey without sharing that feeling."

In 1999, Wolfe published the first of three books in a new series called "The Book of the Short Sun." The action begins decades after the end of the "Book of the Long Sun." Narrated by the character Horn, *On Blue's Waters* tells of Horn's quest to find the original leader of the colonies on the planet Blue in an effort to save the decaying human cities. "Wolfe's prose is masterful and his main characters are well developed," wrote a critic in *Publishers Weekly.*

"I like writing. It's hard work," Wolfe told Baber, "I've tried to do things that seemed to me should be done and nobody had done yet. But everybody who's worth reading is trying to do exactly that." In *CAAS,* he wrote about unfulfilled ambitions. "I want to write a great book, of course; but an author can't say that," he said. "Thus I say instead with perfect honesty that I want someday to live in a rambling white house with 13 rooms on a hillside overlooking the Pacific. But if the

truth be known, to be again what I was when I wanted to be what I am today."

Works Cited

Baber, Brendan, "Gene Wolfe Interview (1994)," *The World's Home Page,* http://world.std.com/~pduggan/wolfeint.html (October 21, 1999).

Batchelor, John Calvin, "Warriors, Gods and Kings," *Washington Post Book World,* October 26, 1986.

Budrys, Algis, review of *The Shadow of the Torturer, Magazine of Fantasy and Science Fiction,* May, 1980, p. 23.

Clareson, Thomas D., *Dictionary of Literary Biography,* Volume 8: *Twentieth-Century American Science Fiction Writers,* Gale, 1981.

Greenland, Colin, "Miracles Recollected in Tranquillity," *Times Literary Supplement,* January 15, 1988, p. 69.

Gunn, James, review of *The Shadow of the Torturer, Washington Post Book World,* May 25, 1980, p. 8.

Hillman, Martin, *London Tribune,* April 24, 1981.

Hutchinson, Tom, *Times* (London), April 2, 1981.

Jonas, Gerald, review of *Calde of the Long Sun, New York Times Book Review,* September 11, 1994, p. 46.

Lerner, Fred, review of *The Urth of the New Sun, Voice of Youth Advocates,* April, 1988, p. 42.

Review of *On Blue's Waters, Publishers Weekly,* September 13, 1999, p. 65.

Sallis, James, review of *Nightside the Long Sun, Los Angeles Times Book Review,* June 6, 1993.

Samuelson, David N., review of *The Citadel of the Autarch, Los Angeles Times Book Review,* April 3, 1983, p. 4.

Sargent, Pamela, *Twentieth-Century Science Fiction Writers,* St. James Press, 1986.

Wolfe, Gene, essay in *Contemporary Authors Autobiography Series,* Volume 9, Gale, 1989.

For More Information See

BOOKS

Andre-Driussi, Michael, *Lexicon Urthus: A Dictionary for the Urth Cycle,* Sirius Fiction (San Francisco, CA), 1994.

Contemporary Literary Criticism, Volume 25, Gale, 1983.

Gordon, Joan, *Gene Wolfe,* Borgo (San Bernadino, CA), 1986.

Lane, Daryl, William Vernon, and David Carson, editors, *The Sound of Wonder: Interviews from "The Science Fiction Radio Show,"* Volume 2, Oryx (Phoenix, AZ), 1985.

PERIODICALS

Analog Science Fiction & Fact, August, 1990, p. 143; June, 1991, p. 178; June, 1994, p. 161; February, 1995, p. 159.

Booklist, July 1, 1975; November 1, 1982; August, 1989; November 15, 1992; September 15, 1994, p. 118.

Chicago Tribune Book World, June 8, 1980; June 14, 1981.

Extrapolation, Summer, 1981; Fall, 1982.

Kansas Quarterly, Summer, 1984.

Kirkus Reviews, December 1, 1999, p. 1854.

Library Journal, November 15, 1990, p. 95; December, 1992, p. 191; August, 1994, p. 139; September 15, 1994, p. 94.

Locus, February, 1990; December, 1993; August, 1994.

London Tribune, April 24, 1981.

Magazine of Fantasy and Science Fiction, April, 1971; May, 1978; June, 1981; September, 1994, p. 16.

New York Times Book Review, July 13, 1975; September 12, 1976; May 22, 1983; November 24, 1985; July 2, 1989; May 13, 1990; May 9, 1993, p. 20; January 2, 1994, p. 22.

Publishers Weekly, September 8, 1989; November 9, 1992; December 20, 1999, p. 61.

Science Fiction Review, Summer, 1981.

Times Literary Supplement, May 18, 1973; January 15, 1988.

Washington Post Book World, March 22, 1981; July 26, 1981; January 24, 1982; January 30, 1983; November 24, 1985; October 26, 1986; October 27, 1987; August 28, 1988; April 30, 1989; January 31, 1993; December 26, 1993; October 23, 1994.*

—Sketch by Brenna Sanchez

Autobiography Feature

Richard Wormser

1933-

STAGES IN THE LIFE OF A WOULD-BE WRITER

Primary Experience

I am in second grade. Television is still an inventor's dream and the computer a fantasy. I am painfully learning to write the letters of the alphabet the old-fashioned way—by hand. I scrunch up in my chair, my face almost touching a sheet of white paper on my desk with evenly spaced, blue parallel lines running from the top to the bottom of the page. Next to it is an inkwell filled with blue-black ink; in my hand, shaped like a claw, I grasp a black, steel-tipped pen as if I were about to attack someone with it. On the blackboard are rows of neatly shaped letters of the alphabet which I agonizingly try to copy on my paper so that they balance on the lines. The signs of my struggle are everywhere. Ink is all over the page, my hands, my arms, my shirt, my face. My "a's" look like "o's," "p's" like "t's," and I am hopelessly lost trying to distinguish "z's" from "q's." Nor can I get to keep the letters on the line. They either slide below it or soar above. Miss Bow, my blonde-haired teacher, parades up and down the rows with ruler in hand peering at our work. She grabs my collar and pulls me upright so she can see my paper. As Miss Bow bends over to examine my letters, I am tempted to pull at her hair to see if the rumor is true that she wears a wig to cover her bald head. Miss Bow asks me if a chicken with ink on its feet has walked across my paper. The class laughs. I think to myself, writing is beyond me. I will never learn how to write.

Today, after having written some fifteen books, forty or fifty documentary films, and many newspaper articles, I still feel I will never learn to write—not as I want to anyhow. The computer saves me the trouble of worrying about whether my p's look like q's, and whether my words will stay in a straight line. But writing remains hard for me. I never seem to say exactly what I want to say in the way I want to say it. The nuances of feelings I want to express elude me. Trying to capture the right words is like trying to catch butterflies. I never quite find the one that will illuminate the truth of the object I am trying to grasp in language. Reading great writers gives me a glimpse of the promised land but does not guarantee that I will ever enter it.

The Reading Years

The books I read as a child are to the mind what McDonald's hamburgers are to the stomach—junk. Comic books. Boys' adventure stories of super-macho idiotic heroes who speak in near-grunts or single-syllable worlds. I love baseball stories, in part, because Babe Ruth lives two blocks away from me. My friends and I often wait by his apartment building to catch a glimpse of him in the late afternoons when we know he will be returning home from his cancer treatments at the hospital. When he gets out of the car, wearing his camel hair coat and cap, much shriveled but still a giant in our adoring eyes, we crowd around. "Hi, Babe!" "Babe, can you come see us play sometime?" "Sure, kid," he says in a voice that sounds more like a death rasp, "Someday."

Richard Wormser, shooting on location in the Oklahoma Panhandle region, about 1983.

When I am in junior high school, I play hooky to go to Yankee games instead of class. To do this I forge my parent's signature on notes excusing me from class. My parent's handwriting is also in the chicken-scratch style of writing so I can imitate it fairly well. My brief career as a forger allows me to see Bob Feller, then the premier pitcher of the Cleveland Indians, pitch a no-hitter at Yankee Stadium. Cleveland wins 1 to 0 on a homerun in the ninth by the catcher. This proves to me that a Power greater than me wants me to see the game. If He didn't, He would have rained it out. Divine retribution, however, is at hand. I leave the ticket stub from the game in my room where my father discovers it. A long period of confinement to my room without allowance follows. Since I am on the verge of flunking most of my courses, my parents decide that no high school will accept me. They send me to a prep school "to make a man out of me."

Prep school is agonizing. My friends at home never make an issue over the fact that I am smaller and physically immature. In the all-male prep school I am sentenced to, the students seize upon my baby-face looks like a tigershark grabs a helpless swimmer. For the first two years of school, I am the target of a thousand jokes. I feel like a mutant, my fragile ego crushed. I am not yet strong enough to make any athletic team above the junior varsity level, and that only because the teams are so short of players, they take anyone that can breathe. To console myself, I turn to books. I graduate from junk reading to novels and books on history. It helps dull the pain and slowly moves me in a new direction. Like a plant, I begin to turn towards some distant, still unseen, sun, not yet aware of its light and warmth.

Awakenings

Whatever writing sparks begin to glow in high school are extinguished in the first two years of college. Having lived in the highly disciplined world of prep school most of my life, the freedom I find in college causes me to "freak out." Late night drinking, fraternity parties, girls, playing cards, sleeping through classes—all the temptations that college life offers. I regard courses as something to get around, not to learn from. By the end of my first year, I almost flunk out of college. The second year I pull up out of my nosedive just enough to keep from crashing.

In my junior year, I take a course in sociology because I have to. I know nothing about the subject or the teacher. His name is Dick Duwors. He dresses like a farmer, wearing jeans and denim shirts when most men professors wear white shirts and ties. He teaches his course with great passion and enthusiasm. Because he cares, we students care. For the first time in my aimless existence, I find thinking as exciting as falling in love. A light has been switched on in my dark mind. I had lived nineteen years in the shadows with no understanding of myself, my friends, my family, school, or what I was to do with my life. Now I find myself wanting to learn. I go from a C-student to A-.

My Bible is a book written by Jack Kerouac called *On the Road*. The book is about a group of young, somewhat mad young men, who wander back and forth across America seeking its spirit. They drive cars, ride buses, hitchhike, meeting the people, experiencing the heart and soul of the country. The people whose lives they describe are not those you read about in the newspapers. They are men and women who live in the small towns of the Midwest or Southwest, divorced women who work in small diners that dot highways like oases, girls who work as cashiers in movie theaters, young men running away from home, truck drivers hurtling across the country without stopping to sleep.

At the end of my junior year, dreaming of California beaches with waves breaking on beaches filled with long-legged, tanned girls, of great mountains and valleys filled with wild animals, of working at different jobs, having unimaginable adventures, I head West for the summer. I have not yet thought of being a writer, but my vision of the world is being shaped by writers and poets whose hunger for life in their youth is my own: Jack Kerouac, Thomas Wolfe, Ernest Hemingway, Eugene O'Neill, Dylan Thomas, Walt Whitman.

I ride Greyhound buses across the country. Four days and three nights. I pass through cities I have never seen, through hundreds of small towns I never knew existed. A constant parade of people get on and off the bus. Poor and well-off, white, black, and Native American. Farmers and soldiers. Grandmothers and mothers overloaded with children. We talk. "Where you from?" "Where you going?" "Where have you been?" "What did you do?" People traveling to weddings and funerals. Some going home after many years away, others running down for the weekend. Soldiers headed back to base. Out-of-work men seeking work. Girls joining sweethearts and wives leaving husbands. People share food, cigarettes, and swap stories. Some drink whiskey from dark bottles. At night, people sometimes tell you their griefs when they cannot see your eyes. You become two disembodied voices talking in the dark, making contact. They speak of children who have died, time spent in prison, the pain of lost love and abandonment, the violence of abusive husbands or parents, the joy of returning home after a long absence, the fear of illness, the resignation to dying.

I arrive in California, stay with friends, and find a job in a Sunkist lemon plant. I prepare wooden crates in which lemons are shipped. (In those days they used wood to pack citrus fruit.) I meet Mexicans for the first time in my life, learn a little Spanish, flirt with the girls, eat spicy food, and talk about their lives and mine. After several weeks, I am on the road, hitchhiking. I head to the National Parks, from Yosemite to Yellowstone. To earn money, I scoop ice cream, wash dishes, become a store detective. Once I travel seven hundred miles with a Texas geologist who offers me a job prospecting for uranium in the Utah desert. He tells me his astrologer predicted he would meet a young man hitchhiking who would make his fortune. He is too old to go himself (he is over seventy). He offers me $10,000 for a year (half up front), all expenses paid, equipment supplied, and 30 percent of whatever I find. I am curious enough to go with him into the desert, where I meet dozens of men all searching for uranium. It turns out that another geologist also searching for uranium sat down in a riverbed one day and went from being a poor boy to a multimillionaire.

I am tempted to stay in the desert. But I know that a city boy like myself is apt to have losing encounters with rattlesnakes, scorpions, tarantulas, and coyotes whose turf

this is, and who probably resent visitors like myself dropping in.

Instead, I head to Denver where I pick up a dealer's car and drive it to Seattle. Along the way, I give rides to several hoboes. Most people think of them as bums, but I learn that they are homeless migrant workers drifting from job to job. They tell me stories of the old days when they worked in the mines, wheat fields, and logging camps of the West. Many had joined the "Wobblies," the name for their union, the I.W.W. or the Industrial Workers of the World. Just before World War I, the I.W.W. was the most militant union in America. It fought against the bosses, led bitter strikes, and tried to organize the working class of America into one big union. Many are well read. They quote from Karl Marx and Friedrich Nietzche. One man advises me to look for work in the logging camps of the Pacific Northwest. I follow his advice and end up in Port Angeles, Washington, on the Northern frontier, where the Straits of Juan De Fuca separate Canada from the United States. I apply for a job as a logger with the Fiberboard Lumber Company. The manager looks me over to see if I am strong enough, then says, "Well, we could use somebody. We just lost a man yesterday." I took it to mean the logger had just quit. I later learn that is not what he meant.

I buy clothes and boots—loggers need to wear special boots with nails so that they can walk on fallen timber. I rent a room in a boarding house with other loggers. We have to get up at 3:30 A.M. to catch a company bus at 4:30. One logger takes me to an all-night restaurant and advises me to eat as much as I can. I'll need the energy. I have steak, eggs, bacon, pancakes, coffee, and toast. I buy several sandwiches for lunch. Other loggers are there. They regard me with curiosity as "the replacement," but say nothing. I board the bus at 4:30. When it leaves the highway, the bus enters Olympic National Park and begins to climb the mountain roads. Day is dawning, and I press my face to the window as the forest is illuminated by the light of the early morning sun. I have never seen a wilderness such as this before. Ancient forests with trees hundreds of feet high. Waterfalls cascading over the rocks to join the rivers below. Deer leap into the brush when startled by the passing bus. A coyote stops, looks at us as we pass, then continues on his way. The camp site is surrounded by mountains. We arrive at a landing which has been cut into the mountain near the top. On the landing is an engine, called a donkey, which powers cables up and down the slope of the mountain. There are several trucks on the landing and heavy equipment used to load logs onto the trucks. Below me is the slope of the mountain, which is pitched at an angle of about 60 to 70 degrees from level ground. The slope is covered with cut timber. The foreman explains to me that my job will be to get these logs up to the landing so they can be loaded onto the truck. Heavy mobile wires called chokers are attached to a main cable system, much like cable cars on a ski lift. The donkey moves the choker wires up and down the mountainside and raises and lowers them. My job is to take one end of the wire when it is lowered, wrap it around a log, and secure it. The donkey then drags the log up the mountain to the landing, where it is loaded on a truck.

The foreman explains that since the crew working below cannot see what is happening on the landing, and vice versa, the operation between the two sites is coordinated by a "whistle punk." The whistle punk is a logger who sits on a tree stump from where he can see both the crew below and the men on the landing. He has a loud whistle which he uses to signal the crew below when the choker wires are being lowered, when the log is ready to be dragged up, and when it is all clear. The foreman impresses upon me that the most dangerous time is when a log is pulled up the mountain. The choker wires are subjected to tremendous pressure and occasionally snap. When they do, they whiplash along the slope, and anyone standing can be cut down like grain in a wheat field chopped by a scythe. When the log is ready to be pulled up, I am to get behind a log and stay there until the all-clear is blown. Now I learn that the man I replaced stood up before the whistle punk blew the all-clear. The log being dragged up suddenly snagged in a pile of timber; the tension on the cable was so intense that it snapped and whipped down the mountain, catching the standing logger full force, thus creating a vacancy on the crew which I now fill.

I expect loggers to be at least six feet, two hundred pounds, and with bulging muscles. It turns out I am the tallest person on the crew at five feet, eleven inches. Most of the crew are small, wiry men, many of them Native Americans from local tribes. A few are college students and high school teachers. I work at the job for about a month,

becoming more and more skilled each day. I am covered with black-and-blue marks from head to toe as I trip over fallen timber. Just as I start to get the swing of my job, the National Park Service closes down the operation. There has been no rain in the forest for almost a month, and there is danger of a forest fire. And so I reluctantly have to leave one of the best jobs I ever had in my life.

The experiences of my days wandering in America always remain with me. In tribute to those nomadic workers who built the West with their back-breaking labor, I eventually write one of my favorite books: *Wandering in America: A History of Hoboes and Tramps.*

Paris Days and the Beats

The next major stage in my life as a writer takes place in 1959. I have finished college, gone to law school, quit, then to graduate school—and still don't know what I want out of life. After I am accepted by the Sorbonne in Paris as a candidate for my Ph.D., I decide to go to France.

When I arrive in France, Paris is almost on the verge of civil war. The struggle is over whether or not France should keep Algeria as a colony or grant it independence. For almost seventy years, France has occupied this North African country. The French who have settled there—known as "colons" or "pied noirs"—are fiercely deter-

No. 16 (third from right) on the basketball team in prep school.

mined to keep Algeria French. The Algerians just as fiercely want independence and are in a state of rebellion. A vicious, bloody war has broken out, and both sides are extremely cruel and brutal. In Paris, the country is divided. The political Left demands that the government withdraw French troops out of Algeria, and the Right wants them to stay. Algerians and French occasionally kill each other in Paris.

I am oblivious to all of this when I first arrive in Paris. The city is so beautiful, the architecture unlike anything that I have seen in my life, that all I do the first few weeks I am there is walk with my face pointing toward the sky, my mouth open to drink in everything I see. I visit museums where I am dazzled by the masterpieces of French art. I explore every little street I find, walk along the banks of the river, take coffee at a hundred cafes, visit bistros at night to listen to folksingers and African American jazz musicians who, fed up with racism at home, have settled in Paris where they are welcome. Sidney Bechet, who some considered the finest jazz clarinetist that ever lived, spent the last years of his life here. A street was named in his honor when he died, and all Paris attended his funeral.

Because I speak so little French, I live in a completely French section of the city, where no English is spoken, and work on the language. After three months, I manage to communicate halfway decently. I am pleased when American tourists occasionally mistake me for a native Frenchman.

Since I am a student at the Sorbonne, a five-hundred-year-old university, I move to the Latin Quarter where it is located. The Latin Quarter is one of the most exciting sections of Paris to live in if you are young and either a student or a writer/artist. The Latin Quarter is also called the Left Bank because it is located on the left bank of the Seine River which divides the city. It was, and to a certain degree still is, the great Bohemian center of Paris. Here once lived many of the great writers, poets, and artists of France. You can visit a house where Moliere, one of France's most famous playwrights, lived in the seventeenth century. In the 1920s, many of America's and Europe's best writers lived here after World War I: Ernest Hemingway, Gertrude Stein, William Carlos Williams, E. E. Cummings.

The buildings in this quarter evoke a sense of France's magnificent cultural and religious history. The most dominant building is the Cathedral of Notre Dame. Not too far away is the Pantheon, where many of France's most famous people are buried. Nearby are the Luxembourg gardens.

I move into the Latin Quarter, but I must find a permanent place to stay. Plenty of small hotels have rooms but they will not allow me to stay more than twenty-nine days. This is because French law at that time requires hotels to reduce the rent in half for anyone who stays more than thirty days in a room. And so every twenty-nine days, I travel from hotel to hotel, carrying my bags, trying to make a deal with an owner to let me stay.

One day, I get into a conversation in a café with Jerry, a young American who has come to Paris to write. He is living in a hotel room where he has made a deal with the owner. He pays more than the law allows for residents but less than the standard rate for guests. He is short on funds and needs a roommate. He offers me a place to stay if I will share the rent. I agree and move in. The hotel has no name and is only known by its address, Number 9, Git-Le-Coeur. Git-Le-Coeur is the name of the street. It literally means "Rest-the-Heart." The hotel is on a tiny street, ten minutes from the university by foot, one minute to the Seine River, seven minutes to the Cathedral of Notre Dame. I am in the heart of the Latin Quarter. Nearby is the Ecole des Beaux Arts, the major school of painting. The streets are filled with small shops and food markets, bookstores, and cafes. Five minutes from where I live is the Café des Deux Magots, where the then two greatest writers of France, Jean-Paul Sartre and Albert Camus, sometimes sit, drink, and talk with their friends and students. (They didn't talk to each other as the Algerian War divided them.) Everything seems pure French. The only visible sign of American culture is a movie theater that plays old American films. The McDonald's-KFC blight is still years away.

After I settle in as Jerry's temporary roommate, he invites me to join him one evening to visit another American who lives in the building. Although I prefer to be with French people so I can learn to speak the language, I agree when he tells me he and other writers will be reading from their works. It blows my mind to discover that these writers are the very people I had read about in *On the Road.* Allen Ginsberg is there. So are Bill Burroughs and Gregory Corso. By sheer good fortune, I am in the same hotel in which some of the outstanding poets and novelists of my generation are living. Awesome to say the least! Several nights a week, I crowd into a small room with dozens of other would-be writers, listening to them read. Burroughs is writing *Naked Lunch,* based, in part, on his drug experiences in Tangiers and elsewhere. When it is published, some critics will call it "obscene," others a "masterpiece." Ginsberg is writing a book of poems which he calls Kaddish (the Jewish ceremony of mourning for the dead). The poems and literature celebrate sexual freedom, drugs, racial diversity, jazz music, the rhythm of which is in their writings. They celebrate the despised and outcasts of the earth—people like the hoboes whom I had met in my western wanderings—and condemn hypocrisy, materialism, American political repression (it was still the McCarthy era in the United States), and racism.

I now try to write but, when I try, I find what I write feeble and tear it up. I meet other would-be writers with different agendas than the Beats. One of them introduces me to Richard Wright, a great American writer and a black man. I often go to the café he frequents and listen to him argue, sometimes with James Baldwin, about whether or not American blacks should invest their energies in fighting for their rights in America or helping the newly independent African countries unite in a Pan-African movement. Wright favors Pan Africa, Baldwin America.

French universities are radically different from American. There are no small classes. You listen to a lecture with hundreds of other students in a large room, take notes, and write a paper. You are assigned a teacher who works with you on your thesis. I enjoy Paris too much to submit myself to the discipline of a student's life, so I drop out of school. I work at a number of odd jobs, including doing translations of French film treatments for American film companies, unloading vegetables in the marketplace, selling the *Herald Tribune* newspaper on the streets, working on the docks as a longshoremen in London, transporting books from Paris

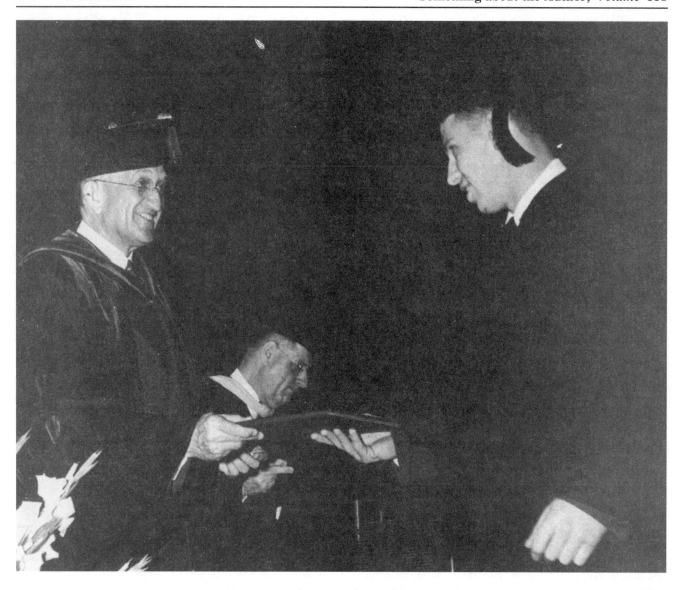

College graduation, Bucknell University, 1955.

to London for book dealers. I have a student card which allows me to eat cheaply and attend movies and plays for free. I have French and American friends. One is an extraordinary folksinger from Oregon who plays a five-string banjo in small night clubs in Paris. One night, a group of us from the hotel, including Darryl, wander into the Algerian section at three in the morning. A group of Algerians, thinking we are French, start to menace us. I explain to them we are Americans and in favor of Algerian independence. Then one of the Algerians sees Darryl's banjo. He asks if he will play. Darryl says yes. They take us to a small club where a group of Arab musicians are playing Arabic music with Middle Eastern instruments. Darryl joins in. He has such a great ear that he can harmonize his banjo with their instruments. It is a terrific night. We all go home at eleven in the morning and collapse. At times, I wander through other parts of Europe. I hitchhike to the South of Spain. I cross the English channel by boat and hitchhike through England, Wales, Ireland, and Scotland. People everywhere open their homes to me, play music for me, let me date their daughters, feed

and shelter me. We talk through the night about all kinds of things. They want to know what America is like. I want to know what their lives are like. Sometimes we gather around a piano and sing. One moonlit night, a man and his wife play a bagpipe concert for me by a lake in the wilds of the Scottish Highlands.

In my last month in Paris, a revolution takes place on the streets. Hundreds of thousands of people gather every night to demonstrate against the war in Algeria. The government is in chaos and cannot function. Police are everywhere. People are fighting on the streets. One night, as I am about to go for dinner in an Algerian restaurant a few doors down from my building, I hear firecrackers in the street. When I get downstairs, the police are every-where. Someone has entered the restaurant and machine-gunned four Algerian men eating there. If I had been there ten minutes earlier, I would have been a fifth victim. I look for my Algerian friend who is a member of the resistance. He has disappeared, and I am told by some of his friends not to ask questions. Suddenly, Charles de Gaulle, the great wartime leader of France, has been asked to take over the country. Some people see him as France's salvation. They believe he will continue the war and win it for France. Others fear that he will turn France into a police state. He will surprise everybody. He will end the war by agreeing to Algerian independence. For doing so, he is almost assassinated.

Shortly after De Gaulle comes to power, I decide it's time to head home. I am in my mid-twenties and have been a student all my life. I haven't the faintest idea of what I want to do. I return by boat. When we approach New York, it is 5:30 in the morning. Dawn is rising in the east, and it is a warm summer's day. People gather excitedly on deck for their first glimpse of the city. For most of them, this is their first visit to America. As the ship glides effortlessly into the harbor, the sun rises behind the city's tall buildings, silhouetting them. The Statue of Liberty stands in the harbor like a goddess, glowing in the reddish-gold early morning sun. The silent passengers seem awestruck as the ship slips past the golden figure of the lady with the lamp. This is what it must have been like in the days when our immigrant forefathers arrived in America and saw, for the first time, the symbol of their hopes.

Writing

In 1961, I return from Paris without a job or any idea of what to do with my life. Several weeks after I return, Bill, a former college professor of mine, calls me. He is now editor of a small-town Pennsylvania newspaper. Would I be interested in working for him as a reporter/photographer? He knows I have never written anything more than a term paper. Nor have I ever taken pictures with anything more than a point and click camera. But Bill has faith I can learn, and off I go to Pennsylvania.

The town is called Shamokin, an Indian name meaning "Eel Creek." For almost a hundred years it has been a coal town in the western part of the anthracite coal region. When I arrive, I feel I have landed on the moon. The landscape is bleak and barren. Almost all of the deep mines are shut down. Coal is still mined but by huge steam shovels that rip the coal from the ground and leave giant scars in the earth, scars which in those days coal companies were not required to heal. Mountains of slag, dirt, and coal have replaced forested hills. At night, these heaps of refuse glow with internal fires as the coal inside them, ignited years ago, continues to burn. The landscape looks like what some people imagine hell to be. In some nearby towns, veins of burning underground coal sometimes cause the street above them to suddenly collapse, occasionally trapping people.

The paper I work for, the *Shamokin Citizen,* is owned by John U. Shroyer, a wealthy dress manufacturer, who is a larger-than-life character. Physically impressive, even though in his seventies, John U., as he is called, is a man of nineteenth-century America with its Victorian values and its beliefs in a Puritan God and rugged individualism. John U. worked himself up from near-poverty to riches in the dress industry. He could have been governor of Pennsylvania, but he took a moral stand on an issue that politically finished him. When he was Secretary of Transportation for the state of Pennsylvania, he was promised the Republican gubernatorial nomination for the next election. During his term of office in transportation, he discovered that a construction company had built a state highway using cheaper materials than specified in the contract. John U. told the contractor to tear up the highway and rebuild it. The contractor was a big contributor to the Republican Party. He told the political bosses what John U. said, and the bosses pressured John U. to drop the matter. He refused. As a result the highway was rebuilt, and John U. was not nominated for governor. He promptly switched to the Democratic party and helped the Democratic candidate win the election by campaigning against the Republican candidate as an independent, thus splitting the vote.

The great thing about working for a small-town newspaper is that you get to explore all aspects of community life. You cover everything from weddings to funerals, city council and school board meetings, fires, automobile accidents, and an occasional murder. I learn to take photographs with my stories. Because the paper I work for is a weekly, I can take time to write my articles. I find I have some talent for feature writing—longer, descriptive pieces that narrate a story rather than deal with an event. When a man kills his retarded daughter, instead of just reporting the facts, I write a long piece about what it was like for the man to live with a retarded daughter, what the pressures in his life were, and what drove him to the desperate act of killing his child. For me, what was more important was understanding what lay behind the violence of his deed, rather than the act itself.

As I drive around Shamokin on my daily rounds, I often pass the last remaining deep coal mine in the area, the Glen Burn Colliery. It employs about three hundred miners, and the coal is mined over two thousand feet deep. I sometimes stop to watch the miners as they emerge from the mines, their cases and clothes covered with coal dust and dirt. "What is it like," I wonder, "to work so far down in the earth?" "How do they mine coal?" "What are their lives like?"

I am dating Sandy, the daughter of a miner who is a reporter for the daily newspaper against whom we compete. Sandy's father introduces me to other miners. I play cards with them on Saturday afternoons in a small bar and listen to them talk about their jobs. I ask my editor to let me write a series of articles on the mines. He agrees but the publisher thinks I am crazy. "This is a coal town," he says. "Everybody knows about the mines." "I don't think so," I answer, "Only the miners know about the mines. To everyone else, mining is as big a mystery to them as it is to me." The publisher reluctantly agrees to allow me to write three articles.

The Glen Burn Colliery is an anthracite coal mine. Anthracite is perhaps the cleanest fuel in the world. It burns without smoke. It is formed from fossils lying in the earth for millions of years and has been subjected to intense pressures taking place in folded rock when mountain ranges were created. It is a dimly lit, almost prehistoric world, where men move about like shadows. There is a constant flow of hoppers carrying the coal to the surface.

Because the mines are so deep, there is constant danger of flooding, and water must be continually pumped out. The air is contaminated with coal dust. Many older miners suffer from what they call "miner's asthma." Their lungs fill with coal dust and, after twenty years, they can barely breathe. Most die relatively young. Although pumping brings a continual flow of fresh air into the deepest part of the mine, miners cannot avoid inhaling dust where they work.

The coal is usually sent to the surface in cars called hoppers, which are driven by electric power. In the section where I am sent, mules pull the hoppers. The mules are born and die in the mines. Because they never see the light of day, they become blind. Yet Floury, the mule skinner who drives them (and who happens to be almost as blind as the mules), guides them through the mine with a sure hand. He has a rapport with the animals no one else has. Where other mule drivers sometimes find the mules stubborn and difficult, they meekly obey Floury.

Mules are used in this section of the mine because there is danger of gas, and a spark from an electric car can trigger an explosion. In the past, explosions occurred with frequency. Methane gas gets trapped in the coal or rock. If the gas is released and ignited by a spark, it explodes. In some explosions, over a hundred men are killed. Another deadly gas is carbon monoxide, the same poisonous gas emitted by cars. In the old days, miners used to take caged canaries with them into the mines. The canaries were placed where they would be the first to be affected by carbon monoxide if it was released. When miners see their canary suddenly drop dead, they rush to get out of the area. Often, there is not enough time and they are trapped by the gas.

I am taken to a room where men dynamite the seams of coal in a large chamber to break it up. To keep the rock roof above them from collapsing, they leave pillars of coal and install timbers as support. Yet the pressure is so great that sometimes the roof collapses despite the support, crushing the men underneath them to death, or trapping them in an isolated section.

The coal is removed from the chamber after it has been dynamited. Once the coal is removed, then the pillars are dynamited so that their coal can also be taken out. This is a highly dangerous operation. Sometimes a fuse may be defective and the dynamite explodes before the miner can leave the chamber. Sandy's father is killed this way two years after I leave the region. The dynamite exploded before he was able to get out, and several tons of rock fell on him, crushing him to death.

The normal circulation of the *Shamokin Citizen* is about 5,500 copies a week. After I write my articles, it jumps to 7,000. Instead of three articles, I write seventeen. The reason has less to do with my skills as a writer and more with the fact that people are fascinated by the mines and by the history of mining in the region. Many of the articles I write are about the past. I locate old miners who remember gas explosions and other mine tragedies. I write about the different immigrant groups who came to the region and where they settled. I even find a ninety-five-year-old man who worked in the mines when the Molly Maguires ruled the coal region. The Mollies were a semi-union, semi-terrorist organization of Irish miners in the 1870s, who fought against the mine owners who exploited them. Most of them were caught and hanged. The miner, whose name is Danny Walsh, used to earn money as a child by singing songs in bars in which the Mollies hung out.

One day, I am assigned to accompany a group of women from a ladies' club, who visit a state institution for the mentally retarded. Two thousand men, women, and

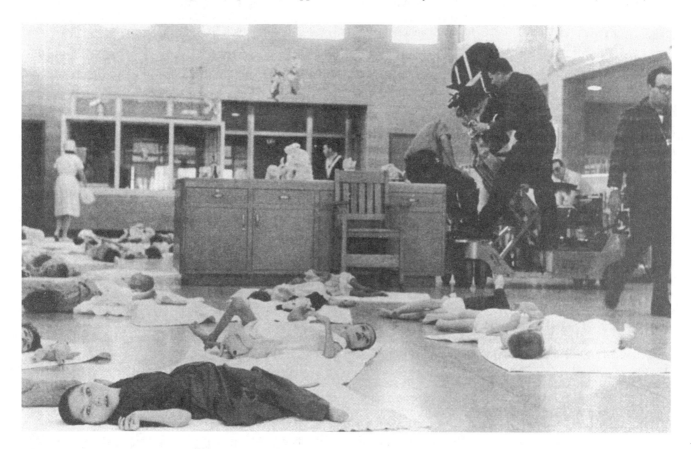

Shooting film in Selingsgrove State School and Hospital, an institution for the retarded, Selingsgrove, Pennsylvania, 1963.

children are living there. Some children are so severely retarded that all they can do is lie in bed all day and stare at the ceiling. Others seem normal. Most have been abandoned by their parents. I write my article, but I am not satisfied with it. It does not do justice to either the people institutionalized there or the staff taking care of them. I want to tell their story, but on film. Since I have never made a film, and since I don't know where to get the money, I work at the institution as an attendant while I write an outline for the film and try to get a grant. Working with retarded children is extremely difficult at first. The hardest part for me is to overcome my prejudices and see past their handicaps. Even in the most severely retarded children, humanity resides, but it is not easy to work with such children day in and day out, year after year.

Smith, Kline and French, a pharmaceutical company, agrees to finance the film I want to make. They also bring in an experienced producer with whom I work closely. When the film is finished, it wins a number of awards. Working on the film shows me how much I don't know about film. I have much to learn. But, at least, I know where I am going.

A Time of Focus: The 1960s

The 1960s is "the best of times and the worst of times," to borrow a phrase from Charles Dickens. The country erupts into a number of social revolutions fueled by the energies and passions of millions of young people, most of them high school and college students. The revolutions target racial, gender, and sexual discrimination. African Americans lead the way with their peaceful demonstrations against segregation, disfranchisement, injustice, and police brutality. Despite the nonviolence of their marches, they are sometimes murdered, often beaten and arrested. Later in the decade, the women's movement emerges as women protest against gender discrimination. Homosexuals also demonstrate against discrimination and harassment because of their sexual orientation.

The anti-Vietnam War movement intensifies these protests. Millions of people demonstrate in the streets against America's war against North Vietnam. Hundreds of thousands of young people drop out of society. Many run away from home to San Francisco and New York, become "flower children" and "yippies," live in communes, take drugs, and listen to the music of Janis Joplin, Jimi Hendrix, Bob Dylan, Grace Slick and the Jefferson Airplane, Simon and Garfunkel, the Band, James Morrison and the Doors, and dozens of other rock and roll bands. The energy of the music matches the energy of the times.

Despite the tremendous civil rights gains and reforms of the sixties, the decade is a violent one. Prisoners stage a revolt against over-crowding and inhumane conditions at Attica Prison. A number of guards are taken hostage. The state police raid the prison, uttering racial curses, and indiscriminately kill over forty guards and inmates. In the South, dozens of civil rights workers are murdered, including four little girls killed in a Birmingham church when a bomb planted by Klansmen explodes.

The main targets of violence are demonstrators. Although the First Amendment of the United States Constitution guarantees Americans the right to free speech, this right exists more in its violation than in its practice. Most local police and politicians have little, if any, regard for free speech, especially when they don't like what is being said. I help make a film on the police riot at the 1968 Democratic Convention in Chicago. Tens of thousands of young anti-war demonstrators are viciously attacked by the police. We film scenes of police smashing people with clubs, blackjacks, and brass knuckles (some of our crews are attacked) on the streets; some police enter hotels and beat people in their rooms.

The instigator of this police riot is the mayor of the city, Richard Daley, an old-time political boss who considers Chicago his personal kingdom. Daley declares war on the protesters, whom he considers enemy invaders. Police arrest thousands, mostly innocent people who happen to find themselves in the wrong place at the wrong time. The charges are so false that almost all of them are dismissed. Some activists are tried and sentenced to prison by an extremely hostile and vindictive judge, but their convictions are overturned by an appeals court which criticizes the judge for his prejudices.

The sixties are a turning point in my life. I learn how to make films as well as discover what I want to make films about: the past and present struggles of people to win the political, civil, and human rights denied them by their fellow Americans, politicians, police, and courts.

In 1975, with the Vietnam War ended and the Civil Rights movement no longer making headlines, the country enters a passive phase. I head to the Middle East as a still photographer to shoot and write a series of photographic stories for a book publisher on the Arab peoples who are usually demonized by the American press. My focus is on family and community life rather than politics.

Despite America's one-sided support of Israel, I am welcomed everywhere I go in the Arab world. Most people I meet have never seen an American. I travel throughout Syria, Egypt, and Jordan. I live in small mountain villages in Syria. I photograph Syrian women, once sheltered in the home, now working in factories and studying in colleges. I live with a farmer and his family in a small rural community in Egypt and show how the end of British rule in Egypt made it possible for him to own his own farm. I wander freely through the village, take pictures of school-children at work, farmers working in the fields, men and women at prayer. I live with a family for several weeks.

In Cairo, I visit Al Ahzar, the oldest university in the world (over a thousand years), photographing and talking with students there. In Jordan, I spend two weeks living with a small group of Bedouins in the desert. I photograph the older people who prefer to live in the desert and maintain the old ways, but who send their sons and daughters to universities. I accompany a hunting party deep into the desert, where I narrowly miss being stung to death by a poisonous snake. In Amman, I sneak into a refugee camp in Jordan and live with a Palestinian family in order to tell their story of how they were forced to leave their land during the first Israeli-Arab war. I can see the deep frustration of young people crowded in the camp, lacking the identity of their own homeland and without much hope for their futures. It is not surprising that their anger will one day lead some to strap bombs to their bodies and, entering an Israeli bus or marketplace, blow themselves up and as many Israelis as they can.

Photographing in the desert, 1975.

Back to the Future: Writing Books

In the 1980s, Ronald Reagan is president and the slogan of the 1960s, "Down with Washington," has been replaced by a new slogan, "Up with Wall Street." A new generation of young people emerge. The era of the Yippie—a name for those opposed to the killing in Vietnam—gives way to the era of the Yuppie—a name for those in favor of making a killing in the stock market. Filmmakers like myself are still trying to make our social and political documentaries. I make a film in Pittsburgh, Pennsylvania, about a group of ministers who are protesting against the massive layoffs in the steel industry in their region. As a result of massive unemployment, there is a dramatic rise of suicide, alcoholism, and family violence among ex-mill workers. I live with the family of one of the ministers, on and off for a year. Some congregations turn against their pastors and try to fire them. They object to ministers using tactics like throwing a dead skunk into a bank to protest that the bank's policies "stink" as far as creating jobs for the unemployed is concerned. When Pastor Doug Roth is kicked out of his church by his congregation, he and his supporters occupy the church building and lock themselves in. I and my crew join him. The incident makes headlines around the world. The state police eventually break down the doors and arrest the minister, who is sent to jail along with his wife and three of his supporters. Among them is a seventy-five-year-old man, Wayne Cochrane, who comments, as he is led off in handcuffs, "It's a damn shame I had to wait until I was seventy-five to fight for my fellow man. Christ was telling me to do this all along, but I was too thickheaded to listen to what He was trying to tell me."

The ministers' campaign ultimately fails. The mills are not reopened. The city of Pittsburgh does little to help those men and women whose fathers and grandfathers once made Pittsburgh one of the wealthiest cities in America. But what the ministers lose in one way, they gain in another. Their struggle, they say, has deepened their Christian commitment and their resolve to continue. Their fight has made them stronger inwardly. They point to Christ and say that if He based his commitment on immediate results, He would have given up almost as soon as He started. Today, they are still battling to improve the lives and well-being of the people of the valley.

One day I discover a book about the Pinkerton Detective agency. Its founder, Allan Pinkerton, was America's foremost private detective in the nineteenth century. The agency had an anti-union reputation and was said to provide police informers, spies, and thugs to break up strikes. It turns out, however, that the agency did not become deeply involved in the labor wars until after the death of its founder, Allan Pinkerton. Pinkerton, I discover, was a labor radical in Scotland before he was a policeman! He had to flee to America to avoid arrest. While he eventually became a detective, Pinkerton also was an abolitionist who hated slavery. He helped fugitives escape from the South, even though he was breaking the law by doing so. He worked closely with the abolitionist John Brown, who, after murdering five slavery men in Kansas, came to Chicago seeking Pinkerton's help. Pinkerton raised money for him and helped some of his associates flee to Canada. During the Civil War, Pinkerton set up America's first Secret Service and recruited men and women to spy on the Confederacy. After the war, he chased train robbers in the West, including Jesse James. Someone suggests I submit the Pinkerton story (which I unsuccessfully try to make into a film) to a book company that publishes books for young adults. I do and they agree to publish it.

After my first book is published, I realize that writing for the young adult market allows me to write about subjects that I care about, and for which there is no longer a strong support for documentary films. Compared to the 1960s, in which America's young people passionately struggled to change America, the 1990s is a time in which most people couldn't care less about improving the world. Perhaps through my books I can reach an audience that is not yet indifferent to the plight of America's dispossessed—those for whom society seems to have no place.

My next two books are about young people and crime. Some years earlier, I had seen a film I hated. It was called *Scared Straight* and showed how a group of men serving life terms in a New Jersey prison try to scare teenagers in trouble with the law into going straight. The teenagers are brought into prison where they are escorted by the lifers. After the tour, they sit on a stage while the lifers yell and curse at them for their dumb ways and warn them that if they *do* come to prison, they will be raped, beaten, and perhaps murdered. The program is very dramatic, but I never have believed that young people change their ways because they are threatened. I meet with the lifers and explain that I want to write a book (and later make a film) that does not focus on violence, but on how life is wasted in prison. This, I feel, will have more of an impact on young people.

The lifers agree, and the prison authorities give me a certain degree of freedom to move about the prison. I spend the better part of a year, off and on, interviewing men about their lives, how they got into trouble on the outside and why, and what has happened to them as a result of being in prison. When the book, *Lifers: Learn the Truth at the Expense of Our Sorrow,* is published, I then make a documentary film based on the same subject. Both the book and the film show that many lifers are intelligent, articulate, even eloquent, with a profound understanding of the world. Given the right circumstances, they could have been leaders in their communities. The tragedy is that they had to discover what they might have been by coming to prison. On the other hand, considering the world in which they grew up—abandoned by fathers, raised by incompetent mothers, surrounded by violence and temptations for easy money from drugs, it is not surprising they fall into criminal life. What begins as shoplifting and car theft, soon develops into burglary, armed robbery, drugs, and murder.

The film and the book also reveal how some lifers channel their anger and energy into constructive lives. Many men become weary of the criminal life after spending many years in prison. Being inside, off the streets, living in a highly structured world helps them re-evaluate their lives. Afraid of becoming burned-out, they often look for something besides crime to give meaning to their life. Sometimes it's education, family, or the love of a woman. Religion is a powerful force. Sunni Muslims and the Nation of Islam help many men change their lives. One man who helps me gain insight into the influence of Islam is Daoud, a Sunni Muslim. Prison, he says, is filled with temptations—drugs and sex, extortion and violence. He admits quite frankly that when he first came to prison, he wanted

to become a drug king. But he turned to Islam instead. It gave him the discipline, meaning, and inner strength he needed to survive the degradation of a prison environment. Charles, a powerfully built weight lifter, finds spiritual meaning in pumping iron. Its values are discipline, health, self-control and self-respect. He has organized a weight lifters club in which members pledge not to use their strength to intimidate the weak.

Some men serving life sentences have not committed serious crimes themselves. Charley's story is a good example of what can happen to someone who falls in with the wrong people at the wrong time and place. He was joyriding in a stolen car when one of his buddies got out to buy some cigarette paper. Unknown to Charley, his friend held up the store and, in the process, shot and killed the clerk. Charley didn't know what happened until his buddy told him what he had done. When Charley was arrested, he was offered a lighter sentence if he would turn state's evidence. Charley refused to be a "rat." Instead, he asked for a jury trial because his lawyer felt that he would receive a lighter sentence for not being involved in the killing. Instead, the jury found Charley equally guilty with the gunman. The judge gave him a longer sentence than the killer, as punishment for his insisting on having a trial rather than cooperating and accepting a lesser plea.

In my next book, *Juveniles in Trouble,* I write about teenagers in trouble. The book points out that what often starts as a small crime can lead someone to death row. What I find amazing is how some teenagers can sink to the bottom of life's barrel and still manage to pull themselves to the top. Carlos is one example. By the time he was fourteen, he was a school dropout and crack addict, who lived in dumpsters, ate out of garbage cans, hustled for drug money as a male prostitute, and tried to commit suicide several times. One night, out of desperation, he landed at Covenant House, a refuge for runaways under twenty-one that also has a drug program. He was so down and out that he agreed to enter a drug program, which he thought he could use for a few days to get himself together and then return to the streets. But a few days stretched to a week, one week became two, two led to four. In the program he heard others tell about their degraded lives and how they were slowly making it. At the same time, Carlos's anger and frustration made him want to quit the program a hundred times. One thing that stopped him was seeing a good friend quit the program and get hooked on drugs again. Carlos knew that is exactly what would happen to him if he quit. Carlos hung on for six months, graduated, went back to school, and got a job. Two years later, he planned to get married. People who knew him in the old days would have said that Carlos could never accomplish what he did. And Carlos would have been the first to agree.

Today, I continue to write about people who, having experienced the worst that life has to offer, are able to pick themselves up, stumble forward, and move out of the darkness of their lives into some light. At the same time, I still write for young people, finding that the ideas and opinions of most adults are hopelessly set in concrete and are all but impossible to break through. In many young people, the concrete, though hardening, has not yet solidified in their brains. Some are still open to new experiences, willing to suspend judgment until they have more understanding of issues, and listen to different sides.

And so I write for those who can make a difference in the world, can change it, and help make it a place where all people can have a chance to live decent and productive lives.

Writings

FOR YOUNG PEOPLE; NONFICTION

Allan Pinkerton: America's First Private Eye, Walker, 1990.
Photographic Book of Cats, Checkerboard, 1990.
Photographic Book of Zoo Animals, Checkerboard, 1990.
Money Book, Checkerboard, 1991.
Lifers: Learn the Truth at the Expense of Our Sorrow, Simon & Schuster, 1991.

Three Faces of Vietnam, Franklin Watts, 1993.
The Iron Horse: How Railroads Changed America, Walker, 1994.
Growing Up in the Great Depression, Atheneum, 1994.
Wandering in America: Hoboes and Tramps 1870-1940, Walker, 1994.
Juveniles in Trouble, Messner, 1994.
The Titanic, Trumpet Club, 1994.
American Islam: Growing Up in Muslim America, Walker, 1994.
American Childhoods: Three Centuries of Youth at Risk, Walker, 1996.
The Rise and Fall of Jim Crow: The African-American Struggle Against Discrimination, 1865-1954, Franklin Watts, 1999.
The Dictionary of the Civil War and Reconstruction, Franklin Watts, 2000.
Defending the Accused: Stories from the Courtroom, Franklin Watts, 2001.
Whistle-Blowers, Franklin Watts, forthcoming.

WRYDE, Dogear
See GOREY, Edward (St. John)

*   *   *

WYATT, B. D.
See ROBINSON, Spider

WYNDHAM, John
See HARRIS, John (Wyndham Parkes Lucas) Beynon

Z

ZAUGG, Sandra L. 1938-
(Sandy Zaugg)

Personal

Born June 5, 1938, in California; daughter of Lanie H. (in U.S. Navy) and Irene E. (a homemaker; maiden name, Freeney) Leach; married Wayne E. Zaugg, August 21, 1961 (died, June, 1979); children: Kimberly K., Edwin L. (deceased). *Education:* Walla Walla College, B.A., 1961; Loma Linda University, M.A., 1988. *Religion:* Seventh-day Adventist. *Hobbies and other interests:* Reading, world travel.

Addresses

Home—725 South College Ave., College Place, WA 99324. *E-mail*—zaugg@innw.net. *Agent*—Barbara Neighbors, Deal Literary Associates, 544 Gorham Rd., Ojai, CA 93023.

Career

Elementary teacher and supervising teacher in Mountlake Terrace and Kirkland, WA, 1961-65; homemaker, 1965-76; House of Neighborhood Services, Redlands, CA, sewing teacher for Mexican homemakers, 1974-76; librarian and music teacher at elementary school in Riverside, CA, 1977-81, elementary teacher and supervising teacher, 1981-83; Far Eastern Academy, Singapore, typing teacher and residence hall dean, 1983-88; Walla Walla College, Walla Walla, WA, associate dean of women, 1988-93, instructor in English as a second language, 1992-96, director of English as a second language program, 1996-99; writer. Goodwill Industries of Walla Walla, member of board of directors, 1991-97; American Cancer Society, member of local board of directors, 1996—.

Writings

UNDER NAME SANDY ZAUGG

The Rock Slide Mystery, created by Jerry D. Thomas, illustrated by Mark Ford, Pacific Press Publishing Association (Nampa, ID), 1998.

Rattlesnake River Adventure, created by Thomas, Pacific Press Publishing Association, 2000.

Work represented in anthologies, including *A Gift of Love,* 1994; *A Moment of Peace,* 1995, and *Touch of*

Sandra L. Zaugg

227

Joy, 1995, all published by Review & Herald (Washington, DC). Contributor of articles, stories, and poems to magazines and newspapers, including *Lutheran Digest, Purpose, Living, Women of Spirit, Evangel,* and *Primary Treasure.* Newsletter editor for local American Cancer Society, 1996—.

Work in Progress

A children's book, *Life without Daddy;* an adult book, *Surviving the Death of a Spouse;* a collection for all ages, *Mrs. Green's Stories.*

Sidelights

Sandra L. Zaugg told *SATA:* "I've wanted to write most of my life, but I didn't have a clue about how to begin. Finally I took some classes in writing and began planning, hoping, dreaming. Then one day I read a recently published book and thought to myself, 'I can write better than that!' My writing life began.

"I love to travel. I've been around the world several times and across both oceans many more times. It's so interesting to go to a new place and meet new people and see new things. One of my favorite places is Brugge, in Belgium. It has funny little boats that run the canals and friendly people—and all the buildings are older than I am! I also am fond of reading and writing, so I read about writing and traveling, and I write about traveling and reading—and I read and write while I travel.

"I have an amateur radio license, but no radio, and wood-carving tools that haven't been used since I began writing in 1995. I love to laugh, play Rook, eat out, and watch the Mariners and the Lakers. I dislike weeding, exercising, washing windows, and eating onions.

"My advice to a 'wanna-be' writer is: don't let anything stop you. Just write. No excuses, no procrastination, no regrets later. One more thing: find a good critique group, and stay open to helpful suggestions."

Of her work in progress, Zaugg wrote: "*Life without Daddy* is for ages seven through ten. It is one girl's story of learning to have fun again and working out how God fits into the picture after her daddy died. It is my daughter's story—sort of. *Surviving the Death of a Spouse* describes one woman's journey to recovery, with a practical guide to common errors, encouragement, and what to expect. *Mrs. Green's Stories* is a collection of short stories suitable for telling in church services, at home, or at school. Mrs. Green is a well-known teacher in Portland, Oregon, and she has been entertaining children and adults for thirty-five years. The stories are historical, from her own family, and include Protestant church history."*

*   *   *

ZAUGG, Sandy
See ZAUGG, Sandra L.